The Untold Stories of Broadway
Volume 2

By
Jennifer Ashley Tepper

Dress Circle Publishing
New York

For information about permission to reproduce selections from this book,
or for information about special discounts for bulk purchases,
please contact:
Editor@DressCirclePublishing.com

Book design by Emily Dew
Author Headshot by Matthew Murphy

Dress Circle Publishing
New York, New York
www.dresscirclepublishing.com

Part of the proceeds of *The Untold Stories of Broadway, Volume 2* will benefit education programs at Theatre Development Fund (TDF). TDF is one of the nation's largest not-for-profit performing arts service organization dedicated to the audience. TDF provide's online information for audience members of all levels of experience, offer affordable ticketing and accessibility programs, and introduce theatre and dance to future audiences through award-winning theatre education programs. TDF education programs serve over 10,000 students each year and are offered at no cost to students and schools. In partnership with over 100 New York City and tri-state area public schools in need of arts programming, TDF's education programs include interactive in-class workshops, playwriting classes, post-performance discussions, mentorship by renowned theatre professionals, and of course, tickets to Broadway, off Broadway, off-Off Broadway and dance performances.

For all the Peggy Sawyers
and all the Peggy Olsons.

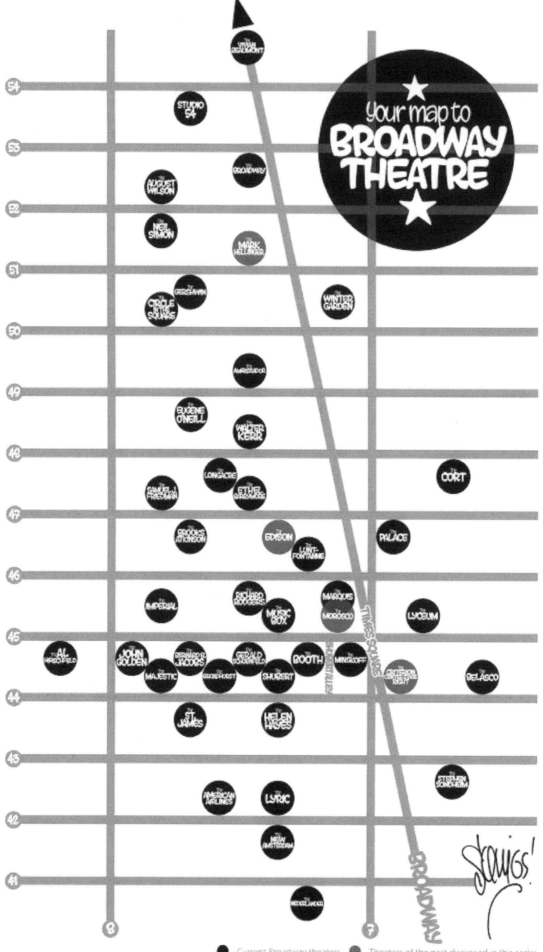

Current Broadway theaters.   Theaters of the past discussed in this series

Table of Contents

The Untold Stories of Broadway Introduction 1

Volume 2 Introduction 4

The Palace Theatre 7

The Barrymore Theatre 53

The Gershwin Theatre 93

The Circle In The Square Theatre 135

The Shubert Theatre 181

The Criterion Center Stage Right 241

The Vivian Beaumont Theatre 255

The Nederlander Theatre 291

Timelines 329

Acknowledgements 341

Volume 2 Complete List of Interviewees 343

In Upcoming Volumes of The Untold Stories Of Broadway 344

The Untold Stories of Broadway
Introduction

When I was growing up in Boca Raton, Florida, people would ask me: What do you want to be when you grow up? I would often respond:

"I want to be the theatre."

I didn't want to be *in* the theatre. I wanted to *be* the theatre. I wanted to live and breathe Broadway.

I lived 1238.6 miles away from New York City, but I was hell-bent on being a part of it someday. I sat in my humid hometown, listened to cast albums, read Playbill Magazine, and circled all of the shows I would see and places I would go.

I moved to New York City when I was 18 years old, and from the moment I set foot in Times Square, I felt like I was home. As far as theatre was concerned, I was living in the center of the universe. I was the luckiest girl on Earth. I'd take the subway uptown from NYU and spend hours just sitting in front of the Neil Simon Theatre. It was where my favorite musical, *Merrily We Roll Along*, had played. It was my place. Being there made me feel connected to the city, even though I was so new. I felt such a strong connection to these places where shows I cherished from afar had actually played.

Every time I entered a theater—Broadway or otherwise—I was hit by a blast of memories, of history, even though I'd never been there before. I walked into the Imperial Theatre to see *Dirty Rotten Scoundrels* and I knew: *Dreamgirls* was here! And *Fiddler on the Roof!* And *Pippin*! I was now getting to live inside the great theatrical tradition that every inch of New York City was steeped in. Even the restaurants and bars and shops— I knew that they were filled with the footsteps of people who had built our theatrical legacy.

When I was a senior in college at NYU, I worked with the *[title of show]* team and helped get that original musical to Broadway. I spent the summer of 2008 at the Lyceum Theatre assisting director Michael Berresse. It was one of the greatest adventures of my life thus far. My time inside the oldest continually operating theater on Broadway gave me a priceless education and a lot of the experiences I had then greatly informed this book series. (You can read about the Lyceum in *Volume 1*!)

Later, while I was working as Broadway director Michael Greif's assistant, we went to see the play *33 Variations* at the Eugene O'Neill Theatre. Michael pointed at the stairs in the back of the orchestra section, and told me a story that had taken place there 25 years earlier during *Big River*, when he had been Des McAnuff's assistant. Experiences like that also planted the seeds for this book series.

For three years, I worked for Broadway producer Ken Davenport. Working on the 2011 revival of *Godspell*, I got to spend a lot of time at the Circle in the Square Theatre. That was a very different kind of Broadway house. Spending time at Circle, putting on theatre in the round in a very incredible modern space, made me think about the uniqueness of each Broadway theater. That was something I wanted to explore in this book series. (You can read about the Circle in the Square in *Volume 2*!)

This series was inspired by my love, not just for Broadway shows, but also for the beautiful, fascinating palaces where they live, and for the sense of community all around them. In a world where historic places are destroyed every day to make room for the new, New York City has the privilege of having dozens of 100-year-old Broadway theaters where show folk and audiences today do the exact same things they did a century ago. A kid hands their ticket to a Shubert usher and walks inside to have their life changed forever. This happened in 1913 and it happens today.

Our Broadway theaters have been home to thousands of shows. They have borne witness to the best and the worst times of peoples' lives. They have been there for the shows that ran years and the shows that closed in one night. Each theater holds secrets. There are secret rooms and secret doors and energy of secrets from the past swirling in the air. When you sit in a seat at a Broadway theater, you are sitting in the exact spot where thousands before you have sat and watched a show. When you move into a dressing room at a Broadway theater, you are sharing a room with the hundreds of show people before you that smeared grease paint on in that same mirror. The 40 theaters between 41st and 66th Street are where every Broadway musical and play has come to life for over 100 years. While the shows change every year, "Broadway" still stands for people telling each other stories in a handful of large buildings in midtown Manhattan. That sense of continuity creates something very powerful in the center of our city that gives it a special sparkle. Broadway is, and has always been, the heart of New York.

Young people who fall in love with the theater often don't realize that there are more options open to them than performing the play, writing the play, or moving the sets. After my first book came out, I spoke with a student who said, "I didn't realize how important the house manager is in making the show happen!" and another who commented, "I think it would be cool now to be an orchestrator." My hope is that the stories in these books can help show kids just how many different options are open to them in professional theatre, how many possible careers they could consider pursuing, within the art form that they love. No matter which they decide on, I hope everyone walks away knowing about all of the important jobs and people that go into making each show happen.

I interviewed over 230 theatre professionals: actors, directors, writers, producers, designers, stagehands, musicians, box office treasurers, house managers, door men and women, advertising executives, company managers, press agents, stage managers, ushers, and so many more. This book contains the stories of legendary artists of the theatre and it also contains the stories of those who are just starting to make a name for themselves. Today's Broadway debuts are tomorrow's Tony Award winners. Some of these interviews are a snapshot of the early career of future stars and some of these interviews chronicle a lifetime in the theatre.

I wanted to chronicle how Broadway, like many types of art, is in the eye of the beholder. One person finds a theater intimate and another finds it cramped. One person loves a show and another hates it. One person thinks backstage is glamorous and another thinks it's a dump. You ask 230 people a question, you get 230 different answers. *Rashomon*, the famous movie about differing memories of the same event, came up a lot during interviews. I've included several instances where people in the same room came away with different interpretations of the same experience.

The Untold Stories of Broadway covers over 70 years of our theatrical past. Stories from those who were there begin in 1943! Even though this work covers as many shows and people and events as it does, it is still a representative rather than comprehensive look at Broadway history. If you get a glimpse of stage management and you wish you knew more, go take a stage management class. If you find yourself wanting to know more about *I Love My Wife*, go buy a book on musicals of the 1970s. I hope that it is a gateway for people to learn more *and* create more theatre.

This series is a love letter to Broadway and all of the people who make shows happen every night, to entertain and enlighten people from all over the world. Just like I craved insight into this world when I was growing up in Florida, I want to provide others who are fascinated by Broadway with never-before-heard backstage and onstage tales. I want to share the history of our Broadway theaters through the personal stories of the people who spend their lives in them.

Every single person interviewed for *The Untold Stories of Broadway* did have one thing in common: we all love the theatre. The good, the bad, and the ugly of it. The great highs and the bitter disappointments, the opening nights and the lazy Tuesdays, the beginnings and the endings, the moments of drama and the moments of comedy, the tears and the cheers.

And we are all part of it—from the fanciest Broadway legend to the kid in Florida listening to her first Broadway cast album.

Volume 2 Introduction

When you take one specific theater and look at its stories over many decades, you get to see a microcosm of all of the ways things have stayed the same on Broadway, and all of the ways they've changed. In this book, you'll hear about what it was like to be an understudy at the Barrymore in the 1940s *and* in the 2010s. You'll get to see how discount tickets changed over several decades at the Shubert. Socio-political issues are chronicled throughout the Palace chapter, with stories involving homophobia, the Republican National Convention, and even suffragettes. From the history of professional women in the theatre to the evolution of sound design, many aspects of Broadway are explored through the stories of those who lived them, within a specific house.

You also get to follow the timelines of Broadway greats as they live out their dreams in the very places they started dreaming them. At the Gershwin, Joe Mantello was changed by *Sweeney Todd* as a kid and then returned to direct *Wicked*. Laura Linney admired the Vivian Beaumont across the street during her time studying at Juilliard and then got to make her Broadway debut there in *Six Degrees of Separation*. When Baayork Lee spoke to Michael Bennett about what theater *A Chorus Line* should go into, they agreed that their dream was for the show to light up a stage they started out on: the stage of The Shubert.

In addition to the theaters, the theaters' neighbors are also an important part of Broadway. What was Charlie's? What was the Pub Theatrical? How has Shubert Alley changed over the years? For every place that's been destroyed, there are others still standing with secret past lives and fascinating histories that date back to the early 20th century. This book explores the untold stories of haunts that are long-gone and also those that you can still walk into today.

This second volume in *The Untold Stories of Broadway* series delves into the topic of not-for-profit theaters on Broadway. The Circle in the Square, Criterion Center Stage Right, and Vivian Beaumont are all theaters that have spent the majority of their lives as not-for-profit. At the current moment on Broadway, four Broadway theaters are owned by not-for-profit companies and present only their productions: the Samuel J. Friedman Theatre (Manhattan Theatre Club), the Vivian Beaumont Theatre (Lincoln Center Theater), the American Airlines Theatre and Studio 54 (both Roundabout Theatre Company). These theaters are partially subsidized by contributed income in the form of government/foundation grants and tax-deductible donations. In the rest of Broadway's houses, commercial theatre takes place: where producers raise the money for their given show and then try to rent a house from its landlord. Different from the nonprofits, commercial shows have to (at least) cover their weekly costs with ticket sales. Commercial shows run for a certain length based on their box office success. The other big difference is that in a not-for-profit house, a season is planned in advance, mostly with limited runs of shows. Further differences are discussed in the chapters herein. The for-profit vs. not-for-profit sides of Broadway are an important aspect of understanding how shows get into their theaters.

Not many people outside of showbiz realize just how different each Broadway theater is. There are physical realities in each space that must be paid attention to by producers, directors, and designers especially in order to make any given show successful. The size, shape, location, and eccentricities of each theater all contribute to its story. In this volume, you'll learn how certain shows "saved" certain Broadway theaters from being destroyed. While the Barrymore, Palace, and Shubert have mostly been considered valuable "hit" houses, the Gershwin, Circle in the Square, Vivian Beaumont, and Nederlander have at times been considered impossible theaters to work in. Which shows changed the fates of those theaters forever? The Criterion Center Stage Right is now long-gone, and the stories inside provide insight into why it was never saved by its perfectly fitted show. From the decisions of producers to the creativity of scenic designers, this book explores how the theater each show opens in can hugely affect its potential success.

At the Nederlander, the "*Rent* wall" still stands. Hundreds of people over the course of the show's 12 year-run left messages in the famous alley on 41st Street, and they can still be read by those who travel there today.

Everyone who works at the Palace knows about the legacy of the Judy Garland dressing room. Those untold stories are shared in this book, and while many know about these sacred spaces, there are just as many sacred spaces that people don't know about. What are the palatial offices on top of the Shubert like? Why do show folk call the Vivian Beaumont bathrooms magical? What are the traditions at the Barrymore? Who's seen the ghost of the Palace? What special rooms make the Gershwin unlike any other theater?

Here are the stories of the Palace Theatre, the Barrymore Theatre, the Gershwin Theatre, the Circle in the Square Theatre, the Shubert Theatre, the Criterion Center Stage Right, the Vivian Beaumont Theatre, and the Nederlander Theatre, eight Broadway theaters that light up New York City. This is the second volume of a multi-volume work that will include all 40 Broadway theaters, as well as several Broadway theaters that are no longer.

Thank you for going on this journey with me and I hope you enjoy this second installment of *The Untold Stories of Broadway*.

Jennifer Ashley Tepper, October 2014

Notes:

For the purposes of this book, "theater" refers to the location, and "theatre" refers to the art form.

The interviews within were conducted between March 2013 and October 2014. In some instances, interviewees refer to the current state of an aspect of theatre, and it should be understood that these reflect a specific moment in time.

While the majority of tales take place in the featured theater, I've left in select excerpts that took place "off site," where I felt they were valuable to a full story. I've also left in some elements of conversational tone that were found in the interviews. As an avid reader, I often enjoy seeing how people truly expressed themselves. Similar to reading a rehearsal script with notes for a now-famous show, sometimes seeing the process adds to the work itself. In that spirit, I wanted you, the reader, to see some of the wheels turning, some of the thoughts trailing...

Each chapter of this book focuses on one Broadway theater and uses personal stories to take you chronologically through the history of that theater. Interspersed with interviewees' stories are my own tales and also some interesting facts and stories that I collected along the way.

The Palace Theatre

Built: 1913
Location: 1564 Broadway
Owner: The Nederlander Organization
Formerly Named: B.F. Keith's Palace Theatre (1913-1932), RKO Palace Theatre (1932-1949)
Longest-Running Show: *Beauty and the Beast* (1994-1999)
Shortest-Running Show: *Home Sweet Homer* (closed on opening night in 1976), *A Meeting by the River* (closed on opening night in 1979), *Break a Leg* (closed on opening night in 1979), *Frankenstein* (closed on opening night in 1981)
Number of Productions: 65

I did my first Broadway show, *George M!* at the Palace Theatre. Al Jolson and Eddie Cantor and Judy Garland had all played the Palace! It was unbelievable to think about. I made my debut where those greats had performed.

When I walked in those Palace doors, it was always overwhelming. Each day, I thought: *I'm in a temple. I'm in a special place that not a lot of people get to be in.* Walking into the Palace stage door is to a performer what walking into the Yankees locker room is to an athlete. The history and greatness that have come before make it a holy place.

-Loni Ackerman, Actor

Introduction: A Hundred Years Of Dust

Austin Nathaniel, House Manager

There is a staircase at the Palace that everyone refers to as the Judy Garland staircase.

In the very back of the orchestra, near the center aisle, there's a secret door to a staircase. I always hear stories about how Judy would stand in the staircase and smoke before making her entrance from the rear of the house for her shows here.

There's also the star dressing room in the basement that was once Judy's. It was Liza Minnelli's when she played here. Right now during *Annie*, Jane Lynch is in there, and soon it'll be Faith Prince.

The offices we're in right now, on the mezzanine level, used to be part of the Nederlanders' main offices. This used to be an eight-story office space, before the giant hotel was built on top of the Palace in 1987. There's a closet at the bottom of the grand staircase here that used to lead to an old birdcage elevator that ran through where we're sitting now. Now, you can walk right into the hotel if you pass through two doors on this level.

As a house manager, I've seen all of it—from pizza in the front row to singing along to the show. Actually, a couple of weeks ago, there was a woman I had to talk to at intermission because a lot of audience members complained that she was singing along with the entire performance of *Annie*. She and her husband were very apologetic and pleasant and said they wouldn't do it during the second act. The next day I arrived to find that their lawyer had contacted the theater and they would be suing for infringement on their First Amendment right to free speech.

People are very attached to the shows that they love and to Broadway in general. Every single show has its own super fan following. I try to be as unobtrusive as possible to those people, but obviously if something is bothering the other audience members, you have to deal with it.

In the old vaudeville days, the Palace boxes were the prime seats, because there was just one person onstage. Now, with all of the light towers and speaker stacks along the proscenium, the front box seats can't be sold because they're terrible angles. I have chairs set aside so in case those spots are ever viable, we can put seats on sale.

The dressing room tower here is actually very separate from the structure of the auditorium. We have some rooms in the basement, but aside from that, the dressing rooms are in this stage left tower, in the back corner of the building. There are eight floors of just dressing rooms, an old elevator, and stairs. On the right side of the proscenium, we're completely hedged in by the hotel structure. The hotel is actually held up by these four stilts: two of them run through our building and the other two are right up against us in the back alley.

With *Priscilla Queen of the Desert*, we had constant bachelorette parties. Sometimes that was really fun. Sometimes though, people could be hard to deal with in the house. A lot of people were not expecting the content of that show to be what it was. It was rough for me personally, being gay. Several times a week, I had to deal with people who were freaking out that the show was gay and they wanted their money back.

I don't expect everyone to know what *Priscilla* is when they buy tickets, but if you can walk past the giant posters of drag queens and disco balls, the pink, glittery painted walls, the six-foot tall lipstick onstage, how do you not know at all what to expect when the curtain comes up?

One night, a woman came out into the lobby after the first couple of numbers, and she was very upset. She was crying. She was visiting New York with several of her friends and she kept saying that she didn't know what the show was and wanted her money back. I tried to be as gentle and helpful as I could, explaining that the show had already begun and I wasn't able to refund the tickets.

She said to me, "I think it's completely unfair that I have to speak to you about it." I explained that I was the manager, and I was in charge, but that she was welcome to write to the producers about it. Then she told me that she thought it was unfair that she had to speak to someone about the complaint who was gay.

I admit that my brain went blank for a second. Then I said, "Well I think it's unfair that I have to stand here and take your complaint seriously."

She started sobbing again and left, which I felt a little bit bad about—but not that bad. *Priscilla* was one of my favorite shows that we've had here, but dealing with that audience was tough. If they had stayed for the whole show, they would have understood that it was actually a very sweet story about a family. But people get caught up about what they get caught up about. It just is what it is. The house staff is not here to change people's minds or lecture them; we're just here to make sure they have the best experience they possibly can.

On the top floor of the auditorium, we have this gorgeous original plaster dome and proscenium. When I first came to work at the Palace, they let me climb on top of it. It was amazing—like being on top of Ms. Havisham's wedding cake in *Great Expectations*. The building is actually a physical cube, and the dome is made from sections of plaster sculpture that are suspended from the flat roof by steel bars. It's been there for a hundred years! It's covered in a hundred years of dust and stuff. There are a series of catwalks that are suspended above the dome, because you can't step on the plaster—you would fall through. It's terrifying and amazing, and you can't help but think about how that's been there for a hundred years. We just had our 100th birthday, and this huge beautiful plaster dome has just been hanging out there for all this time. It's incredible.

———————

Five new Broadway theaters were being built during the 1911-1912 season, including the Palace Theatre, the Shubert Theatre, the new New Theatre, Winthrop Ames' Little Theatre (now the Helen Hayes), and the Julian Eltinge Theatre. The Times *reported, "Two other theaters, one east and the other west of Broadway, on 48th Street, are also projected."[1] These would become the Cort and the Longacre.*

Ten new Broadway theaters ended up being built in one season, leading some to believe the market would become oversaturated. What happened in actuality was that the theatre district moved north, accommodating these new houses, and theaters south of 42nd Street began closing. The New York Times *reported that vaudeville manager Martin Beck and theatrical manager Herman Fehr were the ones building the Palace. It was "planned for productions but may be devoted to vaudeville."[1]*

Several buildings at the intersection of 47th Street and Broadway were demolished to make way for the Palace, although the building on the exact southeast corner could not be obtained, so the Palace was built on L-shaped real estate. At that point, Beck had to agree that the theater would not *show vaudeville after all, because it could not conflict with other vaudeville organizations in Times Square. The Hammerstein company controlled all vaudeville between 34th and 59th Streets.*

Beck, the general manager of the Orpheum Vaudeville Circuit, had wanted a New York theater for a while, and bought this property for $583,000. Today, this would be close to $15 million. Because of all of the commotion over exclusive rights to vaudeville in New York, it was decided that the Palace would be more of a music hall, with acts including ballets, pantomimes, musical comedies and so forth. Beck and Fehr were careful to specify that the programming wouldn't conflict with that at Hammerstein's Victoria. Early reports of this conflict predicted a "vaudeville war" between the two theater controllers, but this never came to pass. The acts in their houses were different, and before long, the Palace took off on its own merits as a premiere vaudeville house, and nothing could stop it.

The vaudeville bill was different each week. The first week included a one-act operetta, a Spanish violinist, balancing acts on wires, and the New York Times *cartoonist Hy Mayer who illustrated while also doing impressions of celebrities. The second week at the Palace had a bill of fourteen acts, including a Polish dancer, a one-act-play, a vocalist, and a family of entertainers. The third week featured "Oriental" dances, a drama, a ballet, an opera, and a play directed by Cecil B. DeMille. The London Palace Girls, imported from the West End's Palace, were a regular act. There were no 'moving pictures', only live entertainment.*

1956/1978/1991: The Palace In Three Decades

Tony Walton, Director/Scenic Designer/Costume Designer

The Palace had an extraordinary appeal to me, even before I worked there: first on *All That Jazz* in 1978, then designing *Woman of the Year* in 1981 and *The Will Rogers Follies* in 1991. In 1956, while Julie Andrews, my wife at the time, and Rex Harrison were the toast of the town in *My Fair Lady*, Julie and I went to see Judy Garland at the Palace. It was an overwhelming evening that I will never forget. Happily, I still have my Playbill for it and can re-experience her performance through the recordings of that legendary night.

At one point, Judy excitedly told the entire Palace audience that Julie was there, and that everyone there should immediately run to see *My Fair Lady* if, miraculously, they could get a ticket! Richard Rodgers, who had only recently been released from the hospital after a cancer operation that had taken away a good part of his jaw, was also in the audience. Judy introduced him, and begged him to come up onstage and play something for her

---

[1] "A Palace Theatre For Times Square." *The New York Times*. 21 Dec. 1911. Retrieved from nytimes.com.

to sing to. He went, very courageously, because he was speaking with much difficulty and his mic'd[2] communication with Judy sounded raspy and hard to understand.

To her embarrassment, when Judy and Rodgers tried to settle on what they should perform together, they discovered that she knew hardly any of his songs! He would suggest a tune, and she would say she didn't know it. Finally he said, "Surely, you know 'Little Girl Blue'?" and assured her that if she got into any trouble, he'd call out the lyric to her. Then, haltingly, Judy Garland performed with Richard Rodgers as her Palace Theatre accompanist, and, needless to say, it was extraordinarily moving.

At that time, Julie and I were close with Rodgers because he and Hammerstein had created the TV musical of *Cinderella* for her. There hadn't been a great deal of optimism that he would survive his cancer, but he did of course. And when he had been onstage with Judy Garland, we were afraid that it might be the last time we'd see him. We were so grateful that turned out not to be true.

We came to know Judy pretty well because she was a regular member of Roddy McDowall's party guests with whom we often used to gather. Roddy would host after–theatre evenings during which we would watch classic movies from his remarkable collection. Nöel Coward was often there, and he and Judy would sometimes perform together! These were extraordinary gatherings, to say the least!

Remembering *Judy at the Palace*, when I had the opportunity of encouraging, and seconding, Bob Fosse's hope to use the Palace Theatre for the opening sequence of *All That Jazz*, I jumped at it. I knew the theater's back wall was spectacular! It was covered top to bottom with rows and rows of old radiators. When one needs to create a scenic version of an old theater's back wall, it is usually necessary to manufacture fake old radiators because the real ones have long ago been trashed. Happily, that was not the case at this legendary house.

I was the co-production and fantasy designer for *All That Jazz*, and when I went with Fosse to the Palace to check it out, I said, "Bob, if we use this theater for the audition sequence, there is a good chance we'll get an Oscar for the design of the movie. Everyone will assume we designed this radiator wall!" As it turned out, I believe I was right. I think that Palace back wall may be the reason we ended up winning the Oscar for Art Direction!

That opening audition sequence in *All That Jazz* was Bob's version *of A Chorus Line*. He was upset with himself that Michael Bennett had beaten him to the punch. Bob had been the first to feature his ensemble members as individuals, but Michael had 'pipped' Bob at the post by coming up with his brilliant notion of making an entire musical about the chorus.

Almost two decades after *All That Jazz*, I designed *The Will Rogers Follies* for the Palace. I remember that Tommy Tune phoned me from a famous old theater he was performing at in St. Louis; the Fox, I think. He said, "Tony! There are some stairs here in the mezzanine that alternate between being a regular step and a longer tread. I was just experimenting with some dance steps on them, and I think these are the proportions we need for the steps on our *Follies* staircase." He gave me the dimensions, and I duplicated them exactly for our huge illuminating staircase. They took up an enormous amount of room, so it was quite a squeeze to fit anything else into what was left of our crowded backstage area.

The Will Rogers Follies had an extended preproduction period while the producers were trying to raise the money and couldn't. Eventually Tommy decided that he wanted to do a tour of *Bye Bye Birdie* with Ann Reinking. After he left it seemed as if we were throwing in the towel on *Will Rogers*. But, suddenly, in the middle of his tour, two things happened simultaneously: our producers raised the needed money, and Tommy realized that we'd been conceiving the show incorrectly. It had always been planned as a sort of *Ziegfeld*

---

[2] mic: abbreviation for microphone; a body mic is a microphone with a small head that is often hidden on an actor, as opposed to a hand-held mic

Presents The Will Rogers Follies, but it should've been Will Rogers' *own* Follies. Then it could take advantage of a Cowboy and American Indian theme; this would connect perfectly with Tommy's own Texan and Cherokee roots.

I was working on a film in California when Tommy had this epiphany and the money was finally raised. Tommy told me, "We have to make the show happen, just as soon as my tour is complete." I told him that I couldn't plunge in right away, as I was I still in the midst of the movie I was currently designing. Tommy wound up persuading the producers to send Willa Kim, the costume designer, Jules Fisher, the lighting designer, and himself to Los Angeles so that we could all collaborate on the new version of the show face-to-face. The four of us gathered around a table beside the swimming pool at Tommy's hotel whenever I could get a break from the movie. We jointly conceived what would become *The Will Rogers Follies* that premiered at the Palace.

It turned out that I was able to do the show, provided that the scenery could be entirely achieved during the rehearsal period. There was an absurdly short amount of time to design, draft, build, and paint the scenery. And actually, because I was so busy designing and supervising the drafting around the clock, I never managed to visit the scenic shop during the building and painting of *Will Rogers Follies*—and that never happens. You need to go there frequently, to check on how it's all going. But on this show, the first time I saw any of the finished designs was when they were actually onstage at the Palace! That was terrifying. It was remarkable that the producers agreed to such a freakish procedure, but it was the only way to achieve the scenic production in the time-frame available. This was also the only occasion I was able to say, "I can't spend time shopping for bids from a range of scenic shops. I only have time to zero in on one that I know and can trust to do a good job for whatever we can afford to pay." Luckily our producers were surprisingly supportive of this shotgun approach and all was achieved without rancor.

So, *The Will Rogers Follies* arrived on Broadway via this lunatic whirlwind process. Bill Mensching, the owner of our chosen scenic shop, would dash into my studio as we were in the midst of drafting a sequence, rip my designs off the table, and holler, "I can work with that!" Even if it wasn't finished! It was an amazing adventure. When the show opened, many of Willa Kim's glorious Tony-winning costumes were still unfinished—especially those for Mrs. Rogers' dream of being shown her beautiful Ziegfeldian gowns, brilliantly bejeweled, as the lyrics describe them, with rubies and emeralds, and so on. At the first preview they were just makeshift and incomplete versions of the costumes that wouldn't be fully finished in all their fabulous detail through many previews. Fortunately, by opening night, everything was entirely completed as we had hoped it would be—and we were rousingly welcomed.

———————

In 1913, the legendary actress Sarah Bernhardt began her run on the Orpheum Circuit at the Palace. It took some convincing to get her to come to America to play in vaudeville, since she considered her French repertoire far above the caliber of vaudeville performers she would need to share a bill with. In the end, she accepted and came to the Palace amidst much fanfare. The Palace managers took pains so that the financial terms were not disclosed. It later was revealed that Bernhardt was paid $500 after each performance—in gold. An eight-foot high safe in the basement held the gold.

Suffragettes waited for Bernhardt outside the Palace stage door, hoping to gain acknowledgement from her, and find out if she supported women's right to vote. She took an American flag from them while exiting the theater during her final week of the run and stated her support as crowds cheered for her. At her final performance, she received 20 minutes of applause and took 17 curtain calls.

In 1915, the Washington Post *reported that The B.F. Keith Palace Theater would stay open all summer, due to its unprecedented amount of success with vaudeville acts. It was called "the most successful music hall in the world."[3] Earlier in 1915, the paper had written glowingly of a bill at the Palace comprised of opera singers, musical comedy*

—————————

[3] "Notes of Stage." *The Washington Post.* 16 May 1915. Retrieved from proquest.com.

performers, comedians, children, and "decorative dancing roller skaters." By the time the Palace's entertainment was being reviewed, most legit papers were referring to it as vaudeville. Every legendary vaudeville act played the Palace, and every emerging vaudeville act had one goal: to make it there. In 1915, Weber and Fields came to the Palace and played vaudeville together for the first time since 1897. In 1927, Fanny Brice did an assortment of comic and dramatic songs and scenes, and a dance in which she showed her comedic ungracefulness. Later, in 1928, her act at the Palace included "My Man." Her time at the Palace provided much inspiration for Funny Girl.

On June 1, 1930, the New York Times reported that the "only remaining straight vaudeville house in the United States is the Palace Theatre in New York."[4] November 16, 1932 was the day that vaudeville died, when true vaudeville at the Palace ended. What happened in between these two dates? The relentlessness of the Great Depression, and the rise in popularity of the movie house.

In 1932, many of the acts were characterized as "old vaudeville favorites" and there was an element of nostalgia in the advertising of all Palace acts. That summer, there was a reduced price, and short films were added to the bill. This caused many old timers to lament that the golden age of the Palace was coming to an end. Once feature-length films were added to bill, people truly began mourning for the end of vaudeville and variety as it once was. By 1935, films had overtaken the Palace.

On October 16, 1932, the New York Times wrote:

> The old order, which changeth with amazing frequency along the mercurial highroad known as Broadway, bowed to the inevitable last week... With the announcement that the Palace Theatre, for nineteen years the Olympus of vaudeville to which every variety entertainer did aspire, would forsake its traditional destiny and become a de luxe motion-picture house there may have drifted up into the night air about Forty-seventh street the figurative smoke of forgotten camp-fires, the careening ghosts of old warriors... The passing of the Palace, a capitulation to its celluloid rival some time during the early Winter, will mean something more to the theatrical world than just another step in the decline and fall of variety. It will give the coup de grace to an honorable slogan- "to play the Palace!" It will extinguish the light which has steadily shone for more than one nostalgic actor in places far from home. It will draw the curtain upon a stage where many of today's top-rank entertainers first endeared themselves to the hearts of their countrymen.[5]

In 1939, the Palace was renovated and given a new marquee as well as a new lobby. In 1949, the owners of the Palace tried to switch the house back to vaudeville, with eight acts and a feature picture four times a day. Each show would be three hours long. All of the vaudeville hopefuls of days gone by gathered on the Palace beach with their old clippings in hand. The area where TKTS[6] now is was once called the Palace beach. It was where vaudevillians would gather between bookings to try to get their next job. The new Palace had a microphone onstage as well as new seats and carpeting. The brass rail had been removed from the boxes and the marble columns in the lobby were gone. The critics did not enjoy the new acts overall and they received unfavorable reviews. Vaudeville kept trucking. In 1951, the Palace management expanded their programs to have ten acts. Then, Judy Garland was announced. Judy Garland's shows in 1951 and 1956 were the highlights of the decade at the Palace.

The return of vaudeville incited eight stars of yesteryear, all women in their seventies living at the Actors Fund[7] Retirement Home, to revisit their old home. All eight had played the Palace and were welcomed onstage after the finale for a bow. One remembered how she had once shared a bill with the current act's father, while today's star

---

[4] "Palace, Chicago, Passed To 'Talkies.'" The New York Times. 1 June 1930. Retrieved from nytimes.com.
[5] "No More Parades At The Palace." The New York Times. 16 Oct. 1932. Retrieved from nytimes.com.
[6] TKTS: the discount ticket booth in Times Square, operated by the Theatre Development Fund
[7] The Actors Fund: a nonprofit service organization that helps all who are in the field of entertainment with everything from medical care to financial services

was in a high chair backstage.

During the 1950s, valiant attempts to continue a vaudeville bill went on, ballets were presented, and headlining vocalists took the stage at the Palace. But by 1957, the Palace was back to just showing movies.

Radio and talking pictures are what killed vaudeville because Americans could see and hear their favorite stars there instead. A century later, it's television that occupies the place once taken by vaudeville bills. The serious plays in the vaudeville bills were similar to today's Law and Order, *with a crime committed or a disguised person who laid the initial groundwork for the plot of the sketch. And much of the vaudeville bills hold similarities to today's reality television talent contests, with animal acts, musicians, gymnasts, and other specialty performers competing for attention.*

1966: Jimmy Nederlander Raised The Money And Bought The Palace

Elizabeth McCann, Producer

I started out working for a guy who managed touring plays. From time to time, we used to play Detroit. And if you played Detroit, you got to know the Nederlander family. They owned many of the theaters there, and occasionally they'd take one of our bus and truck[8] tours.

Jimmy Nederlander decided that he wanted to spread out from Detroit. He was motivated by the fact that he felt that the Shuberts had cheated his father.[9] This was way back in the dark ages, but the Nederlanders had a long memory. So Jimmy left Detroit and bought a theater in Cleveland. He lost money, so he bought a theater in Chicago. Eventually, he heard that the Palace Theatre in New York City was for sale.

For him, the Palace Theatre was it. It was *the* Palace. Part of it was that there had been all of these movies with Judy Garland, all these movies from MGM about vaudeville performers whose dream was to play the Palace. "Two a day at the Palace!" "You gotta play the Palace!" I don't think anybody thinks anything about it being that anymore, but for Jimmy, the Palace meant something.

It was a great house. And it was for sale.

Jimmy Nederlander raised the money in Detroit and bought the Palace Theatre. He was beginning to establish himself in New York. But he needed a theatre manager, and he deliberately didn't want to hire anyone who'd worked for any other big producer. So he hired me.

I met with him, and he said, "Well I've got to talk this over with my partners because they're not sure I really need anybody to manage the Palace. But I want you to do it. I'll get back to you." He didn't get back to me for six months!

I went to work for him, and it was the greatest training I ever had. Jimmy was a remarkably smart man. The Shuberts always specialized in putting theatre on Broadway, but Jimmy believed in filling a theater with whatever you could find. We played around with every different kind of show business at one time or another, from concerts to dance shows. It was a great education for me.

---

[8] bus and truck: a way of referring to a theater tour, since they often literally use a bus and truck to get around the country with the show; often implies a lower level tour than a "national tour"

[9] David T. Nederlander managed Detroit's Shubert-Lafayette Theatre until it was sold off—at which point J.J. Shubert accused him of stealing money from selling off the theater's furniture. This argument escalated into a Nederlander-Shubert feud that lasted for decades—over used furniture originally valued at around $75,000. (Schoenfeld, Gerald. *Mr. Broadway: The Inside Story of the Shuberts, the Shows, and the Stars.* Milwaukee, WI: Applause Books, 2012.)

But it was challenging to fill the theaters at that time. We sit here now and every theater is booked, and every one is doing a million dollars a week. It wasn't like that then. After nine years, I couldn't think of one more thing to put in the Palace Theatre. Jimmy acquired some other theaters along the way, and we would sit there and scratch our heads. We had to hustle.

I think the best time to get into any business is when it's a little down on its luck and when you also have a strong, entrepreneurial boss who isn't going to be shot down. I owe it all to Jimmy. I do. He was always, always there for me. He still is.

———————————

In 1965, rumors began circulating that the Palace might be turned into a "real" Broadway theater for plays and musicals by a new owner. More musicals were playing on Broadway, and the demand for larger houses for them had begun. After a couple bids, the Nederlanders purchased the Palace for $1.6 million (almost $12 million today).

Sweet Charity *was the first legitimate show to play the Palace. The new Palace for* Sweet Charity *would have two bars for alcoholic and soft drinks—one in the inner lobby and one in the downstairs lounge. In 1965, only four Broadway theaters served alcohol: the Alvin (now Neil Simon), ANTA (now August Wilson), 46th Street (now Richard Rodgers), and Mark Hellinger (now the Times Square Church). The state liquor laws had recently changed, allowing theaters to serve. Pre-mixed cocktails were served at most houses due to time constraints, but for some time the Palace only served champagne.*

The Nederlanders were new to Broadway and didn't always play by established rules. For example, at the beginning of the run, the Nederlanders had Sweet Charity*'s programs printed by Stage Magazine rather than Playbill. In 1966, when the Palace opened, its redesign was bold, colored with red and gold, a sharp contrast from the modest, muted shades of Broadway theaters as they had been painted in the mid-20th century. Crystal chandeliers were found buried in plaster in the dressing rooms, and reinstalled in the lobby. The backstage elevator on stage left was installed. Everyone from Mayor Lindsay to Ethel Merman attended opening night of* Sweet Charity.

At first, the balcony seats in the third level were not sold, and that area of the theater was sectioned off. After opening, Gwen Verdon asked the Nederlanders if these seats could be given for free to students, servicemen, and the like, and they complied.

After the Palace, the Nederlanders bought the Henry Miller's Theatre and the Brooks Atkinson. Patriarch David T. Nederlander had learned from and worked with the Shuberts, and his two sons, James and Joseph, did apprenticeships at the Shubert Theatre in Detroit. His grandsons, James L. and J.J. were in elementary school when the Nederlanders began to take root in New York. These days, James L. Nederlander is president of the Nederlander Organization, which owns and operates nine Broadway theaters.

———————————

1966: *Sweet Charity* Reclaims The Palace

John McMartin, Actor

Bob Fosse and I did a musical together called *The Conquering Hero*, which was short-lived on Broadway. Then, we did a musical called *Pleasures and Palaces*, with music by the great Frank Loesser. That one never got out of Detroit.

One night, after a performance of *Pleasures and Palaces*, Bob and I were at a bar together. We knew we were closing and we weren't going to New York, and Bob said, "I want to do something else together." I said, "Oh, wow." And he said, "What's the matter?"

I said, "I've been in two bombs with you now—I thought you wouldn't want to work with me again," and he said, "Well, I was thinking maybe *you* thought that about *me*!"

A little while later, we ran into each other on the street in New York. Bob said, "That show I told you about, I'll send you part of the script." It was the elevator scene from *Sweet Charity*. He said, "I don't know if you'll have a number or anything," and I said, "I don't care if all I have to do is just this elevator scene." Neil Simon wrote it, and it was top-drawer comedy.

We went into the Palace. The Palace was iconic to me, because when I was a kid I would listen on the radio to comics always saying, "Oh, I played the Palace!" It was the pinnacle for them, because it was a top vaudeville house. And I thought: *I get to play the Palace!*

It had just been changed to a legit house, and we were the first play to go in there, so I felt I was entering into theatre history. I was, too, because *Sweet Charity* was a success and a joyous one for me and the company. We all had a great time. I did the movie because of its success, all thanks to Bob Fosse.

I remember during one of the previews of *Sweet Charity*, Gwen Verdon was doing one of the dances, and she stumbled. Bob ran from the back of the house and leapt over the orchestra pit, onto the stage. He broke all the barriers. She was alright, and they resumed, but that was startling.

Like most theaters, the majority of the beauty is out front. But backstage, there was this great wrought iron circular staircase, just like you see in the movies when they make movies about theatre. I was a kid, a young actor, just glad to be anywhere. But to be in the Palace? That was amazing.

I still think: *I played the Palace*!

1966: John McMartin And Joel Grey

Ed Dixon, Actor

I saw the national tour of *Hello, Dolly!* starring Carol Channing that came through Oklahoma City while I was still a kid. It was the first national, they used the Broadway set, and seeing it was one of the most exciting things that had happened to me in my life.

Then, I saved money and came to New York. I saw eight shows in one week! The very first show I saw was *Sweet Charity* at the Palace Theatre, with Gwen Verdon and John McMartin. Later that week, I also saw *Cabaret* with Joel Grey. Then, last year, I ended up doing *Anything Goes* on Broadway with both John McMartin and Joel Grey, who were 82 and 80 years old respectively. That was extraordinary—to have that amazing full circle that took 45 years to complete!

Sweet Charity was very stark, and Fosse's style was different from what I was expecting. In my childish brain, I was actually kind of disappointed because there was very little scenery and I thought all Broadway was going to be like *Hello, Dolly!*

The thing I loved the most about *Sweet Charity* was John McMartin in the elevator scene with Gwen Verdon. It was one of the funniest things I have ever seen in my life!

I got to tell him that, when we worked together on *Anything Goes*. I actually got to go up to John and tell him that he was in the first show I saw on the first day I arrived in New York! He's such a consummate old professional that he just replied, "Oh! That's nice."

1966: Do You Wanna Have Fun?

Peter Link, Writer/Actor

The first Broadway show I ever saw was *Sweet Charity* at the Palace.

I had just come to New York to study at the Neighborhood Playhouse. I was living in the 34th Street Y, which was a horror show, and I never wanted to go home at night. I'd leave school over on the East Side, walk across town, and get to Broadway. Sometimes I would hang out on Broadway all night because it was so fascinating.

One night I was standing in front of the Palace Theatre. I'd just come out of a movie, and there was a crowd going into this show. A guy came up to me and said, "My friend didn't show up. Would you like a ticket?" I told him, "I can't afford it." And he said, "I'll just give it to you."

So he took me in to see *Sweet Charity*, my first Broadway show. He was such a nice guy and in the second act, his hand came over onto my lap. I said, "Oh, no! You've got me all wrong!" He was disappointed, and I felt really bad.

The show was great, and Gwen Verdon was great, but I don't remember much about the second act because I kept worrying the guy was going to try something again. It was an experience! That was my first Broadway show.

————————

In the first half of the 20th century, more stars appeared on the Palace stage than on the stage of any other still-functioning Broadway theater. From the moment that Ethel Barrymore and Sarah Bernhardt headlined at the Palace, the building was indoctrinated as an important home for live entertainment. The Marx Brothers, Fanny Brice, Weber & Fields, Ethel Waters, Al Jolson, Eddie Cantor, Bob Hope, Sophie Tucker, Mae West, Fred Astaire, Bill Robinson, Ethel Merman, Bing Crosby, Jack Benny, Frank Sinatra, Jerry Lewis, Danny Kaye, Harry Belafonte, and, of course, Judy Garland all appeared at the Palace.

In the 1942 Busby Berkeley movie musical For Me And My Gal, *Judy Garland and Gene Kelly play Jo and Harry, who dream of playing the Palace. The two would-be vaudevillians almost make it, but are sidetracked by the events of World War II. Harry is drafted, but he slams his hand in a trunk to avoid the war. Jo finds out and leaves him, but when he goes overseas to entertain the troops and saves lives in a heroic act, they reunite on the stage of the Palace.*

For Me And My Gal *was based on the true story of Harry Palmer and Joanne Hayden. Harry really had been drafted and injured his hand to avoid going to France, just when the two had an act that was about to play the Palace in 1917. "You think anything's going to stand in the way of us playing the Palace this time? Oh no, not even a war!"*

For Me And My Gal *marked the first time Judy Garland played an adult role and received star billing for a film. Almost a decade of Hollywood later, in 1951, Garland had her first huge triumph at the Palace as herself, in* Judy Garland at the Palace "Two-A-Day." *The show ran for 19 weeks, broke all box office records at the Palace, and made Garland the talk of the town. Garland collapsed and was hospitalized a couple of times during her run. At one point, she collapsed mid-performance and Vivian Blaine, star of* Guys and Dolls, *came out of the audience and sang some songs in her stead. The collapses were attributed to nervous exhaustion and a throat infection. She would return to the Palace in 1956 and 1967.*

In 1967, Judy Garland "At Home at the Palace" *was the second production to play a Palace that had now gone legit. The Hollywood starlet even brought her kids with her. Lorna and Joey Luft were 14 and 12, respectively, and shared the stage with Mom for 15 minutes of the act, singing and playing the drums. Garland's 1967 production featured her rendition of the song "For Me And My Gal," magnificently recreated on the Palace stage as the sentimental audience sang along. Her last Palace stint took the town by storm, just as the theater was transforming into the Broadway house it was always meant to be. Her death came less than two years later.*

In the back of the house, just behind the standing room area and the sound console, there's a tiny little door that was put in. Behind it is a staircase that goes down to the basement. Judy Garland would stand in the staircase and smoke, and sneak upstairs to watch scenes that she wasn't in.

The star dressing room in the Palace is in the basement. While its first inhabitant was Gwen Verdon, it is regularly called "The Judy Garland Room". In 2008, her daughter Liza Minnelli occupied it during Liza's at the Palace.... *In between, the dressing room was home to everyone from Lauren Bacall (*Applause *and* Woman of the Year*) to Bette Midler, Diana Ross, Josephine Baker, and Shirley MacLaine. The room has a rich history of diva occupants.*

1967: *Henry, Sweet Henry*

Baayork Lee, Actor/Choreographer

Henry, Sweet Henry was Michael Bennett's second show as choreographer. We only ran for a couple months. One of my memories is of this guy who often waited at the stage door for his wife who was in the show. "Who's he?" "His name is Woody Allen." "Oh, okay."

I played one of the kids at the girls' school. The show was based on a movie, *The World of Henry Orient*, about two girls who were fascinated by this avant-garde pianist. In the movie, it was Peter Sellers and in our show, it was Don Ameche. The two leading ladies were smitten by this musician, and we played their companions at school. Michael expanded the film and included our school ensemble in a lot of moments in the story.

In the opening of the second act, there was a scene I loved where we all sang and danced "Weary Near To Dyin'" as hippies in a park. Bob Avian was our dance captain, and in the song, he had to pick me up and put me on his back. So every time I went home to have dinner with my family between shows, he'd yell after me, "Don't eat too much! I have to carry you!" The opening number, the "Academic Fugue", was also terrific work that Michael created for us. I wish there was footage of that.

The Palace is quite amazing. It seemed to me to be larger than other theaters. There were more tunnels than I'd ever seen backstage, and more space. I was used to theaters like the St. James, with dressing rooms in a tower and stairs going up and up, and mostly being isolated on the top floor. The Palace has dressing rooms all over; they're like little cubby holes.

We closed on New Year's Eve. I remember emptying our dressing rooms, and then trying to cross Broadway, as all of these crowds were waiting for the ball to drop and 1968 to begin.

Henry, Sweet Henry *was the second musical at the Palace, after it re-opened with* Sweet Charity. *The musical had a bright, brassy score by Bob Merrill (*Funny Girl, Carnival, Take Me Along*), and choreography by Michael Bennett. Bennett had recently gotten his first Broadway choreography credit with* A Joyful Noise, *which closed after 12 performances.* Henry, Sweet Henry *also flopped, but it propelled Bennett into a line of hits:* Promises, Promises, Coco, Company, Follies. *In the Palace orchestra pit, creating dance arrangements for Henry, Sweet Henry was a 23-year-old Marvin Hamlisch. Hamlisch admired Bennett's work so much that when they met, he told him he was filing his phone number not under M or B, but under G for Genius. He knew they would work together again. They did—on* A Chorus Line.

Alice Playten stole the show each night as pint-sized villainess Kafritz. She was only 20 years old, and she received a Tony nomination and performed her showstopper, "Poor Little Person", on the Ed Sullivan Show. Playten was used to the spotlight, as she played Baby Louise during the original run of Gypsy—*which is also undoubtedly where she learned how to belt like Merman!*

1968: The First Mega-Mix

Brig Berney, Company Manager

The first Broadway show I ever saw was *George M!*, starring Joel Grey, at the Palace Theatre. I was about five years old.

We were in Long Island for a family wedding and then all of the cousins got to come into Manhattan in a limousine and see a Broadway show. I remember walking into the lobby—it still looks exactly the same today, even though the outside of the theater doesn't.

Even though I was a little kid, I knew some of the music in the show, because in preschool we sang "Grand Old Flag" and some of the others. I remember saying, "Oh! I know this!"

At the end of the show, they basically said: "Well, our story is over but we have all these other songs that we haven't sung by George M. Cohan." Then they did a gigantic medley. Maybe it was the first mega-mix!

During the 1968 season, David Black, producer of George M!, *protested to the League their moving up of the Tony nomination eligibility date for the year. This had been done to allow for more time to prepare for the live broadcast, which was becoming more high-octane, but it prevented* George M! *from being eligible until the next year. In 1969,* George M! *was up against hit musicals like* 1776 *and* Hair *and was not nominated for Best Musical. In 1968, it would definitely have had a shot, as 1968 is still considered to be one of the weakest seasons for new musicals of all time. It is the only year where the Best Musical winner,* Hallelujah, Baby!, *was not even running anymore at the time of the awards. The fact that* George M!—*which wasn't even nominated in 1969—could have won had the eligibility rules not been changed, shows just how circumstantial a Tony Award win can be.*

1968: Hookers And Jetés And Greasepaint

Loni Ackerman, Actor

In 1967, I was studying dance at Luigi's Jazz Center. They had live music while we danced: there was a drummer, there was a jazz pianist, somebody would come in and play saxophone. It was like being onstage!

Sometimes, choreographers would come to class and say, "We're doing summer stock here. Come and audition!" During the summer of '67, Tony Mordente came to class and I said, "Oh God, it's one of the Jets!" I was 95 pounds with long brown hair, because I was in ballet. He said, "Would you come to this audition? It's for a show called *How Do You Do, I Love You*."

I went to the audition, and sang "Rockabye Your Baby With A Dixie Melody", when they were expecting some soprano thing. Their mouths were open. I was fearless! To me, it was like, *Oh, this is another little test.* I knew that I should be in these shows because all I wanted to do was be in a show. I never had the ambition to kill the person in front of me. It was just like, *I should be in these shows because this is where I belong.* I got *How Do You Do, I Love You*, and Michael Stewart, the book writer, was also writing the book to *George M!*

I didn't even have my Equity card[10] yet, and he said, "Come to this audition. It's *George M!* It's a tap audition." I didn't tap; I am one of the worst tap dancers.

So, I went to the first audition. We were onstage at the Palace. We did the tap and they lined up all the bad tappers. It was like out of a movie. I was at the end, the last one on line. And Joe Layton said, "This one stay, thank you, thank you, thank you." He got to me, and I knew he was going to say, "Thank you." I thought, *Well I tried.*

Then I saw Michael Stewart running over to Joe Layton, at the back of the theater—right out of *Smash!* I know he said, "Keep her." I know because there was a silence, and then Joe said, "Okay. Loni, you stay." Everyone was looking.

We did the ballet, and I had never done split fouettés like that in my life. And I never did again! Then, we had to sing. I didn't even have music. That's how naive I was. I sang "Rockabye Your Baby With a Dixie Melody" again. We read. And I got a callback!

At the callback, they said, "Does anybody play an instrument?" I raised my hand, and I said piano, and told them I could play ragtime. They asked if I could play "Alexander's Ragtime Band". My hands did not belong to me that day. It was like the jetés. My hands were possessed!

The next day I got the call that I got the show! I was the second piano player, and I was going to play a dog trainer.

We were in rehearsal, and all of the girls had to audition for the role of the maid who sings "45 Minutes from Broadway." In the middle of the song, the character had to say, "In a minute, honey!" We're all sitting in a row, and I thought, *Oh what the hell?* I did a deep Louis Armstrong-style growl of "In a minute, honey!" I used to do a great Louis Armstrong impression, and that's how I got that role. Some of the girls were not happy with me, but hey, I knew what I had to do.

At that time, on 47th Street, the hookers were in full force. It was high boots and short skirts. Sometimes, my mother would meet me in between shows, because I'd just turned 19. She would walk me down the street to the Palace, and I knew all the hookers! "Hey, Loni! What's happenin' today? How you doin' today? Alright, child!" My mother would look at me like, "Are these your friends?" And I would say, "They're nice!"

I shared my dressing room with Susan Batson and Patti Mariano. The carpet was dirty and old and it had that smell, which I loved. Some people complained about the smell, and I thought: *No, I love the smell of the costumes.* It was like the Met, when I went for class. I would pass thousands of costumes on the top floor and that smell... You know, that smell of standing in the wings. The smell of the greasepaint. *This is all I want.*

With *George M!*, I would sit in the house and they would ask, "Why are you here?" I just wanted to see how the show was put together. I liked hearing the lights click. I just loved that whole world. I never had any ambition to do anything else but be in a live house. That's it.

Richard M. Nixon, President-elect at the time, attended George M! *and was greeted with a standing ovation. He sat in the 5th row with his wife, daughters, and several friends, and went backstage afterward to congratulate Joel Grey and the cast and to accept a vintage George M. Cohan recording from the cast. Nixon commented that he missed going to the theater several times a week, as he and his wife would do right after World War II when they*

---

[10] Equity card: proof of membership in the Actors' Equity Association, the union representing stage actors and stage managers

were living in New York. He told the George M! *cast, "We used to sit in the balcony then, but we enjoyed the shows just as much."*

1968: We'd Squish Out Cigarettes With Our Tap Shoes

James Dybas, Actor

I was in *George M!* at the Palace Theatre. There's this song called "You Haven't Lived Until You've Played The Palace". I think that's true.

The show had these rigorous auditions for Joe Layton, who was directing and choreographing. We did these long dance combinations and all of this tap dancing. We all had speaking roles too, and then Loni Ackerman and I had a dog act.

There was a section in the show where everyone did these vaudeville acts. I had to go down to this place called Animal Talent Scouts, and meet the two dogs we'd be working with, Spot and Frieda. There was a wallaby and all these parrots and snakes. Behind the building, they were keeping llamas. And when I needed to use the restroom, I saw that there were snakes and frogs in the bathtub. Eventually, during the show, I was able to take one of the dogs and have him stand in my hand on his back two feet while I lifted him in the air.

At that time, everyone smoked cigarettes in the wings and you never knew when the fire department was going to come for an inspection. We actually made up a code. When they were coming, someone would say over the loudspeaker: "Lord ___, please report to the stage manager." Then we'd throw the cigarettes on the floor, squish them out with our tap shoes, go onstage and start dancing.

In 1932, while Sophie Tucker was performing at the Palace, a fire was started by a stage lamp falling into a curtain. Patrons panicked and scrambled out of the theater, with several getting trampled or burned. At the time, the papers noted that all 1700 seats were sold out and there were 200 standing room ticketholders in the back of the orchestra. Today, there are rarely more than 30 standing room ticket spots in the back of any theater, including the Palace. Back then, it was more of a ten-deep mosh pit.

1970/2012: Lauren Bacall's Liquor Drawer

Charles Strouse, Writer

I try not to go to opening nights of my own shows because I'm always scared. The first opening night of mine that I went to in New York was *Applause*. That was because our star, Lauren Bacall, said to me, "If you don't come to opening night, I'm not coming either." I said, "You're kidding." She said, "No." So I did go to that opening night!

Backstage with Bacall was wild because every celebrity that I could imagine came to visit. Noël Coward came! I liked to hang around so that maybe she'd introduce me. *Everyone* came. Liz Taylor and Richard Burton would just drop by. Betty Bacall kept a big liquor drawer, because she had a lot of guests.

Betty always spoke out. In fact, I learned a lot from her. I was always lacking in self-confidence, and I used to watch Betty and think: *Wow, I guess that's possible, to really speak your mind to somebody.* She sure could.

At Christmastime one year, my wife and kids and I went to Florida. I came in one night to tell her that we were going away, but that I wanted to wish her a Merry Christmas first. She said, "I know why you're going: so you don't have to buy me a present!" Just by coincidence, I had bought her a present that week, a silver frame from Tiffany's. I brought it out and we had a good laugh.

I love the Palace now too, because *Annie* is playing there. The Palace is beautiful—and not in the way that an apartment is beautiful. Theaters are beautiful because there's a "haunted house" feeling about them. So many people have trod the boards. So much money has crossed hands. So many errors have been made. So many hits have played that could've been misses, and there have been so many misses that could've been hits.

There's a great deal of tradition that holds on with everybody. You're never supposed to say "Macbeth," and people are very serious about that. There are also things you're supposed to say, like, "kiss the wolf" in Italian. I have no idea what that means but people are always saying it. Theatre folks love tradition.

1970/1991: My Dad Wrote It

Amanda Green, Writer

The first Broadway show I ever saw was *Applause* at the Palace Theatre.

I was five. What do I remember about seeing it? My dad wrote it, so I was very proud. I remember there were jokes about homosexuality, which I thought were hilarious. I didn't really understand all of them, but I knew they were daring, and I loved that. I remember the excitement of going backstage. Lauren Bacall was a big star, and it was thrilling to see all of that.

Later, I spent time at the Palace with my dad during *Will Rogers Follies*. I was a fan of Keith Carradine, who played the lead. I'd had such a crush on him as a kid. I saw the movie *Nashville* and I was obsessed with the song he sang, "I'm Easy". I would go into record stores, when there were still record stores, and I'd ask, "Do you have a copy of *Nashville*?" They never did.

I didn't get to know him that well, but I thought he was just amazing.

———————

Two decades later, Keith Carradine starred in Hands on a Hardbody *at the Brooks Atkinson, with lyrics by Amanda Green, book by Doug Wright, and music by Amanda Green and Trey Anastasio.*

During The Will Rogers Follies, *Keith Carradine often made a curtain speech, telling audience members not to drink and drive. This was keeping in character, as Will Rogers would often do the same. The great legacy of* The Will Rogers Follies, *which played 981 performances at the Palace starting in 1991, is that Rogers himself had played that very stage. Much like when, in* Funny Girl, *Barbra Streisand conjured Fanny Brice back to the Winter Garden, where she had once played, Keith Carradine did rope tricks and spoke the wisdom of America's wisest cowboy where Rogers himself had once performed lariat stunts in 1916.*

———————

1970: Listening

Len Cariou, Actor

I was in *Applause* longer than I was in anything else: 15 months.

About nine months into the run, I started feeling odd. Something felt strange to me onstage, and I couldn't figure out what it was.

I called Ron Field and I said, "Do me a favor, come in and see what's going on. There's something wrong and I can't figure it out." He came and he knocked on my dressing room door after the show. I said, "It's still there. It's this funny feeling and I can't put my finger on it. Everything looks like it's the same."

And he said, "I was about to come and congratulate you guys on how good I thought the show was after nine months, how tight it was. The only thing I can think of is that you're maybe not listening as the character. Maybe you're listening as Len."

Nobody had ever said that to me before. I'll be damned if he wasn't right! And it happened to me again on *A Little Night Music*, exactly nine months into the run.

Applause was my favorite of my opening nights, because I have 13 siblings and my entire family was there: my sisters and their husbands, my brothers and their wives, my cousins, my hometown friends. My mother was still alive and she came with her sister. Then, while they were in town for opening, the nominations came out and I was nominated for a Tony! That was a thrill for all of us. It was a pretty heady time.

1970: The House Contractor

Red Press, Musical Coordinator

I didn't grow up wanting to be a music contractor. I don't think that I'm different from most people. You don't ever know where you're going to end up, and a turn at one point in life brings you into a different world.

I was playing shows as a musician and had no thought about being a show contractor. I had done a little bit of contracting outside the theatre, working on jingles and other things. At one point, I put together a big band for the Paramount Theatre, which used to do stage shows. At that time, there were basically two major contractors who did 95% of the work on Broadway.

There was a union rule that each theater had to have four musicians who were hired for every show that was there. They were part of that theater. One of them was a contractor. He didn't hire the whole orchestra; he just took care of payroll each week, made sure everyone showed up on time, and dealt with any problems with the house musicians. The contractor hired for the given show was really in charge.

I did a show called *Applause* on the road; we went to Baltimore, then Detroit. In each town, it changed and changed, and by the time we got to New York, it was a pretty good show. We went into the Palace, where it just so happened that the house contractor was a friend of mine. He was a family friend, and he had just gotten the job as the Palace contractor. Whenever he went on vacation or had to do something elsewhere, he would ask me to take over. Ultimately, he quit, and I became the contractor for the Palace Theatre.

When the Palace Theatre didn't have shows, it had acts. I remember Shirley MacLaine. I remember Bette Midler. And for those, they asked me to hire the full orchestra. I was in a different situation than most house contractors because I was actually hiring musicians—and the producers felt my musicians were good!

There were two women who ran the whole Nederlander Organization at the time: Liz McCann and Nelle Nugent. While I was there, they quit the organization and went out on their own, producing. And since I had worked for them at the Palace, which is a Nederlander house, they knew me. One show they had come in was *Sherlock Holmes*, and they asked me to contract it on Broadway. It was just a play that had musicians, so it wasn't big. But still, I had shifted to being a producer's contractor. Then they got some bigger stuff, and people started to hear about me, and I became successful.

I had a tiny little office at the Palace, in the basement. It was like a single men's room, with enough space for a locker to put my things and a little tiny table. My most vivid memory there is of when *Lorelei* came into the Palace—it was basically *Gentlemen Prefer Blondes* with a different name—and the conductor was Phil Rosenstock. After work, he and I would sit in my tiny office with a bottle of scotch. I like him very much; he was a great conductor.

When I started doing theatre, there were very few women in the pit, except for the occasional harpist. When I hired some women to play *Lorelei*, a man who was one of my house musicians said to me, "How dare you hire a woman! There is a man sitting at home trying to support a family who is unemployed!" I will never forget that. Things were different.

But in that show, I decided to hire women in the pit. As always, the men would bring in magazines of naked women to read when they weren't playing, and the women became aware of it. So the women went out and got a picture of a naked man and they hung it up in their section of the pit. My conductor came in and saw it and gasped, "Who put that picture there?! How dare they! There are *women* in this orchestra!"

———————————

Of every Broadway theater, it's possible that the Palace has had the widest variety of entertainments. From vaudeville to concerts to legitimate plays and musicals, the Palace has seen it all. In 1936, there was a revue called Broadway Heat Wave *featuring female orchestra leader Rita Rio. The Palace was once home to religious services each Lent, led by religious groups. George Abbott's 100th birthday celebration was held at the Palace. In 1918, a rally was held at the Palace made up of theatre folks volunteering to go entertain overseas in France. Several musicians' strikes were held in the Palace. Woodrow Wilson's memorial was held at the Palace.*

In 1925, the Palace held a midnight benefit in support of the construction of the Cathedral of St. John The Divine. Everyone from Al Jolson to Fanny Brice to Will Rogers participated. There was so much interest in tickets that the same show was held simultaneously at the Hippodrome on 6th Avenue near 44th Street, with all performers rushing back and forth between theaters to entertain two audiences.

1972's From Israel With Love *featured 26 performers formerly from the Israeli Army Entertainment Corps. In 1928, the Palace held the* Fur Fashion Pageant and Revue, *staged by the New York Retail Furriers' Association.*

Citizen Kane *had its world premiere at the Palace on May 1, 1941. The* New York Times *review opened, "Within the withering spotlight as no other film has ever been before, Orson Welles'* Citizen Kane *had its world premiere at the Palace last evening."[11] The film was not a financial success at first but became a hit years later due to many critics and filmmakers citing it as the best film ever made and thrusting it back into the spotlight. Prior to its premiere at the Palace, Welles' film stirred up controversy because of the secrecy surrounding its production. Welles kept studio executives off set, and kept the true subject of the film out of the news. This was because its subject was a fictionalized version of American newspaper magnate William Randolph Hearst. Hearst was so angered upon learning the true topic of the movie that he did everything in its power to try to get RKO Pictures to destroy it. When RKO released* Citizen Kane *anyway, Hearst banned newspapers from talking about it and manipulated movie theaters not to play it.*

Orson Welles was 25 years old at the time, and this was his first feature film. After skyrocketing to success in theatre and radio, RKO Pictures gave him an unprecedented amount of control on his first film. It was an original story. Welles wrote it, directed it, and starred in it, and he was unwilling to compromise. Over the next decade and a half, Citizen Kane *caused Welles' career to decline and filled his professional life with obstacles and problems. In the second half of the 20th century,* Citizen Kane *began to inspire a generation of filmmakers with its innovations, as they discovered it. Film critic Roger Ebert called it the greatest film ever made.* Citizen Kane *had been initially*

———————————

[11] Crowther, Bosley. "Orson Welles' Controversial '*Citizen Kane*' Proves A Sensational Film." *The New York Times*. 2 May 1941. Retrieved from nytimes.com.

set to open in New York at Radio City, but after threats from Hearst, Radio City pulled out. The film opened in New York at the Palace instead.

In 1946, Disney's Song of the South *was protested as it played at the Palace. White and black protestors led a demonstration side by side declaring the movie offensive due to its glorifying of slavery. Policemen controlled the demonstration, and made protestors remove a wooden coffin containing a likeness of Jim Crow.*

The Palace began interspersing concert engagements with legit shows. In 1973, David Bowie was even expected to play the Palace. While this run never materialized, others such as Bette Midler and Diana Ross, had great concert success at the Palace in the 1970s.

1970: Chocolate Babies, Nudity, And The Automat

Jeb Brown, Actor

In the autumn of 1970, my mother and father had a pair of tickets to the theatre and my dad was called out-of-town unexpectedly. I became my mother's date and that's how I ended up seeing *Applause* with Lauren Bacall at the Palace Theatre at age six.

My mom didn't really know how the evening would go, but she did know that I was interested in performing. I had seen the movie *Oliver!* the previous year and I was crazy about doing my own snappy version of that musical in my living room for any available audience... babysitters, relatives, etc. My mother didn't know much about *Applause*, but she wasn't concerned; she'd take chances like that and I was the beneficiary of her whimsy. I saw R-rated movies before most of my friends saw any movies, and I loved that. I remember that on this occasion, however, once we got to the theater, she got me a box of candies—the now-defunct and forever politically incorrect concession stand item called Chocolate Babies—just in case.

Well, let's just say that I didn't touch those chocolates. They sat on my lap and I sat mesmerized. I don't remember much from that show except that I loved it. And because of that, my parents started taking me to the theatre on a regular basis. I saw *Two By Two* with Danny Kaye, *Sugar* with Bobby Morse and Tony Roberts, *Two Gentlemen of Verona* with Raul Julia, *Purlie* with Cleavon Little and Melba Moore... a lot of great things.

But I have only flashes of memory from my first Broadway show, *Applause*. Years later, I worked with Lee Roy Reams, who had been in it, and I was able to corner him and ask, "Okay, Lee Roy, did these things really happen onstage?" I was incredulous, because they were mostly sexual memories. I remembered a woman in the party scene in a beaded gown that hung in long strands from her neckline to her ankles. When she walked, the beads would spread and you could kind of see her figure underneath. To a six-year-old, she was naked. And I remembered a scene with men on tables, dancing, and when they jumped in the air, their waiter aprons would fly up and you'd see that they were naked underneath.

Lee Roy set me straight on what did and didn't happen, but to a child's eye... well, those dancers in tight outfits and the whole bit—there was a sizzle about it. That wasn't the only thing I was interested in that night, but the intoxication stuck with me. I also just remember the grand magic of the curtain rising and a story being told and 1700 dressy adults eagerly sitting and watching together. That felt like a big deal.

Before the show that night we went to the Automat for dinner. There was an elderly man who was likely homeless who spoke to us at length and it was my first time having that experience. And that afternoon we had come in early to attend a taping of *To Tell The Truth*, which was a huge game show on TV at the time. I had watched it often, and now there was that celebrity panel right in front of me, so that was exhilarating. I later worked on game shows in L.A., so that experience came full circle as well. There was a lot going on that day. It changed my life.

With its position right in the heart of Times Square, the Palace has been the site of more wild, illicit, or illegal activities than most other Broadway theaters—onstage and off. In 1946, a patrolman rescued a two-week-old baby who was trapped in an unventilated locker in the basement lounge of the Palace. The night superintendent heard the baby's cries, and the locker was opened with a crowbar. If an hour had passed, the baby would have suffocated. He was found with a note from his mother, begging someone to take him and give him a good home. "To whom it may concern. Please won't you give me a home or place me in one? I am a good baby. I don't cry very much. I'm very tiny now but I will make it up to you when I grow up."

1971: Time Steps and Full Circles

Jim Walton, Actor

The first theater that I was in to see a show was The Palace. I saw *Applause*. It was the summer of 1971, and I was 16. My father brought my older sister Joan and me into New York City on a Wednesday, and we saw *Applause*.

We sat on house left of the orchestra. I loved *Applause*. Then we had dinner at one of the two Howard Johnsons that are no longer there. After that, we went to what is now the Richard Rodgers Theatre to see *No, No, Nanette*. We sat in the front row of the mezzanine and I remember we leaned out over the railing, Joan and I. She's a dance teacher now, and we tap danced then so we just thought it was awesome.

It was a perfect day. I'll never forget it. We went to Duffy Square, where TKTS is, and we made sure to tap dance. We did a double time step in front of the statue of George M. Cohan. Just a couple of green Indiana kids and their father. It was very generous of him. I was just remembering that time, not a week ago, when I saw *Annie* back at the Palace. I saw it with my old friend, Lonny Price, and I told him that story.

I just loved the score of *Applause*. Lee Roy Reams was in it and he later became a colleague and a friend of mine whom I've worked with many times. He was this young guy from the Midwest who made it on Broadway. I remember the show being, for a very conservative family from Indiana, a little liberal!

There was "She's No Longer A Gypsy" where all the waiters had on just aprons, and they turned their backs and had bare backsides. I remember our father kind of being embarrassed. And I was going, "What? You can do that?!" It was almost like I didn't know that anyone could ever do that.

Lauren Bacall was in it, and Len Cariou! I, of course, knew who they were. So that was number one. Joanie and I wanted so much to see *Applause*.

And I thought of it because when I went to see *Annie* the other night, I was sitting there watching, and in act two, during the radio show with Bert Healy, what sign lights up over and over? "Applause, Applause!" I just thought, *Well, if I get hit by a bus walking out of here, my life has come full circle.* You know? My father passed six years ago, and so it was interesting to go back there, and with Lonny, one of my oldest, dearest friends.

As far as *Applause*, I don't really remember anything else at all. I just remember the feeling of how much we loved the show.

From the 1940s through the 1960s, the Buitoni Spaghetti Bar was next to the Palace. You walked in, put 25 cents in a slot, sat on a stool, and a conveyor belt brought you spaghetti. The conveyor belt even took your dirty dishes away! There were signs that said "Try it… buy it!" Buitoni Spaghetti Bar was one of the first chains with real brand endorsement in the center of Times Square.

Ted Chapin said, "My brothers and I would go to the Buitoni Spaghetti Bar together before matinees. Most people went to Howard Johnson's across the street, but we loved Buitoni. The waitresses wore shapely vests that said Buitoni, and since we were teenage boys, we enjoyed that just as much as our plates of spaghetti."

The locale is now the Money Exchange booth, but in recent years has been a Body Shop and a Foot Locker.

1975: *Goodtime Charley*

Terry Finn, Actor

My first Broadway show was *Goodtime Charley*. I was in college already. We had a lot of Broadway scores that I used to dance around the living room to, my favorites being *My Fair Lady* and *West Side Story*, but I never saw a show. It just wasn't part of… maybe my parents didn't go out anymore. I was the 5th kid, so by the time I came along, my parents had been there, done that. It was kind of like, *Let's just get through this and get this kid out of the house.*

I remember Joel Grey in *Goodtime Charley*. He was already famous to me because of *Cabaret*. I remember the "Goodtime Charley" song.

That song is the first thing I ever heard Lonny Price sing. I thought that was weirdly karmic. After we were all cast in *Merrily We Roll Along*, we had these gatherings before we started rehearsals. Lonny sat at the piano in his room and Steve Sondheim was there, and at the piano he sang "Goodtime Charley." I thought, *Wow, I can't believe you're singing that song. That was my first Broadway show.*

The 1975 film The Sunshine Boys, *adapted from the play by Neil Simon, follows the story of two former vaudeville comedians—so of course there's a moment outside the Palace. As Walter Matthau walks down Broadway, we can see* Goodtime Charley *at the Palace, and billboards next to it for* Grease *and* Raisin.

1977: Never Again

Neil Mazzella, Technical Supervisor

I bought tickets to *Man of La Mancha* at the Palace, and I ended up sitting in the last row of the second balcony.

My mother turned to me and said, "This is the best you can do?" So, I always made sure I never went to that balcony again, especially now that I work in the theatre!

1978: … And *All That Jazz*

Eileen Casey, Actor

I worked with Bob Fosse on a couple of shows, and I was also in his movie *All That Jazz*.

The movie opens with this audition sequence that we shot at the Palace Theatre. We shot a lot of the movie at the Kaufman Astoria Studios before they were renovated. It was basically a big warehouse where they built this replica of Broadway Dance, Fosse's favorite studio to rehearse in.

We worked really hard on every scene in the movie, we rehearsed forever. Then we were supposed to start shooting, and all of the girls realized we hadn't been called for a costume fitting. Fosse wanted us to wear our rehearsal clothes, and he wanted Cheryl Clark, who was doing this specific moment in "Take Off With Us" to go topless. There was some disagreement.

This was on a Friday afternoon and we were supposed to start shooting on Monday. They gave her an ultimatum and she said she wasn't going to do it. So they called Sandahl Bergman who was on vacation, and she came in, and then we had to rehearse for a whole other week. We taught her the whole number. Everyone kind of went, "Oh, another week's pay? Okay."

Shooting with Fosse was great. It was fun and hard. I had done *Pippin* and *Dancin'* with him, and then there was *this*. After I did *All That Jazz* I said, "Nothing can top this." I mean, what could I do then? I thought: *Everything is going to be so weird, and not as good, from now on.*

The opening scene of All That Jazz *finds Joe Gideon, Fosse's fictional version of himself played by Roy Scheider, holding auditions for a new musical at the Palace. Indeed, the real-life auditions for several of his shows were held there. Fosse also spent time at the Palace professionally, working on* Sweet Charity *and socially, with Ann Reinking during her run in* Goodtime Charley.

The audition scene that opens All That Jazz *gives a glimpse into Fosse's mind as a director, and also gives a glimpse at the Palace Theatre in 1978. When the character makes his exit, there are Times Square billboards for* The Wiz, A Broadway Musical, *and* I Love My Wife *visible outside the Palace doors.*

All That Jazz *was supposed to film for two days at the Palace, but this ballooned to a seven day shoot, due to Fosse's perfectionist nature. Fosse spoke in Schieder's ear through an earpiece the entire time, guiding him through the cattle call with real-time opinions on the dancers. The masterful scene truly was Fosse's own version of* A Chorus Line *but in only 15 minutes.*

In June of 1987, George Abbott's 100th birthday celebration was held at the Palace. Fosse was upset by Fred Astaire's death that day, but he and Gwen Verdon participated nevertheless, alongside Helen Hayes, Kitty Carlisle Hart, Butterfly McQueen, Betty Comden and Adolph Green, Nanette Fabray, Jose Ferrer, Carol Channing, and Harold Prince.

Four months and eight days later, Bob Fosse's memorial was held at the Palace Theatre. John Kander, Fred Ebb, and Peter Allen—all of whom wrote songs that filled All That Jazz—*played the Palace in his memory.*

1979: We Closed On Opening Night

James Woolley, Stage Manager

My Broadway debut as a stage manager was on a show called *Break a Leg*, which played the Palace. It closed on opening night, and starred the great Julie Harris!

When we were in rehearsal, we were laughing so much. We constantly had tears rolling down our cheeks. We thought we had the biggest hit of the century!

Then we previewed at the old Stratford Theatre in Connecticut and at intermission, there was a traffic jam in the parking lot of people trying to get away from us. I don't even know why we came into New York after that.

The day after opening at the Palace, I remember Julie saying, "Do we have to do it again?" And we didn't. We closed on opening night, which was not uncommon in those days.

———————————

In 1979, Joel Grey returned to the Palace for The Grand Tour, *a short-lived Jerry Herman musical. The show was about the unlikely pairing of a Jewish man and an anti-Semitic colonel, as they tried to escape the Nazis. It played 61 performances. Both* Break a Leg *and* Frankenstein *closed on opening night at the Palace, in 1979 and 1981. In the* Times, *Frank Rich described* Frankenstein*'s creature as "a beery lout in a Halloween costume."[12]*

———————————

1979: You Can Feel The History

Harry Groener, Actor

I was born in Germany, and I immigrated to America in 1953. I lived in San Francisco for a while, but when I came to New York, I just fell in love. I said: *This is it.* I fell in love with the city and everything about the East Coast.

My first Broadway show was *Oklahoma!* and I was just in awe of the Palace Theatre. At that time, it had this classic marquee. Now the theater is covered up, with a hotel on top of it. It's encased in real estate. Even though, you still go into the Palace and you stand there and you can just feel the history of it. You can't help but think of everybody that played there, the vaudeville, Judy Garland, the musicals... and there I was, playing Will Parker in *Oklahoma!* on that stage!

Agnes DeMille was still alive and very much a part of our production. William Hammerstein, Oscar's son, directed it. Jay Blackton, who was the original conductor of the original company, was our conductor. I would stand on the Palace stage looking down into the pit and think about how the face looking back at me was the same face that the original company saw. It was stunning.

Agnes was really something. The production was initially supposed to just be a road company. After we did nine months on the road, they wanted to bring us to Broadway, but Agnes said, "Not with these sets and costumes!" We got all new sets and costumes. We came into New York, and had the greatest nine months. It was thrilling.

Richard Rodgers was still alive but he was fading fast. I remember that he was at a performance but I didn't get to meet him.

I don't feel as enamored by the East Coast anymore, as I did when I was doing my first Broadway show. But it's okay. That's just what happens sometimes. You fall out of love.

———————————

[12] Rich, Frank. "Theater: 'Frankenstein' Has Premiere At Palace." *The New York Times.* 5 Jan. 1981. Retrieved from nytimes.com.

1979: The Night After Richard Rodgers Died

Jessica Molaskey, Actor

I moved to the city in 1979, and I got my first audition for a Broadway show—and I booked it. I had gotten my Equity card doing *Oklahoma!* at the MUNY with Mary Wickes, this ubiquitous character actress from the 1940s and 1950s. I saw her in New York, and she said, "I'm coming to Broadway with *Oklahoma!*, and they need one girl, so I'm going to recommend you."

I went to the open call, and there were *hundreds* of people. I had never been to one before. I had a rolled-up copy of "How Are Things in Glocca Morra?" and I went to the head of the line and said, "Mr. Hammerstein is expecting me." They let me in!

Back then, the Palace didn't have the facade on it. I can't believe we ever let them change it! When I first came to New York, I was very active—a lot of us were—in trying to landmark buildings because they were tearing them down right and left. It was like, "What, are you kidding me? How are you going to tear down the Palace?" But they basically did. It was this beautiful, old building. Still, it's pretty intact on the inside. You "played the Palace," and that inside is still there, even if the outside was destroyed.

Agnes DeMille was very actively involved with our *Oklahoma!* We basically did it exactly how it was for the original production. We didn't have mics on. There were mics on the floor, but that was it. We met a lot of the original company when I did *Oklahoma!* and that was really fun.

It was such a beautiful family. As a matter of fact, during the out-of-town run of the show, Marty Vidnovic had a baby and her name is Laura Benanti. Her mom was doing *Brigadoon* down the street at the time. Marty was only on for a few minutes during the show, so he would bring Laura and we would hold her and babysit her in the dressing rooms. It's crazy. I see her now and I'm like, *I held you in my arms in the Palace dressing room, and you're so gorgeous now, you're a star.* It's beautiful when theatre feels like home like that.

Also, the thing about theaters is that you really get to know a lot of the doormen. If I had to go to the bathroom, there's a million theaters where I could just walk in the door. Or if I wanted to sit and watch tech[13] rehearsals for something. You just get to know those people, and they're so sweet.

On New Year's Eve, the day after Richard Rodgers died, we were in the show and we could hear the revelers. The show was long—it came down at 11:15, maybe. They called us in in the afternoon and said "Would you guys be willing to sing 'The hills are alive with the sound of music' at the end of the show, after curtain call?"

It starts out a cappella with the women, and then it builds and builds. But there were all these people out with their noisemakers, because it was only 45 minutes til midnight—and you could sort of hear them coming through. So we just started singing from the verse: "I go to the hills…" I can't talk about it without crying.

We could just hear all of these people outside while we were singing. It was almost like this celestial chorus ushering Mr. Rodgers up. I'll never forget that. Then we had a glass of champagne downstairs, and I walked outside. It was snowing.

---

[13] tech: intense technical rehearsals for a show that involve integrating every element of the production; a time when it is not appropriate to get engaged

1981: "My Husband Has To Smell Her"

Diane Heatherington, Box Office Treasurer

The first show I worked on at the Palace was *Woman of the Year*. The balcony of the theater wasn't opened up at that time. When Judy Garland had played the Palace, they had the whole house open, but when Broadway shows came in, they never used the top balcony.

Then they decided to open the balcony for *La Cage*, because it was such a hit that they needed the seats! When they told us in the box office, we didn't know how to tell people to get up there. We didn't know how to get up there ourselves. We had to go up to the boxes and climb over the bar to get to the balcony, and then climb back down to figure it out!

The Palace had a small elevator off to one side that was only big enough to fit one or two people. It went up to the manager's office. That tiny elevator was always intriguing.

Most of the craziest things I've heard while working in the box office happened at the Palace.

When Raquel Welch came in to do *Woman of the Year*, her husband, André, was her manager so he would come into the box office and hang out and check to see how everything was going. One day when he was there, a lady came up to the window and asked to buy the best seats we had available. I told her I'd be glad to give those to her, and as I was looking, she kept insisting that they just had to be the best seats. She said, "You don't understand. My husband has to smell her."

André got up and went to the window and said, "Excuse me?" The lady started laughing and said, "My husband is just a really big Raquel Welch fan and he told me it's important that he gets to smell her." I said, "Well, this is *her* husband."

One time, during *La Cage*, a woman came up to me at intermission in tears. I asked if she was okay and she told me that everyone at her hotel had told her that this was the show to see, but that it was against her religion. She had a very Southern accent, and I'll never forget that she said, "I can't believe there are homosexuals in there!"

I said, "Are you talking about the ones onstage or the ones sitting next to you?"

Sometimes you just have to wonder how people wake up in the morning and go outside and get around, when they say things like that. Another favorite in the box office is, "What time does the eight o'clock show start?"

———————

Several actors at the Palace spoke about the backstage elevator operator. The Palace is the only Broadway theater that has one. Whoever is operating the elevator has a track,[14] just the same as an actor in the show. "Scene three: go down to second floor, pick up these four people, go to stage level." The tiny elevator travels through the dressing room tower throughout the night, following along with the show.

The Palace also has a front-of-house elevator that takes people up to the mezzanine. Late at night after the show, when there's no one in the theater but the custodial staff and ushers, many of them have said that they've heard this elevator start to move. Rumor has it that the elevator has its own ghost, perhaps an old actor, stagehand, or usher.

———————

[14] track: an assigned set of tasks carried out by a production member in a specific job throughout the course of a performance

In 1927, the head usher at the Palace, Murray Roe, was found dead in Central Park in between two boulders. The beloved usher had been suffering from asthma attacks. Upon his death, the theatre world found out that Murray was the son of the acclaimed writer E. P. Roe. He had inherited a huge estate and been a popular member of New York society and innovative engineer at the turn of the century. In 1905, he was married, and a year later, he was divorced and moved to South America. When he returned to America in 1913, he had lost his fortune. He became a porter and then an usher at the Palace Theatre, where he was cherished for his humility and leadership. Perhaps the elevator is just Murray Roe saying hello...

————————————

1983: The Parade Of Stars

Mel Marvin, Writer/Arranger

One of my favorite experiences was this one-of-a-kind show produced by Alexander Cohen. It was called the *Parade of Stars Playing The Palace.* It was this huge television special shown on a Saturday night on CBS.

I love the Palace. The glamour quotient of playing that show there... the whole thing was spectacular. They took the extraordinary history of the Palace Theatre and celebrated it with all of these stars. Lauren Bacall performed from *Applause*, and Gwen Verdon performed from *Sweet Charity*. They went all the way back to the beginning of the Palace Theatre, so Sandy Duncan and Don Correia played Fred and Adele Astaire. Shelley Winters and Milton Berle and Carol Channing all performed. Berle had been there when the theater was a vaudeville house!

And I got to work with all of these stars, doing the arrangements for the program. I got to go to their homes and to rehearsal studios, and spend time putting together this amazing evening. My favorite experience was rehearsing the *Sweet Charity* number. Gwen Verdon was doing a different cut of "If They Could See Me Now", so I went into a studio with just her and Bob Fosse. I was 40 years old or so, and I was just awestruck playing the piano for these two theatre legends. He treated her like the queen of the world. Watching the two of them work was something special that I'll never forget.

1983: From *La Cage Aux Folles* To *Kinky Boots*

Daryl Roth, Producer

I was lucky enough to make some wonderful friends who worked in the theatre, long before I became a Broadway producer.

One of my most memorable Broadway experiences was taking my son, Jordan, to see the original *La Cage aux Folles*, written by Harvey Fierstein and Jerry Herman. Jerry graciously gave us a backstage tour, including the wig room, the costume room, and the sets onstage. My thrill was seeing the excitement and bright eyes of a young boy who adored theatre and thought he was in heaven.

When I think about *La Cage aux Folles* being one of the early shows that Jordan and I shared, I am grateful for that journey which brought us to *Kinky Boots*.[15]

————————————

La Cage aux Folles was originally supposed to be written not by Jerry Herman but by Maury Yeston. At that point, the show was to be called The Queen of Basin Street. *Lack of financing caused the rights to switch hands, and eventually Herman wound up writing* La Cage. *The show, which played the Palace for 1,761 performances made*

————————————

[15] Check out *The Untold Stories of Broadway, Volume 1* for more on this story.

Herman the first composer-lyricist to have three shows that ran over 1,500 performances on Broadway: Hello, Dolly!, Mame, *and* La Cage aux Folles.

―――――――――

1983: The Razzle Dazzle

Hunter Bell, Actor/Writer

The Booth holds a magical allure to it, but the theater I want to work in the most is the Palace. I've always been so intrigued by the history of it, and the location. The façade is unlike anything else.

I also love the Martin Beck and the Virginia—with all respect to the new names, those theaters are frozen in time for me. They are locked in my heart and brain with those names. And I love the Booth for the intimacy and the Palace for the razzle dazzle.

I saw the original production of *La Cage aux Folles* at the Palace and it rocked my world. I was just a little theatre nerd in the 1980s and it was so big and gay and fabulous—it blew me away. It was larger than life. It gave the Palace this really specific feeling for me that has always lasted.

―――――――――

In the mid-1980s, Aaron Sorkin was a bartender at the Palace Theatre. Originally an actor, he was also a runner for the TKTS booth before he sat down at a typewriter. Much of A Few Good Men *was originally scribbled on cocktail napkins at the Palace Theatre bar during act one of* La Cage aux Folles. *Within a few years, the bartender turned Broadway playwright when* A Few Good Men *opened a few blocks south at the Music Box.*

When actor Peter Krause auditioned for Sorkin's Sports Night, *Krause reminded him that they worked together at the bar at the Palace. Sorkin was the bar manager at that point and Krause was a bartender.*

―――――――――

1986: Condemned Floors

Joe Traina, House Manager

In 1986, shortly out of college, I went to work for the Nederlander Organization. I was an administrative assistant. The offices of Jimmy Nederlander and of Arthur Rubin, former Nederlander Organization vice-president, were across the hall. I'd bring them messages, transfer calls, make coffee, and tend to guests.

At that time, the offices were located in the Palace Theatre Building. Those offices are no longer there because the building was razed to make way for the hotel that was built above it. We entered from the street, walked into the theatre lobby and would take an elevator on the right up to the Nederlander offices. Only floors one through five were occupied because the fire code would not allow the upper floors to be used.

―――――――――

In the 1980 movie Fame, *the character of Montgomery—played by Paul McCrane—lives in a loft inside the Palace Theatre building. When he plays the guitar and sings "Is It Okay If I Call You Mine?" we see a shot of Times Square at night, zooming in on a neon pink sign blinking "Palace." To the right are* Grease *and* Annie *billboards, and to the left, one window has a dim light.* Oklahoma! *is playing below. The character, a student at the High School of Performing Arts, plays one of the most indelible songs from the popular movie musical in a pool of calm, as his dark room is lit up every other moment by the Palace neon. The old* Fame *school, chronicled in the movie, where Monty, Coco and the others danced on cars and dreamed big, was just one block over, on 46th Street.*

The original Palace Theatre building where Monty lived was 12 stories high and very narrow except for two middle floors that were built right over the actual theater lobby. The booking offices of the B.F. Keith vaudeville circuit and the Orpheum circuit were the first to be in the Palace Theatre building. Arthur Hammerstein also had offices there. When the Nederlanders took over the theater in the 1960s, they also took over the offices. In the late 1980s, the theater was empty for about three years so that the Doubletree Hotel could be built over the Palace. The original tower was torn down.

La Cage *had to close for the Embassy Suites Hotel to open. The show was supposed to move to the Hellinger but this was deemed too expensive. A couple years later, the Hellinger would close too.*[16]

1987: When The Names Would Roll

Laura Heller, General Manager

I always try to go to Gypsy of the Year and the Easter Bonnet.[17] They're so special. Broadway Cares/Equity Fights AIDS events really bring us together as a community. The events were started at the Palace Theatre in 1987 during the original run of *La Cage aux Folles.* The cast and crew of that show decided to try to raise some money to help people who were suffering from this new, horrific disease.

I was there from the beginning and saw all of that. There were times when they would roll names of victims during the show and you'd see the names of friends who you didn't realize had died. Friends you didn't even realize had been sick. People would just sob. That's what it used to be about.

A lot of people just disappeared. You wouldn't hear from someone for a couple months, and you'd go, "Oh my God, what happened to him?" Then you'd find out that he'd gone back home. There was such a stigma about it that a lot of people didn't want to stay with their friends. They were forced to go home to families that had rejected them because of their sexual preferences—that's where they had to go to die.

A group of us would get together once a week and decide which of us would go to visit which person's hospital room with food. We all tried to help out. That's how the Stage Managers' Association was started, based on the people who were getting together... it was all stage managers at first. At one point while we were doing this, people in the group started saying, "We really don't have a voice at Equity. Maybe we can get a voice of our own." Then we put together the Association while we were also spending our time figuring out taking care of our friends who were so ill.

The devastation that AIDS had on this industry is unbelievable to young people of today. I just don't think it can be explained. It wasn't just the creative people who died; it was stage managers, technicians, so many others. What theatre is today is completely different because we lost Michael Bennett. But there were so many.

When the names would roll, there were hundreds. It was devastating. It got to the point where anytime you hadn't heard from a friend, you would start worrying about them. And a lot of the time, you would be right, and they were sick.

---

[16] Check out *The Untold Stories of Broadway, Volume 1* for more on this story.

[17] The Gypsy of the Year and Easter Bonnet competitions are annual events held by Broadway Cares/Equity Fights AIDS in the winter and spring, respectively. Each is held in a Broadway theater and involve current shows coming together to raise millions of dollars in support of the organization. Shows raise money through donations at their own theaters, culminating in a showcase. At Gypsy of the Year, cast members from each show (often ensemble members, or "gypsies") perform an original act, ranging from parody songs to choreographed dances. At the Easter Bonnet competition, the variety acts also include custom-made bonnets from each production. Both events attract the biggest stars that Broadway has to offer, who pitch in to help fundraise for those in need.

In 2013 alone, Broadway Cares/Equity Fights AIDS distributed over $10 million to those in need. Their annual events have continued to bring the community together to raise money and awareness for almost three decades.

1994: Broadway Theaters Are Like Superman

Alan Menken, Writer

I remember walking into the Palace for the first time when *Beauty and the Beast* was coming in. It felt like the theater was undressed. You walk in the front door and there are no ticket takers and it's daytime. There are planks of wood all over the place, and half-built sets. People are hammering and shouting and warming up.

Broadway theaters are kind of like Superman. You know, during the day, they're Clark Kent, and it's only when the lights are down and people buy tickets and get Playbills and walk in that it becomes Superman.

I remember thinking: *This is our home for now*. And the Irish pub next door, Langan's: *This will be the regular place we go during the run of this show.*

Then there are the audiences who are your friends and the audiences who aren't your friends. That's a bracing experience. It's like in the movie *A Bronx Tale*, when the bikers come into the bar and create trouble and say, "We're not leaving." Then the door closes and they're told, "Now you can't leave." When you open a show, it feels a little like that. "Now you can't leave. We're going to write whatever we want about you, and say whatever we want. You're on display here now."

1994: A Rookie In The World Series

Rick Sordelet, Fight Director

I've done over 50 different Broadway shows, and worked in almost all the different theaters. *Beauty and the Beast* was my first one.

Beauty and the Beast started at the Palace, and then we moved to the Lunt-Fontanne. There were several fight directors up for that job. I went to school with Rob Roth, the director. At the time, he was 27 years old and he had been a big part of talking Michael Eisner into doing theatrical musicals. He has the cojones of a dinosaur and has never been afraid to share his vision.

Rob had been doing shows in Los Angeles and faxing Michael Eisner to come see his work. He finally got him there, and Michael was impressed. They decided Rob would work on a stage version of *Mary Poppins*. Rob got to work on it, and then Michael met Andrew Lloyd Webber at a party. Andrew Lloyd Webber said to him, "You should do *Beauty and the Beast*. It's a perfect musical, and it would be perfect for the stage." Michael responded, "Yeah, but it's got a teapot and candlesticks and we already have the theme park show."

But Michael started thinking about it and he called Rob. Ideas began percolating, and they realized that if they could start the story just as the people had turned into inanimate objects, they could Imagineer the whole thing.

Rob wanted me to be the fight director but he had to meet with several candidates. In the meantime, Disney asked me to go down to Walt Disney World to help with an arbitration. The actor playing Gaston in their theme

34

park show thought he should get more money because a sequence in the show was a fight rather than a battle sequence. They wanted my opinion.

I was a little worried that being a part of that discussion might hurt me, in terms of getting the job on Broadway. It turned out to be the opposite. I got along well with everyone there, and I ended up looking at their *Indiana Jones* show too. They said, "What do you think? Could you make it better?" and I said, "Hire me and find out!"

That led to me getting a job on the Super Bowl Halftime Show. One of the Disney folks I met on the arbitration was Bettina Buckley, and she called up Rob and said, "I found a fight director I really like for *Beauty* on Broadway." Rob told her, "I already have a guy I really like." She said, "This guy's name is Rick Sordelet," and he said, "That's my guy!"

That's how I got the job. The gods smiled on me. I got my first Broadway job and I've never looked back.

I had done lots of regional theatre, but once we got into tech for *Beauty and the Beast*, I was really surprised by the number of people who were there! There were two dozen computer consoles and everyone was working so hard. And I was really impressed with IATSE.[18] Our guys in regional theaters were really good and worked really hard, but when I got to know IATSE... well, there's a reason that it's called Local One. Those guys are great, and I was amazed by how hard they work. They set a gold standard for how things are done, and for me, it really set a high bar. I felt like a rookie going into the World Series. It was like I was on the Yankees and we were going all the way. It was great.

———————————

In 1991, when Disney's animated Beauty and the Beast *film premiered, chief* New York Times *theatre critic Frank Rich said that it had "the best Broadway musical comedy score of the year."[19] This was part of the catalyst for Disney chairman Michael Eisner to create Disney's theatrical division and begin bringing musicals to Broadway.*

Beauty and the Beast *debuted at the Palace and became the longest-running show to ever play there, from 1994 to 1999. The show moved to the Lunt-Fontanne Theatre to make room for Disney's* Aida, *which played a successful run from 2000 to 2004, one of the longest runs of any musical to not be nominated for Best Musical at the Tony Awards. In between* Beauty and the Beast *and* Aida, *Disney had their most significant artistic triumph on Broadway with* The Lion King, *which opened in 1997 and is still running, making it the longest-running Disney musical on Broadway.* Tarzan *and* The Little Mermaid *had disappointing Broadway runs,* Mary Poppins *had a more respectable engagement, and Disney's two most recent ventures,* Newsies *and* Aladdin, *have been very successful, even playing back to back at the Nederlander and New Amsterdam for a while.*

———————————

1995: An Elementary School Trip To *Beauty And The Beast*

Jonathan Groff, Actor

The first Broadway show that I ever saw was *Beauty and the Beast*. The thing that I remember most about it was that at intermission, one of my elementary school teachers walked over to me and said, "One day, you are going to be in that pit playing your trumpet on Broadway." I played the trumpet in 5th grade.

I had never even been in a real play before, and I remember thinking, "No, I'm gonna be onstage." I was only nine years old but I just had a feeling that I would be acting on Broadway, not playing my trumpet!

———————————

[18] IATSE: The International Alliance of Theatrical Stage Employees
[19] Rich, Frank. *The New York Times*. 13 Nov. 1991. Retrieved from nytimes.com.

1995: I Saw My Second Broadway Show From The Sound Booth

Andrew Keenan-Bolger, Actor

When I got the part of Chip in *Beauty and the Beast*, I was nine years old. My whole family relocated from Michigan to New York for a year. In hindsight, that's a really cool thing my family did for me. It was an incredible sacrifice. Then, after a year, my parents were like, "Okay! It's time for us to go back home." We went back to Michigan.

The Palace is a huge theater. After I got cast, my parents asked if we could see the show. *Beauty and the Beast* was a really hot ticket in its day, and we hadn't been able to get tickets! They told us they were sold out, but we could sit in the sound booth to watch. That's how I saw my second-ever Broadway show: from a sound booth!

The Palace is a token Broadway theater. It feels lavish and it feels ancient at the same time. There's an old-timey backstage elevator that goes up to the 8th floor, and there's an elevator operator to control it! I became really good friends with the elevator operator during *Beauty and the Beast,* and I'd just ride up and down with her. The backstage felt old and tiny, and you were stacked on top of each other. A lot of backstage felt like it was still in its original form—and then you'd get out onstage and everything was cutting edge!

Up until that point, I don't think I had any relationships with adults other than my parents. I got to make those through *Beauty and the Beast*, and that was something really unique to have as a kid. The group that I was doing a show with felt like a lot of big sisters, big brothers, aunts and uncles. I think part of it was working on a Disney musical. You feel so surrounded by families.

I felt so close to my cast, and I had serious conversations with adults that I never would have had just going to school in Michigan. I'm still very close with a lot of those people. A lot of them took me under their wing. There was one guy who played in the pit who found out that I was kind of a musical theatre nerd, and really started educating me. He basically turned me into the musical theatre dork that I am today.

I still see Kerry Butler all the time. She was my first Belle, and it was her Broadway debut as well. She would always come up with really fun things to do backstage for the two Chips[20]—but she'd include everyone. During Thanksgiving, we always had a hand turkey contest. People would go full-out crazy! The makeup people would design beautiful art. They would hang it all on the wall outside the dressing rooms and everyone would vote. There were big prizes. I came in third place for my hand turkey. I really loved working with her. Marc Kudisch was my Gaston. Jeff McCarthy was my Beast. It was a very all-star cast.

I became really close with the swings.[21] There was a woman named Terri Furr, who I still keep in very close touch with. She has a daughter now and her daughter just played Chip in *Beauty and the Beast* at their community theater! Terri recently brought her daughter to *Newsies*. Terri was around the age I am now, when she was doing *Beauty and the Beast*. It was really cool to take a picture of all of us on a Broadway stage. Three generations.

I love the Palace. That backstage… it's painted differently than it was in 1995, but even now when I go to drop things off for my friends who are in shows there, I still get so wide-eyed walking down those stairs.

---

[20] Due to child labor restrictions, many shows featuring children, including *Beauty and the Beast,* hire multiple actors to alternate in one role.
[21] swing: an off stage understudy who covers multiple roles

1995: When Andrew Was Chip

Celia Keenan-Bolger, Actor

I think *Beauty and the Beast* is an amazing show! The fact that my brother was in it... I remember that growing up, my mom's sisters would sometimes say to me, "You came out onstage and I just started crying!" I always thought that seemed weird. Then, when Andrew was Chip on Broadway, I understood.

I felt so proud. I couldn't believe it was happening! I remember thinking, *How did they just carry his head across that stage on a tray? That is definitely his little face and his voice. What is happening?* It was the magic of theatre, and also the magic of feeling connected to someone you love onstage. It was crazy and a genuinely magical experience. I loved that show.

I was a freshman in college, so it was at the peak of all theatre nerdom in my world. I was in a musical theatre program so I knew everything that was playing on Broadway. I just remember feeling so lucky to have an "in" when I would come home to visit, because my brother was part of the theatre community.

There's a place where everyone stands backstage at the Palace. It's not a green room, but it's the place where everybody sort of waits. I would stand there, just to watch Marc Kudisch walk by and Beth Fowler and Andréa Burns and Kerry Butler... all of these people who I was just so in awe of. It made me feel a little bit close to that. It was so special and lucky.

When I interviewed Brynn O'Malley, who was playing Grace in Annie *at the Palace, we chatted in her dressing room just before a performance. I got to see the Palace elevator, the dressing rooms, the backstage. We were chatting away when the stage manager called "half-hour,"*[22] *and on my way out, Brynn and I ended up in that same Palace waiting area, where a cast member was celebrating a birthday. I watched a slew of orphans, Jane Lynch, stagehands, dressers—everyone—all gather under the stage to sing "Happy Birthday". The orphans began chanting some new lyrics to a tune from* Annie. *Brynn said, "Oh, they make up a new song for everyone's birthday."*

As we walked out onto 47th Street, I realized that no one had questioned that I was there. I was just Brynn's friend, standing backstage with her, welcome to be part of the party. As Celia said about standing in the same spot 18 years earlier, getting to feel a little bit close to that was special and lucky.

That's Broadway.

1995: My First Time Backstage

Heidi Blickenstaff, Actor

I grew up in California with Sarah Uriarte Berry, who was the first replacement Belle in *Beauty and the Beast*. I remember going to see her in that show and going backstage afterwards.

It was the first time I had ever been backstage in a Broadway theater, and it was at the Palace. I remember trying to act super cool and nonchalant, like it wasn't my first time, like I had been backstage on Broadway a bunch of times before. But I was kind of dying inside. You know, you dream this dream as a kid and of course it also includes the backstage part: signing in every night and going to your dressing room and being friends with all of the people backstage. All of that was very much in my Broadway fantasy too.

---

[22] half-hour: the time by which actors are required by Equity to be present in the theater; a warning that signals there are 30 minutes until the show begins

Every bit of that backstage was crowded with forks and spoons and dresses, and every kind of prop and flying set piece. I had just seen the show, so I was familiar with everything that had been onstage, but to see how it was stored backstage was really phenomenal. At that point, I had done some national tours and been in big theaters across the country. Most of them are much larger than Broadway theaters; there's more square footage available for theaters downtown in other U.S. cities. But in New York, you really have to be creative to fit everything into the theater.

Sarah showed me the yellow ball gown, and told me how much it cost. It was an exorbitant amount of money. Then she told me that at her final audition, she and the other girl who were up for the part both had to try on the dress. They didn't have the money in the budget to build a new one, so they could change the actress but they couldn't change the dress.

Sarah joked, "I guess I fit the dress better." She was so lovely and gracious that night, very "this is not a big deal" in a humble way. Meanwhile, inside I was like: *Oh my God, this is the biggest deal of all time ever in my life.*

———————

When I was 14 and on my first-ever trip to NYC, all I wanted was to see Adam Pascal in Aida. *Of the musical theatre stars I loved most from cast recordings, he was the one who was leading a brand-new Broadway show that I could actually see. My family got to the Palace, tickets in hand, and according to the big board in the lobby, some understudy named Will Chase was on.*

I started bawling and screaming like I was dying, and I turned red from crying, the way only a 14-year-old fan can. The box office took pity on us and exchanged our tickets for the Sunday matinee, the last day of our trip, when Adam would hopefully be back in the show. At 7:40pm, my mom, sister, and I ran down Broadway, knowing we had to see another show but not knowing what. We walked into the 42nd Street revival just as the curtain was coming up on those dancing feet, and it was one of the most magical theatrical nights I have ever had to this day.

That Sunday, we saw Will Chase give a fantastic performance as Radames. I bought a pre-signed Adam Pascal "Model Prisoner" CD at the merchandise booth and cried into the liner notes the whole plane ride back to Florida, thinking about how I'd just had the most incredible, life-changing week of my young adult life—but missed seeing the one star I wanted to see the most.

I have now seen Adam Pascal perform live plenty of times. I'm the hugest admirer of Will Chase, and am so grateful I got to see him in the role. And I never would've seen 42nd Street, one of my favorite classic musicals, in a production the likes of which Broadway will never see again, if we hadn't visited on a week when Adam Pascal was out sick.

Broadway is seeing stars that you've always wanted to see, live. But Broadway is also Idina Menzel breaking her rib and 200 teenagers crying outside the Gershwin, poor Maureen Moore giving a great performance for a theater full of audience members who wanted a refund, and mercury poisoning, and Linda Mugleston, and a broken foot even with a Tony in hand, and 20 Long Island women screaming outside the Imperial because all they wanted was Hugh Jackman.

I'm glad I turned red and sobbed hysterically in front of three startled Palace box office employees, a lobby full of families going to see Aida, *and everyone on Broadway between 47th Street and 42nd Street at 7:40pm that June night in 2000. It started my long history of embracing every understudy slip that falls out of a Playbill, not knowing to what new theatrical discovery or adventure it might lead.*

———————

2003: Getting To Know The Palace

Craig Carnelia, Writer

It's always a joy seeing my wife Lisa Brescia in the shows she's in. It was a great experience getting to know the Palace so well when she was there in *Aida* playing Amneris for the last year of the show's run. My daughter, Daisy, was 10 or 11 at the time, and we would go see the show often.

On closing day, Daisy and I went backstage after the show. We were out on the Palace stage by ourselves, waiting for Lisa to pack up her dressing room. There was a red deck in that show, and Daisy and I actually laid down on it together. We didn't say it out loud, but we were communing with it in some way. Daisy said how sorry she was to leave this theater, and I said, "Maybe you'll be back in a show of your own someday." You know, she might be!

———————————

A large amount of real estate on the same block as the Palace is taken up by the Times Square McDonald's. America's most ubiquitous fast food chain took the place of a very European fast food chain—Wienerwald—which used to occupy the building. From schnitzel to crocks of beer, Wienerwald served Austrian specialties in a themed environment. In the 1970s, Wienerwald was a favorite Times Square stop for families.

The real estate across 7th Avenue and Broadway from the Palace was once a Broadway house as well. When the Palace was built, the southwest corner of 47th and Broadway was a piano factory belonging to manufacturer Frederick Mathushek. By 1918, the Shuberts had built the Central Theatre there. Richard Rodgers' first full Broadway musical score was heard at the Central: Poor Little Ritz Girl. *Just like the Palace, the Central began struggling, and it turned to movies in the late 1920s. Burlesque and all-girl revues were seen at the theater, and over the years it experienced several name changes, to the Columbia and the Holiday.*

During a return to legitimate theater in the 1950s, the theater housed a hit Yiddish revue called Bagels and Yox. *In 1956, the theater housed its last Broadway show:* Debut, *which closed after five performances. The theater was turned into a movie house, first called the Odeon, then the Forum, then Movieland. In 1989, the lobby became the Roxy Deli and the auditorium became a disco called Dance USA. In 1998, the auditorium was demolished and became the W Hotel. In 2013, the Roxy Deli became a Radio Shack.*

———————————

2004: The Republican National Convention

Jeb Brown, Actor

Years after seeing my first Broadway show, *Applause*, I got to play the Palace in *Aida*. It was thrilling. As a kid, one doesn't differentiate between the theaters, but as an adult, knowing you're in the same place that changed your life as a child...

The Palace is a gorgeous place with a labyrinthian backstage. The intense thing about the joint is that when you get into a run there with a cast of 30 or more, there are at least ten cast members that you never ever see. You're in the elevator, you go to your dressing room, you take the elevator to the stage. *Aida* was fast-moving, and everyone had a full evening, running hither and yon. There weren't a lot of communal spaces. There are narrow hallways. And the show was full of automation. So we all just ran past each other, or didn't see each other at all.

I remember our elevator operator, who spent the whole show going back and forth. For three hours the guy had his own track! The 5th floor to the 6th floor, the 6th floor to the stage, and so on. You wait for three people, you go down, you bring hats up to the 8th floor, go back to stage management. There was a long run sheet for the elevator operator on the elevator wall.

When my wife came to visit me, she was outraged that this poor soul had to spend his career in this tiny elevator. She's not in theatre and she was shocked. Maybe it wasn't a particularly humane thing to have anybody do. Maybe she was right. Showbiz isn't always pretty.

The orchestra was in the pit, but there were also a handful of members in a room on the 6th floor because the pit couldn't fit them all. It felt like the beginning of a time when that was happening; I feel like *Avenue Q,* just a little later on, might have been the first show I was aware of where the entire band was somewhere else.

I wish I had Judy Garland's ghost story from the Palace, but all I can tell you is that the dressing room that was hers has got to be one of the most beautiful on Broadway. Anyone you took backstage while working at the Palace would have to see it. It's just that special.

When I was doing *Aida*, the Republican National Convention was in New York City. It was 2004, and it was a big election. Bush was running for a second term, the Iraq War was pretty fresh, WMDs hadn't been found, 9/11 had happened... there were very strong feelings about whether that guy should be re-elected. It was post-Giuliani NY and peaceful protestors were being arrested all around Times Square... literally netted, in fact. And in the midst of this highly charged atmosphere, we suddenly found out, as a company, that we were going to be performing for a house full of Republican Convention-goers. It was a very intense thing, and there was talk amongst the ranks: *Is there any way we can call out as a company and just not perform?*

That may sound like the height of unprofessionalism, but people were not ashamed to speak out about how they felt at that moment politically. It was a heavy time, and many of us in the arts community felt at odds with the Republican Party as a whole. We wound up doing the show, and it was a good performance, but a very strange one, too.

Aida is a show about interracial romance, among other things, and the way that landed with that particular audience on that particular night was noticeably different than the way it landed eight shows a week regularly, for our four-year run. It was hard to believe we were feeling what we were feeling, but to this crowd the interracial relationship that was central to our story seemed to be received with palpable discomfort.

We had never felt that during the show before. This was in the final year of *Aida*'s run, and when a big show like that has run that long, there becomes an understood spectrum of expected response. And it wasn't an absent audience; they were very much with the story. But there was a real energy shift in terms of how they got involved. They seemed to be resisting the love story and leaning away from the moments where the couple would finally connect against the odds. The show's dramatic arc peaked in those moments, but this audience felt cool at best.

It felt like we were the floor show for this convention that many of us opposed. We were under contract and we had made peace with the idea of doing our jobs and doing them well. But to then have the show received like that... everyone in the company talked about it and processed it at length. It was very strange. It wasn't a small thing.

———————————

In 2006, the Palace was home to Lestat, *the third failed vampire musical on Broadway in half-a-decade, after* Dance of the Vampires *and* Dracula. *The previous tenant,* All Shook Up, *was its aesthetic opposite: a candy-coated Elvis jukebox musical with $19.55 tickets in the balcony in honor of the year the show was set. Just prior to that, Vanessa Williams and Linda Eder had played Palace concert engagements, hearkening back to the diva concert acts of the 1960s and 1970s. Of course nothing was as much of a throwback as* Liza's at the Palace.... *in 2008.*

———————————

2007: Blood In The Water

Michael Rupert, Actor/Writer

In *Legally Blonde*, something happened to me that was actually kind of scary.

We had an elevator room below the stage. The elevator would come up right near the end of the first act, before Elle does "So Much Better". The actor playing Aaron Schultz and I would load into the elevator, it would move up to the stage, and then we'd come out and I'd post the intern list.

During one performance, Bryce Ryness, who was playing the role, and I were getting into the elevator. It was dark, with just a little bit of blue light. Elle's dorm room set was in pieces, leaning against the wall, and in the dark, it fell on me and knocked me to the ground. It was huge and really heavy! Someone had forgotten to bungee cord it to the wall.

This was right before I was supposed to get in the elevator and go up to do the scene! Our head carpenter immediately got on his headset to Bonnie, our production stage manager, and she ran down to talk to me. I had 30 seconds before I had to get in the elevator, or the whole show would stop! My hands were all cut up, and I was bleeding, but I said, "I think I'm good. Let's go."

The first thing I had to do when I got off the elevator was say a line to Christian Borle. I forgot my line! I was so dazed by what had happened that I was like, "Emmett, you gaaa... waaa..."

Christian looked at me like, *Oh God, what's wrong with Rupert? Is he drunk?* I literally appeared to be drunk, because I was so woozy.

When I came off stage for intermission, everyone on staff was there. I felt so bad for the head carpenter, because he felt like it was his fault. Needless to say, after that, there was always a bungee cord around the wall.

2007: I Spent Two Years There

Christian Borle, Actor

Legally Blonde was a joyous, joyous group of people. We all cared about that show so much. That's part of what makes Jerry Mitchell and his shows so special. He really cares about the story and the people. The whole team on *Legally Blonde* spent a lot of time together: in the theater, in their dressing rooms, going out to bars, talking and trying to collaborate to get it just right.

Bill Berloni was the dog wrangler, and I had some bits to do with the dogs that played Bruiser. Bill would bring the dogs to my dressing room at half-hour, and we would have five minutes of bonding time. That was not a bad way to kick off the night. They were so sweet, those dogs.

I spent two years in my *Legally Blonde* dressing room in the Palace. I don't think I will ever have a dressing room as good as that one.

It was on the third floor, on the side. I was underneath Orfeh. There's a big star dressing room downstairs in the basement, which Laura Bell Bundy had. I think most of the stars have it because it's just very close to the stage. Then there are two that are on top of each other that have an anteroom and then a dressing room. It felt like I had a living room!

Because I didn't have to enter in *Legally Blonde* until a half-hour into the show, I had a whole hour in that dressing room. I binge-watched a lot of television. All of *The West Wing*, all of *Six Feet Under*, all of *The Wire*. Re-watched all of *Battlestar Galactica*. It was really quite a time.

———————

The Palace has a long history of animal acts, up through Legally Blonde. *In its vaudeville days, lions, monkeys, and dogs were on deck, and because of this, there was even a dressing room specifically for animals.*

When the theater opened, it had 32 dressing rooms, two backstage elevators, a green room on stage level, and an animal room. There was even an art gallery on the mezzanine level.

———————

2007: You Helped Me Find My Way

Laura Bell Bundy, Actor

Judy Garland was once in the dressing room I had at the Palace, and that's all I cared about. Judy at the Palace!

There are a lot of special doors at the Palace that get you backstage. If I went to see a show there, I could sneak right backstage. Some people say there are ghosts at the Broadway theaters, and I think there are, too—but not creepy ghosts, just spirits of people's lives.

We had all these pre-show traditions at *Legally Blonde*. On two-show days, we did a dance party five minutes before the second show. We had work-out routines we'd do backstage, and we did "Saturday Night on Broadway." At 15 minutes to curtain, the dog would come over to my dressing room and we'd bond. The girls at *Legally Blonde* would have these juice deliveries from Organic Avenue, with tons of bottles of juice, delivered on a Wednesday that would last through the week. I'd also pick a theme for the whole cast each night: Soap Opera Night or Pageant Night. Then there would be flavors of those themes throughout the whole night, backstage and onstage. It kept you on your toes and having fun.

I was onstage for pretty much the entire show of *Legally Blonde*, but I really felt like I got to know people despite the fact that I didn't have a lot of off stage time. There was a great vibe and energy on that show. We felt like such a family. Jerry Mitchell is such a positive person, and he'll cast people over and over who are good people that are great to work with. Because of that, his shows are always fantastic groups. And Jerry's all about hard work and telling a story, but he's also about fun. My best friends, to this day, are girls who were in *Legally Blonde*. I got a support system from that cast that I'm going to carry with me for the rest of my life.

For hundreds of shows, the dogs were amazing. And then there would be a night where a dog puked onstage. Right before the "Legally Blonde Remix", that happened during a performance, and Andy Karl was running out bringing Orfeh paper towels to clean up this dog barf on Broadway.

I lost my wig three times during the show. One time I bend-and-snapped so hard that it fell off. Another time, my wig fell off and I looked at the audience with just a wig cap on and said, "Thank you for coming to see *Legally Bald*!"

There was the night that someone in the front row was eating a bucket of Popeye's fried chicken. Another time, a woman in the front row had a Chihuahua on her lap. At the beginning of the second act, she put out a pee-pee pad in front of her seat, and the dog took a poo right in the middle of the show. This is at a Broadway show!

People don't realize how much the dressers and hair staff end up becoming your best friends. My dresser on *Legally Blonde*, Laura Ellington, really had my back. She was my protector and I could never have done the show without her. We had a routine for everything. We used to joke that dressing me backstage was like a kick-

42

stop at a Nascar race. Everything looked so expertly done because of her, and she was also there for emotional support, like, "Here's a tissue, sorry you went through a breakup."

Your backstage staff is there for everything. It becomes very intimate with the people who are there for you every day, who make sure your clothes are steamed, and that you have everything you need. It becomes so much more than just changing your clothes and doing your wig. You become intimately close with these people They know everything about your life. You can't escape each other, so you just end up talking all the time. You become so close.

People say that the Palace has a ghost, and many think it is Louis Borsalino. Borsalino was an acrobat who fell 18 feet to the stage during a performance in August of 1935. He was reaching for another acrobat's arms and missed. However, he was only injured—he did not die, as many assumed. Palace players who spot the Palace ghost say that they hear someone swinging up in the fly and then they hear screams.

The opening act at the Palace in July of 1926 was an Algerian acrobat named Sie Tahar Ben Belhassen. Reportedly, before going onstage, he said to a stage manager, "They say opening acts always die at the Palace but Sie Tahar no die." On opening night, he was found dead in his dressing room of a heart attack after completing his act onstage. He's much more likely to be the Palace ghost although no one seems to remember him...

2008: The Golf Cart Accident

Charlie Alterman, Musical Director/Conductor

I subbed[23] over at *Legally Blonde* at the Palace, which was crazy because it's this legendary theater—even if it's now buried under the Doubletree Guest Suites Hotel. It's so beautiful, and it was beyond cool working there. I ended up taking over for the associate conductor when he left to do another show. That show was so much fun to conduct!

There was a mishap with the golf cart once. The golf cart is in two scenes. Elle's mom and dad wheel on in it in one scene, and then later on in the show, there's a parade and it carries a group of people around. During that part, it has to actually ride a specific path right on the edge of the stage. And during the two-week run when I was conducting, the actor lost control of the golf cart and it almost drove right into the audience!

The golf cart literally got stuck right at the edge of the stage! The actor veered over, trying to get off stage, and then slammed into the proscenium stage left. The golf cart was hanging over, about to fall into the pit.

People from the audience actually got up and started to push the golf cart back onto the stage! Then, stagehands came out and tried to pull it up, but it was weighted toward the house. So they needed the audience members' help. It was hysterical.

Brilliantly, right around that spot there was a vamp, and Orfeh's character came on. Her line was "Kyle, what's going on?" And she was like, "What the *hell* is going on?" The whole audience lost it. It was amazing. The golf cart was the big story from that show. I can't believe I was there for that.

2009: Recreating *West Side Story*

---

[23] subbed: substituting for members of the regular team on a show; term often utilized to describe "sub" stagehands or musicians

Kevin McCollum, Producer

I have always loved *West Side Story*. I grew up watching the movie and my mother had the album. In 2007, Arthur Laurents came to Jeffrey Seller and me about producing a revival on Broadway. Jerry Mitchell was going to make his directorial debut with it. Jeffrey and I were very interested, and we approached the Nederlanders about working together and giving us a theater.

At that point, Jeffrey and I had an idea to create a television program showing auditions for the show. We thought it was an exciting idea: let's go to Puerto Rico and find the 19 and 20-year-olds who are perfect for the show. Arthur was on board with this, but some of the agents and estates involved with *West Side Story* were worried that it wouldn't look good. They wouldn't do it. To their surprise, we handed the rights back.

To spend $10 million on a revival and not feel like you have the right tools to make it a success is not how I produce shows. We knew that for a *West Side Story* revival, even though it's one of the greatest musicals ever written, we needed to have a new education process, to get into people's homes in a unique way and remind them what the show is about.

The next year, we produced *In the Heights*. I got a call from Arthur. "I know a new way in," he said. "I have a new reason for doing *West Side Story*, something that will give it special relevance today: we create Spanish translations for the Sharks. We make it the first truly bilingual production of *West Side Story*. And I want to direct." We were on board with that idea, and we decided to move forward.

We took the show for an out-of-town tryout in Washington D.C. and we didn't quite get it right. We tried subtitles during some of the Spanish parts of the show. By the time we came into town, I think we'd successfully recreated *West Side Story* for a modern audience and that was exciting. We put timpani drums up in the Palace boxes to give the show a surround-sound feel. Playing the Palace was a treat, and we got to play with audience expectations even though the show was a revival.

2009: The 6th Grade Play

Lin-Manuel Miranda, Writer/Actor

It all started in 6th grade. I was cast as Bernardo in the 6th grade play. I'd heard of *West Side Story*, but I never really knew what it was about. In fact, there used to be a store on 96th Street called "West Side Store-y." *That* was my first exposure to it. Someone explained to me at some point that it was the name of a show.

When I was cast in the 6th grade play, my mom said, "Okay. Well, we should watch it." We watched the movie that afternoon and I was just like, "There are Puerto Ricans in this?!" As someone who grew up speaking Spanish at home and English at school, I was just, like, "I get to be Puerto Rican in my school?" It was a big deal.

I also knew that it was based on *Romeo and Juliet*. We had studied *Romeo and Juliet* in elementary school, so I was really confused when she didn't die. I remember turning to my mom and asking, "It was *Romeo and Juliet*. Why didn't she die?" My mom said, "Because no self-respecting Puerto Rican girl kills herself."

I was blown away by the show. I got to do "America" in 6th grade. Then, as soon as I started directing in high school, I knew I wanted to do *West Side Story*. I had an amazing time putting it together. I don't remember much about my senior year of high school, except *West Side Story*; that was all that I cared about. That was my whole year.

Years later, after *In the Heights*, Kevin McCollum called me and said, "Arthur Laurents is going to call you. Answer the phone."

44

Arthur called and asked, "Can you come over to my house?" So I went over to Arthur Laurents' house down in the Village and he said, "You know, I've always wanted to try this. Here's a draft of *West Side Story*. I've marked up the pieces that I want to be in Spanish. Do you think you could do this?"

I said to him, "I don't know anyone else who could do this but me." I knew that score so well. I knew it the way you know a show when you loved it, and then you directed it, and you mapped out every beat. So I felt very honored.

If it had been anyone else asking, I wouldn't have done it. *West Side Story*'s pretty untouchable! But it was Laurents and it was Sondheim; it was the surviving members of this creative team wanting to try something, and the Bernstein family was really excited about it. It was great.

I had a blast writing it. I wrote it with my dad, mostly, because he came to New York when he was 18. I wanted my work to be Puerto Rican Spanish. I looked through a lot of translations and they were very academic Spanish. I was like, "This is technically correct. But there is no way a teenager in a gang says this shit." I felt that way about a lot of the translations that I read, so I tried to keep it simple.

Steve's whole thing was, "As long as it rhymes where I have it rhyme, use whatever imagery you want. That's the only thing to me. If I'm listening and I don't speak Spanish, I'm going to be checking for that." Keeping the internal rhymes of "I Feel Pretty" and the quintet was the challenge. It was really fun.

I was at rehearsals when the Spanish stuff was being implemented, but I was still doing *In the Heights*, so I wasn't around that much during previews.

I was at the first preview at the Palace, though. It was fun watching Steve and Arthur reconnect over the show. That was fun to see from my bird's eye perspective, because I met with each of them separately. That was great.

––––––––––––

Monday afternoon was the big performance of the week at the Palace during its vaudeville days. Each new bill would premiere on Thursday, and Monday afternoon was when agents and music publishers and bookers attended the show, as well as other industry professionals. Today, shows in previews play Monday nights, and that's when the Broadway industry gathers to see them. Not much has changed there.

––––––––––––

2009: My Shot At Tony

Jeremy Jordan, Actor

I made my Broadway debut in *Rock of Ages* as a swing, and nine months into the run, I booked *West Side Story*. I had a few great auditions to be the first replacement for Tony. When I sang "Something's Coming", Arthur Laurents cried. I couldn't believe that. So I thought I had a very good chance at the job. Then they called me and told me that they were bumping the current standby to replacement and I was being offered the Tony standby position. I wouldn't have auditioned if I'd known that—going from standing by in one show to standing by in another would be a lateral move. So I said no.

Then they came back and told me, "We can guarantee you two shows a week." But I was already doing two shows a week, at least, at *Rock of Ages*, so I turned them down. That's when *West Side Story* came back with this amazing offer: Two shows a week as Tony, principal salary, and I didn't have to show up at the theater the other days. I literally came in twice a week to play the lead on Broadway and that was it. I've never heard of a contract like that!

I saw *West Side Story* in community theatre as a kid. It's one of my top three favorite shows ever. I was so excited to play Tony. It's sometimes a thankless part, because the majority of the attention is showered on the women playing Maria and Anita. Tony gets forgotten in some productions, but I was determined to make Tony memorable. That was my goal for the run. I think I did it. I felt really good about my performance. I felt very lucky I got to play Tony on Broadway before I got too old.

Arthur Laurents and I spoke a lot in the beginning. When I got the part, he took me under his wing and we had a couple of sessions. I went to his apartment and we had a long conversation about the role of Tony. Then I began being part of his weekly sessions at the theater, which were the worst. He would bring the whole cast into the auditorium and give notes, and he would find one person each week to tear to shreds. Then he would praise another actor. He would do it often with two actors who had been on for the same part. There were days when he told me I was the best Tony he'd ever seen, in front of the production's original Tony, Matt Cavenaugh. Then there were days when I was really proud of my performance where he told me I was horrible and had checked out completely from the show.

One time, a note session got particularly heated. Arthur announced that my performance was awful, and I said, "If you don't like what I did, tell me how to fix it." He replied, "Just don't do it like that." I blew up. If you're a director, you're supposed to direct us. He would always tell us we were bad without giving us any clue on how to improve it for him. This time, I called him out on that, and he responded, "You're just trying to assert your masculinity," so I said, "No, I'm just trying to stand up for myself and not be bullied." It was a little loaded, and after notes, I apologized to him. That was the last time I ever saw him.

The show was the first time I got to truly experience and express anguish onstage. I got to express joy and fear… but the end of act one when Riff would die in my arms was my favorite part of the show to do. Tony is freaking out and he shouts, "MARIA!" at the top of his lungs. It was intense, and I loved acting that part of the show.

There's a woman named Pecas who we loved and who worked on house staff at the Palace. She always stood at the stage door when the actors were signing autographs and handed us pens. She was the sweetest. If you were having a bad day, she would greet you with a smile and love. Sometimes there's a generous amount of space between actors and crew, and sometimes there's not. I'm always close with my dresser, but it's nice when you get to be friends with other crew members and house staff too.

The star dressing room at the Palace is cool. There was bright red carpeting in there, which I think Liza had put in during her run, right before *West Side Story*. Matt Hydzik and I alternated using it when we were Tony, but all the stuff in it was his. I went back to the Palace when my wife Ashley Spencer, was in *Priscilla*, and Tony Sheldon had the dressing room. There were hundreds of Playbills lining every inch of the walls.

A lot of people say there are ghosts at the Palace. I did feel a little strange in that dressing room sometimes. But I don't know if I really believe in any of that stuff. There were a few weird noises here and there.

2011: Quick Change

Brittnye Batchelor, Hair and Makeup Artist

The most challenging quick change I've ever had was on *Priscilla*. I had a cue with Nick Adams where he changed out of being a woman into being a boy. It was a lot!

I actually had to stand in the wings with packing tape. The *Priscilla* actors had glitter on their lips, and that's how they got the glitter off. I stood with the packing tape: one end stuck to my hip, the other end stuck to my hand. I was holding a mirror, a face wipe, and a bike light. And the whole thing was really very fast, maybe 15 seconds!

―――――――――

The Palace Theatre in its music hall heyday had a huge issue with scalpers, or "ticket speculators" as they were called in the 1910s. Palace Theatre management and the surrounding police force would arrest ticket scalpers, inform those speaking with them that any tickets they bought would not be honored, and generally discourage would-be customers by reprimanding the speculators.

These days, stand in front of the Palace and you'll be accosted by a different kind of ticket hawker—flyer girls. Young ladies in all black with red tights do "Fosse" moves and hand out flyers for Chicago *while those in princess costumes hand out* Cinderella *material.*

―――――――――

2012: The Idea Of All These Girls

Arielle Tepper Madover, Producer

Annie was the first Broadway show I saw. Allison Smith was *Annie*. My grandmother took me with my three cousins, who were rowdy boys. I don't think they connected to it as much as I did.

I fell in love. I fell in love with the girls. I was an only child, and the idea of all these girls living together was amazing to me. Any time I saw a Broadway show or a TV show where there were lots of kids living together, I thought it was the greatest thing ever. So I just fell in love with that at *Annie*, and then, as the show continued, I thought about the fact that these people were my size, and I fell in love with theatre.

Producing the new *Annie* revival was a dream come true. When I produced *Red*, we were in previews and Jeff Wilson and Wendy Orshan, who were my general managers, came over. They asked what I was doing next and I said I was thinking about doing *Annie*. They said, "Really?! That's a great idea!" It's really the only musical I could think of doing. I love producing plays, but *Annie* was my first show, something I loved so much.

I sort of realized that I'd spent the past 30 years getting to the point where I could produce it.

It's an amazing thing, the show. *Annie* has touched so many people around the world. And to have three living authors around, to tell the story about it, 36 years later... it's incredible.

2012: Circle of Love

Merwin Foard, Actor

All throughout *Annie* rehearsals, James Lapine would start the day with what he called "The Circle of Love." Everybody in, everybody, no matter your job description: intern, Anthony Warlow, didn't matter.

We would make a huge circle, and he would randomly pick somebody out and go, "What did you have for breakfast today? Good, good, good. Did you buy that or did you make that? Great, great, great."

To one of the kids, "Did you have homework? Tell me about your school? What's your mascot?" Just general. Nothing about the show, just about us and our lives. Lovely.

We keep that going even now, because it became a habit. It's not that we all sit in a circle, but we certainly do check in with each other more because we learned so much about each other during that. "How's your little brother doing? Aww, that's so great. What's he doing now? Does he play sports? Okay, wow, yeah."

It's also a testament to the adults as to how smitten we are by these girls. We just want to take them all home and have them as our family, because they are so very, very sweet. So many of them are making their Broadway debuts. The kid who played *Annie* today, Taylor Richardson, is actually the understudy, and she has incredible talent. The traditions we have are mostly about encouraging and being gentle to these kids, and taking care of each other.

2012: We'd Like To Thank You, Herbert Hoover

Michael Starobin, Orchestrator

The opening of the *Annie* revival was quite electric and special. The election had just happened in November. Obama had been re-elected and somehow those politics, coupled with the issues in the show, really electrified the audience.

———————

In 1925, the Embassy Theatre opened on 7th Avenue between 46th and 47th Streets. The Embassy was a premiere movie theatre for refined, high-class audiences. With reserved seating and an intimate design of only 556 seats, the Embassy also boasted an almost exclusively female staff, including its manager. In 1929, the Embassy became the first movie theatre in the United States to show newsreels.

The Embassy movie theater survived as a movie theatre until 1997, when it became the Times Square Information Center. Having been landmarked, the interior of the building retained its original design and features, including beautiful wood paneling and carvings on the walls and an ivory ceiling with gold detailing. The building provided an entrance to an office building containing Actors' Equity headquarters, museum displays about current Broadway shows and history, and helpful kiosks providing information to tourists. In July of 2014, the Times Square Information Center closed. Setting it apart from many other Times Square buildings, the Embassy/Information Center has been only two things for the last 89 years. What will it be next?

———————

2014: Keep Ya Head Up

F. Michael Haynie, Actor

Sometimes when people ask me what the first Broadway show I saw was, I say *Pippin* by accident. I never saw *Pippin*, but I loved that movie. That's why I do theatre: because I saw Ben Vereen as the Leading Player on that VHS. I always wanted to play roles that were played by black actors. I wanted to be Coalhouse in *Ragtime*; I wanted to be Jim in *Big River*. I was just taken by those roles.

I was born in Marietta, Ohio, but grew up in Macon, Georgia. I moved here ten years ago to go to NYU. I had never seen a show at the Palace before we moved in here for *Holler If Ya Hear Me*. I don't usually cross to this side of Broadway. I know that sounds weird and judgmental but I don't mean for it to. I'm a West Side theater person. Most of the shows I see or act in are on the west side of Broadway. Every now and then, I'll venture over to the East Side. So it was interesting to book a show at the Palace.

Of course, when you book a show at the Palace, people say, "Oooh, you're playing the Palace!" It's a theater name you don't forget. I read the Wikipedia entry and learned about how fancy the place was, and then I came here to scope it out and it was covered in scaffolding, and there was nothing up yet about our show. That was anticlimactic.

Our first day at the Palace, I walked in the stage door and was really surprised by all the steps. On the West Side, the stage door entrances are the same, but at the Palace, you have to immediately take steps downstairs. The West Side theaters also mostly have similar color schemes, with all of the taupe paint. The Palace is so red. We were excited that the Palace was getting a facelift for *Holler If Ya Hear Me*, but I was not expecting what I saw when we got into the house. There was sawdust everywhere. It was a mess!

The other Broadway show I've done is *Wicked* at the Gershwin. I played Boq, and this show is a very different experience since I'm standing by. Some days I walk into the audience to watch the show and an usher says, "Excuse me sir, where's your ticket?" I have to show them, "That's me in the Playbill. I'm part of the show, I promise." If we don't have a healthy run, I might end up never going onstage. I keep explaining that to my mom: "Mom, I have a Broadway job, but I may never get to be onstage."

It's a labyrinth backstage at the Palace. During the second preview, I was still getting lost, and had to ask an usher how to get backstage. Usually there's a stage level door to backstage in the audience, but at the Palace, you have to go to the basement, and punch in the door code at a door next to the men's bathroom.

I cover[24] one role in *Holler If Ya Hear Me*, which is played by Ben Thompson. Right now we're trying to figure out if I need to be on a standby contract, which is technically a principal contract, or if the producers are going to move me to a chorus contract. That would mean I would sing off stage every night, and come out and bow, in addition to covering Ben. A chorus contract costs the production less. If I covered more than one role, I would be a swing, which is a third kind of contract—but I can't be a swing, because every other role has to be played by a black actor.

The other day, I was watching the show and taking notes in the audience, and a woman nearby asked me if I was enjoying it. I told her I was, and asked her the same. We began talking and then she said, "Wait—are you a part of this production?" I told her I was, and explained that I was a cover. Then a family next to us joined the conversation, and a woman asked, "Which roles do you cover?"

I just looked at her in disbelief. She must have been about 50 years old; she wasn't someone who had seen Al Jolson perform *Swanee*! This average woman was asking if I did blackface in a Broadway show.

All of the original audition breakdowns for the Griffy standby asked for an actor who was Latino or mixed-race. At some point, I think they realized that they wanted the role to be white. I went in, and I can rap, sing, and play guitar; I'm also as Aryan-looking as it gets. They hired me because of all of those things.

In some ways, what our show is doing has never been done before. That's scary, and it's also a tremendous responsibility. We are fighting on behalf of all hip hop writers and all people who envision hip hop on Broadway. TI and LL Cool J rapped *The Music Man* on the Tony Awards this past year. A lot of people thought it was stupid or absurd. Conan O'Brien started a hashtag: #NoRapOnBroadway. We were shocked by that. The week we started previews on Broadway, there was a trending hashtag on Twitter calling for no rap on Broadway.

Right now, *Holler If Ya Hear Me* has people who are coming who are really interested in a Tupac show. We need to get more of those people in the theater, and also get people interested who might not initially think the idea is for them. All of that is really hard with a brand-new show, especially when you don't feel supported from within the community. When I told my dad, "I booked my second Broadway show—it's a new Tupac musical!" the reaction wasn't, "Oh my God, your second Broadway show!" It was, "There's a Tupac musical?" That's hard.

---

[24] cover: another term for understudy

It's hard to go to work when people on the street are telling you, "Your show is going to close." It might. All shows can do that.

I think this is a compelling story that needs to be told. I think that the music is hard. Some people hear rap and they zone out. They can't hear the words. And the team wouldn't want to dumb it down for those people, because then the rap crowd would come in and go, "Well, this isn't real—this is rap done Broadway-style." You want the show to be legitimate. You want it to be real. You want it to be everything. Any show can be the next *Wicked*, and get bad reviews, and lose the Tony for Best Musical, and then run forever. Any show can be the next *Glory Days*, and close on opening night. Any show can be anything.

When I was in *Wicked*, I had a conversation with a Broadway actress who said, "What is it like being in one of those shows? One of the government shows?" That's what some people think the long-running shows are. But *Wicked* deserves to be running. It tells a great story. A lot of the reason it's been so successful is that it's a family show. Dads can take their daughters to *Wicked*. That's not what *Holler If Ya Hear Me* is. Tupac had profanity in his lyrics, and our director asked our book writer to make the script consistent with that. There are guns and violence in the show. We have an adult musical, which is a hard sell.

I love this community, and all of my best friends are part of it. And I hate shows sometimes, too. I go and see stuff and love things and hate other things. But it's frustrating to see some of the Broadway community be against the show before they even see it. Hatred for a show without giving it a chance sometimes happens, and it makes the community devour itself in a way that's hurtful to everyone.

Some days I'll be watching the show myself and have doubts about a moment. Then a couple days later, I'll be watching Kenny Leon, our Tony Award-winning director, and think: *Oh man, you've been fixing this problem all along and no one knew it. And now this works.* Previews really are previews. But it's hard for actors to look at them that way. Twitter doesn't have an opening day. Everything about the show is public from the moment the first audience member walks in.

I'm kind of fortunate that *Holler If Ya Hear Me* isn't my Broadway debut, because it means that I get to watch 15 other people's Broadway debuts happen. That feels so cool. I saw a couple Broadway debuts happen at *Wicked*, but some of those people had been doing *Wicked* for a long time on tour first, so that felt different for them. Of course it was still cool but it was a different kind of excitement. One told me, "I'm so familiar with the show that it doesn't feel like this big thing."

On the other hand, I saw one of the ensemble members in *Holler If Ya Hear Me* walk onstage at the Palace for the first time. He was in his costume, and he looked out into the house—and I saw everything in his eyes change. All of a sudden, he was Usher playing an arena. He's a great dancer, and he just instinctively started to dance, for himself. Then he pretended to give high-fives to the whole front row and pointed to them. The whole time I was fumbling with my phone because I wanted to capture this moment for him. He didn't see me. Then someone else called his name and he turned and just walked away. I had just witnessed the most private moment of someone going: *I'm on Broadway. This is real.* I got to sit in the audience for our final dress rehearsal and watch 15 people have that experience.

I'm short. I have a high voice. I don't often get to be the dad in the show. But on *Holler If Ya Hear Me*, I get to be the dad for once. I get to be with people on the phone saying, "Mom, I had a bad show today," and when they hang up, say, "No, you didn't have a bad show, it was just that second-performance feeling." People have always done that for me.

Even though I think we have something special, I still have my moments of panic that the show is going to close. I try to keep that away from the other actors in the theater, especially those 15 people making their Broadway debuts. When the company meeting happens and they tell us this is it, I'll know what's happening. Tonya

Pinkins will know. Chris Jackson will know. But those Broadway debuts won't know it's any different from any company meeting.

That's the part I never want for anybody. I don't want this to ever not be magical. Because it is. This is one of the coolest jobs anyone could ever ask for: to work on a Broadway show. Because this show isn't a random production that runs at a random playhouse. This is on a list of shows that made it to Broadway. That's a list that's quite long, because Broadway has been here for a while. But when you look at the 2014 to 2015 Broadway season, for the rest of time, *Holler If Ya Hear Me*, book by Todd Kreidler, lyrics by Tupac Shakur, will be there. It will always be there. We will be eligible to be nominated at the Tony Awards next year.

And then the show might get licensed. Or it might not. The show could run on Broadway and this could be it. It could poof up in smoke after that, and those who saw it on Broadway will be the only ones who ever experienced *Holler If Ya Hear Me*. It will disappear into the temporal memories of live theatre. We're assuming we're going to do a cast recording, but some shows don't.

When I do a show off-Broadway and it's struggling, everyone thinks: *Okay, we'll regroup, maybe go out-of-town, and then try to go for Broadway.* That's not the case here. This is it. This is the big leagues. There's no next step.

I've seen people of every ethnicity and age group come into this theater. Some of them love the show and some of them hate it. But this is a success that we celebrate each day. I hope that when *Holler If Ya Hear Me* closes, whether that's in a month or ten years, the headline is: "Look what this show was able to do." And I hope someone else goes, "Oh, this is a good idea," or even better, "I think I can do this better." That's my favorite phrase in theater, if you really mean it. It's not insulting. I hope a young writer who isn't Tupac, or an amazing established rap artist sees this show and thinks that and makes their own Broadway show. I hope this is some kid's first Broadway show and he goes, "I like rap and I like musicals. There's a place for me." That's all I hope for this show.

On the first truly sweltering day of the NYC summer in 2014, I met F. Michael Haynie at the Palace stage door and he brought me into the catacombs of one of Broadway's most famous houses. In nearly every Broadway theater, the stage door leads to a small room where the door man or woman sits, and a hallway that leads both into the wings and to a set of stairs leading up to dressing rooms. The Palace is different. From the moment you walk in the 47th Street entrance, you must duck your head as you descend steep stairs.

It wasn't always that way. In the heyday of the Palace, headlining performers would describe walking through an iron gate, to a courtyard, with the Palace stage door looming ahead of them. Some say the reason why the stage door setup changed was a fire caused by actors smoking on the fire escape, or someone who was killed when an object was dropped out the window into the old stage door alley. Part of the reason was definitely the new hotel structure.

Once you're in the lower level of the Palace, you see how easy it would be to get lost here. F. Michael tells me that he was still getting lost after a couple weeks. The area where the Annie *girls sang happy birthday, where I imagine young Celia Keenan-Bolger gaping at* Beauty and the Beast *cast members, was filled with* Holler If Ya Hear Me *wardrobe staff, washing costumes for that night's performance. A line of costume bras spins in a circle as two cast members walk by, drinking juice.*

We walk through the lowest level at the Palace, and I'm amazed by the amount of square footage, broken up into little rooms like pockets. A door leads us to a stairwell and suddenly we're in the orchestra seating level, in the back of the theater. There is a "Hip Hop Hall of Fame" in the works that wasn't here a few days earlier. I saw the second preview of the show, and ran into Austin Nathaniel, who gave me a tour of the "new Palace." Holler *had completely changed the layout of the audience, altering the Palace from 1700 to 1200 seats, by creating stadium seating out of the orchestra section. As such, upon entering the house, audiences would see half of the "old" orchestra seats empty, out of view of the stage, with a mural in the style of the show watching over them.*

With the new setup, the first row audience members could sit with their knees up against the stage, and with a small ladder, anyone could climb from the top row of the orchestra stadium seating to the mezzanine. The effect on the Palace was fascinating: the house was more intimate and the action onstage was more immediate, but the theater felt oddly incomplete to me, even from my mezzanine seat. My friend who had never been inside the Palace before, said it felt like a medium-sized theater. What?! The Palace is huge, gargantuan, a Mecca of vaudeville, concerts, musicals. But not in the summer of 2014. Anyone who saw the Palace then saw it as something completely different, with a completely different kind of show inside.

In F. Michael's dressing room, on the 6th floor, I learned that his space had previously belonged to Lee Sellars, who'd played Officer Krupke in West Side Story. *He opened and closed the show. Judith Moore had occupied the room during* Beauty and the Beast, *and Tom Nelis during* Aida. *Their names were all scrawled on the bottom of a drawer in the room.*

And for two months during the summer of 2014, the room had belonged to F. Michael Haynie too. Holler If Ya Hear Me *closed after one month of performances. F. Michael never went on. A couple of weeks later, just as I was finishing up this chapter, I got a text from him: "Glad you're finishing the Palace chapter on our closing weekend. You'll be way up to date on this place." A sad message of its moment, coming from inside the Palace, just as I was wrapping together stories of Judy Garland and Bob Fosse and Cagelles and dancing spoons and forks in that sacred building.*

In April of 2015, the new musical An American in Paris *will open at the Palace Theatre, with a book by Craig Lucas and music and lyrics by George and Ira Gershwin. From Tupac to Gershwin in one season—the Palace still has variety!*

The Barrymore Theatre

Built: 1928
Location: 243 West 47th Street
Owner: The Shubert Organization
Longest-Running Show: *I Love My Wife* (1977-1979)
Shortest-Running Show: *Step on a Crack* (closed on opening night in 1962), *Happiness Is Just A Thing Called A Rolls Royce* (closed on opening night in 1968), *A Place For Polly* (closed on opening night in 1970)
Number of Productions: 186

I've done three shows at the Barrymore now: *Company*, *Speed-the-Plow*, and *Arcadia*. I'm two shows away from matching Ethel Barrymore herself!

I love learning about who has been in the Broadway theaters I'm working in, before me—especially who has been in my dressing room. Who had my dressing room at the Barrymore? Marlon Brando! Sidney Poitier and Laurence Olivier performed in that theater. Katharine Hepburn. Paul Newman. Fred Astaire sang "Night and Day" on that stage. Gene Kelly did *Pal Joey* there. "September Song" from *Knickerbocker Holiday* was introduced on the Barrymore stage. Maggie Smith did *Lettice and Lovage* in that theater, which I saw when I was in college. I saw Jessica Lange and Alec Baldwin in *Streetcar* there, and I got my aisle seat at TKTS! Madeline Kahn was in *The Sisters Rosensweig* there. *Baby* was there, which was special to me because I played Danny when I was 16 at a semi-professional theater in Miami.

The Barrymore is my favorite house I've ever played in. It's the most perfect jewel on Broadway. It has 1000 seats, so it's not too big, but it's not so small that you feel like you're in a small space. It has the beauty of a classic Broadway house. I realized at some point that the classic Broadway houses are perfectly designed. You can give a small performance on the stage of the Cort or the Barrymore and the audience will see it in the last row of the balcony. You can have a gentle moment and people will feel it from there. The Barrymore has intimacy and elegance.

-Raúl Esparza, Actor

When I was up for *Curious Incident*, I kept thinking about how if I got it, I'd be working at the Barrymore. I knew it would be so special to play this theater. On my first two Broadway shows, I had never been to the theaters before I started working in them. But at the Barrymore, I've had incredible theatergoing experiences. I saw *Company* here, which was amazing. Then I saw *Arcadia*, which I loved. This is the Raúl Esparza theater to me! And I get to work here now, too.

-Taylor Trensch, Actor

Introduction: I Started In The Mailroom

Diane Heatherington, Box Office Treasurer

I came to New York in 1977. My first Broadway show was right here at the Barrymore! I saw *I Love My Wife*.

I Love My Wife was special because I ended up working on the show, in the mailroom. I worked in this very room we're sitting in, which used to be the mail office. Every day we'd sit here and hear the whole show. It was a fun musical. The audience was always really lively and the experience of actually talking to the customers on the phone was interesting.

We didn't fill the tickets in those days. We just filled out the credit card information they'd tell us and then it would go to the box office. People would give you all sorts of excuses for why they needed to switch tickets. And they had a hard time saying "*I Love My Wife*". They would always say, "*I Like My Wife*". "It's "'Love'!" That was funny to me.

When I was young, I started working in Miami at Coconut Grove Playhouse. I came to New York on vacation to visit a friend and we walked past the Barrymore Theatre. At the time we walked by, the treasurer of the theater was outside having a cigarette, so my friend introduced us. It happened to be the day after *I Love My Wife* had opened, and Frank the treasurer said to me, "Oh, you work in theatre. Do you know how to do phone orders?" I said, "Yes!" And he said, "Well, here's a pen. Go up these steps and introduce yourself to Louise and I'll pay you out of my pocket until I can get you on payroll."

That was 38 years ago, and now I'm the treasurer of the Barrymore Theatre.

It all just happened to fall into place. I came up here to this room and I've never left. I found an apartment that week in the *New York Times* on 44th and 10th and I haven't left for 38 years. It was $175 a month when I moved in.

Before that trip, I had come up to visit people two other times. The first time I stayed with my friend and my sister on Park Avenue, and the second time I stayed with a friend in Brooklyn who was working as a cab driver. He was too busy working to show me around, and he lived with his father, so the father took me to the tip of Brooklyn and showed me the skyline and said, "That's Manhattan and this is as close as you're getting." I thought: *But I'm so close!*

I knew I wanted to be here. I just fit right into the walk and the pace of the city. To this day, I'm amazed that I live here, right in the middle of it. I just couldn't see being in New York and living in Long Island City, or anywhere else. It's nice being right in the middle of it.

When I first moved here, I was visiting my sister in Pittsburgh and her neighbor asked me where I lived in the city. I told him the West Side and gave him some vague answer, and finally he got it out of me that I lived on 44th and 10th. And he said, "Oh my God, Jane, she's in Hell's Kitchen. Get her out of there. Make her come home!" My sister was alarmed, and I said, "Oh, forget it. It's nothing. Nobody's bothering me. It's a family neighborhood."

Then the first year I lived here was the year of the 44 Caliber Killer. My sister called me up and said, "Are you sure you're okay? You're on 44th Street with this serial killer!" And I told her, "No, no. It's the 44 Caliber Killer, not the 44th Street Killer." That was what my beginning here was like.

There were a lot of hookers. There used to be a parking garage behind my apartment. You'd hear the prostitutes getting beaten up all the time. It was really rough, and there were lots of drugs. 42nd Street was very different. I don't know if I liked it better before. There were a lot of people selling drugs, but at least you could walk through them. Now the streets are so packed that you can't get through anyone. It's just like, "Move! Move to the right! What's wrong with you people?"

After working in the mailroom at the Barrymore, I got into the box office at Circle in the Square. I did an apprenticeship for three years there. Circle was good because they had repertory, so there were new shows all the time, and that was exciting. I got to meet a lot of the actors because they would come in through the front door.

54

Then I worked at the Palace for two big shows: *Woman of the Year* and *La Cage aux Folles*. Once *La Cage* closed, I started bouncing around and I moved to the Shubert Organization. I was bouncing from theater to theater for them. As long as you had your union card and the theaters were busy, it was easy to find work back then. Now it's a little harder.

About ten years ago, I worked my way up to head treasurer. First I worked at all three theaters on the east side of Broadway: the Lyceum, Belasco and Cort. I finally got on this side of the block, which is much better. I don't have any family in the business like a lot of treasurers do; I came up on my own.

From a customer's standpoint, I think that box offices aren't as personable as they used to be. People don't have the same connection of speaking with a person who is actually in the theater they called. Now they dial a ticket service, but it's so much of a business that a lot of the people you speak to aren't even in the city. They don't genuinely know the show or the theater or the neighborhood. They have a script, but it's not as personable. And of course, a lot of people order online. They'll accidentally order online from a broker who charges them way too much money, and then they come to us, confused about why the prices on their tickets don't match what they paid.

After our opening night of *Death of a Salesman*, I ended up talking to Paul Simon and Diane von Furstenberg. Paul put his hand on my shoulder and said, "Well, how are you?" and just started talking to my friend and me. Theatre is like that. Later my friend asked, "What was he talking about?" And I said, "I don't even remember! But Paul Simon was talking to us!"

Another time, an actor came to see *Speed-the-Plow* who had just started a big role on *Law and Order*. He was at the box office picking up his tickets and I told him what a good job he was doing. He thanked me, and from behind him, someone said, "She's right, you're doing a great job!" We looked, and it was Smokey Robinson! He came over and shook my hand under the box office window. He said to me, "You have such an interesting job!" When you meet celebrities at my job, you get to just treat them like they're normal and acknowledge them and say hello. It's nice.

Our offices are under the mezzanine, not backstage. I've never even gone all the way to the top, backstage where the dressing rooms are. The last show before this one was *Chaplin*, and it had a huge cast. Everywhere you went was jam-packed with people and costumes. I was always thinking: *How'd they fit this thing in there?* But I'm glad they did. It was a fun show.

The critics get very hard on certain things. They'll pick at something they don't like about an actor or writer. I don't know why people go by critics' reviews. The reviews of *Chaplin* weren't great but people loved it, and audiences always came out raving. They would come to the box office and say apologetically, "I loved this!" I never know what to say to that. There are a lot of shows like that. You feel bad because you know how much work and passion is put into it and how many jobs depend on it and how many audience members love it—but people only see the reviews. They don't understand.

It used to be that when a show closed with a certain percentage of money still in the advance sales, the box office would stay open for a week so we could give people refunds. That hasn't happened for a long time, mostly because it happens on the internet now, or the credit cards refund automatically. We do get people who show up with their tickets for one show and another show is already playing. People came with their tickets to *Chaplin* and we had to explain that they had been refunded, and *Macbeth* was now in this theater. They were insulted but it was because they didn't read what was sent to them. We can only do so much.

It was exciting to do *Exit the King* with Geoffrey Rush. He was so nice to everybody. He would always be in our alleyway having a cigarette. One day, he saw me walk past and said, "My children are here visiting from Australia, can I introduce you?" I was tickled and honored. He was so kind. He sent all the heads of the departments personal opening night cards.

James Spader was here for *Race*, and on his last day, he said, "Diane, do you remember the first day we met?" I said, "No..." And he reminded me that the stage manager was taking him around, introducing him to everyone. He said, "We met, and the first thing out of your mouth was, 'Are we doing Sunday brunches?!'" And I said, "James, you have to understand, being in the theatre, that's important to us. We need to know what to bring to brunch!"

———————————

Many theaters were built by the Shuberts for their star performers, and named after them. The Ethel Barrymore is the only one of these that's still an existing Broadway theater. The Shuberts also had involvement in the Maxine Elliott Theatre on 39th Street, the Nora Bayes Theatre on 49th Street and others that are now gone.

These days, including the Barrymore, there are three and a half Broadway theaters named after women. Taking into account the Helen Hayes, Vivian Beaumont, and half of the Lunt-Fontanne, all of the theaters named after women are for performers. Helen Hayes and Lynn Fontanne were performers; Vivian Beaumont was an actress and philanthropist. 20 and a half Broadway theaters are named after men—mostly producers, writers or theatre organization owners. Fascinatingly, none of the Broadway theaters currently named for men are for actors.

The Barrymore is a house where important American drama was given life. The original production of Knickerbocker Holiday *found a home at the Barrymore. The original productions and revivals of* A Raisin in the Sun *and* A Streetcar Named Desire *were at the Barrymore.* The Women. Pal Joey. Look Homeward, Angel. Tea and Sympathy. American Buffalo. Hurlyburly. Joe Turner's Come and Gone. The Sisters Rosensweig. *A notable number of these plays were launched at the Barrymore, and then once they'd attained hit status, were moved to less desirable theatre locations.* Look Homeward, Angel *played out the end of its run at the 54th Street Theatre, and* A Raisin in the Sun *moved to the Belasco.*

This used to be a regular tactic of theater owners, when it was cheaper to move shows from theater to theater. It became more expensive as physical productions began to be built for their theaters, and as union rules changed. Interestingly, with the recent movement of productions to off-Broadway following their Broadway runs, such as Avenue Q *and* Peter and the Starcatcher, *this trend has returned in a different way.*

———————————

1943: I Lost My Accent

Joan Shepard, Actor

I was an understudy at the Barrymore on the play *Tomorrow the World*. I understudied Joyce Van Patten in 1943, and last week, she came to see my show in the Fringe Festival! More than 70 years later, we're still in touch.

Up until I did that show, I had quite an annoying, chirpy British accent, since I was from England. The accent helped me get my first Broadway shows, because a child with a British accent would be needed, and I didn't need to be taught.

My mother was no stage mother. She wasn't pushy or ambitious. But she was very smart. She heard about this new play called *Tomorrow the World* that had a great part for a ten-year-old girl. She took me to see the producer, Theron Bamberger. He dismissed me and he told us that Joyce Van Patten was already playing the part. But then he said that he might consider me for the national company, if I could lose the accent. So the very next day, I did. Accent gone.

Joyce Van Patten was terrific in the show. She started out as the understudy. Nancy Nugent, the director's daughter, had the part. They got to Boston, and Nancy got sick, so Joyce went on. She blew everyone away so they moved her up. They kept Nancy as understudy, but that was hard on her so she left. That's how I got the part as Joyce's understudy.

We had understudy rehearsal twice a week, on Wednesday and Saturday. I would rehearse with Richard Tyler, who understudied one of the male leads. He was a very good actor. One day, they came to me and said, "Mr. Bamberger is really considering you for the national company, so we're going to arrange for you to go on during a Wednesday matinee. That way, he'll see if he definitely wants you to do it."

Joyce was furious. I don't blame her. If the shoe was on the other foot, I would've been furious too. That was the only time I ever went on for her. After that, I went straight into the national tour.

At the Biltmore next door, *Kiss and Tell* was playing. That was a big hit comedy directed by George Abbott. The Brooks Atkinson was across the street, although it was called the Mansfield then. I don't remember which shows played there at that time; there were two that closed quickly.

We used to go to the Automat on Broadway, between 46th Street and 47th Street, before shows. My mother and I ate there around the corner, and then went to the theater.

I've been back to the Barrymore and it looks exactly the same. It's amazing. I went backstage to visit someone and the stage door, the alley, all the same. Even the water cooler is where it was.

———————

Ever heard of John Garfield? He was the original male lead in A Streetcar Named Desire *at the Barrymore, before he dropped out during contract negotiations. After a fruitless casting search in Hollywood, an emerging young Broadway actor named Marlon Brando was cast.*

———————

1946: Romantic And Swashbuckling

Elizabeth McCann, Producer

The first Broadway show I ever saw was *Cyrano de Bergerac*, at the Barrymore, starring José Ferrer. It was an overwhelming experience for me. I sat in the balcony. I was a teenager.

The experience taught me something. If you want to get people interested in the theatre, please don't take them to Ibsen. Take them to something that is romantic and swashbuckling and fun, especially for girls. Take them to a play that gives them the glamour of the theatre. Unfortunately, I think very few plays do that today. They are about things like Jewish angst on the West Side—and I think: *I live in the middle of that, why do I have to go see a play about it?*

A lot of contemporary playwrights have been helmed into writing very small plays. If you're Nora Ephron, you can write *Lucky Guy*, with a large cast, but most playwrights are out of luck. Almost everyone seems a bit safe and a little well-intentioned, with a few exceptions, like Christopher Durang. And another thing that's killing the Broadway play is that it's been beaten to death on Broadway by the musicals. It's just not there.

Later on, I produced *Cyrano*, as a double bill with *Much Ado About Nothing* by the Royal Shakespeare Company. Derek Jacobi played Cyrano, and was quite wonderful. Actually, the better production of those two was *Much Ado*, which was glorious. But *Cyrano* sold them. Ours was a very different production than José Ferrer's. I liked it very much, but it wasn't the same as my first experience.

I became sort of in love with going to the theatre. My family didn't have that habit. My family had a tail-end-of-the-Depression-let's-go-to-the-movies habit. So my theatergoing was actually an accident. A cousin from New

Jersey had a spare ticket because her friend got sick, and my mother said, "You've got to go to the theater with your cousin. She's not allowed to go alone." I was pushed into going to the theater, to a play that I couldn't pronounce the name of. I couldn't pronounce "José Ferrer" either. I said, "What is he, Spanish?" I had this typical Irish Catholic attitude about anything that sounded different. But I might never have gone to the theater, if I hadn't been forced into it. That's how it happened.

———————————

During the 1946 production of Cyrano de Bergerac *starring José Ferrer, several matinees featured all of the understudies playing the lead roles, and all of the stars in minor parts. José went before Equity to ask for permission to do these special performances, meant to showcase the unsung heroes of showbiz.*

I got to interview the legendary Liz McCann in her office, inside of the Sardi's building. Directly to the right of the street entrance to Sardi's on 44th Street is an office building entrance. The doorman is always singing, whistling, humming—on this day of June 2013, it happened to be South Pacific, *which I couldn't help note had played its original run on the same block. Of course every person in the Sardi's office building was steeped in Broadway history! An office in this building meant you were one elevator ride from a martini at the most famous theatrical restaurant of all time.*

On the 9th floor, Liz's office was filled with posters of her Broadway shows and memorabilia from years of producing the Tony Awards (and winning eight, too!) As she told me tales of her theatrical career, a hot June breeze blew in the small window facing 44th Street. Liz went from stage-struck kid to right-hand woman for the Nederlanders to a risk-taking producer and general manager in her own right. Along with her one-time co-producing partner Nelle Nugent, Liz was responsible for bringing a lot of dark plays and important work to Broadway, including Dracula, The Elephant Man, Amadeus, *and* The Life and Adventures of Nicholas Nickleby. *Her long-time collaboration with Edward Albee showed the industry a commercial producer excited to take a chance on unconventional plays, because she thought they deserved to be seen.*

———————————

1957/2000: I Auditioned Here In The 1950s

George Nestor, Usher

I grew up in New York, in Queens and later in the Bronx. I was always performing as a kid in school. The first time I ever auditioned for a professional show was in this very theater, the Barrymore, for Lee and J.J. Shubert. The Shuberts were always sending out companies of operettas that they owned. I decided I had nothing to lose, so I worked on my singing, and came up here to try out.

Before I went onstage, I watched a bunch of old-timers audition who had obviously worked for the Shuberts before. I watched a guy with a toupee and elevator shoes and full stage makeup. They were all looking for work and they all came out and sang before me and sounded like experts. I thought: *This is the wrong business for me. These guys are all fantastic!* I couldn't believe the tremendous level that they worked at.

The Shuberts had this guy who worked for them who did everything: he painted scenery, he hired people. He worked for them for years, and he knew where everything was. He was known as Mar Simmons. He read with me, and was rather inane at the lines. I'll never forget that Mr. Shubert said, "For God's sake! Give the man something to play against, will you?"

My father was an elevator operator in a fancy building on 5th Avenue and the producer Elliott Nugent lived there. He was a nice friendly man, and my father talked me up to him, so he gave me an audition. That was how I got a walk-on role in a play at the Barrymore, called *The Greatest Man Alive* in 1957, starring Dennis King. I knew who he was because he was in Laurel and Hardy's *Fra Diavolo* and in the film *The Vagabond King*. The other people in the cast were wonderful: Kathleen Maguire, Russell Collins... just being around them was a thrill.

All of 47th Street was very different back when I started. Down the block was the Strand Theatre, which is no longer there. The front of the Barrymore was different, but the inside is more or less the same.

I started doing little off-off-Broadway shows here and there. I did a couple of off-Broadway plays by Ionesco where Ionesco actually attended the performances and complimented us. That was wonderful. I did a couple of tours. I put together my own little concert group and we did performances off and on until about 2000, when I got into ushering, which puts bread on the table.

I started working as an usher at the St. James Theatre, for Jujamcyn. I worked on and off there, so someone said, "Call the Shuberts, you'll get more work that way," which I did. Then I got into the Barrymore on a regular basis, and that was it. The first show I worked on at the Barrymore was *The Real Thing* (2000) by Tom Stoppard. I didn't like it; I didn't care about any of the characters. I didn't know what the heck they were talking about! Then *Tale of the Allergist's Wife* (2000) came in and was great. That ran for a couple years and had several casts. I loved when we had *Betrayal* (2013), a great play by Harold Pinter, with Daniel Craig and Rachel Weisz.

There are a lot of substitute ushers who come in because people get sick, and other people have friends that they want to get into ushering. Sometimes there are little conflicts. You don't like this one or he doesn't like that one, but mainly it's a well-functioning family. Sometimes it's surprising what you're expected to do within a certain time frame. For example, when I worked *Swing* at the St. James we always had a ton of understudy inserts that we had to jam into Playbills before the house opened. That was kind of tough.

Some shows here have Sunday brunches. We used to have barbecues in the alley during the summer, but then the whole theater smelled like a picnic, so we stopped. That was a wonderful tradition. We have Christmas parties and birthday parties and all that.

Ms. Ethel Barrymore is obviously a very benign spirit. If we saw her walking around, it would be all for the good. I've heard of houses that are haunted, but I just feel that Ms. Barrymore is a kind spirit and her influence on the theater is a positive one.

———————

Ethel Barrymore was part of a great theatrical family, including her father Maurice Barrymore, her brothers John Barrymore and Lionel Barrymore, her nephew John Drew, and her great-niece Drew Barrymore.

Don't Drink the Water, *Woody Allen's first original Broadway play, spent some time at the Barrymore. Allen's Broadway career started with co-writing the libretto for an old-fashioned revue called* From A to Z *that played the Plymouth when he was 24 years old. Songs for the show were written by many early-career legends, including Mary Rodgers, Jerry Herman, and Fred Ebb. After that,* Don't Drink the Water, *a farce about the Iron Curtain, was produced in 1966. It opened at the Morosco, and moved to the Barrymore and then the Belasco, playing a total of 598 performances and launching Allen to even greater successes.*

———————

1977: Showers, Blackouts, And Ray Liotta

Joanna Gleason, Actor

I Love My Wife has a brilliant score by Cy Coleman and Michael Stewart. That show was the source of friendships that are with me to this day. Jimmy Naughton ended up living about five minutes up the road from my husband and me, in Connecticut; Ilene Graff and I have been close friends all these years, and our kids grew up as friends. Then there was the late Lenny Baker, who was amazing. We all just loved each other. That show was pretty special.

Ray Liotta came up to me recently and said, "Do you know that I worked concessions at the Barrymore when you were doing *I Love My Wife*?" I said, "Oh my God, you must have been 12!"

I remember the Barrymore as the most perfect size. It's not known as a musical house—I later ended up doing a play there, *Social Security*—but the Barrymore was intimate and gorgeous for our musical. It was small enough that you could feel the whole house. You got a sense of: *I can occupy this space.* This was before we were all body mic'd!

I climbed three flights to my little dressing room. At first, there was no shower available near me and Ilene. So I made an appointment with Gerry Schoenfeld. There I was, right off the turnip truck, and I made an appointment with the Shuberts! I came in, and he said, "Hi, doll!" and gave me a big hug. I said, "Mr. Schoenfeld, we have no shower!" Within a day, there was a pre-fab shower installed up on the third floor of the Barrymore. That was my doing.

Also, I was on that stage in July of 1977, when there was a blackout in New York. We were standing onstage, doing the show, and we heard the sound of power shutting off. Everything ground to a halt, and everything went black.

We got flashlights from the crew, and told everybody, "Don't panic." By flashlight, we finished a number! The audience stayed in their seats. Then, very orderly, everybody filed out and onto the streets of New York. Everybody made their way home that night in pitch black, together.

New York was fabulous that night. There was camaraderie in the streets. I was renting a place on the Upper East Side, so I walked from 47th Street to 81st Street, through blacked-out New York. It was great in 1977; I don't know how great it would be now. There we all were, hanging in the dark.

––––––––––––––

In 1945, Gertrude Lawrence starred in Pygmalion *at the Barrymore, the last straight play she ever did on Broadway.* Time Magazine *expressed delighted shock that the 32-year-old play was still relevant and, in fact, better than some current shows. In the 1940s, revivals weren't a regular occurrence. While Shakespeare's work and other work considered to be classic were redone in different productions, the idea that a show from a recent decade could come back so soon was the exception, not the rule.*

––––––––––––––

1977: Very Young And Very Old Hat

Ilene Graff, Actor

For *I Love My Wife*, it was love at first sight for me with Joanna Gleason. I had never met anybody as funny or as glamorous in one package. And she was married! It was almost too much. I still feel that way about her, and I tell her so all the time. "You're just too beautiful and too funny, and I can't believe you like me!" She had a certain exotic star-thing about her. She was the catch, and I was the New York actress who just worked. We were a good pair. She had this big dressing room where we hung out.

I remember things about the Barrymore, and then when I go back there, I'm surprised. *The stairs were here?! My room was here?!* I think what I've done is blend some of the theaters together. To some degree, it's magical, and then to some degree, it's really just your workplace. It's where you go to do your job—it just happens to not be an office or a store; it happens to be a theater. Sometimes, looking back on all those years I was doing shows, I'm almost jealous of my younger self and I think: *I would do anything to just peek back and see what it was really like.* Because I suppose my memories are romanticized and probably not as accurate as I think. I wish I could remember certain things better.

There were only four of us in *I Love My Wife*. One of my fondest memories of the run was that during the second act of the show, the boys were onstage together for a certain amount of time while Joanna and I had to be backstage sitting behind a flat,[25] on the floor. Every night, that would be our time to quietly schmooze and gossip and laugh.

———————

The Syracuse Herald-Journal *called* I Love My Wife, *"The first X-rated musical for the whole family!"*[26] *In fact, the show, about two couples who are old friends and consider a foursome, has the tone of a candy-colored sitcom: friendly and innuendo-filled, but not filthy. That was the point: the show brought America's sexual revolution to Broadway by displaying the bewilderment of suburban squares who audiences could relate to—longing for adventure and yet unsure of themselves.*

The show also brought its band into the action as small characters, in a way that was more revolutionary than its sexual content. Harvey, Stanley, Quentin, and Norman had roles in the plot and took the stage themselves, although they also happened to play instruments. Actor-musician shows and roles in musicals would increase exponentially in the years that followed, including the production of Company *directed by John Doyle that would play the Barrymore three decades later.*

———————

1978: Waiting At The Stage Door For The Smothers Brothers

Danny Burstein, Actor

I loved going to high school at the High School of the Performing Arts, and it completely changed my life. I was this kid from Queens, who knew nothing about any of it, and just had an idea that he wanted to be an actor. The year I auditioned, over 4000 kids auditioned for the school. About 128 made it in. I was very lucky.

We had an assignment at the High School of the Performing Arts to interview a theatre professional. And I didn't know anybody. I really knew nobody!

The Smothers Brothers were doing *I Love My Wife* at the time. I went to see the show; I second-acted[27] it! Then I waited at the stage door for one of them to come out. Dick Smothers went very quickly, but Tommy Smothers stood there and signed autographs. I decided to ask him. I said, "I'm going to the High School of The Performing Arts, and would it be possible that maybe I could interview you for a little while?" He said yes!

It was my first time backstage on Broadway. We were at the Ethel Barrymore. I interviewed Tommy Smothers for the better part of an hour. He couldn't have been lovelier. I asked him about what he thought about being in a Broadway show, and what it was like… I can't believe I remember this, but I asked him what he would do differently, if he had to live his life over again.

He said that he wouldn't be so afraid. That he wouldn't hide from people, and that he would just walk down the street and be as normal as possible. I have no idea what I did with any of the things I wrote down, or my assignment that I handed in. But I do remember him saying that. That stuck with me. I try to do more of that now. Some people really do separate themselves. And I just try to be as normal as possible.

———————

---

[25] flat: a flat piece of painted theatrical scenery
[26] Raidy, William A. "Season's Big Musical Overcame Early Troubles." *Syracuse Herald-Journal.* 7 May 1977: 8.
[27] second-acted: as a verb, this means to sneak into a show during intermission and catch only the second act

While the actors in I Love My Wife *spent a lot of time in bed together, real-life couple Hume Cronyn and Jessica Tandy hold the record at the Barrymore, having spent a year there in* The Fourposter, *and even longer on tour.*

1978: Brotherstudy

Walter Bobbie, Director/Actor

When the Smothers Brothers became the replacement stars in *I Love My Wife* on Broadway, the director, Gene Saks, asked me to understudy both of them. Yes, understudy *both* Smothers Brothers. I really needed a job at the time and I said, "yes," loving the challenge but never thinking I would actually go on. Cut to: Tommy Smothers gets the flu. A bad case. Really bad. For at least a week I was Dick Smothers' other brother.

What I remember most vividly is Dick's extraordinary generosity and focus. A lifetime with his brilliant, improvisatory brother Tommy kept Dick in the moment at every moment. Dick was endlessly playful and never seemed disappointed that his brother wasn't there. After my nerves settled, which to my surprise happened quickly, it was a joy to be onstage with a master straight-man who was used to high-wire improv. True spontaneity. Yes, we got all our laughs... well, all the ones in the script. The extra laughs that Dick and Tommy invented nightly were not actually in the script. That was comic genius between brothers. And understudying doesn't cover brotherhood.

Dick made me look good and let the audience know all was well. And except for the few patrons who asked for their money back, all really was well.

After that, I was offered another job understudying a star comic, but I had no desire to test my unique experience against a career of biting my nails in the wings while less adventurous patrons lined up for a refund.

1982: All The Kids Were Cheering

Craig Carnelia, Writer

Putting *is there life after high school?* up at Hartford Stage was a great experience. Since the show was so successful there, we knew it was coming to Broadway—and we had a choice of ten producers! I'm not exaggerating.

The show's experience in New York was misfired in every way, and very painful. Having looked back at it over the years, sometimes by myself and sometimes with my collaborator, bookwriter Jeff Kindley, we see what we did wrong and that there were about three fatal mistakes that we made—and by definition, one will do it.

Our first mistake was made on our first day of collaboration. I was doing *Working* at the time, and Jeff was very aware of it and really liked what we were doing with the material. On our first day on the *high school* show, we asked ourselves, "Do we want continuing characters? Or do we want it to be like *Working*, where people play a number of different characters?" We decided to have them play a number of different characters, and we could've gone home right then. In *Working*, that device suits the material because we're covering a vast span of society and a diversity of jobs. In *is there life after high school?* there was no such justification to have each actor change characters, especially since we were inventing the characters.

We failed, and it's unfortunate because I really like the book Ralph Keyes wrote, that the show is based on. And I really like my score, as do a lot of other people. The shape of the show just doesn't work. It also probably shouldn't have been on Broadway, and our director who had done fine with it in Hartford did not do as well in

New York. Then, when the show was in trouble, he ended up being replaced, but by that point, it was too late. The show was completely misfired, with some really talented people onstage, and a good score. We earned our failure; we made it happen.

It was my first time at the Barrymore, and while that time was vivid, it was not a pleasurable experience. It was difficult. I had an ulcer at the time, in my 30s, which I no longer have. I was in pain—actual physical pain— throughout the process. Plus, the process itself was painful. We needed a director who had done musicals. And Jeff and I should not have made that first fatal mistake.

In fact, many of the producers who saw it in Hartford, and loved it because it was so popular with audiences, said to us, "Gee, I wish there was a story." And everybody who has approached me since about doing something new with it has said the same thing. I'm positive that's the issue with that show. I approached Jeff a couple of years ago about our possibly doing something with it where we would start over and use the idea and some of the score... but it's not really going to happen.

Our time at the Barrymore was vivid and long because we extended previews. We stayed in previews for probably about five weeks, and I was there every day all day. I have many memories of that specific feeling of rehearsing a show in a Broadway theater: the feeling of coming in from the outside and going into this dark, intense place, where there are these pockets of work going on around the house. You walk through the rows and you bump into seats that are down. It's an unreal world, and outside, it's spring. It was so strange to come in from spring into the Barrymore every day and work. It was so intense and we fought so hard for the show after the directors changed. One pleasure I did have after the change was when I redirected "Fran and Janie" myself. I was telling our new director what I thought would make the song work better, and he said, "Just do it." So, I did. It's a special song and I enjoyed having the chance to take good care of it.

The closing performance was bizarre. There were only about 400 people there, in a theater that seats 1100. So, there were only a handful of people scattered in the mezzanine, and then no one on the sides or in the back of the orchestra.

When the house lights dimmed, there was a clicking like I'd never heard before, all over the house. It was the sound of people recording the show in various ways! I was with Scott Rudin, who had seen many of the previews with me and gone through the process with me. The show had no overture, and I remember turning to Scott and saying, "The clicking is like an overture." That's what I remember about our closing performance.

1982: Putting Band-Aids On The Show

Harry Groener, Actor

is there life after high school? was at the Barrymore, and that was a production that was problematic and flawed. The director was not right for the show, there were things wrong with the production, and we had to try to make it work.

One problem was that the book the show was based on was very white bread. High school can be very bloody, but the stories the book told were about love and friendships and cheerleading. So that was what the show was, too.

Craig Carnelia's songs were the best part of the show. They were richer, deeper, and had more to them than the monologues or anything else in the show. Design-wise, it felt like an off-Broadway piece that they tried to make into a Broadway show. That's always a mistake. At first we had a lot of designer costumes and then those went by the wayside, and we ended up with a unit costume with one different piece per character. When the show closed after 12 performances, we got to keep all our clothes.

The original director was fired, and several people stepped in to put "band-aids" on the show. It limped along until it closed. Years later, I saw the show again, at a tiny theater in L.A., with one of my castmates, Jamie Widdoes, who is now a successful TV director. The show worked so much better in a smaller space, but the problems of the monologues not being as good as the songs—that was still there. You can't solve that problem, but a lot of the other problems of the show were solved just by the nature of the space.

I loved working with the people who were in that show, and we still see each other occasionally. David Patrick Kelly works on TV and on Broadway, Jamie is in L.A., Sandy Faison is married and lives in Brooklyn. My wife goes on Facebook and finds out what's going on with each of my friends from *is there life after high school?* We all survived, but it was a difficult birth.

The next musical to play the Barrymore was Baby, *a show about three couples on a college campus who are expecting children: two unmarried students, sports instructors trying to conceive, and an older couple who already have three grown children. All three pairs deal with the upcoming life event and the highs and lows that come along with bringing a baby into the world.*

When Baby *hit Broadway in 1983, it brought the adult musical to a new level. The show was a realistic portrayal of average life events on a Broadway occupied with stories about dancing* Cats, *celebrity* Dreamgirls, *the cartoon characters of* Doonesbury, *the drag world of* La Cage aux Folles, *and the Greek drama of* Zorba. *In fact,* Baby *was in a musical genre of its own, with few peers, although* is there life after high school? *could certainly be considered one, and perhaps even* I Love My Wife, *to a degree. Something about the Barrymore's intimate feel but middle-range seating capacity lends itself to smaller musicals and these often tell a more realistic story than Gershwin-sized or Palace-sized juggernaut productions. The Barrymore was built for musicals about real people.*

While audiences who saw Baby *liked it, it was difficult to get them to buy tickets to this everyday story in the first place. The show was nominated for the Best Musical Tony and ran a respectable eight months, but its most lasting legacy may be its first act finale: a young woman singing on her own about the first time she feels her baby kick.*

1983: The Surge And The Rush

Liz Callaway, Actor

I just remember *Baby* being very intense. It was too exciting for words. I remember being so nervous for the entire time we were running!

Before the first preview, we did an invited dress. My sister came. We went to eat at Mamma Leone's beforehand, and I couldn't eat anything. I tried to have a cup of soup, and I couldn't. It was just so exciting.

One of the most exciting things on any show is the first time you see the marquee. That's always an incredible moment. Seeing the *Baby* marquee was interesting, because they actually made a mistake with the artwork! If you look at the music notes that are in the artwork, it's like they were designed inside-out. That was funny.

Being in the Barrymore Theatre was nice because we were right next door to the Biltmore, where *Doonesbury* was playing. That was fun, because we'd all run into each other. It was a really good season overall, an interesting season.

One of my most vivid memories of *Baby* is that we had our closing notice up practically every week. On Wednesday matinees, the whole company would get Variety and we would read the grosses together. We'd think: *This is the week we're going to close*. I was the Equity deputy,[28] so I had to deal with certain things. We were on salary cuts.

Had I known that we were going to run that long, I would've enjoyed it more! But I really always thought: *Well, this is the end. Oh wait no, this is the end! Okay, well, one more week*. It was not a run where you could relax and just enjoy it. There were many things we did enjoy—I loved the Broadway softball league![29]—but we just never relaxed into the run.

I met my husband through *Baby*. He was a fan, and I remember talking to him after performances. He would wait outside afterward, near the stage door. He came to the first preview because he had auditioned for the show. He's a director now, but he was an actor then, and he thought: *Oh, let's see who got that part*. And then he thought: *Wow, look at her*. He saw the show 13 times.

We finally started dating a few weeks before the show closed. It was funny, because the producers joked, "By the end, he had really good seats!" *Baby* will always have those great memories for me.

Lizzie was my first lead and greatest role. That spoiled me! I thought: *I am going to have a lot of these. What interesting part will be next?* But they don't write parts like that. They're very rare. And it was a great cast, a very special group. The show may have been slightly ahead of its time.

I loved doing "What Could Be Better?" I think that is just the most perfectly crafted song. I loved doing that with Todd. I loved doing "The Story Goes On", of course. "Ladies Singing Their Song" was great. I liked "I Want It All", but that song had so many lyric changes that it was a *lot* of work to remember them all while you were performing.

I remember one night during the show, I started to feel really woozy. I started being not able to see out of one of my eyes. During the first act, I thought: *Oh my God. I'm going blind*. I kept doing the show. That night, I sang "The Story Goes On", thinking: *This is the last time I'm going to be able to see*. It was *so dramatic*.

I got off stage, and someone said, "Oh, you have a migraine!" I thought: "I do? Oh!" I was 22 and had never had one, so I just didn't know. Now my son is 22, and it's amazing and weird to think that I was his age when I did *Baby*. So young!

———————

Much like Baby, Doonesbury *(104 performances) next door was filled with young actors who would go on to great careers, including Mark Linn-Baker, Gary Beach, and Kate Burton. Two of the leads, Laura Dean and Lauren Tom would both have large guest roles on early seasons of* Friends, *playing Rachel's co-worker Sophie and Ross' girlfriend Julie. While* Baby *was based on realistic life events and* Doonesbury *on Gary Trudeau's comics, the kids of both musicals hung out together on 47th Street, and wondered if their shows would run, while a new play called* Noises Off *opened across the street.*

———————

1983: TKTS

Julia Murney, Actor

Because I grew up in the city, I was lucky in that my mom and I would go to TKTS on a whim. That's how I saw *Baby*, that's how I saw *Sunday in the Park with George*. It wasn't because we went, "Let's go see *Sunday in the Park*," we just said, "We'll go and see what's up!"

---

[28] Equity deputy: a liaison between performers and the union, elected by the Actors' Equity company members in a show
[29] Check out *The Untold Stories of Broadway, Volume 1* for more on this.

I loved *Baby,* and then I got the cast album and loved it all over again. Liz Callaway was amazing and Catherine Cox was fantastic and Beth Fowler did this little thing vocally that I inadvertently stole! It's a sort of vocal fall-off. It got lodged in my brain. I loved that show.

———————

I interviewed Julia Murney in her apartment. I interviewed Craig Carnelia in his classroom just before he began teaching. I interviewed Ilene Graff at the Irish Rogue, a 44th Street haunt that no longer exists, and Harry Groener at Hurley's, a 48th Street haunt that does. Danny Burstein and I chatted for an hour on a bench in Riverside Park, watching kids walk by with balloons. With Richard Maltby Jr., I sat in a diner on the Upper East Side, deserted except for him and me, exclaiming about Miss Saigon *and* Ain't Misbehavin'*... and* Baby.

———————

1983: Becoming A Parent

Richard Maltby Jr., Writer/Director

I wish someone had kept a diary during *Baby.*

Right before previews started, we wrote a new ending, but we were in tech so we didn't have time to put it in. We had to tech the existing ending. Then, when previews started, the first thing we did was cut it.

We put two or three new numbers in during previews. John Lee Beatty, our scenic designer, created this moment where a bunch of basinets and high chairs came out on a track, and that lasted a day. Scenes changed completely. I remember someone who came to the first preview, and then saw the show after it opened, and could not believe how different it was.

Because I never watched the show from the very front of the orchestra section, I didn't realize that the show's track was noisy. We got a lot of flak for that, but we just didn't know because we couldn't hear it. You should always try to watch your show from every spot in the theater.

I loved the Barrymore Theatre. I thought it was a great house.

Nobody had wanted to put money into *Baby*. Raising the money was like pulling teeth. We finally got it, but at that point in the year, it was hard to get a theater. Our producer, Jim Freydberg, went to the Shubert Organization and basically said to Bernie Jacobs, "I have my entire life on the line here. I have mortgaged my house. You have to give me a theater." Bernie was a genuinely kind person. He gave us the Barrymore Theatre.

During our last workshop before Broadway, we had a 4th storyline, about a single woman who was going to have a baby without getting married. It was one story too many, so we cut that out, at which point the house of cards that was the structure of the show kind of disappeared. We slowly built it back up, between that workshop and our first day of rehearsal for Broadway.

On the first day of rehearsal, we discovered that our second act was too glum. The characters had all these problems, and it seemed like the show was saying that babies ruin lives. That wasn't what we wanted to say at all! We wanted to write about how babies change your life, change your relationships.

At the end of our first day of rehearsal, we threw out the second act, and started to construct a new one. That ended up giving us a lot of changes we had to make in the first act as well.

We wanted to write about this incredible act of bravery, becoming a parent. An incredible act of bravery that's very ordinary, and happens every day. And we didn't want stories about people who shouldn't be married; that would've been easy. We wanted to tell stories about people who belonged together, who were in good marriages. We wanted to get to the bottom of that specific thing that all marriages have. There's something you don't talk about. A mutually accepted lie of some sort. The baby usually puts that on display, and you have to confront what you actually are to each other. For example, with the characters Nick and Pam and their relationship, Nick is the strong one who always takes care of Pam when she falls apart. What happens when it turns out they can't get pregnant and it's his problem and not hers? Is he able to accept strength from her, despite the premise of their relationship? No, because all of the other elements of his life are solved by the fact that he can be strong in his marriage. These were the kinds of things we were writing about in *Baby*.

Another challenge in writing *Baby* was that, as everyone knows, plays are conflict. Scenes in plays have to have conflict. You scream at me and I scream at you, and that's how we have a dramatic action—except when the issue is a baby. If the issue is a baby, you can't, and you usually don't, yell at your wife, "How could you let this happen?!" You usually say, "Oh, I couldn't be happier!" That changed the dynamic of the show. We had a lot of scenes where there was an enormous amount of subtext, and a surface where no one seems to be dealing with what's going on. That led to a script of *Baby* that sometimes gets productions where nobody goes below the surface! It's funny. Luckily, the score always redeems the show, and the songs eventually get real enough that you can't deny what's going on. But sometimes, people don't dig into the subtext of the book, and they play the show like a sitcom.

We changed *Baby* all throughout rehearsals and previews. We changed a lot. The last thing we did was take the song "Patterns" out, for reasons that we thought made sense at the time, but really didn't. We shouldn't have done that. But we ran the whole season!

———————

Fun fact: at the age of 19, I spotted Richard Maltby Jr. in the audience at a performance of Lennon *at the Broadhurst. All I had with me was a Snapple, so I asked him to autograph it. I still have my Richard Maltby Jr. Snapple wrapper.*

———————

1983: Songs That Haven't Been Written

David Shire, Writer

I was just so happy to be in any Broadway theater for the first time, doing *Baby*, a show of mine. I would've preferred to be in the Shubert, which we were in for our next show, *Big*. The Barrymore is a smaller house. And it's not quite in the heart of Broadway. It's on 47th Street, so it's a little out of the Broadway hubbub. But I would've taken anything! It was so hard to get a theater for a relatively unknown team. I just remember that it was kind of small, and the orchestra pit was not that big. We had the orchestra onstage, in the back, for that production.

On the first day of rehearsal, after six years of workshops, and endless rewriting, the cast read the show. We pow-wowed after it, and we all agreed that the second act was all wrong. It wasn't working. So while Richard was staging the first act, during the first week or so, we were actually also going back to one of our apartments and rewriting the entire second act every night. In a week or two, we had a new second act. That was quite a rewrite. But you always change things during previews.

The end of the first act, "The Story Goes On", is a high point for me and for other people too. Liz Callaway first feels the baby kick and sings that song, which is kind of a unique song. Richard and I like to write songs that haven't been written. As far as I know, no one had ever written a song for a woman when she first feels her baby kick. I think that's why it's such a powerful moment: it was such an unexpected song.

One of my favorite memories is when I'd drop in to see the show by myself. I'd just wander in and see the second act, or curtain call, or something. One of the pleasures of having a show on, especially at that age, was that I could just drop in! I could watch it any time. I used to go in and stand in the wings while they were doing the finale. It was so exciting to be watching it from standing in the wings, like I was in a movie musical.

1983: A *Baby* Baby

Todd Graff, Actor/Director

I never really knew that I wanted to be an actor or a director. At first, I wanted to be a writer. I never went to college and after I graduated high school, I was broke, doing crap jobs. The girl I was living with at the time, Dawn, worked in casting, and a show called *American Passion* came into her office.

American Passion wanted rock 'n' roll kids for the cast; they didn't want actor kids. They wanted people who had never done a show before. And I was in a rock 'n' roll band. My entire band auditioned individually for the show, and two of us got in. All of a sudden, I was an actor.

The show was the inaugural production at the Joyce Theater. It was directed and choreographed by Pat Birch. The cast! It was Jane Krakowski, Martha Plimpton, Robert Downey Jr. *American Passion* opened and closed in one night. But it was in previews for a month, which was lucky because Richard Maltby and David Shire and Jim Freydberg, who were working on *Baby*, all came to see it. That's how I got *Baby*. And Norman Lear, the producer of *American Passion*, signed me to sort of an overall "actor deal," and that started my television career. So even though *American Passion* was a big flop, it was very important for me professionally.

When *Baby* happened, my sister, Ilene, was about to give birth to my niece, who was the first of that generation to be born in our family. We're a very, very close family, and my sister lives in Los Angeles. She gave birth when we were early in previews with *Baby*. There were still changes going in every day, but I had said all along that when my niece was born, I was going to need to go to Los Angeles for a day to see the baby. They were understandably opposed to that, because we were in previews. There was a lot of tension and screaming. But it was very important to me!

Despite them saying, "If you go, don't come back," I left *Baby* and went to meet my niece. I missed two shows. When I came back, everything was fine. It was a big deal for me when my sister came to see *Baby* a couple weeks later, right after she had given birth. That was very emotional.

I never considered myself an actor. I never took any acting classes, and I never really knew what I was doing. It was always fun for me, because I had no discipline. I think the good thing about my playing Danny was that I was always completely in the moment when I was onstage. The bad thing about it was that all the other actors had to deal with this idiot who never knew what he was going to do. As a director now, I wouldn't want an actor like I was, but it was certainly fun for me!

I'm not a dancer at all and I had a hard time learning choreography—and there were two numbers in *Baby* where I had to *dance*: "Fatherhood Blues" and "Two People In Love". We were rehearsing with our choreographer, Wayne Cilento, and it was hopeless because I just couldn't learn it! Then Wayne had the idea of taking Liz Callaway and me out to a club. We went out dancing at a club one night, and at rehearsal the next day, Wayne started pulling out things he had seen me do, by myself or with Liz, when we were clubbing. That's how those two numbers were choreographed. He was nominated for a Tony Award for Best Choreography!

Sondheim came to see the show because he was very friendly with Maltby and Shire. He actually came during that first week of previews, when we were having that big fight about me leaving to go to Los Angeles. After the performance that night, he told Maltby and Shire that he thought the show was great, but that they had to "get

68

rid of that kid"—meaning me. Because I had no chops at all, no technique, if I was upset, Danny was upset. If I was happy, Danny was happy. There I was, in the middle of this horrible situation with the producers, so Danny was just miserable and erratic for the entire show. For some reason, Sondheim thought that was the wrong way to interpret the role! But Sondheim and I subsequently made up.

Liz had a little crush on me while we were playing Lizzie and Danny, and for my birthday, she got the band together, onstage, at the theater, and recorded the Olivia Newton-John song "Make a Move on Me". The lyrics go: "I'm the one you want / that's all I wanna be / so come on, baby / make a move on me." And I was gay, but not out at the time. So she had a crush on me and she recorded "Make a Move on Me" and gave it to me as a gift. I got it and I was like, "This is so cool! You should totally sing pop music!" I completely missed the point, and said to her, "What if you got into a studio? Screw this Broadway stuff! You could do this!" She just looked at me like, "You really don't get it, do you?" I really didn't get it. She literally made me a song called "Make a *Move* on Me". That happened in the theater, on that stage.

Every night I stood in the wings and watched Liz sing "The Story Goes On". Every night. I was the only person in the show who was new to it when we started Broadway rehearsals. I was the only one who hadn't done the last workshop. I didn't know anything about it. We sat down around the table and did the read-through and on that first day, Liz sang "The Story Goes On", just sitting at a table, and blew me out of the room. I couldn't believe how amazing she and the song both were.

By the time she was singing "The Story Goes On" onstage eight times a week, I was thinking: *I love this show. I love it because I'm in it. I love it because it's good. But also, there's something really special going on here. There's something really important and memorable about* this *woman, at* this *point in her life and her career, with her amazing talent, singing* this *song from* this *show.* I wanted to watch it whenever I could, so I did. Every night.

———————

*Nikka Graff Lanzarone, now a Broadway actress in her own right (*Women on the Verge of a Nervous Breakdown, Chicago*) still has her Uncle Todd's show jacket[30] from* Baby. *When the Transport Group presented a concert of* Baby *in 2012, Todd and Liz hosted it, and Nikka sang one of the roles.*

In stark contrast to Baby, American Passion *is a show that the world hasn't heard anything about since its 42 previews and one performance in July of 1983, when it opened the Joyce Theater. Todd may have gotten* Baby *out of it, but both Martha Plimpton (age 12) and Jane Krakowski (age 14) were fired before opening/closing night. Frank Rich in the* Times *observed that the show was a rip-off of* A Chorus Line *only with teenagers pouring out their hopes and dreams to an unseen D.J.*

———————

1983: The Graff Family Of Broadway

Ilene Graff, Actor

My brother Todd was in rehearsal for *Baby* when I was pregnant with my daughter, Nikka. He told them, "My sister is having a baby and when the baby is born, I'm going to LA." They sort of said, "Yeah, yeah, yeah." Then Nikka was born and Todd said, "I'm going to LA to see my niece," and they said, "No, you're not." So he said, "Then I quit." And they said, "No, no, no."

He came and he met the baby and then went back. As soon as I felt I could leave her for a couple of days, I came to New York with my friend Linda to see the show. We sat there, Linda and I, holding on to each other and hysterically crying through the whole thing! There was my little brother, being a big Broadway star in his show,

---

[30] show jacket: most Broadway shows used to create jackets for their teams, with the title of the production on the back

singing like an angel—about having babies! And Liz Callaway? Give me a break! To this day, every time I see her, I say, "How did you *do* that?!"

Baby was just fabulous. I'm so lucky—my family is ridiculous. They're just ridiculous! Can you imagine going to see *Les Mis* and seeing your little cousin Randy originate Fantine on Broadway?! And you get to say, "That's my baby cousin Randy!" It's very exciting. We're very lucky.

1986: Barrymore Brunches

Joanna Gleason, Actor

I was back at the Barrymore about ten years after *I Love My Wife*, for *Social Security* in 1986. I think I had my old dressing room.

We had a fantastic cast—Olympia Dukakis, Marlo Thomas, Ron Silver, Stefan Schnabel—and Kenny Welsh, who one night, was in his dressing room watching the playoffs, and didn't show up at all for our entrance. I came on alone one night!

When we were doing *Social Security*, all of us—the wardrobe crew, the stage crew, the cast—had brunch in the basement together before the Sunday matinee. Sometimes, we had theme brunches! Occasionally, we would do barbecues between shows with the cast of *Precious Sons*, because they were back to back with us, at the Longacre. We shared an alley, so they could look into our windows and we could look into theirs, and sometimes we'd eat burgers together.

1988: August Wilson

Irene Gandy, Press Agent

August Wilson was a very, very good friend of mine. Such a talent.

When we first started working on shows together, I was the only other person of color there a lot of the time. There was an honesty between us.

He didn't go to opening night of *Joe Turner's Come and Gone* because they told him he could only have a couple seats, so he gave them away. And he would only stay at the Edison Hotel. I remember he told me once that as long as he could write, he didn't care if his plays were presented in a basement or a theater.

I'm the founder of the Black Theatre Festival, and I did a lot of work bringing artists together, like August, Ron Milner, Ed Bullins. They were like a family.

When August first started writing, he was told that he had plagiarized his work. He hadn't. He was such a quiet person, and very political through his writing, and wrote so much about families. I don't know any other playwright that wrote the volume of hit plays that he did, other than Tennessee Williams. There were so many great ones, but he told me the play of his he liked the best wasn't his biggest hit, *Fences*. It was *Joe Turner's Come and Gone*. When I saw it revived this season, that was incredible.

I miss him a lot. He was an amazing man.

————————

In the 1970s, filmmaker and auteur Melvin Van Peebles took over the Barrymore with both Aint Supposed To Die A Natural Death *and* Don't Play Us Cheap! *For each of these musicals, Van Peebles wrote book, music and lyrics. In the case of* Don't Play Us Cheap!, *he was director and producer as well.* Ain't Supposed... *came first, in 1971, and had the tagline: Tunes From Blackness. The show used both spoken word and rap to tell stories of black street life, including brutal killings and a corrupt justice system. It was nominated for seven Tony Awards including Best Musical, with song titles like "Funky Girl on Motherless Broadway", "I Got The Blood", and "Put A Curse On You". The follow-up,* Don't Play Us Cheap!, *in 1972, was less successful, and followed a pair of devils trying to break up a Harlem house party. With their immediacy and perspective on black street life in America, both shows bear resemblance to* Holler If Ya Hear Me *(2014). In fact,* Holler *listed its setting in its Playbill as "NOW on MY BLOCK."* Ain't Supposed... *listed "Here. Now." and* Don't Play Us Cheap's *setting was "A couple days before tomorrow. Here." Four decades apart, these shows brought a similar jolt of awareness about the African American experience to the Broadway stage.*

In between the two Van Peebles shows, a musical called Inner City *played the Barrymore. Another experiment in the 1970s hippie musical theatre genre that was birthed from* Hair's *success,* Inner City *was based on a book by Eve Merriam about urban problems in America. In that way, it was similar to its fellow Barrymore musicals of the early 1970s.* Inner City *called itself "a street cantata," but was categorized within Broadway circles as a revue. Today, we would call it a song cycle, as the show has a score written specifically for it. Song cycles first started to enter American musical theatre as a significant, identified genre in the 1990s, with shows like Maury Yeston's* December Songs *and Jason Robert Brown's* Songs For A New World. *But just like those,* Inner City *was an evening of songs by one writer on a specific theme, with moments linked by concept rather than character.* Inner City *was the only Broadway producing credit of the late politician Harvey Milk.*

———————————

1993: Wendy Wasserstein

Tom Hewitt, Actor

Going into *The Sisters Rosensweig* as a replacement was great, because there was pretty much an entirely new replacement cast. We got a full four weeks of rehearsal together, so that was awesome. It was really like starting the show fresh, and we created a new sensibility for the material together. I didn't feel a need to imitate John Vickery, and we all felt that way about the people we replaced.

I have a vivid memory of myself, Amy Ryan, and Brían O'Byrne purposefully standing together, three-in-a-row, and then walking into our first Broadway stage door together. We were all making our debuts! That was fun.

Hal Linden was really nervous before our first performance, and he was a fantastic Broadway veteran! That surprised me. I thought: *Oh Christ, that never goes away? Wow. Welcome to a lifetime of stage fright, Tom.*

Working with Wendy Wasserstein was great. I recently came across this beautiful piece of Wedgwood China that she gave me for opening night. I found it and hung it up, and it brought back great memories. I loved it when she watched the show. She told me I was one of the best actors she'd ever worked with. She kept saying that to me. I loved her.

1997: Cy Coleman

Doug Katsaros, Orchestrator/Writer

Cy Coleman called me one day and he said, "I want you on this new show I'm doing." He called me because I had worked with him on *Welcome to the Club*. It hadn't done well, but we worked together well, and he wanted me on *The Life*.

I ended up being the vocal and dance arranger. The score was incredible from the beginning. *The Life* was about prostitutes, so perhaps that was off-putting to people. But the songs were terrific and Chuck Cooper and Lillias White both won well-deserved Tony Awards. Once we got the show up, it was all just about making what was already good work better. And what always worked was that Cy Coleman music!

1999: The Carol Burnett Blackout

Amy Wolk, Merchandise Manager/On Site Educator

One day, during *Putting It Together*, there was a blackout. Lightning struck and the lights all went out. They came back on, but the whole grid had to be reset. I was there.

While they reset the grid, Carol Burnett came onstage, explained what happened, and answered questions. I watched this happen, and it was like the beginning of *The Carol Burnett Show*! She took all kinds of questions. She told jokes. She yodeled!

The other actors sat on the side of the stage, watching and laughing. They all joked around with each other, and watched Carol.

Later during the run, Bronson Pinchot got injured, and Evan Pappas came in temporarily to replace him. Then, something happened and there was one day where there was no one to play that part. So, Christina Marie Norrup, who understudied the Younger Woman, went on for that role!

When you're in the theater every day, you see stuff happen that no one else ever gets to see happen. You see understudies go on for parts they've never gone on for before. You see technical snafus, where everyone rallies. You see a lot.

2000: An Eight By Ten Glossy

Evan Pappas, Actor

Carol Burnett was my idol. When I was in high school, my friend Joyce and I would write scripts and send them to *The Carol Burnett Show*. They were horrible. We were just kids from Daly City, California who wanted to be discovered.

We would send in these terrible scripts, and we would always get back these eight by ten glossys of Carol or the cast, with a stamped-on autograph and a Xeroxed letter saying, "Thank you for your interest." We kept all of them. It was around 1974.

Cut to 2000, and Carol Burnett is starring in *Putting It Together* on Broadway. They asked me to replace one of the actors, and suddenly I was rehearsing and going to meet her! When I was introduced, I just stuttered. I had never done that! There are two people in the world I have that kind of reaction to: her and Stephen Sondheim. So there I was *in Putting It Together*, singing his music, with her.

I turned into a kid in front of Carol Burnett. I told her the story about Joyce and me writing her fan letters and sending our scripts, and she joked, "Oh, we probably used them!" I said, "Oh no you didn't. We never missed an episode!" She laughed and I told her about the stamped, autographed eight by tens. We chatted a bit more and then I went up to my dressing room.

Not two minutes later, there was a knock on my dressing room door. I opened it, and it was Carol's dresser with a photo of her. On it, she had written: "Evan, This is not stamped. Love, C."

We became great friends during that show. I only got to do it for three weeks, and I only had three days to learn it. And I was onstage with George Hearn, Carol Burnett, Kathie Lee Gifford. They were wonderful. It was just the greatest experience.

I played a character called The Observer, who started at the back of the house each night, and would come down and talk to the audience. Because of that, I spent a lot of time gabbing with the ushers. Whenever I went back to the Barrymore to see shows after that, we'd have the best time catching up.

When my three weeks in the show were up, on my last day, I found out that Carol had been watching me do "Buddy's Blues" from the wings every night. That's when I went: *Okay, you can retire now*. My childhood idol, one of the reasons I went into this crazy business, was watching me do a song from the wings every night? She didn't have to do that. That was amazing. It was worth anything.

2000: The Great Playwright

Fritz Frizsell, Stagehand

During previews of *The Real Thing*, I was the extra sound man for a couple weeks. It was the kind of job where you were constantly on standby. When they needed you, they needed you fast, but most of your time was spent waiting. I was always in the back of the house, behind the curtains that separate the orchestra seats from the lobby doors. So, too, as it happens, was Tom Stoppard.

I have always been a huge fan of his, and after the second day, since it was always just me and him, I summoned the nerve to tell him that I loved his work and that *Rosencrantz and Guildenstern Are Dead* was my all-time favorite play, with *The Real Thing* a close second. We chatted a bit every day for the rest of the week. Somehow no one ever saw us talking. On my final day, I was scheduled to leave at intermission. I packed up my stuff and exited through the alley, where my boss, a bunch of stagehands and Tom Stoppard were, most of them on a smoke break. I bid them all a good night. "Fritz!" Stoppard said. "You're leaving?" Jaws dropped. Tom Stoppard knew my name?

"Yes, Mr. Stoppard, this was my last night."

"Well, it's been very nice talking to you."

"It's been an honor working with you," I said as I left, leaving my boss and brother stagehands wondering just how I knew the great playwright.

Tom Stoppard has spent a significant amount of time at the Barrymore. The original production of Travesties *and the first Broadway revivals of both* The Real Thing *and* Arcadia *played the Barrymore.*

During the original production of The Real Thing, *which played the Plymouth, Cynthia Nixon made history for appearing in both that show and* Hurlyburly *at the Barrymore at the same time. This was possible because both productions were directed by Mike Nichols, who wanted her for both roles. Cynthia's character was in the very beginning and very end of the three-and-a-half-hour long* Hurlyburly, *and in between, she would run through the Edison Hotel and across 47th, 46th, and 45th Streets to play her role in* The Real Thing. *According to Tony Walton,* *who worked on both productions, "They were close, but not <u>that</u> close. She really had to run for it!" Cynthia was 18 at the time. Equity has since changed its rules so that one actor can't play two principal roles simultaneously.*

In 1927, Beulah Bondi appeared in the first act of Mariners *at the Plymouth and the second act of* Saturday's Children *at the Booth.*

———————

2002: A Different Time At The Barrymore

Craig Carnelia, Writer

Decades after *is there life after high school?*, I came back to the Barrymore to work on *Imaginary Friends* with Marvin Hamlisch. When we first heard which theater the show would be in, I thought: *Oh no! Not the Barrymore!* I'm not by nature superstitious, but that was my gut reaction.

I didn't feel that way once the show moved in. The Barrymore is a gorgeous theater, and it was the perfect place for *Imaginary Friends.* The formality and traditional quality of the space that had felt so wrong for the smaller, more casual *is there life after high school?* perfectly suited the world of Lillian Hellman and Mary McCarthy. Also, it was a different time in my life, and I was a happier man. *Imaginary Friends* happened at the end of a very busy time for me, when I had three shows in production over the course of one year. So the show had a great sense of focus about it for me.

My favorite memory from that entire experience took place in Cherry Jones' dressing room. Watching Cherry's process throughout the workshops and productions of *Imaginary Friends* had been a feast and a lesson in itself. But late in our run, she confided in me that a line from one of my lyrics had given her the key to her character. The song was a Shirley Temple-style pastiche with serious overtones. In it, her character says: "All that lonely loneliness is through." I had felt, in studying Mary McCarthy, that that might be what had driven her. Apparently, Cherry agreed.

———————

The 2003 movie Something's Gotta Give *starring Jack Nicholson and Diane Keaton featured scenes at the Barrymore Theatre. Keaton's character was a playwright, and her newest production,* A Woman To Love, *based on autobiographical events that happen to the character in the movie, premieres at the Barrymore. When the film was shooting there, President Bill Clinton was nearby and heard about it—and stopped by to say hello to his friend Jack Nicholson.*

———————

2002: Nora And Marvin And Craig And Jack

Harry Groener, Actor

Nora Ephron was brilliant. I was so sad about her passing in 2012. We got to work together on *Imaginary Friends*, which she wrote along with Marvin Hamlisch and Craig Carnelia.

I was playing Feste in *Twelfth Night* at the Old Globe in San Diego, when my director, Jack O'Brien, took me to dinner and talked to me about this play. He said, "This is the team: me, Nora, Marvin, and Craig." That was it. Just to be in the room with those people, plus Cherry Jones and Swoosie Kurtz? I didn't care what the piece was. I said: "I'm there."

The show was about Mary McCarthy and Lillian Hellman, and I played all the men in their lives. The schedule entailed a workshop, some readings in New York, a production on the West Coast, and then bringing the show to New York. The dates were all laid out, and everything happened the way Jack said it would happen.

Nora was brilliant. She just sat there and observed and wrote and fixed. She was very supportive, and always right there with you as scenes were unfolding. She was intense; there was always a specific kind of intensity about her.

Marvin was a vaudevillian. You'd come in for the first day of rehearsal and go, "Hey Marvin, how ya doin'?" And he'd reply singing: "Hey Marvin, how ya doin'? Ya da la da ba da!" He just always had a song. Everything was a song to him, and he was larger than life. Marvin always enjoyed what was going on; he loved working with people. At one point, I was working with the musical director on a song, and he said to Marvin, "Do you mind if we try this with it?" And Marvin said, "Whoa whoa whoa. Of course I don't mind, but also, I want you to think of me as a dead composer." He meant that he wanted us to have the freedom to do whatever we wanted with the material. He gave us that freedom and then he walked out of the room.

What he was saying was that he trusted us. He trusted people who were going to work with his music. He was a generous and sweet man, and it was an honor to work with him. And it was also so fascinating to see how he and Craig worked together! They were such different people and their work together was incredible. They had such respect for each other, and collaborated brilliantly. They fit together like a handshake. It was great to see.

Then there was Jack, who really is the cheerleader of the American theatre. He just loves the theatre, and he wants it all to work. He creates a safe room for everyone to take their chances in. He's inspiring. He inspired all of us. When he gave notes, they were insightful and brilliantly written in and of themselves. They were like speeches. Working with him was stunning, and I wish I could do every play with him.

Bob Fosse's two closest cohorts, Herb Garder and Paddy Chayefsky, both had their biggest Broadway flops at the Barrymore. Gardner's The Goodbye People *ran for seven performances in 1968, and Chayefsky's* The Passion of Josef D. *ran 15 performances in 1964. The three men lamented these losses as they did with all ups and downs in the theatre: by meeting over sandwiches at the Carnegie Deli. As has been well documented, the deli was practically an office conference room for these great creators of the American theatre, even though their actual offices were a few feet away at 850 7th Avenue.*

2006/2008/2011: tick, tick… *Company*!

Raúl Esparza, Actor

I was cast in the Broadway revival of *Assassins* in 2001. The production ended up being cancelled because of September 11, and it eventually happened years later with a different cast. But because I was cast in *Assassins*, I got to meet Steve Sondheim. A few weeks later, he came to see *tick, tick… BOOM!* because he was Jonathan Larson's mentor. He came to the show with James Lapine, and after that I got a call that they wanted me to come in and audition for the Sondheim Celebration at the Kennedy Center!

They wanted me to audition for George in *Sunday in the Park with George* and Franklin Shepard in *Merrily We Roll Along*. I told my agent, "No way. I want to go in for Charley!" I had dreamt of singing "Franklin Shepard Inc." since I was in college. I never thought I actually had a shot at either role. I had only done one Broadway show at that point. Still, I was thrilled that they wanted me to audition.

Then *Assassins* was cancelled. I was in the middle of a workshop for *Urban Cowboy* when my agent called me: "Honey, they're going to offer you Charley! But hold on. Because I think it's very possible that they're going to offer you George, too." I went from being scared that I would never get to work with Sondheim to suddenly doing the greatest part I've ever played, George, and a part I'd always wanted to play, Charley, in rep with him at the Kennedy Center!

And then I even got to work with Sondheim on Broadway in *Company* four years later. Bernie Telsey thought I would make a good Bobby, and wanted me to meet with John Doyle. So I went to see his production of *Sweeney Todd*. I didn't really get it, but I still couldn't shake the feelings the production had left me with. So I went to see it again, and was completely overwhelmed the second time. Patti LuPone's performance in that production was one of the most powerful things I've ever seen. She played five things at once in her final scene: she realizes Sweeney is about to kill her, and she's fighting for her life, and she's also seducing him—she's truly feeling five emotions at once, and she played all of them. It was a master class. Her body was in his arms and she was physically reaching away from him and screaming, but simultaneously holding his face and trying to caress him. It was unbelievable. I thought: *I have to talk to him. I have to meet the guy who directed this.*

John Doyle and I met and we talked about *Company*. I read the play for the first time on my 35th birthday. They offered it to me a week later.

I had seen *Company* before, but I'd never loved it. It wasn't one of my favorite Sondheim shows. I saw *Sweeney Todd* in California, and the music was insane and soaring. The second act quartet was a sonic explosion of blood. I went to school with Danielle Ferland, so I saw her in *A Little Night* Music at New York City Opera, and I loved that. I saw *Into The Woods* on Broadway right as I was about to start college at NYU, so I felt like that show was a bit about my life at the time, in terms of what I was stepping into and what was ahead of me. I was always afraid of New York, in a way. Sondheim's shows mean different things to you as you go through life, and I loved so many of them for different reasons.

Still, *Company* was not a show that I named as a favorite early in life. I didn't understand its irony and its cynicism eluded me. "Being Alive" never struck me. The show just didn't have an emotional impact on me. I found it to be a very cold, hard piece of writing. Then I started to listen to *Company* on my headphones while I was walking around New York City. I really heard the music, and thought: *Oh! That's what he was doing!* The rhythms of the city are in the score of *Company*. It's a score that takes a certain amount of musical sophistication to appreciate. Something like *Sweeney* hits you hard and wows you, whereas *Company*'s charms are more subtle. They take time.

Working with John Doyle is one of the greatest gifts any actor can get. Our *Company* started at the Cincinnati Playhouse. We rehearsed for six weeks there and did the show. There was no intention for it to move to Broadway. I wasn't planning on that. I had just done *Chitty Chitty Bang Bang* and I really needed to get back to basics. *Chitty* wasn't a great experience. We loved the team, but it turned out not to be the show we signed up for. I actually had a conversation with Steve about my being cast in *Company*. Why would I want to play Bobby? There are better parts I could play—like George and Charley even. I said, "I don't care about that. I want to work with you and John." I knew that going out-of-town and working with this wonderful director, and with Steve, would be healing.

After six weeks rehearsing, I realized that I didn't understand the show. I began to feel like I was learning what it was about every time I watched Elizabeth Stanley, the magnificent girl who played April, and Barbara Walsh, especially. Her character, Joanne is the lynchpin of the show, and Barbara really tapped into what *Company* was about. At one point during rehearsal for "Ladies Who Lunch", John asked me, "What's the most significant thing in this song?" I said, "She's really bitter." He turned to Barbara and asked the same question. She said, "Everybody dies." It's true!

John's rehearsal process is unique. You never do a run-through with John. You run parts of scenes over and over like you're rehearsing scales on a piano. I have a tendency to externalize in rehearsals early on, like I have finger paint and I'm using too much of each color to make black. I make way too many choices to make my performance big, to get past it. John wouldn't have that. He would make me rehearse moments 60, 70, 80 times in a row. Just when you think you're going to lose your mind, something breaks, and a habit goes away that you weren't even aware you had. You just say the words because you're so damn tired and pissed off, and that's when the play really begins. Bobby changed because John helped me break habits.

There's a picture of Barbra Streisand in Martin Gottfried's *Broadway Musicals* book. I got that book when I was a kid. Barbra has her hands up and spread in this gesture like she's reaching for the stars, and I always thought: *That's Broadway.*

Self-consciousness like that implies a certain kind of performance. When I was playing Riff Raff in *Rocky Horror Picture Show*, people started coming to the show dressed as the characters, and would imitate them, but our versions of them. One guy said to me, "I love what you do onstage, and you have that incredible moment where your hands go up and they sort of splay!" I thought: *Holy shit, I'm doing the Barbra Streisand pose!* I think you need that in performance. That bit of Barbra Streisand, or Liza Minnelli. John Doyle taught me to fine tune that instinct. He taught me to trust that it would be there. So did Rob Marshall and Sam Mendes, when I worked with them. I learned how to trust my performance and not over-show.

John does run-throughs for each character. Each character in *Company* got a full run-through for the scenes they were in and the scenes that have information they need, with the staging and perspective changed so that they were the center of the story. We started with Joanne, and then Amy, and then Kathy, who ended up kind of exploding, and my scene with her became one of my favorite scenes in the show. Because of John's run-throughs, everyone in the cast got a chance to star in the show. Everyone became more aware of the show they were doing, and that interplay came alive!

When you're doing a show eight times a week, you have the ability to focus on what someone else is doing, their character, and how you interact with them. And when you do that during the run, you don't change the staging—you just become hyper-aware of what everyone is doing, in a way that can't help but change you each time you tell the story. I broke my habits and got very simple with the character, and then became hyper-aware of everyone else. That made Bobby take on very different qualities for every performance. It became a very still and simple performance, except for the moment it had to not be, at the end.

I didn't know the Barrymore Theatre at all before we were told that that was where we were going to go. We didn't have any inkling we might transfer to New York—and then Steve showed up.

The first time I played the piano during the show was in Cincinnati, in front of Steve. My hands used to sweat so badly that they'd fall off the keyboards! I was that nervous. I went to Mary Mitchell Campbell, our musical director, and asked her if there was something that could keep my hands from sweating. We got this product I thought would help, but it ended up just creating a sort of goop. After one show, Amy Justman said, "There was some kind of paste all over the keyboard!" I felt bad.

In rehearsals for Broadway, Steve would say, "Raúl, can you look up when you play the piano?" I couldn't! I first learned to play piano for *tick, tick... BOOM!* so it's not like I was really a piano player at any point. And playing Steve's song made me a nervous wreck.

George Furth came to see us in Cincinnati. I was nervous about that because he wasn't particularly pleased with our *Merrily* at the Sondheim Celebration. He was vocal about the fact that he didn't like our not using the original script. Then George ended up being one of my favorite people I've ever worked with. He was a great, funny, lovely man.

We were originally on a thrust stage[31] in Cincinnati. The audience was looking down at us, and there was a lot of light work on the floor. All of that had to change when we came to Broadway. We also opened up the backstage of the Barrymore as part of the staging. The theater changed us and our production in a very cool way. For our minimal production of *Company*, the Barrymore was ideal, because Steve's shows all feel like plays that just happen to sing.

Returning to the Barrymore for *Speed-the-Plow* in 2008 and then *Arcadia* in 2011 was great. It is a house that is full of love, from the ushers to the last person in the box office. And Manny the electrician! I love Manny. I actually made fun of him to the audience once during *Speed-the-Plow*. He brought the lights out before the show was over, and then he brought them back up! I joked to the audience that our stagehand must have been smoking something backstage, and he actually came out and said, "Hey!"

When you come back to a theater like that, it feels like a family reunion. Everyone comes out to say hi. I tend to bond with crews because they make the show, and it's always special to come back to working with the same crew again because they're like, "Welcome home!" That's really how it feels.

I do a lot of stuff to my dressing room because of the Barrymore. There are two major dressing rooms there: the stage level one, which is usually a stage manager's office, and a second floor dressing room. There's usually no green room at the Barrymore, and when we were doing *Company*, Steve liked to hang out, so my dressing room became the hang out. It was really cool, and also kind of intimidating for people who didn't know him! I got used to it during *Sunday in the Park* at the Kennedy Center. Before show time, Steve would come into my dressing room as my dresser was putting on my beard, and her fingers would shake while she was doing it because she was so intimidated! Then he would leave and she would breathe, "Oh my God!"

During *Company* rehearsals, I ran into Patti LuPone and I told her how much I loved working with John. She said, "During tech rehearsals, you should walk over to John and say, 'Would you like to come to my dressing room for a cocktail?'" I asked her what he drank, and she told me, "Always have Tanqueray and some tonic for John. Get a lime! And have some almonds around. For Steve, have a bottle of wine." So I started setting up a bar in my dressing room. My dressing room had a very large front room and a second room in the back. I put the bar in the front room. At first it was small. Then I said, "Screw this, it's scary enough to go out there and play Bobby and be all by myself in that world—let's make this a huge bar where everyone can hang out!" Because of Company, I put that bar together in my room every time I was at the Barrymore. I did it at the Cort too! I set up a bar there too, and we started calling it Chez Raúl.

On *Speed-the-Plow*, Thursday nights were our big hang-out night and everyone would stay late in my dressing room. Even Peter, our door man, who is intensely cool, would stay late and have a drink with all of us. During *Arcadia*, we had theme nights! My dresser, the standbys and understudies and I would come up with British Night where we all had Pimms Cups, or a night where all the furniture was missing, or Bean Bag Chair Night, or a night with only drinks from the 1970s and disco music! One night everyone only drank martinis and we were all completely sloshed by the time we left the theater. Before we went to the Tony Awards for *Company*, we all had champagne in my room. Heather Laws' daughter Sammy was there, and the dressers made a little version of Amy's wedding dress for her and put her in it. Heather's little girl was sitting on the sofa of a dressing room bar in this big white wedding dress.

I started having everyone sign a book when they came backstage. There was a night that Annette Bening, Warren Beatty, and Glenn Close came back, and Glenn said, "What the hell? I've worked on Broadway my whole life, and I've never had a dressing room this good!" The character of Bobby is partially based on Warren Beatty, so that night the whole cast hung out with them. It really turned into a party, with music playing and people telling stories. It was like being at a real bar.

---

[31] thrust stage: a stage that extends into the audience on three sides

Moby Dick—Rehearsed by Orson Welles played 13 performances at the Barrymore in 1962. A fascinating piece, the show found actors in an 1800s repertory theatre rehearsing a stage version of Moby Dick. *Another unique show that played the Barrymore was* The Night That Made America Famous *in 1975. A revue with songs by Harry Chapin, the show featured well-known tunes like "Cat's In The Cradle" alongside new songs written expressly for the production. Chapin himself appeared in* The Night That Made America Famous, *and it featured multimedia effects and projections, which were very new for Broadway at the time.*

2009/2012: Broadway Through The Back Door

Sandy Binion, Actor/Dresser

I came to Broadway late, compared to most others. I feel like I slipped in the back door. I'm originally from Ohio. When I was 19, I moved to North Carolina. I was an actor in Charlotte and I sustained myself doing theatre there for about ten years. One thing led to another and I ended up moving to New York to be an actor when I was in my early 30s. For coming to New York so late, I feel like I was relatively successful. I worked on Broadway as a performer and did *Jane Eyre*. I did some national tours. But the people who I was competing with had been here since they were teenagers. I couldn't beat their known-entity reputations. Even so, for a while, I did pretty well. People started to know who I was.

Then I hit a window of time where I couldn't get any work. I was a professional seamstress before I was an actor. One of my friends told me to join the wardrobe union, and I have never looked back.

My first show on Broadway as a dresser was *The Crucible* in 2002. I interviewed with Laurie Bork, the wardrobe supervisor, and she told me she was concerned about hiring me because she'd seen a lot of actors go backstage to work and be miserable. I explained that that wasn't me; what made me miserable was being unproductive. I got the job! I dressed all of the young girls in the show. For a while, I would dress a show and then perform in a show, then dress a show and then perform in a show. I was comfortable going back and forth like that until my dressing jobs got more and more high profile. Then I realized that I was a lot happier backstage, oddly enough.

I've worked as Daniel Radcliffe's dresser on three different shows. I was Tom Hanks' dresser on *Lucky Guy* and Philip Seymour Hoffman's dresser on *Long Day's Journey Into Night*. A lot of the stars I've worked with have only done film before. They come to Broadway and are surprised, because in film, the dressers are not present. They work in a different area and are not as hands-on. I've had film actors ask me, "What is it that you do?" It's easier to tell them what I don't do. Whatever you need, if I'm your dresser, I'm the person you're going to communicate that to.

I was the only dresser on *Race* at the Barrymore. I had a dressing room adjacent to the star, which was James Spader at first, and then Eddie Izzard, but I took care of the whole cast. It was the kind of show where you'd get everyone dressed at the top of the show, send them onstage, and then didn't see them until intermission. At intermission, I'd get them into act two costumes, and then I didn't see them until curtain call. I turned my dressing room into a jewelry studio. It was great!

The most difficult show I've ever worked on was also at the Barrymore: *Chaplin*! That show had the most difficult fast changes. I've never worked on a show that was that hard. I had to get Rob McClure, who played Chaplin, into flying harnesses! Rob was amazing, and Deb Sheridan, the wardrobe supervisor, trusted me to do my own rigging. Since I'm a seamstress, I was able to use my knowledge and be hands-on. The Chaplin tramp suit would have to disappear and then Rob would have to reappear in a three-piece suit.

At one point, stage management came to me to tell me we were going to do an understudy put-in.[32] I told them it would never happen. We needed to have separate rehearsals first just for getting the understudies in and out of costumes. The costume changes were so choreographed! We were very sad to see that show go, but I don't know how long I could have physically done it.

I think every one of our Broadway theaters surprises new people because they come backstage and go, "This is it?" You see the front of these houses and they're so gorgeous with chandeliers, and then you go backstage and realize that that's just not where the money goes. At the Schoenfeld we had windows! A wardrobe room with a window? That doesn't happen. Wardrobe is always on the lowest level, because we go with the washing machines. In the Barrymore, the backstage has been renovated recently, but the wardrobe room is essentially a cage.

When I was a performer in *Jane Eyre*, I had just purchased this abandoned log cabin out in North Jersey. I asked some of the stagehands how they'd suggest fixing something in the house that I wasn't sure about. They basically laughed in my face. I figured out how to do it on my own and took before and after pictures and showed them. They were impressed. They never doubted me after that. Having the resource of the stagehands is amazing, because they know how to do anything. And the people in the wardrobe union are the most creative people I've ever been around. They are inquisitive, curious, kind. They will share information. We all go from theater to theater together, and on so many first days, it's like a family reunion of crew. It feeds me artistically in a way that I was never fed as an actor. As an actor, you do what you are told to do. In the crew, one person is dying wool, another is making a map. I'm a jewelry artist in addition now, because it complimented the work I was already doing.

I'm extremely blessed by the career that I somehow stumbled into. My mother taught me how to sew when I was ten. She said, "Do you want new clothes for school, Sandy?" I said yes, and she said, "There's the sewing machine." I learned, and I loved sewing. When I moved to North Carolina, I did an apprenticeship with a tailor for two years. I managed a dry cleaners and did all of the alterations there, and I worked for a high-end ladies' store and then an interior decorator. I did theatre there in Charlotte while I was also doing all of that.

I always tell young actors to have other passions. I see actors who aren't working, who have no other reason for being. It's the most heartbreaking thing in the world. I used to wonder if I didn't succeed completely as an actor because I had other things that entertained me. I didn't eat, sleep and breathe acting. I just think you have to have other things in your life that fulfill you.

I've always been thankful because my mom taught me to do a lot of things, and I can do them all. Right now, I'm in the process of taking a little less work as a dresser so I can spend more time as a jewelry artist. I would love it if my jewelry was part of the costumes for a Broadway show.

———————

The Barrymore was home to Philip Seymour Hoffman's last Broadway show, the revival of Death of a Salesman, *which broke all box office records at the theater in 2012. He played Willy Loman in a performance the* New York Daily News *called "vivid... expert at expressing Willy's soul-crushing sadness"[33] only two years before his death.*

———————

---

[32] put-in: a rehearsal for a replacement or understudy; the only time that they get to run their role in the show with all of the other actors, costumes, scenery, the orchestra, and so forth. Most replacement and understudy rehearsal happens with stage managers or resident/associate directors, in a more informal setting.
[33] Dziemianowicz, Joe. "Theater Review: '*Death of a Salesman.*'" *New York Daily News.* 15 Mar. 2012. Retrieved from nydailynews.com.

2012: Running In The Aisles

Hayley Podschun, Actor

Picking a favorite Broadway theater is like picking a favorite child! They all hold such amazing memories. I might actually have to say the Barrymore, where I did *Chaplin*. I liked it because it's one of the smallest houses I've ever been in, and partially because of that, the cast became such a family. Every show I've ever done has been a family, but in *Chaplin*, every crew member knew the family of every person onstage, and the orchestra was friends with the dressers, and everyone *really* knew each other. We grew to love each other.

We were proud of the show, and we were proud of each other. Also, *Chaplin* was my first original Broadway cast of an original Broadway musical, and that's special. I think the Barrymore will always hold a special place in my heart.

Rob McClure started this tradition by accident, when he wasn't really warmed up for the show one day. He started running in between every aisle of every seat in the theater, from the orchestra to the mezzanine. I quickly joined him, because I felt like I wasn't getting enough cardio in the show, and I wanted to warm up too. Then, before every performance, we would run the theater, through every aisle, up through the two little boxes on top, behind the curtains. We'd run and then we'd both end up in the boxes, stretching and asking each other about our days. It was our time to check in with each other.

Now I'm touring with *Wicked*, and I've been carrying on this tradition in every theater I can, before every show. And Rob is at the MUNY[34]—and he even ran all the seats there one day! It's just this cool little tradition we both really loved, and it's neat to go through every seat because somebody's going to be sitting in each of those seats, watching you perform soon after! You feel like you're seeing the theater from each perspective, and it gives you this little energy from the audience before the show even starts.

———————

On the mezzanine level at the Barrymore, there's a series of rooms on house left. This was once where people could stand to smoke and watch the show at the same time! A couple of Broadway theaters still have these areas, although most have been converted to bathrooms, merchandise stands, bars, or more audience space.

———————

2012: Slide Whistle Hooligan

Shannon Ford, Musician

Chaplin was a multi-percussion book. So I was basically doing the work of three percussionists. I played a drum set, timpani, xylophone, bells, blocks, and whistles, all in one show. It was hard work, because I mostly play just a drum set.

I did the workshop of *Chaplin*, and the percussionist only played the drums. I thought the show would be relatively easy to play. Then Larry Hochman, the orchestrator, did a great job creating the parts for Broadway, from an artistic perspective. But there I was, playing the hardest book I've ever had to play! In one song, I had to play xylophone, hop back to the timpani, and then tune the timpani for a different note in the middle of a musical phrase.

I also remember that in the Barrymore, on the 5th day of tech, we were all delirious from the process of working for 14 hours while only really rehearsing for 30 seconds at a time. At one point, we were watching Rob McClure who played Chaplin do his part on the high wire over and over. There was one part where he did a

———————

[34] MUNY: The Municipal Theatre Association of St. Louis—America's oldest and largest outdoor space for musical theatre

handspring on the high wire. The 40th time he did it, I decided to grab the slide whistle, and I made this loud cartoon sound to go along with his move.

I thought it would be funny and would break the tension, but I kind of got yelled at, and then there was total silence in the theater. I was like the third grade kid who got called to the front of the class. I put the slide whistle away and waited to be fired. Now, it's the conductor's favorite story; he makes fun of me for it all the time.

2012: Ten Days To The Barrymore

Beowulf Boritt, Scenic Designer

When I started designing *Chaplin*, I knew we were going into the Barrymore. As the scenic designer, you don't always know that in advance. What's interesting about Broadway proscenium theaters though, is that if you know whether you're going into a small, medium or large sized house, a lot of the basics are the same. The prosceniums are the same, but the depth and wing space varies a lot.

Chaplin was designed to fit in the Barrymore. However, because of the way plans for the show came together, it was designed in about ten days! That's really fast.

Because of how long it takes to build scenery and get it set up in a theater, the set is well on its way before a show ever gets into rehearsal. In *Chaplin*, there's a big number in the first act that chronicles Charlie Chaplin's rise to fame. The director Warren Carlyle had broken it into three beats, with each step being one part of Charlie's climb up the ladder, including meeting and marrying his wife.

Charlie Chaplin was always chasing women, so the theme of the number was naked women everywhere. I designed the first beat with these deco naked ladies swimming through the air, the second beat with these naked lady planters, and the third beat, the New Years Party, with a glitter curtain and banner that said "Have A Fabulous 1921" with a picture of a girl sitting on the moon.

In rehearsal, what had been a three-beat number turned into a four beat number, as the show changed and Chaplin married his wife during that section. However, we didn't have the scenery to accommodate this, so for the first few previews, the actors had to play the wedding scene in front of this Happy New Year banner. It didn't make sense, because the wedding was supposed to be taking place months later.

There were so many other things with the show that we were trying to work on, that nobody had identified this as a problem until I said, "This doesn't make any sense!" We reworked the artwork for that last beat, and there wasn't enough time to get it repainted, so we had to get a printed version that could be turned around in a few days. It was sort of the same image, but it said "Have a wonderful life!" or something of that sort.

The piece of scenery is there for probably only about 30 seconds. But because the show moves so fast, it actually did help make that one moment clear. Then, at the very end of the sequence, one of the actors swung by and tore the banner down, just as Chaplin's life began to fall apart. It was a nice image.

2012: I Was Mistaken For A Crew Guy

Michael Mendez, Actor

I made my Broadway debut in *Chaplin*. The first day we moved into the Barrymore, I was just overwhelmed. I was in the ensemble and shared a dressing room with two of the other guys in the cast. Just to see my name on

82

a dressing room door on Broadway… it was unreal. We had a couch! The first time I walked onstage, I just couldn't believe it. I started to cry a little bit, but didn't want other people to see.

The first day of our tech rehearsals, I was wearing a t-shirt and shorts. I was sitting off stage, waiting in the wings to go on, and one of the crew guys came up to me and asked, "Dude, can I have your flashlight?" I was like, "What?" "Your flashlight!" There was a pause, and then he said, "Oh, you're IN the show!" I thought: *Awesome. Guess I don't look like everyone else in the show*. That was funny. I got mistaken as a crew person on my first day.

The first preview was nuts! It was such a fast process: two weeks in the rehearsal room, two weeks in the theater, and then previews. I was excited because I wanted everyone to see how great Rob McClure was in the show. And that first curtain call was something I'll always remember. I was bowing with Broadway veterans! I'd done shows off-Broadway and regionally, but something about Broadway just felt magical and unique.

During one part of the show, I played a homeless guy, and I came up with a specific moment where I gave a girl a flower. They ended up cutting it during previews, because it drew a little too much attention away from the song going on at the time. And that's okay; it should have been cut if it was pulling focus. But I liked that moment, because it was the first thing I brought to the show that was different from the guy who had done all of the workshops.

Having famous guests at the show was awesome, but most of the time, I was too scared to go meet them. We heard that Al Pacino and Robert DeNiro both came. The one person I did say hi to was Nathan Lane. I saw *The Producers* when it first opened, and he's always been an actor who I've admired and wanted to model myself after. And it was also fun to meet friends of the cast who came backstage—like Sutton Foster!

When we were at the Barrymore, *The Performers* was at the Longacre. Their theater was right behind ours, and we always kept our window up, so sometimes we could hear them. One day, we heard Cheyenne Jackson singing in his dressing room, so we thought it'd be funny to yell, "Cheyenne! Cheyenne!" He yelled back, "What? Who is this?" And we shouted, "*Chaplin*!" He said, "Who?" and closed the window. Broadway theaters are packed together!

Being part of the cast of *Chaplin* was the first time I really felt like part of the theatre community in New York. We all started the show onstage, so we had a tradition before every performance where we'd all go onstage and form a circle, put our arms in the center, and yell, "Go *Chaplin*!" Then, Wayne Wilcox would come in the center of the circle and do a little dance to the overture. By the end of the run, Zach Unger, the little boy in the show, would do the dance with him. They had lifts and moves. As soon as it was over, we'd all run to our places and start.

I was surprised that there was no green room at the Barrymore! We did THNOB, or "Thursday Night On Broadway," where we'd all have a little celebration after the show, but we had to do that crowded into a hallway somewhere. And for birthday celebrations, we all had to invade Rob's dressing room.

The stage door was interesting for me. I'd get a lot of fans of my sister, Lindsay Mendez. A lot of them came in *Godspell* shirts, and they'd be like, "Michael! *Godspell*!" Or, I'd be signing, and overhear someone saying, "That's Lindsay Mendez's brother." I'd call her and joke, "I hate you. Every day I walk out, and people only want to talk about you!" But really, it was great. I liked meeting Broadway fans who were excited that we were both in musicals.

We knew about our closing date six weeks in advance, so it was sad, but we were prepared. Rob spoke at our curtain call, and then we all took a piece of the set and signed it for him. It was emotional; I didn't expect to cry, but I did. You just end up thinking: *Am I going to get to experience this again? Or is this going to be the only time?* You hope not, but at the same time, you just never take it for granted. I knew the whole time that this was a privilege and something really special. A lot of my friends haven't gotten to do this. I always knew it was a special chapter in my life, one that I was lucky to live. And then it was over. But I'll always have the memories of it, and I got to meet a lot of great people.

2012: My Little Brother

Lindsay Mendez, Actor

My younger brother Michael and I are both performers, and I always wanted him to have the opportunity to perform on Broadway. I knew he would get it someday and it was only a matter of time.

When I made my Broadway debut in *Grease*, it was fun to involve him. He's shy, but he got to know every cast member and learned the ropes. It was like that with every show I was in, although I think he always felt a little strange about it.

Then Michael got his first Broadway show: *Chaplin*. He was finally *in* it and now he's much more comfortable around my shows too. It was a big step for both of us.

Seeing my little brother make his Broadway debut... I cry when I think about it. I got to take my mom. My mom got to see him do that. She passed away soon after, and she was so happy she got to be there for that. I will always be grateful we got to see it together.

Chaplin was such a special show for Michael, with a great cast of people. He always says that he's so glad he had that experience, that one time, and even if he doesn't get to do it again, it was enough for him.

It means so much to me that my brother and I are both out here doing this. We're from California, and we took dance together growing up, and did shows. I got to watch him have this dream while we were both kids. To have the support of a family member who really gets it, to navigate through this city and this business together is so special. It's awesome to have a sibling who is right there with you.

———————

I interviewed stage manager Sally J. Jacobs while I was working on Macbeth. *She told me that at the Barrymore, where she worked on* A Streetcar Named Desire, *the crew got every show at the theater to sign the curtain rods on closing night. "If the stagehands don't ask you to do that, I'll be very surprised! It's been going on for decades." After the last performance, I was occupied with our closing party, and I never got to find out. Guess I'll have to wait for my next show at the Barrymore.*

———————

2013: This Feels Real

Krysta Rodriguez, Actor

Filming scenes from the TV show *Smash* at the Barrymore was so cool. I had not really spent a lot of time in the Barrymore, so in that way, it felt very real. *Hit List* was my main association with the theater.

The weird thing was that we weren't allowed to film on the stage! We filmed in the audience, in front of the theater, at the stage door, on the fire escape... but there were union crew guys there, guarding the stage. It felt like: *I'm supposed to be here and feel like this is my theater, but there are these differing definitions between the television version of what that means, and Broadway's version, and they don't really mix.*

84

It still felt very real. I remember the day that we went to the Barrymore for the first time, and there were pictures of us outside the theater. We were taking pictures together. It was like our marquee had gone up in real life!

A lot of the *Smash* experience was like that. When the Tony nominations came out on the show, I remember someone said, "This really feels like I'm getting a Tony nomination!" And people who didn't get Tony nominations were depressed. We were all watching the announcement to see who was nominated and who wasn't, and these real Broadway stars were announcing it. Because that's actually an aspect of most of our lives when we aren't on *Smash*, we'd get wrapped up in it sometimes and forget it wasn't real.

2013: This Fake Musical

Jeremy Jordan, Actor

We filmed scenes from *Hit List* at the Barrymore, and it was really cool to shoot across the street from the Brooks Atkinson, the theater I made my Broadway debut in. *Smash* put up an entire fake front-of-house[35] at the Barrymore, so there were *Hit List* critics' quotes and posters with our faces on them. I've never been so excited to see my face outside of a theater. When we saw it for the first time, I just remember thinking: *Our show is so bad-ass! Oh my God!*

I've had my picture outside the theater before, on real musicals, but it was so much more thrilling with this fake musical! I can't explain it. It was just really fun.

———————

In the Barrymore, you can see down the fire escape to the Longacre stage door exit and fire escape. In an emergency, a star could exit through these connected fire escapes, but in actuality they're much more often used for pre-show shenanigans between casts in the two theaters.

In 2013, I worked as part of the marketing team for the Broadway revival of Macbeth, *which starred Alan Cumming... in all of the roles. While* Chaplin *was the show to immediately precede us,* Smash *spent several weeks filming scenes surrounding the fictional Broadway musical* Hit List *at the Barrymore before* Macbeth *moved in. As* Hit List *starred and featured songs by several of my friends, including my best friend and collaborator Joe Iconis, I spent many nights across from the Barrymore, watching the action. One particularly blustery early spring night, Joe and I sat at the old-fashioned Rum House, sipping whiskey and watching as Jeremy Jordan and Katharine McPhee, as Jimmy Collins and Karen Cartwright, played a scene at the Barrymore stage door. What if* Hit List *was real? I couldn't help but think this all throughout 2013. What if Joe's songs were really on Broadway now?* Hit List *was special, because it was the closest we'd get to that—for now.*

Within a month, Alan Cumming was going up in the cherry picker[36] and putting the Macbeth *marquee on top of the Barrymore himself, as our team ran up and down 47th Street, taking photos. (Alan really did do everything in this production!) We were welcomed into the Barrymore with open arms, and as I did my job, creating promotions for the show, monitoring how audiences reacted to our creative signage in the lobby, and working on online content with my colleague Steven Tartick, I also explored every corner of the 85-year-old Barrymore. One afternoon, while Steven set up a camera to capture the stagehands building the set for a time-lapse video, I ran to the bathroom, and ended up running up half-a-dozen flights of stairs, needing to see every floor backstage. They were painted white and mostly looked the same, although the rooms at the top were a bit cleaner and obviously used less frequently. There were no time-lapse videos when Joanna Gleason had these showers put in, or even when Craig Carnelia noticed the appearance of bootleggers. But these walls were still here, and these doors, and yes—*

———————

[35] front-of-house: the portion of a performance venue that is open to the public, not just those who have purchased a ticket
[36] cherry picker: an elevated work platform that is used for many different purposes, including putting marquees in place

85

even these fire escapes. Later in our run, I would lean out a dressing room window and hear the actors from First Date *at the Longacre debating where to eat dinner after their show.*

During tech for Macbeth, *I sat alone in the darkened mezzanine, watching it all, imagining that this is just what it must have felt like to be in tech for* The Life *or for the original* A Streetcar Named Desire. *The first show I ever saw at the Barrymore was* The Glass Menagerie *starring Jessica Lange during my freshman year of college, so I associated the house with Tennessee Williams, and yet I also grew up knowing that two of my favorite cast recordings had been of shows born at the Barrymore:* Baby *and is there life after high school? To me, the Barrymore meant intimate musicals about real people and important American drama—and now it meant Shakespeare and fictional musicals too. A few months later, I would co-produce a live concert version of* Hit List *at 54 Below. A fake life at the Barrymore led to a real life at Broadway's supper club.*

On opening night of Macbeth, *I watched Liza Minnelli and Bernadette Peters walk our red carpet, I got dressed in a Barrymore dressing room, and we all received gifts from Alan: soap engraved with "Cumming" and notes that said "Be large in mirth." I watched the first ten minutes of the play from the old "smoking room" on the side of the mezzanine, and then stood in front of the theater, the formerly bustling street now deserted, staring at our front door signs: "Warning: You are about to enter the Barrymore Theatre. The producers ask that you please refrain from speaking the name of the play you are about to see while inside these walls." Old theatrical lore coupled with modern marketing. I walked down 47th Street, heading to set everything up for our opening night party, but was halted by the Brooks Atkinson, darkened to my left. My favorite musical of the season,* Hands on a Hardbody, *had closed there a week earlier, after only 28 performances. I took a moment of silence for the empty theater.*

A month later, I sat with my best friends Joe Iconis and Lauren Marcus in their 47th Street apartment, one block west of the Barrymore and Friedman and Brooks Atkinson. With a group of our pals, we watched the Barrymore cast of Hit List *sing Joe's song "Broadway, Here I Come!" on the* Smash *finale—as their Tony Awards performance!*

I could see the Barrymore from their apartment window.

For a brief period of 2013, 47th Street was the home of a Broadway show I got to work on, one of my favorite musicals ever, and the fictional hit that got my best friend's songs on national television. We raised our glasses to all of this on the May evening that Smash *ended. Then we got drunk on good whiskey and bad wine, and after yelling for a while about the future of musical theatre, my friends and I stormed 47th Street. Long after midnight, we pulled the 8-foot by 6-foot* Hands on a Hardbody *signs off the doors of the Brooks Atkinson, hollering and laughing and crying (that was me). I said goodnight to the Rum House and the* Macbeth *marquee and brought my stolen* Hardbody *signs home. They hang on my wall as a reminder of my favorite year on 47th Street.*

2000-2014: A Stagehand's Career

Philip Feller, Stagehand

In 2005, I started working here at the Barrymore Theatre as the house property person. I'd been a production prop man in 2000, on *The Tale of the Allergist's Wife*, here at the Barrymore. Before that, I'd certainly installed scenery and automation for shows here, but 2000 was my first time on a Barrymore running crew. When the position of house prop man[37] vacated in 2005, Mr. Entin and the Shubert Organization were so kind as to offer it to me. *I know the office and the theater and the building – I'm grateful to go there.* I had been the property man at the Belasco Theatre, a wonderful building, since 1997. My first show here at the Barrymore was *The Glass Menagerie*. Come February, it'll be ten years.

---

[37] In each Broadway house, there is a house crew that works on every production. In addition, each production often brings in their own running crew.

My grandfather, Peter Louis Feller, was an immigrant from what was then Austria-Hungary. He arrived in New York in 1906 and became an apprentice carpenter and then a master carpenter. Large segments of the city were occupied by German-speaking artisans, so within one week of his arrival, through a German newspaper, he'd found work at a German owned theatrical shop. He started working his way up.

My grandfather got his Local One IATSE union membership by working all day in the scenic shop—either Ryzick's, where he started out, or Vail's, where he eventually moved—and then going to be the extra man on the fly floor[38] at the old Metropolitan Opera at night. After working for eight years, he got into the Union in 1914. He worked primarily as a scenic shop carpenter until he retired in 1945.

The Stagehands Union was founded in 1886 in New York City. We members have been fortunate to be protected and insured by this organization. Our predecessors had great foresight and determination to create safe working conditions, good compensation, and pension and annuity plans. And we have largely lived and worked in an era of labor peace in our industry.

My father, also named Peter Louis Feller, was born in 1919. He got into the Stagehands' Union in 1937 when he was a teenager. His brother Frederick Sr. was a stagehand and foreman, and *his* son Freddy became a scenic carpenter. My brother got into the Union in 1968 and worked automating the movement of sets and flying units. He was the first to integrate computer controlled automation on Broadway, for *Tap Dance Kid* in 1983, and went on to engineer and build the larger musicals, with his company Feller Precision, for many years. I've been in the Union for 42 years. It wasn't unusual for theatrical families to flourish, with several generations of sons becoming stagehands. Especially during World War I, the Depression, and World War II, if your father was a carpenter, you probably became a carpenter.

My father was a brilliant, ambitious young man. He grew up in a working-class immigrant household during the Depression, and he wanted to go to college. My grandfather was hardheaded and roared, "What do you want to go to college for? You don't even know what you want to do!" My father graduated valedictorian from high school and then went and parked cars for a summer at Jones Beach. He decided he would try to be a stagehand for a while. He was foreman at the shop he was working in by the time he was 21. He was smart and worked hard. Seeing war coming he enlisted, and was inducted (and married) April 1st, 1941.

While my father was in basic training in the army, Irving Berlin was starting a unit to present *This Is The Army*, his new army revue. My grandfather had built sets for Berlin's World War I show, *Yip Yip Yaphank*, and Berlin saw the name "Feller" on a list of recruits with theatrical experience, and had my father transferred over from the infantry. It rapidly became clear that he was the most skilled technical person there, so he was put him charge of the carpentry department of *This Is The Army*.

Five years later, when my father returned from the war, he began working on shows with many people he'd gotten to know in the army—writers and directors and producers who respected him. He was appointed production carpenter on many projects, and in 1948, he formed his own business, National Scenic, with partners Jo Mielziner and George Gebhart. He bowed out of that shop in 1950 to return to production carpentry. In 1957, Dave Steinberg, the shop owner, invited him to take over managing Imperial Scenic Studio in Fort Lee, New Jersey. He did that for five years before deciding to go into business for himself. Of course, the scenic shop business is a tough one. It's a seasonal business. Sometimes you get lots of shows and sometimes none. Sometimes there are shows that go way over-budget or shows that flop immediately, and perhaps can't pay their debts. There were about seven shops at the time, and Feller Scenery rapidly became dominant in the New York area.

In 1962, when my father started the Feller Scenery Studio, he gathered a lot of highly qualified guys who he'd been working with for years. One of his particular talents was to evaluate a person's skills and limits and know

---

[38] fly floor: a platform high above the stage where stagehands control equipment

where to put them where they would excel and become invested in the process. A lot of great people from that time came to work with him, and the studio gave birth to a new generation of technical theater professionals, including Ted Wondsell, Gene O'Donovan, Bill Mensching, Jerry Harris, and Sam Gossard. Feller's was the place to work on the big projects, to get invaluable experience. Pete Sr. would always give people just a bit more than they'd done before, so their skills would expand. He had a temper, but he would also explain to you what you did right and wrong.

Up until Feller Scenery, the technical and physical elements for theater were built and supplied by separate businesses, each doing only either scenery building, or scene painting, or lighting, or sound, or costumes, etc. My father's dream was to amalgamate all of these techniques and technologies under one roof, ideally, in proximity to the theatre district. All the elements could be assembled, evaluated by designer and director, even rehearsed on, prior to the load in at the theater. This helped set designers increase the complexity of their shows, as directors and the public demanded a more cinematic experience. Katherine Wiley Feller, my mother, opened Costume Associates (which continues to operate, led by the great theater artist Nino Novellino, as Costume Armour) to build costumes. My brother Peter started Feller Precision. TheatreSound and Four Star Stage Lighting were also under the umbrella. Their collective achievement was to build and deliver all the technical elements a show might require.

My folks took us to see shows all the time. I think the first one that I saw was *Call Me Madam*, which my father won a Tony for in 1952.[39] I also saw *The Pajama Game, Fiorello!, The Most Happy Fella*. I got to be around a lot of the great musicals when I was very young. *West Side Story* was one that struck me as being particularly brilliant. My cousin Fred Feller was the production carpenter and my father built the show.

The job of running a scene shop was all-consuming and as a kid, I saw that my father was always working and often exhausted. But he and Katie loved their work. We also got to have great theatre people over to our house. I remember Jo Mielziner coming over for dinner, along with other great designers of the day, including Boris Aronson, and the young Peter Larkin and Robin Wagner. On Saturdays, I would go visit the shop my father worked in and I'd get $5 to sweep the shop. It was a time for myself and my brother to connect with Dad, and eventually when I was old enough, I would work in the shop when they needed extra hands loading trucks. In 1964, I started subbing as a stagehand on Broadway. The first show I worked on was *Fiddler on the Roof*, the second *Cabaret*.

When I started working on Broadway, there were no women stagehands. There were some scenic artists who were women, but they were few and far between. Gradually and thankfully that changed, and now there are more and more women in technical theater. Laura Koch, very accomplished and skillful, is the house prop person at the Broadhurst, and got her start with my dad. Heidi Brown at the Imperial is very experienced and talented. The electricians at the Hirschfeld and Schoenfeld are women. My co-house head at the Belasco for years was Leslie Killian, and she's fantastic. It's great that the number of women is growing. These changes have taken a long time. I think we've perhaps made more progress than other industries that involve manual labor. It's an interesting business, because it does involve manual labor but it also involves craft labor, and the talents of mechanical invention and improvisation. Stagehands have to merge a lot of different skills, and everyone has the opportunity to synchronize their experiences and to offer something unique to a show.

When I started out, almost all stagehands were in the business because it was a good union job. They were working class guys who might just as soon have been working on a skyscraper, on the subway, in the fire department. There is no security in this business... a show can close at any time. But you work indoors, mostly, and many of us have spent our careers working two jobs, shop and show. Some of my co-workers had scorn for theatre, in the 60s, and there were anti-gay sentiments, anti-black sentiments, anti-Semitic sentiments. Now, come on! No gays, no blacks, no Jews? There would be no theatre! Still, in those days, one could hear lots of comments. You couldn't walk down a fly floor without someone making a derogatory comment about a

---

[39] Peter Feller Sr. won a Tony Award for Best Stage Technician. This category existed from 1948 to 1963.

minority group. I had long hair. Stagehands would yell, "Faggot!" at me. Thankfully, some of those people were changed by their exposure to the wonderful and creative diversity of our industry.

The Vietnam War transformed a lot of people. Working class unionized white male stagehands had been, oddly enough, part of Nixon's constituency. By 1978 or so, many young stagehands long hair, or didn't care if you did, and were becoming more aware of the necessary alliance of unionism and a progressive perspective. There was a vast cultural shift throughout the country from the mid-1960s to the mid-1970s. Just as the country rejected the war and sexual repression and bigotry so did the working men (and increasingly, women) who ran things behind the scenes on Broadway.

I was an assistant carpenter running automation for many years, usually in the larger theaters that can handle musicals. I worked at the Minskoff, the Gershwin, the Broadway, the Imperial, the Martin Beck, the Winter Garden for *Cats*. Then I went to the Belasco, and worked on great productions as house props, including *A Doll's House*, with the great British actress Janet McTeer. I will end my career at the Barrymore, which is also a small (1100 seat) play house. The Barrymore is a beautifully symmetrical, proportioned house. There isn't a bad seat in it.

I worked on *Exit the King* here with Geoffrey Rush and Susan Sarandon. I've been going to the theatre since 1952, and that was one of the top five shows I've ever seen. The stage was practically bare, with very few scenic elements; it was all in the magic of the words and performances! Like most people working on a collaborative art form, stagehands always like to think our job is essential. But you can do a great show without scenery, in a black box! Everything we do: the scenery and lights and props and sound are all to augment and aid the presentation.

It's a lot of fun and hard work and long hours, building sets and solving problems that arise. As stagehands, we always want lots of room in order to put the equipment in and move it around and not be crushed against a wall each night, but that can be avoided with some good decision-making. At the Barrymore there is very little room off stage left, so in planning the scenic and property activity we put most action and storage to work from stage right. We've had some big shows in here. *Chaplin* was physically huge for the Barrymore.

Since I was an automation carpenter for years, there were parts of a prop man's job that I didn't know about. It's the house property person's responsibility to deal with audience seating in the theater, and to help set up the dressing rooms and the wardrobe department, for each new production, as well as work eight performances a week.

People who work in any building on Broadway become a short-term family for the run of the play. You see these people six days a week, if not more. You're seeing them late at night; sometimes you're seeing them early in the morning. You're doing eight shows a week where you're dependent on them doing their job and they're dependent on you doing yours. Hopefully you get along with them, and most of the time you do. You create a family with professional and personal bonds. And then those bonds are severed the day that the show closes. At the Barrymore in recent years, we have hosted limited-run productions. After four months everybody walks out the door. We empty the stage of the physical structures that have defined and divided it. It is like moving to a new apartment, or even demolishing a house. It's an emotional week, the load-out, because the crew and cast have all grown to admire each other, to be close to each other. Sometimes you keep in touch, but it's really over on closing day.

Right now, we're about to close *A Raisin In the Sun*. It's been a great show to work on. Anika Noni Rose is an incredible performer and person; Denzel Washington is just terrific. Everyone in the cast is. It's a modern classic, a great play, and we have tremendous actors in it, so it's moving, heart-wrenching, every night. There's a moment when Ruth Younger says, "There ain't no black people living in Clybourne Park," and Mama Younger tells her daughter-in-law, "Well, there's gonna be some now!" Every night: BANG! That moment makes working 100 hours a week worth it.

The next show coming in here is *The Curious Incident of the Dog in the Night-Time*. I've read the book it's based on, and it's narrated by an autistic boy. I'm looking forward to it.

I'll do whatever is needed. I'm always just glad to come in and have a job and be around other folks who also like what they do. By the end of each production, I'm always tired but also looking forward to the next show. I'm happy to be at the Barrymore, and very grateful to the Shubert Organization, and Local One of the IATSE. And most of all to my parents, Katherine and Peter Feller, and my brother Peter. They taught me all I know, which is a small portion of what they knew.

2014: The Curious Incident Of The Alternate In The Night-Time

Taylor Trensch, Actor

I have been stalking this play since its inception in London. I loved the book, *The Curious Incident of the Dog in the Night-Time,* so much, and I love the director and playwright who adapted it, so I had been following it like the theatre nerd I am. The day that it was announced for Broadway, for the Barrymore, I remember dreaming about if I got to do the show. It would be the first Broadway theater I worked in that I'd seen shows in before. I got an audition and I kept thinking about that.

For characters like Eva Perón in *Evita* or Peter Parker in *Spider-Man* or Christopher Boone in *The Curious Incident of the Dog in the Night-Time*, an alternate is hired to share the main role because its demands are so enormous. In this case, the actor playing the lead never leaves the stage and role is also very physical with lots of screaming. With an alternate, neither actor becomes exhausted from doing the show eight times a week, and the two actors understudy each other when they're not onstage. Right now, we're in previews and I haven't been told yet which performances I'll be going on for. I'll have a regular schedule once we open, but for now, they're just trying to make sure I'm ready before I go on.

Because there are so many brilliant physical sequences by Steven Hoggett and Scott Graham in the show, we spent the first half of most rehearsal days just doing physical work, including a boot-camp style workout and rehearsal of all of the movement sequences. During that portion of the day, Alex Sharp—the other actor playing Christopher—and I would rotate in and out so we both felt capable doing the physical parts of the play. For the second half of the day, we'd come back and work on the text with Marianne Elliott, our director. For most of that, Alex would rehearse and I'd take notes. Our tech process was entirely with Alex because he was performing before I was so they wanted to make sure he was prepared. Now that we're in previews, I'll have my own tech process and dress rehearsals and then my first performance. Hopefully I won't barf on anyone.

On our first day of tech, we walked in the stage door, down the alley and there was a taxidermy dead dog just lying there, next to a tray of stale bagels. That was a special experience. Then a spokesperson from the Shubert Organization came and spoke to us about Ethel Barrymore. I've been hoping I might see her ghost, but nothing yet. Her image is everywhere in the lower lobby, so I know who to be on the lookout for.

I have my first private dressing room! I like to pretend it was Elizabeth Stanley's dressing room during *Company* or Anika Noni Rose's dressing room during *A Raisin in the Sun*, but I doubt it really was. There are so many floors of dressing rooms! Almost everyone has their own room with a big window. I was so excited to open my window and hang out of it and see the streets of New York, and when I opened it, there was a brick wall. The wall just couldn't be closer to my window. That was hilarious. I spend a lot of time in my dressing room while the show is going on, running my part by myself simultaneously with the action onstage.

I just love being in the Barrymore. My top theatergoing experiences have been in tiny spaces, and it's thrilling to be in a theater so small. You can just feel the audience when you're onstage. The theater works especially well for this play both because it's a small cast and because you want the audience to feel like they're in Christopher Boone's mind. I think the Barrymore invites you to do that.

Lately, I've been watching the show from a different view in the house for each performance. That's been tons of fun. The show itself is brilliant, but it's also fun to watch audience members experience it for the first time. I inadvertently yelled at an audience member the other night. She saw my photo in the Playbill so she started asking me questions and wouldn't stop loudly asking me about props all throughout the show. I had to shush her. There's this box in the show that lights up different colors and becomes different objects. She kept jabbing me and gasping, "Oh my God, it's an oven! Oh my God, it's an aquarium!" Yes, I realize that, and I love the box too, but why don't we quiet down and watch the beautiful performances, lady?

I'm terrified to go on. I have yet to run the show in its entirety and I know my first performance will be in a few days. There are a lot of lines, all this physical work, and the character even builds this huge train track onstage throughout the show. On top of that, I'm playing a character with an impediment. He thinks and sees the world in a different way than I do. Trying to filter all of my own thoughts through that and also remembering to do my job and stay in the right place and not fall off the stage as the upstage wall travels downstage... it's going to be scary!

———————

Taylor Trensch played Christopher Boone on Broadway for the first time four days after this interview. As one Twitter fan said, "Taylor Trensch's performance is out of this universe. I've never felt so heartbroken (in the best way) by theatre."

———————

My Home

Diane Heatherington, Box Office Treasurer

I've always felt very connected with this theater, the Barrymore. This is my office now, and it used to be the mailroom. These are photographs that I took. These are photographs from a friend of mine of Ethel Barrymore, the theater's namesake. You try to make it sort of like a home. You take care of it. You see things that are wrong or broken down and you try to fix them. People are spending a lot of money to be here, and you feel bad if things aren't right.

Each theater I go to, I always take it very personally. I always get involved in the place. That's okay. You spend a lot of time at work and it becomes like home. If you don't get along with the people you work with, it's miserable. I'm happy. I like my crew and I like this theater. It means something to me: starting out here and now being here as the treasurer. In the circle of life, it all comes around.

When I was a kid, I didn't know what I wanted to do with my life. I grew up in Pittsburgh and went to Catholic School for 12 years. All I knew was that I didn't want to stay in Pittsburgh. I didn't want to be a secretary in a mill. I moved down to Florida for five years and had odd jobs there. I was working in a clothing store there and this guy who ran the Coconut Grove Playhouse used to come in all the time. One day he said to me, "Why don't you go up to the theater and see if you can get a job? I can't just give it to you, but why don't you fill out an application?"

I did, and that's how I got started. I didn't really know about the theatre, but I just sort of fit in. I like working with money and figuring out how to get people to show up to see a show. It's very important: the marketing of theatre and how to make people aware that the show is there. Then I just came here for vacation and never left. I fell in love with New York City. It's a good place. You see people who want to run for the hills; they can't take the dirt. I just sort of fit in.

We don't usually do Sunday brunches at the Barrymore because some of our crew thinks it's messy. But on *Elling*, we did. We only ran one week but Denis O'Hare made everyone waffles. I thought, "Wow, why can't this show run?" At some theaters, you do holiday things. It's like a family, and that's good. Some people go, "Oh you get involved with the people backstage?" You don't have to, but I like it. You spend a lot of time here. It's good.

The Gershwin Theatre

Built: 1972
Location: 222 West 51st Street
Owner: The Nederlander Organization
Formerly Named: Uris Theatre (1972-1983)
Longest-Running Show: *Wicked* (2003-Present)
Shortest-Running Show: *The Red Shoes* (closed after five performances in 1993)
Number of Productions: 76

I remember seeing *Sweeney Todd* and *Pirates of Penzance* at the Uris, which is now the Gershwin. I remember seeing *Cyrano* there, and Derek Jacobi swinging on the stage. I even remember watching a dress rehearsal for the Tony Awards there one year! I was so excited. I watched Angela Lansbury trying to figure out her mark while they adjusted the lighting. It was wonderful. The theater is huge!

-Laura Linney, Actor

Introduction: I Knew I Wanted To Be In This House

Greg Woolard, Door Man/Usher

I started ushering on Broadway ten years ago. The first show I ushered was *A Raisin in the Sun* at the Royale. After that, my boss told me I could pick which theater I wanted to go to. "Would you like to move to the Majestic, the Rodgers, or the Gershwin?" Without thinking, I said: "The Gershwin!" After it came out of my mouth, I thought: *Why did I say Gershwin? That theater has the longest of the three shows!* But I just knew I wanted to be in this house somehow.

My first time seeing a show at the Gershwin was in 1977. I was in the front row in seats 117 and 118 to see Yul Brynner and Constance Towers in *The King and I*. Then, Thanksgiving week of 1980, I saw Angela Lansbury and Len Cariou in *Sweeney Todd*. I saw so many shows here before I worked here: *Singin' in the Rain, Starlight Express*... you name the Gershwin show, and I probably saw it!

In my mind, the Gershwin and the Minskoff are sister theaters. You almost don't know which one you're in. They look the same because they were both designed to be modern. Stagehands who come here are always saying, "You're one of the few houses that has an elevator! We love working here!" We have elevators, and we also have an escalator. All of the older Broadway theaters are right on street level, but we look like a theater that was designed later on.

I've worked at either Circle in the Square or the Gershwin for over 30 years now, either as a flyer boy, usher, or door man. The streets around us have evolved, and there are new restaurants popping up all the time. But there's always our corner deli here on 51st and 8th that has been here forever.

It still breaks my heart to look across the street and see that the Mark Hellinger Theatre is not the Mark Hellinger Theatre anymore. That was the home of *Dear World, Rags, Sugar Babies, My Fair Lady*. That theater was legendary. It's the kind of house that producers are looking for now, with a huge amount of seats. It's exactly what they want, but it wasn't then, so it was sold. I saw *Grind* there. I saw that production of *Oliver!* with Patti LuPone.

When I first got the door man job at the Gershwin, I was always saying to my friends, "Don't call me Pops!" In the old movie musicals from the 1920s and 1930s, the door man is always called "Pops."

Everyone has their idea of what the job of door man is. Essentially, I make sure no one comes into the theater who isn't supposed to be here. I try to be as helpful to the cast and crew as I possibly can. I keep my eye on everything. I work in tandem with our security crew each night with the stage door after the show. I page people to come downstairs when they have visitors. If it's raining, I'll announce on the intercom, "Ladies and gentlemen, cast and crew, you're going to need an umbrella tonight." We have no windows backstage, so they might not know. We treat each other like family here. Every day when I come in, the first thing I do is make a list of everyone who's got mail. Then when they come in, I'll let them know. I make sure that when food gets delivered, it gets to the right person. A lot of times, people will order food after the show starts, so I'll sign for it, and they run down after a scene to pick it up.

The internet has really changed everything about being a fan of Broadway. Somebody will come to the stage door and say, "I can't believe so-and-so's going on!" And I'll say, "Well you know more than I know!"

There are a lot of traditions here. The cast of *Wicked* sometimes has a theme for put-in rehearsals. When someone new is going into the show, they pick "Star Wars" or "pajamas" and everyone has to dress up accordingly. There are cookie contests. The cast and crew really are a family here, and it's amazing to me how much they bring me into that. I'm down here, and they're up there, but if it's somebody's birthday, I'm always brought a piece of cake.

Yesterday, somebody came in with a piece of luggage from Kennedy Airport with a name on it that was not remotely familiar to me. My answer could've been, " This isn't ours, take it back to Kennedy." I could've chosen not to deal with that. But it had the right address on it, so I found a phone number. I dialed that phone number and it turned out that it did belong to a staff member. I will always go the extra mile to be helpful in any way, shape, or form I can.

Not long ago I went over to Lost and Found and raided them of about 12 umbrellas so that if it's raining, I've got some to hand out to people. I don't know that every stage door man feels it's their job to do things like that, but I enjoy this. This is a great job for me to retire on and I look forward to coming to work every day. Just about every person says goodnight to me by name when they leave. That makes me feel like I'm doing something right.

---

*While the Gershwin and Circle in the Square are considered buddy theaters, sharing a block and an alley, they're not actually connected. There is no way to get from one theater to the other when you are backstage. From 2005 to 2008, David Stone, producer of a show in each house (*Wicked *and* The 25th Annual Putnam County Spelling Bee*), had to go outside in order to run back and forth between the two—and from 2011 to 2012, writer Stephen Schwartz (*Wicked *and* Godspell*) did the same thing.*

Even though they're not connected to each other, the two theaters are both connected to the Paramount Plaza building. When real estate moguls the Uris brothers built the structure in 1970, they were required by the city to include a theater as part of the new edifice. The Gershwin first opened as the Uris, and the whole building was erected on the spot where the Capitol movie palace once stood. The Capitol was one of Times Square's premiere movie theaters in the first half of the 20th century—it is where The Wizard of Oz *debuted in New York, and where* Doctor Zhivago *had its world premiere. In the Capitol Theatre, there were several signs that proclaimed: "Smoking In The Balcony Only." The Capitol's neighbors included Shapiro, Bernstein & Co Music Publishers, and the Rismont Tea Room.*

As well as its two Broadway theaters, the Paramount Plaza complex is home to a 48-story office building, a parking garage, several ever-changing restaurants, an Equinox gym, a subway entrance, and an outdoor seating area.

1972: The First Large Broadway Theater In 41 Years

James Dybas, Actor

The Uris was the first large Broadway theater to open in 41 years! Being in *Via Galactica* was a big deal because we were opening the Uris.

For *Via Galactica*, Sir Peter Hall was coming from London to direct. Our composer Galt MacDermot had just had a huge hit with *Hair*. The librettist, Christopher Gore, later had a huge hit with *Fame*.

Auditions were in August of 1972, and after I was cast, I was sitting in Central Park when I suddenly decided to start a journal about *Via Galactica*. My first entry was on Tuesday, September 5. I wrote:

> I sit here in anticipation of what a week from tomorrow will bring. I walked past the Uris Theatre today and asked one of the workers if I could see the inside. He was on top of some scaffolding, some forty feet above the lobby and he said, "Sure, go on up." One of his coworker buddies joked and said, "Hey, he could get me some discount tickets."
>
> As I walked in the orchestra section of the Uris Theatre, the enormity of it hit me like a ton of bricks. Stucco to be exact. I caught my first glimpse of the caramel, gold white interior. I made my way down to the stage, row by row, touching and enjoying the feel of the dark gold velvet covered seats. I didn't know what to look at first. Should I run up to the balcony? Jump up on the stage? See what the backstage facilities were like? See the upper lobby?
>
> Sure enough, I was backstage before you could say, "*Via Galactica*." I checked out all three floors of dressing rooms, all with brand new Formica sinks. Lavatory with shower and light bulb-lined mirrors. "Which one of these will I be in?" I wondered. Up two flights, more dressing rooms with lots of green and yellow walls, which were clean, free of cracks and gook. Brand new. Down two flights and I'm now in the wings. There are all kinds of wire hanging from the roof of the stage and men working on it. Looks like circus rigging. Damn it, I can't go on the stage. Back down to the upper lobby. On the way out I rip out an upholstered armrest from the orchestra section seat. It hadn't been cemented on yet. What a souvenir to have for years to come!

Later that day, I went to a trampoline lesson. We all went to the YMCA to do trampoline training for our Broadway show. To simulate space, we were jumping around, and to let you know we were all from different planets, we wore makeup on our faces that was red or pink or yellow or blue...

At first, we thought we were going to need to do all kinds of trampoline tricks in the show: front flips, back flips, different landings. But then, during rehearsals, there were all these accidents, so the trampoline action was cut down. The coolest part of the trampolines was that there were these six large ones on the stage—but when they weren't being used as trampolines, the stagehands would change them into hardwood stage panels from underneath. Characters would be walking around normally, and then suddenly, we would start to sing a number in space, and that's when we'd be bouncing around seamlessly on trampolines. For 1972, that was some stagecraft!

There were many injuries while we were rehearsing on the trampolines. I made a home movie backstage during rehearsals, and there's one part where several actors are walking up the stairs to the mezzanine, and you see an eye patch, a leg in a boot, an arm cast, a bandage on someone's head. The cast looked like war veterans. Nothing very serious happened, and every day, the director would say, "If you don't feel comfortable doing this, don't. We can make adjustments." But people wanted to.

There was also a huge ladder on our set, that zig-zagged up. In fact, it went all the way up to the fly floor. They hadn't finished the theater yet, so they took a sledgehammer and knocked a big hole through the cinder blocks so we could get from the top of the ladder directly into the dressing rooms on the fly floor level. The zigzag ladder was this giant sparkling silver stairway to the spaceship that really looked magnificent.

One day, in rehearsal, a lot of people got on top of the zigzag ladder and it probably hit its weight limit. The ladder plummeted. It was terrifying. People were crying. A headline flashed through my mind: "Ten Actors, First Casualty of New Theater." Luckily, everyone was fine. When we came in the next day, Peter Hall, our producers, and the stagehands union were all there and we had a discussion about safety.

I remember one night, a couple of us from the cast along with the writer, Christopher Gore, went to see a preview of *Pippin*. The lights came up on Ben Vereen as the narrator—and I just saw Christopher turn green. The narrator of our show was a black man as well. That was the turning point when the writers really decided: our story should be told by a child. A 12-year-old girl in the cast, Irene Cara, was made the new narrator. Of course she later had a big hit record with *Fame*, which Christopher wrote.

At one point in the show, we had this big spaceship that looked like a dragon that went out over the audience. During one preview, people in the audience started screaming. It turned out that oil from the dragon was dripping on their heads!

I understudied Keane Curtis. He was a wonderful actor, and the role he played was just a head. He had no body, and his head was in a box. So he had to sit scrunched up for the whole show, with only his head out, and mirrors around it.

Peter Hall kept encouraging us, and telling us how much better the piece was getting. And the audience reactions really were varied; some people loved it, and others hated it.

The back curtain was made entirely of ping-pong balls strung together, three rows deep. John Burrey, the scenic designer, arranged for slides to be projected on the ping-pong balls. It was an amazing concept.

I still have part of my original costume from *Via Galactica*. My main character was this space clown, with goggles on his head and these big balloon pants.

1972: Five Bodies To Fill Seats

Mana Allen, Actor

Long before TDF[40] or other discount ticket services, the word would go out among the theatrical community to fill seats that weren't sold at full price.

My family got tickets to shows in trouble because all the stagehands knew that my dad, a stage manager, had

---

[40] TDF: the Theatre Development Fund, a not-for-profit organization that supports shows and audience development through many programs, including discounted tickets for those in the arts, not-for-profit sphere, and low income brackets

96

five bodies they could count on to fill that many seats.

Via Galactica is one I really remember seeing with my family when I was 16. I loved it. I remember the ping-pong ball curtain, because they did projections on it. I remember the music and the trampolines. I remember thinking that Raul Julia was so handsome even though he was painted blue and I remember the beautiful girl painted gold who he was forbidden to love! I also remember going backstage after the show. The stagehands told my dad that the show was going to close soon, and then they let us hold the props. They let my little sister hold a prop baby that was as heavy as a real child. We thought that was so cool and then they let us jump on the trampolines. That probably wouldn't happen today.

Later, volunteering at the New York Public Library for the Performing Arts, I met Barbara Cohen Stratyner, the curator of the museum there. She told me that she put herself through college as a stitcher in Broadway costume shops and she actually helped on that *Via Galactica* ping-pong curtain! She told me, "I helped string those ping pong balls with a lot of other people."

Equity used to give out tickets too, sometimes with directions... That's how I got to see *Carrie*. When we picked up the tickets they said, "You can have these tickets if you promise not to laugh in inappropriate places."

Throughout Broadway history, certain shows have altered theaters to accommodate their own unique physical needs. From The Rocky Horror Show's *"renovation" of the Belasco that ripped out the box seats in 1975 to* Rocky's *boxing ring that altered the Winter Garden seating in 2013, musicals that theater owners believe will be hits have often been given permission to change the theater they will call home. The 1972-1973 season saw a significant number of these theater-altering productions. Trampolines were built into the deck[41] of the Uris for* Via Galactica. *The stage of the Broadway was covered in dirt and mud for* Dude. *At the Brooks Atkinson,* Lysistrata *erected ramps all over the theater. This was an era where Broadway was trying to evolve along with the times and become more experimental in show content* and *form.*

The Uris actually has one of the most often reshaped stages. Several designers have chosen to build sets out over the audience in order to make the large theater feel enveloping and inclusive. However, this is actually an option already built into the theater: the original architects made it possible for the deck to be turned into a thrust or dismantled. Later on, the Uris would be transformed into a roller rink for Starlight Express *and a playground of rain for* Singin' in the Rain.

1972: *Via Galactica*

Harvey Sabinson, Press Agent

Via Galactica! The original title was "*Up!*" and it was going to play the Uris Theatre, which had just been built. It is now called the Gershwin.

They built a weird marquee that came out perpendicular to the theater, and the name of the theater was on the bottom of the sign.

I said, "If you put the title up there, it's going to read '*Up!* Uris'"

I didn't think that was appropriate.

---

[41] deck: another term for the stage area

Over the course of writing this book, four different people told me they were the one responsible for the name change from Up! *to* Via Galactica. *Just like* Rashomon, *everyone has their own version of the story. Any history book ever written was written based on memories—and it's important to remember that no history book has ever been 100% true. Each person has his or her own truth.*

1973/1979: Orchestra Comrades

Jack Gale, Musician

There's a joy and a feeling of comraderie that develops when you're part of a show's orchestra because you rely on each other so much. Sometimes, the conductors don't have the show under control, and the musicians make sure together that the show sounds good, even if the stick is thrown down at the wrong time. On the other hand, sometimes a great conductor can save the day.

In 1973, I was playing *Seesaw*, which starred Michele Lee. Donald Pippin was the conductor, and Skippy Redwine was the associate conductor. One night, Michele's understudy was on and she started this long, dramatic song by coming in eight bars early—but she wasn't aware of it. It looked like a hopeless situation, but Pippin got her attention and got her to slow down, and Redwine crouched over the top of the piano he was playing, got everyone's attention and sped us up. After about 20 seconds, we were all in the same place, and the show went on like nothing had happened. It could have been a train wreck. I was astonished by that. That's the ingenuity and professionalism of Broadway musical direction and conducting on display.

In *Seesaw*, there was a very risqué opening number with all of these scantily clad girls, dancing provocatively and making a lot of noise. The point was that Ken Howard played the lead character, a Midwestern guy who was shocked by all of this, and on the button of the number, a cop came in and said, "All right! Move it along!" There was a moment of silence and then he said, "Didn't you hear me mister?" and that always got a big laugh because you realized that he was talking to this guy, rather than to all these women, disturbing the peace.

One night, we had a special guest in the show. Ken Howard, who was a movie star, looked just like New York's mayor at the time, John Lindsay. That night, Lindsay came on during that scene, and stood nose-to-nose with Ken. It was quite a memorable performance!

The most exciting musical I ever played was *Sweeney Todd,* in 1979, at the Uris. I hated the idea of the show when I first heard what it was about: cannibalism and all that horrible stuff! I didn't want to take a job playing it, but I needed work. And then I got there, and the show was musically thrilling and turned out to be a masterpiece. We had a huge pit! The orchestra pits get smaller and smaller as they add seats into the theaters. That makes a good reason to not hire as many musicians. But on *Sweeney Todd*, it was a large orchestra.

1973: Everyone's Traveling On A Crazy *Seesaw*

Michon Peacock, Actor

When we did *Seesaw* in Detroit, the producers were not happy with how it was being received. They brought in Michael Bennett with a totally different concept, along with his entourage. The ensemble had to re-audition for Michael. Some of us were kept, but many were fired during the Detroit run. We rehearsed the new version during the day and performed the old show at night. Not a good situation... Grover Dale had been the choreographer, and I was the dance captain[42]—but of course, that would change, too.

Once we were back in New York, Michael asked why I was standoffish with him. I told him the truth about how I felt he handled the situation in Detroit. He did try to explain but admitted he wasn't at his best. We did begin to build a better working relationship and would talk periodically. Though I really wasn't dance captain any more, I was happy to help him work with Ken Howard in teaching him how to waltz.

Then right after we opened, he asked me to come up to his office at the Uris. The Uris was huge! Incredible dressing rooms, wide hallways, rehearsal space and office space not to mention the massive stage and overwhelming number of seats!!!

Michael said he was pretty concerned that the show wasn't going to run, so he asked if I'd help him do something about it. "Like what?" I asked. He told me he had heard I practiced Buddhism! He said he chanted sometimes, too. I was kind of surprised. However, then he said, "There's one thing we haven't done: we haven't chanted about this. I think we should all chant together. Aren't there some other people in the show that are Buddhist? Could we do something like that at your apartment?" I said, "Yes, sure!" But I was a bit freaked out as I was still rather new to this myself.

I had this old, teeny apartment in the Village on West 4th Street. I asked a couple of members from my Buddhist group to support because I didn't know who would actually come and be able to chant for an hour. It was pretty amazing as Michael, Tommy Tune, Michel Stuart, Merel Poloway, and others were all there—sitting or kneeling on the floor chanting. They were great. Michael never left my side. There were eight to ten of us and we chanted for an hour.

Later, Michael motioned for me to come into the kitchen and said, "I just got a call that tomorrow night Mayor Lindsay is coming to the theater and he's going to stand in for Ken Howard in the opening number. Publicity!"

It was amazing. I have the front-page pictures from *The Post* and *The Daily News* of when the mayor stepped into "My City", our opening number. It was a huge publicity success and we ran! Some of the cast asked, "Is it because we chanted?" Well… the power of unity, determination and energy shouldn't be underestimated in any endeavor, right?

———————

I interviewed Michon Peacock at the Cosmic Diner on the northeast corner of 52nd Street and 8th Avenue. Near the end of our chat, she pointed out the window. "Oh! There's Eileen Casey. I did Seesaw *with her." 40 years later and a block away, there we were.*

———————

1973: Hiring And Firing

Eileen Casey, Actor

I did *Seesaw* at the Uris and the Hellinger. Originally, Ed Sherin was directing, Grover Dale was choreographing, and Lainie Kazan was the star. We went out-of-town to Detroit and got really bad reviews.

Wayne Cilento was in it, and it was his first Broadway show. Every time I turned around, he was stretching. He never stopped! He later became a choreographer and choreographed *Wicked* at the same theater.

---

[42] dance captain: the member of the cast who assists the choreographer in maintaining their work during the course of a run

Out-of-town, Joe Kipness, one of the producers, let Ed and Grover go and brought on Michael Bennett. He let Lainie go and brought in Michele Lee. Tommy Tune came in to play a role and help with choreography. We all had to re-audition for Michael on the stage of the Fisher Theatre. He let some of the chorus people go, and I was kept. Then we re-vamped the whole show—everything. It was a whole different show by the time we came to the Uris.

1973: A Jewish Girl From The Bronx

Randy Graff, Actor

Growing up, there was a show that was an "ah hah!" moment for me. My mom took me to see Michele Lee in a preview of *Seesaw*. She was playing this character, Gittel Mosca, who was a Jewish girl from the Bronx.

I so identified with her, being a Jewish girl from Brooklyn. That show had an interesting effect on me. I thought: *If she's a Jewish girl from the Bronx and can be in a musical, then I can be in a musical too.*

Some years later I was doing a reading with Michele Lee, and I told her that she had such an influence on me. You know, I didn't even think of her as Michele Lee. I saw her as Gittel Mosca, that role that I could do too.

———————

In 1974, the theater housed nine special productions that could be better described as special appearances. Sammy Davis Jr., Anthony Newley & Henry Mancini, and the Fifth Dimension all played the Uris.

*After opening with an outer space epic (*Via Galactica*), the Uris housed a modern New York City musical (*Seesaw*), a classic operetta (*The Desert Song*), and a new-old show (*Gigi*). Gigi was one of the first shows in Broadway history to go from a movie musical to a stage musical, spearheaded by the same creative team. (This would become a far more popular trend later on!) Gigi only ran for 103 performances at the Uris, but as of this printing, it is planned for its first Broadway revival in 2015. None of the first four shows at the Uris recouped, so in 1974, many special productions and concerts gave the theater their best shots.*

Next, the Nederlanders attempted to turn the Uris into a successful house by integrating several ballets and operas such as Treemonisha *and* Porgy and Bess *into the playing schedule. While dance and special events kept the house open and in use, they often had very short runs and did nothing to prove that the Uris could be a successful house for Broadway shows.*

———————

1976: *Porgy And Bess*

Jack O'Brien, Director/Writer

I was the last person hired for the revival of *Porgy and Bess* in 1976, and I was the director. The show was completely cast, and ready to go.

They had wanted Hal Prince to do it for the Houston Grand Opera, and he was booked. Meanwhile, I was working at the American Opera Center at Julliard with a conductor, John DeMain, who happened to be the musical director of Houston Grand Opera. He found me to be clever, and one day, out of nowhere, he said to me, "Who should direct *Porgy and Bess*?"

To be frank, I didn't know the opera very well. I remembered the movie, and I said without batting an eye, "A black woman." He asked why, and I said, "Because it seems to me that the most interesting character in the piece is Bess. In the 1920s, in order to survive, she had to get into proximity for protection with the strongest man in the community. Originally, it was Crown. Then, she found Porgy and found love with a crippled person. It seems to me that a contemporary black woman would have some cognizance of what that would be like."

It was an interesting answer; I'm not quite sure where it came from. He asked, "Do you know any black women directors?" I told him I did, and I recommended Vinnette Carroll, who I had worked with briefly and who had an urban arts organization. She did things like *Your Arms Too Short to Box with God* and other revues, but she took months and months to create them.

They went to Vinnette and offered her the show. And she said, "Yes! How much time do I have?" They said, "Three weeks." And she said, "Honey, I couldn't do that in three months." So they hired me, and it made my career.

———————————

In between Gigi *and the theater's next tenant in the genre of Broadway musical, 27 separate special productions played the Uris. In 1977, the first Broadway revival of* The King And I *opened at the Uris starring Yul Brynner and Constance Towers.*

During that production, Yul Brynner started a significant Uris Theatre tradition. In recreating his role of the King of Siam for a revival of the show, he began a long history of actors doing "second chance" performances of roles that made them famous.

Cathleen Nesbitt recreated the role of Mrs. Higgins, which she'd played in the original production of My Fair Lady, *in the 1981 revival at the Uris. Also at this theater, Lonette McKee had the distinction of playing Julie in both the 1983 and 1994 revivals of* Show Boat. *In 1983, when Angela Lansbury recreated Mame at the Uris, alongside her were Jane Connell, Anne Francine, Willard Waterman, and Sab Shimono, all of whom had been in the original production. In 1990, Topol brought back his* Fiddler on the Roof, *which he had done on film and in London. The Uris became known for not just revivals of shows, but revivals of actors bringing back celebrated roles.*

———————————

1977: Yul Brynner Was Two Inches Tall

Joe Traina, House Manager

The first Broadway show I saw was *The King and I*, on May 10, 1977, at the Uris Theatre, which is now called the Gershwin Theatre.

Yul Brynner and Constance Towers were in the show, and we sat in the last row of the theater. Yul Brynner was about two inches tall from my view. My friend's mom took us. After that, I went to see shows fairly frequently!

1977: De Wickedest Critter In De World

Jack Gale, Musician

In 1977, I played *The King and I* at the Uris, starring Yul Brynner. There's a famous scene in *The King and I*, where Anna teaches the Siamese children to put on this charming performance of the story of *Uncle Tom's Cabin*. It's an amazing part of the show because, the way it's written, it casts a light on the situation that the king is actually in with his slaves, and how he's mistreating them.

One line in the scene is spoken by this little Siamese girl, Topsy, who says, "I specks I'se de wickedest critter in de world!" It's a famous line from the show and from the actual novel, *Uncle Tom's Cabin*.

The conductor for that production was known to be somewhat high strung and difficult. I really enjoyed working with him, but there were those who didn't. One night, when he walked into the pit, a young horn player absentmindedly played the Death March. The whole orchestra was shocked, and the conductor looked very angry. It seemed like something terrible was about to happen, when the third trumpet player suddenly said, "I specks I'se de wickedest critter in de world!" It was so funny that even the conductor laughed, and the whole thing was resolved in a really humorous way.

All of those guys are gone now, but I've always remembered that, even decades later, because it was just so like the theatre. It was great that a musician took something from the show that was said every night and used it to help another guy out.

———————————

When it opened in 1972, the Uris was the first new Broadway theater built since the Vivian Beaumont in 1965. But prior to the Beaumont, the last time Broadway had gotten a new theater was in 1928! Between the opening of the Barrymore in 1928 and the Beaumont in 1965, hundreds of new Broadway shows opened but not a single Broadway theater. Directly following the birth of the Uris and Circle in the Square in 1972, Broadway also expanded when the Minskoff was built in 1973. Since then, there has been one more new Broadway theater built: the Marquis in 1986.

In the summer of 2014, rumors began circulating that the Shuberts would build a new Broadway house on 8th Avenue between 45th and 46th Streets.

———————————

1979: Previewing *Sweeney Todd*

Len Cariou, Actor

In *Sweeney Todd*, the pie shop was made incorrectly. It was made out of steel instead of aluminum, and it caused many problems. We never got through tech. When the first audience was there, we still had not teched the end of the show because the set kept breaking down. It was locking in a certain position and we couldn't turn it. So we had to stop—even in the first preview—and the stagehands had to come out and take over from the company who were supposed to be moving the set.

After the first preview, Stephen Sondheim met me at my dressing room door and said, standing there, "They understood it. They actually f---ing got it!" We had a great embrace and congratulated one another. The show was too long, we knew that, but it may be the best musical ever written in the history of the world, and we knew that too. Leading up to the first preview, it was all: *Are they going to get it? If they don't get it, it's going to go all for naught.* That's the way Broadway is. But they got it.

I left the theater that night, and I went to Joe Allen. Joe came over to me, sat down, and said, "I hear you have a lot of trouble with your show." I said, "Well, yeah, we had tech troubles but the show is fine." And he said, "Oh, I heard from so-and-so that it's no good at all." I asked, "He was at the first preview?" And he said, "Yeah, he was there."

I was very angry. I said, "Well, if you believe that asshole—" I mean, in the first place, why would you come to the first preview to criticize? And in the second place, if you're in this business, how do you not see what *Sweeney Todd* is? I said, "This is a piece of genius theatre, Joe, so when you see him again, tell him I said to stick it up his ass. Because if I see him again, I'm going to punch him in the nose."

We had to deal with some things, and they remade the pie shop out of the proper material and the rest is history. Great history. But it was a difficult time and, you know, we also had the very famous preview when the catwalk fell to the deck.

In the middle of the second act, Mrs. Lovett and I are looking for Toby because I realize that he knows what's going on, and we're going to kill him. It's just the two of us on the bare stage with follow-spots, and we come out of a trapdoor from the basement. During this part of the show, the catwalk moved upstage.

I came out and we were singing, "Nothing's gonna harm you, not while I'm around. Toby, where are you?" Then, I heard a very strange sound, a metal clicking sound. There was only the two of us. While I'm not singing, I hear more noise coming from above us. I look up, and the bridge—made of steel, must have weighed three tons—was starting to descend onto the set. Very slowly.

Angela Lansbury was over there, and the blocking was that she'd go back upstage. I saw that, and I walked over and grabbed her by the arm. I didn't say anything, I just grabbed her by the arm and I took her downstage. She followed, and we kept on singing. She was clearly wondering, *What's going on?*

Lo and behold, it all came crashing to the stage. We had to stop and stagehands had to come and lift the wall back up. I went out on the stage and said, "Take two."

"Epiphany" was just amazing to perform every night. And I could actually see people in the first few rows. It scared the shit out of me.

1979: We're Going To Have To Find It

Larry Fuller, Choreographer

Sweeney was a very difficult show, stylistically. When Hal gave me the original script, and I first read it, only half the first act had been musicalized. The rest of it was the play that Hugh Wheeler had written, based on the original script from London. Christopher Bond wrote the melodrama that Steve had seen in London, in a fringe theater. Steve had come to Hal with the idea to musicalize it.

Hugh Wheeler wrote a whole new script, which was absolutely wonderful. Hugh never got as much credit as he deserved. When I first read it, I said to Hal: "How the hell are we going to do this? I mean, is it going to be a real kind of horror story? With real-looking body parts, and things hanging on meat-grinder with the oven on? Or is it going to be more obviously artificial parts of mannequins and stuff like that?"

Hal said, "I don't know, Larry. We're going to have to find it." That's what we did during the rehearsal period. Then the actors really found it, with the audience, during the three weeks of previews.

I remember at one point during rehearsals, I asked Hal if he was having any fun doing the show. And he said, "No." I responded, "Neither am I. It's just such difficult material." But then it was *so* rewarding. It is, I think, Steve's masterpiece. But nobody thought that at the time. Even though *Texas Chainsaw Massacre* was doing great business at the movie house, people were shocked to see something like that on the Broadway stage.

During the first preview at the Uris, I was standing in the back of the orchestra, and there were maybe 300 people in that huge orchestra section. I was watching the beginning of the show, and I thought: *We are in the wrong theater. It's too big. We should be at the Broadhurst. With wooden scaffolding and rope pulleys and things, splashing the first three rows with blood. It should be right in their face.* It was so huge, that theater.

The bus and truck was more intimate. I thought it was, conceptually, design-wise, the better version. Then, mini-*Sweeney* was years later at the Circle in the Square, and I missed the ensemble very much. Because the sound they had was just so stunning. That hugeness was perfect for the show.

———————

Sweeney Todd was the first of the Harold Prince-produced shows that didn't have the customary out-of-town pre-Broadway tryout, as the cost was prohibitive. In Larry Fuller's interview, he spoke about the artistic value of trying out aspects of a brand-new piece in front of an audience. Sweeney Todd's choice to preview in New York was indicative of a huge way that the development of new shows was changing.

As more shows swapped out-of-town tryouts for longer New York preview periods in the 1980s, public scrutiny during New York previews became more rampant. Shows couldn't incubate and revise and better themselves away from the public eye of the most major theatergoing city in the United States. And audiences felt that if they were going to pay the ticket price of a Broadway show for a preview (which many more of them were, since there were so many more New York previews!), they expected a finished product.

Broadway shows were "killed in previews" from bad word-of-mouth in a manner that hadn't previously happened as often. Some people attribute this to the change in quality of shows in the 1980s but the truth is that not only did fewer shows have the benefit of getting things right out-of-town first, but that content-wise, they were also contending with immediate and extreme scrutiny as they tried to improve in New York.

While working in front of an audience is still just as instructive and helpful to a piece, there's no more (semi) privacy in New Haven. Theatre professionals were once able to try out a new show in front of an out-of-town audience who understood they were getting an unfinished product, and were happy to be part of the process. Maybe a critic or two would take the train in and report "No Legs, No Jokes, No Chance" (as Walter Winchell from the New York Daily Mirror did about Oklahoma!)[43] but mostly, shows would get a chance to develop based on audience reaction before being widely judged.

Creative professionals started to find ways to adapt, with longer workshop processes and labs. Then, in the early 2000s, when the internet came into greater play in the Broadway community, everything changed again. Now, word-of-mouth for a show in development could reach from New York to Iowa to Hawaii instantaneously—yet another difficulty for creative professionals to grapple with. It barely mattered by the early 2000s, during the era of Seussical and Taboo, whether you previewed in New York or Toronto or Miami; word-of-mouth could spread as quickly as the click of a mouse.

How has this immediate scrutiny really changed which shows succeed and which don't? Well, shows with bad initial word-of-mouth that spreads quickly have a harder road to overcome in order to go on to a long successful run. And yet there are always exceptions—such as Wicked! ... But more on that soon.

As Richard Rodgers once said, "I wouldn't open a can of sardines without taking it to Boston first."

———————————

1979: Meat Pies For Lunch

Joanna Merlin, Casting Director/Actor

I'll never forget the first day of *Sweeney Todd* rehearsal. The whole cast assembled to read through the script. They were reading and Steve was playing and it was just amazing. Then we broke for lunch and Steve provided the lunch for everyone: meat pies. Nobody wanted to eat them, but of course we all did!

I remember something that Steve said about Angela Lansbury that somehow stuck in my mind. There was a performance of the show where Angela was knocking on the door, and nobody was answering like they were supposed to. Steve said to me that Angela was the kind of actress who would have kept knocking until her fingers bled—she has that kind of energy and intention and commitment. I think that was probably true.

---

[43] Wilk, Max. *OK! The Story of Oklahoma!* New York: Grove Press, 1993. 17.

1979: God, That's Good!

Ken Billington, Lighting Designer

Sweeney Todd happened during the days before everyone would just give a standing ovation automatically at the end of a Broadway show. And at the first preview, there were people standing and screaming right next to people who thought it was awful. A very famous agent came up to me at intermission and said, "I hope you got paid in cash." He thought it was the worst thing he had seen. Now, arguably, it's one of the great shows of the 20th century!

It was exciting. I always knew, from the first reading in Hal's office, that it was a major piece of musical theatre. We put it together quickly, and when we got to see it onstage in front of people, it was incredible.

There were those who hated it, maybe because it wasn't *My Fair Lady*. I think that's sort of standard with Stephen Sondheim. People really like his work or really don't like it. When we opened in London, we were a mega-flop at the Drury Theater. *Sweeney Todd* closed there within four weeks! Half the critics said how terrible it was, and the other half said it was a masterpiece. And all these years later they revive it all the time over there, as they do here.

1979/1993: A Future Scenic Designer At The Uris

Anna Louizos, Scenic Designer

Sweeney Todd was very memorable to me. It was at the Uris Theatre. Now it's called the Gershwin, but then it was called the Uris. It was very exciting because I got half-price tickets and I got to see it in previews.

It was very big. It was a big, vast space. Eugene Lee's design had a big bridge that tracked up and down, and this huge backdrop that was a reproduction of a lithograph of a factory. So it had a very dark, industrial feel to it.

I was an assistant designer on *The Red Shoes* later, at the same theater. I was mostly working in the studio with Heidi Landesman, who was the designer, and building model set pieces, drafting. I wasn't in the theater much on that one.

1979: I Didn't Connect

Don Stitt, Actor

I didn't really connect with *Sweeney Todd* at the Uris. I was in row M of the orchestra, so it wasn't that I couldn't hear or see. It wasn't that it wasn't good either, but looking back, I think it's such a cavernous space that it was the distance.

For me, the TV version brought the show to life more than the original production. The immediacy of the camera made me feel the story was better told on TV. I love *Sweeney Todd* now.

1979: MR. SONDHEIM, MR. SONDHEIM!

Ann Harada, Actor

I saw *Sweeney Todd* the day it won the Tony Award. I was 15. We were in town for a week and my parents were like, "You can see a Broadway show every night this week if you want." I yelled, "Yes please!"

So I saw *Sweeney* at a Sunday matinee, and then the Tony Awards were Sunday night, and I watched them in our hotel room. The next day I was walking down the street, and I saw Stephen Sondheim get into a car with some beautiful woman.

I literally hollered, "MR. SONDHEIM! MR. SONDHEIM!" and he turned to me and he said, "Yes?" and I said "THANK YOU!" I was crying. Oh my God, it was so embarrassing!

———————

The Gershwin is home to the Theater Hall of Fame, the only nationally recognized hall of fame honoring lifetime achievement in the American theatre. Each year, eight new theatrical luminaries are voted in, based on their credits and contribution to the art form. When audience members enter the Gershwin Theatre, they take escalators up to the rotunda level, where you can enter the orchestra section. This level is adorned with giant wall plaques which list the names of all Hall of Fame honorees, as well as their photos and even mementos from their shows, such as props or scripts. There are items from everyone from Bernadette Peters to Lynn Fontanne. As a special bonus, there are also some retired scenic pieces from Wicked *on display. If you're seeing a show at the Gershwin, arrive early so that you can take in all of these pieces of history!*

———————

1980: Replacements

Evan Pappas, Actor

The first Broadway show I saw was *Sweeney Todd* with Dorothy Loudon and George Hearn.

I was a Sondheim junkie, I knew every note, and I was sitting there, finally seeing it realized. Finally! I remember thinking, *Ah, these are the two replacements for Angela Lansbury and Len Cariou.* I didn't know yet who all these people were. I learned later that George Hearn was a huge Broadway star. But I remember saying to my friend, "Wow. They're really good." Some people think that if you're not the original then you're not as good, which I learned to be so untrue.

Then, 20 years later, I got to work with George Hearn on *Putting It Together.* I was in my early forties at the time, but I was like, "It's George Hearn! It's George Hearn!" I couldn't wait to tell him that that was my first Broadway show. He is the sweetest man in the world.

1981: Better Ask Rex

Penny Davis, Wardrobe Supervisor

We were at the Uris for *My Fair Lady.* Well, it was the Uris then. The Gershwin now. And Rex Harrison was Henry Higgins.

One time, our Pickering and Doolittle—Jack Gwillim and Milo O'Shea—went away on their days off. They both went to California, and when they came back, they got snowed into Chicago. Each of them got snowed in, even though they were traveling separately! They called and said they weren't going to be able to go on, because they were stuck in Chicago. So, they put the two understudies on. Luckily they were two separate people!

We began the show, and at 8:30, they both appeared at the theater! The stage manager got flustered. Instead of saying to the men, "Glad you're home safe, see you tomorrow," he went to Rex, in the middle of a quick change in his dressing booth off stage left, and said, "Pickering and Doolittle are here now. What should I do?"

I was there, so I saw this happen. Rex was bewildered, but he knew everybody thought he liked to be in charge, so he said, "Put them on!" We had already seen "Get Me To The Church On Time". We were coming up to a whole series of quick changes for Pickering.

The dressers started frantically trying to switch everything to the right rooms. If you know that theater, it's like... well, if you forget something, it's easier to just go buy a new one! It's a huge backstage, a block long. Rex himself acknowledged afterwards that it was stupid. But it should not have been Rex's decision.

Cathleen Nesbit was Mrs. Higgins. She was a trip! She was a dear, dear woman, but pretty senile by that time, and had to have a keeper. You never quite knew what she was going to do once she got onstage. One night, some of the cast was invited to a dinner party after the show, and so when she went onstage for the little scene right before "Ascot", she said, "Jack! Jack!" to Colonel Pickering. "Are you going to the party tonight? Jack! Are you going to Mrs. So-and-So's party tonight?" He bowed and then said "Yes, madam, but first we're going to Ascot." And then they scooted her off stage!

One of the most charming things was that a fan found a picture album of Cathleen's first American tour of the Abbey Theatre in the 1910s, at a flea market, and sent it to her. I was sitting right outside her dressing room in a little alcove when she got it. She never really remembered my name, but she liked me. And I liked her, and would always do little nice things for her. She said, "Young lady! Young lady! Come here, I want to show you something!"

The scrapbook was filled with all these incredible pictures. She had a long term affair with the famous poet, Rupert Brooke, and he died very young. He was in the scrapbook. With awe she said, "This is me on the ship coming over from Ireland, and that's Rupert." She pointed out and remembered every single person in each photograph including the actress, Peggy Wood. It was such a wonderful, sweet moment. It made me think about who she was, and the career she had. She was forever. She did so many different things, had such a body of work, it was extraordinary.

From December of 1981 to January of 1983, Annie *played the 4th and last stop of its multi-theater original Broadway run at the Uris Theatre. At the curtain call of the final performance, the creators took the stage of the Uris and announced that an* Annie *sequel would open on Broadway soon.*

Annie 2: Miss Hannigan's Revenge *tried out in Washington D.C. and attempted to open at the Marquis Theatre in 1990 but closed out-of-town. A second shot at a sequel,* Annie Warbucks, *tried to get to Broadway but landed off-Broadway in 1993.*[44]

---

[44] Check out *The Untold Stories of Broadway, Volume 1* for more on this story.

1982: Little Redheaded Kid

Hunter Bell, Actor/Writer

The first Broadway show I saw was when I was on a trip to New York when I was little, with my mom, brother, and grandmother. We went on a theatre weekend, and the two shows we saw were *Dancin'*, and then *Annie* at the Uris.

I loved *Dancin'*, and I had no idea that it was sexual, or "Fosse-style"; I was just so happy to be seeing a show! The next night, we saw *Annie*, which starred Dorothy Loudon and Allison Smith at the time. I had a 101-degree fever, but I begged, "Please, please, please, still let me go!" I got to go, and I was probably hallucinating there in the Uris Theatre.

I was out of my mind, I loved *Annie* so much. It's because I loved the show that I remember the Uris so well. And it was such a weird name. I remember as a kid thinking, *Why? Why would you call a theater that?*

1982/2002: My Equity Card And Beyond

Merwin Foard, Actor

When I first moved here to go to school, it never occurred to me that theatre was something I could do. At the time, as a voice major at Manhattan School, I was looking at an operatic career. Then they told me, "You're gonna have a heck of a career in your mid-forties." I was 19! I thought, *I'm not gonna wait around*, so I started auditioning.

Occasionally people would post on a bulletin board open calls that were happening. I saw this open call notice that *Show Boat* was looking for legit voices, and had an age range that I fit. They wanted tall men because Donald O'Connor was going to star in it. He was 5'5", so they wanted him to look kind of impish. I fit all the criteria.

I talked with a couple of the other guys in the opera department. We went down to the cattle call. Thousands of people showed up at the Equity Building on 46th Street! They brought us into the room, 25 at a time and said, "You and you, stay. Everybody else thank you very much." They were just going by physical type alone, having no idea about what we'd done, our resume, our talent.

Being a student, I was wearing a really sweet little button-down collar shirt, a V-neck sweater and horn-rimmed glasses. I looked very preppy. I got typed out. My buddies were also typed out. We left. "So much for that, let's go back to school."

But I couldn't accept that. Because if you read the casting call, I was the perfect fit. They just didn't know that! When you got typed in, you went outside to the monitor and gave him your information. The guys were like, "You can't embarrass yourself. You have to leave with us." And I said, "No, I will hate myself if I don't at least try. If I sing for them and they don't cast me, fine. But I can't let them think by my look that I can't do what they want." They were like, "You're gonna burn bridges." They left, shaking their heads.

I took off my glasses, took off my sweater, put in contacts, and went out to the monitor. I told him I was typed in. He gave me a card, I filled it out, and I sat there and waited. Finally, it was my turn to sing. They only wanted to hear 16 bars.

I sang Cole Porter's "Night and Day". There were probably 12 people behind the table. I finished singing and they asked if I knew "Ol' Man River". I sang.

I got the job and got my Equity card and said goodbye to school. At this point, I was a first semester sophomore.

Show Boat toured for 11 months then opened on Broadway at the Uris. I left it to do the *Mame* revival with Angela Lansbury. So my mom and dad came to two Broadway openings within three or four months of each other. And they just said, "Merwin Jr., are you going to be doing this all the time? Should we come up from Charlotte all the time for different opening nights?" I said, "You might! If we're lucky, if we're lucky!"

Angela Lansbury had in her contract for *Mame* that she would play the Uris Theatre where she had done *Sweeney Todd*. We toured *Mame*, and waited to see what *Show Boat* did. Rumor was it wasn't going to last, and if it closed, I would just come right back in to the Uris.

Then *Show Boat* closed. We were about six months into this *Mame* tour in Philly and we came flying back into New York with a rickety touring set, no PR,[45] no advance box office sales, and threw the show up at the now-Gershwin Theatre. It only ran a few months because it just couldn't get an audience fast enough.

That theater's backstage is enormous! The size of it was really shocking to me. And it's a maze! From backstage to the dressing rooms to what floor you were on... the hallways just keep going. It was remarkable. And then onstage looking out at 2000 seats. It's daunting to see that many people.

It felt great to be back there for *Oklahoma!* 20 years later. There was a security guy at the front of the house at the Gershwin named Steve. He was so friendly! He remembered me from the other shows that I'd done, because I'd done *1776* there too. When I went back with *Oklahoma!,* he greeted me with open arms. I was like, "Oh my gosh, you remember?" He was like, "Of course I do!" Whenever he saw me, he would always yell my name and give me support. And then the backstage guys! You'd see these fellas and I was amazed that they held their same job show after show after show. They still had the same house electrician or the house carpenter or the house props guy at the Gershwin. It was great to reconnect with them and remember, "Oh yeah sure. That was you? Oh yeah, now I remember you." Very cool to share that bond. When a show like *Wicked* plays that theater, you're so happy that they're not having another random show that's going to come in and close— because it's a hard house to sell. You're happy for them that they have a mega-hit where they can actually sit back and relax and retire and not have to think about other jobs in between shows at the Gershwin. That's great.

I'll never forget closing night of *Mame* there. We worked so hard to try to make that show run. Angela Lansbury actually called a company meeting and asked if we as a company would agreed to take half our salaries to keep the show running, until we could gain momentum. Angela Lansbury was saying that, so of course everybody said, "Yes ma'am, anything for you, yes!" It didn't happen though.

Angela's favorite flower is a sterling silver rose. If you ever see them, they're a beautiful, deep lavender color. I ordered 16 of them.

The curtain call of *Mame* had all of the guys in beautiful foxhunt outfits: red cutaway coats, white pants, knee boots, with very sharp little top hats, white gloves, and riding clasps. We came out dancing to the title song and we bowed in an angled line. Angela would pass each of us and gesture to us as we went down on one knee. We'd drop down, drop down, drop down...

I gave everyone the sterling silver roses. On the final curtain call we all sang "Mame" and as we got on one knee, we each held a rose up to her. By the end, she had 16 guys each offering her a rose. She had a bouquet of roses. She was crying and we were crying, it was ridiculous! We couldn't even sing.

---

[45] PR: public relations, anything related to press and media attention and opportunities

While Merwin was in Show Boat *at the Uris, he was in* Mame *at the Gershwin. It was less than a month later, but the theater had a whole new name, christened during the 1983 Tony Awards.*

The 1983 Tony Awards opened with a visual of a Pan Am flight zipping through the clouds—presumably on its way to the Uris. Then they moved to a performance onstage from the cast of My One and Only, *with the names of the night's celebrity appearances announced in white type simultaneously. The first name? George Abbott. The list of names is overall alarmingly theatrical: Cleavant Derricks, Bonnie Franklin, Florence Lacey... sure, those folks are mixed in with Laurence Olivier and Lena Horne, so there are certainly "names" involved that are known worldwide, but everybody who participated was deeply connected to the theater.*

In fact, each presenter during the 1983 Tony Awards announced the nominees in their category while wearing their costume from the Broadway show they were currently performing in. In contrast, the 2014 Tony Awards included many more nationally "famous" presenters with only marginal ties to Broadway—but to be fair, Broadway in 2014 was attracting many more of these people to its stages. In 1983, there weren't large numbers of mainstream celebrities stopping in to Broadway for a season here and there like there are today. In 1983, celebrities like Gloria Estefan and Tina Fey weren't developing musicals for Broadway—and of course, we are lucky to have them, so why not feature Broadway's biggest names in the action? The biggest names on Broadway are changing, so the biggest names at the Tony Awards are too. There's a positive side of each era: in one, it's truly inspiring to see those currently on Broadway receive the spotlight for one night on national television; yet in the other, it's truly inspiring to see the biggest names of film, television, and music believe Broadway is an important part of the entertainment industry and aim to be part of it. Hopefully, future Tony Awards can bring us a balance between the two.

But in 1983, the Tony Awards had a homey glow. The proceedings felt so friendly at the Uris that Lilianne Montevecchi called out to Stephen Mo Hannan to make sure she'd pronounced his name correctly, and he called back to her affirmatively from the audience for all to hear. Debra Monk and Margaret Lamée, two of the actors from that season's Pump Boys and Dinettes, *were the "trophy girls." George Abbott commented, "You give me the feeling that I'm among friends." And the Uris... and then the Gershwin... embraced them all.*

After the Best Musical award was given out, Laurence Olivier appeared and declared, "It's really splendid when theaters are named for people who've made creative contributions to our wonderful business—and what more creative and talented contributors can there ever have been than George and Ira Gershwin?" And with that, the lights went out on the Uris, and up on the Gershwin Theatre on Broadway.

1983: I Watched The Whole Show Come To Life

Hal Luftig, Producer

I went to grad school at Columbia's theatre program. One of the great things about that program was that a whole chunk of its curriculum was internships and observerships, with the idea that the student would get first-hand experience. A lot of times it was unpaid, but it was valuable experience nonetheless—and I came to that program without any experience.

My undergraduate degree was in psychology and journalism. When it came time to go to college, my parents, who were great, said, "We love that you love the theatre, but you should get a degree that you could actually use." So I did. I got an undergraduate degree in something totally unrelated and was miserable. For two years I worked out at *Newsday*, the Long Island paper. I was an assistant copy editor, and I just hated it.

So I finally went back to school—at Columbia—and I had no experience or exposure to anything in the theatre. I dove into the internship pool head first. I did an internship at the Manhattan Theatre Club for casting. I did an internship at Serino/Coyne for advertising. I did an internship at the Shubert Organization where I learned house management and box office procedure. And then I wanted to be a producer, so I thought, *Gee I should do that too!*

Columbia found me an internship with Mitch Leigh and Manny Kladitis. At the time, they were producing the first revival of *Mame* with Angela Lansbury, 17 years after the original.

I was pinching myself because I had *seen Mame*! Somehow, I sat in the very first row. I was ten years old and in the first row watching Angela Lansbury in *Mame*. It was phenomenal.

The first day of rehearsal, I was assigned to whatever was needed by the stage manager. After half the day, I got up the courage to go up to Angela and say, "Ms. Lansbury, I am so pleased to meet you and I saw the original when I was ten years old"—which thinking back on it now, was probably horrifying for her, because I was a 24-year-old, so she must have been like, *Thanks a lot kid*! I just gushed on and on and on.

I'll never forget that she was sweet as pie. She just smiled and smiled at me as I spoke to her. Then she leaned in and said, "Can I just tell you something?" I said, "Sure!" I had on a striped shirt, and she said, "I can't look at stripes. I have this visual thing where stripes make me dizzy. So it is lovely, lovely to meet you and I am so happy that you're on this production and I look forward to working with you, but sweetie could you not wear stripes?" And I was mortified! I almost burst into tears.

But it was really, truly wonderful. It was the first time I had ever seen a show put together. Yes, I got coffee and filed and made copies, but the stage managers were all wonderful to me. I think they saw a zeal in my eye and knew why I was there. I watched the whole show come to life and be constructed, and I was in heaven.

I'll never forget when they staged the whole "Mame" number for the first time. I just sat there and I blubbered like a two-year-old, because you know, I was this ten-year-old kid all over again, watching Angela Lansbury relearn how to do *Mame*. It was thrilling.

The thing I remember most about the Gershwin is how huge it is backstage. Huge! The stage entrance is on 51st Street, and most of the dressing rooms are on the 50th Street side. You have to take the elevator and run across to the other side of the stage. What I remember most was opening night, because flowers and gifts kept coming in, and because I was the production assistant, I was delivering them to each room, running around, exhausted. I spent hours going up and down, running across the stage, bringing things to different floors, and running back. That was my first time backstage at a Broadway theater.

I used to stand in the wings once the show was up and running. They were so gracious to let me do that, and I learned so much about how a show runs backstage. It's something that I do to this day with any show I'm producing. I don't micromanage, but I think it's very helpful for a producer to see the show from backstage so he or she knows how everything works. It's part of my job, but it's also *fascinating* to watch everybody! Scenery being moved by stagehands, dressers stripping actors and putting new clothes on them...

One time at *Mame*, I was backstage watching that happen. Mame is on in every scene, and each time she has a new costume that's more fabulous than the one that came before. I'll never forget that I was standing in the wings, and Angie turned to me, in her underwear, while they were getting her dressed, and she said, "Are you having fun?" I said, "I'm having a great time!" She said, "Good." And she winked! I'll never forget that.

It's incredible just how many of Broadway's most successful producers and other professionals started out as interns and gofers. Hal Luftig has produced over 25 Broadway shows to date, and won Tony Awards for Kinky Boots, Thoroughly Modern Millie, *and* Annie Get Your Gun. *And he started out getting coffee and making copies!*

1986/2003: I Was Just On Broadway!

Eddie Korbich, Actor

My Broadway debut was in *Singin' in the Rain* in 1986. I was hired to replace an actor who was going to perform on a cruise.

A week before my actual "opening night," the stage manager said to me, "You want to ride the trolley across the stage in the 'Beautiful Girl' number? You can wear your jeans and we'll get you a shirt and tux top since you'll be sitting down, but you'll get a taste of Broadway before you go on for real." Well, duh—yeah!

So that night I was sitting on the trolley in the wings. Everything was dark and the sound was muffled and I remember the other actors saying hi and smiling at me. Then suddenly the trolley started to move and when we cleared the proscenium it physically felt like a flood of light burst out at me with this huge brass sound from the orchestra—it was everything you dream of. I couldn't believe it. I just kept thinking: *I'm in a Broadway show, I'm in a Broadway show.* I mean, I saw *Sweeney Todd* there. It was the same moment we had rehearsed onstage, but everything was totally different.

When I came off stage, everyone was looking at me and smiling. I couldn't move my face out of this goofy grin and I was saying, "I was just on Broadway!" over and over. I couldn't help it. I went down to wardrobe to get out of my costume, and I said to them, "I was just on Broadway!" A few weeks later, I was sitting there hanging out with the dressers and the wardrobe mistress said to me, "That first night was our favorite. You made us remember why we got into this business."

Later, I did *Wicked* at the Gershwin. I covered the Wizard and Dr. Dillamond. That show is really like a machine, where every cross has to be planned out in advance. You can't cross behind the stage during certain sections; everything is planned out to the second.

I have a philosophy as an understudy that many actors probably do not agree with. I think your job is really just to make the show go on as smoothly as possible and not have an ego. You're an actor and of course you're creative, but really you need to not ruffle anything, not reinvent the wheel. If I need to go on for Dr. Dillamond, I do Bill Youmans doing Dr. Dillamond. You can't mess up the rhythm of the show, of what the show is. You need to fit into the show correctly, and that becomes a creative exercise in itself. It's completely fulfilling and interesting. And of course, even though you're doing someone else, you're still you. Hal Prince taught me that, but that's another story.

Singin' in the Rain in 1985 had the largest rain sequence to date of any New York show. The rain fell on a 20 by 40 foot section of the stage. Ironically, the Uris was the first Broadway theater ever built to not have an asbestos fire curtain. Instead, there was a water curtain.[46]

---

[46] Check out *The Untold Stories of Broadway, Volume 1* for more on this.

1987: Disheartening

Michael John LaChiusa, Writer

I remember subbing once for *Starlight Express*—but we weren't in a pit, we were in a part of the building that felt as though it was four blocks away, watching a monitor, playing synthesizers. I thought: *This is so disheartening. This is so dead. This is dead to me.* And I never did it again. It wasn't my thing.

1987: Real Rock 'n' Roll

Steve C. Kennedy, Sound Designer

I worked in the Gershwin for *Starlight Express*. It was amazing but crazy. We were there 24 hours a day putting the show in. And there were accidents, nights we had to halt the show, people almost being killed. But we opened it. It didn't run long, but it was one of my favorite shows.

Starlight Express was real rock 'n' roll. There were electronic drums, and the band was up in a room by themselves, completely isolated. You'd walk in there and you couldn't really hear anything except the sound of fingers on keyboards. Everybody had headsets on. And then suddenly, a trumpet would come in! It was quite exciting.

1988: A Telegram From Helen Hayes

Bryan Batt, Actor

Framed on my wall, in my house in New Orleans, is a telegram from Helen Hayes. She happened to be at a local community theatre production of *Godspell* I was in, so I got to meet her. Later, at a party in her honor, she met my parents and they struck up a friendship. She actually convinced my skeptical father to support my move to New York to try to become an actor.

When I got the job in *Starlight Express*, Helen Hayes sent me a telegram saying, "Welcome to Broadway. May you have a triumphant stay," and I just realized that last Friday was the anniversary of that day. The telegram was on Friday the 25th of March, 25 years ago, so that was my Broadway debut.

I was a nervous wreck because—forget that I was on Broadway—I was on *roller skates*! I had this very difficult, physical dance number in the second act, which was with actual acrobat street skaters, who could do anything on roller skates. I just willed myself not to fall down. I had to learn how to do coffee grinders and handstands and cartwheels, all this stuff on skates. I wasn't as strong a dancer as them, and I remember just praying. My father had recently passed away, and I thought a lot, *I wish you were here, Daddy. Get me through this.*

I was so nervous, but it was also magical. On my first night, the stage managers brought me champagne and all my friends and family sent me flowers.

At the top of the second act, there was a number where I was at the front of a "train" of skaters, and the guys behind me always wanted to roller skate very fast. I got slammed into the metal gates of the set many times. My knuckles were always scabs while I was doing the show. There was one night when I was in the show when I took a big fall and rolled off the side of the stage! I stopped myself, and finished the song with my legs dangling into the audience. You know in the cartoons when you see Tom hit Jerry over the head with a hammer, and then the stars circle around his head? I actually understood what that meant!

There was another time when our skate coach, Michael Fraley, saw that one of the bridges did not make a connection, but I didn't see it. I was about to plummet one story to the deck, and I was skating fast. He had to do something to stop me, so he punched me! I wasn't hurt, but I would have been really hurt if I had fallen.

The Gershwin was cavernous, but then later on, I did four shows at the Minskoff! The best thing about those newer theaters is the bathroom and shower situation. You often will actually have your own bathroom and shower in a theater like the Gershwin or Minskoff. At first, during *Starlight Express*, I shared a dressing room with Michael Scott Gregory, and then later with Keith Allen. Keith was a hoot, and he insisted we had to decorate our room to the hilt. We made it really beautiful, so it became a great place to hang out. That room became like a true second home, and from then on, I made every dressing room my own.

1988: Roller Skating!

Laura Bell Bundy, Actor

My first musical was *Starlight Express*. I remember getting last-minute tickets with my family at TKTS. I was five or six years old, visiting New York. I remember that we were in box seats on the mezzanine level, and I spent the whole show leaning over the box.

I was totally enthralled. Roller skating! I had no idea what was happening in the story, but everything was exciting: the movement, and the singing, and the love story. It was other-worldly. It scared me, and it made my imagination go wild.

1990: Broadway Is Downton Abbey

Michael Berresse, Actor/Director

I was on the road for a full year and a half with *Fiddler on the Roof*. We did a national tour and took the show to Japan before we came to Broadway, which was unusual. That was my Broadway debut, in November of 1990, at the Gershwin.

I was disappointed by the Gershwin. My experiences seeing Broadway shows were that the exteriors were old-school and pretty, and oddly sandwiched in the world of New York and modern society. Then, you would step in, and be inside this magical realm and have a really romantic experience. I always thought, *Someday, someday, someday.*

When that day came, it didn't have that romanticism. The dressing rooms were modern and clean. I later came to find out that they were much nicer than other dressing rooms on Broadway, but the auditorium just didn't have that history to it.

Then, they brought in that recreated Boris Aronson *Fiddler* set, and I went down during tech and saw it. It was that moment when I thought: *Well, okay. When the houselights come down and I see the integrity of the production, it'll be just as fantastic as I fantasized being in a Broadway show would be.*

At the time, the Gershwin was considered a bit of a stepchild of Broadway. There was that feeling, like: *Okay, you made it to Broadway, but it's at the Gershwin.* Now, it's become an entirely different thing! *Wicked* has transformed people's idea of the theater, and now lots of people want to play there.

I've never had a conversation about this, but I really do feel that there's a hierarchy of integrity in terms of the Broadway theaters. Partly it's because of their histories, partly it's because of the productions they've had. It's almost like Broadway is a giant mansion, or an English country estate, and there are some theaters that feel "upstairs" and some theaters that feel "downstairs." It's like Broadway is Downton Abbey! There's a real feeling about who goes where, and why.

My perception is that the Booth is sort of the guest room for visiting royalty, like a foreign celebrity. The St. James is the Lord's bedroom. The New Amsterdam is for the lost dauphin who comes to visit, when the glory of his lineage is restored. The Gershwin was always sort of like the staff's dining room to me.

The theaters actually feel like their own communities, and the diversity is what makes them so functional. I have had the great good fortune of working pretty much all over the mansion. And some of the rooms that you would expect to have the big canopy bed and view over the moat were not necessarily my best ones. I think that if you're lucky enough to work in New York, in these theaters, over an extended period of time, it's like getting to know your house really well and learning to appreciate every aspect of it. You like the secret nooks and crannies. You like the grand ballroom, but you don't want to live there all day every day. You also want to spend some time downstairs, or up at the Beaumont, the carriage house.

1990: Everyone Was Dressed Up But Me

Krysta Rodriguez, Actor

The first Broadway show I ever saw was *Fiddler on the Roof* in 1990. I was six years old, and my family was on a trip. When I was younger, my parents sold the house and quit their jobs and we got a motor home and traveled around the country for an extended period of time.

We parked in New Jersey and took a day trip to New York to see a show. I was so excited. I was wearing shorts and a tank top, and probably like six different tube socks scrunched up. We got to the theater, and all these girls were in pretty dresses. They were so fancy, and I was mortified. I didn't want to go inside because I was like, "I'm the only one at this theater who's not dressed up and everyone's gonna be looking at me!"

I remember, profoundly, the experience of the lights going out and realizing that nobody could see me anymore. It didn't matter what I was wearing because we were all experiencing something together. When intermission happened, the magic broke, and I was like, "Ugh! Everyone's dressed up again!" Then the lights went down again, and I was okay. I had a very special experience, even at such a young age, at my first show.

1990: New York, Broadway, AIDS

Michael Berresse, Actor/Director

Doing *Fiddler* at the Gershwin felt a little bit like we were an afterthought of Broadway. There was this feeling that New York was just a stop on the tour that we'd been doing for over a year, and I felt a little like nobody wanted us there. I also felt like it couldn't have been that legitimate of a show, because it was my first Broadway audition and I got it. In retrospect, I realize that I was very young and all of these perceptions had to do with my own insecurities more than anything else. I look back now on how amazing some of the people in the show were, and the lasting impact they had on my life, and how incredible the show itself is.

We started touring the show in 1989, and came to Broadway in the fall of 1990. I've lost several friends from that cast. It was still an era where a lot of young gay men were dying.

One of my closest friends in *Fiddler* was Keith Keen, who had done *Dancin'* and *La Cage aux Folles*. When I met him he was already ill, and he did our show throughout the course of his deterioration from AIDS. He did the show to the point where he had gone blind in one eye, and was having trouble walking. He was very physically compromised, trying to do *Fiddler* with a 104-degree fever, and he was still cracking jokes, making people laugh, doing weird dances in the dressing room. He singlehandedly brought more joy and life into that production than any other person, despite the fact that everyone knew he was dying. The team modified his track enough so that he was still able to do it. Two weeks before the show closed on Broadway, he had a seizure and had to finally leave.

The day before the show closed, between performances on a two-show Saturday, Keith's lover, Jay Brown, asked a couple of us to come and see Keith to say goodbye. At that point, he was nonresponsive. He was at home in his bed, and he died that night. The show closed the next day. Part of me felt like Keith was using that *Fiddler* chapter to sort of close the book on his life as well. It was okay to let go because everyone else was moving on as well. I think that three other men in that company also eventually passed away.

It was a strange reality for me. It was the horror of an era, combined with the dawning of a joyous new era for me, having just gotten to Broadway. That time is a very, very important part of the ghosts that live in these theaters. For me personally, the Gershwin will always remind me of the souls that were lost during that time. Every theater you step into has a distinct personality. It's partly because of the design, and partly because of its age, but I think, most of all, it's because of the human stories that have gone before.

That's what I remember when I remember the *Fiddler* chapter. I was so naive. I was so ignorant of New York, Broadway, AIDS... all of it was so foreign to me, and it was a really rapid education. In a heartbeat, there was the drama, the loss, the success... the show won the Tony Award for Best Revival. It was a strange combination of all these things slammed into a short period time. In a strange way, I look back on it now and see that it was great preparation for everything that's come after.

1993: Jule Styne

Red Press, Musical Coordinator

I worked on several shows with Jule Styne as a musician in the 1960s and 1970s. Later, after I became a contractor, he was doing a show called *The Red Shoes*. His general manager wanted me to contract the show, and Jule said he wanted to talk to me about it.

I knew the movie, *The Red Shoes*, and all of its classical ballets. I had worked at the New York City Ballet, the American Symphony Orchestra, and the Philharmonic. But I figured: *Okay, Jule Styne knows me as a gypsy musician, not as an orchestra contractor. He wants me to go meet with him and prove myself.*

The general manager and I went to Jule's apartment on 72nd Street and 5th Avenue. He welcomed us and we went into his study, where this was this big, beautiful piano. Jule sat down and began to play us the songs from the show he had written. He played and played, and at the end he said, "You're hired!" I never said one word.

———————

The Nederlanders were open to filling the Gershwin with any show that might work. The tenant just prior to Fiddler on the Roof *was* Bugs Bunny on Broadway. *The show celebrated famous animators and cartoon characters, and was an amalgam of cartoon footage, live characterizations, and an orchestra performance, in honor of Bugs Bunny's 50th birthday.*

In 1993, the Gershwin housed Raffi and then Yanni.

———————

1994: Elaine Stritch In Her Underwear

Marty Bell, Producer

One of my jobs on *Show Boat* was to take care of Elaine Stritch. We wanted to make sure she always had what she needed, and she needed a lot of attention. I ushered her through the whole run in Canada, where we played before we came to Broadway.

One Monday during our out-of-town run, I was in my office when the phone rang. It was Elaine, and she said, "Marty, do you mind if I need my driver today?" I said, "Why do you need your driver? It's your day off." And she told me: "Well, I was homesick last night and I had the driver take me to New York."

This was the driver who was supposed to just take her from the theater home to her apartment in Toronto each night! He had just driven her all the way to New York because she asked.

Elaine would just sit around her dressing room in her underwear. She didn't care who came in! I spent two years talking to Elaine Stritch in her underwear.

1994: They're Closer Than I'm Ready For

Gavin Creel, Actor

I saw *Show Boat* as my first Broadway show and it was at the Gershwin Theatre.

I knew it was the biggest house on Broadway, and I remember thinking the theater was really small! I was from Ohio, and I grew up thinking that Broadway was going to be huge, massive houses, and that the people were gonna look so tiny, and it was all going to be very far away and untouchable. I remember thinking, *Wait, they're way closer than I'm ready for them to be.* I thought it would be like Radio City times two. I don't know why, but growing up in Ohio, I just thought, *Well, it's not going to look like an auditorium in my town. It's surely going to look like something from the moon, or something from heaven.* And it wasn't. I felt like my seat was really close.

I also remember being confused when the lead actress came out of the stage door. "Wait a minute, where are all the photographers and limousines and the throngs of fans?"

I saw *Passion* next, right after that and there was nobody at the stage door. Jere Shea just hiked his backpack up on his back and walked down the street. I was so confused.

1994: That Huge Boat

Ben Rappaport, Actor

The first Broadway show I saw was the revival of *Show Boat* at the Gershwin. I have a very specific memory of the boat itself. It was my first show, so I didn't know what to expect in terms of how large it was going to be, compared to school or community theatre.

That boat was full-sized. It was incredible. There was an effect where they used the lights to create waves that looked real. And I couldn't believe they fit that huge boat into a theater. I wasn't aware that shows could be that size or use tricks of stagecraft that way. It blew my mind.

1994/1997: I Used To Sneak In

Ken Davenport, Producer

The Gershwin is not only big onstage, it's big off stage—including upstairs. It's one of the few theaters that has a rehearsal room, or it did when I was there as the Associate Company Manager on *Show Boat* and then *Candide*.

The first show I ever produced rehearsed in that Gershwin rehearsal room. On Mondays, the day off, I used to sneak in with my cast of a workshop called *Prime Time*, which was a television theme song revue. One day, we set off the alarm and then ran down the street.

The stage management and company management offices for *Show Boat* were upstairs too, because the cast was so big. There were 74 Equity members!

I put rehearsal rooms into my office not only to rent them out, but because it reminded me of what we had in the Gershwin. That was very helpful to us on those shows. It was just so convenient.

1995/2002: Rodgers And Hammerstein And The Gershwins

Ted Chapin, President of The Rodgers & Hammerstein Organization/Past Chairman of the American Theatre Wing

When Oscar Hammerstein's centennial came in 1995, *Show Boat* was playing at the Gershwin. We knew we wanted to do an event, but I don't remember how we arrived at the rather audacious idea of putting together a huge event right on the stage of the Gershwin.

It was a one-hour presentation at noon, on Hammerstein's actual birthday, with Broadway performers singing his material, and the public was invited, free of charge. The great thing was that Garth Drabinsky, the producer of *Show Boat*, loved that kind of stuff, and he even put a plug in some of his weekly *Show Boat* ads for the event.

The event was on a Wednesday, and the house manager was appalled that we were starting at noon. They had a matinee at 2pm, and we were told that if the show wasn't over by 1pm, he would put up the house lights. We did fine by that. We're theatre people. We understood what that meant. It was a fantastic event, and we had a great collection of people.

The irony of all ironies is that, seven years later, it was the Richard Rodgers centennial, and which show of his was playing on Broadway? *Oklahoma!* And where was it playing? The Gershwin.

We held an event in Rodgers' honor, using the same idea. It was absolutely magical. Laura Benanti, who was in *Into The Woods* playing Cinderella at the time, did a song from Rodgers and Hammerstein's *Cinderella*. Louise Pitre, who was in *Mamma Mia!* at the time, sang "It Never Entered My Mind" half in French, because she's French-Canadian. I remember Barbara Cook was slated to sing a song, and that morning, our stage manager, Lauren Class Schneider, came up to me and said, "Uh, Barbara Cook is asking when she sings her second song?" And I said, "Whenever she wants." That was an easy answer. And it was the right answer. So Barbara Cook did two and knocked them out of the park. There was even a wonderful moment, when I introduced Barbara and then introduced her accompanist Wally Harper. I looked over, and Wally was mouthing "thank you" to me.

We got to celebrate the centennials of both Richard Rodgers and Oscar Hammerstein in a theater named after George and Ira Gershwin.

1995/2002: Oh What A Beautiful Mornin' On The Deck Of A Show Boat

Bert Fink, Press Agent/ Senior Vice-President of The Rodgers & Hammerstein Organization

It's very funny that when Richard Rodgers and Oscar Hammerstein each had their centennials, they were linked by a theater named after George and Ira Gershwin! Coincidentally, when each man had his 100th birthday, he had a musical playing at the Gershwin.

In 1995, for Hammerstein's birthday, we presented a concert on the set of *Show Boat*. It featured Liz Callaway, who was in *Cats* at the time, this wonderful young talent from *Carousel* named Audra McDonald, and even some singers from *Show Boat*. We used some audio recordings from Hammerstein himself. It was pretty low tech.

One special sequence we did had Ted Chapin reading the words from the opening scene of *Green Grow The Lilacs*, which *Oklahoma!* was based on. Ted read, "As I walked out one bright sunny morning, I saw a cowboy way out on the plain." Meanwhile, you heard Doug LeBrecque in the distance singing "There's a bright golden haze on the meadow…" and you could tell how the playwright had given Hammerstein the inspiration. And there was something wonderful about hearing "Oh What A Beautiful Mornin'" sung on the deck of a show boat.

We put the event together with Livent, and at one point we were talking about the ticketing and how we were going to seat people upstairs. Someone at Livent snickered at me and said, "You'll be lucky if you fill half the auditorium." Well, when you announce a free concert on Broadway, you do! We had lines around the block and we filled the Gershwin Theatre. It was a wonderful turnout and a great way to give back. The concert was called "Something Wonderful."

Seven years later, we had a companion concert called "Something Good" to celebrate Rodgers. This time, we filled the Gershwin and we even had to turn away about 300 people. On the set of *Oklahoma!*, we had Lea Salonga, who was in pre-production for *Flower Drum Song,* sing from that show, and *The Boys From Syracuse* cast members, who were in rehearsal, sang too. Patrick Wilson sang "Oh What A Beautiful Mornin'" and since Laura Benanti was playing Cinderella in *Into The Woods*, she sang from Rodgers and Hammerstein's *Cinderella!* At one point in the program, we announced cast veterans from all of the Rodgers musicals, going backwards. We started with *I Remember Mama* and *Two By Two*, and went all the way back to Celeste Holm and Joan Roberts, who were there from the original company of *Oklahoma!* We also had a dancer named Jonathan Bush from a 1950s off-Broadway revival of *Oklahoma!* participate and we received a letter from his nephew— President George W. Bush. The program ended with Barbara Cook singing "Wonderful Guy", Laura Benanti singing "Something Good" and the cast of *Oklahoma!* singing "You'll Never Walk Alone" and "Climb Ev'ry Mountain".

When Richard Rodgers died, there had been a funeral but no memorial. There was no public event. A lot of people said to me that even though it was years later, the concert felt like it was, in essence, his memorial. It was a beautiful event that I'm very proud of.

1998: *On The Town* At The Delacorte And The Gershwin

Annie Golden, Actor

The Gershwin was massive. We went in there for *On the Town*, after having started at the Delacorte in Central Park.

I originally auditioned for the role of Hildy, but George C. Wolfe called me at home and offered me a non-singing role, Lucy Schmeeler. And I said, "For you and the summer festival at the Delacorte? Yeah! Of course!

When else am I ever gonna get in there, George?" He replied, "I just wanted to make sure you were interested in a non-singing role. I love your attitude," and so he got me into the Delacorte.

He confided in me that people would leave the theater and go, "Okay, you've got Annie Golden in your show, why is she not singing?" Under the pressure of that, George asked the team, "How about Annie Golden as Lucy Schmeeler sings eight bars of the most beautiful ballad in the show?"

So there I was, onstage at the Delacorte with Adolph Green and Betty Comden and Kevin Stites and Todd Ellison. We were at the piano, and I did a sneeze in character, and then they gave me a bell tone. I sang: "When you're in love, time is precious stuff, even a lifetime isn't enough," for their approval, to see if George could put it in. They loved it and they said yes! That you could have royalty like that sitting there at the Delacorte with you in your street clothes, with Belvedere Castle behind you, working on a show? That was remarkable.

In that same scene, the nightclub would disappear and the two lonely hearts, me as Lucy Schmeeler and the elegant Jonathan Freeman, were left alone. Then she sings, he sneezes. He caught my cold. One time, in the park, a raccoon came up to us in the scene. Jonathan Freeman saw the raccoon. If I had seen the raccoon, I would have run off! The whole audience was laughing and Jonathan just stamped his foot, and the raccoon went.

Then we took *On the Town* to the Gershwin and it was mega. The Gershwin was cavernous. It was the first time I had my own dressing room right off the wings. My nephew was born at that time, so I arranged to have a telephone in my dressing room to get the news. Mary Testa and I are like sisters, so we had adjoining rooms, and the door was always open. It was kind of beautiful. It was dreamy stuff. It was a wonderful time. That was the Gershwin, cavernous and yet homey and a great group.

1998: We Don't Belong Here

George C. Wolfe, Director/Writer/Producer

On the Town is a very frothy show. At the Delacorte Theatre in Central Park, I was able to locate this other kind of emotional verve that was underneath it. And you can't get more perfectly frothy than the New York skyline and a proscenium built by God! The park is so warm and embracing, and the scale of *On the Town* made sense there. The Delacorte is surprisingly, bizarrely intimate.

There was a gap before we moved the show into the Gershwin, which turned out to be a difficult fit for the show. *Sweeney Todd*, which played there brilliantly, was a machine in many respects. *Wicked*, in it's own way is also a machine, in that they both move with incredible levels of efficiency. *On the Town*, on the other hand, is this silly, odd, wonderful homage to New York. The performances were wonderful, but they belonged in a smaller theater.

Personally, the journey of that show came at a significant time in my life. When I did *On the Town* in the Park, I was on dialysis and next to nobody knew it. In the interim before we moved into the Gershwin, I had a kidney transplant. The Broadway production was the first show I did after that. Sometimes I think that because I was very very sick when I first did the show, the park production was infused with this "I'm not dead!!! I'm alive!!!" energy. I didn't want to acknowledge how sick I was, because I was afraid it would overwhelm me, so I just worked—and I think that came through in the show.

I do have the best memories of Betty Comden and Adolph Green. Adolph was one of the sweetest human beings ever, and Betty was so smart and elegant. It was a joy. They were thrilled with my take on the material, and I was thrilled to be working with them.

1999: A Normal Kid From Long Island

Harrison Chad, Actor

I did *Peter Pan* on Broadway when I was six.

I grew up on Long Island, and when I was younger, my cousins and I used to put on shows at family gatherings and seders. My uncle had a friend who was a talent manager, and he always told my mom, "Your son has a great face for acting."

I had never done anything even slightly show business-related. I played soccer with my friends. I was a normal kid from Long Island. My mom decided to take me to this talent agent, and I was more than willing to go—it sounded fun. That day, they sent me out on an audition for an Oscar Mayer Weiner commercial with Cal Ripken Jr., and I got a callback. I didn't even know what that meant—I was six! I lost out to this other kid, Gideon. Later on, Gideon would *always* be the kid I'd see at auditions.

I thought going into the city and auditioning was so much fun. At one point, I got an audition for *Peter Pan* on Broadway. It was a touring company with Cathy Rigby that was going to come to New York for three months. I auditioned for the role of Michael, having never sung professionally. I had never even done a school show!

It was the first audition I had ever been in where there was more than just a camera and two people. There were literally 15 people across the table. My six-year-old self went up to every single person and shook their hand. I had no teeth at the time! I sang the song, did the dance call, we drove home and—this is weird—but I remember that I was upset because we hit a pigeon on the Long Island Expressway.

I got it. I got the understudy job. It was incredible! *Peter Pan* was in the Gershwin, which is humongous. Everybody in the cast was just wonderful. The engagement was during the summer so I didn't have to miss any school. That was great, because my parents were always sure to make it so that acting was like a varsity sport for me. I went to public school and didn't miss much; school was important. When I was in *Peter Pan*, I got a job as the voice of Boots on "Dora The Explorer" and all of this turned from being "this thing that I might do" to "this thing that I love doing." I kept auditioning after that. It took on a life of its own, and it became my life.

I got to go on in *Peter Pan*, so I did make my Broadway debut at the Gershwin when I was six! I knew I was going to go on, so my family, my friends, and people from my hometown all came to see the show. It was a matinee. I was so nervous. I still have an image in my mind of the scrim[47] coming up and looking through the audience—because Michael has the first line of the show. The scrim went up and I remember just looking out before my line and thinking, *Whoa, this is crazy!*

The flying was incredible. After the show we rented out Ellen's Stardust Diner, and all of my friends and family went out and had a huge lunch. My teachers came, my friends came, my Hebrew School teachers came—it was ridiculous!

The Pub Theatrical at 1633 Broadway, on the corner of 51st Street, was a popular hub for theatre folk for years. Part of the Uris and Circle in the Square building, the restaurant was known for always letting theatre folk sit as long as they wanted. Sondheim: A Musical Tribute *had a huge after party there. The Council of Stock Theatre's "Straw Hat Awards" were given out in 1973 by Cary Grant at the Pub Theatrical. (Anthony Perkins and Maureen Stapleton were two of the recipients.) The Actors Fund held fundraising bazaars at the Pub Theatrical.*

---

[47] scrim: a somewhat transparent material that behaves similarly to a show curtain, but allows audiences to see a degree of the stage behind it

An advertisement in the May 1972 Playbill for Jesus Christ Superstar *said: "Get a real taste of Broadway at Stouffer's new Pub Theatrical restaurant," with the P, U, and B in a font both industrial and hip, at different levels. In the "Uris Building, S.W. Corner of 51st and Broadway." This would've been right across the street from* Superstar, *which was at the Hellinger.*

The opening night party for Via Galactica *and for the Uris itself was even held at The Pub Theatrical, where Ethel Merman was heard to say, "I think I'm going to study the trampoline."*

1999: A Cup Of Fairy Dust

Craig Carnelia, Writer

The first time I went to the theatre with my daughter Daisy, I took her to see Cathy Rigby in *Peter Pan*. She was very young, definitely under five years old. We went backstage, because I had a number of acting students in the show and they ended up introducing us to Cathy. She gave Daisy a cup of fairy dust, which she ended up taking home.

But the most significant memory I have of that day is when Daisy and I walked out from the stage left wing, onto the stage of the Gershwin. Daisy looked out into the huge, empty house, paused, and started to tap dance. She didn't know how to tap dance. But she had some idea that this was what you did when you were on a Broadway stage.

2003: Changing The Theater's Reputation

Nancy Coyne, Advertising and Marketing Executive

The opening nights that I remember are the ones for shows that became landmarks. That's what I want to do; I want to make shows that have legs, that have the ability to run and run, and become landmarks so that tourists visit them.

Tourists come here now and they want to see *Wicked*. *Wicked* is a landmark. I've enjoyed opening nights the most in theaters whose reputations were changed by the show. The Martin Beck Theatre was regarded as "nothing runs at the Martin Beck," and when Frank Langella opened there in *Dracula*, all of a sudden the Beck was a highly regarded theater. That was one of the shows that I worked on when I was at The Blaine Thompson Agency.

When *Wicked* went into the Gershwin, I thought, *Oh no! It's so big, it's so hard to sell the Gershwin.* I'd just worked on the Cameron Mackintosh production of *Oklahoma!* in there. It was not a conducive theater. Then *Wicked* moved in, and changed the fate of that theater.

I love that *Wicked* changed the fortune of the Gershwin Theatre. It made it a hot house, when before, people just did not want to book the Gershwin.

It needed a huge hit. Not just a hit, a HUGE hit. And it got one.

Dracula *was the reputation-changer for the Beck/Hirschfeld, and* Wicked *for the Uris/Gershwin.* Rent *saved the Nederlander. (But more on that later.) It makes one think about the Mark Hellinger... Legend has it that Andrew Lloyd Webber wanted the theater very badly for* Sunset Boulevard *in the early 1990s, but it had just been leased to the Times Square Church. It would have been the perfect match. If only the theater had held on a little longer, it might have gotten its own savior.*

———————

2003: How We Got The Gershwin

David Stone, Producer

Before *Wicked*, I had actually worked at the Gershwin years before when I worked for Barry and Fran Weissler on the production of *Fiddler on the Roof*, starring Topol, which played there in 1990.

Even earlier than that, I saw the original production of *Sweeney Todd* at the Gershwin. I saw *Singin' in the Rain* there. Once I got into the industry, I saw everything at the Gershwin. I thought—as many did—that it was huge, almost unplayable in a way. I thought that only *Sweeney Todd*, which was enormous, had ever really played the space well.

Marc Platt is my producing partner on *Wicked*, and he spends most of his time as a film producer in Los Angeles. Earlier in his career, he worked with Sam Cohn at ICM and had a relationship for years with Bernie Jacobs and Gerry Schoenfeld of the Shubert Organization. As a result, when we were looking for a theater for *Wicked*, his first instinct was to talk to the Shuberts.

At that point, I had been around long enough to know everyone, and I said, "I'm not sure that's going to go well..." But, we went to the Shuberts. Gerry, of course, said, "I'll need to read a script, and I'll need to come to a reading, and I'll determine our interest at that time." And at our first New York reading of *Wicked*—which was probably as much for Gerry's benefit as anyone's—he left at intermission. I really loved the man and, over the years, I grew close to him. But he just didn't connect to the show at all. And, not incidentally, he had also recently passed on *The Producers* and *Hairspray*.

Next, we went to Jujamcyn. I was about to do *Man of La Mancha* at their theater, the Martin Beck, and I was renting office space from them at the time. They really only had one theater that might have been appropriate, so we went there. Rocco Landesman was not available, so he asked us to meet with Jack Viertel. Jack basically said, "You can't have this many scenes in a stage musical. This isn't some sort of movie!" Marc was understandably offended. *Wicked* had the same number of scenes that *My Fair Lady* and *Guys and Dolls* had.

I said, "Let's go to Jimmy," and Marc said, "Oh, I don't know." His experience in the 1980s with the Nederlanders was that they weren't the Shuberts. We went in and met with Jimmy Sr., Jimmy Jr., and Nick Scandalios. I had been very close with them for years—personally and professionally.

Jimmy Sr. says, "Tell me about this show, *Wicked*." Marc says, "Well, it takes place..." and he starts doing his flawless pitch. Within 30 seconds, Jimmy says, "Yeah, that sounds great." He turns to me. "Listen, kid, I've always liked you. What theater do you want?" I said, "Well, this one would be great, and if not, that one." He said, "You got it!" Marc looked at me and said, "That's it?" And I replied, "That's it."

It's not that the Nederlanders don't have good taste. They certainly do—and sometimes they help to make the biggest hits on Broadway happen. But what Jimmy's whole career has been about is finding *people* he believes in—writers, directors, producers—and just trusting them. That was the point. For decades, his success has stemmed from him simply saying, "I like you. You're the jockey, I don't care right now about the horse. I believe in you. Go." That's why we got the Gershwin.

Now, the Gershwin was not the theater we necessarily wanted, but based on shows that were closing, the Gershwin was what the Nederlanders had available. When I realized that this was where we were going to bring *Wicked*, I sort of cried myself to sleep that night. I was really upset. I was very concerned that the show would not work in that theater.

But we had an ace in the hole in that we had Eugene Lee as our set designer. He had done *Sweeney Todd* and *Show Boat*, both at the Gershwin, and he understood exactly how to do a show in that space. He knew to push the stage out, and how to make the theater feel intimate, to the extent that the Gershwin can. Joe Mantello, our director, really relied on him in this area. It cost a little more money, but it was so important: the way that Eugene made the theater part of the show by putting the vines and the gears on the side, and the way he brought the audience into the world of the show.

Obviously, now we can all say that the Gershwin is the best thing that could ever have happened to *Wicked*. In terms of the physical production, the ticket sales, and the merchandise, it has been the best possible theater. *Wicked* sells twice as much merchandise as the second-highest merchandise-selling show on Broadway, primarily because of the way the lobby is laid out. Yes, the Gershwin was certainly the perfect home for us.

We work very hard at maintaining *Wicked*. I'm very flattered when professionals like Ted Chapin come to the show and say, "My God, it's as good as opening night, if not better!" We really care about maintaining the quality, and we're all over the show all the time. There's Joe and two associate directors, Wayne Cilento, our choreographer, and two associate choreographers, and I'm around a lot. The technical supervisor is there all the time; our designers go back in. It's a full time job for many people who maintain it. We have some actors who have been there since the beginning, and that continuity is great. And then we have new actors all the time, who challenge everyone with their different energy. Crew and musicians tend to stay in great, steady jobs, as they should. But there's some changeover there as well and it's healthy.

When *Spelling Bee* ran next door, having two shows in two theaters right on top of each other was great for me. *Spelling Bee* ran for three years, and *Wicked* was running that whole time. I could go see this enormous show with a million moving parts and have to travel all over the theater to see the 100 people working on it. And then I could go downstairs and see this little show where basically the entire cast and crew was sitting in the green room. The shows were both wonderful and original and exciting—and you couldn't ask for two more different experiences. To run from one to the other at the same performance was culture shock for me. It kept me grounded about how shows are crafted, how unique they all are.

Having the Gershwin and Circle in the Square right there together was thrilling—for me, for the audiences coming out of the shows, and especially for the companies of the shows themselves. The thing about Broadway versus the West End is that there's no theatre community like that over in London. Maybe there's a theater here, and a theater there, and some of them are slightly near each other. But, people don't see each other's shows. They don't go to Joe Allen or Angus or see each other outside the building. They're not interested. They all just go home after the show. They don't socialize. They don't have Broadway Cares. They don't have these events. They don't have union meetings. They have no particular concern about the bigger picture. They simply care about the show they are in at the moment. And their gardens.

It's a cliché, but it's no joke: this is an industry first, but this is also a community. Stagehands and performers support each other's shows and benefits on their one night off. We raise more money for charity than the West End does, by a huge margin. We develop new work together. This is a *community*, and we want to see each other socially and professionally. And it's very important how the Broadway theaters are clumped together. That's what encourages all of this activity in the first place.

The Gershwin holds 1280 seats in the orchestra and 660 in the balcony. At the time the theater was built, its designer, Ralph Alswang, felt this would maximize potential profit for shows there, as most audience members want an orchestra seat. Even though the last row of the orchestra at the Gershwin is much farther from the stage than the average mezzanine seat in a Broadway house, to a potential ticket buyer it is merely a coveted "orchestra seat." This mindset truly paid off when Wicked *finally transformed the Gershwin into a hit house. The production* *constantly breaks its own box office records, and at the end of 2013, became the first show ever to gross $3 million in one week on Broadway.*

One of the most incredible aspects of Wicked*'s success is that the show had a troubled out-of-town tryout, and received a negative review in the* New York Times *when it opened in 2003. After showering love on only Kristin Chenoweth, Ben Brantley called the score "generic" and the show "lopsided," "overplay[ed]," and a "technicolorized sermon."*[48] Wicked *is that rare show that gained such great word-of-mouth and popularity among the people that it overcame a bad New York Times review.* Wicked *is that rare show that could fill the Gershwin.* Wicked *is also that rare show that has infiltrated popular culture, with its songs sampled as part of hit pop music and television shows.*

1979/2003: The Boy From Rockford, Illinois

Joe Mantello, Director/Actor

The first Broadway show I saw was at the Uris Theater, now the Gershwin, where *Wicked* is playing. I came to New York with a group of friends who were fellow community theatre aficionados in Rockford, Illinois, and we saw seven or eight shows.

The first show that we saw was *Sweeney Todd* at the Uris. We dressed up for it, and I can still remember going up those escalators and thinking that everyone else was dressed very casually. I was surprised by that.

I still remember where our seats were. They weren't great seats, but they were pretty good, midway up in the house. And *Sweeney Todd* started with this incredibly loud, piercing, shrill whistle and the banner dropping. I remember jumping in my seat—and we were off!

I remember Eugene Lee's brilliant set, I remember Mr. Prince's incredible direction, and I remember thinking that it was astonishing. I had never seen anything on that scale before! We did a lot of community theatre in my hometown, and there was also some professional theatre as well, so I wasn't a complete novice—but I had *never* seen anything on that scale. I was so dazzled by the stagecraft of *Sweeney Todd*.

There was a moment, directing *Wicked*, where I thought, *Well, isn't this fascinating that here I am, back at the Uris/Gershwin Theatre and Eugene Lee is the set designer!* There was something so satisfying and full circle about it.

It was my job, and I showed up every day to work on the show. I would do the things that I was expected to do, and the things that I wanted to do. But then, every once in a while, the boy from Rockford, Illinois would kind of peek out, and take stock of it, and awe would set in.

2005: Writing *Heights* At *Wicked*

Lin-Manuel Miranda, Writer/Actor

Alex Lacaimore and I wrote a lot of *In the Heights* backstage at the Gershwin, listening to *Wicked* and those orchestrations. Alex was conducting the show at the time.

---

[48] Brantley, Ben. "THEATER REVIEW; There's Trouble In Emerald City." *The New York Times*. 31 Oct. 2003. Retrieved from nytimes.com.

My second date ever with my now-wife Vanessa was to *Wicked*. I used the one fancy hook-up I had at the time—Alex—to get us tickets. "Emergency house seats." I spent way more money than I had to spend.

Right before the show started, Alex turned around and pointed at us. Then he turned back to the orchestra, and started the—BUM BUM BUM BUM BUM—overture, and the show began. I'll never forget it.

2005: Hurricane Katrina

Bryan Batt, Actor

I'm from New Orleans. I live there part-time, and so many of my friends and family are in New Orleans. When Hurricane Katrina happened in 2005, my brother lost his house. Many friends of mine lost family members. Their homes were flooded horribly, beyond repair. My friends in the theatre emailed me, and said, "What can we do?" And I thought: *What do we do in the theatre but put on a show?*

Within two weeks, a ton of my theatre friends organized a Broadway fundraiser to help Hurricane Katrina victims. My friend Tony Galde, who I had done *Starlight Express* with years earlier, was doing *Wicked* at the Gershwin. The whole thing was put together at that theater. They asked me where I wanted the money to go, and I picked charities I thought were great, that were really helping the victims.

They asked me to open the Katrina Benefit Concert with "Do You Know What It Means To Miss New Orleans?" I don't know how I got through it, but I did. It was one of those moments when theatre comes together, like no other community does, to do what we do. Every show participated. It was the first major fundraiser for victims of Katrina.

———————

This event raised over $200,000 for Hurricane Katrina victims, and featured performances from Liza Minnelli, Ben Vereen, Bernadette Peters, Idina Menzel, Bebe Neuwirth, Patrick Wilson, and dozens of other performers. Many casts of Broadway shows—including Wicked, Light in the Piazza, Hairspray, Rent, Avenue Q, *and* Spelling Bee— *performed.*

Ben Vereen, who was at the Gershwin then, starring in Wicked, *issued the statement:*

> *On Monday August 29th, 2005, Hurricane Katrina ravaged the Gulf Coast like no other storm in recorded history. For hundreds of thousands of people just like you and me, life will never be the same again. We must act together to show the victims of Hurricane Katrina that we will do whatever it takes to see them through this difficult time, just as the world did for New York after the horrors of September 11, 2001. When ticket sales hit an all time low and businesses were struggling to keep their doors open, our fellow Americans rallied around our city. They came to stay in our hotels, eat at our restaurants, shop in our stores... and they came to see our shows!*

———————

The Elphabas

2006: Caissie Levy, Actor

Rehearsing for *Wicked* was weird, because I went in alone. I was replacing someone in the ensemble and covering Elphaba, and I was the only one rehearsing. I had to learn every dance number—all the partnering and the lifts—and also all of Elphaba's material.

They have a rehearsal room on top of the Gershwin, and I learned the show up there for three weeks, and then was put into the ensemble. I didn't go on for Elphaba for another five months. When that finally happened, it was an out-of-body experience. It was just amazing. I had a bunch of friends who came to see me, and my boyfriend-now-husband was there. I remember feeling really prepared because I'd had five months, and everyone at the Gershwin was so supportive of me. The ensemble girls' dressing room celebrated with me, and I felt so much love and so much terror. As Elphaba, you don't have a moment to breathe during the show, so you don't have time to think about it. That role is so incredibly satisfying.

2007: Julia Murney, Actor

While I was playing Elphaba in *Wicked*, a girl sent me a letter asking me to write the words "Defy Gravity" for her. She wanted to get a *Wicked* tattoo. Months later, I came out the stage door, and she was there, with this beautiful butterfly and the words "Defy Gravity" on her leg.

Wicked is the kind of show with a huge, creative fan base. I have a whole box of "Elphabears" that sing *Wicked* and drawings and a million other things that I didn't want to throw out. I can't hang them all over my home, because I don't have room. Part of me thought it would be cool to auction them off for Broadway Cares, but of course I don't want to hurt anyone's feelings!

One night, during curtain call, someone ran down the aisle holding a giant sign over their head that said "I <3 JULIA." Sebastian Arcelus leaned over to me and whispered, "What are you, Justin Timberlake? Is this Madison Square Garden?" I certainly have not had to contend with that to the degree that some other actors have. When I saw *How to Succeed* with Daniel Radcliffe, girls were screaming out, "I love you, Harry Potter!" He was such a pro and stayed in character. I have so much respect for the stars, for the people with rabid fanbases. They handle it. They figure it out, and they're graceful and gracious. I admire that a great deal and try to use that as an example. If they can be that, I can be that on my own, way down the ladder. And the *Wicked* fans are great! It could just get crazy sometimes.

For example, coming out of the Gershwin stage door was a craft in itself. As Elphaba, you have to shower the green off first, so there are all of these people who have waited for a while for you—and all of the other actors have gone home long ago. It would sometimes take an hour to sign and take photos with everyone. Some nights, if it was very very crowded, I would make an announcement that I could only sign and not take posed photos, and I remember once seeing someone roll their eyes at me! Of course, you want everyone to have their magical experience, but the stage door is not part of your actual job. And while you love that people have a connection to that show, sometimes they don't want to meet you, what they want is to meet the green girl. They feel disappointed if you have to go quickly or aren't what they expected.

In this particular day and age, people really do not realize how distracting cell phones are to actors onstage. Some gentlemen have phones that have a constant blinking light, and when they stick it in their front shirt pocket, you can see it throughout the entire show. What we can see from the stage is pitch black, and then a light... a light... a light. When I would go up in the cherry picker for "Defying Gravity", I would just see phones and recorders everywhere.

That's the other thing with *Wicked*: you can't stop the bootlegging. If there's a night where you feel a little sick, and you decide you go on anyway, but your voice isn't at it's best, you still know there will be a recording on YouTube by 11:30pm. It's sometimes hard, when that's in your head, to stay focused on the story.

When I was a kid, one of my neighbors was in the original cast of *Sweeney Todd*, and for my birthday, he walked my friend and me into the Gershwin—it was the Uris then—and sat us in the back of the orchestra! So I was once a kid in that theater, and I got to see Len Cariou and Angela Lansbury. Back then, it was a more loosey-goosey situation, where you could walk down to empty seats when the show started, so we were going to do that. Then, that whistle at the top of the show went off, and we both looked each other and said: "We're not moving." We were too scared!

2011: Donna Vivino, Actor

I've been in *Wicked* on Broadway for almost two years, as the Elphaba standby. The first time I went on, I had four days' warning, so I got to invite people. Before I joined the Broadway cast, I had been doing the show on tour. I remember running out of breath the first time I did the show on Broadway. Elphaba is more taxing physically in New York because of all of the running around you have to do, but vocally, it's easier because you're not changing climates and finagling theaters with different acoustics.

The Gershwin is enormous. People get lost. The standby dressing room is on the third floor, and if you're one of those tracks, you can go to work at the Gershwin for weeks and not see anyone except for onstage. That's how much room we have. There's this big photo of Angela Lansbury and Len Cariou in *Sweeney Todd*, because that played the Gershwin, and we always joke, "Pray to Angela." And there's a rehearsal room upstairs that we call our frat room. Wherever I go next, I'm sure it will feel small.

Some people are shocked that I have to be there in the theater, as the standby. For a while, they let standbys be "on a beeper." It's up to the stage manager's discretion on each show. These days, I leave right after act one as long as there's another cover in the building. If there's an emergency during act two, the cover, who is also in the ensemble, goes on.

There's no cell reception in the Gershwin, so if you're backstage, you really have to interact with those around you. It makes it a more focused place to work. I really like that I go into that big cement block and know I'll be shut off from the world except for the people in Oz.

I was Cosette in *Les Mis* and worked with our *Wicked* stage manager, Mary Beth, when I was just a kid. When we were rehearsing for *Wicked*, she was tearing up, and I said to her, "I even have a broom again!" She went, "And a bucket!"

The green room at the Gershwin is great. There's a television and we play board games. Sometimes we'll all be watching the show happening on the monitor in real time, and sometimes we'll all be watching *Dancing With The Stars*.

The Gershwin has spoiled me. It's this big, modern theater. The wing space is so huge, I can't believe it. In the 4th floor rehearsal room, there's a treadmill and a piano, and people will even have yoga classes on Wednesdays between shows. The Gershwin is a luxury resort.

1996/2013: Lindsay Mendez, Actor

The first Broadway show I ever saw was *Show Boat* at the Gershwin. When I was 12, my dad had to take a business trip to D.C. and he took me with him. On our way from California to D.C. we stopped in New York, because I had a friend from home who had been cast in the musical *Big*.

The first night we were in New York, the night before we went to see Carrie in *Big*, my dad said, "Let's go to TKTS." We ended up with tickets to *Show Boat*, and it was my first Broadway show—right here in this theater.

I remember watching "Ol' Man River". That was my favorite. I just couldn't get over how big and grand the show was. My father sang along the whole time, so that annoyed me, as a 12-year-old. But I also remember sitting there and feeling very moved.

We sat in the center orchestra section. I remember the seats were blue, and I remember walking down the aisle. This theater is so special, because there are all of these displays in the lobby. I remember thinking: *Every Broadway theater must be this cool.* They are, but not in the same way as the Gershwin.

I worked at Circle in the Square during *Godspell*, and that theater wasn't my favorite. It's down underneath the ground so it's dark with no windows. The dressing rooms are small, and there's no green room—except for Hunter Parrish's dressing room, which we all turned into a green room. Now that I look back on how challenging his role was to do eight times a week, it means even more that he opened his dressing room to all of us.

My dressing room at the Gershwin is lavish. I know that if I star in another Broadway show, I will never have as big of a dressing room. We have a green room here, but I also keep the door to my dressing room open like Hunter did. My room becomes Grand Central sometimes, with people coming in to hang out. I know a lot of Elphabas close it, because you have to conserve your energy to play this part, but I try to leave it open. I love that I have enough space to do that. At Circle, I had the smallest space. I loved working there, but in certain places you're more comfortable, and it's nicer.

Also, since it's *Wicked*, I never check the grosses to see if I'll have a job next week, or worry that an audience wasn't very good. The audience is always full, passionate, and stoked to be here. That's so neat: to have an audience that's already so into the story before it even starts. You don't have to win them; they're already there. Personally, because the last show I did was in a 300-seat theater, it's been a good challenge to play up to a huge balcony here. You have to lift your body. I'm still working on that.

As soon as I make my final exit, I get in the shower and scrub all the green off. It takes about 25 minutes for me to come out. The stage door can be great and terrible at the same time. I find it great that people want to express that they enjoy the show. People want to get their programs signed, and I think that's really cool. I love talking to fans of the show and doing that for them.

Back when I stagedoored, I didn't even have a camera, and that just wasn't part of the culture of Broadway the way that it is now. Now, everyone wants to take a picture with Elphaba. Sometimes, they might want to take a photo with Lindsay, but most people want a photo with Elphaba. It's a challenge because you've just scrubbed all this green off you, and your voice is tired, and you're taking pictures for an hour and talking. I do love meeting these great fans, who are so sweet and wonderful, but there are nights when you just have to go home and rest.

When Derek Klena and I did *Dogfight* together, directed by Joe Mantello, it was the best working experience of both of our lives. We got so close to Joe, and learned so much from him. I feel like I learned everything about being an actor from him. The thought of working with him again on *Wicked* was thrilling. I would work with him every day for the rest of my life. And with Derek... well, *Dogfight* was a hard show because it was hard story to tell, for both of us. It could have been a great working relationship, or it could have been really awkward. And we became such good friends. I couldn't wait to be in the show together every night.

When they talked about putting us in *Wicked* together, it was so exciting. It was Derek's Broadway debut! I will keep this leading man forever. I love every moment of working with him. We rehearsed *Wicked* together for four weeks. Joe came in and worked with us like old times. Doing a show like this, you can start to feel isolated, because the role is so hard and solitary—you're playing a loner and an outcast—and you have to live like a monk. But I feel like I'm always out there with my family. I feel so supported by everyone here, and that stems from Joe and Stephen Schwartz, and all of us wanting very much to be here.

"Defying Gravity" used to scare me—with the physical act of being above people's heads and singing those notes—but now I love it. It's the best ending of an act ever, and it's so exciting to be performing it live. The song is great, and every night, the flying is thrilling. It shocks people, and makes them feel something. And I feel so f---ing lucky to be Elphaba when I'm singing it.

———————

When the Uris first opened, it was one of the largest, most technologically advanced performance venues in all of New York City. That said, the first actors at the Uris were the most excited about... the showers. The majority of Broadway theaters were built in the first third of the 20th century, when accoutrements such as elevators, escalators, and showers were considered luxuries. But the Uris has all three! Those showers came in handy later when the cast of Wicked *had colored makeup to shower off quickly. The* Via Galactica *cast were the first to get good use out of the showers—they had colored makeup too!*

As columnist Earl Wilson wrote when the Uris opened, "Everybody kept mentioning the showers in the dressing rooms which shows you that a lot of actors must not have been bathing regularly."[49]

———————

2011: Maintaining The Wigs

Brittnye Batchelor, Hair and Makeup Artist

The first Broadway show I saw was *Wicked*, in the Gershwin Theatre. I was 21 years old, and it was my first time in New York, ever. I came here on a trip with my mom during spring break of my senior year of college.

It was magical. It was exciting. I remember looking onstage and thinking: *I want to be involved*.

Later on, in 2010, I was working on the *La Cage aux Folles* revival. I became friends with a makeup artist who filled in for me when I was sick. She was also a makeup swing on *Wicked*. As soon as *La Cage* closed, I was looking for work and she recommended me for *Wicked*! I had done it as a local, so that helped me get hired. When the tours travel, they bring their people, but they also bring in local hair and makeup people, because it saves money.

I kept thinking I was going to get lost during my first time backstage. It was so exciting, knowing I was back there. It's a maze!

My mom actually came to see the show again and, coincidentally, it was a year from the day that we saw it together. Because I was working on it, she got to sit in the pit with the orchestra, so that was exciting.

We do eight shows a week, but on top of that, we have to make sure the wigs all look perfect. Outside of the show, I usually have between 4 and 16 hours a week of work, maintaining the wigs.

I'm a hair stylist on the show, and I'm also called an internal swing, which means that if the hair supervisor, hair assistant supervisor, or makeup supervisor is out, then I fill in for their specific tracks. The hair supervisor works on Morrible, Fiyero and Nessa, the hair assistant does Elphaba and Glinda, and the makeup supervisor paints the green girl green. In my regular position, I do makeup and hair for the ensemble and for Boq.

I used to love walking under the stage in the basement because there were all these pictures that had to do with the history of things that had been in the theater. It's not like that now, because they've painted, but we still have the *Wicked* mural.

———————

[49] Wilson, Earl. "Plush Theater Has Showers For Actors." *Beaver County Times*. 24 Nov. 1972. Retrieved from news.google.com.

People are always surprised to learn that making Elphaba green only takes about 25 minutes. We paint her with an actual paintbrush! She gets green, and then there's the beauty makeup on her face, for contours and eyebrows.

When snafus happen during the show, it's always hectic. If Elphaba gets something in her eye and part of the green makeup needs to be redone, it's a challenge because that makeup artist is on a very set track throughout the course of the show. He has to do the monkey masks, any of the facial hair, and scheduled touch-ups throughout each performance.

2012: I Never Auditioned For *Wicked*

Taylor Trensch, Actor

I never auditioned for *Wicked*. I auditioned for *Dogfight*. I was so excited to go in for that show because I love Joe Mantello's work. After the audition, I didn't hear anything for a while, and figured I didn't get the show. Then my agent called me and said, "Remember when you auditioned for *Dogfight*? Well, they'd like you to be in *Wicked*."

I had seen the tour of *Wicked* in Tampa, Florida, where I'm from. When *Wicked* came to town, it was sold out, as it always is, but my friends and I waited outside the theater, hoping we could buy someone's spare tickets. We were lucky because these kind old ladies had extra tickets and we bought them—then they came back and told us that they were so happy that young people were so excited about theatre that they wanted to give us our money back. That's how I saw *Wicked* for free!

Before I was cast as Boq, I had never seen *Wicked* at the Gershwin though. I remember walking into that lobby for the first time; it's unlike any other lobby you've ever seen. There were so many people there, and all these little girls in pink and green dresses. I was baffled that I was a part of this enormous show. It's a show and it's also a tourist attraction. People come to New York to see the Statue of Liberty and *Wicked*. It's really exciting. That was my Broadway debut!

While I was at the Gershwin, *Godspell* was our neighbor at Circle in the Square. That was exciting because Hunter Parrish was playing Jesus. As young lads, we lived in California at the same time and took acting classes together. We were little actors trying to break into the biz. I remember how excited we were when he was cast in the movie *Sleepover*, which was his first big project. Now we were both on Broadway in theaters next to each other.

My dressing room was on the second floor, and I shared with Tom Flynn, who played Dr. Dillamond. On one end of the theater, the stairwell had this beautiful painted mural, and on the other side, the stairwell had the signatures of every actor in *Wicked*. I remember always noticing Brynn O'Malley's signature on the wall, because she signed it: "The Nessa With Bangs."

I loved performing for so many little kids. I have two young cousins who came to see the show who couldn't have cared less about me. They were so excited about the two witches. I think one of them actually shoved me out of the way to get Jackie Burns' autograph.

The *Wicked* stage door is really an amazing experience. No one waiting there cares about anyone except the witches, which is hilarious and humbling and kind of great. I loved seeing girls and boys recognize Jackie and Chandra Lee Schwartz, who were playing Elphaba and Glinda. It would take little kids some time to adjust to the fact that Jackie and Chandra were not painted green or in this big blonde wig, and once they realized who they were, there was this mixture of joy and total embarrassment. Every night, children would scream waiting

131

for Jackie and Chandra to come out, and then when they did come out, they would run away, too shy to get their autographs.

2012: I'll Be Boq

F. Michael Haynie, Actor

I went to see *Wicked* to see George Hearn as the Wizard. Since *Sweeney Todd* was life-changing for me, I really wanted to see him. I loved the show, and I thought: *I could really play that Boq role.* In 2006, I went to a random call for the show. I was non-Equity at the time, but I went in. I thought I did well, but I didn't get a callback. Then I went in another time for Boq and got typed out for it! I thought: *Okay, I guess I shouldn't go in for Boq after all.*

Then in 2008, during my last semester at NYU, I got a phone call from Bernie Telsey's casting office. They said, "We need you to come in for Boq." I thought: *Oh my God! I'm going to book it! This is it.* I went to the audition, and the guy who came out of the audition room before me looked like a doll. He looked like what I imagined the ideal Boq was in my head. I suddenly knew he was going to get it, and he did. I walked into the room and immediately got the sense that the people behind the table had already picked. That was the last time I ever got called in for *Wicked*.

A few years later, I was doing *Dogfight* off-Broadway and my mom was in town to see it. We were at lunch and I got a call from my agent. "F. Michael, there's an offer coming your way from Telsey's office for *Wicked*." "Really?! Which tour?" I asked. "The Broadway company." I was going to make my Broadway debut.

Bernie Telsey is like the Willy Wonka of New York—not because he looks a little bit like Gene Wilder in the movie, but because he really wants to take the most deserving people up in the glass elevator. He's started and helped more careers than anyone else.

That night, I got to the theater for *Dogfight* and saw Joe Mantello. He told me, "We wanted to get *Dogfight* open first, but we figured it out during tech. David Stone and I were sitting there and went, 'Should we make F. Michael the next Boq?' 'Yeah, of course we should.'" I have no idea if Joe and David even knew that I had actually auditioned for *Wicked* and not gotten it before. I was almost scared that if I talked about that, they would change their minds.

The night after I started rehearsals for *Wicked*, I got two tickets to see the show. I took my friend Alex Wyse— he later ended up playing Boq too! I got a little teary walking into the theater that night, knowing I'd be up there on Broadway two weeks later. They were the longest two weeks of my life. I felt ready to do the part the next day.

My Broadway debut was on a Tuesday. And it was just a regular Tuesday for everybody else. People called out. I did the show for the first time with the Glinda standby, Kate Fahrner. People in the theater came up to me and said, "Where's Etai? Are you Boq tonight? Cool, nice to meet you." My three best friends—Drew Gasparini, Andrew Kober, and Alex Brightman—were in the audience that night, and that was great and scary, because Alex played Boq for two years! But for lots of people, it was just a Tuesday.

I did the show with seven different Elphabas, seven Nessaroses, five Glindas, five Fiyeros, three Wizards, three Morribles and four Dillamonds. I did 312 performances and never missed a show. My understudies both loved and hated me.

Lindsay and Derek came into *Wicked* too, so it was a *Dogfight* reunion. I got notes from Joe, but it was a different process than a few months earlier, when we'd all developed a brand-new show together and talked about the characters. Part of going into a show like *Wicked* is discovering your take on the role yourself. A couple nights I walked off stage and thought I was the worst actor on the planet. You have to try things within the structure of the show and figure out what works for you, without having any kind of conventional rehearsal period.

Wicked was the most amazing Broadway training. I learned about being part of a huge success that had nothing to do with me. The standing ovation I got every night didn't have to do with me. It had to do with Christopher Fitzgerald and that original company and what Joe Mantello, Stephen Schwartz, Winnie Holzman, and David Stone did all those years ago, that we've been able to be part of. And granted, the current performances are amazing, but the reason for the audience reaction is the empire that has been built. Every day that I have lived in New York City, *Wicked* has been running.

Getting your costume for *Wicked* is unique. You go to a warehouse on 38th Street, and there are rows and racks of the costumes that have been worn by every principal in the history of the show. They're only missing Idina Menzel's dress, which is at the Smithsonian, and Shoshana Bean's dress, which is on display at the Gershwin. When I went to the warehouse, they told me, "We're making costumes for you, but they might not be ready for six months." I was only on a nine-month contract! The Boq track has five pairs of shoes. One of them you only wear for the opening number, and they are knee-high dragon scale LaDucas[50] that are under a huge cloak. The audience barely even sees them! But that's why *Wicked* is *Wicked*.

I have never lost it onstage worse than I did during my last show at *Wicked*. I don't know why. Maybe it was because it was my Broadway debut. Maybe it was because I'd made friends. Maybe it was because I was scared about the future. It's hard to leave when your show has 2000 people standing up and screaming their brains out every night. During the performance, I looked at my Nessarose, Catherine Charlebois, and sang my line, "Nessa, Nessa, surely now I'll matter less to you, and you won't mind my leaving here tonight." Catherine looked up at me with her big brown eyes, and I just thought about how nice she'd been to me. She was the first person I talked to when I found out my contract wasn't being renewed and I was leaving the show. I never got the line out. I just sobbed. I couldn't form words. Lindsay Mendez was staring at me from the wings too. I got off stage and was furious with myself.

I wasn't sad. I was happy about other projects I was working on. I had gotten to achieve something I dreamed of. But all of a sudden, I felt like I was losing something really big that I loved. I was a principal on Broadway. I had the responsibility of carrying on a show that people saw ten years ago, and keeping up its integrity. Not everyone feels like that, and it's sad. Some people check out in a way that they don't on a new show. Every single person in the cast of *Holler If Ya Hear Me* is present. They understand that they're part of the risk, and part of the reward, and they feel ownership. There's something about the government job that makes you feel like you have the right to go, "Eh, I'm just in *Wicked*." But no, you're not. You are part of most people's *Cats* now! There's a whole generation of people whose first Broadway show was *Cats*, and now there will be a new generation whose first Broadway show was *Wicked*. And *Wicked* is a great show! It's magic.

My dream someday is to originate a role on Broadway, to create something new. On *Wicked*, I knew no reviewer was going to come and say, "F. Michael Haynie is the reason this show is closing" or "F. Michael is fantastic," but I got to be a part of this amazing production. On *Holler*, I get to actually see what Broadway previews are like, what opening a show is like, while I standby for someone who is originating a role. Hopefully someday I'll get to do that an original show and be the first person to play a part—any part. I don't have dreams of Tony Awards—unless they make an Ensemble Tony Award. They really should! Equity is having a harder and harder time deciding which roles are principals, because shows are changing. And ensembles deserve recognition. Being in the ensemble is an amazing thing.

---

[50] LaDucas: the premiere flexible character shoe of the dance and theatre world

1998/2014: How It All Comes Together

Mary Testa, Actor

I'm here at the Gershwin now, playing Morrible in *Wicked*. It's so big. After I come down the stairs screaming, "Wicked Witch!" I used to go around, come downstairs and go around the changing room back to my dressing room. One day I thought: *Why aren't I just going through the changing room?* So I tried that, and now if I'm even a moment too early, there are rolling racks with costumes and I have to jump out of the way. I changed the rhythm of a moment. *Wicked* runs like a huge, well-oiled machine.

I always marvel about how it all comes together. Everybody pulls their own at their job so that this huge show can happen, and I'm always kind of dazzled by that. Sometimes I'm walking from one end of the stage to the other for an entrance and I think: *Wow. I don't know if audiences realize just how many people are behind the show, pulling off each cue, timing everything.*

I was here in 1998 for *On the Town*, and my dressing room was on the other side of the stage. Annie Golden and I shared what is now the drum room. Actually, we had these adjoining rooms. Mine was closer to the stage, but hers had a doorbell. I wanted a doorbell! I went out and bought a doorbell. It went "Ding dong," even though our doors were really open to everyone most of the time.

Betty Comden and Adolph Green were around, and they were great. Adolph's eyesight was failing, but he was the most enthusiastic person there. He would always sit in the audience and watch, and then after a number, you'd hear him yelling, "Great! Great!" You always knew when Betty was there too, because her presence was lovely, but she was quieter. They were in their eighties. They seemed fragile.

I like to watch "Defying Gravity" from the wings. Hearing the audience shriek at the end of the number is very exciting. *Wicked* is just incredible. It's amazing that after ten years, it's still packed. Audiences scream at the beginning, when the show starts, and they scream at curtain call every night. *Wicked* really affects people of all ages. It's great fun to be part of a show where you can feel the audience enjoying it so much.

The Gershwin stage door is halfway down 51st Street. Once you enter, there's a hallway with an elevator on the right. When I interviewed Mary Testa, I was waiting for this elevator to take me to her dressing room on the stage level when I struck up a conversation with the door man. Before I knew it, I had set up a meeting to interview Greg Woolard the next week.

The elevator delivers you to the stage left wing. The majority of the principal dressing rooms are on stage right, and this is where I interviewed Lindsay Mendez in 2013 and Mary in 2014. Down this hallway and through a door to the stairwell is the famous Wicked *mural. Created by several long-time* Wicked *cast members, the mural spans several floors within the stairwell and colorfully depicts different scenes from the show!*

Multiple stairwells throughout the Gershwin have special meaning—the stairwell entrance by the stage door is filled with the names of every person who has departed Wicked, *in order. The first name is Taye Diggs, who briefly played Fiyero during its first year. As you walk up the stairs, you see Joel Grey, Ben Vereen... there are hundreds of names. Ensemble members who have gone in and out of the show have their names there a dozen times. For three flights, these stairs tell the story of* Wicked's *comings and goings for over a decade.*

In the part of the Gershwin you get to see, the Hall of Fame walls are covered with the names of the theater's most famous. In the part of the Gershwin you never get to see, the stairwell walls are covered with the names of the first company that has truly made the Gershwin its long-time home.

134

The Circle In The Square Theatre

Built: 1972
Location: 235 West 50th Street
Owner: Paul Libin and the estate of Theodore Mann
Formerly Named: Circle in the Square/Joseph E. Levine Theatre (1972-1974)
Longest-Running Show: *The 25th Annual Putnam County Spelling Bee* (2005-2008)
Shortest-Running Show: *Glory Days* (closed on opening night in 2008)
Number of Productions: 96

I saw *True West* starring Philip Seymour Hoffman and John C. Reilly at Circle in the Square, and it was one of my favorite experiences in the theatre ever. I remember walking into the lower lobby and seeing all of the pictures of past productions on the walls. I thought: *This is where* real *theatre happens. Art happens here! Kevin Spacey in* The Iceman Cometh *and Lynn Redgrave in* Saint Joan*.* Then we moved in for *The 25th Annual Putnam County Spelling Bee*, and those portraits in classic plays were juxtaposed with our signs that said things like "No Spitting In The Auditorium" and "Piranhas Are Good Sports"! It was hilarious. Circle in the Square commemorated all of these prolific classical actors in their lobby, and then there we were, playing 11-year-olds in a new musical, decorating the place with construction paper.

-Celia Keenan-Bolger, Actor

Introduction: Student, Janitor, Broadway Star

Eric William Morris, Actor

I moved to New York in 2004 and started theatre school at Circle in the Square. Not everyone knows this, but Circle in the Square Theatre School has classes five days a week, 9am-6pm in the basement of the same building that the Broadway theater is in.

The theater is two floors below ground level, and the classrooms are on the basement level, below that. So, I went to school in the same building that Broadway shows were going on in—and three or four stories below the parking garage for *Wicked*.

When I first started class, *Frozen* had just closed, and by the spring of my first year, *Spelling Bee* opened. It got nominated for a lot of Tony Awards and was there for the next three years. We had these seminars on Monday nights where a working actor would come in and talk to us, and I remember Deborah Craig from *Spelling Bee* came in a little after they opened.

Even though they're in the same building, the school and the Broadway theater are not actually affiliated. However, I got a job at the theater because I went to school there. I got to know a woman named Kelly Varley, who was the liaison between the two. The school is a two-year program and at the end of the second year, you get to do a final project on the stage of Circle in the Square. When I was in my first year, a bunch of people dropped out of the project, so I filled in and did two shows on the set of *Spelling Bee*. Kelly was the stage manager and we got along well.

I was working as a waiter at Blue Fin in Times Square while I was going to school. Then, someone had to pull out of their job managing the infrared headsets and being the janitor for *Spelling Bee*, and Kelly asked if I wanted that job. It fit better with my school schedule, so I started working there.

For almost two years, that was my job. I was the janitor and headset person at *Spelling Bee* for the rest of my time as a student and then for eight months after I graduated while I was also going to as many auditions as I could.

I had one of my first Broadway auditions to understudy in a show called *Coram Boy*. I got an appointment on a Wednesday for that Friday. I was called back the following Monday night, which was the day rehearsals had started. The director was British and had flown in for the first day of rehearsals, so she was seeing understudies that night. I found out the next morning that I got the job and would be making my Broadway debut. Not even a week had passed since my original audition!

When I got cast in *Coram Boy*, I had a janitor shift at Circle in the Square that night, and I decided to keep working. For two weeks, I was rehearsing a Broadway show during the day and cleaning up the candy that Jose Llana threw around the theater during the song "My Unfortunate Erection" every night. One of the main parts of my job at *Spelling Bee* was picking up that candy. It actually took about two hours after the show ended to clean that theater and make sure I got all the candy.

Coram Boy was a good experience but it closed after 30 performances. I never got to go on for either of the roles I understudied. After that, I got some film and TV work, and I did *As The World Turns* for a while. Then, I started bartending in Astoria. I made a lot of money doing that, but I was exhausted all the time. Kelly let me know that there was a new show coming into Circle—*The Norman Conquests*—and if I wanted I could have my old job back and pick whatever shifts I wanted.

It was funny to see the different audiences between *Spelling Bee* and *Norman Conquests*. The infrared hearing sets that I was in charge of are basically hooked up to the sound system, so that people who have a hard time hearing can get some help through earphones. My job was to take their ID or credit card and issue them a headset, and then make sure they checked it back in and got their collateral back. During *Spelling Bee*, I averaged two per show, so I wasn't very busy in that department. Then, during *Norman Conquests*, I had about 35 for every performance. Although *Norman Conquests* was also amazing, *Spelling Bee* drew a younger, hipper crowd. During *Spelling Bee*, I could kind of leave while the show itself was going on, but during *Norman Conquests*, I'd stick around because during the first act, invariably at least one person would come back really angry that their headset didn't work.

One time, there was someone taking pictures in the theater who wouldn't stop. My boss, the manager of the theater, really went to the length of the law and took the camera and pulled the film out. The person was throwing a fit, saying that they were going to sue, and I literally had to stand in between this angry person and my boss. There were moments like that all the time.

In 2009, I was working at *Norman Conquests* when I got an audition for *Mamma Mia!* I had a callback and then two months went by and I didn't hear anything. I took a week off to go to the beach with my family, and got a call from my agent. I had just had a second callback for *Spider-Man* the previous week, so I thought the call was about that. My agent said, "Hey, remember that *Mamma Mia!* audition?"

I got the part of Sky in the Broadway company of *Mamma Mia!*, but that didn't start until late August, so I was able to finish my job at *Norman Conquests*, which was nice.

Circle in the Square is right across from the Winter Garden, where *Mamma Mia!* was playing, so every day, I'd walk past the *Mamma Mia!* marquee on my way to work and think: *What the hell is that going to be like?* I had been seeing that *Mamma Mia!* marquee every single day since I started school in 2004, because it had been playing across the street for that long. And I had never seen the show!

136

It was a rare and very cool experience to walk by that theater every day and know I was going to get to be in the show. There's something special about having a big job coming up and feeling like, *Whatever. I can do this for a few more weeks. I can clean the theater. I can clean the toilets.*

Mamma Mia! was a blast, and playing Sky was great. It was also really funny because I went back to do one of those seminars at my alma mater and all my old teachers were like, "We see the poster of you across the street every day!" That was really neat.

I did a benefit at Ars Nova the other night, and Celia Keenan-Bolger was in it too. She couldn't remember why she recognized me, and I told her it was because I used to clean her dressing room. I used to sweep under her table, and then last week we were sharing a microphone. She was like, "You've got to be kidding me!"

I want to do a show at Circle in the Square someday so badly. I have to. I want it to be in the round and I want it to be a show where a set piece comes out of the stage, like *Godspell*, so that it shuts down Room 115, which is the Shakespeare classroom right underneath the stage. Everybody gets really flustered when that happens.

I want to do a show at Circle one day, but I don't want to do a show where anything messy happens in the audience! I won't even leave a crumb behind in a movie theater anymore. I know what it's like to bend over and pick up everybody's garbage at Circle in the Square.

————————————

The Circle in the Square theatre company was founded in 1951 by Theodore Mann, José Quintero, Jason Wingreen, Aileen Cramer, and Emily Stevens, with the idea of doing great plays in repertory in the round. The group set up their first theatrical locale at 5 Sheridan Square, and thus, the off-Broadway movement was born. The venue was a former nightclub, so the company could not get a theatrical license—instead, they had a cabaret license. Because of this, Circle in the Square theatre company's first production, Dark of the Moon—*about a witch in Appalachia— had to serve cookies and punch and set up cocktail tables in order for the show to go on.*

Circle in the Square was truly put on the map in 1952, when they revived Summer and Smoke *by Tennessee Williams, which had flopped on Broadway in 1948. Critics agreed that the company was doing extraordinary work. Following this, the company received much-desired permission to revive Eugene O'Neill's* The Iceman Cometh, *which had also flopped on Broadway less than a decade earlier. The production was majorly acclaimed and led O'Neill's widow to allow the company to stage the American premiere of* Long Day's Journey Into Night, *which then won the Pulitzer. Circle had established itself as an important part of New York theatre life.*

In 1960, Circle in the Square theatre company moved to a second location, at 159 Bleecker Street. The company continued to produce important revivals of less appreciated works as well as classic plays. In 1963, Paul Libin became the managing director. In 1972, based on their admirable body of work, Mayor John Lindsay invited the company to open a new theater on 50th Street and Broadway. While Circle had produced shows on Broadway before, they now had a permanent home there. The new Broadway house opened as the Circle in the Square/Joseph E. Levine Theatre, in honor of the movie mogul who vowed to write a large check to the organization. When he never came through, his name was quietly removed from the marquee. During the 1970s, Circle in the Square produced shows in both their downtown and uptown homes.

Uptown, Circle in the Square—still led by Mann and Libin—continued to do important revivals and classics in the round (and thrust). The theatre school of the same name, begun in Greenwich Village a decade earlier, also moved to 50th Street. Circle in the Square Theatre School is the only accredited performing arts institution associated with a Broadway theater.

*The company inhabited its Broadway home for more than 25 years, until it went bankrupt. In 1999, the theater's first "rental"—*Not About Nightingales—*was produced, and from that point on, the theater became a coveted spot for any Broadway show desiring unconventional staging. With 776 seats, Circle in the Square is the only Broadway* *theater for shows "in the round" and one of only two, the other being the Vivian Beaumont, that can be configured as a thrust stage, where the audience surrounds the stage on three sides. Since 1999, Broadway's 4th smallest theater (after the Helen Hayes, Samuel Friedman, and American Airlines) has been a successful home for unconventional musicals and plays, from* Spelling Bee *to* The Norman Conquests.

1972: They Were Still Laying The Carpet

Nick Wyman, Actor/President of Actors' Equity Association

I got bitten by the acting bug in 7th grade. We did a skit about Benedict Arnold in my social studies class. The girl I was in love with, Nancy McCune, played my wife. At the end of the skit, I died, and Nancy took the blanket on me and used it to cover my face. Because I was so tall, when she covered my face, she uncovered my toes. That got a big laugh from the audience and I thought: *This is what I want to do.*

I went to acting school at Circle in the Square in the fall of 1972. It had just moved to 50th Street, and they were still laying the carpet when I began school! They had this great thick carpet with the Circle in the Square logo: a dark gray circle inside a red square, and then a red circle inside a dark gray square, alternating. I stole a chunk of it to make a chessboard at one point.

When I started school, they were just premiering the first production at Circle in the Square: *Mourning Becomes Electra* starring Colleen Dewhurst. And of course, *Via Galactica* was opening at the Uris next door. Years later, I did *My Fair Lady* at the Uris. The two theaters' stage doors are not close together, so there's not a lot of interaction in that regard. But as I became more involved with the unions and Broadway events as the President of Equity, I continued to interact with Ted Mann and Paul Libin at Circle in the Square, just like I did when I was in school. There's a continuity and joy to that. The Broadway family is very tight.

Circle in the Square Theatre School boasts many famous alumni, including Kevin Bacon, Gina Gershon, and Molly Shannon. Former student Philip Seymour Hoffman would go on to make his Broadway debut at the theater in True West, *and former students Winnie Holzman and Idina Menzel would go on to create the biggest hit of the theater next door,* Wicked.

By night, Circle in the Square is a glamorous Broadway house, replete with stars in the audience and onstage. By day, Circle in the Square is filled with stretching, singing, studying students who occupy every inch of the space. When I worked on Godspell *at Circle in the Square, I would often encounter dance classes in the lobby, vocal warmups in the backstage hallways and lunching teenagers—talking with passion about Broadway shows—in the upstairs alley. They are the only students who get to study Broadway, on Broadway!*

1973: *Uncle Vanya*

Christopher Durang, Writer

I remember paying $10 for standing room for *Uncle Vanya* at Circle in the Square. It was a wonderful production that Mike Nichols directed, that starred George C. Scott, Julie Christie, Nicol Williamson, Lillian Gish and Elizabeth Wilson. Wilson was especially moving as Sonia, although they were all terrific. I remember exactly how it felt to stand in the back of that theater.

Mayor John Lindsay was given a special Tony Award in 1973 for his great contribution to Broadway. Because he put a bill into effect that would give builders of major high-rises in midtown special treatment and bonuses if they

built a legitimate theater on the premises, he is directly responsible for the existence of several theatrical venues, including Circle in the Square, the Uris/Gershwin, the American Place Theatre, and the Minskoff. The only other time a Tony honor was given to a mayor was to Mayor Michael Bloomberg in 2013 for his dedication to New York City tourism.

———————

1973: The Color-Changing Costume

Tony Walton, Director/Scenic Designer/Costume Designer

Uncle Vanya at Circle in the Square was one of my favorite productions to work on. It was directed by Mike Nichols at one of his extreme peaks, and featured an extraordinary all-star cast, all of whom were perfectly fitted to their roles.

Yelena was played by Julie Christie, who was a dear chum. She actually lived with us throughout rehearsals and the run of the show. My wife, Gen, used to be terrified when Julie'd go to work every day on a bicycle. She was a Brit and not used to pedaling on what seemed to her the wrong side of the street! Julie was unexpectedly daunted by the brilliance of her castmates. She had never really thought of herself as a classical actor, despite her Oscar-winning brilliance in films. She never stopped working on her role and became increasingly dazzling as the run progressed. At the beginning of the play, Julie made her entrance through the audience and just drifted, slowly trailing her long lace skirt and her parasol behind her; floating the whole length of the forestage and disappearing upstage without saying a word. It was an amazing directorial choice by Nichols.

When this entrance occurred at the first preview, Warren Beatty—who was smitten with Julie and sitting right near her point of entry—let out an extraordinary gasp, audible to everyone, as she floated onstage. It was very touching seeing the tears spring to his eyes and no surprise that he and Julie eventually became an item for quite some time.

Circle in the Square is a very challenging space—better suited for fashion shows than for drama. For *Uncle Vanya*, the first act had to suggest a garden exterior, which could be instantly transformed to represent the interior. Designing a wall upstage that could work equally well for both the exterior and the interior of the house was quite a challenge We also needed furniture that could serve believably in both settings as it wasn't possible to have entire settings move on and off there. So bearskins were thrown over the oak seating and lace or paisley table cloths were added to the garden tables to suggest appropriate furniture for the interior.

I created a window over the double door entryway that was based on the windows of Chekhov's Russian summerhouse. It was draped with a canopy that could be dappled with sunlight through leaves and then be dropped out of sight for the interior. I created a leaf gobo[51] for our lighting designer, Jules Fisher, that is still being used to this day. I think it may now be called "Realistic Leaves," and features the illuminated gaps between the leaves rather than the leaves themselves.

At Mike Nichols' suggestion, Jules had student apprentices lying, unseen, up in the grid on mats. Each manipulating a lamp that functioned as a tiny follow spot on the actors' faces and followed them wherever they moved. It looked as though the actors faces were aglow with auras of light around them. No one ever figured out how that was done!

To focus on these remarkable faces even further, I created the costumes without much color, or in a very deep shade. There was nothing brightly hued in them at all, except for Julie's white lace gowns. So that all that anyone was fully conscious of was the faces. If there were interesting costume details, they were just there, not screaming to be noticed. Lillian Gish, surprisingly, did require some extra attention. She came to her first fitting,

———————

[51] gobo: a device placed within a lamp to control the shape and look of its illumination

saying, "This is going to be very interesting for me because I've always designed my own costumes. Wait! ... No... I tell a lie! Not for *Birth of A Nation*! My mother designed those."

I showed Lillian my designs. She was playing the old nanny, so of course I had her in dark wool and muslins with a little white accent here and there. Seeing my sketches, she burst into tears and said, "No, no, no! Russian peasant women never wore anything dark! Being adopted as members of the family, they wore delicate clothing in pretty pale pastel colors." Ray Diffen, in whose costume shop the clothes were being made, said disbelievingly, "Really, Ms. Gish?" To which she replied, "Have you ever been to Russia?" He said, "No, but I've seen *The Cranes Are Flying*!" (That was a Soviet movie about World War II.) "Well hold your tongue then!" said the adamant Ms. Gish. Shortly thereafter, Ray absented himself from further dealings with our great lady.

I told Lillian placatingly that I would try to figure out a solution. And very fortunately, at this point in the 1970s, weightless, beautiful Thai silks had been turning up in New York. They were gorgeous and as light as tissue paper. I got a lot of those silks in pale lilacs and mauves, which I hoped might be acceptable to her, and we made her delicately flowing costumes in those colors. Lillian was entranced with this and floated around the fitting room murmuring, "You see! You see!"

I warned Nichols that something bizarre was going to be appearing on Lillian at the first dress rehearsal, and asked him to warn the company to be discreet. I told him I would take care of it gradually. Each night, we would take her costume away from her dressing room on the pretext of adding some embroidery detail or other. And each night we would dye it down a tone or two. During the photo shoot, the photographer said, "I love your costume, Ms. Gish." And Lillian charmingly replied, "I do too dear, but the strangest thing is happening to it in the dressing room overnight, I think it must be oxidizing or something!" In the photos, her costumes appear to be virtually black!

Cathleen Nesbitt, the original Mrs. Higgins in *My Fair Lady*, who I knew well, was in that production, too. Although seriously arthritic, she was the opposite of Lillian. I had found these beautiful antique bootlets for her, and they turned out to be tight and uncomfortable. "Don't worry," I said, "We'll find something else." "No, no. I love them!" she said, "If necessary, I'll have another toe or two taken off."

George C. Scott was a magnificent Astrov in our *Vanya*, and bizarrely, I had been appointed to be his admiring watch dog on matinee days as there was always a risk that he would get badly pickled between shows. There was a little restaurant in the lower area of the theatre complex that we'd go to. I would try to get him to tell me stories of his career to keep him from getting too interested in the booze, but mostly he'd talk about what an impossible line of work he was in, and that he would feel obliged to mercifully kill any of his children who became interested in joining the acting profession.

Julie Christie, Lillian Gish, Cathleen Nesbitt, George C. Scott... and that wasn't all. The production also starred the remarkable Nicol Williamson, Elizabeth Wilson, and Barnard Hughes, under the inspired direction of Mike Nichols... Quite a group!

1978: Watching In The Voms

Jerry Zaks, Director/Actor

Once in a Lifetime was so much fun. I played various small parts, and the show was directed by Tom Moore, who directed my first Broadway show, *Grease*. One of my jobs was to keep crossing the stage, hollering, "It's the retakes, it's the retakes, I'm telling you: it's the retakes. What is it? The retakes!" I was in farce heaven, and I was also understudying two of the leads, George and Jerry, played by John Lithgow and Treat Williams.

I got notice about a month ahead of time that Treat would be missing several performances. I lived and breathed nothing but his role for that month. As an understudy, you often don't get your chance, so I was fiercely determined to get it right. I had a wonderful first night in the role. I got to play opposite John Lithgow, and we got big laughs! Because we were at Circle in the Square, we could see what was going on backstage through the voms. And what I remember most of all was seeing the rest of the cast in the voms watching us. That was cool.

"The voms" are the affectionate name given to the exits from Circle in the Square's stage to the backstage area. "Vomitorium" is the proper term for a passage that goes underneath the audience to get backstage. Contrary to popular belief, this term has nothing to do with vomiting and is an ancient Roman term for a space where people could make a swift exit.

Audiences enter the Circle in the Square through an upper lobby located near 50th Street, in a mid-block alley that also contains the audience entrance to the Gershwin. After entering this lobby, audiences take an escalator to the mid-level lobby, where three doors lead to the auditorium. (A staircase also leads to the lowest lobby, with bathrooms and a photo gallery of past shows.)

Upon entering the performance space, audience members walk down another set of stairs to their seats; Circle in the Square is truly underground. But walk straight forward after entering from the far left or far right door, and you will reach an "EXIT" door that leads directly backstage. The voms—a story lower, on stage level—lead backstage as well. In fact, open the door in between the womens' room and mens' room downstairs and you will be backstage on stage level as well.

Godspell *was in the round, so there was a set of risers with seats over the area that would be the stage for a show done in thrust. Underneath these risers was a dark, long storage space for props, costumes, sound equipment, and cast members' water bottles. Several surprise entrances happened both through the riser vom and the vom across from it. In one bit during* Godspell, *all cast members had hats and canes to dance with, except Judas. A stagehand entered from a vom and handed him a plunger. The voms are great for surprise entrances and exits.*

1978: The Christian Science Monitor

William Ivey Long, Costume Designer

My Broadway debut as a designer was creating the costumes for Liviu Ciulei's production of *The Inspector General*, at Circle in the Square.

As luck would have it, exactly when the show opened, there was a newspaper strike. There were absolutely no reviews! Isn't that funny? My first show on Broadway where I was an assistant, *Me Jack, You Jill*, closed in previews, and my first show on Broadway where I was a designer had no reviews.

Except for the *Christian Science Monitor*. They were the only ones who reviewed the show. I became a wild fan of the *Christian Science Monitor*, and I have been ever since.

30 years later, the *Christian Science Monitor* called me and wanted to do an article about my designs for *Little Shop of Horrors*. I said, "Absolutely! *Anything* for the *Christian Science Monitor*!"

1982: An Audition

Terry Finn, Actor

I had an audition for *Present Laughter* on the stage of Circle in the Square. I missed out by a hair. That would have been spectacular. It was Nathan Lane's debut! I remember George C. Scott was laughing and laughing during my audition. I thought I nailed that one. And then I got home and they said "Well, you're great, but..."

1983-2003: Circle In The Square Made Me A New Yorker

Greg Woolard, Door Man/Usher

I'm from North Carolina. I always loved cast albums but I didn't get to come to Broadway until I was in college. My first Broadway show was *A Chorus Line* at the Shubert. Of course, I knew every word of the show before it began because I loved the recording so much. I remember being enthralled by the Shubert Theatre itself, and being in disbelief that I was actually seeing the original cast.

I moved to New York in May of 1981. I worked here for a year and a half. For a while, I sold Chipwiches on the street! Then I moved home and taught school for a year. I decided I needed to come back, so I returned to New York in June of 1983 and I've been here ever since.

When I was here in 1981, I made a bunch of friends, so when I came back, I was visiting one of them who worked at the half-price tickets booth. One day I told him I was worried that I might have to move home and teach for another year, because it was so hard to find work in the city during the Reagan recession. He said, "I think they need someone at Circle in the Square." They were in the middle of a production of *The Caine Mutiny Court-Martial*.

I ran to Circle in the Square. They put a hat on me, sent me back to TKTS with twofers[52] and flyers, and I never looked back. From that day until the strike of 2007, there was not a week where I didn't work for a theatrical general manager and have a paycheck. About two weeks after I started working on *Caine Mutiny Court-Martial*, Joe Namath went into the cast.

The next show that came along was *Heartbreak House*, starring Rex Harrison, Amy Irving, Rosemary Harris, Dana Ivey, and Philip Bosco. They weren't going to need anyone at TKTS for that show, so they put me to work in the subscription office.

After working at Circle in the Square, I was connected with Albert Poland, general manager of *Little Shop of Horrors, Steel Magnolias*, and other shows downtown. I worked for him. He was good friends with Cameron Mackintosh, and when Cameron called him and said, "We need somebody for *Les Misérables*," he gave him my name. I had two interviews and didn't get hired. Then, on my birthday in 1989, they called me and hired me. They had me go out to the booth not with twofers but with flyers, just letting people on the line know that they could get tickets if they went directly to the box office. I stirred up a lot of business and really blew it out of the water for them. Every week when we'd check in, I'd ask, "If you're going to let me go, can you give me a week's notice?" And they'd say, "Let you go? You're the reason why we're not at the half-price boards. You're doing great!" They kept me there until I retired from it, 20 years later.

I don't go down to Times Square anymore. I don't get any pleasure from seeing what's there now. I was there when the theaters were torn down to put up the Marriot Marquis. These days, it's a completely different place. Of course there are people for whom Times Square still has that caché, but not for me. I still think about the old

---

[52] twofer: slang for "two for one" tickets, i.e. discount tickets

Howard Johnson that was there on the corner, and all of the other things that are no longer there. There's nothing now that's like what Times Square used to be.

Part of why I think I was good at my job is that I'm a good old Southern boy. I'm just polite to everybody. People were always coming back and saying, "I remember you!" One time I was in line at the Leicester Square half-price booth in London, on a trip, and people came up to me and said, "You work in Times Square! I've seen you!"

One day, I was in the Circle in the Square offices when the phone rang. I picked it up and a voice said, "Hello, this is Madeline Lee Gilford." Without even thinking, I replied, "Madeline Lee Gilford who wrote the book that I'm reading right now, *150 Years In Show Business*?!" She said, "Yes!" And I told her, "I am reading your book at this very moment!"

Jack Gilford was in town, and she was trying to get him tickets to see our production of *Heartbreak House*. I had no tickets at all but I told Madeline that she should call our house manager, Bill Conch. She did, and he managed to get her into the show. She actually called me back to tell me! So I said, "If I meet you in the lobby, could you sign my book?" "Of course I will!" She was happier than I was. She was the sweetest, nicest woman.

A couple years later, in May of 1985, Bill and I decided to go on a trip to Europe. Jack Gilford was doing a show called *Look to the Rainbow* at that time, a revue of E. Y. Harburg. I dropped off a note for Madeline at the theater, saying that I knew she probably wouldn't remember me, but we'd met at Circle in the Square and I was really looking forward to seeing the show. The night we saw it, we were brought backstage, where Madeline said, "Oh, Jack is so pleased that you're here!" We spent time with them and ate strawberries.

When Kevin Kline was at Circle in the Square for *Arms and the Man*, he would come down to our office on Saturday afternoons and visit. He loved telling stories and I'd ask him tons of questions. He'd sit there and I'd say, "Tell me what really happened with *On The Twentieth Century*." He'd just done *Silverado* which kind of put him on the movie map.

Frank Langella and Amy Irving both visited, too. I loved asking them questions. I needed to know this stuff! I didn't realize at first that you weren't really supposed to talk to them. They came to us and never seemed to mind. I got to know Raul Julia when he did *Design for Living* with Frank Langella and Jill Clayburgh, and I later ran into him at the Cannes Film Festival. He was promoting *Kiss of the Spider Woman*, and he recognized me. That was amazing.

I basically worked at Circle for three years straight, and then left and branched out a bit. I came back in 1987 for *Coastal Disturbances*. I still get a kick out of telling people, "I was on a softball team with Annette Bening and Tim Daly." Nobody knew who they were during *Coastal Disturbances*, but of course they became big stars later.

Later on, when I started ushering, my first job was on *Metamorphoses* at Circle in 2002. After that came *Life (x) 3* with John Turturro and Helen Hunt. After that show closed, nothing else was coming in right away so I drifted away and started freelance ushering. I worked at *Movin' Out* and at Avery Fisher Hall a lot.

Now that I'm at the Gershwin, it's interesting because we're kind of connected to Circle in the Square, but really, we're a street apart. Our stage door is on 51st Street, and they exit through their lobby onto 50th Street.

We had all of our opening nights at Luchow's, right in our little complex. Theresa Merritt would always come, because she was friends with Ted Mann. Ted was also friends with Vanessa Redgrave, at a time when it wasn't popular to be friends with Vanessa Redgrave. In fact, she was supposed to do *Heartbreak House*, but the uproar over it made it impossible,[53] so Dana Ivey wound up playing the role.

During *Heartbreak House*, I would babysit Rosemary Harris' little ten-year-old daughter. She turned out to be the great actress Jennifer Ehle!

I have been blessed. I walked into the lobby of the Circle in the Square without a job and this lady came up to me with a cap and said, "Go. Here are some flyers, here are some twofers. Go." And I just adapted to it. I was so glad that the job would keep me living in New York City, because that was my ultimate goal. I have been blessed with friends I've made through the theatre jobs I've had. My best friends, my honorary family, are people I met through TKTS. One of my good friends that I met through TKTS got me my Equity Card because his family staged industrials and they let me stage manage.

I've done a lot of different jobs by necessity. It's what kept me in New York. One job just led to another. Something was saying: *We're going to make sure you stay in New York. We're going to make sure you stay employed. We're going to make sure you stay in the theatre.* This was in the days before you went on the internet and found listings and applied for jobs. You just heard from friends, "Oh, so-and-so is hiring over Christmas." That's how I came up. It's very different now.

———————————

The Circle in the Square subscription office was downstairs, backstage. At Circle in the Square, there are offices on the same lower lobby level as the bathrooms. There's also the door that takes you backstage to the dressing rooms. On a level below that, there are now classrooms, and that's where the subscription offices used to be along with Paul Libin's office, Ted Mann's office, and the development office. At that time, Circle in the Square was a not-for-profit Broadway theater, like the Friedman, Vivian Beaumont, Studio 54, and American Airlines today. (At the time the theater opened, the only other Broadway non-profit was the Beaumont, which mostly housed not-for-profit productions... but more on that later.)

Unlike most other theaters, Circle in the Square has no formal stage door. Actors exit through the right side of the upper lobby, and stanchions are often put up outside to create a stage door-like area. As box office treasurer Diane Heatherington told me, "Circle in the Square was exciting to work in. Since they played shows in rep while I was there, the casts were always changing, and the front door is also the stage door so everyone said hello to me when they came and went. It was nice to work like that!" In cases where stars need to sneak out, there is a door on the right side of the mid-level lobby that leads to the Paramount building. In the 1980s, actors would use this private hallway to get to Luchow's for opening night parties.

Luchow's is one of the most legendary Manhattan restaurants of all time. The German establishment lit up 14th Street near Union Square from 1882 to 1982—for exactly a century! The epitome of the American dream, Luchow's was created by an immigrant named August Luchow who bought the restaurant where he started out as a waiter. Since Union Square was a hub of the entertainment industry (Luchow's neighbors were the Academy of Music and Steinway Hall) the restaurant became the center of the action, frequented by every major actor, writer, musician, producer, composer, and other creative personality who came through New York City. Victor Herbert is said to have founded ASCAP[54] at Luchow's, and it was a dining spot for everyone from Sigmund Romberg to Theodore Roosevelt to Kurt Vonnegut to Florenz Ziegfeld. The German dishes were delectable, the imported beer flowed (except during Prohibition!) and the opulent décor and boisterous music engendered an atmosphere of celebration year-round. By 1982, Union Square had changed significantly, and Luchow's was forced to close. The building was demolished and NYU's University Hall went up in its place.

———————————

[53] Redgrave sued the Boston Symphony Orchestra for cancelling a contract with her due to her political activism; the litigation became complicated and many in the arts were against her point of view on the matter.
[54] ASCAP: the American Society of Composers, Authors, and Publishers

Luchow's, intending to capitalize on its theatrical clientele, moved uptown to the theatre district and relocated, for the first time in a century, to the lower level of the 51st Street and Broadway corner of the Uris/Paramount Plaza building, where the Pub Theatrical had once stood. Confident advertisement proclaimed: Luchow's Opens On Broadway! Many Circle in the Square and Uris productions had their opening night parties at Luchow's—and Singin' in the Rain *even had a barbecue in the Luchow's courtyard! Luchow's advertised relentlessly and even created partnerships with several Broadway shows whereupon ticket buyers could get a package that included tickets and dinner. Despite all of this, Luchow's uptown location closed quietly in the late 1980s.*

Mars 2112, an outer space-themed restaurant opened in the spot in 1998 and closed in 2012. The tourist attraction was notorious for welcoming its customers with a simulated journey through space. The venue, occupying 35,000 square feet in the heart of Times Square, is currently empty and waiting for its next tenant.

*In its 40-plus years as a Broadway theater, Circle in the Square has been home to only nine musicals: four original (*Anna Karenina, The 25th Annual Putnam County Spelling Bee, Glory Days, Soul Doctor*), and five revivals (*Where's Charley?, Pal Joey, Sweeney Todd, The Rocky Horror Show, Godspell*). It has been home to 87 plays. In April of 2015, Circle will get its 10th musical:* Fun Home *by Jeanine Tesori and Lisa Kron. Notably, it is the first musical at the theater with an all-female writing team. The only female musical theatre writer to have worked at Circle previously was Rachel Sheinkin, who wrote the libretto to* Spelling Bee.

Part of the reason for this lack of musicals is that Circle in the Square's mission as a theatre company was to focus on classic plays and revivals of worthy drama. The first musical at Circle was Where's Charley? *in 1974, starring Raul Julia, and the second was* Pal Joey *in 1976. While these did foray into musical theatre, they were true to Circle's ongoing ambition to show audiences a worthy work by a prolific writer that hadn't been seen in New York in a while.*

Pal Joey's *leading role has the distinction of having been played on Broadway by Gene Kelly, Harold Lang, and Bob Fosse, and then by Frank Sinatra in the movie version. However, in the show's two most recent Broadway outings, it was played by the promoted understudy after the star left the production during previews. Why did stars Edward Villella and Christian Hoff play a first preview of* Pal Joey *but not an opening night? Joey Evans is quite a demanding role for an actor-singer-dancer, and both understudies, Christopher Chadman and Matthew Risch, were promoted amidst much drama. Villella, star of the New York City Ballet, couldn't sing the show, and Hoff, recent Tony Award winner, couldn't dance it. Turns out that the complicated show requires a true triple threat.*

When cynical theatergoers complain about the recent proliferation of musical revivals on Broadway and what this says about new musicals, their opinions are unfounded. The amount of musical revivals has not notably expanded. The 1970s saw 39 Broadway musical revivals (including these two at Circle) and the 2000s saw 40.

In 1989, Circle in the Square's next musical was a transfer from the York Theatre Company, a Sweeney Todd *revival deemed "Teeny Todd" for its intimate size, quite the opposite of what the original production had been next door.*

1989: Throwing The Cage

Jim Walton, Actor

Our revival of *Sweeney Todd* at Circle in the Square was a great production. I loved being in it. I had seen the original and loved Victor Garber's performance as Anthony, so to be cast in that part was thrilling. To get to hear the music every day was unbelievable!

My memory that sticks out from the show is about something really terrifying that happened. In the show, Anthony sings "Johanna" and then he meets Johanna and gives her this cage of birds. Then, Judge Turpin and the Beadle come, kick Anthony out, and break one of the birds' necks to kill it. They give him the empty cage back, and he sings, "I'll steal you, Johanna…" He vows to come back and get her.

At Circle in the Square, there's a vomitorium, which is the main entrance where the actors enter and exit the stage. After I sang the song each night, I was supposed to throw the cage into the vomitorium. I did it every performance, no problem. I played baseball; I know how to throw things. It had to be a pretty exact throw, because there were people sitting on either side of the vomitorium. So, every night at half-hour, I would practice throwing the cage. It always went smoothly.

Then one night, near the end of previews, stage management came to me and they said, "We have a new cage for you. It's a little smaller." That was fine by me. They told me I couldn't practice throwing it before the show, because they didn't want it to get beaten up at all. What I heard from that was: "The *New York Times* is here." I ended up being right.

That night, during that part of the show, I was holding this new cage. I was singing and then I took a step and threw the cage toward the vomitorium. It felt odd coming out of my hand; it felt lighter and I hadn't gotten to practice with it. The cage hit the floor, and in slow motion I saw it bounce up, hit a banister, and fly right toward a woman's head in the front row. I couldn't watch it because I had to pick up my bag and exit. I felt terrible for the woman, and I knew the *Times* and all the other critics were there. I waited until I knew I had ten minutes before my next entrance, and I went into the stairwell and sobbed. I was so upset with myself.

At the end of act one, I got a note backstage. It was from the woman the cage had hit! She had written me the kindest letter saying, "Please don't feel bad. They gave me a drink and comped my ticket. I know it was an accident!" I found out that the cage had hit her and put a gash in her forehead. I have this horrible feeling that I'll meet a woman with a scar one day and I'll say, "Hi. Did you see *Sweeney Todd*…?"

The next day, I found out that Frank Rich, the *New York Times* critic, had been sitting on the other side of the bannister, equidistant from where the woman was sitting. If the cage had hit the banner the opposite way, it would have hit Frank Rich!

1989: Every Door In New York Flew Open

Eddie Korbich, Actor

Someone played the record of *Sweeney Todd* for me in college, and I was absolutely hooked. I played it non-stop. The next time my parents and I went on a trip to New York, I wanted to see it so badly. I remember that my mom really wanted to see *Sugar Babies*, and when we were walking into the Uris Theatre, she saw Ann Miller jump out of a limousine in a green jumpsuit across the street at the Mark Hellinger and I felt really bad that I talked them into *Sweeney*.

But we all loved it! We saw Dorothy Loudon, George Hearn, and Ken Jennings. We sat in the mezzanine, and I remember feeling so overwhelmed. I said to my family, "Someday I want to play Tobias. Someday someday someday." I thought Ken Jennings was incredible.

When I finally moved to New York, I lived in Astoria and all I did was audition. One day, my roommate Monica told me: "They're doing *A Little Night Music* at Bergen Community College in NJ and you should audition." I wasn't right for Henrik, but I played the cello so I figured: *Why not?* And I knew that they were doing the show six months later at Equity Library Theatre.

That doesn't exist anymore, but it was a magnificent venue to perform at. It was at 103rd and Riverside, and the shows were an amazing showcase for actors, designers, directors, everyone—and everybody in New York

146

came! You didn't get paid; you got $5 a day for a subway token and a sandwich. After the two weeks were over, you got a list of everyone in the industry who came.

So I went in for both the Bergen Community College production of *Night Music,* and later, the Equity Library one. I ended up getting both! I used my time at Bergen to really perfect my cello playing and it was one of those times where I felt I had a plan to advance my career, that if I got completely familiar with Henrik in this production I could hopefully nail the audition for the New York production, and I felt amazing when it worked out. The Equity Library show was a sellout. Sondheim came to see it, and then we heard the production was going to move off- Broadway! Unfortunately, they denied us the rights because there was a possible Broadway production in the works, and that was it.

Susan Schulman, the director, later did *Sweeney Todd* at the York Theatre. We loved working together, so she called me to come in. I got Tobias. And then we moved to Broadway.

It felt like every single door in New York flew open for me at that moment. That was it. Doors that had been closed before opened. That was 1989.

I remember opening night on Broadway. At the party, I was thanking Sondheim and shaking his hand, and calling him Sir. He shook his head at me and laughed and said, "Eddie, what's all this 'Sir' stuff? Call me Steve."

And there I was, playing Tobias in *Sweeney Todd*, in the theater right next to where I'd seen it.

1989: My First Broadway Show

Christian Borle, Actor

The first Broadway show I saw was the *Sweeney Todd* revival at Circle in the Square. It was so exciting. *Sweeney Todd* was my favorite musical of all time before I even saw it.

When I was in middle school, I had an amazing teacher named Timothy, who gave us quizzes every week on different musicals. We watched *Sweeney Todd* in his class, and that's when I really started to get the theatre bug. He was one of the most influential teachers I ever had, and he was also the first person I ever knew who died of AIDS.

Because of him, I was obsessed with *Sweeney Todd* all throughout middle school and high school, and then I actually got to see it live on Broadway. The production was amazing and it was horrifying.

I had watched the show on videotape many times, so I noticed all the things in this production that were different. I saw the Judge's "Johanna" verse for the first time, and for that scene, he was on a rotating platform and the entire cast was sitting around it. Every time he whipped himself, they clapped to signify a whipping sound. It was very effective.

I also remember that I was sitting under a speaker, so every time they did the factory whistle, even though I knew when it was coming because I knew the score backwards and forwards, I leapt out of my seat. At intermission, I asked if they had any novelty razors that squirted blood and of course they said no. That was my first whirlwind New York adventure.

1995: The Exotic Cousin

Laura Linney, Actor

I loved Circle in the Square. I loved that theater. A lot of people didn't. It had a bad reputation when I worked there, because people thought the theater was like a basketball court. It's in the round, but elongated, so the auditorium is the shape of a long pill. I thought that worked really well for our production of *Holiday*. And I went to college with a theatre in the round so I was used to playing those sorts of diagonals.

I just loved the history of the place. I loved that Colleen Dewhurst had worked there a lot! Josie Abady was the co-artistic director when I worked at Circle in the Square, and she was wonderful. I enjoyed coming to work there every day. One funny thing was that my dressing room had cigarette burns everywhere: on the tables, in the shower. I guess whoever I inherited my dressing room from was a big smoker!

Broadway rarely closes, and we had enormous blizzards during the run of *Holiday*. I have memories of getting out of the subway and trying to make my way to Circle in the Square in four feet of snow. I had a conversation with the box office treasurer during that time that totally changed the way I look at a theatre schedule. We had performances on Christmas Eve and Christmas and I went to him and asked, "Is anyone really coming? Does anyone go to the theatre on Christmas?" And he told me, "Yes, and let me tell you something. Most of them are single seats. We are two-thirds full for both performances, in single seats." I never feel bad about performing on a holiday now. I look at it very differently.

Broadway is interesting geographically, because there's a whole different culture when you're in a show on 45th Street, with all of those theaters and show folk grouped together. Then there's a different feel if you're working in a theater "on the wrong side of the street."[55] But no matter what the theater's reputation, each theater has a different history and that's what makes working on Broadway exciting. There are even newer theaters that are building up their own history, and you get to be part of their beginning.

Circle in the Square is sort of like your exotic cousin that people don't know how to talk to, but once you figure it out, you discover he's really great. Some directors just don't know how to use it well. It takes a particular type of director to know how to use a unique space like that, and also material that lends itself to the round. Of course, it's a different experience for actors too, to be completely surrounded by the audience. There's a certain psychology that comes with having a back wall, where you feel less exposed. Circle in the Square is exhilarating. When you're up there, you're up there. There's nothing protecting you. Ironically, there's also no stage door at Circle in the Square, so you have to go out the front! Sometimes, you might feel shame and want to sneak out the back, but at Circle, you have to show your face because the front door is also the back door.

I love that Circle in the Square is more appreciated now. I was so scared for a while that they would knock it down, or something would happen to it. It comes and goes as far as popularity, but it's such a great theater. I'm so happy for it when there are good shows going in, like I know there are now.

1996: Hanging Out With Al Pacino

David Gallo, Scenic Designer

The first show I designed on Broadway was *Hughie* at Circle in the Square. *Hughie* was the first of a series of one act plays that Eugene O'Neill was working on when he died. They were all meant to be explorations of a character describing a deceased person. Only *Hughie* was completed.

---

[55] Widespread in the theatre community is the theory that the theaters on the East Side of Broadway—the Stephen Sondheim, the Belasco, the Lyceum, and Cort—are at a disadvantage because of their location.

The play took place in a flea-bag hotel in Times Square in 1927. Al Pacino played the lead role, a man who stumbles into his hotel after a four-day drinking binge and describes the previous night clerk at the hotel to the new night clerk, played by Paul Benedict.

Hughie was the perfect debut for me. As well as starring in the play, Al Pacino directed it, and it was his theatre directing debut. I was Al's guy, so even though I was a young designer, I was able to get things done by telling the grizzled old stagehands, "Al wants this, Al wants that," and they responded to that pretty well. It was a good collaboration artistically as well. It was basically me and Al Pacino hanging out for hours talking, walking around Times Square, exploring cheap Hell's Kitchen hotels, things like that. The creation was deeply personal, and he got to look at it as both the character and as the director while I slowly added the environment and visuals.

Initially, it took forever to get the job. I went to four or five what I guess you would call interviews with Al, but each quickly turned into a design meeting. We designed the show specifically for Circle, and I remember the reviews said that the show dealt with the space better than it had been dealt with in the past.

We removed one of the seating sections. The theater is perma-round now, but back then, you could only take out one end and have this ludicrously long thrust. You had two options: panorama window or thrust. We were creating an environment for one guy, and he had to be able to negotiate that space—and it's also a play with a single entrance. And no exit. A guy stumbles onstage drunk at the top of the show and then no one ever leaves, although the character talks about leaving for the entire 55-minute play. It's a challenge for a designer, because you have to have an entrance and imply a distinctive exit, and with the layout the play used, Circle in the Square only had one vomitorium. Don Holder, our lighting designer, did amazing work.

Hughie *was Circle in the Square theatre company's second-to-last show in its Broadway home, before* Stanley *became the last in 1997. In the late 1990s, at risk of going bankrupt, Circle scrambled to infuse the company with new life by gambling on new leaders, Josephine Abady and Gregory Mosher. Abady had a two-season run as co-artistic director before she was forced to resign. Having previously overseen a successful overhaul at Lincoln Center, Mosher attempted to change Circle's non-profit system from a policy where subscribers would purchase the season's four shows at once to a policy where members would pay a yearly fee in exchange for priority to attend the shows they'd like, at a member price.[56] This plan was not financially successful quickly enough, and Circle in the Square theatre company folded.*

The theater lay dark for almost two years before its first commercial production, Not About Nightingales, *opened in 1999. The show notably embraced the space, and critics proclaimed that the production "solved" some of the theater's previous problems. In the meantime, Circle in the Square almost became the Broadway home of another not-for-profit company: Manhattan Theatre Club. MTC considered this move but wound up choosing to breathe life back into the Biltmore Theatre instead. Following the* Not About Nightingales *rental, from September to December of 1999, Circle in the Square was used to film* The Chris Rock Show. *Briefly, from the mid to late 1990s, all of the historic photos and posters from past productions were taken down from the Circle in the Square lobby, with management supposing they could not get a current hit if the theater was seen as focused on the past.*

When the house was moving from not-for-profit ownership to becoming a Broadway theater for rent by any commercial production, there was a chance the theater could be scooped up to become a television studio—luckily, this foray into television with The Chris Rock Show *was short-lived.* True West *and then* The Rocky Horror Show *took over the space, showing how legit commercial productions could make the unique theatre*

---

56 Evans, Greg. "Mosher/Square Deal To Reinvent Circle?" *Variety.* 9 Sep. 1996. Retrieved from The Entertainment Industry Magazine Archive.

space come to life. From that point forward, Circle has continuously been a coveted Broadway space for smaller shows with immersive concepts.

———————

2000: The Floor Show

Tom Hewitt, Actor

Very early on in *The Rocky Horror Show*, we had to figure out how to deal with audience participation. People were very enthusiastic, and they wanted to participate in the same way that they did with the film.

For instance, when Dr. Scott—played by Lea DeLaria—makes his entrance, during the movie, you traditionally throw toilet paper. A couple weeks into the run, there was a performance where Lea entered and the stage was festooned with rolls and rolls and rolls of toilet paper. Toilet paper as far as the eye could see. The stage was WHITE.

It became clear that we were going to have to deal with this because we couldn't do any of the planned set changes or choreography with that amount of toilet paper. The cast started picking it up and throwing it back to the audience, which just created a whole other level of chaos. Rolls were thrown back and forth and it got out of hand. We actually had to stop the show and kind of deal with it. Then, the audience caught on that it had to be cleaned up in order to go on with the show.

It was shortly after that performance that participation chips began being sold. A participation chip meant that you got a paper bag containing confetti, a boa, a flashlight, and some toilet paper to throw.

Funnily enough, audience members didn't really interact with me; the character of Frank 'N' Furter sort of commands a certain amount of respect. The situation was more problematic for Jarrod Emick and Alice Ripley. During "Over at the Frankenstein Place", the audience had squirt guns inches from their faces. They were sometimes unexpectedly doused with water while they were singing.

The audience reactions to *Rocky Horror* would also change seasonally. They were different during the holidays. When I got a Tony Award nomination, there were definitely Tony references yelled at me, mostly about how I was going to lose to Nathan Lane for *The Producers*. It was hysterical. Then when Luke Perry came into the show, the audience would yell *90210* references.

I loved the proximity of the audience, and how they could also see each other. That was part of the fun of the show. I think my favorite moment was the few measures before my entrance in "Sweet Transvestite", especially early on in the run, because people didn't know where I was coming from! That music would start and they knew my character was about to enter, but they were all in anticipation, not knowing from where. Then, a giant chandelier lowered from the ceiling. That just tickled the pants off of me! The anticipation of the audience was delightful; it was a great, fun feeling in the theater. It had nothing to do with me; it was built into the show.

The Rocky Horror Show was my first experience backstage of being separated from people. I got the big part, so I got a relatively big dressing room. It was on the bottom floor, next to the stage management office, and it was actually two dressing rooms put together. I loved it because it soon became a quick-change room for other people, and my door was always open so people stopped by a lot. It was awesome to have constant visitors. Joan Jett had a fast change in my dressing room, and we'd always chat. That was the best.

The most exciting person who came to the show, for me, was Lily Tomlin. I just adored her when I was a kid. One of my survival tactics for not getting beaten up was being able to do imitations of Ernestine and Edith Ann, two of her characters from *Laugh-In*. I could really do impeccable Lily Tomlin imitations as a kid! People would ask me to do them. It was one of my first "performing" things. Anyway, she was doing *The Search for Signs of*

Intelligent Life in the Universe at the same time as we were doing *Rocky Horror*, so I got to be on Broadway at the same time as Lily Tomlin. I would run into her at award events and each time, she would say to me, "Hello, Tom Hewitt." She would say my full name every time I saw her.

2000: The Pantless Man

Fritz Frizsell, Stagehand

The first day Tom Hewitt showed up at Circle in the Square for *Rocky Horror*, he introduced himself. I said "Actually, Mr. Hewitt, we've worked together before." He looked at me a little quizzically, and I clarified: "*Pericles*, on The Acting Company tour in the early 80s." He looked at me in mock dismay, and responded "Oh, no, my dear! We are both of us far too young to have *ever* done such a thing!"

One day during production, B.H. Barry, the renowned fight director, was teaching a sword-fighting class in the lobby. Several stagehands had to pass through, and an impromptu battle broke out, the students with their swords, the stagehands with crescent wrenches and whatever other tools they had handy. Everyone ended up on the floor in hysterics, B.H. laughing hardest of all.

Dick Cavett, the narrator for *Rocky Horror*, always started act two with a monologue, and his usual opening joke was the story of how excited he was when he got the call for *Rocky Horror*. He went on to describe how disappointed he was that it wasn't for the part of Frank 'N' Furter—because, he said, "I have the legs for it."

One night, at that point, a man in the audience shouted "Yeah? Let's see 'em!"

"What, you want me to drop my pants? I will if you will," Cavett replied. And the man, who was in the first row, stood up and dropped his pants. Of course, both follow spots went straight to the pantless man, leaving Cavett in the dark. The stage managers gave the follow spot operators a lot of leeway in that show, but they weren't too thrilled with us that night.

2000: Sacred Space

Raúl Esparza, Actor

The first Broadway show I ever saw was *Broadway Bound* at the Broadhust, and the first Broadway musical I ever saw was *Into The Woods* at the Martin Beck, which is now the Hirschfeld. I guess you know you're getting older when you call the theaters by their old names. I sentimentally call the Neil Simon the Alvin all the time, just because that's what the characters call it in *Merrily We Roll Along*.

I'm from Miami and during my senior year of high school, I had come to visit some friends at Columbia University, where I'd applied. I wanted to see *Les Mis*, but it was sold out, so I ended up seeing *Broadway Bound*. I remember thinking how small the Broadhurst seemed to me, after being used to giant touring houses in Florida. I also remember Elizabeth Franz, who was spellbinding. Jonathan Silverman was in that show, and later on we did an episode of *Law & Order* together, so I got to tell him, "You were in the very first Broadway show I saw! You inspired me!"

When people say that to me now, I feel two things: I feel old, and I feel incredibly lucky to be part of that line. That's something you really feel in the theatre, that strong sense of passing things down from generation to generation. You don't feel that with film and television work, unless maybe you're on a legendary soundstage, like the old Warner Brothers lot where you can say, "Wow, this is where they shot *Casablanca*!" The theatre has

151

a whole different sense of energy, because wherever you go, you know: *Look at what used to be done here, look what I'm a part of!*

I've always felt a little like theatre is a religious event. There's a sacred space between the actors and a sacred space between the audience and the actors. And what's sacred isn't the stage or the house; it's the space between people and the energy that lives there. The theatre is a conversation. I can come up with a performance in my living room, but it doesn't matter if it doesn't bounce off other people. These theaters are the places where, for a century, conversations have happened.

In theatre, you are engaging with audience members who are right in front of you, and you feel them. Whether it's a show like *Rocky Horror Show* where they are responding vocally and physically, or a show where they're quietly listening, there's a human connection happening. And you can meet that person afterward at the stage door. You can see them walking down the block. Theatre is unlike anything else for that reason—and Broadway is that, plus it's this incredible conglomeration of multiple spaces that house so much human energy every single night. You know that within ten or so blocks, so many people are having the same experience at the same time. The buildings seem to have a history of their own that the walls hang onto. I think each theater feels haunted—in a good way—by the shows that came before.

During *Rocky Horror Show*, Jarrod Emick said to me, "If you want to get psyched and remember why you're here, walk through Shubert Alley every day on your way to work." I did, and every day, I would see those posters of which shows were happening simultaneously with ours. I'd see people going to every show on Broadway, audience members and theatre folks. I was in some way part of all of that, even though I wasn't in all of those shows. Every night I would remember that I was in a part of town where theatre had been done for over a century—that's a lot to live up to! And while there are walls dividing us, every night at 8:05, all the curtains go up and all of these different stories are happening at once. Right now, where we are, I can see *Phantom of the Opera* and *Bullets Over Broadway* and *Mamma Mia!* and *Matilda*—and tonight, they'll all happen, within a few feet of each other. There's an almost carnival atmosphere to it.

The Rocky Horror Show was the first show I performed in on Broadway. The director, Christopher Ashley, said that part of the reason they hired me is because I sounded the most like Janis Joplin at the audition! Doing that voice eight times a week was insane. So while I was doing *Rocky Horror Show*, I really had to scream-sing or not sing at all. There was no middle voice available to me.

One day, between shows, I almost got into a fight with a guy at Starbucks. I hadn't taken off my makeup, and I had this fake eye. A middle-aged man was so upset by my appearance that he told me I looked like a freak. I would've punched him if my friend hadn't stopped me. People react very strongly to makeup. A similar thing happened when I was doing *Cabaret* at Studio 54, but this time it was to Katrina Yaukey, who went to the grocery store between shows. She had bruises and track marks on her arms—drawn with makeup—and the cashier leaned over and whispered to her, "Girl, you'd better cut back!"

At first, I was scared of the show. I didn't understand the whole transvestite thing. I had seen *Rocky Horror* in Miami, and it frightened me—then, after I got into it, I completely fell in love with it. Now, I've done many shows where I've had to cross dress, and it doesn't faze me. I learned—first from *Rocky Horror*—that cross dressing onstage is all about power: sexual power and also the power you get from playing with audience expectations about gender. You don't know how that's going to play on Broadway. But the uglier and more exposed you are, the more power you have over the audience. It can make you feel incredibly strong onstage. *Rocky Horror* is such a fun, sweet show, but you do have to have that undercurrent of the dark side of power.

Our costume designer, David C. Woolard, had the idea that my character, Riff Raff, was unfinished, physically. He was conceived as an incredibly sexual alien robot, so there were little holes in my costume. My nails were painted silver, and then the polish continued up my hands, so it looked like half my hand was metal. I had my navel pierced at the time, and I stuck a safety pin through it. Both of those things were probably a bad idea! I also played around with staining my teeth with blood. Jarrod always quotes me about that, saying, "Yeah, I tried that—it tasted like shit and it didn't land."

David also gave me assless chaps as part of my costume, but I had to wear underwear with them. Sometimes I would do "naked" performances where I would go out there without the underwear and be like: *Screw it, I'm making the audience see everything they're supposed to see!* We also did one naked rehearsal, an understudy put-in, where everybody took their clothes off. The whole cast rehearsed in their underwear, and I played the role of naked audience member who sat there and was offended. I was butt naked, sitting there muttering, "This is terrible, all these kids! This is the worst thing ever!" There's a picture somewhere of me walking out of the house, naked, shaking my head, while the rest of the cast is performing onstage, and you can see one of our dressers doubled over with laughter in the background.

The backstage at Circle in the Square doesn't really feel like a theater; there's an industrial, almost jail-like quality to it. Plus, you're underground so there's no fresh air or light. It has a fortress-like quality, which can get to you. But there's a lot to love about it, too. It's such an intimate theater, like the ones I was used to performing in regionally. 700 seats feels manageable: the last row is only a few feet away. You can really connect to the audience. For *Rocky Horror*, it was perfect. I was also surprised by how malleable the theater is! Every time I've seen a show there since, the space has changed. Our designer, David Rockwell, went all-out and put mannequin body parts and red fabric on the walls, creating this old movie theater atmosphere. Circle in the Square may not have the grandeur and beauty that other Broadway houses have, but there are things about it that are great—it can be a very transformative, exciting black box.

I'll never forget *Rocky Horror*'s final dress. It was one of the most exciting performances I've ever been a part of. It was less than a week before my 30th birthday, and I was feeling pretty buzzy that I was about to make my Broadway debut, and I didn't know how it would go. Rehearsals were very different from other shows I'd worked on, and I was really nervous.

The people in that cast are among the finest people I've ever worked with. Lea DeLaria and I did *Broadway on Broadway*[57] together before we'd even started rehearsals, so she heard me sing before anyone else did. When I performed "Time Warp" for the first time in rehearsal, the whole cast jumped up, and Lea was like, "What did I tell you?! Who IS this guy?!" The whole cast was so supportive of it being my Broadway debut, and going into that dress rehearsal, I just really wanted to show everyone what I could do.

We hit the stage for our final dress rehearsal, and nobody really knew what to expect. We had been directed to perform the show like it was a train that just would not stop at the station, so the audience couldn't jump in. They had all brought their props like they were going to see the movie version, and they were going to participate! There was toast flung, and toilet paper thrown, and all of these things that eventually were banned, because they were unsafe! The people at our dress rehearsal were total die-hard fans—they were dressed up, and they were going crazy for us.

Jerry Mitchell gave me the best first entrance any actor could ever hope for. During "Over At The Frankenstein Place", I rose up through the middle of the cast, singing. Our musical director had created an obbligato line[58] that wasn't in the score, for Riff Raff to hit a high B, and that was the moment when the whole set collapsed on itself—the proscenium smashed, the floor started to turn, and flood lights blinded the audience. The audience lost their minds! They started screaming like they were at a rock concert. I thought: *Holy shit*—this *is Broadway?!* Then, I got to do "Time Warp", and that blew the roof off the place even more. That dress rehearsal was the first time I performed on Broadway, and it was unforgettable.

––––––––––

[57] *Broadway on Broadway*: a free concert in the center of Times Square featuring Broadway shows
[58] obbligato line: in musical theatre, is often used to mean a vocally dramatic, optional or added part of a song

153

When I was writing The Untold Stories of Broadway, Volume 1, *I was thrilled to land an interview with Broadway actor Raúl Esparza. Not only had I loved Raúl's voice on cast recordings for over a decade (*The Rocky Horror Show*!* tick, tick... BOOM! *Taboo!), I had seen him give mind-blowing performances (*Company*! The Homecoming! Speed-the-Plow*!)—and also meaningful interviews where he spoke about the Broadway theaters themselves. I couldn't wait to ask some questions of this brilliant mind. The day of our interview, we were supposed to meet at Sardi's at 3pm. Raúl only had half an hour for the interview, as he was in the midst of a hectic shooting schedule.*

It was pouring rain, so I arrived a bit early, giving myself time to dry off my sopping wet clothes and shoes. One of the popular, stalwart bartenders on Sardi's second floor, Jeremy Wagner, kept me company while I squeezed rain out of my hair and waited for Mr. Esparza—for an hour. Due to some crossed lines of communication, he thought the interview was on another day altogether. When that day arrived a week later, he was called in to shoot Law & Order, *and after that, my first book was due—sans Raúl Esparza insights. I was disappointed.*

For book two, I was determined to make the long-awaited Esparza interview happen. Almost a year later, we set a time and place to try again: Sardi's, of course, this time at noon. I walked down sunny 44th Street on a June afternoon, and as my hand went to open the famed large wooden door, I noticed a sign: Closed For Private Party. I thought: Oh GOD. What if Raúl Esparza only wants to do the interview at Sardi's? What if—

Mid-thought, there he was, walking up 44th Street toward me, on a block where actors have met journalists for over a century. Raúl Esparza gave the sign a glance and said, "Should we go to Angus McIndoe instead?" We walked to the theatre haunt a few doors down, and it was uncharacteristically empty. We sat by the open windows in the quiet restaurant, with the light of the sun and the lights of the Majestic and the St. James streaming in.

tick, tick... BOOM! *was starting performances at Encores! during the upcoming week, and before the interview even started, we began chattering about it. Raúl was seeing the dress rehearsal and had spoken with the new company about his time in the original cast; I was putting together a concert of unknown Jonathan Larson work that would take place prior to a performance. He told me about his favorite song that was cut during previews—I told him it would get its first public performance since those previews, in the concert! The whole exchange, which couldn't have taken place a year earlier, opened up the conversation and lent the proceeding interview a congenial sense of being on the same wavelength.*

We spoke for an hour and a half, and it was one of my favorite conversations about theatre I've ever had. "I really enjoyed this," he said, as we stood on 44th Street, and I could tell that this legendary actor, who has done hundreds of interviews, meant it. He is truly one of the sharpest minds, one of the most gifted artists, and one of the most nerdy theatre geeks, of our time. I walked past Sardi's and it wasn't raining at all.

2001: September 11th And December 31st

Liz Larsen, Actor

Because of September 11th, *The Rocky Horror Show* was forced to close down. But our producer, Jordan Roth, wanted to open it again. A lot of shows at that time tried to forge through and reopen.

In the hiatus, Alice Ripley had gotten another job, so her cover, Kristen Lee Kelly—who had been playing Columbia—moved into her role. They needed to get a new Columbia quickly so that they could get the show back up. At one point, I had done three shows with Chris Ashley, the director, in one year. And one of my dear friends, Terry Mann, had replaced as Frank 'N' Furter about a month before the show closed down. So, Terry apparently said to Chris, "Just call her. Don't even audition her—I think you should really just call her." Chris said he would, so Terry gave me a heads up on a Friday afternoon. I didn't believe him. On Monday morning, I got a call. It was a great offer. I couldn't believe it. Terry and Charlotte d'Amboise, his wife, are my guardian angels and my best friends. They have been for so long. They facilitate so much happiness and so many good, creative opportunities in my life. That's what's wonderful about having best friends in the theatre, who are also like family.

We had a unique schedule with a 5pm and a 9:45pm show every Saturday and then a 1:30pm matinee on Sunday. New Year's Eve fell on a Saturday, and Terry and I were furious, because nobody in the cast showed up. Some people had an attitude about it: *I'm not going to Times Square on New Year's Eve to do that crazy show and then try to get home after midnight!* But Terry and I are professionals, so of course we showed up. All of the understudies were on, and we had to cut a couple of tracks. At one point, I was at the edge of the stage and a woman reached out and grabbed a chunk of my hair! I had this crazy, spiked, pink-orange hairdo. She leaned over to her friend and said, "See, I told you it was real!" I think she was tripping. I told the stage managers what happened, but before they could get to her, she started crawling around on the floor. It was anarchy!

There was a lot that was crazy, but I truly think I have never loved a cast like I loved the people in that show. I got to work with Terry, my best friend. Daphne Rubin-Vega is like nobody else; she is so soulful and beautiful. And Matt Morrison! He had originally been hired to play Rocky, but decided to pursue this boy band thing. When that didn't pan out, he came back and was in the chorus. And then we got to do *Hairspray* together later. He played Link Larkin, and the rest is history! But during *Rocky Horror*, I'll always remember him being the sweetest, nicest gentleman to me and to everybody. I was this mom with kids and there I was having scenes where I had to hump him onstage. And he was so respectful! He's just a great guy.

After The Rocky Horror Show, *an innovative play called* Metamorphoses *was next on the Circle in the Square stage. Adapted from the classic Roman poetry of Ovid which retold Greek myths,* Metamorphoses *set each story in an onstage pool. Creator Mary Zimmerman premiered the work at Northwestern University in 1996. In fact, when it got to Broadway in 2002, some of the student actors who had been with the play since the beginning were still its stars.*

The nine myths retold in the show were thousands of years old, and yet they resounded wholly in a modern New York that was still reeling from September 11, 2001. The larger-than-life themes of death, love, chaos, survival, and tragedy proved themselves timeless. When Orpheus bargained with the Gods to try to bring his bride Eurydice back from the dead, or when Zeus and Hermes granted a mortal couple's wish to die at the same time, audience members could be heard sobbing.

The 27-foot wide pool at the center of the production served as a metaphor for natural disaster, for primal love, and for eternity. Zimmerman brought intellectual and academic subject matter to life in a production that was broad and full of overly physical elements, including the water that would splash all over the first few rows of the audience. And although the staging was modern, the audience layout gave the feel of classic Greek and Roman theatre, marrying the new to the old.

2004: Commercial Audience

Bernie Telsey, Casting Director

We did *Frozen* at our theater at MCC, and it was wonderful. We got the reviews to move it uptown to Circle in the Square, so we made that happen. Even though we had the reviews, all of a sudden there's a challenge to get 600 people into your show each night as opposed to 200.

Frozen was such a dark story that it was a challenge to find an audience. Getting the show up wasn't a challenge, but it was hard to find an audience quickly without a lot of marketing dollars. The show was great, but I don't think we ever found its commercial audience.

2005: T-H-A-N-K-S, Wendy Wasserstein

Sarah Saltzberg, Actor/Writer

My best friend Kelly had this best friend from high school, Michael, who was Wendy Wasserstein's assistant. I always told them, "I need to work for her! I will do anything. I just want to be around her because she's so talented." At one point, she needed a weekend nanny, and I took that spot. Her daughter, Lucy Jane, was two at the time. I remember that the first weekend I was there, I was making eggs and toast and Wendy told me, "You're such a great cook!" And I thought: *Oh my God! It's just eggs and toast!* But she was so amazing, and she never cooked.

I had been working for Wendy for a little while when I started working on this theatre piece downtown called *C-R-E-P-U-S-C-U-L-E.* We did a performance of it and got some great reactions. So we decided to mount it again, and this time we kind of actively pursued a couple young producers and backers[59] and invited them. I got pretty aggressive about calling and emailing, and a bunch of them came to see the show—but it didn't work out. I also invited Wendy, and she came to see the show, all the way on the Lower East Side, with her niece, Pamela, and Pamela's boyfriend. There was no fourth wall,[60] and I remember watching her and not being able to tell if she was having a good time or a terrible time! There was some original music in the show at that point, but there was also some recorded music, and we ended the show with "Luck Be A Lady". After the show ended, I hugged Wendy and told her how much it meant to me that she came, and she said, "The show is so great! But you cannot end it with "Luck Be A Lady". And I really think you should call my friend Bill Finn."

I didn't grow up on musicals, but I knew who he was, of course. I said, "Do you really think he would be interested in working on this show?" And she replied, "Well, I don't know if he would be interested in doing it, but he works at NYU, so if nothing else, he could recommend somebody that might be interested in writing the full score."

So we met with Bill Finn. We had made a tape of *C-R-E-P-U-S-C-U-L-E*, so we showed it to him. He fell asleep during the screening of the tape. And at the end of it, he woke up, looked at us, and said, "I know exactly what this is about. I'm going to start writing these songs now."

We were nobodies. We were just putting on a show to do a good show and have some fun. Then Bill got involved and suddenly we had some real fire power behind us. I think he really identified with the characters. I think he kind of missed them. And suddenly, he brought Rachel Sheinkin in to write the book. We had sort of been doing an improv show, within a structure, and she really made it into the book of a musical. We had created the show when spelling bees were first becoming more popular to watch on TV, and serendipitously, they were getting even more popular. Jay Reiss had written most of the sentences and definitions, and Dan Fogler and I helped with some of them—but that's why Jay has the additional material credit.

When we did the show that was really *The 25th Annual Putnam County Spelling Bee* for the first time, at Barrington, I remember seeing a five-year-old sitting on the lap of his grandma, and they were both laughing hysterically at the same thing, but probably for different reasons. That's when I knew the show was going to be successful.

Fast forward to the green room at Second Stage and David Stone, who had been involved since Barrington, telling us, "We're moving the show to Broadway." Nobody said anything at first. We were all dumbfounded. He looked confused, and then said, "Hmmm, I thought you guys would be a little more excited?" And that's when we all burst into tears at the same time; everyone in the green room was just sobbing. It was 7:27 before an

---

[59] backers: another term for investors in a production
[60] fourth wall: the imaginary wall that separates the stage action from the audience

8pm show, and everyone was a mess. I think we started the show late that night. Dan and Jay and I had been working on the show for so many years at that point. I remember when the show was downtown, Jay had turned down a writing job on some TV show like *Dawson's Creek* in order to stay with the production. His manager was furious at him, but he said, "I just feel like there's something that's going to happen with this show and I have to stick with it." I realize now that if he had left to go do that writing gig, *C-R-E-P-U-S-C-U-L-E* wouldn't have happened. It wouldn't have moved on.

And then we were so fortunate to have the rest of the cast come on board and be so creative and willing to play, in the spirit of the show. There wasn't a bad one in the bunch, and these are my greatest friends now. It was such a magical time. I went out for drinks with Carmel Dean and Jay a couple weeks ago, and Carmel was like, "God, I think about that time now, having had other experiences in the theatre, and truly nothing will ever come close in so many ways to that time that we had." It's so true. We had an amazing time together. And it wasn't just how much we loved our show and each other—it was also how we felt every night to look in the house and be bringing such joy to people.

2005: We Grew Up Undeniably

Celia Keenan-Bolger, Actor

If you had told me when I was performing in a cafeteria in the Berkshires that *The 25th Annual Putnam County Spelling Bee* would move to Broadway, I would have laughed in your face. I never thought that could ever happen. But there was *something* about the show. People loved it.

Then all of a sudden the show was moving to Second Stage, and we were going to get to work with James Lapine! This was James Lapine who I had been so obsessed with, James Lapine who created *Sunday in the Park with George*, James Lapine who I read about in books. And at Second Stage, I thought the same thing: *People really* love *this show.*

I remember the day that David Stone, our producer, gathered us in the Second Stage green room. He said, "I want to give you the rundown of what's going to happen. We're going to extend until February here. We're going to take a hiatus. We're going to get the set ready for Circle in the Square. And then we're going to open on Broadway in April."

It was silent. Nobody said anything.

David said, "I thought you guys would be happy about this?" And we all started screaming and sobbing at once. We were just shocked—genuinely shocked.

Now I'm older, and I feel like when I work on shows, everyone is thinking: *What's the story? What's the enhancement money*[61] *doing? Are we moving to Broadway?* None of that was part of my trajectory on *Spelling Bee*. It was just pure and ignorant. I ran into another room and called my dad, and yelled, "You can't tell anybody, but *Spelling Bee* is moving to Broadway, Dad!" Sarah Saltzberg and Dan Fogler and Jay Reiss had all created this thing off-off-Broadway that was now on this huge journey, and the next stop was Broadway. They never thought that was possible. I remember so many people crying that day.

On opening night, Bernadette Peters was there. I couldn't believe it. Of course, I had been as obsessed with her for my whole life as I had been with James Lapine. I remember thinking: *In what world do I get to perform and Bernadette Peters is in the audience?! How do I get to do this for my job?!*

---

[61] enhancement money: money given to a not-for-profit production by a commercial producer who is hoping to develop it for its next step

157

2005: Ice-Breaker

Todd Buonopane, Actor

At one point, the cast had just finished a run-through of *Spelling Bee* and James Lapine was not happy. The note session was *very* tense. In the middle of an awkward silence, Jesse Tyler Ferguson suddenly whispered, "Bernadette *said* you'd be like this." The tension was immediately released and everyone laughed.

2005: I Decided I Would Turn It Down

Beowulf Boritt, Scenic Designer

I made my Broadway debut designing the set for *Spelling Bee*. I did the show at Barrington Stage before James Lapine was even attached to it. It was a busy summer for me. My agent at the time, Ron Gwizada, was Bill Finn's agent as well, and he got me an interview with Bill to discuss the show. After the interview, I was offered the job. Then, I read the show and listened to this demo tape of Vadim Feichtner plunking out the tunes. The script was in very rough form, because it was really developing with a lot of improv. And I thought: *This is the stupidest idea for a musical I've ever heard. Adults playing children? Audience interaction?*

I decided I would turn it down. I'm eternally overbooking myself, and I thought: *This is a good choice. The show doesn't pay much, and it's at a summer stock theater. I'm so busy already this summer.* I told my agent I wasn't going to take the show. He was sort of quiet for a minute and then he said, "You know what, Beowulf? You really need to do this show." It was the only time he ever said that to me, and he was right.

After Barrington Stage, James Lapine came on board and some of the team changed. But James interviewed me and hired me for the Second Stage production. We didn't know exactly what would happen, but James was shaping the show and producer David Stone came on board—so there was always this chance we could go to Broadway. I designed the show for Second Stage, keeping that in mind. My set for off-Broadway would have fit into just about any Broadway theater except one.

Lo and behold, *Spelling Bee* got a rave in the *Times*! Almost immediately, we were out there looking at Broadway theaters. We had been hoping for the Music Box, but for some reason, we couldn't get it. Then James called me and said, "They want us to look at Circle in the Square." That was a terrible idea! The set wouldn't fit. I'd have to completely redesign the show.

Then we walked into Circle in the Square and I thought: *Oh my God, this is perfect.* We got the idea of setting the show in a basketball court/auditorium, which wasn't part of the show off-Broadway. But Circle in the Square kind of conjures up ideas of an old gymnasium. I said to our general manager, "You know, this means we can't use any of the old set." And they said, "We know. We have a new budget. You have ten days to redesign the show."

I dropped everything, hired a bunch of assistants, and we cranked out a new design. Since then, I've learned that it's actually not so uncommon. Later, I designed *Chaplin* in ten days too. But it was a roller coaster on *Spelling Bee*. It was my first Broadway show! And because until then I had done a lot of shows on my own in little theaters, rather than working as an assistant to bigger designers, I'd actually never done a Broadway show in any form until I was designing my own. It was a huge learning experience for me, but luckily the whole team was so supportive and really helped me.

At one point in the show, Jesus appears to Marcy Park. Off-Broadway, we had him entering crucified on this giant cross. I thought it was funny—and my Catholic in-laws thought it was the funniest thing they'd ever seen. But I think because it was a show written and directed by a bunch of Jews, they got nervous about having a crucified kid, so we cut that.

So the cross came over to Circle in the Square, and it sat in the lobby all through tech. There's a hilarious photo of the master electrician for Circle in the Square, Stewart Wagner, who is this big tall guy with a beard and long hair, lying on the cross in a loincloth he'd found.

On the whole, the show had the same feel on Broadway as it ever did. We adjusted things because of the shape of the theater, but it just enhanced the audience experience.

2005: "Come On Over, I Need Help With This Next Show"

Carmel Dean, Musical Director/Conductor

My journey to Broadway started at NYU. Bill Finn was one of the adjunct faculty members there, and he came in as a special guest lecturer. I heard that he often used students as assistants on projects, so I went right up to him and told him, "I really love your work. If you ever need anyone, let me know."

He called me right away! He was writing a song that he was submitting to be used by *The Caroline Rhea Show*, which ended up not getting selected because it sounded like a song from *Falsettos*. It was a great song, but just not the song they wanted. But I helped him get the song written out and put together for submission, and I did it very quickly so he was impressed. Because of that, Bill asked me to work on his next project, which was the show *Elegies: A Song Cycle*. He got them to hire me as associate musical director when they did the show at Lincoln Center. It was my first professional gig!

Around that time, I was graduating from NYU and Bill had become like my uncle. He just called me up one day and said, "Come on over, I need help with this next show." He told me the plot and started playing music, all the while asking, "Can you arrange this for six people? Can you do this or that?" It all started just like that, and that's how I got my first job on Broadway, as an associate conductor and vocal arranger, working on *The 25th Annual Putnam County Spelling Bee*.

Like many jobs on Broadway, it was born out of a personal relationship and then just evolved. I never had an interview or auditioned to be part of the show. It happened organically. We did the show out-of-town, and then off-Broadway at Second Stage. I remember the day that our producer, David Stone, called a company meeting in the Second Stage green room. We all had an inkling we might be going to Broadway, because the show was doing well, but we weren't sure.

He sat us down and simply said, "We're going to Broadway." Everyone screamed and screamed! For almost all of us it would be our first Broadway show—including myself, and Vadim Feichtner, the musical director. And most of the team on the show was the same age, all mid-20s, so it was really exciting because we felt it was our time to debut together.

Spelling Bee was so fun to work on. It was such a laugh fest. And it was a blast to have the audience volunteers every night! Our creative team built the show in a way so that it was almost foolproof, no matter what happened. They structured the piece so that there were set moments where Jay Reiss and Lisa Howard could pull the show back to the script. It was a show where we just never felt like: *Oh my God, it's the 8th show of the week.*

We had these "Adult Performances" which basically turned into crazy shit-shows of: *Who can be the most offensive and ridiculous and rude?* But they had funny moments. During the Adult Performances, there was a hilarious moment during the number "Pandemonium". The kids would just throw stuff everywhere, and the vice-principal and Rona would try to control them, and there would be this big build toward the end of: "Life is pande-, pande-, pande-, pandemonium!" And then the song just stopped, everything was quiet... and during the Adult Performances, you'd suddenly hear: *Bzzzzzzzzz*. It would take the audience a moment to realize what was going on, and then they'd just lose it. And that's the moment when Rona would go over, grab her vibrator and put it back in her purse. On Broadway! We were lucky to get to have fun and play around like that.

They had to build a treehouse for me. Vadim was onstage playing the piano, and the reed, cello and percussion players were in front of him. But I was playing synth, and they couldn't fit me onstage. So they built me this floating treehouse above the drums. In the beginning, I had all these fancy ideas of putting a bucket there that I could pulley up and down, to send things to the drummer. That didn't happen, but Jose Llana would climb up and say hi, and the stagehands would throw me things. It was fun!

In Sheffield, Massachusetts, we literally did the show in a cafeteria at the local high school. Then we moved to Second Stage, with a proscenium, and then to Circle in the Square, where we did the show with a thrust stage. The show really evolved to embrace each space. On Broadway, Chip got to walk around and throw his candy, and there were so many moments of audience interaction when people really felt involved because the story was all around them.

Of course, we also turned the lobby at Circle in the Square into what looked like an elementary school hallway. It was great because we didn't compromise the actual space and the history; we didn't knock a wall down or anything. But we took the walls and made them ours with posters and decorations. There was a large picture of me in the 3rd Grade with a gap-toothed smile and lettering that read: *Vote Carmel For Cafeteria Monitor!* So many people buy tickets to a Broadway show without really knowing what they're in for, and this was a way of really telling people what they were going to experience from the moment they walked in the door.

2005: National Spellers, Gin, And Dirty Jokes

Jose Llana, Actor

I'll never forget when the runner-up of the actual National Spelling Bee came to see the show. He was spelling all these words correctly, but we had to get him out so that the show could continue! He was on his 8th word, and we finally made up some weird word so he'd misspell it.

At that moment, the audience turned on us! You could tell they felt: *You shunned this little boy! You made him lose again!* After that, it ended up being the worst audience we ever had.

There was also a time that we had a guest speller who had clearly gone to the bar and had five drinks. He came onstage, and he reeked of gin! He wasn't listening when he was supposed to, and he talked at random times, and just stumbled around. It was very awkward.

There were a lot of great mishaps during *Spelling Bee*. The potential for something silly and stupid to happen was so high. We always just made it part of the show.

The adult nights at *Spelling Bee* actually turned out to be pretty stressful! They were a great thing for a cast of improv actors, but they weren't as fun as we thought they'd be. The audience would come expecting this R-rated thing, and we wouldn't want to disappoint them, so we'd front-load the performance with all these sexual and disgusting in-your-face jokes. Then, after the first 45 minutes, the audience was just exhausted by it. The last half of the show isn't as funny, and at that point, they didn't really care and it seemed slow. They didn't care

160

about Olive or Barfee, they only cared about the next dirty joke. Those shows were a great lesson in comedy writing. They were fun, but that was a problem with them—it was basically like performing a brand-new show, without any rehearsal, and hoping for the best.

2005: *Spelling Bee* Ten Times

Andrew Keenan-Bolger, Actor

I saw *Spelling Bee* ten times. It was my favorite! My sister was in it, so I got to see all these different versions of it. I saw it in a rehearsal studio, I saw it off-Broadway, I saw it on Broadway. Then, I got to be in the show on tour! It was interesting to be there from the genesis of the show, through all these different productions, and then end up getting to play Leaf Coneybear.

Opening night, Circle in the Square had such an electric audience. I think that was my favorite time seeing it. The action between the stage and the audience was so connected—there was so much participation! Opening night with celebrity guest spellers was hilarious.

2005: My Broadway Debut Alongside My Best Friend

Todd Buonopane, Actor

I first saw *Spelling Bee* at Barrington Stage Company because Celia Keenan-Bolger is one of my best friends from college. I thought: *This is something I could be in someday!* At that point, we didn't know it was going anywhere at all. Then, it moved off-Broadway, but they could only afford two understudies: Willis White and Lisa Yuen. Willis and Lisa couldn't conceivably cover all of the characters, so Vadim Feichtner, the musical director, was the cover for Barfee, and if the actor playing vice-principal Panch ever called out, James Lapine was going to go on.

Then, the news came that *Spelling Bee* was transferring to Broadway! I went in for the second male cover track—for Barfee, Coneybear, and Panch—four times. At the same time, I was in the final workshop of *In My Life*, playing God, and that was about to go to Broadway as well. Joe Brooks, who directed and wrote it, wasn't letting us out to audition for anything else. We just weren't allowed. My first three auditions weren't during times when I had rehearsal, but my final callback for *Spelling Bee* and our final Broadway workshop of *In My Life* were—and they were both at Ripley-Grier Studios! The stage manager said to me, "I'll call 'ten minutes' five minutes before your audition, and we'll just hope for the best!"

I walked into the audition room, and there were 25 people there: James Lapine, Bill Finn, Tara Rubin and her associates, every producer of the show. I said hello and then told them: "Just so you know, I'm rehearsing this workshop down the hall. I'm not in a hurry or anything—I just wanted to tell you in case you come looking for me." Then James joked, "You can leave now."

Everyone laughed, and I thought that was hilarious and not terrifying, so I continued. I've heard since then that James likes to scare people a little bit in their auditions to see how they react, so I guess I passed that test. I was pretty happy with how the audition went, but then I sat in the hallway for a while with the three other actors up for the track and thought about what James said. When they let all of us go, I figured I didn't get it. I hadn't gotten in trouble with *In My Life*, so at least there was that.

On lunch break, I went to Macy's to buy something to wear during our workshop presentation. I called Celia and I remember saying to her: "I really think I blew it. I don't think James liked me—oh hold on, I have another call—"

And that's when I found out I got the job. In the middle of Macy's, with Celia on hold. I started bawling my eyes out.

It's one thing to make your Broadway debut, and it's another to make your Broadway debut alongside your best friend. I also felt so lucky to be doing it as an understudy because the whole experience really helped me understand the mechanics of Broadway.

We were one of the last shows to open before the Tony Awards cut-off, and nobody was calling out at the beginning of our run because all of these voters were coming. Dan Fogler as Barfee was our favorite to win the Tony, but one day he got food poisoning. Because of the voters, it was decided that he would go on anyway, but I would sit in the wings in costume, and if he came off stage and tagged me, I would go on. Dan ended up making it through the show, so I didn't make my Broadway debut that night.

Later in the run, on New Year's Eve, we had a 2pm show, but Jesse Tyler Ferguson thought it was a 3pm show. The stage manager couldn't reach him, so I got dressed up as Coneybear. Jesse finally got there at two minutes before show-time, but it was too late for him to go on so he just watched the show from the back. I'm glad I didn't know that at the time, because I would've been even more nervous!

I was happy but scared when I first got the job, but our whole team was amazing and I buckled down and worked my butt off. Since I covered four roles, I had to learn four harmony parts. I'm not one of those people with natural musicianship, so I had to work really hard to get all four harmonies in all of the songs. I ended up being good with all of the parts by a certain point. Though the cast of *Spelling Bee* was brilliant, a lot of them had not been in a musical before—so while everyone tried to sing their part, some people eventually switched, or would get confused. The rule became: When you're on, start at a part, but if you hear a harmony not being sung, sing that. I got really good at jumping around.

It was a unique show to understudy, for sure; I covered all these leading roles. I was lucky in that I looked like Barfee, my sensibility was Coneybear, and when I slicked my hair down and put on glasses I looked like Karl Rove in a way that worked for playing the vice-principal. I fit into the show in the way that they needed me to. Understudying like that forces you to be brave. And someone at the time gave me a great piece of advice. They said: "Your first performance as each character will be good, because you're good. Your fifth performance will be great. You have to forgive yourself for not being great the first time you do it, because you haven't gotten the rehearsal time. Your rehearsal time is in front of a Broadway house." *Spelling Bee* really made me the bravest performer I could be.

Grabbing audience members each night was fun, and the show never got boring. I remember this one time where an audience speller got voted out, and when Mitch Mahoney patted him on the back, a huge puff of dust came off him! When that kind of stuff happens onstage with your fellow actors, you can talk about it backstage or laugh about it, but not with an audience member. There was one performance when Jesse farted on the bleachers, and it was so loud that half of the audience heard it and yelled, "Ewww!"

The Broadway understudy community is so good to each other. Whenever someone popped their cherry with a certain character, we would get them flowers and decorate their dressing room door.

2005: Our Ritual

Sarah Saltzberg, Actor/Writer

I remember walking around Circle in the Square and being told, "This is where the show is going to be." That whole time was like a dream. It happened so quickly, and was so overwhelming and unexpected, but at the same time, I always knew the show was special. People responded to it no matter who they were.

There was a whole process for choosing the audience members who would come onstage and be part of the show. Staff in the lobby would interview people and select who the audience spellers would be, and then there was still 30 minutes before the house opened. So sometimes, the people who were picked would get nervous and go get drinks! We'd be onstage dealing with people who were totally sloshed. And then there was the time I went to grab the hand of the audience member I was in charge of, and I couldn't get a grip on it. In character, I hissed, "Gimme your hand!" Then I looked down, and… she had no thumb.

The original Broadway cast went through such an unbelievable experience together. We'll always be close, because of that. So many of us were making our Broadway debuts, including me, and we all worked to make each other comfortable. I would get really, really nervous about forgetting the words to my song. It was strange, but my ritual, from the first production on, was always staring at the fire extinguisher. I would stare at that part of the set, and sing my song three times before it happened. Derrick Baskin had to do a cross around the same time, and wordlessly, we worked out this thing where he just knew when I was done with the second time through it, and then he would pass. We never discussed it; it just silently became our ritual that we did together. When we got to Broadway, we'd still do it, and we added in slapping hands as he crossed. He did that through the whole run. I think he knew that if he didn't cross in front of me at that time, I would freak out. But we literally have never talked about it, to this day!

Our cast always hung out together in the green room until the 15-minute call, and then we'd go upstairs and get into our costumes. We had so much fun together, but we didn't have a lot of time backstage, since we were mostly onstage for the whole show. So instead of having backstage rituals, we had little games we'd make up while we were onstage at the Bee. Dan and I sat next to each other, and we started saying hello in character, just in the background. That turned into us in a restaurant, with him taking my order. Still in character, he'd say, "Okay! What do you want today?" And I'd be like, "Umm maybe pancakes, and if you have any soy bacon, that would be great." He would pretend to write it on a pad. This was in the middle of the show, but we were doing it like kids would do it, like Barfee and Logainne would do it.

Nobody ever recognized me when I was leaving the theater, because I looked so different than my character, so sometimes I would be in the house after the show and overhear something like, "Why did that girl have two dads?" And I'd hear a parent answer, "Well, some people have two dads, and some people have two moms, and some people have a dad and a mom." That happened more than once. And I remember feeling so excited that we were starting conversations like that.

My character, Logainne, was the most controversial of the characters. Not often, but sometimes people did leave, either during the political speech, or when they realized she had two dads. Since *Spelling Bee* was licensed, I've gotten some letters from people saying things like, "I want to do *Spelling Bee* at my school, but the principal is uncomfortable with the two dads theme. How do you think I should approach this?" And my reaction is always to say that it's the job of the people who educate young people to not just have tolerance but to have respect and admiration for everybody. This is your opportunity to show this alternative family, that has flaws like any other family, and you have the right to do that, if it's a public school. You have the right to start a conversation with your community.

At a master class a couple weeks ago, a woman actually came up to me and told me that she was one of the people who had written to me. They ended up doing the show! It was a school in the south. I asked her, "How did it go?" And she said, "It was great! It was totally great."

2008: Good Old Glory Type Days

Nick Blaemire, Actor/Writer

I wasn't at the first preview of *Glory Days*, which I wrote, because I was performing on Broadway in *Cry-Baby* at the same time.[62] There was one night a week that I could be at a performance of *Glory Days*, because the shows had a slightly different schedule.

After our run in D.C., we had about four days of rehearsal in New York and then moved into a Broadway theater. Looking back at it now, I can't believe we said yes to that crazy situation! I would never change it, but I do remember walking into Circle in the Square and just thinking: *Wow. 680 seats of humans and concrete.*

Despite how stressful it ended up being, I could not imagine a more fun situation. If I could do it for the rest of my life and have to run from one Broadway show I was in to one I had written? Of course I would. That was amazing.

Jesse Vargas, who was orchestrating, was running back and forth from *Saved* at Playwrights Horizons. None of us knew that *Glory Days* was going to happen, and then at the last minute, we got the theater. So we would walk back and forth to our other theaters and talk and make changes in the show. I remember sitting in the audience a lot with James Gardiner while he worked on the book. He had the brunt of the work because he only really had two and a half weeks of previews to do everything he needed to do.

Every night before the show started, the four guys—Steven Booth, Andrew C. Call, Adam Halpin, and Jesse J.P. Johnson—would sing "Good Old Glory Type Days". They always killed it! They were the best singers. They had almost inherent perfect pitch as a group, and there was this amazing vibe they had together, always, from the beginning. James and I loved watching that from the audience every night, at the end of our day of rehearsal.

It was such a great group of people. Even though it was high pressure, every time I was in there, I always felt good—until we found out that we might not open. It's very odd. Some of my *Glory Days* memories feel clouded because of *Godspell*. Since I was there so much longer with *Godspell*, I associate Circle in the Square with that show a lot in my head.

When I was doing *Cry-Baby*, I was living with my friend, Ryan Watkinson, in his aunt's apartment. I remember our *Glory Days* director, Eric Schaeffer, calling me there, and saying, "We're moving. We're gonna move to Broadway. We just have to raise some money. We have to figure it out together." I said, "Alright!" And I started thinking about who I knew. We put together a very long list. Every morning from 7am to noon, I would make calls and write emails to people, and then I'd go to *Cry-Baby* preview rehearsal. I'd go back to calling and emailing whenever I was on a break. Between Eric and me, we raised about $1.3 million in about two weeks. And it was the best pitch in the world: "Hey, friends of my mom, this is your favorite family friend who is getting the opportunity of a lifetime." It wasn't my 7th show. It was this insane once-in-a-lifetime, I'm-23-and-getting-a-chance-for-my-show-to-go-to-Broadway moment.

The producers promised they'd raise the other half: the other $1.3 million—but they couldn't do it. We knew that was going on. Eric was like, "Who else should we call? What do you think we should do?" He was amazing. He is one of the most kind, supportive guys. About a week into previews, one of the producers pulled me

---

[62] Check out *The Untold Stories of Broadway, Volume 1* for more on this story.

outside and said, "Hey, I think we have the last $400,000. Here's the thing: this potential investor wants you to change the age of all of the characters from 18 to 25. He wants the show to take place after college instead of after high school." I said, "What do you mean? But that's not the show." And he told me, "That's our only option. Otherwise we're not going to capitalize and we can be sued." You can get in trouble for going into previews without the full capitalization, and we'd already done that.

I pulled James out of the theater and we had a conversation. We decided that we'd rather close the show than make that change. We were too far into it, and didn't have enough time to change the show that way, even if we'd wanted to. This was literally right before our *New York Times* photo shoot, where we were supposed to be hanging out and having fun outside the theater.

Then Eric came through with more money from an investor, and the father of one of my best friends from college invested a healthy portion of money. Of course, everyone who invested lost everything. He still says he spent more money on me than he did on his daughter's wedding. We got the money, and closed the gap just in time, before we would've had to close in previews. Right after that, Broadway Across America called. They said, "We saw the show, and we really like it. We'll keep it open through the summer, if you can keep it open until a week after opening." We thought: *Amazing! That's going to save us.* And then the producers couldn't keep the show open for more than eight hours after we got our reviews. It was a very big learning experience. Broadway Across America are also the people who brought *Hands on a Hardbody* to Broadway and pushed it through that incredible gauntlet of its first five weeks, because they believed that was the right thing to do, to give the show a chance to be seen. And it is. That was a thing I learned: know who you're trusting with your baby.

We opened *Glory Days* on a Tuesday night, and I had a Wednesday matinee of *Cry-Baby*. So I went home early, and everyone else stayed out and partied until 3am. I got up, went to my matinee, and didn't hear anything from any *Glory Days* people. I had no idea how anyone on the team was reacting to or thinking about the reviews. No one checked in. That day, I had to go to University of Michigan showcase rehearsal because the students were performing "Good Old Glory Type Days" as the closing number with new lyrics that I had written. So I was sitting in their rehearsal at Chelsea Studios when I got a text from James that said, "We're closing. Come to the theater."

It was already the headline on Playbill. I walked to Circle in the Square from Chelsea Studios with people passing me on the street saying, in a snarky voice, "Sorry!" I got to the theater and the cast was sitting in the lobby. They were all stunned and angry. And they were so talented and deserving of more of a chance than that. The producers couldn't look us in the eye. They said, "We'll see you again. You guys are all so talented." I was thinking: *This is not a reading, you jerks.* My hard feelings have faded a lot since then. I was pretty pissed at the time.

We got a call two hours later from the *New York Times*, asking "Do you want to do a blow-up story?" We said, "Maybe in a week!" Then I went back to the Marquis and performed *Cry-Baby* that night.

Everybody was amazing. There was a tremendous outpouring of support and joy and love from the community. Out of the hundreds of emails and phone calls and cards I received, I most remember Matt Cavenaugh's note. I had never met him. He was doing *A Catered Affair*, and he sent me a cigar and a handwritten note. It basically said, "Hey, I don't know you, but I think you're doing a really hard thing and a brave thing, and welcome to the world. Congratulations. I'll be at the next one." I'll never forget that. It was a very complicated time.

2008: An Insider Experience

F. Michael Haynie, Actor

During my senior year of college, my friend Alex Brightman invited me to the final dress rehearsal of *Glory Days*. He was one of the standbys in the show. I remember getting to the lobby and them saying, "You're on the list." The list! There wasn't even a ticket. I felt like part of such an insider experience.

Then I sat there at Circle in the Square watching *Glory Days*, and I lost my mind. It was exactly the kind of show I wanted to do, and could see myself doing. The show starred four young white dudes who were all tenors and sang this modern rock score. I saw four roles I would love to play—and actually could. I grew up wanting to be Ben Vereen, but I knew that wasn't really possible. This was something possible for me.

There's a whole generation of people around my age who were born in the 1980s and saw *Cats* as their first musical. I did. That's cool in one way, but imagine the people whose first musical was one of the few previews of *Glory Days*—or the one real performance. You know what I mean? That's *really* cool. They were the only people who ever saw it.

2009: Three Show Days

Amy Wolk, Merchandise Manager/On Site Educator

I loved working on *The Norman Conquests*. That might've been the greatest show I've ever worked on in my life. I watched it all the time, by choice. We did these three show days: 11:30am, 3pm, and 8pm. Sometimes, that theater feels like a dungeon! You never see the light of day, because the theater is downstairs with no windows—and we really never saw light, because of how many shows we did in one day.

I could've watched *The Norman Conquests* 100 more times. I was sad that it was a limited run, and I was so sad to see it go. I was the only merchandise person who worked it, so I was really their person. Everyone working on the production was so nice. They were all from Britain and thrilled to be there together doing that show they believed in on Broadway. They were just so happy to be there—and everyone loves working on a show like that.

———————————

The Norman Conquests, *an import from the Old Vic Theatre in London, was comprised of three separate plays by Alan Ayckbourn, each taking place in a different area of a house, during one dinner party. With the subtitles "Table Manners," "Round and Round the Garden" and "Living Together," each third of the piece stood on its own, but also filled in gaps from the storylines of the other two. The production was a rare case where Equity allowed an entire British cast to be brought to Broadway intact.*[63] *This choice paid off in the terrific critical and audience reception of the production and also a 2009 Tony Award for Best Revival of a Play.*

———————————

---

[63] American and British Actors' Equity Associations often work together to make equitable exchanges enabling artists from each country to work in the other.

2008: Prepare Ye

Jennifer Ashley Tepper, Theatre Historian/Producer

One extremely hot day in July 2008, director Danny Goldstein came to see *[title of show]*.[64] I had met Danny a couple times before at some concerts and events. We didn't really know each other, but I thought he was very nice, and a good director. It was so cool to me that he was going to make his Broadway debut directing *Godspell*, starring Gavin Creel, at the Barrymore that fall! I'd loved *Godspell* since I saw the national tour in 2001. Since Danny was pals with the *[title of show]* gang, he came backstage at the Lyceum. I told him how much I loved *Godspell* and how much I was looking forward to seeing his production.

Danny mentioned that the 2008 *Godspell* revival would have an SDC[65] observership position.[66] He told me I should apply, that I'd be perfect for it. Susan Blackwell assured him that I came highly recommended. I thanked my lucky stars, dropped everything, and ran straight home to put in my application.

To the left of our *[title of show]* stage door, there was a MetroLight[67] for the upcoming production of *Godspell*. It declared "Prepare Ye" scrawled in bright purple on a white background. My best friend, our *[title of show]* intern, Leah, and I would wave at the *Godspell* sign every day as we exited the stage door, for good luck. When I didn't hear back about the SDC position, I wrote to Danny, and he said they'd picked someone else for the observership.

I was sad. It seemed like a dream, my summer on Broadway with *[title of show]*. While I wasn't naive enough to believe magic would strike twice so rapidly, all I wanted was to bounce around Broadway shows, working and learning and breathing the dusty theater air.

Then, the Barrymore production of *Godspell* was cancelled. Well... "postponed," as we say in the theatre world.

From an August 2008 press release:

> *Composer Schwartz added, "I take comfort in my belief that productions happen when they are supposed to. The cast and creative team was poised to create a terrific production and I have no doubt it will be just that when its time comes."*

> Godspell *is the latest casualty of the new theatre season, which has already seen postponements and/or cancellations of the revival of* Brigadoon, *the Harry Connick Jr. vehicle* Nice Work If You Can Get It, *and the revival of Ntozake Shange's acclaimed play,* For Colored Girls Who Have Considered Suicide When the Rainbow Is Enuf.

> Godspell *had been scheduled to begin previews Sept. 29 at the Ethel Barrymore Theatre with an official opening for Oct. 23. In addition to Creel and [Diana] DeGarmo, the announced cast included Joshua Henry as Judas with Uzo Aduba, Andrew Arrington, Sara Chase, Celisse Henderson, Morgan James, David Josefsberg, Telly Leung, Kyle Post, Dana Steingold, Maria Thayer and Daniel Torres.* [68]

I was devastated for everyone involved with *Godspell*. I couldn't believe it had been cancelled entirely. I was just sad that I wouldn't get to see it.

---

[64] This is not a typo. *[title of show]* is actually the title of the show.
[65] SDC: the Stage Directors and Choreographers Society
[66] observership position: an opportunity for emerging directors and choreographers to observe a master in their field throughout the rehearsal process on a specific project
[67] MetroLight: a poster lit up from behind, usually displayed around methods of transportation, such as in parking garages, subway stations, or bus stops
[68] Gans, Andrew. "Broadway Revival of *Godspell* Postponed." *Playbill*. 19 Aug. 2008. Retrieved from playbill.com.

2011: Unlike Any Other *Godspell*

Ken Davenport, Producer

In my first meeting with Stephen Schwartz and Danny Goldstein, when I said to them, "I want to produce this show," I also said, "I have two conditions."

I knew we needed to have a star—they hadn't planned on having a star in the previous version. And I knew that we needed to be at Circle in the Square. Because to bring *Godspell* to Broadway, it needed to be unique, exceptional—unlike any other *Godspell*.

Luckily, they both loved the idea. And of course, *Godspell* had to be in the most unique theater on Broadway, the only theater in the round!

A year later, *Lombardi* was still playing and we were getting antsy, so I said to Stephen, "Okay. We can think about other theaters." He replied, "No. We belong at Circle in the Square. It's perfect." We waited it out until *Lombardi* closed, and we got the theater.

We wanted to make Circle in the Square part of *Godspell*, and *Godspell* part of Circle in the Square. We had the idea to make the lottery seats this mosh pit where people sat on pillows that eventually became props in the show. *Godspell* is essentially about a guy telling stories, so why not make it look like story hour? Then we thought of putting the musicians all throughout the audience. That wasn't something Broadway had done, and it really made the audience feel even more like they were onstage. It was a huge challenge for the sound department, but a group of very talented Broadway professionals took an idea that they were excited about and made it work.

My first time at Circle in the Square was to see Spelling Bee. *I won the ticket lottery with some college friends during my freshman year, and sat in the front row. This was in May 2005, and in May 2011, I was eagerly awaiting my first chance to actually work on a show at Circle in the Square. I had been working for Broadway producer Ken Davenport for a year, and our main focus was getting our revival of* Godspell *to the Great White Way. Early on, it became clear that Circle was the only place for the unique production, so we were waiting for the current show,* Lombardi, *to close so we could move in.*

Godspell *would be the first-ever Broadway show made possible by crowd-funding. In other words, thanks to a lot of work with lawyers, Ken had gotten some SEC[69] rules altered so that* Godspell *could welcome investors who were putting as little as $1000 into the production under the collective producer umbrella of "The People of Godspell." (This may sound like a lot, but $25,000 is the lowest threshold for many current Broadway productions!)*

In the show's song "Beautiful City", the lyrics tell us that we can build a beautiful city "brick by brick, heart by heart." This motto of community became our concept for the production—for the direction of the production, and also for the producing model, for the way we were going to get Godspell *to Broadway together. Hundreds of theatre-lovers would have their first chance to be inside a Broadway show as a real part of it—as investors. Just like the characters in* Godspell, *we would build something worthwhile together out of many small pieces. The serendipitous gleaming red bricks in the Circle in the Square/Gershwin alley reminded me of this concept every time I walked by 50th Street, and looked up at* Lombardi *on the marquee. (And the concept was a blessing, until we decided to give over a thousand people engraved bricks for opening night! That was heavy.)*

------

[69] SEC: The U.S. Securities and Exchange Commission, which governs the ins and outs of investments and markets

I couldn't wait. Godspell *would be the second Broadway show I would work on, after* [title of show]. *The creative team was in place, and the financing was on its way. As I learned while working in a producer's office, one often needed a Broadway theater in order to fully finance a production. So all we needed now was the right theater at the right time. With limited theaters on Broadway, sometimes shows are dependent on other shows closing within a certain time frame, or else they might not happen at all—and often don't. This system makes it difficult for producers and others involved with productions not to circle around their desired theaters like hawks circling their prey. In the end, we truly didn't wish ill on Lombardi; we just waited impatiently to find out our fate.*

On May 3, I was sitting at my desk at Davenport Theatrical, on the third floor of 250 West 49th Street. I was working late, when at 9:42pm, I saw a new headline on BroadwayWorld.com. I G-chatted Ken immediately.

"Lombardi posted closing!!"
He responded: "WHEN??"
I typed back: "MAY 22!!!" as I simultaneously yelled the date out loud in the empty office.

It was official: we would be part of the honorable line of shows that had called Circle in the Square home since 1972. Godspell *would be performed where Ted Mann and Paul Libin brought their dream to Broadway, where Raul Julia and Raúl Esparza had both brought the house down, where the work of Tennessee Williams and Eugene O'Neill was given new life. On May 22, Lombardi closed, on May 25, Ken announced that* Godspell *would open at Circle in the Square in the fall, and on May 26, I stood on 50th Street in my "Marquee Raising" outfit (don't pretend you don't have one, too) and watched our* Godspell *key art[70] become nestled underneath* Wicked.

As I worked with our team on advertising schedules and financial plans, I constantly day-dreamed: who would be our ten *Godspell* performers?

2011: *Godspell* And Laura Nyro

Liz Caplan, Vocal Supervisor

The second show I ever saw was the original off-Broadway production of *Godspell*. I was 13 or 14 at the time, on a school trip. I wasn't a musical theatre geek; I was a hipster kid and really into singer-songwriters, especially Laura Nyro. Then I saw *Godspell* and loved the music. I thought: *This is strangely like Laura Nyro! Wow, musical theatre can be sort of in the pop vernacular.*

That's what got me more interested in musical theatre: knowing that it could be like *Godspell*. It started me on a new path. Decades later, I was introduced to Stephen Schwartz by Harris Doran, and I was absolutely tongue-tied. I never get tongue-tied! I could meet Mick Jagger and calmly say hello. But this man's music actually changed my life.

We said hello, and Stephen said, "Liz Caplan, I know that name." I told him, "Well, I teach all of the Elphabas in *Wicked*." And he said, "I have so much to be grateful to you for!" I told him how I saw *Godspell* at the Promenade when I was a kid.

Then, a few years later, 40 years after I saw *Godspell*, there I was, working on the first Broadway revival of the show. One of the most poignant experiences of my career was being in the recording studio, working on those songs for the cast album with Stephen, Charlie Alterman, Danny Goldstein, Ken Davenport and the whole cast. I was teaching these songs that had affected me so much: "Day By Day", "All Good Gifts", "Save The People".

---

[70] key art: the official artwork associated with a specific production of a show

When we were walking out at the end of the day, I finally felt like I'd gotten to be good enough buds with Stephen to say: "*Godspell* really changed me, because I was the hugest Laura Nyro devotee when I went—" And he exclaimed, "Ah, Laura Nyro! She was my inspiration! I was so inspired by all of her ideas and riffs when I wrote *Godspell*!"

After *Godspell*, a few years later, *Pippin* came out. I saw it on Broadway about 20 times when I was 16 and 17 years old. I went every month because I loved it so much—I saw every cast. Then last year, I got to teach Patina Miller as she rehearsed the Leading Player role for the revival—and she won the Tony for it! These last few years in my life, I felt like these circles were completed that I never could've imagined as a little kid, loving Stephen Schwartz's music. It was an amazing reward after feeling like I stuck with things and kept pursuing what I loved for all these years: like someone tapped me on the shoulder and said, "You're back. You're home."

———————

During the summer of 2011, we held a lot of auditions for actors to appear in our Godspell. *Four of the ten cast members would be held over from the production-that-never-was in 2008: Uzo Aduba, Celisse Henderson, Morgan James, and Telly Leung. But we needed a Jesus, a Judas, a "We Beseech Thee," a "Bless The Lord," and so on. And we needed four swings!*

Months earlier, Ken and I had taken a road trip to see a middle school production of Godspell *in Massachusetts. Even before the show was announced, our office was heading out to locales all over the northeast to talk to schools and community centers about* Godspell. *This was part of our grassroots outreach. In the car, Ken and I were listening to different cast recordings of the show: original New York production, 2001 tour, Israeli cast. I suddenly burst out with, "We have to cast Nick Blaemire! We have to, we have to!"*

Nick was someone I knew that the creative team was championing, and I added my voice to the crowd. "Can you imagine how much energy he would bring to it? He would be amazing! Nick!" When the audience leapt to their feet for Nick at Circle in the Square, I would often think of this shrill line of pleading that happened somewhere between the Upper West Side and the Massachusetts turnpike.

Lindsay Mendez was another object of early pleading. My co-workers and I would often blast YouTube videos of Lindsay wailing with her unbelievable pipes and discuss how much we wanted her to be in the production. It happened! We had our "We Beseech Thee" and our "Bless The Lord."

We also had an open call, where, in the spirit of community, absolutely anyone could come audition for Godspell. *Along with our casting agency, Telsey + Company, my co-worker Ben and I set up a day of auditions at the Actors Chapel on 49th Street. The line, comprising mostly of non-Equity hopefuls and recent college grads, snaked down 49th toward Food Emporium, all the way up 8th Avenue, and wrapped around 50th Street. During the most crowded point of the day, the end of the line was on Broadway, almost creating a full square around an entire city block. The open call saw over 1000 performers audition for* Godspell, *and a few made it very close to the final cast.*

Rounding out the cast were Hunter Parrish as Jesus, Wallace Smith as Judas, Anna Maria Perez de Taglé singing "Day By Day" and George Salazar singing "Light of the World." Joaquina Kalukango, Eric Michael Krop, Corey Mach and Julia Mattison were the swings. As any one of them would tell you, it was a close group of kindred spirits who became great friends and who fit together well, onstage and off.

Of the 14 actors who wound up in Godspell, *two were very close to not being cast. In one role, we almost had an actor with some name recognition. At the last minute, it was decided not to offer that person the role, in favor of the genius performer who won out with sheer talent. In another role, we did cast a different actor—but his contract didn't pan out, paving the way for one last day of auditions—where we found and cast someone amazing, who would make their Broadway debut in* Godspell.

———————

2011: Come Sing About Love

Nick Blaemire, Actor/Writer

Stephen Schwartz is a hero of mine, so seeing him at the theater every day for *Godspell* was pretty great. He's a master of his craft. He's an opinionated man. He knows what he wants and what he likes, which is good. If not everyone in the room is in agreement, he's a great chairperson in terms of a tie-breaker opinion.

Stephen hated our run-through of *Godspell* in the rehearsal studio. He brought a bag of Red Hots and was eating them in the corner, and then spilled them all in the middle of the run, which I've always felt was out of anger. Of course it wasn't. He just thought we hadn't yet figured out how to do *our* version of the show. That was probably true. It was our first run-through and we were very nervous.

After that, he demystified himself very quickly. He was brilliant and gave great notes. He also said a lot of normal, human things, and we all just came to love him. But this is a guy who had his song covered by Michael Jackson. He wrote several of the most popular musicals in the world. This is the same dude, sitting next to us, eating Red Hots. It's one of the great things about celebrity and fame. We're all just people. A lot of people wear their celebrity as this kind of shadow, but he doesn't. He doesn't dress like a superstar or act like a superstar. He just kind of proves that his reputation is based on talent by being himself.

I remember the moment when Danny told me he wanted me to sing "We Beseech Thee" while bouncing on a trampoline. I thought: *Why me? I'm not an acrobat.* Plus, Stephen had seen me play guitar in my audition, so he said, "I want you to play guitar while you jump." We tried it in rehearsal and it was *hard*. I didn't feel great about it; I was very self-conscious. But I practiced every day, and I fell in love with doing it. It was this fun challenge I had to beat every night.

On closing night of *Godspell*, I felt exhausted and a little off my game. I had started *Dogfight* rehearsals, so I was rehearsing every day and then doing a different show at night. It was double-show duty at Circle in the Square for me again. I had been having back problems from jumping and landing on the wooden stage, and my voice was tired. I had started to get self-conscious about "We Beseech Thee" again.

Then the song started, and it just took off. That night, there were five minutes of applause after "We Beseech Thee". We had to stop, and we just stood there together for five minutes. We all smiled at each other and at the audience and felt: *This is amazing. How grateful are we for the talented people we got to spend time with, and for everyone who made this thing.* It was a "holy shit" moment.

For all of the things that Broadway is and isn't, that you think it's going to be when you're younger, that was a perfect moment in time. For a show that I thought was going to be received better and wasn't, here was this indication of how much people loved it. It broke through all of the snark about Broadway that exists, and once more proved why I love it, why we do this. Not because of the applause, but because that still happens. Even though it's the 2010s now, and people are texting in the middle of the show, you can still win them over if you really throw yourself into the show the way that everyone in our cast continued to, despite our fatigue and body and voice injuries. It was all about energy and joy and passion for putting on a show.

Our *Godspell* gang was the greatest group of people. Everyone in that cast wanted to be the alpha, which was hilarious, because it's a show with a bunch of ensemble members. Also, the show is typically done with a bunch of improv comedians and most of us were mainly singers. We were all out of our comfort zones, and trying to be funny. Because of that, we came through with some hilarious stuff that ended up in the show and also a lot of terrible jokes. We made this "Bit Graveyard" that we hung on the wall next to the Sign-In Sheet. You had to write anything of yours that was cut on there, to retire it officially. My Robert DeNiro impression. Wallace's armpit farts. Celisse's "Nobody knows the trouble I've seen…"

After the opening number, we all had a really quick change—and I was covered in water. George and Telly and I always had a memorable time changing into these completely cumbersome clothes with new mics when we were all wet. The whole cast had a tradition of getting McDonald's and eating it together at the theater in between shows on Sundays. Hunter Parrish eventually became the ringleader of that. He became one of my favorite people in the building. He went from being the quietest guy to such a leader and a great force of positivity. Sometimes it was almost like we had to remember to keep the fun onstage, because we were having so much genuine fun with each other off stage that when the show started, we'd be a little tired. That was awesome. A great "problem" to have with a cast.

At *Godspell*, everyone was running around so much and losing so much weight, so we ate a lot of junk food! I shared a dressing room with Telly and we'd scream pop songs together and pound Red Bull. That theater is a great backstage to hang out in. There's no green room, so everybody has to stop by and hang out in each other's dressing rooms, which is fantastic. At the Marquis, there's a green room, but during *Cry-Baby*, people didn't like hanging out there much. Everyone pretty much stuck to their own dressing room. *Godspell* was a hang-out fest.

I think I can say without being too cocky that Telly and I had the "cool dressing room" to hang out in. Hunter's dressing room was a great hang-out spot too, and it was bigger and swankier, but he had a lot to do to get ready for the show, and we didn't. George and Julia were both a floor up from Telly and me and they were two of my best friends on the show so I went up to visit them a lot. Then there was the loudspeaker. Before the show, Celisse or George or Hunter would get on the loudspeaker. There were a lot of dirty jokes. I remember Lindsay coming to mine and Telly's dressing room, and having heart to hearts with us about her auditions for *Dogfight*, and what was going to happen. After performances, we'd all go to the musicians' dressing rooms upstairs and have post-show drinks. There were really good rituals in that theater. It was a seamless sort of backstage-onstage life.

One day, someone pointed out the backstage mailboxes to me. There were the *Glory Days* boys' names. They had left them there on the mailboxes, and that was awesome. Then I remembered how Jesse Johnson had decorated to the nines what would become Celisse and Lindsay's dressing room in the middle of *Glory Days* previews. I was like, "Jesse! We have to find out if we're like making it through this before you decorate." He bought a TV. He got a rug. He cut people's hair in there. It was hilarious; the room looked like a 1970s fantasia.

Coming back to Circle in the Square was great. People were so cool to me about it. I always felt a little uncomfortable because I never wanted to bring it up or seem like I was bragging about it. But people would bring it up to me, like, "Is it so cool that you've been here twice?" And it really was. I would get choked up about it. There was a picture of *Glory Days* in the lower lobby, on the wall, next to pictures of plays with Philip Seymour Hoffman and Al Pacino and Dustin Hoffman.

Circle in the Square is such a cool theater. I remember seeing *Spelling Bee* there, and *The Miracle Worker*, and *Lombardi*. I even saw *Metamorphoses* there when I was younger. When I saw that, I thought: *Wow, I can't believe they put water onstage!* And I got to be in water onstage in that same theater. I saw two different sound designers try and succeed at making a rock show work in a theater with concrete walls. I got to work with Ted Mann twice! And Paul Libin and Susan Frankel… they bought me drinks during *Glory Days* and remembered me like I was family when I came back for *Godspell*. Circle in the Square is a magical place.

2011: Lucy Trying To Get Into Ricky's Show

Charlie Alterman, Musical Director/Conductor

The biggest challenge of doing *Godspell* in the round was... not getting caught goofing off with Lindsay Mendez! Truth be told, we were always doing bits—but they were very much in the spirit of *Godspell*. We were always in character, but we would find these moments where we could do something with a prop, or have a silent bit with an audience member.

The tricky thing about being in the round is that there's really nowhere to hide—and in *Godspell*, basically no one ever leaves the stage! You couldn't clear your throat without it being part of the show, and you had to be 100% engaged at all times. When I conducted *Next to Normal*, even though I was onstage, there were times when I was not in the light, so I could find my bottle of water or eat a Ricola or write down some notes about what had just happened that I wanted to work on later.

It was a challenge, and it was also thrilling. I was inspired to stay engaged during that show. And I can be a ham, so I started to feel like Lucy trying to get into Ricky's show. During our rehearsal process, someone would be like, "Oh, how are we going to get the drum to—" And I'd yell, "I could hand it to him!" I found myself becoming more and more part of the action.

One thing that surprises me about audience members is that some of them are not afraid to interact with you while you're playing, especially during exit music! I always want to be receptive, but sometimes a theatergoer will start speaking to me, and I'm just thinking: *Can't you see I'm playing the piano, and conducting, and I have headphones right now?!* I don't think they realize that the conductor is still working, even though the show has ended.

During *Godspell*, we loved jamming out at the beginning of intermission, with people waving at us and taking photos onstage with us. A lot of the interactions were great. Then there was one woman who literally came up to me and said, "So who do I call to get a job in one of these pits? My son is a piano player!" She started talking to me about it and asking questions while I was still playing!

So many amazing people came to see *Godspell*, and it meant a lot to have real conversations with them about the show afterwards. On opening night, that original Toronto cast came together. I had worked with Martin Short on *Fame Becomes Me*, and at intermission, during the jam session, I felt someone grab me from behind, and it was him. He gave me this big bear hug! It made my night. Paul Shaffer came back later to do an appearance in the show playing the act two intro, and I was told, "We need you to come in and rehearse with Paul." *Rehearse with Paul Shaffer?! What the hell am I going to tell him that he doesn't already know?!*

We really had a lot of celebrity visitors, for a production that was very much an underdog and only ran for eight months. Darren Criss had a couple friends in the show, so he came to see us when he was doing *How to Succeed*. The scene at the stage door was insane. Not since the Beatles touched down at JFK! I'll never forget talking to Angela Lansbury after the show. Things like that really do have a big impact. You feel like you're sharing your work with people who understand it. It's not that stars matter more, but there's something about showing this piece you're proud of to Angela Lansbury, who is at the top of the business, and has had such experiences. She had insightful things to say to us about the show, beyond "I loved it," and her words meant so much to us.

2011: The Drummer Dunk Tank

Shannon Ford, Musician

Every show sets the band up differently. More and more, the rock musicals have been isolating the musicians, because of the volume level we have to play at. Shows get creative with arranging the band members to get the sound they need. As a drummer, I'm almost always in my own area.

When I did *Brooklyn* at the Schoenfeld, half the band was in the basement and the other half was off stage right. It was the first time I ever looked at a conductor on a video screen rather than in front of me. I had headphones on. It was like doing a recording session eight times a week. And since then, that's become pretty standard for shows I've been part of.

For *Godspell*, I was in a little box like the guy in the dunk tank at the county fair! The whole band was spaced throughout the audience, which people loved. The guitar player was sitting next to a theatergoer and the bass player was sitting next to a theatergoer, and so forth. Audiences don't usually get to interact with the musicians and see them play up close, so it was special. As for me, the show designed this 8' x 10' box that I had to climb a ladder to get into.

The musicians all had talkback mics so we could communicate with each other. Since I was isolated, I could use it the most, without anyone hearing it. I had a plastic box with sound effects that I would play during key moments of the show after we got comfortable in our run. It was basically a second show! And oddly, it kept me focused on the show. Every musician playing a show has tons of downtime. You'll play for seven minutes, and then there'll be a ten minute book scene. In *Godspell*, that was true because there were all of these parables. If I was just sitting there listening to the same parable in the same place every night, my mind would wander. The sound effects helped me stay active. For example, after I finished playing "Prepare Ye", I would think: *I have five minutes free here. Let me try this sound effect tonight, in this spot of the parable, because last night the other one didn't get a laugh from the band.* It kept us all connected and creative during downtime.

I loved my little dunk tank during *Godspell*. I really had the best seat in the house. Since the actors had so much opportunity to improv every night, I loved watching what they'd come up with. I was never bored. I felt like a paying customer!

During tech rehearsals, we had a major injury, we watched Jesus get crucified in his underwear on Yom Kippur, and I got my last Coke.

Morgan James, our "Turn Back O Man", was jumping on the trampolines we used for "We Beseech Thee", when she sprained her ankle. One of our swings, Julia Mattison, went on for Morgan's role through previews and until a few weeks after opening night. (On opening night, Julia sat in Zach Braff's lap during her number and ad-libbed, "I'd like to get into those scrubs!") Julia would go on to play all five female roles during the run of the show.

The crucifixion was masterfully staged by our team on what happened to be the holiest Jewish holiday of the year. I watched Jesus rehearse dying safely in his harness ten times, in lieu of attending synagogue that year. (At the post-first preview party, I got some awkward stares when I unthinkingly yelled, "The crucifixion was wonderful tonight!")

During a particularly stressful moment at the theater during tech, Ken barked, "I need a Coke!" Mindlessly, I dashed to the local pizza joint, Famous Amadeus, and got one large fountain soda for the boss man. Upon running it back to the Circle in the Square, he clapped me on the back and said, "Jen, you could've sent someone else out to get this. I think your days of running out for Cokes are behind you." I had never for a second minded a beverage run on any production—but I felt his comment signified some rite of passage.

Leading up to opening night, there was a flurry of constant Godspell *activity both at Circle in the Square and at our office, one block over. Some of my jobs included creating a* Godspell *display for the Times Square Visitors Center, working with our marketing team to create "Godspell Girl,"[71] and getting gallons of grape juice on trade. As Director of Promotions, a big part of my job was to obtain valuable items, marketing and advertising for the production in exchange for tickets. The "wine" that thousands of* Godspell *audience members drank at each intermission was one fun item that I got a company to trade us that actually saved us quite a bit of money each week!*

I was also in charge of our opening night party at Planet Hollywood on 45th Street, which, shortly after, was partially sold and transformed into another restaurant, making us the last Broadway show to celebrate opening there. Our Godspell *drink menu included: Coors Light of the World, Day by Day Drop, We Beseech Thee-Tini, Turn Back O Manhattan, and Save The People Punch.*

2011: They're All Comedic Icons Now

Telly Leung, Actor

Opening night of *Godspell* was insane. Our production was in the round, and it's such an intimate house that we could see everyone in the audience. And we knew everyone there!

The entire original Toronto cast of *Godspell* was at our opening night, sitting in a row together: Paul Shaffer, Andrea Martin, Victor Garber, Eugene Levy, Martin Short... all of them. It made me so proud to know that our company was following in the footsteps of such incredible people, that our show had this amazing history and lineage that we're now a part of. Every time we did anything, I would see them all talking out of the corner of my eye, and pointing to us. They were elbowing each other, remembering what it was like for them decades earlier in Toronto, and enjoying it so much. It's something I'll never forget.

And then they all came backstage together, to meet us! I remember watching the moment that Nick Blaemire met Martin Short. Martin Short was like, "Hey, you're 'We Beseech Thee'! I was 'We Beseech Thee'!" And in my head, I was like: *You're not "We Beseech Thee", you're Martin Short!*

All of them congratulated all of us and we connected over *Godspell*. They didn't come to the opening night party that night, and Stephen Schwartz told me, "They wanted to go have a little party just by themselves, because they're barely ever all together." I thought: *Perfect. That's exactly where they should be.*

There's something about *Godspell* that creates a family like that. I suppose that's the reason I do theatre: for the family. I grew up as an only child. I didn't have brothers or sisters, and when I look back now on Broadway shows I've done—especially *Godspell*—those are my brothers and sisters. They're like family to me. If anyone from *Godspell* called me, I would drop everything and be there for them in a heartbeat. I saw that closeness with the Toronto cast, too. They're all comedic icons now—but at that moment, they weren't. They were the *Godspell* cast of Toronto, and they were just kids again, starting out together.

I look forward to the day that our cast can do that too. I can't wait for us to all get together and see the *Godspell* revival 30 years from now. I can picture me in the audience sitting there elbowing Nick Blaemire and Lindsay Mendez and Hunter Parrish and Uzo Aduba like, "Remember that?! Remember when we did that?"

---

[71] Godspell Girl was a concierge for the production who helped patrons have a more enjoyable experience by answering questions, running the ticket lottery, and being a friendly, consistent face at the theater.

On our opening night we created a tradition. Because everyone in our cast was on a principal contract, we didn't get to have a gypsy robe ceremony.[72] So Lindsay, our stage manager, David O'Brien, and I came up with the idea that we would baptize our Broadway newcomers instead. It seemed to fit in with *Godspell*. We filled spray bottles with water and sage oil and each of us Broadway alums baptized a Broadway newcomer. For Anna Maria, who idolizes Lea Salonga, we said, "Anna Maria, we baptize you in the name of Lea Salonga and all the fierce Asian divas to come, that you will join their ranks." Then, we gave the spray bottles to the Broadway debut kids and said, "Now it's your turn. Take the sage water and bless the theater." They ran around and sprayed every corner of every spot of the theater. Little did we know that this sage water was making the stage slick, but our props manager, Owen, caught that and made sure the stage was mopped again before the performance started.

2011: Love And Kindness Crowns Thy Days

Lindsay Mendez, Actor

Opening night of *Godspell* was really special. We had worked so hard for so long, that I started feeling like our show was never going to be born! So it was thrilling to finally open on Broadway.

Hunter Parrish's last show was also special to me. *Godspell* was such a labor of love for the cast and inner circle of people who put it together. I've never been part of a show that was an ensemble like that. We loved each other like a family—and we fought like a family! Through it all, we were really connected. Hunter's final performance felt like the beginning of the end.

There are certain shows where casts can rotate and new cast members can come in quite easily, and then there are shows where it's really difficult. With *Godspell*, ten actors create their show together, and then you have to try to fit replacements into something that fundamentally isn't their show. It's different than *Wicked*, where there's a distinct character and each person gets to take the character's journey in their own way.

When Hunter left, I remember thinking that I was ready to move on as well. I knew that things were going to change, and the whole experience of *Godspell* for me was about those ten people. Then, Corbin came in to play Jesus, and he was amazing! But the day of his first performance, I was offered the lead role in *Dogfight*. So it was all meant to be.

———————————

Godspell opened to mostly negative reviews in November 2011, but we were determined to make our show run. Throughout the process, our team remained determined to uphold Ken's goal of "doing things no one else had done before." After opening, we tried a lot of different ideas in that category that we thought could help the show gain new fans. One of these was "tweet seats," where a selected group got to sit in the last row during a performance and live-tweet the performance. The event was covered in the media and became a divisive topic in the theatre community. Were we embracing technology positively, something that Broadway is often slower to do than other forms of entertainment? Or were we condoning cell phone use during theatre?

Throughout the show, our actors threw confetti into the audience, our musicians handed guitar picks with "Godspell" on them to kids sitting near them, and our act two opener and other improvised sections of the show changed based on current events and happenings.

I got to write an article for The Dramatist, *the journal of the Dramatists Guild,[73] and interview both Ken and Stephen Schwartz about "The People Of* Godspell," *and how our production was shaped by the "community-*

———————————

[72] Check out *The Untold Stories of Broadway, Volume 1* for more on this story.
[73] Dramatists Guild: professional association of American playwrights

produced" model. "People invest in small businesses all the time," Ken told me. "But many think that producing a Broadway musical is an elite thing. That it's only for a select few. I knew that if we could change the model and make it possible to invest in Broadway at a more affordable level, there would be people from all over, excited about the opportunity to take part in making a Broadway show happen."[74] Indeed, throughout the run of the show, we brought our "People Of Godspell" into the theater to fill them in and get their opinions on everything from public appearances to budget cuts to social media marketing. The "People Of Godspell" included priests, moms, cast members from the original production, teachers, door men, Broadway composers, aspiring young theatre producers, and many more. Godspell was the first community-produced show on Broadway.

Another unique event was "Godspell Cast of 2032." For the second time, I got to run a Godspell open call—but this time it was at the theater and involved children age 6 to 16. We cast ten kids to play miniature versions of our cast and sing a medley at curtain call. It was amazing to see them take the stage in small costumes that matched our production's costumes perfectly. Later on, several casting directors told me that they discovered child performers from our event or the YouTube video thereof. Several of the kids later performed on Broadway in A Christmas Story, Matilda *and* Les Misérables.

2011: The Future of Broadway

Ken Davenport, Producer

"*Godspell* Cast of 2032" was one of the most successful events we ever did. We had this idea—and I will go on the record and say that I borrowed it from one of the first shows I worked on, which was *Grease* in 1994. We had a competition to find the "*Grease* Cast of 2004" in 1994. So we thought we'd have one for *Godspell*—and the turnout for ours was ten times bigger. I think it was a sign of the times. Theatre is "cooler" now.

I remember getting a text from Jennifer Tepper from the theater in the morning, saying, "Ken, there are 200 people here." That was early in the morning before we'd even started auditions, and it didn't stop all day. Hundreds and hundreds of kids came to audition. It was incredible.

People ask me if I go to my shows all the time, and the truth is that I go to the last five minutes a lot. I go to watch the audience. I love to see their reactions and their joy. I want to put a smile on their faces the way that *Les Mis* and *Phantom* put a smile on my face when I was just starting out.

That day at auditions for "*Godspell* Cast of 2032," I saw all of these kids so excited at the thought of being involved in a Broadway show. That was great. There are two things I remember the most: Little Gaten Matarazzo coming in and auditioning with "Grenade" and blowing us all away. And this little girl who walked onstage and just burst into tears. She was petrified. It was too much for her, but she so wanted to do it anyway. I walked her to her mom and we got them free tickets to see the show that night. I remember thinking: *I don't know if I could have done this as a kid.* I was in shows when I was five, but to wait in line with hundreds of other kids, in a Broadway theater? It was a lot of pressure. It was inspiring to see them.

Like many productions, Godspell *was waiting on Tony nominations to decide its fate. We ran from October to June, doing somewhat respectably in the grosses given our low weekly overhead, and picking up steam. Since* Godspell *is a beloved title, our production brought a lot of parents to the theater, eager to share the show with their kids. Since we had many popular young actors in the show, we found under-30 audiences flocking to the show and sharing positive word-of-mouth.*

---

[74] Tepper, Jennifer Ashley. "People Of *Godspell*." *The Dramatist*. November/December 2011.

My sister, Jessica, and Godspell *co-worker Blair shared an apartment on 51st Street during the run of* Godspell, *with a fire escape overlooking what we called "Schwartz Alley." Many nights we would watch audiences and cast members come and go from* Godspell *and* Wicked, *overhearing their comments on the shows. "Mom, was Jesus that cute in real life?"*

2012: Serendipity In The Square

Corbin Bleu, Actor

In 2012, I planned a trip to New York with a friend of mine. She was coming from Italy, I was coming from California, and we were going to meet in NYC. She ended up not being able to come, so I almost cancelled—but then I decided to go anyway. I was actually dating a girl from Toronto at the time, so I called her, and asked if she wanted to come down to New York and hang out. She did, and that was kind of the beginning of our relationship—so the trip set a lot of things in motion.

We decided we wanted to see a Broadway show. I didn't even pick *Godspell*; I was talking to Jim Caruso, a friend of mine, and said, "We're going to see a show tonight. What are you up to? Do you want to see anything?" And he said, "Oh, I actually have tickets to *Godspell*!" I had never seen it before, and thought: *I would love to see that!* When I got to the theater, I saw that Anna Maria Perez de Taglé and Hunter Parrish were in the show. I knew Anna Maria through Disney, and I had met Hunter through Zac Efron, because they did the movie *Seventeen Again* together. I was astounded that I actually knew two people in this Broadway show!

The show went by in a blur. By the end, I was weeping. I leaned over to my now-fiancée and said, "This is one of my favorite shows ever. I can't believe I've never seen it before." It was beautiful, and I was extremely emotionally overwhelmed and moved by it, especially since I'm a Christian. Jim Caruso said, "I know the director, Danny Goldstein. Let's go backstage and see if he's here."

We went backstage, and it just so happened that Danny was there that night. I later found out that Danny wasn't at the show often that far into the run; it was just chance that he was there that night. I started gushing and telling him how much I loved the show, how obsessed I was with *Godspell*, and how I couldn't believe I didn't know it. And as I was saying all of this, he—well, he seemed weirded out that I was there. He was very nice, but he seemed kind of baffled.

I bought the album, went home, and couldn't stop listening to it. The next day, I got a call from my manager. He says, "Apparently you went to *Godspell* last night?" And I asked, "How did you know that?" He tells me, "The director wants to meet with you." "What? I just met him!" Apparently Hunter Parrish was about to leave, and they were looking for someone to play Jesus. My manager told me, "You showed up last night, just a few hours after the director was talking about you playing Jesus."

I met with Danny, and he told me the exact same story: the day I saw the show, the creative team had discussed the idea of me playing Jesus! "It was strange," Danny said. "I wasn't sure if someone had called you without telling me, or what happened!" It all suddenly made sense. It was fate.

When *Godspell* first happened, they had actually wanted me to audition for the role of Judas. I was working on a movie and the show didn't fit into my schedule, so I couldn't. And here it was—it was all because I was meant to play another role.

The next thing I know, I'm playing Jesus on Broadway! It was a great process, figuring out my vision for the role. We worked on ways to make my portrayal my own, and different than Hunter's, while still upholding exactly what the cast had created. My first night was wonderful. I remember looking into everyone's eyes and connecting. It felt so natural.

178

The first show I ever saw at Circle in the Square was *The Miracle Worker*. At the time, that was the coolest thing I'd ever seen. I had never been to a theater in the round before, and I loved it. I thought, "God, I would love to work here." When I returned to see *Godspell*, the vibe of the theater was even more amazing.

I think I'm spoiled now. I always thought if I could work in any Broadway theater, I would pick Circle in the Square, and I got to do it. There are challenges with theater in the round, because you have to be constantly on, but that makes it more fun. You know that no matter where you are, no matter what you're doing, someone in the audience is watching *you*. No matter what's going on in the show, you have to be completely natural and in it.

You know what? If I could work in any Broadway theater, I would want to go back to Circle in the Square again.

2008/2012: Full Circle

Jennifer Ashley Tepper, Theatre Historian/Producer

When *Godspell* closed, we held a tag sale and sold props, costume pieces, promotional items, furniture from backstage… we made over $10,000 selling items that other productions might've thrown out—and fans walked away very happy, with *Godspell* tissue boxes that said "Bless You!" or George Salazar's old shoes.

We even sold the onstage piano. After the final performance ended, my last job at the Circle in the Square was to chase Stephen Schwartz around with a giant Sharpie so that he could sign the piano.

One item that we didn't sell all of was the *Godspell* lottery pit pillows. The giant plush pillows, deep red on one side with either clouds or fire on the other, were sat on and held in the air by hundreds of Broadway lottery audiences during the run. A couple months later, after Hurricane Sandy, I walked by a shelter on 10th Avenue and noticed that they were looking for bedding and pillows. Later that afternoon, there was a room at a hurricane shelter that looked just like the *Godspell* lottery seats at Circle in the Square.

Show business is a crazy place, where there are so many things you can't control. All you can do is work hard, be true to yourself, and believe. In 2008, the planned production of Godspell was "postponed," so in their honor, I decided to steal the "Prepare Ye" poster on 46th Street which I saw every day when I left *[title of show]*.

One night, after everyone had vacated the stage door area, I planned to un-hinge the Metrolight frame and yank the poster out. It would be much more beloved in my apartment than it would be in a dumpster after the next advertisement went up, and the *Godspell* revival-that-never-happened was forgotten. I was stealing in protest of the unfairness of Broadway.

I got two giant silver screws out of the top of the display, when I heard someone yell, "HEY! What the hell are you doing over there?!" My partner-in-crime Leah and I ran. We ran until we got to 46th and 8th and then we stopped. I held my hand out and showed her the screws. We both laughed hysterically.

When I walked into Circle in the Square for the first time in 2011, to put up a sign that said "Prepare Ye" for our revival of *Godspell*, I brought those two silver screws in my pocket as a reminder to never give up hope. Some productions take longer than others to get to Broadway.

After *Godspell*, the next production at Circle was *Soul Doctor*, a musical about the life of Jewish songwriter and activist Shlomo Carlebach. With the subtitle "Journey of a Rockstar Rabbi", the show had both major similarities and major differences from *Godspell*! Next was *Bronx Bombers*, a new play about the Yankees, with characters including Yogi Berra, Reggie Jackson, Mickey Mantle, Joe DiMaggio, Derek Jeter, Lou Gehrig, and

Babe Ruth, created by much of the same team as *Lombardi*. In 2014, Audra McDonald won her 6th Tony Award for *Lady Day at Emerson's Bar & Grill*, a revival of a play with music about Billie Holiday. That marked the third show in a row at Circle in the Square portraying the story of real figures in recent history.

During both *Soul Doctor* and *Bronx Bombers*, friends working on the productions told me that they were still finding *Godspell* confetti throughout the theater. Every show leaves something behind spiritually, but it was nice to know that twinkling silver pieces of ours were actually embedded in the carpet.

––––––––––––––––

At the time that it opened, Circle in the Square was quite a daring venture. The company was tapped by the Mayor to bring to Broadway something that was missing: legit, classic drama, in the midst of the reigning blockbuster musicals and sitcom-like comedies of the early 1970s. Despite its critical acclaim, the Circle company always teetered on the brink of financial ruin, but they managed to bring their brand of top notch drama to the Great White Way—featuring casts starry enough to sell at Broadway prices—while still maintaining their artistic integrity. All this at Broadway's first real theater in the round!

In a 1972 New York Times *feature, Mann commented, "The backdrop in our theater is the faces of your fellow audience [members], encompassing the play with the vitality and passion of human life. The audience is a breathing, sweating, thinking, laughing, crying segment of the unfolding drama. Each individual becomes an emotional power affecting the actors, just as his presence in the living room of his home tempers the interaction of friends and family... We've embarked on a terrific but dangerous rocket that could veer in any direction. But better to try and do what you believe in than what you believe the public wants."*[75]

Circle in the Square has a lot to owe to critic Brooks Atkinson. When the original Circle house was being designed, Atkinson told Mann that the focus should be the stage, not the audience. The Broadway home duplicated the design of Circle's Atkinson-advised off-Broadway home, with the stage as the first thing you see when you walk in the theater. Indeed, that irregular layout is what has made the theater thrive, whether under the auspices of the not-for-profit company or presenting commercial work.

"The Broadway area is on the threshold of new change," said Mann in 1971. "Smaller houses are reappearing in the district with the reduced seating capacities which will permit more specialized plays to be produced."[76]

The Circle in the Square has not one but two tenants lined up at the time of printing. The River, *a wildly dramatic new play about a man in a remote cabin starring Hugh Jackman, will open in fall 2014.* Fun Home, *a coming-of-age musical with a central lesbian character adapted from a graphic novel, will open in spring 2015.*

––––––––––––––––––––––––

[75] Carmody, Deirdre. "For a New Theater, a Nostalgic Gala." *The New York Times*. 26 Oct. 1972. Retrieved from nytimes.com.
[76] Segers, Frank. "See Theatres In Office Buildings For 'Serious Plays' In Mid-Times Sq." *Variety*. 17 Mar. 1971. Retreived from the Entertainment Industry Magazine Archive.

The Shubert Theatre

Built: 1913
Location: 225 West 44th Street
Owner: The Shubert Organization
Longest-Running Show: *A Chorus Line* (1975-1990)
Shortest-Running Show: *The Selling of the President* (closed after five performances in 1972)
Number of Productions: 213

The opening scene in *The Producers* is in front of the Shubert. It's that iconic theater. It's like the masthead of Broadway.

If there were a statue of what Broadway looks like, it would probably be the marquee of the Shubert and the alley. And it's like being inside the White House. You know very well what it looks like from the outside, but then you get backstage.

Backstage was a different story. If it rained more than a drizzle, the quick-change booth stage right would get flooded and wardrobe would put a tarp up over it. Broadway!

But nothing beats it. The Shubert is the best. It's like a haunted playground. I don't mean to disparage it—I'm talking about it with tremendous admiration, respect and appreciation. Of course there are going to be things like that—the old girl has been there since it all began.

-Steve Rosen, Actor

Introduction: The Shubert Ghost Light

Rose M. Alaio, Door Woman/Actor/Educator

When the show is over, after everyone has left the theater, I complete all of my rounds and turn off the lights—except for one. Then it's just me and the ghost light and the ghosts. I say goodnight to them every night. I say, "Goodnight. I love you!" Last year, we lost a stagehand. T.J. Manoy was 29 years old and worked here before he died of meningitis. His father, Tommy Manoy, is head carpenter here, and his brother, Joey Manoy, is the fly man. I feel T.J.'s presence here every night. Now, I say good night to him, too.

Prior to getting this job, I was working as an Infrared rep. I distributed listening devices to patrons from 1992 to 1998, and supplemented my income with some TV acting jobs and a teaching job in Harlem. One night, I was working at the Booth Theatre and the house manager, Renee, mentioned that the Shubert Organization was actively looking for female "door men." I thought: *Me? A door man?! I couldn't possibly be qualified! Could I?*

I reluctantly went to the interview and was asked, "What makes you think you can be a door man?" I suddenly realized my qualifications. I had been working as a theatre and soap opera actress for decades, so I knew the business. I had been working as an Infrared rep for six years, so I would be able to recognize the majority of "theatre people" who came in the door. I had taught school in Harlem, so I could hold my own in confrontational situations. I *could* do this! The next day, they called me and said, "You're training tomorrow." On December 15, 1998, I officially became the night door woman at the Shubert Theatre, the jewel in the crown of the Shubert Organization, and I've been here ever since.

I actually saw *Over Here!* at the Shubert many years ago. The show starred the Andrews sisters. At one point, Patty Andrews stopped the show and said, "We're sorry, but there is a slight fire off stage right." I saw the smoke billowing onto the stage! She continued, "We have it under control. We just have to stop and get rid of the smoke. We'll start again in five!" When I got this job, I remembered that story. I went to stage right and said to myself: Now where was that fire? Is there a big trash can over here? I imagine they smoked and threw a cigarette butt in a trash can in the wings.

Chicago was the first show that I was here for. It moved to the Shubert from the Richard Rodgers. Karen Ziemba was Roxie; I love her! Bebe Neuwirth came in a few times to reprise her Tony-winning turn as Velma. What a pro! We had a gazillion Billy Flynns, from the hysterical George Hamilton to the wonderful Michael C. Hall to Chuck Cooper, who could hold a note forever! Brent Barrett was my favorite, and he was here the longest. *Chicago* was here with us for four years, and then it moved to the Ambassador to make way for *Gypsy* to come to the Shubert.

Many people have said it, and it's true. The overture of *Gypsy* is a great work in itself. When *Gypsy* was here, we had a 24-piece orchestra in the pit. The orchestra was full and magnificent and reminiscent of what Broadway used to sound like. Mr. Schoenfeld would always come down from his office during *Gypsy*, to take people into the pit to hear the overture. I miss him so much! He loved theatre. Just before the performance started, you'd see him open the door to the orchestra pit, and the light from the basement would pour out into the auditorium. Because of the light, patrons sitting in the mezzanine or balcony could see into the basement! Randy Morrison, one of our stagehands, would always run to turn off the lights. Mr. Schoenfeld would always stand in the pit, close his eyes, and listen.

After *Gypsy*, we had *Forever Tango*, followed by Monty Python's *Spamalot*, followed by *Blithe Spirit*. Simon Jones was in *Blithe Spirit*, and his wife, Nancy Lewis, had done public relations work for the Monty Python franchise. So, Simon and I continued singing the songs of *Spamalot* in the theater during *Blithe Spirit*. Every once in a while, as Simon was coming down the steps from his dressing room, I would sing: "Some things in life are bad, they can really make you mad!" He'd continue with me: "Other things can make you swear and curse." One time, as we got to, "Always look on the bright side of life," Angela Lansbury came out of her dressing room, singing along and kicking! She's so agile, and she has a wicked sense of humor. Angela is one of my favorite people in the universe; I've learned so many life lessons from her.

Memphis was our next show. I loved it! It was an important show with a great message. Now, we have *Matilda*, which I also love. And God bless Matthew Warchus! For *Matilda*, he had the Shuberts raise our balcony seats so that everyone can see the show better from the balcony. Now the balcony seats are great! Every audience member has wonderful sight lines, and they also get the magic of the phenomenal lighting by Hugh Vanstone. Everyone can see all the wonderful moving patterns on the floor of the stage from the mezzanine and balcony. Similarly, on *Spamalot*, the theatre experience for everyone was very much enhanced because director Mike Nichols, a genius and teddy bear rolled into one, had the Shuberts sound proof the theater's back doors. Clout!

I like to watch special parts of just about every show from the wings. In *Matilda*, "When I Grow Up" is a favorite. The big kids alternate with the little kids on the swings. It's wonderful. And during "Revolting Children" each night, I'm always standing here cheering the cast on. The kids are incredible.

Every Halloween, it doesn't matter if there are kids in each show or not; every theater participates in trick-or-treating. All kids who are currently on Broadway are escorted around to all of the Broadway theaters by their guardians, and I'm always the one who gives them candy. I even dress up as the same thing each year: I'm a retired fairy godmother.

It's great seeing someone making his or her Broadway debut walk through the stage door for the first time. They made it! Sometimes, there's a little bit of an adjustment period before those debut actors understand they need to be team players. Everybody is here for the same reason, and we're all a part of it and we're all equal parts of it. Most people get it, thank God. A few never get it. They have an overblown sense of self-importance and think that they should be treated accordingly. I never want to see those people again. Luckily, they're in the minority!

There are those who think that a door man's only job is to let certain people in the backstage area and keep other people out. It's so much more than that. I represent the Shubert Organization, but I also represent whatever production is here at the time. My main job is to make the building safe for people, so that they can relax and do their job. With very few exceptions, no one gets in here after half hour and no one gets in here if they are not on the guest list. Through the years, I have been called a pit bull, while others have found me to be warm and welcoming. *How can I represent both the theater as well as the production and protect them both?* That's always on my mind, and I always do my best.

———————

Rose's famous "guest seat" at the Shubert—mentioned in at least a dozen interviews—is a pillow on a trash can, right next to the Shubert stage door. You sit there, you chat with Rose, and you greet people coming and going through Shubert Alley. People from Memphis *have put on their shoes there, people from* Spamalot *have eaten snacks there, people from* Chicago *have rested there between dance numbers. Everyone from the Matildas to Bernadette Peters during* Gypsy *has occupied Rose's guest spot. It's the most famous seat at the Shubert Theatre.*

———————

1948: Floperetta

Joan Shepard, Actor

I was in a musical called *My Romance* at the Shubert that closed in less than three months. It had music by Sigmund Romberg, who also wrote *The Student Prince, The Desert Song*, and other hit operettas.

I got *My Romance* because of the Shuberts themselves! J.J. and Lee had heard of me because I had been on Broadway and I was also a Quiz Kid.[77] They were impressed with that. At that point, I had no agent, no nothing, so they just called me directly, right out of the blue. I was 15.

When the Shuberts called, they asked if I could come in to J.J. Shubert's office. He spoke with me for a few moments and then said, "Yeah, perfect. Okay." J.J. was short, fat, brusque, but nice enough. Lee was the scarier brother. He would later come around to the theater once in a while and just glower at people. He never spoke, but he was an intimidating presence.

I had a non-singing role in this big musical, so that was interesting. I was in the prologue and epilogue, which buttoned the show. My role was the granddaughter of this actor named Lawrence Brooks. He was the lead in the original production of *The Song of Norway* on Broadway! He was a lovely guy with a terrible gray wig.

My dressing room at the Shubert was on the third floor. It was nothing much, but you don't need much to put on a show.

After two months at the Shubert, *My Romance* moved to the Adelphi. A new play by Maxwell Anderson, who had written *Street Scene* and dozens of other Broadway shows, wanted the Shubert, and we'd fallen off our money mark. The Adelphi was off the beaten track, on 54th Street east of Broadway. We ran there for one month after spending two at the Shubert.

———————

---

[77] Quiz Kids: a popular radio and television show of the 1940s and 1950s that featured smart kids answering difficult questions

In 1881, an impoverished peddler named Duvvid Szemanski emigrated to the United States to escape the pogroms against Jews in his town, Shervient, in the Russian Empire (modern day Lithuania). He left his wife and six children in order to forge a new life and send for them when he had enough money. Upon arriving in New York, Duvvid told American officials that he was "Duvvid Szemanski from Shervient." This somehow became "David Shurbent," and eventually the family name became "Shubert."

A year later, David, his wife, and his children were setting up a new life in upstate New York. They lived in poverty and often accepted charity from other Jews in the community. In order to make ends meet, the oldest boy, Levi (later Lee) found work as a "newsie," selling papes in the street outside the Wieting Theatre in Syracuse. Soon, his younger brother Sam joined him.

David's alcoholism was getting worse, so the brothers eked out an income for the family any way they could. Levi became an errand boy for the Wieting Theatre's manager, John Kerr, and would carry soup from John's house to his office. Sam was often sickly, and one night he was coughing outside the theater when Kerr invited him inside to see the show. Sam's entire world was transformed. While the brothers had found a way to get by in theatre-adjacent jobs, it was that performance of a third-rate tour of The Black Crook that was responsible for Sam Shubert being truly bitten by the theatre bug. Soon after, Sam was granted a role as a child actor in a Belasco touring production, and then his sales abilities allowed him to obtain work as an usher who would also sell drinks and souvenirs. Sam quickly soared from these humble beginnings to head usher to box office treasurer to theatrical tour producer. It was Sam's love for the theatre that brought his brothers Lee and J.J. fully into the show business arena as well.

In 1900, the brothers began making their mark on New York when Sam leased the Herald Square Theatre. They began successfully acquiring theaters and producing shows. At this time, the theatre district was still in the process of moving to Times Square—a move that the Shuberts would truly make possible later on by building many new theaters in the area. Sadly, in 1905, just as the Shuberts were beginning their rise from poor immigrants to the most powerful force in American theatre, Sam was killed in a train accident. He was only 26 years old.

In 1911, it was announced that Lee and J.J. Shubert were planning on building a brand-new theater on land they had obtained on 44th Street. The new building would also house offices for the rapidly growing Shubert business. It would be called the Sam S. Shubert Theatre, after their brother.

As the Shubert was being built, so were nine other theaters, including the Palace, Longacre, Cort, and new Shubert neighbor, the Booth. The Shubert and Booth planned the special advantage of offering patrons entrance via a private road that cut from 44th Street to 45th Street. On the other side of this road was the Hotel Astor. The private road was praised for making the theaters much easier to access than others in the area. It would come to be called "Shubert Alley."

Today, 44th and 45th Streets are the busiest blocks of Broadway. But in 1913, with the Shubert and Booth playing their first shows, there was no Broadhurst, no Majestic, no Plymouth, and no Royale. The blocks of 44th and 45th Streets between Broadway and 8th Avenue were lined with dozens of brownstone homes with storefronts on their bottom floors. Today, 44th and 45th Street are the busiest blocks for Broadway shows. At this point, the Shubert and Booth were just starting the legacy of the theatre district's most bustling streets.

By the 1920s, the Shuberts owned, operated, managed, or booked over 1000 theaters worldwide. They had entered the business as poorly educated Syracuse boys without a dollar to their name, and had succeeded in breaking up the Theatrical Syndicate,[78] as well as reinvigorating the art form with new shows and new places to present them.

1956: My First Day In New York

Larry Fuller, Choreographer

The first day I was in New York was in September of 1956. I stayed with a dancer I had worked with the season before at the St. Louis MUNY Opera. He was the same age as me, and he had come to New York a year earlier and gotten into the original *My Fair Lady*.

The first full day I was in New York, he said, "Come with me. I'm taking you to the final dance audition for *Bells Are Ringing*." The show was—astoundingly—directed by Jerome Robbins and choreographed by Bob Fosse. Wow. It was the callback—the final dance audition—and he got me in, somehow.

I think there were about 17 of us, and they only needed eight. We did a lot of dancing. I got down to the final group, and we stood there in a line a la *A Chorus Line*, right in the Shubert.

Jerry and Bobby—I got to know them later when I worked for them—were standing in the center aisle, just under the shadow of the balcony, so you couldn't see their faces but you could see their silhouettes. I stepped out and said my name. That was all they wanted you to do. I could see in their body language that they were having a very vehement disagreement about me. I was told to step back, and everyone had their turn stepping forward. Then we were told who should stay, and who should go. I was one of the guys that got cut. I always wondered whether it was Bob Fosse or Jerry Robbins who liked me, or didn't like me.

A year later, Jerry cast me as the Jet swing in the original *West Side Story*, because I was age-appropriate for that show. Maybe I was just too young for *Bells Are Ringing*. I looked like a baby at the time. Then I ended up working for Fosse as well, on *Redhead*! My first day in New York ended up having a huge impact on my career.

1959: Mr. Pidgeon

Robert Morse, Actor

I was 28 years old when I did *Take Me Along* at the Shubert.

Walter Pidgeon was in the show, and I always called him "Sir" or "Mr. Pidgeon." He'd say, "Boy, call me Walter!" And I'd reply, "Mr. Pidgeon, I could never do that. You discovered radio! You dress so beautifully, with that flower in your lapel. I must call you Mr. Pidgeon." We kidded around a lot.

On opening night, we all gave each other presents. I went over to his dressing room, because he said he had something for me. I knocked on his door. "Mr. Pidgeon?" "Who is it?" "Bobby Morse." "Come in."

I opened the door, and Walter Pidgeon was peeing in his sink! Afterward, he told me, "You must understand: I'm from the theatre, and in the old days, there would be only one bathroom backstage. You'd be on the third or fourth floor, and many actors would pee in their sinks." I said, "Wow, what lore! That's interesting."

---

[78] The Theatrical Syndicate (or simply "The Syndicate") was run by six men who owned a large amount of theatrical real estate across the country. Together, they colluded to form a monopoly and would prohibit theatre companies and artists from booking any theaters not owned by them.

There was a point during *Take Me Along* where I was off stage for about 15 minutes. A lot of times, I would go all the way up to the second balcony and watch the show with the audience. They never recognized me. I always got away with it. Some nights I would sneak next door to the Broadhurst and watch *Fiorello!* for ten minutes. I was good friends with Tom Bosley.

Tom actually took me to Sardi's for the first time. We started going together between shows on matinee days. He told me: "If you tip the maître d' every few times you're here, he'll take care of you. Also, they want actors in the front so that people can see us!" The service was always great, and one time I decided to come in with $10 and hand it to the maître d'. He thanked me and sat me in front. I told the waiter that I had tipped the maître d', and he said, "That's not the maître d', that's Vincent Sardi!"

———————

Sardi's originally occupied the spot on 44th Street where the St. James now sits. Sardi's and the Shuberts go back a long time; Sardi's used to send dinner across the street to Lee Shubert's office above the Shubert Theatre every night. When Sardi's was booted from their original spot, the Shuberts came to their rescue. In 1927, they took land that belonged to them further east on 44th Street and turned it into a new office building, with Sardi's occupying the first few floors. The Shuberts had originally intended to build a small theater there.

Since Lee Shubert and J.J. Shubert did not get along, Lee's office remained above the Shubert and J.J.'s was in the Sardi's building. (Lee even had an elevator built into the Shubert, which was allegedly used often to bring the prettiest chorus girls up to his office!) The brothers ruled over their empire while staring daggers at each other out their windows. Over the years, many Shubert employees—including future heads of the Shubert Organization, Gerald Schoenfeld and Bernard B. Jacobs—practically wore foot marks into 44th Street, running back and forth between the offices.

———————

1961: *Bye Bye Birdie*

Ted Chapin, President of The Rodgers & Hammerstein Organization/Past Chairman of the American Theatre Wing

The first Broadway show I saw was *Bye Bye Birdie* at the Shubert Theatre, in the days when shows like *Bye Bye Birdie* could open at the Martin Beck—which is now the Hirschfeld—and then move to the 54th Street, and then to the Shubert. It was less expensive to move a show around then.

I saw it in May 1961, when I was ten years old. It starred Gretchen Wyler and Gene Rayburn.

Everyone was looking at this guy sitting in the audience and during intermission people came over to talk to him. I had no idea who he was. It turned out that it was Durward Kirby, who was sort of like an Ed McMahon type personality; he hosted *Candid Camera* and *The Garry Moore Show*. I also remember wondering why all this music that was not on the cast album was part of the afternoon!

I was dazzled by it, in ways that I expected to be dazzled. My father always told a story that I turned to him and said, "Where has this been all my life?!"

———————

Sir Johnston Forbes-Robertson, the celebrated and then-recently knighted British actor, opened the Shubert with eight classic plays in repertory, including Hamlet, Othello, *and* Caesar and Cleopatra. *The first musical to play the Shubert was* The Belle of Bond Street *in 1914. The* New York Times *review opened: "When the audience at the Shubert Theatre last night for* The Belle of Bond Street *saw Gaby Deslys make her entrance clad in a simple blue gown such as is suitable for any humble errand girl of a bonnet shop—in a musical comedy—its members began to be extremely anxious. The general impression is that something must be wrong... Things did not get fairly started until the gowns began to appear."[79]*

The second musical to play at the Shubert, just a few months later, was Madam Moselle. *During a performance, one of the leading actors, Jack Henderson, accidentally punched his dance partner, Helene Novita, in the face. She ran off stage with her nose covered in blood. She later returned to the stage with bandages on her face and resumed the show, but even this style of gumption couldn't save* Madam Moselle *from closing after just nine performances, leaving the Shubert empty for its first summer on Broadway. Much like the previous show's* Times *review, this one's was also an indication of very different times for musical comedy on Broadway: "Madam Moselle, the first of the summer musical comedies which have been threatening Broadway ever since the warm weather set in, made its appeal to the tired business man last night at the Shubert Theatre. Unless that individual is very, very tired the appeal will probably not be granted."[80]*

As we can see, musical theatre has changed quite a bit since those days. The Shubert's most recent tenants have featured many ladies in plain dresses telling the story of rock music in Memphis, *and audiences full of demographics other than the "tired businessman" seeking avant-garde subversive musical entertainment with* Matilda.

The Shubert's first big musical hit was Maytime *in 1917, an operetta which went on to be the second longest-running Broadway musical of the decade.* Maytime *wasn't supposed to open at the Shubert—all plans were in place for the charming romp to open at Broadway's Casino Theatre. The Casino was a grand theater on 39th and Broadway, but* Maytime *was unable to open there due to the construction of the "new Broadway subway line." Subway construction was responsible for giving the Shubert its first musical smash, which would go on to play 492 performances.*

1962: My Dad Worked There

Mike VanPraagh, Stagehand

My dad worked a lot at the Royale, which is where I now work. I remember being here as a kid when he did *Cactus Flower* in 1965 and *The Man in the Glass Booth* in 1968.

Earlier than that even, my dad worked on a show at the Shubert called *I Can Get It for You Wholesale*. It was around 1962, and it starred Elliott Gould and Barbra Streisand. I was eight years old.

One night, I was sitting in the wings at the Shubert, when Elliott Gould came running off and handed me this box. He yelled, "Here, kid! Hold this for me." It was an AM/FM radio with this little earphone. My father looked at me and laughed and said, "You see what he does with that?" I didn't understand.

And he said, "He listens to the basketball scores onstage, during the shows!" That was my start in theatre.

While known as a musical house, the Shubert has housed many acclaimed plays as well. In 1939, The Philadelphia Story *saved Katharine Hepburn's flailing career and also saved the Theatre Guild,[81] who were on the verge of bankruptcy. The show was a huge hit and also at the center of a legal controversy: the Guild, producers of the show, wanted their own box office staff to be able to sell tickets at the Shubert, due to the intricate nature of their subscriber system. The Shubert insisted that its own box office employees must be utilized. For a while, before this*

---

[79] "Gaby Deslys in *Belle of Bond St.*" *The New York Times.* 31 Mar. 1914. Retrieved from nytimes.com.
[80] "*Madame Moselle* Mildly Amusing." *The New York Times.* 24 May 1914. Retrieved from nytimes.com.
[81] Check out *The Untold Stories of Broadway, Volume 1* for more on this.

was settled, those who wanted to purchase tickets to the show that put Katharine Hepburn back on top would have to walk to the Guild Theatre on 52nd Street to buy passes to let them into the Shubert on 44th Street.

1963/1976: Falling In Love With Broadway, From *Here's Love* To *A Chorus Line*

Liz Larsen, Actor

My family went occasionally to see Broadway musicals when I was a kid. We saw *Here's Love*. "That man over there is Santa Claus, I know, I know, I know!" We saw *Mr. President* when I was three! They really took me early.

Once I got to be about 12 or 13, I fell in love with this kid who was a couple years older than me. He was gay but didn't know it. We were obsessed with musicals, so on Friday nights, our parents would drop us off at the bus station and we would take the bus from Pennsylvania to New York, go see a Broadway show, and then come back. A couple times we even got to stay over in the city. I can't believe they let us do that!

We would always wait at the stage door for people to come out, and we'd talk to them and get autographs. We saw *Grease* together. We saw *Pippin* together. We saw *Godspell* together.

There was a time when we stayed over and saw a matinee of *A Chorus Line*. We waited forever for Donna McKechnie to come out! We waited and waited and waited. Finally, she came out. I think she was running out to get something to eat to bring back to the theater. It was literally 7pm when she finally came out. And she came out in a cape!

It was a black cape. We were like, "You're so glamorous, you're so glamorous!"

1966: The Garden Of Eden

Tony Walton, Director/Scenic Designer/Costume Designer

I had worshipped Mike Nichols for years, largely because of his work with Elaine May. They were performing their show, *An Evening With Nichols and May* at the Golden, when my then-wife, Julie Andrews, was starring in *Camelot* at the Majestic. Every time that I went to pick up Julie after the show, I would get there early. And because the Golden and the Majestic had adjoining stage doors, I could sneak into the Golden and watch the completely improvised miracles that Mike and Elaine ended their show with. They were devastatingly brilliant, and they used no tricks! They would always take the first suggestion that was thrown at them by the audience to improv, though we all assumed they'd wait to hear the easiest thing to respond to, and focus their improvisation on that, but they didn't! Every time I saw them, I was completely flabbergasted by their talent.

Mike and I got to be friends during this time, and *The Apple Tree* was the first of many productions that we worked on together for Broadway, off-Broadway, and the movies. This Jerry Bock/Sheldon Harnick show was supposed to be directed by Jerome Robbins, but after a while he left the project and Mike came on board.

Right before we started work on *The Apple Tree*, I took a rest and relaxation trip to Gorée Island, off the coast of Senegal, with my Mark Twain paperbacks in hand. It was quite remarkable there, and I got to stay for a while in the ruins of what had been the French Governor's mansion. It had been badly damaged by a fire but the servants' quarters were still usable, and everything seemed to be made of beautiful, blanched driftwood. I was very inspired by this, and created my design for Mark Twain's Garden of Eden based on it. Mike, who had just filmed his first Hollywood feature, *Who's Afraid of Virginia Woolf?*, said to me, "But Tony, you're creating the

Garden Of Eden out of driftwood, instead of fabulous vegetation and creatures and waterfalls? How often do you think you'll get to design an Eden?" I thought: *Wow! Well, he's Mike Nichols, so he must be right!*

The Apple Tree is made up of three acts, each with very different and unrelated stories, so the overall design idea was that each act would have a different physical approach and yet be tied together by a strong stylistic scheme. After throwing out the driftwood idea, I decided to design each act featuring glowing, three-dimensional sculptural elements. For example, for the Garden of Eden, I created the flora and fauna elements with giraffe heads and such popping out of them. We sculpted these and then created a mold from the sculpture that could be converted into opalescent translucent pieces that were then painted with dyes and lit from behind to look like sort of three-dimensional stained-glass windows. A variation of that creative process was used for all the scenery for each act.

The show starred the unforgettable Barbara Harris as well as Alan Alda and Larry Blyden. They rehearsed the way one does in the theater, with ladders and saw-horses representing any elements needed for the stage action. As I watched them, I thought: *Isn't this working wonderfully?* I went to Mike and said, "Everything is coming along great but I'm worried about the Garden of Eden scenery we're creating in the shop right now." He said, "Why? … don't you trust me?"

Before long, we were in tech in Boston, lighting these glowing, sculptural 'Garden of Eden' set pieces. During this, I was watching as Jerry, Sheldon, or Stuart Ostrow, our producer, went separately up to Mike and whispered in his ear. At the end of each day, Mike would murmur to me variations on, "Sheldon is nervous that our colorful set pieces are making it hard to focus on our Adam and Eve." Eventually at the final dress rehearsal, Mike suddenly turned to us all and said, "You know what? I fear you may all be right! Tony, we're going to have to come up with something more along the lines of the design you originally showed me."

I dashed out of the theater to the nearest hardware store and got some old broom bristles, sandpaper, and little red pins, like the kind you push into maps, to use for the apples. Back at the theatre, I grabbed ladders and saw-horses and created a makeshift setting, while hundreds of thousands of dollars worth of scenery was being thrown into the theater's side alley. Our producer, Stuart, was graceful enough to say, "Well, it was the most beautiful $250,000 I ever threw away!" God bless him!

Even with our simplified Eden set, there still wasn't enough room backstage to store the scenery for all three acts! So we built a sort of tarp tent in the alley so the scenery from the other acts could be put out there while the current one took place. It was such a juggling act that we were relieved and thrilled to get to Broadway's Shubert. By then I had created a simpler 'driftwood' Eden, everyone was happy with it, and we could actually fit everything inside the welcoming Shubert.

1968: I've Never Seen This Before Or Since

Lonny Price, Actor/Director/Writer

My family wound up seeing *Golden Rainbow* twice because Eydie Gormé wasn't in it when we went. Marilyn Cooper was her understudy and she was terrific.

What I remember about that experience was—and I've never seen this before or since—the curtain went up before the overture and Steve Lawrence came out. He said "My wife is sick," and the audience went "Ughhhh!" He continued: "But I want you to meet this incredible girl, also from the Bronx." He brought Coopy out, and she took a bow. He said, "She's terrific, you're going to have a great time. Eydie's sorry she's not here but please stay, I promise you're going to be glad you did." Then the curtain came down and they did the show.

It was so friendly. It was so smart because those were his fans and he treated them like friends.

There was a kid in *Golden Rainbow*, Scott Jacoby, and he was great. I was probably nine at the time and he was probably 11. What I remember is that I wished I was doing what he was doing.

I remember a lot about the show. I loved the set. The floor went up and made a ramp. It was very "musical comedy." It has a very good first act and the second act is... But I enjoy it. I like the music, too. It's a cool album. It's got great musicians on it. And Marvin Hamlisch's dance arrangements! It's very-of-its-time, but I love it.

1968/1975: The Music And The Mirror And The Stairs And The Alley

Donna McKechnie, Actor

The Shubert is in a beautiful location and it has this amazing glow of history surrounding it. You always feel like important decisions are being made upstairs in the offices and like great shows are happening below, onstage.

The first time I worked in the Shubert was on *Promises, Promises*. The backstage is nothing special, but when you're onstage and look out into the house, it's just the perfect theater. It's not too big or too small. It feels expansive, but the audience also wraps around the stage, so it feels intimate. *Promises, Promises* was the first show I ever worked on that had computerized scenery. I was so used to working in stock where stagehands were pulling ropes, and this felt far more modern.

We had some trouble out-of-town but by the time we came to the Shubert, the show was in good shape. I loved doing the dances and was pretty wrapped up in the production, without much of a real idea of how it would be received, although I hoped we'd do well. Then we got all these great reviews, and there was my name in the *New York Times* review! I'd never been singled out with praise in the *Times* before, so that was huge to me.

I had this tiny dressing room all to myself on the third floor, and I don't think anyone—myself included—thought that anyone of importance would be coming to visit me. But after that review, so many people did! One night, I was running down the stairs to leave after the show and I saw Shirley MacLaine coming up the stairs. I snuck a peek at her. Then I whispered to our door man, "Oh my God! Did you see? That was Shirley MacLaine." He told me, "Yes, she wanted to see you. I sent her up." I was so mortified that I could not go back upstairs. I just left the Shubert. Shirley MacLaine climbed three flights to meet me, and I ran away!

During *Promises, Promises*, Jerry Orbach had the star dressing room, which is the one right on stage left near the stage door when you come in. It has two rooms and a private bathroom, and is the nicest room backstage at the Shubert by far. When *A Chorus Line* came in, there were no stars, so that room was turned into the stage management office. My dressing room was on stage right. There was one long flight of stairs that led to a large room on the second floor. We set up a partition in the middle, and myself and Patricia Garland, who played Judy, had the first half of the room. Robert LuPone and another one of the male actors took the second half. It was a great room to visit with people in after the show.

On the night my father died, I thought: *I have to go to work.* I was delirious, but I didn't know what else to do, or how to cope. My legs shook throughout the entire show, but I got through it. I was trying to be present, but I felt like my body was fighting me. That was the night that Laurence Olivier, who was one of my favorite actors, came to see the show. It was such a tragic moment, but it was wonderful to meet him. The experience was very surreal. I spoke to Gwen Verdon about it afterward, and told her how horrible I felt that I just didn't know what else to do but go to work. She told me that when her mother died, she did the same thing.

Shubert Alley was a popular place to hang out in the 1960s and 1970s. My most memorable time in Shubert Alley was on the night in 1983 when *A Chorus Line* became the longest-running musical on Broadway. Michael Bennett had all of the companies from all over the world come together to do this special performance of *A*

Chorus Line together. Of course, there wasn't enough room for all of us at the Shubert, so we filled the entire Booth Theatre as well. There were *A Chorus Line* cast members all over the backstage, onstage, auditorium, and lobby of the Booth, and as we all ran back and forth between the Shubert and Booth, in our top hats, we would pass each other in Shubert Alley. After the show, all of Shubert Alley was covered in this white tent and hundreds of dancers and people who were involved in the show or just loved it stood in the alley and drank champagne together.

1969: Sangria And Sewing In The Second Act

Eileen Casey, Actor

When I was in *Promises, Promises* at the Shubert, the chorus girls had most of the second act off. We would have little parties in our dressing rooms. We'd make sangria and chat.

One night, during the show, one of the girls even ran out to the Singer's Sewing store at Rockefeller Center. She went up there to get fabric and patterns during the show! It's now the Met Museum shop. That's how much time we had in the second act. I would sometimes go across the street to the Piccadilly Hotel and coffee shop and have a snack. Now, the Minskoff is there.

We had a great time dancing in the first act. In "Turkey Lurkey Time", I was on top of a desk, and it was fantastic to dance alongside that group, with Baayork Lee and Donna McKechnie. Then, the second act came and we just kept busy and waited for the curtain call.

———————

Shubert Alley has been both gathering place and shortcut for theatre people for over a century.

These days, Shubert Alley is often utilized for annual charity events which the whole community participates in, including the Broadway Flea Market, where all Broadway shows sell their wares to raise money for Broadway Cares/Equity Fights AIDS, and Broadway Barks, which finds homes for dogs and cats in need of adoption. Stars in the Alley, also held there, is a free annual concert that celebrates each season's shows, often called a Broadway block party.

In 1925, the first Broadway block party was held in Shubert Alley, when the companies of seven current Shubert shows held a joint party following their performances, lasting until 3am. There was a Charleston contest and even Al Jolson was there. This year, when you get an autograph from Audra McDonald and eat a cupcake made by the cast of Wicked *at the Broadway Flea Market, remember that you are celebrating Broadway where the casts of* The Student Prince *and* Is Zat So? *once did.*

When the road between the Shubert and Booth Theatres and the Hotel Astor was first built, it was both a fire exit and a luxury for patrons. It was much narrower than the alley we know today. Hotel guests could peer out their fire escapes to watch actors depart the Shubert and Booth stage doors. In the 1930s, Shubert Alley became a bus terminal for commuters to New Jersey. A brick waiting room was installed on its eastern side, and show posters were put up on its western wall to attract the attention of travelers. The bus terminal lasted less than a decade, but the posters have been part of the alley ever since.

In 1967, the Hotel Astor was demolished and the Minskoff building—including the Broadway theater of the same name—was constructed in its place. Today, Shubert Alley counts as its eastern neighbors the family restaurant Junior's as well as the parking garage that is part of the Minskoff structure.

———————

1970: I Misremember Some Things, But I Really Wanted This One To Be True

Ilene Graff, Actor

I recall my audition for *Promises, Promises* far better than I recall almost anything else I've ever done. People come up to me and say, "I was a guest on Mr. Belvedere, don't you remember me?" and I think, *No, not at all... not only do I not remember you, I don't remember the episode!* But I remember my audition for *Promises, Promises*, when I was 21, more vividly than anything else in my career.

I was onstage at the Shubert Theatre. It was magical. I had just graduated from college and was doing summer stock on Martha's Vineyard. The Fran Kubelik understudy, Patti Davis, who was also one of the four pit singers, was leaving to do *Applause*, so they needed a replacement. The musical director, Artie Azenzer, mentioned this to my dad, and he said, "Ilene could do that!" So, Artie got me an audition.

I got permission to leave summer stock for the day, and I came to New York and went to the Shubert Theatre. It was the morning before a Wednesday matinee, and when I got there, the ghost light was still onstage. The whole theater was starting to be set up, there were ushers all around, and it was like a movie.

I came out onstage and sang "Knowing When To Leave"—and I nailed it. The hustle and bustle stopped and the theater went absolutely silent. Someone in the audience called out, "That was terrific. Thank you very much." Artie asked me to do some scales with him, and then they sent me back. A couple days later, they called me on Martha's Vineyard and told me I got it. Everyone I knew went berserk. I was 21 years old and I was going to be in a Broadway show!

I'm still friends with Artie to this day, and a few years ago, I asked him, "Is my recollection of my audition accurate?" Because I remember it being so much like a movie. He said, "Your memory is right. Everyone was blown away. It was a magic moment on the stage of the Shubert Theatre." And I said, "Good, because I misremember some things, and I really wanted that one to be true."

I've never done that well at an audition since. I think it was the ignorance of youth, just that attitude of: *I'm going to go and get it!*

1970: My Sister Was In *Promises, Promises*

Todd Graff, Actor/Director

My sister, Ilene Graff, was the understudy for the lead role in *Promises, Promises* at the Shubert. When she went on, the whole family went to see her do it. I absolutely loved it. I loved her.

I remember just how amazing it was—I was in this giant Broadway theater and that was my sister up there! That was 1969, so I was about nine years old. And then I went to Philadelphia to see her do *I Love My Wife* in the pre-Broadway try-out and then saw that a few times in New York. I saw her do *Grease* many times, like a *dozen* times, on Broadway. I was her biggest fan.

———————

Todd later put the song "Turkey Lurkey Time," which he'd first loved as a nine year old, in his movie Camp, *about misfits at theatre sleepaway camp.*

———————

1970: "You All Had Better Be Nice To The Kid!"

Ilene Graff, Actor

In *Promises, Promises*, I covered Jill O'Hara and then Jenny O'Hara. I didn't go on for many months, because people didn't miss shows then. But I had lots of understudy rehearsals with our stage manager, the legendary Charlie Blackwell. He was David Merrick's production stage manager, and he also wrote *The Tap Dance Kid*. He was incredible. You just looked at him and automatically you felt a two-way street of respect. He was a mensch and he was charismatic and professional. His notoriously difficult boss adored him.

One day I got to work for half-hour and they said, "You're on!" We didn't have a constant way of being in touch via phones then, so you didn't know you were going on until you got to the theater. I said, "I'm ready!" I called my parents and they made it in from Queens, and my uncle made it in from Brooklyn. It was exciting, and it went well. I felt like the audience was on my side. During the time I was there, I went on fewer than ten times. I always felt prepared, because when you rehearse once a week for a year, you're ready to go on!

Our cast spent a lot of time at Joe Allen, Jimmy Ray's, and the Edison.[82] The pit singers would always go to the Piccadilly Hotel coffee shop, which was on the other side of Shubert Alley, to run and get food and bring it back to the theater. I'd always see Alan Bates there, for some reason. It was right before he did *Butley*, and we'd stare at him, ordering his cheeseburger at the counter, the same as all of us.

Promises had the first covered orchestra pit, and it was the first time an orchestra was mic'd in that sophisticated way. That was what Burt Bacharach wanted. It was a huge orchestra, packed with musicians. We had strings and a harp and French horns, and it sounded different than anything else that had been on Broadway. The four pit singers were right next to the conductor, so we could see everything. I was glad to be a pit singer and understudy. I don't think I was ready to really be in the show at that age. I don't think I was good enough yet. And that experience really taught me how to be in a show.

Plus, I got to be in the band, and that's where my heart is—with the music. I'm just a singer in the band, so I loved being in that pit. They all accepted me, and there was a lot of, "You all had better be nice to the kid!" I was the kid to them, because I was years younger than the youngest band member. It was terrific. I made life-long friends in that pit.

The pit singers shared a room with wardrobe, and Gene Wilson was our wardrobe supervisor. He was legendary. He did *Hello, Dolly!*, and he was as legendary as Charlie Blackwell. Everyone knew Gene Wilson. Being in a room with him was such an education in theatre. It was crazy to sit in that room downstairs, and sort of be in the show, but not really, and sort of be in the band, but not really. We'd be watching all the girls walk by in their "Turkey Lurkey" costumes and we were always just so excited to be there, sitting in that room with Gene. He'd tell us about all the Dollys: who he loved and who he couldn't stand, and why. It was a crash course on how to be in a show and behave in a way that people would respect. I certainly learned that in the basement of the Shubert Theatre.

I made $140 a week, and I was able to save money from that. Even though we look at what ticket prices were then and they seem quaint, our top ticket price for a Saturday night was $15 and that was a lot of money then!

I never interacted with David Merrick; my interaction was with Vinnie Liff, our casting director, and Biff Liff, his uncle and our associate producer. I didn't even have an agent! Vinnie and Biff offered me the bus and truck. I remember talking to them on the payphone at the Shubert. I turned it down, because I didn't want to leave my boyfriend. Biff said, "Are you holding out for the national tour?" I didn't know what that meant: holding out.

---

[82] Check out *The Untold Stories of Broadway, Volume 1* for more on this.

And I didn't know how a national tour was different from a bus and truck! Then he called me back and offered me the national tour.

———————

Jill O'Hara originated the leading female role in Promises, Promises *on Broadway, and her sister Jenny O'Hara replaced her. The two were said to be the first sisters to ever replace each other on Broadway! In addition to the O'Hara sisters and Ilene Graff, another person who played Fran Kubelik on Broadway was Lorna Luft, in her only Broadway role. Ironically, the first person ever offered the role was Lorna's sister, Liza Minnelli, who turned it down.*

———————

1971: Leonard Bernstein Wanted To See Me

Louis St. Louis, Writer/Arranger/Musical Director

In 1971, I was auditioning for *Jesus Christ Superstar* and for Leonard Bernstein's *Mass* at the same time.

I had 12 callbacks for *Superstar*, for the role of Judas. After a while, someone said to me, "I think we've been auditioning you for the wrong role. You should be auditioning for Herod." I decided they were right, and came in the next time wearing a kaftan and an Ethiopian beanie and a pair of Corky's wedges—a large women's size that you could only get in the Village.

The audition was at the Shubert. I went in the stage door, and changed into my getup in the Shubert restroom. They called me back again for Herod.

By the time that happened, I was on my third callback for *Mass*. My third audition was for the maestro himself, Bernstein. I did a gospel rendition of the song, "I Cannot Fail the Lord", in two tempos. Leonard Bernstein got up on his chair and started dancing. I was astounded. When I finished, Bernstein grabbed ahold of me and said, "You have to be in this!"

I got it. He offered me a spot in *Mass* right there.

We went to the Kennedy Center and began rehearsing this huge endeavor. One day in rehearsal, I counted off before my number and the conductor said, "Excuse me, Mr. St. Louis, if you don't mind, I'll do the counting." I apologized, but after rehearsal, the stage manager told me that Mr. Bernstein wanted to speak to me in the morning.

I thought I was going to be fired. I went to see him the next morning at nine, and said, "Maestro?" And he said, "Prompt. I like that. Call me Lenny." I told him I couldn't do that, and he told me, "You'll get used to it. Call me Lenny."

"Lenny, am I being fired?"

"No," he said. "I'm already onto you. I saw you teach yourself your own solo. You're a natural-born arranger. I'm going to make an exchange deal with you. You can do *this* section the way you actually feel it, and then right here, I want you to do this the way it's written."

Later on, he signed the sheet music to my solo, and wrote: "You have an extremely bright future." I'll never forget him conducting opening night. It was unbelievable to behold! It really, really was. It was a great experience, and it taught me a lot. It never would have happened if I had gotten *Superstar*.

I did end up back at the Shubert in 1974 for the show *Over Here!* I did the arrangements.

194

1958/1972: *The Selling Of The President*

Jack O'Brien, Director/Writer

The first Broadway show that I saw was *Auntie Mame* at the Broadhurst, and Greer Garson had replaced Rosalind Russell. I was 18. My father had died the previous autumn and my mother took my sister and me on spring vacation to New York where we saw *Auntie Mame*, a play called *Time Remembered* with Richard Burton, Helen Hayes, and Susan Strasberg, *My Fair Lady, Two for the Seesaw* with Anne Bancroft and Henry Fonda... and *Bells Are Ringing* with Judy Holliday.

They were all extraordinary, but Judy Holliday in *Bells Are Ringing* at the Shubert was transporting. I'd never seen anything like that.

Years later, a show I wrote, called *The Selling of the President*, played at the Shubert. I wrote the lyrics and co-wrote the book, and Bob James wrote the music. Bob and I won an award in 1961 from BMI, [83] for Best Collegiate Musical. We moved to New York with the idea of becoming a writing team. Sylvia Herscher was a 'chemist' at EH Morris Music Company, who put people together. She found a property for us, a book called *The Selling of the President* by Stu Hample. It was going to be a show, and we were going to write two or three campaign songs.

The producer John Flaxman hired Ellis Rabb, my mentor, to be the director. We did a production out at ACT in 1970, and Ellis hated the book. He fired the original writer, Stu Hample, who was doing the libretto, and cut almost the entire book out. We ended up writing more songs and it became this musical with only a trace of book.

We kept working on the show, and Ellis was fired. The producers decided that since I was the lyricist, maybe I could pull together some semblance of a book that involved some of what we did in San Francisco, and incorporated all of the songs. I had about as much experience as a political satirist as my Norwich Terrier! I had some schooling though, and I did it.

We went out-of-town again, with Robert Livingston as the director. He was then fired. John was operating out of the Prince office that time, and he was sure that either Hal Prince or Michael Bennett would come to our rescue. They didn't.

They put me in and had me direct some of it. Because I knew the script and was helpful, the company loved me, and it was decided that I should direct it. But tons of people came to help. Pat Birch came and did a number. Ron Field came out and staged a number. But by the time it opened, it was basically just me. Then the lighting designer got hepatitis!

It was really awful, but there were some nice things about the show. "Stars of Glory" was a nice song. The song "Take My Hand," was recorded by Sammy Davis Jr. and was on the flipside of "Candy Man", so I did get a little bit of money from it. Clive Barnes in the *New York Times* dismissed the score as a Sargasso Sea of mediocrity. But I found out later that when people auditioned for *Les Mis*, and they needed big belt ballads that weren't familiar, they used "Stars of Glory". So nanner, nanner, nanner!

––––––––––––––

[83] Broadcast Music Inc. (BMI) has hosted the Lehman Engel Musical Theatre Workshop since 1961. This group class cultivates the work of musical theatre composers, lyricists, and librettists.

The Selling of the President *closed after six previews and five performances at the Shubert Theatre in 1972. At the time of printing, the Shubert has been a Broadway theater for 101 years, and that is its shortest running show of all time. The musical was based on a best-selling book with the same title that chronicled the marketing of Richard Nixon during the 1968 presidential campaign. The musical took this idea and told the story of the fictional 1976 presidential campaign of George W. Mason.*

The conceit was that presidential hopeful Mason was locked into a TV studio, his campaign controlled by a computer whiz kid, an advertising exec, a TV producer... Mason never actually appears before the people or discusses issues. He is marketed just like a product would be. Ironically, Terminex, the insecticide brand, actually put money into the show in exchange for commercial placement. The authors were against this, which led to an arbitration with the producers.

The show was written by Bob James, Stuart Hample, and future Tony Award-winning Broadway director, Jack O'Brien. Variety *wrote: "Under circumstances likes this, it's sometimes considered sporting to omit the names of the leading players. They presumably read the script and heard the numbers, however, and nobody forced them to become accomplices. Also, they're being paid, at least briefly."[84] The best review of the show came from the* Village Voice, *who called it "Not that bad!"[85]*

Though O'Brien and James never became a hit musical theatre writing team, O'Brien has hired James to create music for his shows for years. As recently as 2009, James wrote original music for Impressionism, *a Broadway play O'Brien directed.*

1973: Send In The Clowns

Joanna Merlin, Casting Director/Actor

When the original production of *A Little Night Music* was rehearsing at the Shubert, one day I stepped out to get some lunch. I brought back food for myself and for Paul Gemignani. When I got back, he was the only one there. Everyone else had left the theater.

Paul said, "I want to play you this new song that Steve wrote for Glynis. It's called 'Send in the Clowns'".

He sat down at the piano and played it for me, right there at the Shubert. It was the first time I ever heard it.

Many famous songs have premiered on the Shubert stage over the years. "Brother Can You Spare a Dime?" was first heard at the Shubert in the revue Americana. *"My Funny Valentine," by Richard Rodgers and Lorenz Hart, was immortalized in* Babes in Arms, *which opened at the Shubert in 1937.*

Although the show originally opened at the Barrymore, Fred Astaire made his last Broadway appearance at the Shubert in Gay Divorce, *where he introduced the Cole Porter song "Night and Day." Ingrid Bergman also played her final performance on Broadway at the Shubert, in a 1975 revival of the comedy of manners,* The Constant Wife.

---

[84] Morrison, Hobe. "The Selling of the President." *Variety.* 29 Mar. 1972. (Hobe Morrison was the father of stagehand Randy Morrison.)
[85] Novick, Julius. "President for Sale." *Village Voice.* 30 Mar. 1972.

1973: My 11 O'Clock Number By Stephen Sondheim

Len Cariou, Actor

A Little Night Music was at the Shubert. I remember what a wonderful theater it was, just perfect. Then they said that we were going to move to the Majestic and I thought, *That's death, isn't it? Death!* We had a few hundred more seats, and I remember thinking, *Boy, this is a mistake.* But it wasn't. It was a fine show at both the Shubert and Majestic.

When we were first rehearsing for *A Little Night Music*, I commuted back and forth from Minneapolis. One day, Hal Prince came to me and said, "Len, your character, Frederik, gets the 11 o'clock number. Steve Sondheim hasn't written it yet, but it's your song." I was pretty excited by that. Actually, at first, I didn't even know what the hell that meant. I was a rookie! Then someone told me it means the penultimate song, usually the signature number of the show. Wow!

I was waiting, impatiently waiting, and two weeks went by, and three weeks went by… still no song. We didn't rehearse the scene because there was no point in rehearsing without the song. Finally, there was nothing else to rehearse except that scene. Because of changes that had happened naturally as the show evolved during the rehearsal period, our original scene no longer worked. We all got together and rethought things, and then our bookwriter, Hugh Wheeler, went and wrote a new scene.

We worked on the scene, and Hal said, "Well, let's call Steve." I said, "Can I call him? You know, it's my song." I called him, and he said, "I'm coming down." Steve got there and we played the scene for him. He was very mysterious. Then he suddenly left. We all just stared at each other. And Hal said, "That's Steve."

About three days later, Steve came into rehearsal and he sat down at the piano. He looked at me and said, "Sorry, Len." I said, "What do you mean?" And he said, "Well, your character doesn't sing this anymore, she does." He began singing "Send In The Clowns."

Needless to say, I was gobsmacked. Now I do the song in concerts and say, "This is my song and I'm going to sing it!" And Steve certainly got me back with songs in *Sweeney Todd*.

———————

In addition to Babes in Arms, *Rodgers and Hart opened many of their shows at the Shubert. Their very first Broadway credit was writing one song for a Shubert Theatre show called* A Lonely Romeo *in 1919. They also spent time at the Shubert with* I Married An Angel *(1938),* Higher and Higher *(1940),* Pal Joey *(1941), and* By Jupiter *(1942). Hart had actually gotten his start in the theater translating German plays into English for the Shubert brothers.*

In 1938, Rodgers and Hart's musical The Boys From Syracuse, *based on Shakespeare's* The Comedy of Errors, *played Broadway. It inadvertently coined a new nickname for the Shuberts, who were indeed "boys from Syracuse."*

The writing team of Richard Rodgers and Oscar Hammerstein II only did one show at the Shubert: Pipe Dream, *in 1955 their shortest-running collaboration.*

———————

1973: A Visit And Letter From Ingmar Bergman

Harold Prince, Producer/Director

When you've been around in the business as long as I have—it's almost 60 years now—you've probably gotten some letters from people who liked a show that you did. Often, they're from the people who you'd least suspect.

One letter I received that was exciting came from Ingmar Bergman. Bergman wrote *Smiles of a Summer Night*, which *A Little Night Music* was inspired by. I was looking through the mail one day, and I saw a letter from Bergman, saying how much he liked *A Little Night Music*. The letter very carefully stated: "*Smiles of a Summer Night* is mine, *A Little Night Music* is yours, and that's a very good thing. I didn't have to feel critical. I could appreciate it for what it was."

When Bergman was coming to see the show at the Shubert, I got a message saying that he was attending a performance and that he did not want to go backstage, nor did he want Steve or me to come to the theater. So, we didn't. At intermission, he told the manager of the theater, "I would really like to meet the entire company." They lined up onstage, and every single member of the company got a kiss from Ingmar Bergman. Then he wrote letters to Steve and me.

1974/2003: The Tony Awards At The Shubert

James Woolley, Stage Manager

My first job in the theater was as Peter Cook's dresser, and that led to a job with Alexander Cohen.

Alex had an office on the top floor of the Shubert, and I said to him, "I have a lot of time during the day. Can I come work for you?" He said yes, and that started a very long relationship. I adored Alex; he was funny as all get-out.

I did the seating for the Tony Awards for 25 years, and we did a lot of them right here at the Shubert. I look at the Shubert now and wonder *How did we ever do it here?* But those were the days before you had thirty investors listed above the title.

The dress code at the Tony Awards in those days was strictly-enforced black tie. I have this absolutely vivid memory of Alex in front of the theater one year. Some guy arrived in a black suit and a black tie and Alex happened to be standing there. He put his hand in his pocket and pulled out a wad of money. He gave it to the guy and said, "Get out." Black tie meant black tie to Alex.

The Tony Awards were always fun at the Shubert. Everyone made a little bit of fun of Hildy Parks, Alex's wife, because she made them all have a theme, but if you watch the old tapes, it was so entertaining! The Tonys weren't advertisements like they are now. I thought this year's were great, but they used to be very different. I didn't start working on the Tonys until 1974, but they told me that during the first year, they couldn't *give* tickets away!

Later, when I became a stage manager, I did *Gypsy*, with Bernadette Peters, and *Spamalot*, both here.

During *Gypsy*, Bernadette had a throat infection during previews, and had to miss some shows. Not only is she the greatest lady to work with, she really has to be close to death before missing a show. She was very sick! Michael Riedel vilified her in the press every day, so, after opening, she only missed three shows. Once, she went on with her bad throat, and kind of let the audience know, *Look, I'm in trouble here.* After the first act curtain came down, we thought she'd go home.

She didn't. She came back. The second act starts in the desert, and she's standing onstage when the curtain comes up. I will never forget that ovation in my life because the audience thought, *Oh, thank you for coming back*. That is a true star. That is a trooper.

———————

Alexander Cohen was a prolific Broadway producer who worked on the Great White Way from the 1940s through the year 2000, and had an office over the Shubert. While the Tony Awards began in 1947, Cohen gave them new life when he became their producer and was responsible for their first television broadcast in 1967. He produced the Tony Awards for 20 years, bringing new recognition to Broadway and showing all of America what it had to offer.

Prior to Cohen's leadership, the Tony Awards had been held privately in locations including the Waldorf Astoria, the Plaza Hotel, the Hotel Astor, and the Rainbow Room at Rockefeller Center. They were broadcast on the radio. Under Cohen, the first Tony Awards show to be broadcast on television was also the first to be held at a Broadway house: the Shubert Theatre. In addition to the 1967 awards, the Tonys were also held at the Shubert in 1968, 1974, 1976, 1977, 1978, 1979, and 1985. In the other years leading up to 1997, they were held in a variety of other large Broadway houses, until in 1997, the Tonys were presented at Radio City Music Hall for the first time.

Cohen innovated Broadway in many ways: he introduced Broadway's first telephone reservation system, he introduced the use of credit cards in box offices, he spearheaded the "I Love New York" television campaign, he was instrumental in raising funds so that both the Actors Fund subsidized housing in Manhattan Plaza and the Actors Fund Retirement Home could thrive and provide services to those in need. He did all of this from his office on top of the Shubert where he worked until he died in 2000.

———————

1974: The Andrews Sisters

Louis St. Louis, Writer/Arranger/Musical Director

One night, when *Over Here!* had been running for about three months, the creative team went to the Shubert to take notes. *Over Here!* starred the Andrews sisters, Patty and Maxene Andrews, and they did not get along. One made $10,000 a week in the show, and the other made $7500, which made for a lot of bad blood.

That night, there was a major argument and Janie Sell went on for Patty. At the end of act one, there was a big commotion in the wings and then suddenly on comes Patty Andrews! The audience went berserk, because they knew something was wrong. There were three Andrews sisters onstage! It was hysterical. We found out later that the commotion in the wings was: "I've changed my mind, I'm going on!"

1974: No Signature Style

Patricia Birch, Director/Choreographer/Actor

We were so happy to be at the Shubert for *Over Here!* We loved it. Our team was coming right off *Grease*, which was still running. During that time, I had four Broadway shows running at once: *Grease, Over Here!, A Little Night Music,* and *Candide*. But though that was the case, I was always a little off-center in my approach. I had all these shows, but I wasn't the "Broadway girl." I was considered to have an alternative aesthetic. It was thrilling to get to bring that to so many people all of a sudden.

Working with our *Over Here!* cast was always great. Ann Reinking and John Mineo were wonderful in the show. The Andrews sisters knew how to do it. They just knew how to strut their number, sell it, and then button it and do another. They were tasteful. We had a lot of work to do out-of-town but we straightened it out together. One problem we never solved were the treadmills we used onstage that would suck actors' shoes in!

Some people say I have a signature style, but I don't think I do. Fosse had a signature style, and in each show, he would adapt it. I don't think I do that. I believe strongly in staying completely in the genre, in the period, in the vocabulary of each show. I love finding out what the emotional language is of the era that I'm choreographing, whether it's 1940s all-American big band swing, like *Over Here!* or summer in 1900 Sweden, like *A Little Night Music*. Some dancers have said that my signature style is focusing on relationships or expressing joy onstage. I think it's finding the emotional language of each show's time frame and lifting each style of dance to be theatrical.

I loved working at the Shubert each time. When you work at the Shubert, you feel like you've arrived.

1974/1992: When You Get Onstage, You Can Feel Everyone

Jessica Molaskey, Actor

The first Broadway show I saw was *Over Here!* when I was really little. It was in the Shubert. Ann Reinking was in it, and John Travolta. I remember thinking Ann Reinking was the most astounding-looking creature I'd ever seen. It was great. I loved it.

I came in with a school trip. I grew up in Connecticut and going to New York… well, one assumed that if you went to Times Square you would die. Back then, it wasn't like it is now.

There's something about the Shubert. I did *Crazy for You* there. The backstage is small, so that's hard because it doesn't provide the space to get really familial, like the Broadway Theatre does. I did *Les Mis* at the Broadway for a really long time, and there was a big green room, and we just lived there. People would lounge on top of each other. But the Shubert is great because when you get onstage and you look out, it's perfect. It's the perfect house. You can see everyone, you can feel everyone.

John Travolta got his start playing Doody in the first national tour of Grease *at the age of 17. His sister Ellen came along on the tour as chaperone to comply with child labor laws. Travolta was quickly promoted to the role of Doody in the Broadway company, and then* Grease's *creative team plucked him from that cast to originate a role in their new show,* Over Here! *at the Shubert. He played the role of "Misfit" and originated a Sherman brothers song called "Dream Drummin'", which he croons sweetly on the original cast recording.*

After Over Here!, *John relocated to Hollywood and within a few years, he had landed both* Welcome Back, Kotter *and* Saturday Night Fever, *the roles that would put him on the map as a star. In 1976, the magazine* Stage and Television Today *reported:*

> *Robert Stigwood has signed the successful and precocious 22-year-old Broadway and television actor, John Travolta to star in three of his films. Travolta began his stage career at 16 in* Bye Bye Birdie,[86] *and went on to appear in* Grease, *which he will film with Stigwood, the musical* Over Here! *and a revival of Somerset Maugham's* Rain. *This summer he toured in* Bus Stop *with Anita Gillette, to rave reviews. He is reported to receive mountainous fan mail daily for some of his previous character portrayals.[87]*

---

[86] Travolta played Hugo Peabody in a summer stock production.
[87] *The Stage and Television Today.* 21 Oct. 1976.

Travolta was only 24 when he played Danny in Grease *on the big screen.*

In 1982, composer Jule Styne and lyricist Susan Birkenhead were at work on a musical called Shubert Alley, *about the family that revolutionized Broadway. To play Sam Shubert, they were looking for "a John Travolta type." The musical never materialized.*

1974: Ann Reinking's Fall

Jack Gale, Musician

When I was playing *Over Here!*, the orchestra was onstage on a treadmill. This was so they could move us on and off stage for some of the larger choreographed numbers.

One night, Ann Reinking was doing the jitterbug out in front of us with John Mineo. He was slinging her over his head, and he went to catch her like he always did, but this night, she fell all the way to the floor and landed on the back of her head. I was petrified; I thought she was dead.

We kept playing, but the audience must have seen it. Then she jumped up, all hunched over, and walked off stage. I found out later that thankfully, she had the instinct to bend her head around, and she actually landed on the top of her back. She was out of the show for a while, but we were so glad she was okay.

The power of the Shubert Organization stayed in the bloodline for a while. J.J.'s son, John Shubert, ran the company in the 1950s and early 1960s. With John, J.J., and Lee Shubert all gone by 1963, a cousin named Lawrence Shubert Lawrence Jr. took over until 1972. At that point, long-time Shubert attorneys Gerald Schoenfeld and Bernard B. Jacobs took charge and they held the reigns for over three decades.

As well as being theater owners, the Shuberts were producers of Broadway shows until the 1940s. Over the next few decades, the organization stopped producing and almost went under several times as lawsuits and ineptitudes ran rampant, especially during Lawrence's time in charge. Schoenfeld came on board in 1950 and brought Jacobs on in 1958; the two managed many tricky legal situations for the Shuberts.

As press agent Harvey Sabinson remembered, "The only guy in my time I ever saw with a trapdoor window was Gerald Schoenfeld in the Shubert offices. He would always look down and check out what was happening on the stage of the Shubert Theatre." Sabinson worked at the Shubert many times, including on Take Me Along *in 1959 and* I Can Get It for You Wholesale *in 1962.*

When Schoenfeld and Jacobs took over officially, they began a series of changes that would help Broadway theatre thrive. The Shubert Organization began producing again. They began supporting artists they believed in, and making shows happen with the potential to bring in younger and more diverse audiences. They managed their position as Broadway landlords strategically by carefully booking shows, regularly refurbishing their theaters, and collaborating with other theater owners more successfully than their predecessors. Schoenfeld spearheaded the earliest campaigns to clean up Times Square. Jacobs became like a father to Michael Bennett, and ushered in A Chorus Line, *one of the first shows of their regime, which would boost the Shubert empire back onto the top.*

1963/1968/1975: It's Gotta Be The Shubert

Baayork Lee, Actor/Choreographer

My first time working with Michael Bennett on Broadway was at the Shubert Theatre, on *Here's Love*. We were both gypsies in the chorus. That's one of the reasons why years later when we were doing *A Chorus Line*, I said, "Michael, we have to have the Shubert! We have to have that theater. It was the home of our first show together."

We also did *Promises, Promises* together there. Three shows at the Shubert with Michael: *Here's Love, Promises, Promises...* and then *A Chorus Line*.

I met Michael when we were kids, but it was during *Here's Love* at the Shubert that he first announced to all of us that he was going to be a choreographer. I always remember that.

At the time that there was talk of moving *A Chorus Line* from the Public Theater to Broadway, we were doing a Milliken Industrial.[88] Michael said, "I have a meeting with the Shuberts." He told me that they were thinking about putting us in the Winter Garden, because David Merrick had the Shubert, and I just kept saying "It's gotta be the Shubert. That's our theater!" I remember when he told me that we got it.

At the Public, it felt like the audience was literally in our laps. Then we got to the Shubert and thought: *Wait. How are we going to do this?* It wasn't intimate in the same way at all. That's what Michael really had us working on for Broadway. He wanted it to still feel intimate, even with two balconies. It was a challenge.

I remember sitting in the house with Michael before we started performances, and him saying to me, "We're here. Look."

Everything felt so homey and family-oriented at the Public. They had this green room with a sofa for us and it was so cozy. Michael and Joe Papp allowed me to go to the Public's scenic warehouse and I got a couple of sofas and chairs and a rug for the Shubert, so we had a hang-out room there, too. Then there was so much hang-out area that we didn't have anywhere to warm up! At the beginning of *A Chorus Line*, our warm up area was the lower lobby.

A Chorus Line was like group therapy every single day. It was very intense. We danced every morning, and then every afternoon, Michael would sit us down and all of these stories would come pouring out again. Everybody had their moment of breaking down. But it was wonderful.

I had been in the dressing room right downstairs from the stage door for three years during *Promises, Promises*. I was the dance captain, so I spent tons of time in that room. I would be at the theater all day: auditioning people, putting new people into the show. I used to grow avocados and the vines would snake around the dressing room pipes. It was home! So I asked Michael to put me in that room again. During *A Chorus Line*, that's where all the covers were. I loved having my same place, with them.

In our dressing room, there was a connecting door to the Booth! That was great because in the second act of *Promises, Promises*, we didn't have much to do, so we would go up and watch whatever show was at the Booth. We had a lot of time, and I was always the one to say, "Let's do this! Let's do that!" Lynne Taylor-Corbett and I

---

[88] Industrials, which hit their peak of popularity in the 1950s to 1970s, were performances created by companies or organizations selling certain products, that utilized theatrical talent. The Milliken Industrial was held from 1956 to 1980 at the Waldorf-Astoria and presented fabrics to textile industry executives and buyers through skits and numbers by Broadway performers. Industrials often paid performers well, and they were a great source of income between theatre gigs. Several of the Milliken Industrials were choreographed by Michael Bennett.

would produce shows in our dressing room. People from the cast would come in with something they were writing or something that they wanted to sing and we would put together shows. Lynne was leaning to play guitar so she'd play different songs. We entertained ourselves.

In 1983 when *A Chorus Line* took over the record of longest running Broadway show from *Grease*, we had this huge show to celebrate. Only Michael Bennett could do what we did. At that point, *A Chorus Line* had companies in Australia, London, New York, Chicago, L.A., Las Vegas, Stockholm, Argentina, Mexico... Michael brought together people from every company and gathered them on Broadway. It was unbelievable. I watch the video and it blows my mind, the way he's smiling.

It was difficult in 1990 when *A Chorus Line* closed and the marquee came down. There were lots of tears and they auctioned off all the clothes. That was really sad to see. Somebody walked away with a hat, and somebody walked away with a vest, and somebody walked away with a red dress.

There was this little coffee shop across from Shubert Alley that's gone. Oh! You know what else is gone? Howard Johnson's! That's where we'd all meet when we didn't get the show, to drown our troubles in a chocolate malt and then go to class. We'd meet at Howard Johnson's! "Did you get it?" "No." "Did you get it?" "No." "Let's go." "Howard Johnson's." "Yeah." Everybody could use the bathroom there. Now they go to Starbucks.

Michael was a visionary. He got a five-picture deal right after *A Chorus Line* opened. *A Chorus Line* was choreographed and directed so cinematically, and that was always in his mind. I think if he were living today, he would definitely be a movie director. He'd still do musicals, but he would also be directing movies.

Every time the original *A Chorus Line* dancers get together, we don't miss a beat. We all went through the same experience—it's like *Rashomon*! We were all there, we all went through it, but everybody has a different point of view. "Do you remember..." "Well, I remember, but it was like *this*!" We're getting older now, but we're still family. We bonded for life, and *A Chorus Line* was the glue.

I just love the theater. I love the ghost light! Sometimes after shows, I would come down and yell, "GOOD NIGHT!" to the theater. There was always that kid in me, loving the theatre, loving to watch them put that one ghost light up. I haven't heard a lot of ghost stories, but of course I think there are actors still in the theaters. I'll probably be roaming around the 44th Street theaters myself someday.

It was the best time. Of course, you don't know it when you're living it. But when I look back? It was the best time.

I went back to the Shubert to see *Matilda*. The theater is the same.

———————————

At first, Michael Bennett thought he might want A Chorus Line *to be at the Barrymore. The Shubert Organization thought they might want* A Chorus Line *to be at the Winter Garden. After touring all of the Broadway theaters and discussing, Michael Bennett and everyone else working on* A Chorus Line, *including the Shubert Organization, concluded that they wanted the show to be at the Shubert.*

There was only one problem with that: David Merrick had the Shubert booked with the Tennessee Williams play The Red Devil Battery Sign. *Although Bennett had figured out that the Shubert was the perfect house for* A Chorus Line, *he took the Broadhurst.*

Priscilla Lopez, A Chorus Line's *original Diana Morales, had actually auditioned for* The Red Devil Battery Sign— *and booked it! Here she was finally with an offer to do a "real play," which she had wanted for a long time. Her agents told her to take it. She didn't.*

Then, The Red Devil Battery Sign *closed in Boston.* A Chorus Line *opened and ran at the Shubert for 15 years.*

1975: Air Versus Sound

Abe Jacob, Sound Designer

When *A Chorus Line* first started at the Shubert, it was the summer of 1975 and it was quite warm in New York. The air conditioning system at the Shubert kept things decently cool, but it was very noisy. It wasn't a problem until we got to the section of the show with Paul's monologue.

At that point in the show, the air conditioning made so much noise that Michael Bennett said he couldn't hear Sammy Williams in the back of the theater. Should we put a body mic on him for his big monologue?

I hesitated. I didn't want to do that, for fear it would change the realness of that moment in the show. I made a suggestion that during each performance, when "The Music and the Mirror", the number right before the monologue ended, we would turn off the air conditioning. Nobody would notice the motors shutting down during the loud applause that Donna McKechnie got each night. Thankfully, the Shubert Organization said yes and let us do it! The controls for the air conditioning systems were in the basement, and we had an intercom line set up between the stage manager and the engineer who turned off the air.

And so, every night of *A Chorus Line*, we would turn off the air conditioning during "Music and the Mirror". The Paul monologue was quiet and real and you could hear it with just the foot mic reinforcement on the stage. And after the Paul monologue, when the actors started to do the tap combination, we'd turn the air conditioning back on!

It was interesting because I think it also increased some of the tension in the theater. The audiences became a little uncomfortable because they got a little warmer. Then the monologue ended and it got cool again, and they never knew how carefully it was all orchestrated every night.

Most of the musicals I had done before *A Chorus Line* had an uncovered pit. The *Chorus Line* pit was covered over, but it was acoustically transparent. It was just covered with black scrim to prevent any light from interfering with Tharon Musser's design.

From the time of *A Chorus Line* on, from 1975 to about 1980, a bunch of us—designers, stage managers, not so much the actors but other people working on shows in the area had this tradition of Saturday lunch at Sardi's. We would go and have a big round table in the front part of the room. Mr. Sardi was always there. Bob Borod, the production stage manager at *Equus* would come, and Lisa Adler, who was a stage manager—a whole bunch of us.

1973/1975: City Visits To The Shubert

Brig Berney, Company Manager

I grew up in Baltimore, and my parents and I would sometimes drive up for three-day weekends. We'd come up Friday afternoon after I got out of school, see a show or two or three and then go back Sunday afternoon.

On one trip, when I was 13 or 14, we had Saturday matinee tickets to *A Little Night Music*. My father bought me the cast album so that I could listen to it in advance, and I didn't have a clue what was going on. I kept whining to him about how I wanted to drive out to Great Neck to see my camp friends after the show, and he kept

avoiding the question. Finally he said, "We can't go to Great Neck because we're seeing another show at night—
Pippin."

So I went to a Saturday matinee of *A Little Night Music*, and it was gorgeous. I still remember those floor-to-ceiling Plexiglass painted panels and how things would disappear behind them and come out in front of them. Somehow, after the show I talked my way into the stage door and met Hermione Gingold. I got her autograph on a souvenir program. She had a tiny little teacup dog, and she asked me to hold him so that she could sign my program. That night, we went to *Pippin*. I was just over the moon. The two shows were both so different and so exciting.

Another time, I was coming to the city with my parents on a Saturday and we got caught in traffic on the New Jersey Turnpike. We had tickets for *Chicago* that afternoon that we had ordered through the ticket agency, Mackey's. It was right next to where the little bar at Sardi's is right now. It used to be a cubbyhole ticket agency. These were in the days where you would order through a broker, but you didn't have to pay until you got there.

We finally got to Mackey's that day, and they told my dad that they'd had to release our *Chicago* tickets. They couldn't hold them any longer because we'd passed the pickup deadline. It was about 1:40pm, so we were pretty much out of time. Then the guy said, "But I have two tickets for a new musical playing across the street. It just started performances and it's about a group of dancers auditioning for a Broadway show..."

My mother didn't think it sounded very interesting, but there I was, a teenager with tears welling in my eyes because it was matinee time and we'd made it to New York and couldn't see a show. So we went across the street—and it was the original company of *A Chorus Line* at the beginning of previews, fresh from The Public Theater. This was before the word about *A Chorus Line* reached us in the hinterlands of Baltimore, so we knew nothing about it.

The seats were great, in the middle of the orchestra. My mother and I laughed and cried and hugged and cheered at the end. In the beginning of the run, people were practically tearing seats out of the theater, there was such sudden excitement about the show. It was a day that changed my life forever. And it was by a total fluke that we were there!

When I finally got to live in New York in 1978, to go to NYU, I saw *A Chorus Line* all the time. I would go and get a standing room ticket every few weeks. Whenever anyone came to visit from out-of-town, and they wanted a jolt of real theatre, we'd go to the Shubert.

Mackey's ticket agency, on 44th Street next to Sardi's, was just one of many of its kind. Broadway used to be rife with ticket agencies, which, before the Internet, diversified the methods of ticket-buying. The first very popular agency was Leblang's, located from 1894 to 1938 in the basement of Grey's drugstore at 43rd and Broadway. A pioneer in entertainment ticketing, Joe Leblang was an immigrant from Budapest who opened up a neighborhood cigar shop. Theatrical press agents asked if they could hang show posters in his store window—in exchange, they would give him free tickets. Leblang accepted, gathered all of the free tickets from his fellow store owners, and began selling them to customers at half of the market price.

Soon, Leblang moved to the basement of the popular Grey's drugstore in Times Square, officially opened as an agency, and began amassing an empire. Dozens of theaters started sending Joe any tickets that were unsold in their balconies at 6pm. Leblang's began selling about 3000 tickets every night.[89] If you wanted to see a show for dirt cheap, you would run over to Grey's basement. Tickets would actually lower in price as it got closer to show time. If you waited long enough, you could see a show for just a few cents, as long as you were willing to run to the theater a few moments before curtain. Before long, other brokers began to pop up in the area, following Leblang's

---

89 Atkinson, Brooks. *Broadway*. New York: Limelight Editions, 1985.

lead. Mackey's was one of the most prominent, along with McBride's and Tyson-Sullivan, the broker which had desks in dozens of Manhattan hotels.

These agencies very much affected how business was done on Broadway. They would buy blocks of tickets to each show and re-sell them with a premium tacked on. At first, show producers would work directly with the agency brokers, and an agency's agreement to buy large ticket blocks for the first few weeks of a run was the way many productions were financed. Ticket brokering agencies were essentially providing front money for shows. This ended in the 1930s as the ticket broker agencies became more regulated. In 1943, Mackey's was caught selling balcony tickets to the smash hit Oklahoma! *with a premium charge of 75 cents. Ticket regulations stated that 50 cents could be the highest premium tacked onto a balcony ticket for any show. As punishment, Mackey's was not allowed to have any tickets to* Oklahoma! *for one week.[90]*

Leblang's faded out a few years after World War II. There were too many competitive ticket brokers, and there was less product. Other agencies, like Mackey's, lasted well into the 1970s, when they started being usurped by business being done at TKTS, the Theatre Development Fund's half-price ticket booth in Times Square.

1975: Serino/Coyne's First Client

Nancy Coyne, Advertising and Marketing Executive

In one year, I transferred from Catholic University in Washington to NYU in New York, *and* I got married. I did everything in one fell swoop: I transferred schools, I got married, I moved to the city, and I never looked back.

My first job was giving guided tours of Lincoln Center. Then I got a job at a radio station writing copy for their smaller clients. Someone from the Broadway ad agency Blaine Thompson heard my radio spots and called up the radio station and asked for my name. Then Blaine Thompson hired me to write radio and television copy for their Broadway shows! They had a monopoly on the business, so everything on Broadway was theirs.

The thing that changed me, personally, was working on *A Chorus Line*. I got my first hint of a show that I would call a landmark, and I thought, *Oh God, this is what's really gratifying! You work on a show and it runs and runs and runs and runs. You feel a part of its success.* That's when we opened our own agency. After about three years, three of us left and opened our own shop: that's what Serino/Coyne is today.

A Chorus Line was our first client, and we developed a really good strategy for keeping shows like *A Chorus Line* and *Cats* and *Phantom* and *Les Misérables* and *Mamma Mia!* and *The Lion King* running for a long time.

I remember seeing the second preview of *A Chorus Line* downtown. My daughter was a baby, I was newly working at Blaine Thompson, and an account executive was going to the first preview. He said, "Do you want to be my date for the first preview?" and I said, "I can't, I don't have a babysitter."

He came in the next morning and he said, "You missed history." I asked, "Really?" and he said, "You have to go tonight." I got a babysitter, and I went to see the second preview. I thought, *Oh my God, how lucky did I get? I work in the medium I love—advertising—for a medium I love—the theatre—and the specific task at hand is to sell a musical that I think is perfect!*

To me, for a great musical, there needs to be a point of identification, and the fact of the matter is that we've all been on that line. We've all gone on job interviews, we've all auditioned, and some of us feel like, in advertising, when you pitch a show, the pitch process is auditioning. I knew that *everyone* would identify with one of those

---

[90] Pulaski, Jack. "Legitimate: Mgrs., Equity Take Drastic Steps Vs. Ticket Brokers in Overcharging." *Variety* 154.3 (29 Mar. 1944): 45.

people auditioning. That was good to know. Everyone has been wronged, not as much as Jean Valjean, but enough that anyone could relate to him. That's the key to a great show.

Working on *A Chorus Line* had difficult moments. I was very young and very new to the business, and they didn't think they could trust me yet. When we did the TV commercial, I hired a great film director, Bob Giraldi, but Michael Bennett was a great director, too, and the two of them didn't hit it off. I ran interference between them, and Michael and I became good friends. I said, "Wait until you see it all put together, and then you'll know." He did, and he realized that the commercial was one of the things that kept *A Chorus Line* running so very very long.

It's not easy to film a commercial in Broadway theaters. There are a lot of unions and they're very scrupulous about their members being covered—which is, of course, what I'd want my union to be, too, if I were a union member. Very few outside production companies ever try to shoot in a Broadway theater to make a commercial for Coke or Pepsi. They'd rather go build a set anywhere and have control over it, rather than doing it at a theater where the union is so strong that they are in control. But by the same token, it is a conducive atmosphere; once you accept the rules and don't fight them, and work with the unions, shooting in a theater can be great!

As a new agency, those early years are a wonderful time. For anyone starting a business, those early years are when you do everything you can. You leave no stone unturned, you haven't got a cynical, jaded bone in your body, and you try everything.

We learned over the next two or three years what worked. Then, Joe Papp called and gave us *Pirates of Penzance.* That was big. After that, we got *Annie!* Then Cameron Mackintosh came into town and sort of reinvented the agency, because he handed us a couple more hits that were just as big as *A Chorus Line: Cats,* then *Les Misérables,* and then *Phantom.* 1-2-3. That changed us. Plus we had an AT&T account that was more lucrative than any show by far, and it enabled us to hire some really good people.

The first temporary space we had was in 146 West 46th Street, the Equity building. There were eight of us. There was no receptionist; we all took turns answering the phones. Six months later, we moved into this space, 1515 Broadway, and we've been in this building ever since!

We were originally on the 4th floor, and when Times Square was a wasteland, we were looking to move out. The building said, "We'll move you upstairs!" and they moved us up here to the 36th floor and helped us build out the space. It was a very strategic move for the agency, and with more space, we were able to hire even more people.

Some houses on Broadway are considered "musical houses" or "play houses," based on their having presented a majority of one or the other type of show. The Shubert is one of the "musical houses," and as such, it has spent decades being filled with chorus gypsies of exactly the variety depicted in A Chorus Line.

After years in the chorus, Kelly Bishop gained attention and a Tony Award as the original Sheila in A Chorus Line *before moving on to a film and TV career in such roles as Emily Gilmore on* Gilmore Girls. *In 1968, a pre-name-change Kelly Bishop ("Carole Bishop") had made her Broadway debut as "Dancer, Cat-Girl" at the Shubert in* Golden Rainbow. *Her second show was in the Shubert as well: in the chorus of* Promises, Promises. *Pamela Blair, the original Val in* A Chorus Line, *made her Broadway debut in the chorus of* Promises, Promises. *Both ladies began collaborations with Michael Bennett at the Shubert that would culminate in him inviting them to originate roles in* A Chorus Line *later on.*

Who else started out in the chorus at the Shubert? Estelle Parsons was an ensemble member and understudy in Whoop-Up *in 1958. In 1959, Valerie Harper made her Broadway debut as "Lady Entertainer, Townswoman" in*

Take Me Along, and occupied a small sliver of a Shubert chorus dressing room at the age of 20. Future Tony Award-winning director-choreographers Rob Ashford and Casey Nicholaw were both in the chorus of Crazy for You *at the Shubert in 1992.*

In 1928, a 25-year-old ensemble member in the Shubert musical Ups-a Daisy *received faint praise for his turn as a comic butler—he was named Bob Hope.*

1975: An Early Impact

Michael Greif, Director

The first Broadway show that really affected me was *Man of La Mancha*. I was very young, but I recognized that it was a serious musical, and I somehow intuited that the show was about transformation and theatrical imagination. I liked that just a suggestion of a location could evoke a whole setting.

My parents took me to the annual musical as a kid, but I started going on my own early in high school. When I was a senior, I got an internship at the Manhattan Theatre Club and that's when I began traveling more and more to the half-priced ticket booth and to the Public's discount ticket line. In the mid to late 1970s, I saw many great and some not-great plays and musicals. One of my favorites was the environmentally-staged *Candide*, directed by Harold Prince. I only managed to get tickets to that because there was a snowstorm. It was so immediate and thrilling—and much like the good environmentally-staged shows we are seeing today.

During the summer of 1975, I saw an ad in the *New York Times* for *A Chorus Line*. I was working in the kitchen of a sleepaway camp in Cold Springs, New York, but something said: *You have to see this show now.* That fall, I sat very high up in the Shubert with my entire family who I insisted accompany me, and everything about *A Chorus Line* blew me away. The craft and artistry were immediately apparent, but its content too spoke very directly to me. It was all about the person who is often relegated to the "back" being glorified and honored. I loved that it was about the tribe or the group. I know still that the work I'm attracted to and most appreciate is always about some kind of tribe or community.

I must have seen *A Chorus Line* at the Shubert 100 times if not more. I was that teenager who would get standing room once a week for a Wednesday matinee. I saw it *a lot.*

15 years later, I was preparing for my first play at the Public at the time that *A Chorus Line* was closing. At my request, Joe Papp got me a ticket so I was able to attend the final performance.

1976: I Lie About My First Broadway Show

Chris Boneau, Press Agent

The first Broadway show I ever saw… well, I actually lie.

I was about to say it was *A Chorus Line*. I was sitting in the Shubert way up high, on a college group trip. I was 19 or 20, and I was the overachieving student who actually organized the trip. A friend and I called this company called "Backstage on Broadway." They organized tours where you got to see shows and also talk to professionals like casting directors. They said, "You can see three Broadway shows," and we were like, "No, we want six." I think we drove them crazy. They're not in business any longer. I don't think we were the reason, but you never know.

We managed to see tons of shows by trading in the orchestra seats that the company had gotten us for cheaper seats in the balcony. Seeing *A Chorus Line* that far up didn't diminish it. I was happy. It didn't matter where I was sitting when I saw it.

But actually, my first Broadway show was *for colored girls who have considered suicide/when the rainbow is enuf* at the Booth. On our trip, we all agreed that we would lie from then on because our second show was *A Chorus Line,* and it was just so much cooler to say that.

I loved *for colored girls*, but it's just not the show people remember, like *A Chorus Line*.

1976: Future Cassie

Charlotte d'Amboise, Actor

One of the first Broadway shows I saw was *A Chorus Line* at the Shubert. I was 10 or 11, and I remember waiting in the alleyway watching all of the actors come out, thinking they were all so cool. Then I got on the bus, and one of the cast members was on it! It was the actress playing Connie, and she just got on the bus to go uptown between shows.

I couldn't believe I had just seen her in a Broadway show, and then we were both riding the bus. I never forgot that.

―――――――

30 years later, Charlotte originated the role of Cassie in the Broadway revival of A Chorus Line *at the Schoenfeld Theatre.*

―――――――

1977: And I Knew It Was What I Wanted To Do

Danny Burstein, Actor

The first Broadway show I ever saw was *A Chorus Line* in the Shubert Theatre. I was 12 years old.

It wasn't the original company, it was a replacement company. It was the first time I was in a Broadway house, and it knocked my socks off. I remember being completely overwhelmed, and the fact that they cursed was so cool to me. It was outrageous and sexy and fun. It made the whole idea of being an actor go up another level. And I knew it was what I wanted to do.

I remember very pretty girls. I remember incredible dancing. I remember the finale. I remember their gold outfits. And that incredible score. And then, they kept repeating over and over again: "ONE! ONE!" It was thrilling.

1980: I Knocked On The Stage Door And They Put Me In The Show

Evan Pappas, Actor

I came to New York for the first time on a ten-day junket. I saw 13 Broadway shows in ten days. I was 21 years old. 21! I was doing a show called *Beach Blanket Babylon* in San Francisco.

During the ten days I was in New York, seeing all the shows, I went to Charlie's. It was a famous theatre bar. I went with some of my friends I knew from San Francisco, who had moved to New York. We went one night after a show, and there was a guy sitting there, named Jim Young. We were all talking and he said he was in a show. And I was like, "Oh my God, you're in *A Chorus Line*!"

He said, "You know, they're looking for a new actor for the role of Mark. You're perfect. You have a baby face." I said, "Oh yeah, right. Like they're going to see me." He said, "Just go knock on the stage door tomorrow. But don't tell them I sent you, because I don't want to get in trouble."

So I knock on the stage door the next day, and I say, "Hi, I'm from San Francisco, and I heard that you're looking for a Mark."

T. Michael Reed, the dance captain, comes out and says, "Hold on a second." He goes back in, and brings somebody else out. They literally look me over. This is at the stage door. I had the balls to knock on the stage door and say hi! They said, "Can you come back tomorrow at noon?" I went, "What?!" I was getting on the plane that next day at four or five to go back home. Then I said, "Okay!"

Well, I didn't know what a "headshot and resumé" was. I kind of had dance clothes. I was more of a singer and an actor, but I was learning to dance to try to make myself a triple threat before coming to New York.

Then I went, "Oh shit. It's a matinee day. There's a matinee. I've got to get a ticket!" I got the last ticket, way over house right. Who was on the stage? Bebe Neuwirth at 19 playing Sheila. Cheryl Clark was Cassie. And I was writing things down, just watching the guy playing the role of Mark.

After, I ran across the street, to where the Marriott Marquis is now, which used to be the Piccadilly Hotel. My friend Ron Wells was a bartender there. I went, "Ron! Ron! I have an audition for *A Chorus Line* tomorrow!" He said, "Only you come to New York on vacation and get an audition. We're here for years, and can't even get a Broadway audition." I said, "I don't have music. I have nothing."

At that moment, Tony Geralis, who was the musical director of *A Chorus Line*, walked into the Piccadilly with Cheryl Clark. And Ron said, "Tony, come here! This is my friend, Evan Pappas. Tony Geralis." We greet each other and I say, "I'm auditioning for you tomorrow." And Tony's like, "Really?" I say, "I don't know what to sing. I don't have any music." And he says, "What have you done?" I said, "Well, I just finished playing Tony in *West Side Story*." He says, "I'll bring the score."

So, I go to the audition the next day, on the stage of the Shubert. I dance. I sing "Something's Coming." And I read for Mark. They say, "Would you read for Paul?" So I read the monologue. I didn't know what the hell I was doing!

I left there with a job. The first bus and truck. I went home with a job.

———————————

Charlie's was a popular hang-out for theatre folks on 45th Street between Broadway and 8th Avenue. Its heyday was the 1970s and 1980s. Once a night, the waiters would famously perform a number from a popular show that season. In 1988, Charlie's closed and the eatery was renamed Sam's. Sam's provided much the same ambiance, even adding in 10:30pm and 12:15am cabaret shows, until it closed in the early 2000s, when the building it was housed in was demolished.

In the late 1980s through the 1990s, Sam's carried on the tradition of Charlie's. The place was shoulder to shoulder with Barrymore's and Frankie & Johnnie's for many years. All three were intimate haunts with brick walls and show posters, frequented by theatre folk in the know. Sam's was said to have a hidden "peek" slot in one of the brick walls, a holdover from the restaurant's Prohibition days. During a real estate boom, the land that all three stalwart theatre dining establishments were built on was sold with intentions of building a high-rise hotel in its place. The market crashed before the demolition could get to Frankie & Johnnies', but the other two are gone.

When I told actor-turned-director-and-producer Don Scardino that Sam's had been demolished, he reacted: "No! It's not there anymore? I didn't even realize. It's criminal that they tore it down. I used to go there all the time and see George C. Scott sitting at the bar in the middle of the afternoon. You'd be talking to somebody, and there would be Jason Robards, just walking into the Theater Bar."

The Theater Bar? Yes. It turns out that the place had a history of serving Broadway folks that stretched even farther back to the 1920s when it was simply called the Theater Bar, or sometimes "The Theater Tavern" or "The Theater Bar and Grill." In 1947, Billboard *reported: "The Theater Bar and Restaurant [is] a haven for actors, musicians, writers, etc. Proprietor Louis Bergen has for 26 years made it the favorite meeting place of the less affluent legit workers, many of whom he staked to meals and loans. His spot never achieved the glamour of Sardi's among visitors to the Great White Way, but many headliners of today can recall when they received aid from Louis Bergen in their struggling days."[91] In fact, famous actors would often send checks to Louis at Christmas to thank him, and he would pay it forward by using these checks to feed the new crop of emerging artists.*

Louis Bergen started out as a bartender at the Garden Hotel bar near Madison Square Garden, one of the wild places that provided Eugene O'Neill inspiration for the saloon in The Iceman Cometh. *Bergen, a poor German immigrant, worked there at the turn of the century, when the young O'Neill would frequently carouse with the showbiz and circus men who drank themselves broke. As the theatre district moved north, so did Bergen and O'Neill. When O'Neill's* Iceman *premiered at the Martin Beck in 1946, the cast and crew would frequently cross 45th Street and dine at Bergen's Theater Bar. Bergen was beloved by all who knew him and feared by those who didn't; he was known to kick out a new customer or tourist in order to serve a regular customer. He had his staff take phone messages for actors who couldn't afford a message service; actors would often hop up from their chairs and help him when he took a turn serving at the bar. When Bergen retired in the late 1940s, he left much of the place to his bartender, Pat Sapienza. The Theater Bar stayed in the family for many years and when desperate advertisements began offering discounts in the early 1970s, they were signed "Sammy Sapienza."*

Many people I spoke to had remembrances of the once-popular joint. Theatrical workers today generally travel farther west for their pre-show or post-show hang-out spots, as most restaurants within a block of Broadway have become catered to tourists. This place was actually referred to as an "intermission bar" because those in the know would dart over and actually grab a cocktail at intermission.

Ken Billington, the Tony Award-winning lighting designer who made his Broadway debut in 1967 said, "When I started in the theatre, everyone went to a place called The Theater Bar, across from the Golden." Actor John McMartin remembered, "The Theater Bar is gone. That's where all of the young struggling actors would go. If you were just starting out, you'd go to see your contemporaries. Beer was 15 cents. I remember when they raised it to a quarter. It's a parking lot now."

Randy Graff told me, "The first time I ever went backstage at a Broadway show was when I saw my cousin Ilene Graff play Sandy Dumbrowski in Grease *at the Royale. I thought:* This is the life I want. This is so cool. This is my fantasy. *She lived in a brownstone on the Upper West Side. She was even dating one of the musicians. After the show she took me across the street to Charlie's. She ordered something off the menu, and I tried to order it too, but I pronounced it, 'kwee-chee.' She had ordered quiche!"*

————————

[91] "Louis Bergen Quits Showbiz Eatery." *The Billboard.* 24 May 1947.

1982: I Make More Money In The Dressing Room

Evan Pappas, Actor

I did *A Chorus Line* on the road from 1980 to 1981, and then I gave my notice. I said, "I've got to go, I've got to get to New York now!" And then they moved me to the Broadway company. It wouldn't have happened if I had waited six months. But I had played Larry, Al, Paul, and Mark on the road and at that moment, they needed someone to cover those roles on Broadway.

I was a kid. I learned so much. I made mistakes. It was a fabulous time. I was understudy to four roles. And I loved it that way, because it kept me fresh. I was always on for a different role. Sometimes I would be Paul two nights, Al two nights, then Larry two nights. I would be moving all over the place. And I'd get double paychecks! They wanted me to go on the line a number of times, but I'd always say, "No, I make more money in the dressing room. I've been on the line for a couple of years. I want to stay fresh this way." Most people would say, "Yes, I've got to have the principal role." I was like, "No." I wanted to learn. I was taking acting classes and voice lessons constantly. I knew my days were numbered in *A Chorus Line* and I wanted to go back to working on becoming a leading man.

42nd Street was down the street. Those people would all come hang out with us in Shubert Alley. It was fun; we'd meet people from different shows. We would watch shows come and go. It was so long ago. *Amadeus* was next door for a while!

Times Square was dirty! So dirty! I remember walking to the subway back then, as soon as you went from 43rd to 42nd, that terrifying little strip towards the subway... 42nd Street was just horrible. It was a viper's den. We would walk in big groups.

Because I was in *A Chorus Line*, people were only looking at me as a dancer. When I left, my agent convinced me—and I think it was the right decision at the time—to take *Chorus Line* off my resume, because casting agents and directors were only looking at me as a dancer boy. I eventually put it back on.

———————

Michael Bennett's A Chorus Line *Playbill bio, in its entirety, read*:

> MICHAEL BENNETT (Director, Choreographer) *has danced in the chorus of the following Broadway shows:* Subways Are For Sleeping, Here's Love, Bajour.

———————

1983: The Cool Girls And My Almost-Not First Show

Anne Bobby, Actor

The first Broadway show I ever saw was *A Chorus Line*. I was a sophomore in high school.

There was a theatre group you could join at school, and they got to see a Broadway show every couple of months. It was considered "cool" because you left on Wednesday at 11am and skipped class. Plus, everyone got to be all dressed up because they knew they were going into the city.

When I was finally old enough, the first show the theatre group got tickets for was *A Chorus Line*! I signed up for tickets but I had just missed the cut off. I was the first person who got refused. The day of the show, I walked into school and all the girls came up to me, dressed up, and they said, "Well, so-and-so is sick, and you were the first person on the rejection list." So I got to go in my little Catholic schoolgirl uniform to the Shubert Theatre to see *A Chorus Line*.

212

It was the best day of my life up until that point, because I got to go! I got to go! We sat all the way up in the nosebleeds. It was awesome.

The theater was so much larger than I had ever imagined a Broadway theater could be. And I felt such history. I sat there and I remember looking at the "At This Theater" part of the Playbill in the dark. *A Chorus Line* was good, and I was very into the story, but there were moments when I just found myself looking around and thinking, *Oh my gosh, look what played here. Look at what happened here.* I felt such continuity.

I was that kid who went home that night, and just went, "All I ever want to do is be on one of those stages." It sounds sort of cliché, but it really is true. That is what it was like for me. And the Shubert. I mean, what better theater to go to for the first time? It was something else.

And who knew I was going to work with Marvin Hamlisch on *Smile*? Wow. Only three years later I would actually get to be on Broadway, singing his music.

1984: I Slept Through The Dirty Words!

Steve Rosen, Actor

First Broadway show I ever saw… it's under debate! I'm sure we could go back in time and look at the ticket stubs. During the weekend that my family came to New York when I was six, we saw *A Chorus Line* and we saw *The Tap Dance Kid*. I don't remember which was first.

A Chorus Line was at the Shubert which is where I ended up doing my first Broadway show. We had listened to *A Chorus Line* a lot in the car, growing up, and I really wanted to be awake and aware so I could see and hear an adult sing the phrase: "tits and ass." The song "Dance: Ten; Looks: Three" had dirty words in it and I intended to laugh my head off. Sadly, I fell asleep in the middle of the "Montage" and slept straight through to the finale. I was six! I was in a dark room and I was stuffed full of hot dogs and pretzels.

But I do remember exactly where I sat. When I was lucky enough to do *Spamalot* at the Shubert, I always looked at that spot. Directly in front of where I lifted my mud mother skirt and yelled "dee," during the "Laker Girls"… that was right in front of the seat that I had sat in when I was six.

1985: The 10th Year Of A Chorus Line

David Loud, Musical Director and Supervisor/Conductor/Actor

I've never worked in the Shubert. I've always wanted to work in the Shubert. The Shubert is where *A Chorus Line* played, and I stalked *A Chorus Line* when I was a little boy and dreamed about it. I even dreamed that I was in it, which was ridiculous. I'm not a dancer. But I loved *A Chorus Line*.

I didn't stalk a lot of shows, but I really stalked *A Chorus Line*. I probably saw it five times. *Sweeney Todd* was the other one. Every time I had $30, I would go see *Sweeney Todd*.

There was a time late in the run of *A Chorus Line* when I wanted to see my friend Diane Fratantoni playing Morales at the end of the run. I had standing room in the back. *A Chorus Line* started.

There was always a quick blackout, and then the lights came on and the stage was full of people. It was magical. It happened right at the top of the show. And as the house lights went out, I saw an older usher lean down and put her program over the aisle light, which she could reach. The effect of it was to make the blackout even blacker.

I asked her about it after the show. I said, "What was that thing you did? You put your program over the aisle light." She said, "Oh, Michael Bennett asked us to do that." And so there, in what was, like, the 10th year of the run, she was still doing that. It was this little piece of stagecraft that Michael Bennett had asked those ushers to do to make that first blackout a little bit blacker, to make that trick work.

———————

Michael Bennett also asked the musicians of A Chorus Line *not to tune up in the pit before the performance, as it would remind the audience that they were at a show.*

———————

1988: I Need To Be In New York City

Brian Yorkey, Writer

I grew up in Seattle, so I applied to schools that were all out there. Columbia was the only school I applied to that wasn't on the West Coast. They offered me no financial aid, but something in me said: *I need to be in New York City.*

Just about every show I saw when I got here blew me away and made me want to write for the theatre.

One very important show to me was *A Chorus Line.* When I saw *A Chorus Line*, I knew the music already, but I didn't know the story.

I've heard a lot of men say this, but Paul's story really changed my life. It was my freshman year and I was just in the process of coming out... those were different days!

I actually saw *A Chorus Line* a second time with a guy who ultimately would become one of my first boyfriends. He wasn't out at the time either, but we had each sort of figured out that the other was gay. Sitting together during that was an electric experience.

A Chorus Line had been running for 12 years at that point. It had been running for many, many years, but it was still so thrilling to me.

———————

When A Chorus Line *closed at the Shubert in 1990, it had played 6137 performances.*

———————

1990: When Ya Do It Right

Don Stitt, Actor

I played a character in *Buddy* based on Alan Freed, the guy who coined the term "rock 'n' roll." It was a sweet gig, too, because my featured spot was only about five minutes long, and all I had to do was talk. I was the emcee of a rock concert, done "in one" as the old-timers say, or, in front of the main curtain. It was really to cover for a scene change. I did a little stand up comedy to warm up the audience, and then I brought on the rock 'n' roll stars, and went outside for some air.

The stage manager, a dry wit named Peter "Mumfie" Mumford, had asked me how they could communicate with me if they needed me to "stretch it out" for any reason. I told them to do what they do in the comedy clubs:

put a red light on the front rail, and as long as the light is flashing, I'll keep talking. I helped write the material, and then I had some other stuff I would do if I needed to fill, like a Chubby Checker impression.

For hundreds of performances, that was the way it went. A four or five minute bit, bring on the "stars," go into the alley to chill, come back in half an hour to play the congas, and bow to a standing ovation. For $1500 a week. It was a great job! The show went like clockwork, and most nights I had the stage of the Shubert to myself for four or five minutes.

But one night, I did the usual, and the light was still flashing. I went into the backup material—but the light was still flashing. *No problem*, I thought. *I'm a pro.*

So I launched into my standup act. That bought me another six minutes or so. And the light was still flashing!

I went over to one of the backup singers, Jill Hennessy, and I adlibbed with her—to limited comedic effect—and the light was *still* flashing. So, I said, "Let's see what's going on backstage at the Surf Ballroom tonight." And I stuck my head through the opening in the center of the front curtain.

Doc, the head carpenter, snapped, "Get back out there!"

I was on the stage of the Shubert Theatre, the light was still flashing, and I had run out of ideas.

So I did something that we do in clubs all the time, but which I'm pretty sure no one else had ever spontaneously done in the middle a Broadway play before. I jumped off the stage, went over to the first guy on the aisle, and I said:

"Hi, what's your name?"
He said, "Mike."
I said, "Hey, Mike, where ya from?
He said, "New York."
Hell, we're all from New York, but we were supposed to be in Clear Lake, Iowa.
I said, "All the way from the Eastern Seaboard, ladies and gentlemen!"

It got a laugh, *and* the light went out. Now all I needed was a clean segue back into the show and I was home free. I said, "Say, Mike, what brings you from the Big Apple all the way to Clear Lake, Iowa?"

Mike said those three magic words. "Rock 'n' roll."

I said to the audience, "Are you *ready* to rock 'n' roll?" Well, they were sure as hell ready to rock 'n' roll, because they'd been listening to me for 12 minutes. So they roared back their approval as I clambered back up on the stage, and I said, "Ladies and gentlemen, boys and girls, put your hands together for a larger than life welcome for that larger than life rock 'n' roll star, Mr. Jaye P. Richardson, the Big Bopper!"

They cued up "Chantilly Lace", and I hit the wing. I was about ready to wring someone's neck, but the entire stage crew had lined up to give me a standing ovation. It seems that they had set up the bandstand on the wrong spike marks,[92] 18 inches upstage of where it was supposed to be. They had to unplug the instruments, strike the instruments, collapse the bandstand, move the bandstand, reassemble the bandstand, restore the instruments and plug everything back in. It had taken them 12 minutes. I had done 12 minutes with a five minute set. It's the only time in my life that I ever got to be Robin Williams.

---

[92] spike marks: spots where tape has been used to denote the placement of a person or item onstage

The producer, director, and musical director all happened to be in the audience that night, so I lingered by the stage door, hoping for a "Nice job" or "Good work." But they were so angry about the tech malfunction that I hadn't even registered in their collective consciousness. They all walked right past me without saying a word. I was terribly hurt by it, so I mentioned how I felt to Mumfie.

He said, taking a drag off an imaginary cigarette, "Mis-ter Stitt... you've been in show business long enough to know...nobody says anything to ya when ya do it right!"

As I left the theater that evening, I cut through Shubert Alley, and I saw that Mr. Bernie Jacobs, president of the Shubert Organization, was getting into his limo. He stopped and got back out. He walked toward me.

"Very good. Very good." He shook my hand, smiling. "Good job." He walked briskly back to his limo. As he closed the door, he said, "Thank you."

For years after *Buddy* closed, whenever Mr. Jacobs would see me in the alley, he would brighten visibly. Perhaps he'd even wave or shake my hand and ask me, "What are you doing now?"

If anyone asks me what my proudest moment in 48 years of show business was, I would say it was the night that I saved the day at the Shubert.

1992/2005: Bruce Adler, Monty Python, And I

Harry Groener, Actor

One of my favorite parts of *Crazy for You* was the duet I sang with Bruce Adler, "What Causes That?" Bruce and I did four Broadway shows together: *Oklahoma!, Oh, Brother!, Sunday in the Park with George,* and *Crazy for You.* Four! That's just unheard of. He was a dear, dear friend, and I miss him. I really miss him.

People always told us that it looked like the number took forever to put together, but it really didn't. It was just Bruce, me, and Susan Stroman in the room, and Susan—to her credit—left us alone a little bit, to figure it out. Bruce and I had a short hand. We could collaborate without having to explain much. We finished each other's sentences.

"What Causes That?" was this iconic number in the show, and the whole conceit was that these two characters just happened to behaving as mirror reflections of each other. They couldn't be surprised by it; they weren't discovering it. The humor was that they were conscious of it, but their focus was on the women they were sad about. We were drunk and singing about Tessie and Polly, and doing all of the same things. Then the point came when we each sat down in a chair and took a bite of a hot dog, and then really looked at each other for the first time.

We looked at each other. And we chewed. And chewed. What you expect is for the two characters to go: *Is this a mirror?!* But we still don't do that. We look, and look, and look. And then take a second bite of the hot dog. It got a huge laugh because the song wasn't about being mirrors. We didn't care. It was just about the girls. We made that very clear. Bruce was really something.

One day years later, I got a call that they were interested in seeing me for *Spamalot.* I'm a Monty Python nut, so I was thrilled.

After spending three years at the Shubert on *Crazy for You*, I got to know a lot of people there. Then I came back a decade later, and it was like coming home. A lot of the stagehands, the front-of-house crew, and the box office staff were the same. It was just great, and the show was a ball.

216

I'm one of those Monty Python fans who would be at a party and have a grand time remembering certain scenes, and quoting lines with friends—and then I was actually onstage, saying Monty Python lines for real. It was a bizarre, fantastic experience. It was a celebration of silliness that made a lot of people very happy.

1992/2005: Full Circle

Casey Nicholaw, Director/Choreographer/Actor

I loved that *Spamalot*—my first show as a choreographer—was in the Shubert, because that was where I did *Crazy for You*, my first show as a performer. That was really cool to me, a full circle. It made me so emotional on opening night! Susan Stroman sent me a bottle of vodka for opening night of *Spamalot*, and I burst into tears. Being acknowledged by the person who gave me my Broadway break was really amazing.

I learned so much from directors and choreographers when I was a performer. In *Crazy for You*, on the second day of rehearsal, there was a great thing that director Mike Ockrent did. We each had a half-hour appointment with him as an ensemble member. We talked about the town of Deadrock, where the show takes place, and what we would want our position to be in that town. We all wrote little bios. So if I said, "I'm a go-getter, eager kind of guy," he was like, "Okay, then you're the guy who'd be cleaning up in this scene." I think that kind of specificity is fantastic when you're directing a show, and I got that from him. I thought it was the coolest thing, and also, you felt really important when he took that kind of care.

When I auditioned people for *Spamalot*, it was so fun. It was the best thing to see their faces! Mike Nichols said, "I leave it to you. You pick the people you want, I just want to come in and take a look at them and say okay." So we had the auditions and then I knew who I wanted to cast. So at the callbacks, it was just those people, but they didn't know it.

It was on a Broadway stage, because Mike wanted to see that. They were all walking in, and I know that feeling from being a performer. I watched all the dancers walk in the door and go like, *Is this it? Is this all the people that are here? Does this mean...?* That was great.

It's funny because at the first preview for any show, you're sitting there nervous, like, *How are they going to respond? I pray to God, I pray to God.* And some first previews are shocking. There's the whole cheerleader thing in *Spamalot*. My associate and I thought: *This is going to go, we're definitely going to end up cutting this.* And the minute it started, the audience just went ballistic. We looked at each other in one of those moments where you go, *Oh my God, this is landing so well! I can't believe it!*

1992: The Pink Girls

William Ivey Long, Costume Designer

I'm told that in subsequent productions of *Crazy for You*, the girls that come out of the car are always dressed distinctively. If they're not "the pink girls," they're "the blue girls." They're always wearing a similar silhouette for coming out of the backseat of that car, just the way we designed it.

It's something that's become identified with our show, and I love that.

1992: Returning To The Shubert For *Crazy For You*

Don Stitt, Actor

The Shubert is my favorite. There's no theater in this town that even comes close.

I've been in some nice theaters, but there's a reason that the Shubert is the flagship. They renovated the theater after *Buddy* closed and when I went to the first preview of *Crazy for You*, with my TKTS ticket, I didn't know what to expect. I walked in and the house staff all clustered around me and we chatted. I thought: *Oh, isn't that great? They remember me!*

But after that preview I went, *And they're never going to remember me again because this is the best show I've seen in ten years, and it's going to run forever.*

1996: The *Big* Kids

John Weidman, Writer

I guess *Big* is the only show I've ever done that had a significant number of kids in it.

Throughout the preview period, we were in rehearsals at the Shubert working on the show, and down in the lounge, school was going on! I'd come reeling down through the lobby, headed for the men's room, and kids would be on the floor, learning algebra. It was a very odd juxtaposition of different experiences.

1996: The Entire Premise Of The Show

Richard Maltby Jr., Writer/Director

Just before we opened *Big*, Mike Ockrent, the director, went, "Oh my God, this is so crazy. We've got this whole company of kids and in the last scene there's just the two of them."

He said, "What happens if Billy brings the kids back with him? So they're all there and they witness Josh's transformation back." And I thought, *The entire premise of the show is that none of the kids know he transformed in the first place. And now you're now gonna send six kids back to their houses who are gonna tell their parents, "That kid turned into a man and then turned back!"?* But Mike was determined to do it and that's what we opened with. Then another kid came in and put a quarter in and said he wished to be big.

That was the end of the show, but I thought it was silly. It was strange because we didn't sit around asking what the show was about. We weren't able to make sure everyone was on the same page.

1996: That Sub Sounds Terrible

Jason Robert Brown, Writer

Big had two particular effects that were actually controlled by the keyboardist in the pit, and my first job on Broadway was subbing for Brian Besterman on that particular keyboard book. One of them was in the first act when they danced on the keyboard. The keys on the keyboard lit up, but the sounds were actually controlled by me in the pit.

I was playing a whole bunch of notes that just sort of corresponded to wherever the actors were putting their feet onstage. I'm sure that now there would be a better way to handle that particular technology, but at the time it was all coming from me.

It sounded terrible if you listened to what I was actually playing, because it was only meant to correspond to the actors' feet. There was one day that I was practicing in the pit and I had the volume up just so I knew what I was doing. One of the other musicians heard me practicing and actually went to Paul Gemignani and said, "Gee, I don't know about that sub in the pit because it sounds like he's playing something terrible."

Then, in the second act, I also played when they were pulling straws in and out of soda cups. As they pulled them out, there would be straw noises, and all of those sounds were also made by me. As a private joke of the keyboard programmer, there were also a series of fart noises that were built into the keyboard, so that if your hand twisted in the wrong direction, the kids onstage would be doing something rather different than it looked like they were doing.

1996: *Rent* And *Big*

David Shire, Writer

When *Big* was out-of-town in Detroit, we did endless rewriting. Our director, Mike Ockrent, was always changing things. One song would be a replacement for another. I once counted all the songs we wrote for that show, and it came to 54 songs. And I guess it must have been a dozen that were written in Detroit. Which isn't the most fun city to be in in the first place!

Getting to New York was like: *Oh my God. We finally have a show at the Shubert.* To many, it's the premiere Broadway theater. And it was all kind of brand-new at the time—freshly painted and everything. And right on Shubert Alley. I thought: *What could be better?*

Then, *Rent* opened, and of course that dominated the conversation. We got mixed reviews and we only ran six months. So it was kind of a bittersweet experience.

On opening night, I was there with my son, who was ten years old, maybe a little younger. Because the seats were scarce, he was sitting farther down front, and my wife, Didi Conn, was in back, and during the show, they mentioned "foreplay." He came running back to Didi, and said, "What's foreplay? What's foreplay?" And she said, "It's what comes between pre-play and post-play." Which didn't clear it up at all. But I think she may have fully explained it later.

1996: A Kid Who's Having Fun

Jake Epstein, Actor

My first Broadway show was the musical *Big*, and I thought it was amazing. I was really young and on a family vacation; my parents took us to see the show on a whim.

I was like, "What is this?!" There were kids who were singing and dancing! It was such a great experience for me to see that. There were all these kids my age doing amazing things.

My family used to drive from Toronto to South Carolina for vacation once a year. That was the first time that my dad said, "Hey, let's go through New York." My sister was doing theatre at that point, but I wasn't. But we both loved *Big*; we *really* loved it. All we both wanted to do after that was see shows and buy cast recordings.

219

It became a family tradition. Everyone is busy, so we don't go to South Carolina anymore, but to this day, we all meet in New York for one weekend every year to see as many shows as we can.

1996: The Legends Of The Shubert

Frank Vlastnik, Actor

When I first moved to New York, my mentor was Vinnie Liff. He was a casting director who cast tons of shows, including *Grease* and *Over Here!* He did all the British imports like *Cats, Starlight Express, Les Mis, Miss Saigon, Aspects of Love*, and *Phantom*. He did a lot of great American musicals like *City of Angels, Kiss of the Spider Woman, Ain't Misbehavin'*, and *Dreamgirls*.

I did my college internship with Vinnie and he really took me under his wing. Then, years later, he cast *Big*, and it was the first Broadway show I was ever in.

Vinnie unfortunately died of a brain tumor ten years ago. After he passed, his partner and a group of 12 of us wanted to scatter his ashes in the theatre district—and it's totally illegal. Still, we all took a handful of ashes. Some people went to Sardi's and put them in front of the door, and some people went to *Phantom*. I went right to the Shubert stage door, because he got me in there and that's where I wanted to remember him. That's where he belonged.

I'd been in the Shubert so many times before *Big*, because from the time I moved here in 1987 until 1990 when it closed, I'd get standing room to *A Chorus Line* for $10 at least once every two weeks. When Donna McKechnie came back, I went every week! I lived down the street, and I'd go to the Roy Rogers or the Pizza Hut in the Minskoff walk-through, and then get a $10 ticket to *A Chorus Line*. I would always go on a weekday, because there would be a couple empty seats and one of the ushers would always come by and say, "Take any seat that's open, honey!" Then, after *A Chorus Line* closed, I saw *Crazy for You* probably four or five times.

Still, I had never been backstage there. And I had never really gotten to explore. Then, we moved into the Shubert for *Big*, and on matinee days, I'd sometimes go up into one of the boxes, when the theater was quiet, and take a little nap there. They had just renovated, so there was this beautiful, soft carpet, and I'd bring a little pillow and just nap in the Shubert. It was magical. There were lots of special places like that in the theater. Our men's ensemble dressing room opened up to the roof and the fire escape, so we had plants out there.

We had tried out in the Fisher Theatre in Detroit, and that felt like a football stadium! The mezzanine was so far away; I think it overhung row P, where most mezzanines overhang somewhere around row J. We really had to play the show as huge, and send everything "out there." The day that we did the walk-through of the Shubert, we were so relieved. We immediately knew it would help the show that the audience was right there.

I met an actor named Ken Kercheval at one point. He was on the TV show *Dallas* and did a bunch of Broadway shows as well. I met him when he was in Los Angeles while I was a reader for *Sunset Boulevard*. He was Larry Blyden and Alan Alda's understudy in *The Apple Tree* and when I met him, I said, "Mr. Kercheval, can I ask you a question? Were you there at the Shubert when Barbara Harris had her famous sort-of meltdown?" He said, "I was onstage with her!"

Alan Alda was sick, so Ken was doing *The Apple Tree* that night with Barbara. She started saying, "I see a tree, I see a cow, I see people, I see all you people..." and Jerry Adler, the production supervisor and stage manager, ran from the standing room at the Shubert, down the side aisle, through that pass door, and got up onstage yelling, "Bring it in! Bring it in!" They wanted to bring the curtain down because Barbara was obviously having a very difficult time with it.

220

Then he told me that they got Carmen Alvarez, Barbara's standby, and made the announcement: "Ladies and gentlemen, we're having a bit of a problem. Please hold." Carmen Alvarez went on for a bit while they called Phyllis Newman, who did the matinees. She came down from Central Park West. That night, Ken did the show with three different women. That's just another great Shubert story.

There was a quick-change room and a prop room stage left at the Shubert during *Big*. We had so many quick changes in that show! I had one that was very fast after the carnival scene, into the Port Authority scene where I played this homeless man called "Matchless," who asked everyone for a match for his cigarette.

Very early on in previews, I was standing there literally jumping out of one pair of pants and putting on a pea coat and little goatee, when a dresser said, "Well, Frank, how does it feel to be in a place of Broadway history?" I said, "What do you mean?" And he said, "This used to be the star dressing room at the Shubert. This is where Judy Holliday was when she did *Bells Are Ringing* for two and a half years. This was her room."

It had become a quick change room. So all of a sudden, I was thinking, *Well, if it used to be the star dressing room, this is probably Glynis Johns' room from* Night Music *and Lilo's from* Can-Can! I wondered, *Which Andrews sister got this?* because I knew they didn't get along during *Over Here!* And it had to be Jackie Gleason's for *Take Me Along*! I started thinking about all the shows, and I almost missed my entrance!

After *Big* closed, I went back to see *Chicago* there and I went backstage to see someone I knew. That room was still a prop room, because Bebe Neuwirth dressed downstairs in the wardrobe area during *Chicago*. Then I went back to see *Blithe Spirit*. A friend of mine had bid on and won a dinner with Angela Lansbury after the show as part of a fundraiser for The Actors Fund. After the performance, we went back and had champagne in her dressing room before eating with her at Orso. It was one of the greatest thrills of my life. And that room had turned back into the star dressing room! Angela had our old prop room turned back into a real star dressing room, with a little seating area, and drapes. I thought: *Good. This is what it should be. This is what should be at the Shubert.*

1997: Covering 21 Different Jobs

Fritz Frizsell, Stagehand

I've always loved *Chicago*. I worked *Chicago* for years, as sub followspot operator. It was really interesting seeing the different casts going through and how the performances would change as it ran. Michael Berresse was great in his original role as the hilarious cad Fred Casely, but when he played lawyer Billy Flynn, his speech in which he essentially threatens Roxie with death if she doesn't pay up and take his instructions seriously was chilling. Mamie Duncan-Gibbs and Deidre Goodwin were amongst my favorite replacement Velmas and Sandy Duncan was a riotous Roxie.

It was during that time that I was subbing on seven shows simultaneously. Seven! I think they were *Contact*, *Beauty and the Beast*, *Cabaret*, *Chicago*, *Follies*, *Rocky Horror*... I can't remember the seventh—*The Producers*, maybe? I was covering 21 people's tracks.

There were two weeks in a row where I did at least nine performances each week in five separate venues: two show Wednesdays, Saturdays and Sundays, plus I think one week had an Actors Fund show jammed in, making it a ten performance week.

One Sunday I was called while at a *Contact* matinee. They needed me to cover someone on that night's *Beauty and the Beast*. Due to the two shows' schedules, there wasn't time for me to make it. *Contact's* matinee ended after *Beauty and the Beast's* evening show had already begun, but it was an emergency and we didn't have a choice. Immediately after my last cue at *Contact*, I flew the 20 blocks downtown and made it to the Lunt just after the show began. Many times, I've done two different shows in one day. I've also done two different jobs on the same show on the same day.

Covering so many jobs, you can get confused as to which follow spot you're running. One time I was doing *Chicago* with another sub operator in another last-minute emergency situation. Neither of us had been there for a long time. The other sub is a very good operator, one of the best. We both knew all three spot jobs on the show, but because it had been so long, half the time I was doing his cues and he was doing mine—but we never missed a cue and no one was ever left in the dark. It's such a joy to work with someone like that, in a challenging situation and have everything go so perfectly, with the audience none the wiser of the craziness going on behind the scenes.

Before intermission of Padlocks of 1927 *at the Shubert, the chorus kids carried its star, Texas Guinan, out of the theater on their shoulders. She would cap the act one closing number by pointing across the street and yelling, "Go eat at Sardi's, suckers!"*

Texas Guinan was a legendary entertainer, owner, and hostess at a series of speakeasies, including the 300 Club on 54th Street. She was known for her catchphrase "Hello, suckers!" and for presiding over New York nightclub life as "The Queen of the West," a nickname given to her after she appeared in silent films as the first cowgirl of the U.S.A. (She even did all of her own stunts!) In Padlocks of 1927, *she also turned the Shubert into a raucous party, calling out audience members she knew by name, introducing herself to others, and encouraging those onstage and in the house to throw confetti at one another. She would later turn the speakeasy scene into a party as well, serving booze during Prohibition to the most exciting members of society and show business before each club was raided and padlocked—then she would open a new club. In various ways, Guinan was responsible for the careers of everyone from Walter Winchell and Ruby Keeler.*

Guinan is also responsible indirectly for the career of Mae West. West's first film appearance was in Night After Night *in 1932, playing a character based on Guinan. Guinan had been up for the role, but was eventually deemed too old to play herself. Earlier, a 25-year-old Mae West had actually played her largest role on Broadway to date at the Shubert, in the 1918 musical* Sometime, *where she introduced the shimmy to the Great White Way and played a racy woman who got in between the romantic leads. Another echo of Guinan's legacy at the Shubert came with* Chicago: *the character of Velma Kelly is said to have been modeled on her.*

1997: We Want Billy

Michael Berresse, Actor/Director

When I was doing *Chicago*, Bill Clinton came to see the show. It's the first time a President came to a show I was doing. There was all this security, and we all had to go through metal detectors just to get backstage. They ushered him in and he had all these people sitting around him. It was exciting.

It never occurred to me that the audience would also know that Clinton was there, and that there would be some fascination about him. So for the beginning of the show we felt a little bit like, *Hey, we're over here, watch the stage please!* Then, they kinda forgot and were watching the show.

Then, we got to Billy Flynn's entrance. All the girls came out and were writhing around the stage in their black underwear singing "We want Billy!" They just kept repeating it and repeating it and repeating it, and the giggles started in the audience… because of course Bill Clinton was there.

The girls kept repeating "We want Billy!" and in the audience, this roar of laughter started to build and build. The audience felt like the song was no longer about Billy Flynn. The whole story had become about how Billy Flynn became Bill Clinton. That was pretty funny.

The 1976 Tony Awards were a triumph for A Chorus Line, *with the show taking home ten statues. Never had the "second place" musical of the season been a more distant second.* Chicago, *with 11 nominations, went home empty-handed. Those involved with the production were heavily disappointed, and some even called out sick for a few days following the Tony Awards. Even though the original production of* Chicago *ran for 936 performances, it is now considered ahead of its time, as the revival has run for over 7400 performances and is still going strong. It is now the third longest-running Broadway show of all time, having even surpassed* A Chorus Line! *The revival of* Chicago *spent six years at the Shubert, from 1997 to 2003. It first played the Richard Rodgers (where the original opened)[93] and has now been at the Ambassador for more than 11 years.*

2003: A *Gypsy* Quick Change

Josh Marquette, Hair Designer

Quick changes are my favorite thing, just because they get your adrenaline going. When you're in tech and for the first couple of previews, they start out as the most horrifying thing ever. Then after a couple of weeks, you're having entire conversations during a quick change! You don't even have to think about it. It's no pressure, but it's so fun. It's your 30 seconds with the actor for that day.

30 seconds is the shortest change you can have and actually get one wig off and another wig on. I had one with my friend Dontee Kiehn in *Gypsy*. We had a quick change where I'd be standing in the dark, and my hands were full. I had a light in my mouth and a hat in this hand and a wig in the other hand. I had to get her wig off, get the new wig on, and put the hat on. And the hat was an apple, with these beaded wires coming off of it.

I'd be standing there, hands full, ready, and she would run up in the dark. At the time, I used to wear a lot of those shirts with snaps all the way down the front. So she'd run up and she'd rip my shirt open and there was nothing I could do! And I couldn't even snap it up as soon as I was done, because I had to get the hell out of there to get off the deck, and my hands were full. So I'd have to walk around the theater with my shirt unbuttoned like a jackass. She did that to me forever.

One day, Dontee went out onstage, and I was watching the show on the monitor. I was like, "What? What is that?" She was out there and they were dancing. Her costume had a garter with an apple on it, and she had something hanging from her apple, something black.

She said later that she was dancing and she felt something brush her leg. She thought it was the back of her costume, so she brushed it off and kept dancing. Then she felt it again, and looked down, and the bra she wore to the theater that day was hanging from the apple. She just picked it up, threw it off stage, and danced.

The first few rows had to have been like: *Why does that character have a bra hanging off her?!* It's live theatre. That's why. It's awesome.

---

[93] Check out *The Untold Stories of Broadway, Volume 1* for more on this story.

2003: Together Wherever We Go

Amy Wolk, Merchandise Manager/On Site Educator

The Bernadette *Gypsy* was the first time I felt like the merchandise staff was specifically included as an entity in the building during a show. We were invited to all the parties. Everybody in that place was a family. That was the first time that ever really happened to me. It's happened since, but that one was a really big deal.

Gypsy people were awesome, because they would have parties in the basement for holidays. There were huge parties in the lower lobby of the Shubert. I have pictures of Bernadette Peters hitting a piñata for Cinco De Mayo. And Secret Santa was really big there. I love when theaters do Secret Santa, and invite the front-of-house to participate. That doesn't always happen, but on BOTH *Gypsy*s, that happened!

The most explosive audience reaction I ever saw was the night after Bernadette Peters did not win that Tony for *Gypsy*. That next night, I have never seen anything like that. The show was amazing. The audience went berserk for her. They wanted to show their support.

My merchandise booth for *Gypsy* was in that corner—that stupid corner at the outside lobby of the Shubert. It's the windiest place on Earth! Every time they'd open the doors, my stuff would fly all over the place, which made me crazy. But everyone filed by my door. Right by me. Everybody. Mia Farrow and Kate Winslet had a whole conversation in front of my booth. Once, Tom Hanks stole a keychain from me, and then was like, "Teehee, I brought it back!" Often, the merchandise booth is hidden somewhere in an upper mezzanine, but at the Shubert, you're as central as the theater itself.

We used to love hanging out at Barrymore's. It's very sad that that's not there anymore. We used to love it, and I miss it. Barrymore's was on 45th Street, right next to where Frankie and Johnnie's is now. The Frankie and Johnnie's front used to be the Barrymore's back room. And I don't know that it was ever closed! It seemed like it was always open, 24 hours a day.

We used to go there a lot *during* the show. You could always get a burger, eat it during act one, and get back in time for your intermission. Or people would go after, and you could meet friends from other shows there. The people in the store, the people who sold merchandise, and the people in the cast—we would all just end up at Barrymore's, sitting in the back over a plate of tater tots.

We always went to Barrymore's, except on Monday nights, when we would go to Don't Tell Mama. We would hang out back in one of the cabaret rooms, and this guy, who was a boyfriend of one of the girls in the cast, would just sit there and play the piano all the time. And it was Gavin DeGraw! He turned into Gavin DeGraw. I was like, "We knew that guy!"

You never know who people are going to be. I've said that forever. My old roommate is in *Mamma Mia!* We started working at the Theatre Circle store together. And people I went to NYU with... Matt Morrison used to have the voice lesson before me. All these people! They all work, and I see them all the time.

I also used to like the cafe under the Marquis, where the Starbucks is now. It was called Ooh La La, and I was obsessed with their muffins. They would give you a discount if you worked in theatre. The Starbucks will too, which makes it about as expensive as any other Starbucks.

Then there's the guy at the Starlight Deli on 44th Street, who gets all the hats. He has a hat from every Broadway show! I always bring him a hat from the shows I work, and he gives me a sandwich in return. He's very upset if there's no hat. I'm always like, "We need a hat for this show. I need a hat for the deli guy!"

2003: Three Strippers On A Balcony

Julie Halston, Actor

The most moving experience I've ever had was opening the stage door on the very first day I got into the Shubert Theatre to do *Gypsy* with Bernadette Peters and Sam Mendes.

Opening that door and walking onto that stage, knowing we were opening such a fabled, amazing Broadway show as *Gypsy* was very moving. I think *Gypsy* is the best musical ever written, and it was the first musical I ever got to do on Broadway. I get teary just thinking about it. On my first day, I stood on the stage, with the ghost light on, and looked out, and just thought about how I was going to be doing "You Gotta Get A Gimmick" right there. It was amazing.

Every night, before the show started, I would stand in the wings on stage right in my first scene costume, and listen to that incredible overture.

The three strippers—myself, Kate Buddeke, and Heather Lee—had a dressing room with a balcony overlooking the street. We loved going out before showtime and looking at the crowds gathering. On opening night, we were hanging out the balcony, seeing Tom Hanks, Kate Winslet, and all these limos. One night, we were on our balcony and saw Cher. "You guys! Cher is coming tonight!" It was very cool.

2003: We Are Powerless

Ken Davenport, Producer

I was the company manager of *Gypsy* at the Shubert during the blackout of 2003.

I remember staring at my computer screen doing payroll. It was hot. I had a little $5 fan and it suddenly stopped. I looked up and out the window, and I watched the lights go out. The blackout rolled right up the streets, 41st, 42nd, 43rd... I thought, *What the hell is that?* And then the office went down. We tried to figure out what was happening on the radio. We had to go and cancel the show and deal with that.

We had no way of communicating with the staff, so I went to the theater to tell people in person that there wasn't a show. As company manager, I tried to help people get home. That was a crazy night.

When you work at the Shubert, you're in the flagship. Their executive offices are upstairs, so when you're a company manager, you get to see Phil Smith[94] come down and cash his checks at the box office. There's something about being in the facility that's special.

2003: Obsessed

Tim Federle, Actor

I made my Broadway debut in *Gypsy* at the Shubert. I had been obsessed with *A Chorus Line* in high school, and I had been obsessed with Bernadette Peters, and there I was, making my Broadway debut where *A Chorus Line* had played, in a show starring Bernadette Peters. It was almost too good to be true.

---

[94] Philip J. Smith is currently the chairman of the Shubert Organization.

On the first day of rehearsal, the legendary, spectacular standby (and leading lady in her own right) Maureen Moore came up to a bushel of us little fresh faced children at the meet-and-greet. She asked us all our names. Maureen was standing by for Bernadette, and she had made her Broadway debut in 1974 as Dainty June in the Angela Lansbury *Gypsy*. I remember her saying, "Is this your first Broadway show? You know you're doing it in the Shubert Theatre? You know it's *Gypsy,* right? It's all downhill from here."

In some way, she was right. There was something about that experience that was never topped. It was one of those unique times when the whole group knows they're part of something special. And I consider the Shubert to be *the* great Broadway theater.

Sam Mendes made the unusual choice of having the whole first week of rehearsal with no singing. I think it may have been because Tammy Blanchard had never sung, but I'm not sure. It was strange but I look back on it now and think: *What a brilliant director.* Our first week of rehearsal was a lot of sitting in a circle, reading the lyrics, and throwing pillows at each other, like we were Ohio State theatre majors.

About five days in, Bernadette was in the middle of the scene at the top of the show before "Some People" and Sam called out, "Should we do this?" The first time that we all heard Bernadette sing "Some People", we were sitting two feet away from her in a theatre games circle. She never marks,[95] which I think would surprise people who think she might be protective with her voice. Bernadette Peters sang out "Some People" loudly and brilliantly and for the first time. The minute she was done, Sam said, in the understated way that only British people can, "Shall we have a tea?" That was his way of sending us on a 15-minute break.

I walked very slowly to the New 42nd Street Studios exit door and ran out to that long cement stairwell to cry. When I got there, Chandra Lee Schwartz, who was making her Broadway debut and went on to play Glinda in *Wicked*, was there too. We grabbed each other and started jumping up and down. All these years later, whenever we see each other, we say, "Remember that time?"

I was so starstruck by Bernadette Peters. Near the end of the run, my mom came back to see the show one last time and when I took her to meet Bernadette in her dressing room, I said, "Bernadette, this is my mom, Lynn. We are such fans." I said "We are such fans" after I had been working with her for nine months!

I remember walking into the Shubert on the first day and seeing Anthony Ward's set being lit. Only half the set was onstage, and half was flown out, and the lights were half on. Jules Fisher and Peggy Eisenhauer lit the show, which was old-school and exciting. I actually stole a plot point from that day for my book *Better Nate Than Ever.* All of the other boys were running around and squealing, and I was just standing there, reverent, taking myself too seriously because Priscilla Lopez performed *here.* Donna McKechnie did her turns *here.* For me, it was like walking into a church because of *A Chorus Line.*

During tech, I found this "Naughty Baby" lyric sheet on stage left that Michele Pawk had pasted to the wall when she did *Crazy for You.* Her husband, John Dossett, was our Herbie, and I remember pointing it out to him.

I understudied David Burtka, who played Tulsa, and went on for him about 15 times during the run. David didn't miss a lot of shows, and I never went on unexpectedly. People were rarely out of that production. Also, we ran for over a year and only two or three people left the cast. That's pretty extraordinary. The first time that I went on as Tulsa, I was very nervous, and Tammy Blanchard really helped me. When you're onstage with her, she has these laser beam eyes and she doesn't break character. She was the calm in the middle of a storm. She's special. I've never been part of a cast like that, before or since. We actually just had a reunion a couple weeks ago, after all these years.

---

[95] marks: rehearsing the basic ins and outs of a role without doing so at performance level

There are certain dressing rooms at the Shubert that are more coveted. When you walk in the stage door, and walk past Rose, you first get to what is usually used as a stage management office. On *Gypsy*, that room belonged to Bernadette Peters. Joel Grey designed her dressing room, and it resembled a sexy Jewish dentist's office. It had grass cloth wallpaper and constant steam everywhere. The Farm Boys had the basement dressing rooms, and the Hollywood Blondes were upstairs.

At the Shubert, everyone wants the dressing room that's stage right, up a long set of stairs. People bitch about going up and down the stairs, but there's a famous balcony up there on the dressing room fire escape. When a show runs long enough, eventually you see a picture of its chorus boys planting things. That's when you know a Shubert show is a hit: when the chorus boys create a garden in Shubert Alley.

There are two meaningful plaques that flank the Shubert Theatre.

The first is close to the Shubert stage door: "Shubert Alley: Dedicated To All Those Who Glorify The Theatre And Use This Short Thoroughfare." This plaque was dedicated in 1963, to celebrate the 50th anniversary of the theater.

The second was placed inside the Shubert lobby in 1991 to commemorate the long run of A Chorus Line. *The plaque was the culmination of a fundraising drive led by Gary Stevens and Alan George, who wrote the fascinating book* The Longest Line: Broadway's Most Singular Sensation: *A Chorus Line.*

The bronze inscription proclaims: "Shubert Theatre, Home of A Chorus Line, *The Longest Running Show in Broadway History." (At the time, it was, having since been passed by* The Phantom of the Opera, Cats, *the revival of* Chicago, The Lion King *and* Les Misérables.*)*

2003: Bernadette Peters Included Us

Tony Massey, Merchandise Manager

I've worked on two shows with Bernadette Peters: *Annie Get Your Gun* and *Gypsy*. I think she is the most beautiful, charitable, wonderful person I've ever worked with in this business. She is great. And her assistant, Patty, is amazing. Nobody has a better assistant.

When we worked on *Gypsy* with Bernadette, she gave everyone in the theater a Christmas gift, and she included us on the merchandise staff. She gave us these stunning Tiffany ornaments. She's just one of those people. She wouldn't forget the front-of-house, including the merchandise people. She made sure the bar staff was included in things, too.

That group on *Gypsy* was the most inclusive group I've ever worked with in New York. There have been other groups that were very close, that I enjoyed, but *Gypsy* was special. And Bernadette Peters set that tone from the top down. It felt like everyone wanted everyone else to be a part of it. We had great parties in the lobby at night. There were parties just because, and everyone was invited.

A couple years after we'd worked on *Gypsy*, I went to see *The Pajama Game* at the American Airlines. I was standing there in the lobby before the show with Amy Wolk, and Bernadette and Patty came in. Now, out of context, I wouldn't necessarily expect Bernadette to know who I am. But she and Patty came over and both said hello to me and Amy. Then, Patty had to go check on tickets, and there we were, standing alone with Bernadette Peters. Even though we'd worked on shows together, it was a different moment. It was a social situation, and it was just us, having a little conversation. People kept coming by Bernadette, and they would just say, "Oh my God, we love you!" or "You're so amazing!" Great things, and she deserves all of that. One woman stopped and said, "I loved you in *Annie Get Your Gun*." And Bernadette turned and pointed to Amy and me and said, "They worked on it too!"

The moment when Bernadette Peters included us and what we do as part of the process—and pointed that out to someone—was so great. It was a moment that I'll never forget. We stood there with her, and she put us all in the same boat. We were all part of this show. *Just because I was the star, it's not the most important thing. We were all part of making a show we loved happen.* It gives me goosebumps even now, because it was just amazing that she understood that.

There are people in this business that aren't like that. Sometimes producers forget that we're a part of this, too. The front-of-house staff is right there on the front lines. Your show is important, and it got people into the theater, but the face of your show is also the ushers and the bartenders and the merchandise staff and the box office. It's all of those people who the audience interacts with during their theater experience. Unless you wait at the stage door and maybe get an autograph, we're the only people you'll actually interact with in the theater. Some producers and some stars really understand that.

2004: Whaddaya Got For Us?

Hunter Bell, Actor/Writer

One of my most memorable auditions on a Broadway stage was for *Spamalot*. I got a callback, and that was on the stage of the Shubert. It was a huge deal to me, and Mike Nichols was in the audience. I didn't get the job, but I spent the whole time thinking how much like a movie it was. It felt like *A Chorus Line* or *Tootsie*, like what you think a Broadway audition will be like, when you're growing up.

I walked out on the stage of the Shubert, and in the dark, I heard someone say, "Okay, Hunter, whaddaya got for us?"

2005: *Gunga Din*

Larry Hochman, Orchestrator

During *Spamalot* at the Shubert, we had many revisions during previews. Then there came a point when we were frozen.[96] It was only about three days before opening. We'd already recorded the cast album.

I came in to watch the show, and it was early so I went to the dressing room of the conductor, Todd Ellison. It was in the basement corridor.

I entered the dressing room and he said, "Oh, it's Mike Nichols again. He's talking about some thing with the overture." He's rolling his eyes, as if Mike Nichols has lost his mind. "Now he's talking about *Gunga Din*." I cut in, and I said, "*Gunga Din*! That's exactly what we should do! I know what he's talking about!" "You do?" He couldn't believe it. So Todd said, "Let's go up and find Mike. He's in the stage manager's office."

We ran up to the stage manager's office of the Shubert, and who's there, of course, but Mike Nichols and Eric Idle. Mike sees me, and I just say to him, "*Gunga Din*! We should do that!" He looks up, elated, and he says, "You know that?"

---

[96] frozen: the point of the creative development process of a show when it is decided that changes can no longer be made, and the show at that moment must be the final version; usually during the last week of previews

228

I said, "This'll sound really weird but I actually have a recording of it." The reason I have a recording of it is that in 1976, I spent a couple of hours here and there hanging out in Stephen Sondheim's brownstone with him because we're fellow record-collectors—and he played me what he claimed was the funniest thing he'd ever heard. He got a copy of it off the TV: *Gunga Din*.

This was a Wednesday night. By the very next day, I had done a whole new routine for the show. It's called the Prelude in *Spamalot*. There are instructions to the trumpet player like, "This is the beat that the conductor shoots you with a gun. Though badly wounded, you continue to play the next phrase." And then there's a final instruction, "With your dying breath, you manage to squeak out one last note."

It's not on the *Spamalot* album, but it was performed that night, and that's how it remains today.

———————

The conductor's basement corridor at the Shubert has an entrance with a couple steps up, followed by a couple steps immediately down, for no apparent reason at all. It's affectionately called "the conductor's speed bump."

———————

2005: The Joy Of *Spamalot*

Rose M. Alaio, Door Woman/Actor/Educator

I barely watched the Pythons on TV during my youth. So, when I heard *Spamalot* was coming, I rented the film it was based on. I hated it! It was stupid and had no ending. *And this is coming into my theater!* Then rehearsals started and all I did was laugh. It was brilliantly maniacal.

The show starred Tim Curry, Hank Azaria, David Hyde Pierce, Christopher Sieber, and Michael McGrath. What a cast! They are all funny, funny men. During intermission of the invited dress rehearsal, with tears rolling down my face, holding my stomach, I stood up and walked over to Eric Idle. I told him, "You are one sick puppy." He said, "Oh, thank you, Rose!" That show just uplifted everyone, both onstage and off.

At one point during the run, a woman came to the door. Her name was Ann Gestring and she had just seen the show. She said, "My son is in Iraq and he loves the Pythons. He's so excited about *Spamalot*." Company members immediately put a basket together, containing the *Spamalot* CD, t-shirts, and the program. We gave it to her, and she sent it to Iraq.

Her son, Lieutenant Craig Gestring, sent back pictures of a Jeep in the middle of the desert. Attached to the antenna, blowing in the wind, was the *Spamalot* t-shirt we'd sent. He wrote us saying that he was playing the CD full blast in the desert. Months later, Craig came to the show with his wife. What an incredible man. His wife's name was Susan, and she was in the Air Force. I asked, "Where did you meet? You're in the army and Susan is in the Air Force." He replied, "In jail." This man had the Python sense of humor! That's why he loves them so much.

The reason Craig joined the army was that his brother was in the World Trade Center when it was attacked. He was hospitalized in New Jersey, and his room overlooked the smoke that billowed from Ground Zero for months after. Craig looked at Ground Zero from his brother's hospital window every day, and then he did two tours in Iraq. Craig brought his brother to the Shubert to see *Spamalot* too. They were both doing great.

Theatre can be curative. Theatre is so many things.

2005: King Arthur's Strongest Knights, All For One And One For All

Steve Rosen, Actor

Spamalot was my first time in a play where I had a fancy body mic, and a wig cap! I had been doing cool underground theater, but was never in anything that had a budget before.

I was casting director Tara Rubin's audition reader[97] for a couple of years. Tara was a huge mentor to me starting out. I was the reader for the first national of *The Producers* (I met Mel Brooks!), *The Frogs* (I met Sondheim!), *Bombay Dreams* (I had to learn a Hindi accent!), *Jersey Boys* (I got kissed by lots of pretty ladies!) and then I was the reader for *Spamalot*—and I got hired! The reader got the job.

The Shubert has a view from the stage that I can still see when I close my eyes. I did *Spamalot* for two years. It was incredible to think that there were so many people out there sitting in an environment that felt so intimate. It was smaller than the theater that we were in for the Chicago try-out so it didn't have that *Oh my God, look how big it is* feeling to it. In fact, it was like, *Oh my God, they're right there!*

Every Sunday after the show, we would go up to the men's ensemble dressing room—stage right upstairs—and do Shot Night! Someone would be in charge of making a fancy shot, and after the last show, we'd all meet up there for a toast of "Good week!" The first year of that show, it was so loved and all of us were having such a good time with each other. I was so young and erroneously thought: *Every show I do is going to be like this!*

We were so happy to be there that we'd stay for hours after our 8th show of the week. There's a fire escape that goes into that alley between the Broadhurst and the Shubert, and in the springtime, there were benches set up there and buckets for ashtrays, and crew guys would go up there for a smoke break. It was this incredibly peaceful place where you realized, *Unless I was in this show, there's no way that I'd ever be allowed to go here—I'm probably not allowed to go here now!*

One day Alan Tudyk and I closed out shot night. After everyone left, we decided to start climbing up the fire escape of the Shubert, until we got up to the roof. It was before camera phones so the only proof is in our memories. We were like, "We are standing in a place that no one ever goes!" Now I'm sure that after I tell you this story, and it gets printed in a book, there will be cameras—but it was like being by yourself, standing on the nose of the Statue of Liberty! It was like a kid who loved Broadway's dream. It was like landing on the moon.

We did "Dollar Friday." John Bolton brought that ritual to the show. Every Friday, to the tune of "Dreamgirls", we'd sing: "Monday we're off 'cause there's no show, Tuesday we're back and ready to go, Wednesday we do it not once but twice, Thursday's payday and that's just nice! And now it's Dollar Friday. Dollar Friday. Dollar for a girl and dollar for a guy day. Dollar Friday. Dollar Friday. Do do do do do do tonight!"[98]

Then John would go around with a bucket, and everyone would write their name on as many dollar bills as they wanted and put them in. Everyone in the theater was invited to do it—from backstage to front-of-house. He would go up in the grid and make sure to get the crew guys and he would go down in the pit to get the orchestra. Then, during intermission, he'd reach into the bucket, and pull a dollar out. Whoever's name was on the dollar bill would win all the dollars in the bucket. "Dollar Friday!"

It was always great because if they said, "Dollar Friday goes to... Meredith in wardrobe!" there would be a "Woooo!!" from the basement that you could hear throughout the entire house. David Hyde Pierce and Hank

---

[97] audition reader: someone who assists at an audition by reading roles opposite the actors in consideration

[98] I interviewed Steve Rosen at Worldwide Plaza, where he actually performed this song for me. Passersby may have thought they were experiencing an audition for an environmental production of *Forbidden Broadway* at Blockhead's.

230

Azaria—two of the finest human beings I've ever met, and two of the finest actors you could ever hope to work with—they felt the right thing to do for Dollar Friday was to put in one $100 bill each, to sweeten the pot for everyone else. Because everyone knew these $100 bills were in there, everyone started putting in more money. When David and Hank left the show, it went from, "This week's Dollar Friday is $503!" to "This week's Dollar Friday is $26!"

Spamalot liked to gamble. I ran a *Survivor* pool. Some of us were really into *Survivor*. I was a nerd about it so I would type up a recap every week of quotable quotes. Later, some people were like, "I don't watch *Survivor*, I just did it because I have a terrible gambling addiction and I really enjoy reading your things every week, because they're funny."

Christian Borle was the master of making things interesting backstage. He's such a thoughtful, funny, creative dude, so if you passed him at the same time backstage every day, it would become a game. We had dressing rooms next to each other, and it was such a blessing to go through that first experience next door to him.

He really made every day hilarious. We had a tradition where every time he rang this bell, I would run into his dressing room as a Southern person and say, "Chicken and ribs are done?!" I remember the last day he was at the show, he rang the bell, I ran into his room as usual, and out in front of me was an enormous plate of chicken and ribs! We had a feast together and that was lovely.

There was just a real family feeling backstage at the Shubert during *Spamalot*. I had another great tradition with Hank Azaria. I was Concorde and he was Lancelot, and after the scene where I got shot by the arrow, we had the same 11 minutes off until the next scene. Hank is a mensch and every night, we'd go up to his dressing room and drink from his refrigerator that was stocked with Diet Dr. Brown Cream and Black Cherry sodas.

The show itself had so much going on, that there wasn't a lot of time during performances to fraternize, but there was this built in 11 minutes where the two of us were off stage. Because of that, the people I really bonded with were whoever played Lancelot. After Hank left, Alan Tudyk took over, and I explained to him that Hank had left his refrigerator stocked purposefully because there was a part of the show where we would go drink a soda together. That was great. When Steve Kazee came into the show as Lancelot, we did the same thing and became great friends.

My dressing room was on the 4th floor, and if you went all the way up the stairs, you'd get to a locked door. We thought maybe it was Narnia, but every once in a while, we'd be getting ready for the show and suddenly, three guys in suits would come down the steps. We realized the door led to the Shubert offices over the theater!

Because of the confetti canons we used in *Spamalot*, there were cameras you could control backstage that were trained on the audience. Because of that, we could see exactly who was in the house. If your mom was there, everybody would be watching your mom watch the show. We could train it on people! So if there was a celebrity there, we'd be like, "Oh, Mario Batali thought that line was funny."

Spamalot was insane in terms of celebrity visitors. One night, George Clooney, Rob Lowe, David Hasselhoff, and Judd Apatow were all there. On the same night! It was the day before *The 40-Year-Old Virgin* opened, so Judd Apatow must have been in town for the premiere. It was amazing to meet that dude the day before he had his first big hit movie. He reached icon status basically by the end of the weekend!

You know who gives great backstage? Liza Minnelli! Big surprise, right? She kept coming back to the show, and the second and third time, she got on the PA system and announced, "Hey, you crazy kids, it's me, Liza May *Minnulli*. I'm gonna be onstage in a minute, and I want to see each and every one of you gypsies and I want to give all of you a big hug because you've changed my life and I love your show."

That was a moment. We're in our dressing rooms at Shubert Theatre and Liza May *Minnulli* is calling us to the stage, because *she* wants to give *us* hugs.

There are traditions on Broadway that date back a century. People have been heading to Sardi's on opening night for 90 years! From the gypsy robe to "Dollar Friday," the traditions bond us all together, through decades and across streets. When Tevye sang "Tradition!" I'm pretty sure he was talking about "Shot Night" and opening night telegrams. That's one of my favorite of all of the Broadway traditions—on opening nights, theatre folks used to get piles of papers from Western Union. This tradition lives on in an altered form: now, every time a show opens, the Broadway theater that is their home gets a pile of papers wishing them luck signed by the full cast from every other show on Broadway.

I personally save one from every Broadway show I work on. I still have opening night telegrams from A Chorus Line *to* [title of show], Follies *to* Godspell, *and more. Broadway is a community that brings humans together every night to tell a story to other humans—and wishes each other well from right down the block. That is our oldest tradition, and one that no one else has.*

2005: The Whole Thing Was Magical

Christian Borle, Actor

On *Spamalot*, the whole thing was magical. It was as exciting as you imagine it would be, with all those people. I learned so much watching everyone, especially Tim Curry and David Hyde Pierce and Hank Azaria, in terms of playing comedy for a live audience. Before that, my instinct had always been that you always keep driving the action forward so you can get the laugh.

In the "not dead yet" scene, they'd drag me on and banter over me and I would interject "I'm not dead." I kept jumping on laughs—and I started to notice that *they* just sat and let the audience laugh. And laugh. Once they were laughed out, the audience would be free to hear the next line. And then they would laugh some more. So I learned to relax a little more watching them.

One of the most amazing things that ever happened to me was that when I went to Chicago to do the out-of-town run, I was on a "pink contract," an ensemble contract. Equity came and saw that my part had grown, and they decided to make the role a principal contract.

By that point, there wasn't room backstage to give me a dressing room. So I was in an ensemble dressing room, which was pretty tight—with great, fun guys. But when Hank heard that there was no place for me, he offered his dressing room. It was a teeny little hallway of a closet of a dressing room, and he just said, "Well, come be in my dressing room! This doesn't make sense. Come hang out with me, and we'll have fun!" I don't think that a lot of people would've done that. We had a very good time. We would play Nerf Basketball in the hallway. In New York, I shared a wall with Steve Rosen, and we had all kinds of crazy fun.

Spamalot was such a hot show when it opened in New York. It was so full of fun people coming to see it, and they would announce who was waiting onstage to meet the cast! Every night, there was someone very exciting. In the face of every fun, fancy person who came, the biggest applause and "whoop" that I heard from the cast backstage was for Harvey Korman and Tim Conway. When they came, the people backstage just went nuts. And they were so sweet and gracious.

I remember the night that Nancy Reagan came to the show. I'm a Democrat, and not a Reagan fan. People were surrounding her—and that was the same night that Lauren Graham was at the show. Sutton Foster and I were obsessed with *Gilmore Girls*; we couldn't get enough. That was probably the first show I ever binge-watched.

And Lauren Graham was standing off to the side by herself! I was like "I don't care about Nancy Reagan. I want to meet Lauren Graham!" I was really starstruck.

————————

During Spamalot, *there was a true changing of the guard. Bernard B. Jacobs and Gerald Schoenfeld, heads of the Shubert Organization, both passed away during the run of the show, and Philip Smith and Robert Wankel took over the offices above the Shubert.*

————————

2009: Put It Back!

Rose M. Alaio, Door Woman/Actor/Educator

Memphis was an important musical with an important story, and the producers of *Memphis* were great. They wanted as many people as possible to be able to see their show. They won the Tony, and only raised the price of tickets by $5. Usually, producers raise it a lot more!

I loved *Memphis*! During previews, David Bryan and Joe DiPietro worked on the show together every night. There was one scene where a white D.J. played "The White Tones" and then the lights would go up on a black D.J., playing rock 'n' roll. One night, they tried the show with the white D.J.'s scene cut. No one was happy about it. After the show ended, I chased down David Bryan and pleaded with him: "Put it back!" I said, "Did you ever see the movie *Seabiscuit*? It's about a horse and the country. By cutting that scene, you just took the country out of *Memphis*!" He told me that they agreed and were working on putting it back in the next night.

The show also did focus groups. And they sent the two standbys to other states to perform songs from the show—and that worked! Busloads of people came to the Shubert because of those performances. Those producers were smart, and the message of the show could not be beat.

2009: *Memphis* Lives In Me

Chad Kimball, Actor

My first experience at the Shubert was with Montego Glover. We were given the task of picking our dressing rooms for *Memphis*. They had just put up the show's gigantic poster outside the Shubert, which took up the entire front and side of the theater. We just looked at it.

After working together since 2003—auditioning together, kissing in that final callback, and then getting it—we had spent *seven* years getting there! So we were looking at that poster, and we both just started crying.

The fact that they stuck with what worked instead of going with star names, that was incredible. We were so involved with David Bryan and Joe DiPietro and Chris Ashley in writing the magic of what the show was, and the producers knew that. There were five of us that stayed, from the first production in North Shore in 2003 to Broadway. It was just a dream come true. We picked our dressing rooms, and I met Rose, the door woman. That was my first time at the Shubert.

To be able to be in the Broadway theater where *A Chorus Line* had been was just magical. Angela Lansbury had my dressing room during *Blithe Spirit*. And David Hyde Pierce during *Spamalot*. Only Make Believe, an organization that introduces theatre to children in need, had a benefit at the Shubert while we were there. They asked if one of the guest stars could use my dressing room on my day off. I asked who, and they said Ian McKellen would be using my dressing room.

I wrote a note to him on my mirror, in marker, and he wrote *me* a note! I have it framed. "Chad, thank you for the loan of your room. Enjoy your triumph. Ian McKellen." The next year, it was Jeremy Irons, and he wrote me a note, too. So sweet. Cool, cool, cool!

At one point in the run—we had been doing it for a while—we were still giving it our best, but I think that people were getting a little antsy. We knew that this big group of kids was coming to see the show,

We did the curtain call, and then the first "Steal Your Rock And Roll". All of a sudden, we see these kids standing up and doing the choreography! And singing louder than we are! I don't think there was a dry eye on that stage. Unbeknownst to us, they had been learning the choreography for weeks!

J. Bernard Calloway put it quite succinctly. We did a talkback afterwards and he said, "That was probably one of the most special moments in my life," with tears in his eyes. And it really was, it just really was. We were buoyed for weeks and weeks from those kids, and I still watch it on YouTube.

I counted how many minutes I was off stage, and of the entire show, I was off stage for 11 minutes and 45 seconds. And those weren't moments where I could just sit down—those were quick changes, and then I was back on again. It was hard to navigate, and then it was even harder with the nerve damage that I sustained. I lost some lung capacity and really felt it in my ribs. There were a lot of things that I couldn't do, and I tried and tried and tried because I loved that show. I should've taken a leave of absence; instead, it just got to the point where I couldn't do eight shows a week. The producers understood that, so we started a schedule where my standby Bryan Fenkhart would do matinees. It was just a lot of work. The role has gotta be somewhere in the top five list of most difficult male roles ever—and it was the love of my life and I *still* want to do it again someday.

The last performance was a tough day. My dresser Jim Hodun was my best friend. He was with me every second of the show. He knew when I was hurting and when I couldn't pick myself up, he'd be there spurring me on to win the race. I didn't pick him to be my dresser, but it just worked out that we were kindred spirits. He's still my best friend, I'd do anything for him. And sometimes I'd think: *I'm in pain. But I want to see Jim, he'll make me feel better.*

I had a receiving room, and then my dressing room, and there was a little door in between. He was very by-the-book, and said that dressers are supposed to sit in the hallway. But we were such great friends and I said, "Jim just sit in here! If you don't sit in here I am going to be very, very upset." My favorite thing was making him laugh. At first he was very serious, not a laugher, but then we just had the greatest time.

---

*Chad is a 44th Street Broadway Baby. He saw his first Broadway show there (*The Who's Tommy *at the St. James), made his Broadway debut there (*The Civil War *at the St. James), appeared in* Into The Woods *and* Lennon *(at the Broadhurst), and then landed* Memphis *at the Shubert. (By the time you read this, who knows? Chad may be starring in* Phantom.*)*

When I asked him if there was a Broadway theater he would want to work in that he hadn't yet, Chad's answer was unique: "I want to work in the Booth so I can go back to the alleys connecting the theaters!" My jaw dropped; it was the first time I'd heard of such a thing. Chad described the catwalks that connected the back sides of the Shubert, Booth, Broadhurst, and Schoenfeld. At my excitement, he suggested, "Why don't we go there now?"

And with that, on a sunny May afternoon in 2013, Chad Kimball and I walked from Worldwide Plaza to the Shubert Theatre, where he asked if a friend of his, a security guard he became close with during Memphis, *was in. He wasn't. "Oh, it's alright!" I assured him. Chad was un-deterred. "We'll come back tomorrow! You've got to see it. It's incredible."*

The next day, true to his word, there we were walking around the four levels of catwalks that connect four of the most famous Broadway theaters. "When we first moved in with Memphis," *Chad told me, "I would always come out here to relax. I could hear* The Merchant of Venice *next door, with Al Pacino." He pointed at the Broadhurst. "It's probably the only place in midtown Manhattan where you're completely blocked off from any sound." He was right. It was completely quiet, although we were surrounded by* Matilda, Lucky Guy, I'll Eat You Last: A Chat With Sue Mengers, *and* Orphans. *I wondered if the little girls crossed paths with Tom Hanks, Bette Midler, and Alec Baldwin out here.*

"It just kind of became mine, you know? I would come out here between shows and think about all of these theaters and who had been in them." Chad's sentiments about the backstage catwalks made me wonder who else had spent time out there. Since all four theaters had been built by the Shuberts, I learned that it was their intention to have these passageways for easy access throughout.

The theater back side alleyway is not the only fun way to end up somewhere unexpected at the Shubert. A pass door in house right leads to four steps that take you directly to the stage right wings. In the ladies' room, there's an outer area with a door that says "Employees Only." Open it, make a left, and you're backstage.

2013: The Kids' Time Capsules

Deborah Abramson, Musical Director/Conductor

The kids of *Matilda* have a lot of traditions with each other, which makes me happy. I have a few myself. After "Revolting Children," I go out to where the kids cool off after that number, and I hang out with them for a bit. Then when it's time for them to come back in, I stand in the wings during the bows. I noticed that Marcia McIntosh, wardrobe, who I knew from *Ghost*, always got herself a cup of water after her final cue. I didn't want to feel in the way, because I still hadn't figured out where I belong at the Shubert, so I thought, *Okay, that's what I'll do. Whenever I stand here, I'll have a cup of water ready for Marcia.* We do that now, and I hope it's the beginning of many tiny traditions.

The children's dressing room is at the top of a very, very, very high staircase. You can see the whole staircase from the wings. That staircase is now half-covered with photographs I've taken of the children. Bobby Wilson, the head guardian, laminated them and taped them to each stair. Many of those children have moved on now, but we get to see their faces every time we climb up to that room.

Heather Tepe, one of our swings, did *Gypsy* ten years ago at the Shubert. And *those* kids made a time capsule and put it under the carpeting in one of the rooms. When we got there to start *Matilda* tech, she found it!

I just saw Leon, who's our incredible day door man—he's downstairs in the hair room. He brought down a bicycle to work on; he's adjusting bikes for a whole bunch of different people in the company, and then on Monday they're going to go for a ride and he's going to show them how to switch gears. I have a great video of him on opening night coming outside to wish all the kids good luck, as they were all getting their "Maggot" t-shirts and taking happy selfies.

I like to think and to hope that at *Matilda*, we're building a home for a while. During *Ghost*, when I went to Office Depot to get containers for our locker room, I cried. Because I thought, *I don't know how long we're going to be here.* And I hated that. So on *Matilda*, I've been very careful. But I've finally settled down enough to cautiously help build as rich a home as I can.

There's always confetti on the floor after the show, and there's always a few stray pieces before each show before the house staff get to it. There's one little girl in the cast who takes two pieces, folds them up, then slides them into a secret place in the set before every performance. It's for good luck. I love that. And I hope they're still there when they take it apart.

2013: During Wednesday Matinees, I Can Hear The Show In My Office

Robert E. Wankel, Co-CEO and President of The Shubert Organization

The Shubert Theatre was built so that the Shubert family could live on top of it. The floor we're on right now was once Lee Shubert's apartment. This was the master bedroom. I still have the original bathroom, including the original tiles and a barber's chair.

We've renovated this floor, but much of it still looks very much similar to how it did when it was built. I redid this office after Gerald Schoenfeld passed away in 2008. Next door is Phil Smith's office, which was originally the sitting room. It still has the original ceiling.

The dining room was on this floor, and it was two levels. We've turned the downstairs level into a file room, but the upstairs part is very impressive. It has a chandelier and a little orchestra area, so you can bring in a group to play.

The front part with the piano used to be the office. Then what's now the office was the apartment. Lee Shubert's brother J.J. Shubert lived across the street, in our second building. We have portraits on the walls that belonged to them, original oils of their parents.

Back when *A Chorus Line* was here at the Shubert, we had this trap door in the floor that we could peek through, and we'd watch the show from there. It's still there, but it's closed now. At the Lyceum, the trap door is sort of on a low part of the wall, but the one we have here is literally on the floor. I don't think it was originally designed as a trapdoor—it appears to have been created for the old lighting bridge, and then turned into a trapdoor to watch shows from.

These days I'll walk down one flight into the balcony and watch *Matilda*. The balcony seats at the Shubert are wonderful. I also used to go down quite a bit to watch *Memphis*. I like to see the audiences' reaction to our shows. On Wednesday matinees, I can hear it from my office.

The very last interview I did before my first book was published was with Robert E. Wankel, current President of the Shubert Organization—called Bob by all who know him in the industry. A non-descript entrance in Shubert Alley led to an elevator which took me up to the Shubert offices in the fall of 2013. I kept myself from allowing my jaw to drop as I saw the waiting room and outside office. Dark, polished wood, hundreds of old books, a shiny grand piano—the Shubert offices, where Lee Shubert once made deals that built Broadway, and where the current leaders now preside, was every bit as magnificent as you'd expect.

I was led into Bob's office, where we spoke about all things Shubert, from the Ziegfeld Follies *to* A Chorus Line. *He even told me that there was a barber's chair in his bathroom where Lee Shubert used to get haircuts! As I was graciously given a tour of the entire office, I looked out a window and saw Sardi's across the street. I knew I was looking out a window that Lee Shubert once used to spy on his brother.*

A staircase from the Shubert offices led up to a conference room that had once been a dining hall, and down to... the mezzanine of the Shubert Theatre! As Bob told me he often snuck down to watch a few moments of Matilda *on matinee days, I knew that Gerald Schoenfeld had done the same during* Gypsy, *and Lee Shubert during the original production of* Kiss Me, Kate.

After the interview, I went—where else?—to Sardi's. I told Sean Ricketts, great-grandson of Vincent Sardi Sr., who currently runs the place with a neighborly smile, where I'd just come from. He offered to show me the other half of the Shubert office history: J.J. Shubert's offices, which had of course been above Sardi's. We took the elevator and Sean pointed out J.J.'s old working space, now bustling with workers busy with their own Broadway-related jobs. I looked out the window at the Shubert across the street.

———————

2013: Vomit And Maggots At Broadway's Classic House

Taylor Trensch, Actor

The Broadway theater I had in my head as a child looked like the Shubert. It's this big, classic, authentic place.

Matilda kind of spilled into *The Glass Menagerie* because our show was a bit louder. I remember watching Cherry Jones leave the Booth stage door on her bicycle. I bumped into Tom Hanks once, who was leaving the Broadhurst after a performance of *Lucky Guy*.

We entered and exited through the audience often during the show. Children would scream as we'd pop up behind them, but adults would actually scream more. And so many people puked during the show! We crossed through the lobby to get back to our dressing room, and so often we'd collide with someone pouring sawdust over some child's vomit on the stairwell or in the lobby. Usually it would be after the point in the show when the character of Bruce eats an entire chocolate cake. That was visceral for people and inspired some projectile vomiting.

For *Matilda*, one section of the women's bathroom was roped off while the show was going on and that's because there's a door there that leads backstage, and we'd enter and exit through it during performances. It didn't stop patrons from using that bathroom during the show, though. I had a lot of laughs with Lesli Margherita over bathroom noises.

The cast of *Matilda* was filled with kids so we had secret handshakes and chants. Every show began with all hands in a circle, and yelling "One-two-three-MAGGOTS!" Throughout the show, there were also little traditions before entrances between an adult and a child. A lot of Broadway shows do "Happy Trails speeches" when someone leaves the show, and the ones on *Matilda* were the best because they were delivered by nine-year-olds! They made me cry like an infant.

One of my favorite things about working on Broadway is walking though the stage door. It's such an exciting feeling every day, no matter how tired you are or how hard you feel like the show might be that day. Just walking through a Broadway stage door makes you feel great, especially at the Shubert because it's in Shubert Alley!

Every door person I've been lucky enough to work with has been so kind and funny. At the Shubert, there is Rose, who is just a pillar of strength and beauty. She loves animals as much as I do, and she makes everyone laugh. The door person is the first person you see when you come to work, and if they are happy to be there, it makes your life better.

2013: The Theater Is Never Cold And Never Empty

Rose M. Alaio, Door Woman/Actor/Educator

I saw Frank Rich, former theater critic for the *New York Times*, with his wife outside the theater last week. I know him from the time I was distributing headsets at *Angels in America*. That show changed people's lives. He came several times; he loved it. In fact, the picture of the ghost light on the cover of his book is from the Walter Kerr Theatre. I told him how wonderful *Matilda* is, and he said that he was seeing it in a couple of nights.

He came back before the show to say hello, and I told him how much his recent article in *New York Magazine* moved me. It was about Clayton Coots, the company manager he also wrote about in his book. I read it, and couldn't stop crying. Coots was his friend, and he was a tortured person. He had once written to Frank: "Happily, I am well adjusted to life enough to keep cheerful and 'up' but there are times I'm not and I get terribly lonely as I am today. The theatre is dark, it's cold and empty and I come here, for there is nowhere else to go." It made me so sad that he felt like that. I feel like the theater is never cold and empty.

When Bertie Carvel first came to the Shubert to play Miss Trunchbull in *Matilda*, he asked me to tell him the story of the ghost light. He told me they don't really have the ghost light tradition in London. I had him read the introduction in Frank Rich's book about the different ghost light theories. One theory is that if there aren't any lights in a theater, ghosts can take over. That's fine for some people. I go with another theory: that the ghost light is there for the ghosts of the characters who have gone before—not the people, the characters. Those spirits are all over the place.

Sometimes I'll take an actor onstage after their final performance, turn off all the lights, and leave only the ghost light. I tell them, "Say goodbye to your character." Then I walk off stage and let them have their moment.

Robert Urich was a wonderful actor who played one of the many Billy Flynns when *Chicago* was here. He was married to Heather Menzies, who was in *The Sound of Music* movie. Robert did the show and then had to leave, because he had cancer. We were so glad when he returned, but then he got sick and had to leave the show yet again. Right before he left, I took him onstage, and I turned all the lights off. I said, "Say goodbye to your character. To Billy Flynn." He looked around the theater, and he looked all the way up. I left him alone. After a while, Robert came off stage and said, "Thank you." The next night, he came back to see the show with his wife and then came backstage to ask me if I could turn the ghost light on for her to see. I did, and the two of them were alone on the stage for a while. Sadly, he passed away about a month later. What a dear human being.

After the final curtain came down on *Gypsy*, Bernadette Peters and I were onstage and I turned all the lights off and told her, "Say good night to Momma Rose." She looked at me and said, "Good night, Rose!" I said, "Not me! Your character!" I love her. She's the real deal—a genuine and good person.

Ironically, I was just voted the Best Stage Door Person on Broadway and was presented with the 2014 First Annual Ghost Light Award! How cool is that?!

I love theatre. I respect and love people who love theatre. Most of the time, everyone comes through the stage door to do their job and have fun. They're called "plays," after all.

2013: A Beautiful Theater That Isn't Dark Very Often

Randy Morrison, Stagehand

The Shubert is where I work now, and it's my favorite Broadway theater.

I've been here for 22 years or so. I got to the Shubert right after *A Chorus Line* closed. Before that, I was bouncing around from theater to theater, doing sound. When you work on the theater staff in the sound department, you usually do the wireless mics backstage. Those people are called the house guys. The sound person who comes with the company usually mixes the show out front. Those people are called the road guys.

For a while, I was a road guy. I would do a show through the load-in and then I would get laid off. Every theater seemed to already have enough house guys on staff to run the show.

When I got to the Shubert, *A Chorus Line* had just closed, and the next show, *Buddy*, was loading in. *A Chorus Line* didn't have any wireless mics; they only had foot mics and shotgun mics.[99] Because of that, there was no house sound man at the Shubert. So there was finally a spot for me. I became the Shubert's house sound man, and I've been there ever since.

The Shubert is a very nice theater, the premiere house of the Shubert Organization. Everybody on the crew is wonderful, and it's a beautiful theater that isn't dark very often. I really like working there.

We work a lot up in the ceiling. If you're seeing a show at the Shubert and you look up, you can see the decorative plaster. A lot of people don't know this, but that's not the roof of the theater. Above the plaster, there's an area with all of the cables that run all over the theater. Then there's also the grid iron, right above the stage. It's not for the faint of heart; you have to climb a ladder straight up.

At the Shubert, there's always a problem with our very small backstage area. It's about 10 to 15 feet on each side. It's really hard to get any set into the theater! And I remember during the musical *Big*, there was a big set for the F.A.O. Schwartz scene and they couldn't fit it through the loading doors. The set had to be cut in half in order to get it into the theater.

The fly floor is along the right and left side of every theater. There are a series of ropes on each fly floor, which are set up differently depending on each show and its set pieces. The flymen control all of the scenery that comes in and out from above by using the ropes that have been set.

Back in the old days, before the ropes were controlled by electric winches, you needed more flymen in each house. Each rope had a colored cloth attached to it, and there was a series of lightbulbs to instruct you, as well as a big cue sheet that had a list of orders like, "Flyman two, rope 21, move from out position to in position." When your cue came, the stage manager would make the colored light shine, and you'd take the right rope and line it up with the lock.

The reason for the different colors was because sometimes you'd have cues coming one right after the other. So it would be "21, red. 22, green. 23, blue." You'd have three guys working that scene change—or maybe just one guy jumping from rope to rope. These days, because of the electric winches that control the cables, there's less of that. We only have two flymen at the Shubert, and one sits at a console. The ropes are controlled by computers, so the whole business has changed.

But it's still a fun business. You have to adapt. You can't just be stuck in the old way of doing things, because everything changes. You have to ready for that. Sound has changed enormously since the old days, too. Everything has.

––––––––––––

Randy Morrison passed away on December 29, 2013, five months after our interview. Known for his Hawaiian shirts and his generosity of spirit, Randy worked in sound at the Shubert for 23 years. During that time, he also took thousands of photos of others working on various shows at the Shubert—another passion of his. A member of the stagehands' union since 1974, Randy is very missed by the Broadway community, and especially by everyone at the Shubert.

––––––––––––

---

[99] shotgun mics: the long microphones that often hang from above; they pick up sound from the front but not the back or sides

I'd Rather Be At The Shubert

"I've never had a show in the Shubert Theatre. I love that theater. I think it's the best theater in the world and maybe one day I will have the privilege and the honor of presenting some of my work in that theater."
-**Maury Yeston**, Writer

"I would like to work in the Shubert, because the Shubert doesn't have turkeys. Shubert shows run."
-**Merwin Foard**, Actor

"Good theatre can happen anywhere, but I'd rather be the guy doing good theatre in the Shubert Theatre."
-**David Gallo**, Scenic Designer

The Shubert brothers were the epitome of the American dream: poor immigrants who built an empire and revolutionized their field. The Shubert Theatre is their crown jewel house and it is also emblematic of the Shubert's greatest act of humanity: their love for their early-departed brother, Sam.

In 1917, another successful theatrical team of brothers, John and Lionel Barrymore, were co-starring in a play called Peter Ibbetson *at the Theatre Republic (now the New Victory). Lionel left the show for a plum role in a new play at the Shubert called* The Copperhead. *It would turn out to be one of the biggest triumphs of his career. John wanted to see his beloved brother perform this new part. Knowing that the Shuberts were notoriously stingy, he told them that he would buy out the house at* Peter Ibbetson *if he could take a night off to see Lionel in the role. The Shuberts agreed. A few days later, John went to the Shuberts with a check.*

"No. No," the Shuberts told him. "We had a brother once, too."

The Criterion Center Stage Right

Built: 1989
Closed: 1999
Location: 1530 Broadway
Owner: B.S. Moss Enterprises/ Roundabout Theatre Company
Longest-Running Show: *1776* (1997)
Shortest-Running Show: *Stand-Up Tragedy* (closed after 13 performances in 1990)
Number of Productions: 40

The Criterion was sad. It was rough going there. Now it's been turned into a Toys"R"Us, an office building, and the Bond 45 restaurant. It's like the theater disappeared! I did several shows there too. The audience was on a corner. How strange.

-William Ivey Long, Costume Designer

In 1895, theatrical impresario Oscar Hammerstein I (grandfather of the important writer of the same name) built an entertainment complex on Broadway between 44th and 45th Streets. It was called the Olympia, and its existence was a huge signal that the theatre district was moving uptown to Longacre Square. (The area would be renamed Times Square a decade later when the New York Times *set up offices there.)*

At the Olympia, a theatergoer could buy a 50 cent ticket, and gain admission to a theater, a music hall, a concert hall, a billiard hall, a roof garden, a café, and a bowling alley! 19th century entertainment seekers were so excited about this that the Olympia was mobbed by thousands when it opened, with patrons trampled and fire marshals called to the scene. The theater within the complex was called the Lyric, but when Charles Frohman took over the lease in 1898, it became the Criterion. In 1914, the Criterion became one of Times Square's first major movie theaters, and was briefly renamed the Vitagraph Theatre. Meanwhile, the very first editions of the Ziegfeld Follies *were being presented in the roof garden space.*

The entire Olympia complex was demolished in 1935. A brand-new building was constructed in its place, containing retail space, the International Casino, and the new Criterion movie theater. The International Casino was not a casino at all; it was a "theatre restaurant," offering dinner and deluxe revues and featuring every amusement from comedians to orchestras to circus acts. Within a few years, the International Casino closed and Bond clothing store moved into much of the building's space, erecting large signage in the center of Times Square. This signage at times included the messaging "Every hour, 3490 people buy at Bond," featured a giant electric zipper, and boasted the site's noteworthy clock inside the "O" of "BOND," which would be a trademark of the area for years to come. Meanwhile, the Criterion was hosting notable film premieres. Crazily enough, considering the patterns of evolution in Times Square today, the new building was far shorter than its predecessor, the Olympia.

In the late 1970s, Bond clothing moved out and the building was empty for a while, a languishing relic in the center of a dirty, crime-ridden theatre district. In 1980, the ever-indefatigable building was given new life when the Criterion was converted from one major screen to a five-screen movie complex, and the Bond store was converted to one of New York's largest disco and rock venues, called the Bond International Casino, a reference to the live entertainment of the past. When The Clash played the Bond International Casino at the height of their popularity in 1981, thousands stormed the venue, causing the same chaos as had happened on the same spot in 1895 when the Olympia opened.

In 1989, portions of both the casino and movie theater complex were taken over to make way for a Broadway theater—the first legitimate house on the spot since 1920—and a new cabaret space as well.

———————

1989/1997: Adorable Art Deco

Tony Walton, Director/Scenic Designer/Costume Designer

When the Roundabout was going through the design process for their new theater, the Criterion Center Stage Right, artistic director Todd Haimes invited a bunch of Broadway designers to come and take a look at the space. The whole venue was adorable because it had been an art deco-styled department store. They told us that the architect had designed the new theater space so that the stage would be in the corner of this huge hall. Every one of us hollered, "Please don't put it in the corner!" How could there be wings or flies? Where would the orchestra go? Alas, they still designed it that way, which made it an incredible challenge to fit a multi-set show into that very restricting corner.

After a while, we realized that the only way to present a multi-set show at the Criterion was to use a revolve, and just reveal sections of the scenic pie while changing the ones concealed behind it. This was a basically traditional, old-fashioned way of designing for a multi-set show. There were still no flies, so the elements for each change had to be squeezed into the virtually non-existent wings. The only thing I ever successfully flew in there was on a roller, and it was the giant parchment for the signing of the Declaration of Independence in *1776*.

It was interesting to transfer *1776* from the small Criterion to the Gershwin, one of the biggest theaters on Broadway! We created a reducing frame for the giant stage by including Philadelphia buildings to the left and right of our main set, and continuing them onto the side walls of the theater. Also, decorating those daunting walls with grandly oversized flags of each of the states represented in Congress. We were too big for the Criterion, and too small for the Gershwin, but we were able to tailor the production specifically for each space.

1989: *Chris Durang and Dawne*

Christopher Durang, Writer

We did a "cracked cabaret" called *Chris Durang and Dawne* at the new Criterion Center cabaret space in 1989, and that was really fun. The show was meant to run for about three weeks, but then we got great reviews and ran for three months. When you walked in, there was the Roundabout's Broadway theater to the right, and then there was a cabaret theater to the left.

It was a great cabaret space, with chairs and tables with little lanterns on them. We could move around a lot onstage, even though we could only enter or exit from stage left, and there was room for a three-piece band.

This cabaret (or club act) came about when I was asked to perform at a benefit for Olympia Dukakis' Whole Theater in Montclair, N.J. in spring 1989. Olympia had been in my play *The Marriage of Bette and Boo*, and had been especially hilarious as Soot in that excellent production. She had asked me to appear at her theater's benefit the previous year and I did a short solo. But when she asked me to come for the second year, I asked her if I could bring ten minutes of a three person "club act" that was in my mind, and she said sure.

I had these new two friends—John Augustine and Sherry Anderson—and we were walking down the street one day and I was humming to myself as I often do; I'm pretty sure I was humming "Bali Hai", when John and Sherry suddenly began improvising a harmonic back-up. Their sudden "accompanying" of my humming struck all three of us as funny.

242

So first I thought we should do an act where the juxtaposition of songs was weird and funny. Michael Jackson's song "Bad" was current at the time, so we started the act with them singing it, and then introducing me. I entered and sort of spoke the lyrics to "Bad". Then we segued directly into "Bali Hai" from *South Pacific*, and the juxtaposition of the songs was very crackpot. At that point, I announced that I was Chris Durang, and pointed to John and Sherry and said, "This is my back up group 'Dawne'." Then I added "I used to be a playwright, but it was too hard. I'm hoping being a lounge singer will be easier." And I said we had been traveling around the country from Ramada Inn to Ramada Inn, and it's been horrible. "The Criterion Center is definitely the nicest place we've been so far," I'd say next.

Let me explain Dawne slightly. There was a group called Tony Orlando and Dawn. Tony was the lead singer, and his back-up were these two attractive women who were called "Dawn." They had, oddly, a made-up shared name. I always found that weird. They were known in the 70s and 80s, so our audiences did get the reference.

Our show was this odd mixture of Broadway musical songs performed in the wrong context, like "Surrey with the Fringe on Top" done as a rap song, or doing the dramatic "Aldonza" from *Man of La Mancha* as a trio. We would sing the overwrought lyrics: "We were spawned in a ditch by our mother who left us there!" while shaking our fists and singing in unison. We pretended we had a manager who forced us to do rock songs that we didn't like, and then I sang the heavy metal "Welcome to the Jungle" while John and Sherry gyrated like crazy. I'm totally wrong to sing that song, and have good enunciation as well so you heard every word—"I want to watch you... bleeeeed!"

I wanted John and Sherry to have a section for themselves, so at one point, I told the audience that I was tired and needed to rest on the Equity cot. John and Sherry brought on a cot, and I lay down and pretended to sleep while John and Sherry had their own "dog medley." (For those who don't know, it's a requirement that any Actors' Equity show must have a cot in the actor's dressing room.)

In the course of my career up to 1989, I got good reviews for my play *Sister Mary Ignatius*, and then I got good reviews except from the *Times* for *Beyond Therapy*, and then I had three other plays in a row that got very mixed reviews. So I was feeling kind of down on things, and then I was asked to do this cabaret in New York, triggered by my having done it for fun at Olympia's benefit. I thought to myself: *It'll be good to have a whole bunch of different critics reviewing me—it will be the cabaret reviewers rather than the theatre reviewers.*

Ironically, what happened is that the reviews from the cabaret critics were awful! The *New York Post* headline was "They Shouldn't Give Up Their Day Jobs." I was expecting more bad reviews, and then all of a sudden, the theatre critics' reviews came out—I didn't even know they had been invited—and they all gave the show rave reviews, including the *New York Times*! What was funny is that the good reviews for *Sister Mary Ignatius* had really helped the show to transfer, and helped me become financially stable as a writer. The good reviews for *Chris Durang and Dawne* were delightful to receive, but we were all paid $125 weekly. John thinks it was more like $200. Still, this wasn't a money maker for us. But of course it was very fun to perform. (John is still my partner after all these years.)

Of course, *Chris Durang and Dawne* was in the 10:30pm "experimental" slot at the Criterion Center cabaret space. At 8pm, they had famous people like Chita Rivera, Ben Vereen, and Nell Carter. I do remember that lots of theater people came to the show. Stephen Sondheim came to see us, and Herbert Ross and Lee Radziwill, and Carol Channing and Tommy Tune came separately but came backstage together, and standing side by side with big smiles they both were as tall as trees.

Over the next ten years, we sporadically did various versions of the act. We never did it again at the Criterion Center, though; the cabaret room there closed.

———————

The Criterion Center was the brainchild of Charles B. Moss Jr., grandson of the theatrical entrepreneur Benjamin S. Moss, who built in 1924 what is today known as the Broadway Theatre, as well as the original Criterion movie theater in 1935. Carrying on his family's legacy, Charles aimed to create an entertainment center featuring a 499-seat Broadway house called the Criterion Center Stage Right,[100] a 436-seat cabaret theater called the Criterion Center Stage Left, and a dining lounge.

The first three shows at Stage Right, the Broadway house, were an intergalactic musical called Starmites, *a political farce called* Mastergate, *and the theater's shortest-running show, called* Stand-Up Tragedy. *After those three individually produced shows, the theater was leased by Roundabout Theatre Company in 1991.*

1989: Superhero Girl's Big Break

Liz Larsen, Actor

Starmites was a beautiful show. But the problem with it was that it should've stayed small. We did it at Classic Stage Company's theater, which was a black box, with a set made out of platforms and boxes. It worked wonderfully, because everybody in the audience could invent their own vision of what Interspace looked like. People created an outer space world in their own imaginations.

Then we found out we were transferring to off-Broadway. We were really excited, and figured we'd be going to a 200 or 300 seat theater. Then all of a sudden, our producers had a meeting with the owners of the Bond Clothing building, who had just renovated it into a legitimate theater. They decided we were moving to Broadway, to this brand-new theater with 499 seats.

All of a sudden, this teeny show with no set and this small feel is going to Broadway. We were on a special contract, where we were all paid less than Broadway salary, which wasn't great. But I was very grateful for my big break. Playing the lead in that show, I really had to strap the production to my back and go. The leading actress played two halves of the same character, and it was an exhausting, huge role.

We got into the Criterion, and it didn't feel like a theater. It felt like a building. The architects who had redone it were used to renovating clothing stores. Everything that could go wrong went wrong. First, when we were in previews, the fire curtain[101] came down and drenched everything. We had to shut down the show for four days, so all of the orchestra parts could be redone. There were no computers so all of these hand-written scores were just wrecked. Then, there were all of the injuries. There were broken legs. We had to hire extra swings. And the sicknesses! People couldn't talk; people couldn't breathe. It ended up that there was asbestos in the theater. It was high drama all around.

We were trying to rewrite the show every day, and we were all exhausted. We had these flashpots[102] on the set that were very expensive for *Starmites*, but looked like crap to the audience. Creating a fantasy world on a budget is very difficult. Things were falling out of the sky. We were jumping out of the way of flashpots. One night Sharon McKnight was onstage and the "Cruelty"—which was this giant 400-pound symbolic electric guitar, made out of mirrors and pipes—crashed down onto the stage. She jumped out of the way—if she hadn't, she would've been paralyzed.

Our director, Larry Carpenter, had a wife who was very spiritual. She decided there was a bad energy inherent in the theater, and we needed to cleanse it. They called in this Indian prayer guy, who brought in all this sage. We were in the middle of a rehearsal day, and the heat in the theater was broken, and we were sick. We were

---

[100] As of this printing, a theater must have at least 500 seats to qualify as a Broadway house.
[101] Check out *The Untold Stories of Broadway, Volume 1* for more on this.
[102] flashpot: a special effect in theatre used to create smoke, fire, or colorful sparks

all told to gather around this Indian healer. He began chanting, and said, "In order to cleanse this space, I shall say the name of an animal. If you think you're that animal, raise your hand."

He said, "Frog," and Gabe Barre raised his hand. The frog was the most generous of animals. Someone said they were a rabbit, and they were told that they were an adorable, loving spirit. The guy said, "Polar bear," and Victor Cook raised his hand because he was dressed all in white. He was told that a polar bear had more talent than the environment he was put in. Great. Finally, there were only one or two of us left. The guy said, "Thunderbird." I thought: *Okay, maybe that's perfect.* My mom had a powder blue Thunderbird car when I was growing up. So I stand up, and the Indian healer says, "Thunderbird. You're the most flawed, narcissistic animal. You think you can fly to the sun, but when you try, it burns you and you die on the ground." I was in tears. It was hateful, and I felt like that was what was happening to me on *Starmites.* I was trying so hard to fly to the sun, but everything was going wrong. I never forgot that day.

My dad hired a bus from my hometown to take everyone to come see *Starmites.* That was huge. My mom is a theatre person, but my dad isn't. And yet he hired this giant bus, and had the whole day catered. I arranged for the theater bartenders to stay late, so we could all have a drink and snack afterward. It was an amazing night because my dad reached out. When I was growing up, my dad owned a rock 'n' roll club. It seemed like he was always saying: *You're really corny. Can't you like Janis Joplin or someone hip?* Because I loved musicals. And this was him saying: *I get it. Theatre. It's okay. And I'm proud. I brought a bus.*

The Criterion Center Stage Right was Broadway's smallest theater when it opened. Ticket prices for Starmites *ranged from $25-$40 and the theater had the sense of being a casual, intimate experience, still on the main stem. In 1991, Roundabout Theatre Company took over the theater, producing on Broadway for the first time. Roundabout was founded in 1965, and began its life as a not-for-profit in the basement of a supermarket on 28th Street near 8th Avenue. They inhabited several off-Broadway spaces in Chelsea and Union Square before launching their Broadway presence with the Criterion.*

The first Roundabout show on Broadway was a revival of the Harold Pinter play The Homecoming. *The first Roundabout musical on Broadway was a revival of the Joe Masteroff, Sheldon Harnick, and Jerry Bock musical* She Loves Me.

1993/1997: The Theater Was Like A Piece Of Pie

Kathleen Marshall, Director/Choreographer

My second Broadway show was *She Loves Me* at the Criterion Center. I was an assistant choreographer. I later choreographed *1776* there.

The space made for a wonderful experience for the audience, because it was sort of like a little amphitheater. It was odd because there wasn't any proper fly space. The whole theater was kind of like a piece of pie, if you can picture it. The audience was like the curve of the pie, and backstage actually came to a point. You had to figure that out. Both shows I did there had turntables, which was not a coincidence. That was a good solution to the fact that there was not proper wing space.

For *She Loves Me*, the orchestra was on this top platform, but for *1776*, the orchestra was actually lined up along the two walls. The conductor was at the point upstage, facing downstage. Although we couldn't see them, they were all behind the set. They were situated like they were on a bus, one behind another, in a "V," facing the conductor. That theater was fun, but always a design challenge.

1993: A Feline Broadway Debut

Anne Bobby, Actor

I loved the Criterion so much. It was the cruise ship theater.

That staircase! I would walk in and there it was, a cross between *The Love Boat* and the grand staircase in the film *Mommie Dearest*. It was a marble staircase with a brass railing. I just loved that theater. It was fantastic.

I loved that there were two theaters in one building, and another show was always next door. It was what I imagine majoring in theatre in college felt like. There was always another group of show people around, more people to meet, another show going up.

It was one of the last theaters I could smoke in. It had a great green room. The only challenge with that theater was that there was no door to the stage. There was no real barrier to backstage, so you had to keep it down a bit. It was never a problem, until one day when I was doing *White Lies*. I had a kitten, and I'd gotten him neutered. His name was Pen, and I had to pick him up between shows on Wednesday, or he would have had to stay over at the vet. So I picked him up and then had no time to take him back to my apartment downtown.

I had permission to keep Pen in my dressing room, and the vet told me he was out of it and was just going to sleep, so I figured it would be fine. I was getting dressed to go onstage for the show with this big dress and hair, and just as I opened the door to the dressing room, Pen shot out and made a beeline straight for the stage. Everyone watched this kitten leaping, dashing across the green room, headed right into the wings.

I have never seen stagehands move as fast as they did to try to prevent Pen from meeting Nancy Marchand onstage. One of them almost caught him, and then he started to run under the stage. Another stagehand divebombed under the stage, and he came out with my little hissy kitten!

I thought I was going to get fired. But everyone was just on the floor, laughing. It was a strange moment because it all happened in complete silence! Pen was a very cute kitten. And he almost made his Broadway debut.

_____

High-class in every way, the International Casino on the east side of Broadway between 44th and 45th Streets featured an elaborate spiral staircase made of marble, bronze and granite. One side of the staircase had a bar built into the banister, so that visitors could travel from floor to floor without taking a break from ordering cocktails. During its era as a clothing store, the staircase was Bond's centerpiece, making the store different from any shop a tourist might visit in their hometown. In the venue's disco days, the staircase flashed bright lights and played music as each stair was stepped on. Everyone who worked at the Criterion theaters remembers the one aspect that made them unlike any other Broadway house: the gorgeous staircase.

_____

1993: I Always Wanted To Direct

Walter Bobbie, Director/Actor

For 20 years, I was a working New York theatre actor who always wanted to direct. Like many successful colleagues, I never studied formally. I was mentored. My training was passed down by acting under the guidance of a superb roster of directors: Tom Moore, Ellis Rabb, Andre Ernotte, Gene Saks, Dan Sullivan, Graciela Daniele, Stephen Porter, Gerry Gutierrez, among others, and most particularly Jerry Zaks. As I was acting, they were my ongoing master class in directing.

Jerry Zaks and I were both in the original production of *Grease* in the 1970s. I marveled as I watched Jerry's transition from working New York actor to four-time Tony-winning director. And ultimately, Jerry had an impact on my career far more significant than any mentor.

After casting me as a replacement in *Assassins* and Lincoln Center's *Anything* Goes, Jerry cast me as Nicely Nicely in his smash revival of *Guys & Dolls.* It was a major hit and a joyous experience (once we got through the first really tough weeks of previews.) I ended up singing "Sit Down You're Rockin' The Boat" in the Macy's Thanksgiving Day Parade and on the Tony Awards Broadcast. It was an exhilarating time.

Early in the run of *Guys & Dolls*, Ted Chapin and the Rodgers & Hammerstein Organization approved me to direct a revue of Rodgers and Hammerstein songs at Rainbow and Stars.[103] I asked Jerry for a three-week leave-of-absence from my great role in his smash hit to direct a cabaret revue... and he said yes. God bless him.

For some reason, every major New York theatre critic came to see *A Grand Night For Singing* at Rainbow and Stars, and basically said, "This show is wonderful. And Walter Bobbie can direct." I was blown away. Todd Haimes offered me an opportunity to do an expanded version at Roundabout on Broadway. Another stunning gift. The legendary Tony Walton designed the set (he had just done *Guys & Dolls*), the beloved Marty Pakladinaz designed the clothes, Natasha Katz did the lights. Overnight, I was a New York director. It wasn't a transition; it was a mitzvah.

Offers came quickly, including Encores!, followed by its artistic directorship. Then I directed *Chicago*, which began a whole new life in the New York theatre where I had been in training for 20 years.

What still amazes me is that friends in the community who endlessly heard my actor rant "...but I really want to direct," showed up for me when opportunity knocked, including casting director Jay Binder. When I got the job directing the Encores! premiere of *Fiorello!*, we called Jerry Zaks to play the lead. That was followed with calls to Philip Bosco, Adam Arkin, Faith Prince, Gregg Edelman, Liz Callaway, Donna McKechnie, and the beloved Marilyn Cooper... that was our first cast at Encores! The costume designer was William Ivey Long. John Lee Beatty did the set. Chris Chadman (*Guys & Dolls)* choreographed. And Rob Fisher was my artistic partner and music director. What newcomer could ask for anything more?

My directing career isn't a template for anyone, especially actors wanting to transition into directing. The only thing I do know is that when those calls came after 20 years, I had a phone directory full of the most elegant theatrical talent in New York City and they were willing to back me up. And that has continued.

My story is an old-fashioned showbiz dream. I hung in there and good fortune came my way. I cherish it.

———————

The line of distinction was thin between Stage Right and Stage Left; Roundabout's Broadway space sometimes hosted revues (including A Grand Night For Singing*) and the cabaret space sometimes presented musicals (including* Suds, *which was a musical "soap" opera in a Laundromat). The two spaces were even close in size. In 1995, the cabaret space officially became the Laura Pels Theatre, Roundabout's first off-Broadway theater in the Times Square area.*

———————

---

[103] Rainbow and Stars: a now-closed cabaret room that was located on the 65th floor of Rockefeller Center

1993: A Grand, Old Broadway Theater

Jason Graae, Actor

The Criterion was this grand, old Broadway theater. I did *A Grand Night For Singing* there, and I felt like it was very glamorous. It didn't have a lot of character, and yet it was right there smack in the middle of Times Square, so it felt like an event to be there.

We did the show at Rainbow and Stars, and it was a huge hit. All of a sudden we were moving to Broadway and it was so exciting. One of the most exciting things to me was that Tony Walton was going to do the set! He built all these gorgeous curtains—floor-to-ceiling beautiful, deep blue curtains. The cast moved them around to different configurations and they were heavy!

There was one moment where Lynne Wintersteller sang "Do I Love You Because You're Beautiful?", and the magic of it took you away. Then we all had to help her shove this giant curtain across the stage. It looked beautiful, but moving those curtains had its hilarious moments. Also, we were nominated for Best Book of a Musical, even though the only lines in the show were my ad-libs.

We did new things with a number of Rodgers and Hammerstein songs. It was an amazing idea that Walter Bobbie had: to take songs that everyone was accustomed to hearing a certain way, and put a twist on them. I got to sing the ballad "Love Look Away", which I would ordinarily never get to sing; it's typically sung by an Asian woman. I did "Shall We Dance" with Lynne, and it was fun because it was about a guy taking a girl out, who he didn't realize was a foot taller than him. It was me and Lynne and Martin Vidnovic and Vicki Clark and Alyson Reed. Everyone was so good, and we had a really good time. Fred Wells did these spectacular arrangements that really made the show hop.

1993: Christmas Cake

Fritz Frizsell, Stagehand

I worked on *A Grand Night For Singing* at the now-defunct Roundabout Criterion Center. There were only two followspots on that show, me and the young house apprentice. I had to teach him how to run a light. Fortunately he was a quick study, for it was a demanding show; it needed to have three followspots instead of two for proper coverage. Not having enough followspots to cover all the actors is a common problem because it's a cost-saving measure for the production. Another followspot means another employee to pay. We were paid $300 a week. Sometimes having one less followspot saves the company money, but the show often suffers as a result—somehow, either way, we manage. We always do.

On opening night, we got to the ladder that we climbed to get to our catwalk—and there was a little box there, tied to the ladder at eye-level. It was a cake from Victoria Clark for us, just a little token of appreciation. She was the only one who had thought of us.

1994: Someday, Somehow, Somewhere

Laura Linney, Actor

The Criterion had that great stairwell! There was this huge circular stairwell in the lobby because the space had been an old department store. I loved that. There was something sort of wonderful about how it made you feel that theatre could invade any place. Theatre could invade an old department store and turn it into a Broadway house.

248

It was interesting to work there. The Criterion Center was technically on Broadway so it had the feeling of being in the middle of everything, but it also felt not-as-fancy as other houses. The theater had no sheen of commerciality to it! That was sort of nice.

I did a production of *Hedda Gabler* there that wasn't very good and was badly received. So I learned a lot while I was at that theater! Our show was three hours long and problematic the whole way through. One of the other actors, Jeff DeMunn, and I struck up a really nice friendship. He played Jorgen Tesman and I was Thea Elvsted. Those two characters have a moment at the end of the play where the deaths are happening, and they are huddled together in the back of the action, at a desk. Every night, we'd get there and be like: *Oh thank God, we made it to the desk!*

There was one night of *Hedda Gabler* when Barbra Streisand was doing a concert and it was being simulcast in Times Square, and blasted on the jumbotron. Because our show was so long, it dovetailed with the concert. So we were at the end of a performance of this troubled *Hedda Gabler* when all of a sudden, seeping through the walls, comes Barbra Streisand's voice singing: "There's a place for us…" I thought: *Oh Jesus, please Babs, I hope you're right!* I'll always remember that. It was surreal, and sort of made sense, given the craziness of that production.

1993/1995: Where The Criterion Used To Be

David Loud, Musical Director and Supervisor/Conductor/Actor

In all the old pictures of Times Square, you see this big "BOND" sign. That's where the Criterion theaters were later on.

The Criterion Center Stage Right was created out of an old retail space. When you walked in, you went up a curved staircase and into this second-story lobby. The theater was semi-circular and the audience embraced the stage. It was an intimate house without a bad seat in it—you felt very close to the stage from wherever you were. Both shows I did there—*She Loves Me* and *Company*—had the orchestra behind the action. In *She Loves Me*, we were exposed at the top of these steps onstage. In *Company*, we were hidden. That's a difficult way to conduct a show—behind the actors, communicating via video cameras. It requires more trust and hope.

During *She Loves Me*, Boyd Gaines would race up the steps after he sang "Tonight At Eight", and he would collapse right next to me. Every night, I would say, "Good job!" under my breath. One night, I had a bad page turn or something, so I didn't say it, and he came to my dressing room after the show, panicked that he had screwed up the number horribly. Of course, he hadn't—he never did, he was wonderful. But when you get into that kind of rhythm on a show, you go insane when you don't get the approbation you need. Apparently, he'd been thinking about this for the whole rest of the performance.

During *Company*, Boyd had terrible problems with reflux. His understudy, Jim Clow, went on for him shockingly early in previews, at a time when he hadn't even been rehearsed yet. He was amazing. I remember frantically working with him to polish up his music performance while he was being fitted for costumes and while other actors were coming in and saying, "Now when you hold me in this scene, you have to make sure you touch this part of my arm." I don't know how he did it. He ended up performing many previews and really saving us.

In 2005, there was a throwback to tenants of earlier days when the restaurant Bond 45 opened on the 45th Street side of the building. The name itself was a reference to the old Bond clothing store and eventual disco venue, and the restaurant's style evoked Times Square in the 1920s through the 1940s.

249

Bond 45 has flourished, becoming a favorite of Broadway's top producers and stars. The Italian steakhouse even has brass nameplates engraved with the monikers of the celebrities who dine at each table most often. In 2009, 33-year-old Jordan Roth (formerly the little boy who loved La Cage aux Folles *so enthusiastically in the Palace chapter!) became the youngest leader amongst the Broadway theater owners when he was named the new president of Jujamcyn. Jordan gave interviews about his new position while at his favorite table at Bond 45, ushering in a new era of Broadway with signs of old Broadway all around.*

———————

1995: There Wasn't A Moment I Didn't Love

Charlotte d'Amboise, Actor

The Criterion Center seemed kind of corporate, or like a convention center. The entrance didn't feel like a normal theater entrance, but there were things that were nice about it.

I did *Company* there, and I loved my dressing room because I shared it with Jane Krakowski and LaChanze. We had the best time, and grew to be very close. Deb Monk and Kate Burton were right next to us, and I'd hang out in their dressing room all the time and listen to their stories. They were brilliant and I so looked up to them.

I loved doing that show, and the company was so close. George Furth and Stephen Sondheim were around all the time. There wasn't a moment I didn't love. I was 31 and I got married that year. My husband, Terry Mann, was doing *Beauty and the Beast* down the street. It was just a really great year.

1995: A Smaller Marquis

Danny Burstein, Actor

The Criterion Center felt a little bit like a smaller Marquis Theatre: modern and corporate and new. It felt a little like being out-of-town, even though you were on Broadway.

It was a good theater for *Company*, and a perfect-sized house. After our planned run was over, we were all set to move to a commercial run on Broadway at the Brooks Atkinson. The marquee had gone up, and posters were everywhere—and then the show was cancelled, one week before we were supposed to start rehearsal. There were issues with the producer; he made certain demands that Scott Ellis, Stephen Sondheim, and George Furth didn't jive with, and the whole thing was cancelled. It was heartbreaking, because we all loved the show—and I had a kid on the way. It was a very important time in my life. But those are the breaks; that's the business. One day, you're up, and the next day, not so much.

George Furth was lovely. He was fantastic and a genius. I did *Merrily We Roll Along* off-Broadway first, and worked with him there. He was unlike anyone I've ever met—he was this child-like character, but also a bit like an old woman. He was brilliant and funny, and constantly having these little tiffs with people. I remember one time when Jim Clow went on for Boyd Gaines. Boyd had an issue with his throat, so Jim jumped into playing Bobby with almost no rehearsal. What he did was outrageously hard. We were in previews, and after the show I remember George grabbed him backstage, and hollered, "Jim, you were incredible! You have the constitution of a lesbian!" That was George.

———————

In its ten short years as a Broadway theater, many notable people made their mark on the stage of the Criterion Center Stage Right. Helen Mirren made a spectacular Broadway debut, winning a Theatre World Award in a 1995 revival of the Russian comedy of manners, A Month In The Country. *The late Eli Wallach and the late Julie Harris both played their second-to-last Broadway roles of their long careers at the Criterion, in* The Price *and* The Glass

Menagerie. *Boyd Gaines played his second, third and fourth Broadway roles and won a Tony Award for* She Loves Me. *Christopher Plummer and Jason Robards tackled* No Man's Land *and Frank Langella appeared in a play called* The Father. Breaking Bad's *Anna Gunn gave her only Broadway appearance to date in Jean Anouilh's* The Rehearsal *and* The Office's *Rainn Wilson played a featured role in the 19th century work* London Assurance. *Jerry Stiller, Billy Crudup, and Paul Giamatti acted in* The Three Sisters, *and Blythe Danner acted in* The Deep Blue Sea. *An innovative production of* The Lion in Winter *starred Stockard Channing and Laurence Fishburne, and a revival of the classic musical comedy* Little Me *starred Martin Short and Faith Prince. Film and TV actresses Ashley Judd and Calista Flockhart both made their Broadway debuts, in* Picnic *and* The Glass Menagerie, *respectively. Frank Wood made his Broadway debut and won a Tony for* Side Man, *one of the few Stage Right shows to then transfer to a commercial Broadway theater and run.*

Liam Neeson and Natasha Richardson met and began an electric affair that led to marriage while co-starring in Anna Christie. *Steven Spielberg reportedly visited Neeson backstage after seeing the production and it was that visit at the Criterion Center that convinced him Neeson could star in his next film:* Schindler's List. *And it was Richardson's relationship with the Roundabout because of* Anna Christie *that led to her leading role in the acclaimed* Cabaret. *Richardson wasn't the only notable actress who played the theater that met a tragic end; the Criterion Center Stage Right also boasted the only Broadway appearance of the late Brittany Murphy, who received rave reviews in* A View From The Bridge.

1997: Conversations With Congressmen

Merwin Foard, Actor

I did *1776* at the Criterion Center, and it felt very modern and industrial. There were two theaters in one building. Both houses were intimate, and the main space had this panorama feeling in the audience. When you were onstage, you could really see the audience and they could really see you.

Scott Ellis, who directed *1776*, had us entering from pass doors, on the sides and back of the house. We walked through the aisles, which came forward and then forked to the side and then came forward again. You could really mingle through the audience and have conversations with your fellow "Congressmen" before getting on the stage for the overture to start.

We transferred the show to the Gershwin after three months, and we really missed some of the environmental elements from the Criterion. We were all thrilled to be moving to a bigger theater, but actually playing the show felt shocking. We went from one of the smallest houses on Broadway to the largest. They actually brought the back of the house in at the Gershwin, and cut off about 500 seats in the mezzanine to make the place seem more intimate. You can't really make the Gershwin intimate, but it did stretch the run of the show. We ran about a year, while other shows Roundabout had already booked played the Criterion. What a funny, oddball space.

1997: I Miss It

Michael Mayer, Director

The Criterion Center Stage Right was a thrust theater. You entered the theater from above, so the closest thing to it that still exists on Broadway is Circle in the Square.

It was a true thrust stage, not a theater in the round that could be adapted. What was exciting for me was that I had a concept for our production of *A View From The Bridge* which involved a Greek amphitheater feel. That was exactly what the shape of the theater was reminiscent of, although, of course, in a much smaller size.

I had worked for five summers at the Hangar Theatre in Ithaca, which had a similar dynamic, so I understood it: how to create entrances from the voms and utilize the whole house. The theater was very environmental, like the Hangar. I liked that. It didn't have much character, so it was really about whatever you brought into the space.

I did a lot of work at the Criterion: *A View From The Bridge, Side Man, The Lion in Winter*, The best thing about it was this feeling of immediacy. The theater felt immediate because it adapted to be about whatever the show was at the moment. Still, it was tricky because no matter what show you were doing, you were sort of aware of the non-specific 1970s retro style of the theater. But I miss it. I'm sad there isn't that kind of theater anymore on Broadway.

1997: No Crossover

David Gallo, Scenic Designer

The Criterion Center Stage Right was this bizarre triangle. It was a great theater to watch a show in, and even though it was kind of a pain in the ass it often lent itself to unique designs. The relationship between the actor and the audience was kind of awesome. But the stage itself could be very problematic. It was in the corner of the room. It was impossibly shallow and there was no crossover so you had to build your own into every set because it was impossible to get to stage right otherwise. And that in itself was nearly impossible, because you needed every damn inch of depth in that theater just to do your show.

Right now, the space where the Criterion stage used to be is where the Tyrannosaurus Rex is at Toys"R"Us. The humor of that never escapes me.

I designed *A View from the Bridge* there as well as several other productions. *A View from the Bridge* had a cast of 30-something people. All throughout tech, the director Michael Mayer would be saying, "Who wants to go into the hole?" That's what we called this tiny pocket stage right where actors would have to hide for entire scenes so that they could enter. There was no real stage right or access to it. And unfortunately we had decided against losing depth to a crossover.

Tony Walton was the one who figured out the room really well. He does a lot of great work everywhere, but every time you saw something he did at the Criterion Center, you just went: "Wow." He just got it.

The space had this quirkiness. It didn't have a consistent center line. It wasn't symmetrical; it was much bigger on one side than the other. But there were cool ideas you could execute there. On *View from the Bridge*, we took the backdrop paint treatment all the way to the back of the house on the theaters side walls. They let you do things like that there. You couldn't easily paint the walls of the Broadhurst or the Lyceum.

In 1998, Roundabout produced a hugely triumphant revival of Cabaret *on Broadway, starring Alan Cumming and Natasha Richardson. Needing a somewhat seedy locale to match the show, the production brought back to theatrical life the old Henry Miller's Theatre on 43rd Street, which had in recent years been a discotheque. Because of Roundabout, the Henry Miller's was used for a show for the first time in a decade in a half. It would later house* Urinetown *(2001), which desired a run-down space as well. The theater, which originally opened in 1918, was gutted between 2004 and 2009. When it reopened, the Henry Miller's was renamed the Stephen Sondheim Theatre, and operated by Roundabout. It currently houses* Beautiful, *a hit jukebox musical about the life of Carole King, that is a commercially produced rental.*

Cabaret moved from the Henry Miller's (which was incidentally renamed The Kit Kat Klub, only during its run) to

Studio 54, where it became the first Broadway show to premiere there in almost 60 years. Because Cabaret was so successful at Studio 54, running for over five years, Roundabout took over ownership of that theater. Its second production there was the Broadway premiere of Assassins in 2004, and it currently houses the return of the very same production of Cabaret that closed a decade ago.

In 1999, Roundabout was evicted from the Criterion. Because of the real estate boom and clean-up of Times Square, the space became much more coveted. The Roundabout lease was supposed to last until 2010. In 2001, the landlords welcomed their newest tenant: Toys"R"Us.

Luckily, in the meantime, artistic director Todd Haimes had been looking at other Broadway spaces. Just as they found out they were being evicted, Roundabout was making plans to lease and renovate one of 42nd Street's crumbling theaters, the Selwyn. The newly renamed American Airlines Theatre opened in 2000 with a revival of The Man Who Came To Dinner. By 2004, Roundabout was also renovating and re-opening an off-Broadway space: the new Laura Pels Theatre, on 46th Street.

The Criterion Center Stage Right was Roundabout's first Broadway home. It brought them to Times Square where they breathed life back into the Henry Miller's (later Stephen Sondheim) Theatre, Studio 54, and the American Airlines (earlier Selwyn) Theatre. Who knows what might be next?

The Vivian Beaumont Theatre

Built: 1965
Location: 150 West 65th Street
Owner: Lincoln Center Theater
Longest-Running Show: *South Pacific* (2008-2010)
Shortest-Running Show: *In The Summer House* (closed after 25 performances in 1993)
Number of Productions: 112

I love that big theater up at Lincoln Center... the Beaumont! You could drive a tractor trailer truck into the backstage area, park it, and then drive another one in easily next to it. The backstage is humongous—and air conditioned, which is incredible. I only worked there as a sub, but I was always impressed by the size of the backstage.

-Randy Morrison, Stagehand

I've always wanted to work at the Vivian Beaumont. I know it's a Broadway theater, but it somehow feels separate from the others. If Broadway theaters are vowels in the alphabet, it's the "and sometimes 'y.'"

I love the space. I think of it, and I immediately think of the *Carousel* set, or the *South Pacific* set. I love a theater that has depth, and I love when directors can do scenes upstage and kind of pull people from the audience in. People have to lean in. That always happens at the Vivian Beaumont.

-Robin De Jesús, Actor

The Vivian Beaumont is one of my favorite theaters to work in. It is one of the newer ones that was well-designed for adaptability. The stage can be fully utilized for sweeping vistas like those seen in *South Pacific*, *War Horse* or *Coast of Utopia*, or it can be closed down for the smaller, more intimate stages like those of *Contact* or *Ann*.

It is a huge theater, onstage and off. It has three catwalks and two grids. An actor in *Light in the Piazza* wore a pedometer one night and discovered that she walked (and sometimes ran, off stage, in order to make it to an entrance on time) three miles during each performance.

Its load-in dock door is a wall that can open up so that a truck can back into it. No need to load or unload trucks in the rain or snow. More importantly, no more pushing heavy roadboxes past the people on the sidewalk. Much safer for all parties concerned, and certainly more convenient for us.

-Fritz Frizsell, Stagehand

Introduction: A Larger Idea

John Weidman, Writer

I have loved working at Lincoln Center Theater. For a couple of reasons.

The most important one is that it's not like working in a rented space. Because it's an institutional theatre, it's got a life and a vitality that's constantly going on all around your show. There's usually something on the stage below you or above you, depending on whether you're in the Mitzi Newhouse or the Vivian Beaumont. And there's a whole staff which is dedicated not just to your project, but to a larger idea of what the season's about, and what the next season's going to be about.

It's very comforting. There's something very satisfying about having the boundaries of your particular show expanded, to include more theater. Greg Mosher was the artistic director there when we did *Anything Goes*, and André Bishop when we did *Contact* and *Happiness*. And Bernie Gersten was there the entire time. The personnel, the staff there are wonderful. You feel you have a connection with the creative teams and the business staffs throughout the building, so that I always felt like I was part of a family that embraced not just my show, but me as an artist and what I was interested in. You don't get that if you're in a commercial Broadway house. Some may, but I haven't. I feel no relationship to the Winter Garden—except as a member of the audience—when I return to it.

And there's another thing that's great about the Beaumont. If you have a hit, you can stand just inside the doors at the head of the aisle and watch, not just the show, but the audience *watching* the show. You're not standing behind them, as you would be in a proscenium house, you're actually looking into their faces as they look at the stage.

With shows that were designed to make people happy—shows like *Anything Goes* and *Contact*—it was especially great to be able to have that experience. Often, with *Anything Goes* and then later on with *Contact*, I would conspire to find myself in the neighborhood during show time and I would slip into the theater and stand in the back and just watch people watching the end of the show or the end of the first act.

They'd feel good, I'd feel good, and then I'd leave. And often, when I did that, I'd look across the theater and see that Bernie Gersten had come down from his office, and was standing at the head of an aisle having the same experience I was.

So it was like that. Everybody's in the same building, the producers are down the hall, they're working on other things, but they're also taking care of your show. It's a great place to work.

―――――――――

Lincoln Center is the only cultural complex of its kind in the United States. Located mainly within a rectangle between 60th and 66th Streets and Columbus and Amsterdam Avenues, it consists of venues for music, dance, theatre, film, education and more. Lincoln Center's inner circle of venues includes 30 indoor and outdoor spaces. Among them are the Vivian Beaumont Theatre, a Broadway house (opened in 1965); the Mitzi Newhouse Theatre, an off-Broadway house (opened in 1967); Avery Fisher Hall, home of the New York Philharmonic (opened in 1962); the Metropolitan Opera House (opened in 1966); the David H. Koch Theater, home of the New York City Ballet (opened in 1964); the New York Public Library for the Performing Arts (opened in 1965); and the Juilliard School (opened in 1969). In 2012, Lincoln Center Theater opened its smallest space, the Claire Tow Theatre, which is dedicated to producing new work with all tickets priced at $20. The Claire Tow Theatre is a sign that, even now, the scope of the enterprise called Lincoln Center is still expanding.

In the 1950s, the area known as Lincoln Square, north and west of Columbus Circle, was blighted by poverty and crime. John D. Rockefeller III spearheaded an effort, along with architect Robert Moses and the city of New York, to clean up Lincoln Square and revitalize the area. The center of the project, which officials hoped would create a ripple effect of positive change, was the Lincoln Center of the Performing Arts. In 1956, the New York Times *stated the center's intentions: "By bringing the performing arts into proximity, the center will focus the city's and country's attention in a grand and striking way on their value to our lives, emphasizing for all a fact that some know to be true—that the modern American wants the things of the mind and heart as well as material substances. By giving the arts up-to-date, completely equipped quarters, the center will open up to them new opportunities for raising their standards and achievements. By providing a unifying concept, the center will encourage the arts to learn and draw inspiration from one another.*[104]

The Vivian Beaumont may be the only Broadway theater outside of the immediate theatre district, stretching from 41st to 54th Street, but it certainly has a family of artistic neighbors all its own.

1967: My First Job

Ted Chapin, President of The Rodgers & Hammerstein Organization/Past Chairman of the American Theatre Wing

The Unknown Soldier and His Wife was the first job that I ever had. We moved into the Vivian Beaumont Theatre, and I was blown away by it. The Beaumont is an extraordinary structure because it was built to house a repertory company. It has the largest stage on Broadway.

The Beaumont stage goes from the middle of the block all the way out to 65th Street, and it was made that way so there could be four or five physical productions stored there. Even by the time the theater opened, when the company was still called the Repertory Theater of Lincoln Center, the decision was made to not run it in repertory; it would house one show and then another show.

I remember walking into that theater and seeing this vast stage, and this auditorium that clearly lent itself best to a thrust stage. It was fascinating, and unlike any other Broadway theater. Also, when the theater was built, they put in these large panels at the front of the stage itself that were designed to fly down and shape the proscenium or provide a backing to the thrust stage. They were run by 1967 computers. But they never worked correctly, so they were put in the "up" position, where they still are to this day. They are just ignored, but if you look up, you can see them.

Before I worked at the Beaumont, I had walked into the theater with my father[105] when the Repertory Theater was rehearsing their first show. There was a turntable and an annular ring, and they were testing how to use the panels. Everyone stood to the side while they tested one, and it came down and crashed into a prop bed. I, thought, *Well this will be difficult!* But they figured it out; the Beaumont had its own needs, and it took many years to figure out how best to make it work.

When *The Unknown Soldier* moved into the Beaumont, the Repertory Theater of Lincoln Center was doing a production of *Galileo* with Anthony Quayle, so the stage floor was covered in these pebbles in concrete. It was rough on everyone's feet, so we had to put padding over all of it for our rehearsals.

As the gofer, I was stationed off stage right, where there was a stage manager's desk and a phone with a light—because they had to turn the ringer off. There were times when they were waiting for a phone call, so I would just sit there and watch the phone but could also see the stage. All I wanted was to be wherever they were actually working.

The Beaumont is a rabbit warren of levels and staircases and corridors. Just to find your way around is very tricky! The stage door was in a different place back in 1967, and once you walked inside, it was hard to figure out where you were going. While we were there, the backstage had all of these beautiful wool carpets in the corridors and dressing rooms. Then during a June thunderstorm, the sewer on the corner of 65th and Amsterdam flooded and all this sewage came into the carpeting backstage. The smell was unbelievable, and all

---

[104] "Symbol of U.S. Culture." *The New York Times.* 23 July 1956.

[105] Ted's father was Schuyler Chapin, who was vice-president of programming at Lincoln Center at the time, and would later become the Commissioner of Cultural Affairs for New York City under Mayor Rudolph Giuliani.

these beautiful carpets were pulled out and thrown away. I think that was the end of wool carpets at the Beaumont!

Because the Beaumont is its own community, there was something very cool about having a show live in that space, and taking over one part of Lincoln Center. One of my favorite places in the theater was this booth in the back of the auditorium, on house left, where all the computer-generated lighting equipment was. A man named Eisenhauer had invented this sort of IBM punch-card-generated computer lighting machine. It was very exciting, totally untested, and not very reliable. Then on the audience right side, there was a booth where director John Dexter and I would go, and I would take notes for him during the show. It was fascinating.

Anybody who's worked on a show knows that the first time an audience comes in, there are always going to be surprises. There are things that the company has laughed at in rehearsal that the audience doesn't think is funny. Then there are things that haven't landed in rehearsal that the audience howls at. In *The Unknown Soldier*, Bob Dishy played a scientist and Brian Bedford played a general. The two had a scene in the first act, and then one in the second act. In the first act scene, Bob got enormous laughs, which no one was expecting, least of all Brian. John Dexter turned to me and said, "Just wait until their scene in the second act." I thought: *Okay, I wonder what he means...*

In their scene in the second act, Brian suddenly used this stutter which he created on the spot, and he used it to pull the attention of the scene back to him. When it was over, John said, "You'll never see that again." But John understood the mentality of actors, and he knew that since Brian was surprised in the first act that the scene wasn't about him, he had to yank it back from the other actor. Once the first performance was done, Brian accepted the balance of the play, and never did the stutter again. It was an interesting lesson for me to learn.

More than 40 years later, I was back at the Vivian Beaumont with the *South Pacific* revival. In my role at the Rodgers & Hammerstein Organization, I try to make myself available when needed but not stick my nose in where it isn't wanted. There aren't a lot of people in the exact spot I'm in within the theatre—I feel like I'm part of these shows, but I'm not a lawyer, I'm not a member of the family who owns the material. I'm a hired hand, but I bring a lot of experience and I think I can be helpful. It's always nice when others feel that way and welcome me in. It's fun when that happens.

When *South Pacific* was previewing at the Beaumont, they reinstated the song "My Girl Back Home", which had been in the movie but cut from the show originally. I emailed André Bishop about that, and told him that I thought because they put the song into the story in that place, there might be material in the next scene that provided information that was covered already in the number. He wrote back and said: "I can't believe how supportive you are of what we're trying to do, instead of saying 'You can't do this or that.' Your notes are in support of the production we are trying to do. Thank you."

If I make an observation like that, it's because I've been around all of these shows for so long. The collaborators on that revival were so smart that it was an honor to open up our drawers at the organization and say, "Here is everything that was ever *South Pacific*," and trust that they'd make the right choices. Then sometimes it was valuable to see a choice they made and really think about how Rodgers and Hammerstein and Josh Logan ended up where they did, and how changes in one part of the show could affect something they'd set up in another part. That's where revivals get fun.

The Vivian Beaumont Theatre was named after Vivian Beaumont Allen, an actress and philanthropist who donated $3 million for the theater in her name to be built. Sadly, she died in 1962, three years before the theater opened. Similarly, Al Hirschfeld died just five months before a Broadway theater was renamed in his honor, and August Wilson died 14 days before a Broadway theater was renamed in his. All three honorees knew about the plans to name theaters after them but unfortunately they passed away before the theaters were named.

258

From its opening in 1965 until 1973, the Beaumont was occupied by the Repertory Theater of Lincoln Center, a company under the leadership of Elia Kazan and Robert Whitehead that focused on plays with social and emotional significance. Prior to the Beaumont being ready for their use, the Repertory Theater of Lincoln Center functioned in a downtown space called the ANTA Washington Square Theatre. The company presented their first six productions there before moving to their permanent home, including two Arthur Miller premieres: After The Fall *and* Incident At Vichy. *When the Beaumont was ready, the company left the ANTA, which—having been approved as a Tony-eligible house despite its location—was a prime candidate for new Broadway shows. Only one played there—the original production of* Man of La Mancha—*before the land was sold to a buyer with deep pockets: NYU. They turned it into a building for their School of Commerce that today is called the Stern School of Business.*

Meanwhile, uptown, the Repertory Theater of Lincoln Center, now under the direction of Herbert Blau and Jules Irving, opened the Vivian Beaumont. Its inaugural show was a revival of Danton's Death, *a play set during the French Revolution whose production addressed issues of both that time and the current day.* Danton's Death *featured one of the first Broadway performances from James Earl Jones and an acclaimed, sprawling set by designer Jo Mielziner, who had also designed the theater itself. In 1967, Blau resigned, saying "The climate is no longer right for me to do what I came to do in the form I had in mind."*[106] *Irving remained until 1972, but the theater was also rented to several commercial productions, including* The Unknown Soldier and His Wife. *At its start, the Repertory was harshly judged by the theatrical community for not staging many American plays, new or old. This changed when they began producing the work of writers such as Sam Shepard, William Saroyan, and Tennessee Williams in the late 1960s.*

In 1973, the Repertory Theater of Lincoln Center was dissolved, amidst a bout of dissatisfaction over the way the company was being run. From 1973 to 1977, Joseph Papp took over the Beaumont with Public Theater productions, aiming to focus on adventurous new work. During this time, the Beaumont saw plays including Boom Boom Room *by David Rabe, about a troubled go-go dancer's affairs and* Short Eyes, *about prison life. After the failure of several original works, Papp changed his repertoire to revivals before the Public vacated the Beaumont in 1977. The Public's patrons vocally preferred the company's home in the East Village.*

———————

1977: A Mind-Expanding Time

Michael Greif, Director

In high school, I expanded my range of theatergoing. I saw the most extraordinary group of plays produced by the Public at Lincoln Center, including *The Cherry Orchard* at the Vivian Beaumont. I will always be grateful that I learned Chekhov could be presented with such beauty, toughness, humor, and emotional immediacy.

I will never forget *Streamers* downstairs at the Mitzi Newhouse, that same year. That play scared the shit out of me. I felt as though I was right in the middle of the action. It was a very dynamic and mind-expanding time for me, seeing those shows. They played a great part in forming my theatrical sensibility.

———————

The Vivian Beaumont sat empty from summer of 1977 when the Public departed, until late fall of 1980, when the newly founded Lincoln Center Theater Company presented a revival of The Philadelphia Story, *starring Blythe Danner, and featuring the Broadway debut of 14-year-old Cynthia Nixon.*

From 1980 until 1986, when the present iteration of the Lincoln Center Theater was formed, the Beaumont was mostly empty. (In 1983, it did briefly play home to an 80-minute version of the famous opera Carmen, *which won a*

———————

[106] Martin, Douglas. "Herbert Blau, Pioneering Theater Director, Dies at 87." *New York Times*. 7 May 2013. Retrieved from nytimes.com.

Special Tony Award.) From 1986 onward, the Vivian Beaumont was programmed under the artistic leadership of Gregory Mosher and Bernard Gersten, who were the first to truly realize the magnificent potential of the venue. Their opening production was a play called The House of Blue Leaves.

―――――――――

1986: Physical Realities of the Space

Jerry Zaks, Director/Actor

I was originally an actor. I worked as an acting member of the Ensemble Studio Theatre. One day a friend of mine, Bill Cwikowski, came up to me and said, "I just read this play. I want to play the lead and I want you to direct it." He had no particular reason to think I could direct, but I read the play—*The Soft Touch*, by Neil Cuthbert—and it made me laugh, so I said yes.

We cast the play with all people I knew, and we did four unpublicized performances. It was great! It was the first time in my life that I was involved with anything in the theatre where I wasn't onstage, and I loved hearing the laughs from the back of the house. I also enjoyed plotting out bits of blocking and business that would make the play better. That was the beginning.

After that, I fell in love with the Christopher Durang play *Sister Mary Ignatius Explains It All For You*. I found it in a stack of plays at the Ensemble Studio Theatre and picked it up and couldn't stop laughing. I called Chris and told him I'd love to direct a production of it, and he said yes, so we did it at the Ensemble Studio Theatre. A year later, André Bishop produced our show at Playwrights Horizons and it was so successful that it transferred to a commercial off-Broadway run that lasted for almost 1000 performances. It was a wonderful play, and it made people take note that I was a director.

The first three shows I directed on Broadway were all at the Beaumont: *The House of Blue Leaves* in 1986, *The Front Page* in 1986, and *Anything Goes* in 1987. I was proud of each of those shows for very different reasons, but the one thing I was proud of on all three was that we showed the community that the theater was a workable space. A lot of theatre artists used to complain that the Beaumont was an inhospitable environment for theatre, but we deflated that myth. The fact is that it's a wonderful space to work in; some people just failed to make it work for their productions and used the theater itself as an excuse.

My 4th Broadway show, *Lend Me A Tenor*, was elsewhere, and then I came right back to the Beaumont for *Six Degrees of Separation*. I love that place! And I've seen so many incredible productions that fit the theater which I've had nothing to do with: *Act One* was fantastic! And *Coast of Utopia*! And *South Pacific*! I'm thrilled that really talented people have continued to make it sing with great theatre. If you listen to the Beaumont, you understand. There are some physical realities of the space that you have to pay attention to in order to maximize the audience experience. For example, don't put any really important action upstage of the proscenium line! It becomes remote. Even in the best seat in the house, that part of the story becomes distant. The Beaumont is a wonderful house to create tableaus in, and utilize for long entrances. But there's a lot of onstage space that truly can't be used for anything critical to the story. There are seats on the far sides, and you have to block the whole show so that it's likely to be enjoyed by audience members even in the "worst" seats. If you pay attention to the audience experience, and create a good play, the Beaumont is joyous and wonderful.

The House of Blue Leaves actually started in the Newhouse. We thought: *Do we dare take this upstairs at the Beaumont?* All of a sudden, one day, we realized that the Beaumont is just like the Newhouse except bigger. We went for it. Moving the show a couple steps upstairs was my big break—my Broadway debut. After it was a hit there, we moved *Blue Leaves* to the Plymouth. I had to adjust the blocking for a proscenium house, which was fine; that created new challenges in how to focus the play for everyone working on it. Having to re-energize with a new challenge like that after a show has been running for a while is a positive thing.

260

1987: Designing For *Anything Goes* (In Other Shows)

Tony Walton, Director/Scenic Designer/Costume Designer

In 1987, I designed the set and costumes for *Anything Goes* at the Beaumont, which starred Patti LuPone. I was very fond of that Jerry Zaks production and extraordinarily fond of Patti. She was the first person I ever went on my knees to, when she first did *Evita*. I literally knelt and bowed deeply to her after the show. Wow! She's also the only person I have ever seen get a standing ovation at intermission. That was on *Master Class*. There's no one like Patti. I was very excited to do an *Anything Goes* that would be created around her Reno Sweeney.

The show was going to have the standard three-month run at the Vivian Beaumont, so it had to be inexpensive, but there was no real way to do it effectively on the available budget. So, I tried to take advantage of elements that already existed at the Beaumont, such as the basement below the stage, in which I was able to place elevators that could bring up different changes of set, and serve as actors' entrances. I also tried to design pieces for preceding productions that I could then adapt for *Anything Goes*! I did *The Front Page* the year before, also with Jerry Zaks, and we decided we wanted that play to take place mostly on the forestage, in order to make the journalist's office setting seem like a little claustrophobic rat's nest. We thought it would be fun to create an extremely grandiose foyer for the Chicago Criminal Court building which contained that office—so that you could hear people entering with acoustically boosted, echoing footsteps on the splendid marble floor, as a vivid contrast to the stuffy scruffiness of the journalist's den. This foyer turned out to be a very useful idea because I could design a grand pair of staircases that I could then use for *Anything Goes*. They were the same pieces architecturally and structurally, but I refinished them with glossy white paint and brass for *Anything Goes*. I also re-used multiple pieces of deco-styled furniture that had been part of other productions I'd done at the Beaumont and on Broadway!

We were doing this Cole Porter musical revival at a time when his position in the small group of great American musical comedy creators had faded a bit. In order to redress this, Gregory Mosher and Bernie Gersten had declared that they wanted our production to be a kind of celebratory cocktail to Porter; at the end of the show, during the curtain call, we actually flew in a big and very endearing photo of him for the whole cast to turn to and applaud.

The acoustics at the Beaumont were very tricky. There was a 'sweet spot' in the dead center of the forestage. An actor speaking in that spot, would hear his sound bounce back at him, and feel he was yelling and instinctively lower his voice. This was solved for *Anything Goes* when some German sound experts came in to experiment. Intriguingly, they built various speakers, pointing at the stage, into the lower risers of the audience's staircases; these new speakers bounced their amplified sound at the forestage 'stern' of the ship. In order to reflect the sound as brightly as possible, we built the ship's stern out of curved sheets of plywood and treated it with high gloss paint. We did a similar thing behind the band, who was on the upper deck of the ship's setting. I designed a giant oval smokestack there that powerfully reflected the band's sound. These acoustic adjustments made the music fill the theater as it never had before. Altogether, it was a grand production!

1990: The Happiest Understudy On The Planet

Laura Linney, Actor

I grew up around theatre because my father, Romulus Linney, was a playwright. I loved everything about it. From listening to him type a play, hearing a furious torrent of activity on the typewriter in the next room, to sitting in rehearsal halls to going to shows and taking it all in. I can remember being a very small child at the Herbert Berghof studio and the Actors Studio, just watching everyone work.

I went to Juilliard, and then I ended up making my Broadway debut right across the street at Lincoln Center. My first professional job was in *Six Degrees of Separation*. I graduated and just went a block over to understudy Robin Morse and Mari Nelson in the play, which was originally at the Mitzi Newhouse. It moved to the Vivian Beaumont, and when Robin left, I replaced her. I made both my off-Broadway and Broadway debuts at Lincoln Center!

I was the happiest understudy on the planet. I loved it. It was the perfect first job for me. I got to watch this amazing production come together and explode. I had known John Guare since I was a little girl, so there was a familiarity there that was special.

I would crawl up in the catwalk and watch the whole show from up there, all by myself. There was a moment that I waited for every night: a monologue that John Cunningham had about losing a painting if you paint too much. I loved watching Stockard Channing onstage every night. She gave this performance month after month and just when you thought it couldn't get any better, it would flower and drop a whole other level on you. It was amazing.

One of my favorite memories of *Six Degrees of Separation* is of being in the catwalk while Katharine Hepburn was in the house. I spent the whole show watching Katharine Hepburn with her collar turned up and her hair in that bun, watching Stockard. It was thrilling. I just sat all the way up there and watched it all.

I loved working at the Mitzi and the Beaumont. They're such great theaters with really fantastic dressing rooms, too. I took so many theatre history courses at Brown, where I did my undergrad before Juilliard. I was geeky, geeky, geeky! There's so much to learn about these places. They have a lot to give.

―――――――――

In 1992, André Bishop took the reigns from previous Lincoln Center Theater director Gregory Mosher, and teamed up with Gersten. He brought his compatriot from Playwrights Horizons, musical theatre producer Ira Weitzman, with him. The two men were known for nurturing the voices, both musical and dramatic, of a new generation of writers, including William Finn, Christopher Durang, Wendy Wasserstein, A.R. Gurney, Craig Carnelia, Lynn Ahrens, and Stephen Flaherty. They brought this sensibility 24 blocks north, where under their auspices and Gersten's, the Vivian Beaumont began to present original musicals for the first time in its history.

―――――――――

1992: Like No Other Year Of My Life

Ira Weitzman, Musical Theatre Associate Producer at Lincoln Center Theater

The first show I worked on at Lincoln Center Theater and the first new American musical to be done in the Beaumont was *My Favorite Year*, by Lynn Ahrens, Stephen Flaherty, and Joe Dougherty. We were in tech, and I was still just getting to know the building and the stage and what it meant to do a musical on a thrust stage. It's quite different than a proscenium in every way.

One day during tech, I looked up at the stage and saw a man who wasn't a part of the production. I didn't know everyone in the building at that point, so I didn't think about it too much. Then I looked a little closer and I thought: *That is Jerome Robbins. That is Jerome Robbins standing onstage of the Beaumont in the middle of* My Favorite Year *tech. What is he doing here?!* No sooner did I realize it was him, then like an apparition, he disappeared.

Sometime later, we got a call from Jerome Robbins asking if he could come meet with André Bishop and me. When we met he told us that he had been thinking about doing a revival of *West Side Story* with a different approach from the original. He was thinking about doing a new production where the Sharks were black and the Jets were white, and he was thinking about doing it in a nontraditional theater space.

262

There is literally a football field worth of space backstage of the Beaumont. It's a thrust theater, but there's a proscenium arch from which the thrust protrudes, and upstage of that is a huge amount of space. A lot was stored there during *My Favorite Year*, but there was still tons of empty space. Robbins was interested in setting up that upstage space so that the theater would be an arena. He wanted to have people watching *West Side Story* from bleachers in that area, making the theater into a space in the round. He had just walked in during *My Favorite Year* tech to case the joint!

That production of *West Side Story* didn't end up happening in the Beaumont, but if it had, it certainly would've been one of the most exciting things to happen to me up until that point. Robbins did do a workshop of that *West Side Story* in the Hammerstein Ballroom before it was refurbished.

––––––––––––

When he was telling me this story, I truly thought Ira Weitzman was going to conclude, "I saw the ghost of Jerome Robbins telling us what to do to fix My Favorite Year*!"*

––––––––––––

1992: Challenges And Hits And The Size Of The House

André Bishop, Producing Artistic Director of Lincoln Center Theater

Long before I started working at Lincoln Center as the artistic director in 1992, I saw many shows there. I was an audience member during all of the different administrations of the Beaumont. The original Kazan-Whitehead repertory company never got into the building—they functioned downtown. I certainly saw a lot of the Irving Blau productions. I saw some of the Richmond-Crinkley productions, like *The Philadelphia Story*. I saw many Papp-Gersten productions, like *Threepenny Opera* and *The Cherry Orchard*. And then when it was Mosher-Gersten, I saw virtually every production they did here. I had been at Lincoln Center a fair amount.

The first show I did at the Beaumont was *Four Baboons Adoring The Sun*. That was a show I had meant for the Mitzi Newhouse, but our director, Peter Hall, wanted a bigger space to do a more elaborate, mysterious and magical production. I gave in, but I don't know if that was the wisest thing. I think the play is small and perhaps it would have come off better in the Newhouse.

There haven't been shows completely planned for the Mitzi that ended up at the Beaumont, but there have certainly been times when I've initially imagined that a show we're working on would occupy our smaller house and it's gone to the larger. I also initially had an idea that *The Frogs* should be in the Mitzi Newhouse. Steve Sondheim and Susan Stroman ultimately wanted it to be in the bigger theater. I felt it was a small show and should've been done in a smaller way than we did. But the plans for that were embryonic.

My first musical at the Beaumont was *My Favorite Year*. That was a show we had developed at Playwrights Horizons, and it transitioned to Lincoln Center along with us. I didn't quite realize what the pressures of a big musical in the Beaumont would be, versus a big-ish musical at Playwrights Horizons. The show wasn't quite ready for the Beaumont, and we learned that musicals with a lot of physical comedy really shouldn't be done on a thrust stage.

The most challenging productions we've done at the Beaumont have mostly been the musicals. You're always working on a musical. *Marie Christine, Light in the Piazza, Parade*... we worked demonically on those shows. Musicals are always the most significant challenge, text-wise. *The Coast of Utopia* presented a lot of challenges in production, too, because it was three long shows in repertory. They were great and they were popular, which we had no notion was necessarily going to happen. I would say *Utopia* has been our greatest production challenge.

Sometimes, you think audience members are going to hate something, and then they are so loving and appreciative that you can't believe you felt so negatively about them. And sometimes, you think audiences are going to love something and they don't. Usually, with any show, I can tell at the end of the first preview how it's going to turn out three weeks later on opening night.

With a show like *Contact*, I knew from the end of the first preview at the Mitzi Newhouse that the show would be successful. You could just tell. At the end of the first preview of *South Pacific* at the Beaumont, I knew we had a huge hit. There have only been a few exceptions. With *Light in the Piazza*, we got an attentive, okay response at the first preview, but by opening, we were getting a fantastic response.

———————

The Mitzi Newhouse is a very unique off-Broadway theatre. As some have noted, it is essentially a shrunken version of its upstairs sister, the Vivian Beaumont. This makes it easier than usual to arrange an off-Broadway-to-Broadway transfer, since the two houses are run by the same company, in the same building, and are similarly shaped. Shows that have moved from the Mitzi to the Beaumont over the years include The House of Blue Leaves, Six Degrees of Separation, *and* Contact. *Other Mitzi Newhouse shows have moved to off-site Broadway venues, such as* Sarafina! *(1988, Cort),* The Sisters Rosensweig *(1993, Barrymore), and* Vanya and Sonya and Masha and Spike *(2013, Golden).*

The Mitzi Newhouse first opened as The Forum in 1967, and was renamed in 1973. In intermittent years when the theaters were not doing well, the Mitzi was sometimes used as a film house. Interestingly, one Tony Award-eligible show played at the theater: Streamers, *in 1976. While the Mitzi is not a Tony-eligible house, this play had a special exception made after significant campaigning.*

The Beaumont and the Mitzi share a lot of backstage area, so if you're doing a show in one house, chances are that you will interact with the other.

———————

1992: Upstairs, Downstairs

Lynn Ahrens, Writer

One of the special things about Lincoln Center is that there's almost always a show running upstairs and a show running downstairs. You're in the same hallways, you're passing the same posters that line the halls. You have this feeling of community, of being part of the history of a place that has held so many shows, and you know that your own show poster will soon go up on the wall there, too. It's a wonderful, communal feeling. By now we have four posters on those walls.

My Favorite Year was "the first American musical" to be staged in the Beaumont. Up until that time, there was no orchestra pit. Instead, there was a mechanism under the stage that had originally been built to allow the stage to be reconfigured into a thrust or a proscenium. But over time, and with underuse, it had eventually frozen and was now unworkable. We watched them do the excavation to remove this giant piece of machinery—the hole went down about three stories! When they'd finished it, the Vivian Beaumont had an orchestra pit, and the first show to use it was *My Favorite Year*. I remember the thrill of seeing our first large orchestra playing, watching Ted Sperling conducting, and realizing for the first time that the conductor was driving the show—sometimes fast, sometimes slow, keeping it on the road, keeping all the performers and musicians in synch. I remember watching him trying to catch Lainie Kazan's unpredictable first notes—every night her performance differed, and every night his arms were poised to drop on a moment's notice to catch her first note, which she sang whenever she felt like it.

The first preview of *My Favorite Year* was pretty memorable. Our rehearsal process was a little dicey, and by the time we got to the first preview, we'd never been able to have a run-through of the show—so we postponed. When we finally got our first preview up, the show ran three hours and the sets were toppling! We knew we had to start chopping things away—it was traumatic, and not a happy night. We got off to a bumpy start, and it wasn't the end of the bumps.

Later in the run, Tom Mardirosian was performing his number in the show, called "Professional Showbizzness Comedy". He was bound and gagged, hopping all around, and at a certain point in the number, he was loaded onto a rolling cart and pushed through a paper brick wall. It was meant to be a comedy number. But on the night I'm recalling, they pushed him through the wall and he rolled off the cart and couldn't break his fall because his hands were tied. He took his curtain call that night with a black eye! It was awful!

On the night we closed, I have a vivid recollection of the snow coming down, and Tim Curry (who had played the tipsy Alan Swann) now tipsy himself. He went weaving off into the snowy night, accompanied by a helpful assistant who had been delegated to get him safely back to his hotel room—it was life imitating musicals.

1992: The First Original Musical In The Theater

Stephen Flaherty, Writer

We did the show *My Favorite Year* at the Vivian Beaumont, and it was the first original American musical that had ever been done in that theater. It was thrilling.

The first day I was at the Beaumont, Bernie Gersten said something to me I never forgot, "Oh you lucky boy! You enjoy every moment that you are in this theater—I wish I were in your shoes because this is your first day getting to work here. You're going to have wonderful days and horrible days, but cherish the bad with the good." And I did.

It was a somewhat rocky birth with *My Favorite Year* but it was such fun writing for Andrea Martin, who was making her Broadway debut in our show. She was my idol growing up; I loved watching Second City TV. She was a writer on the show and would give these amazing comic performances. In our show, she was playing a female comedy writer and sometime-performer in a world of men. I thought: *This is who she is!*

We foolishly wrote a number called "Professional Showbizness Comedy", which we thought had funny jokes on the page. Well, we looked at the audience during that number and it was like an oil painting. They were just sitting there, like that scene from *The Producers*. We wrote and wrote like crazy during previews, trying to fix it, and meanwhile the clock was racing towards opening night. Finally I thought, *You know, we have to go to the source. Let's talk to Andrea.*

We brought her in and said, "Clearly this number is not working. What can we do to help you? What do you think is funny?" And she said, "...Well, I think small dogs walking across the stage on their hind legs is funny, and I think..." And she went from there. In the rehearsal room she started to play with various props she had in a box. So she did a gypsy moment with a tambourine, and then a comic strip tease, and then did some stand-up ("Use your hands.") It dawned on Lynn and me: *This is what the number should be. It should be about Andrea Martin being inventive and creating on the spot, because* that's *who she is: an improv gal. And her character is, too!* We totally scrapped the old number, all except for the title and a little of the tune, and put in a new one that was tailored specifically for Andrea.

Of course, when you're in previews, your rehearsal time is very limited. Tom Mardirosian was playing King Kaiser, the star of the fictional TV show, and he had to do the number with her. But he couldn't learn this entirely new piece. And we had these singing and dancing clowns that had to stay, according to Thommie Walsh, our choreographer. So we had to think: *How can we do this number for Andrea where Tom doesn't speak or dance?* Suddenly, Lynn came up with the brilliant idea of making the King Kaiser character a hog of a performer, who lays down the law, saying that Alice Miller, Andrea's character, is only allowed to have one gag in their act. So, Alice literally binds and gags him so he can't sing or dance, and she takes the number hostage. That's how we were able to give Andrea the opportunity to do her tambourine bit, her comic striptease, her jokes… she did everything but set herself on fire.

The minute that the new song went into the show, the whole second act jumped. Two nights before the critics' preview, the audience started standing up in an ovation after the number. It literally stopped the show and it was Andrea Martin's first Tony Award. It's nice to say that. She was my comic inspiration and now she's my pal, too.

One thing I learned from being at the Beaumont is that comedy is not necessarily at its best on a thrust stage. Who knew? Andrea explained it best by saying, "I do my snappy punch line and then I'm walkin'… I'm walkin'… I'm still walkin'. That wing seems like it's five miles away." There was something about the space that wasn't quite right for the comedy of the show.

My Favorite Year was the last original cast album to be recorded at the RCA Victor Studio, which then became the IRS building. Oddly enough, the highest note in the score is the very last note of the overture. It's a trumpet hitting a high C. We recorded everything out of order, and did all the instrumental pieces last so that we could let the actors go. So the very last moment in the recording studio was the trumpet hitting that brassy, Broadway high C—and then they shut off the lights and that was the end of RCA Victor Studio.

I think RCA was on 43rd Street near 6th Avenue, it was in the 40s for sure. You walked in there and you saw photos of Zero Mostel recording *Fiddler on the Roof*, and the cast of *Ain't Misbehavin'*, and people actually recording all of these great records that I grew up listening to, the records that would inspire me to write for the musical theater.

The character in *My Favorite Year*, Benjy Stone, is a Jewish kid from Brooklyn, but he's really a Catholic kid from Pittsburgh. That's who I was. His story, his yearning, was mine. That's why I wanted to write the show.

We later did three wonderful shows downstairs in the Mitzi Newhouse. In 2005, we did *Dessa Rose*, which was the story of a black woman and a white woman who had both really existed, but in history had never actually met. The show was based on a novel by Shirley Ann Williams and it was this interesting piece about two strong women and how they helped one another and counted on one another.

It was very expansive music, the most expansive I had ever written. I think of *Dessa Rose* as a companion piece to *Ragtime*, and it may very well be the closest I'll ever get to a folk opera. And so my expansive, big show was in the little theater while upstairs in the big theater, the Beaumont, there was this intimate show, *The Light in the Piazza*!

It was such a rich musical season with those two shows running together in the same building. I remember a review that said, "The two greatest love stories currently being sung on the stage are both at Lincoln Center: *The Light in the Piazza* and *Dessa Rose*." I had never really thought of our show as a love story, but you know, it is. It's about these two women who grow to connect with one another in such a surprising, unexpected, loving way. And so I liked that review. And I liked that spring where we both shared Bernie and André's magical theater.

1992: Or Maybe I Remember It Exactly The Way It Was

Evan Pappas, Actor

I got to do the second reading of *My Favorite Year* at Playwrights Horizons, because Ira Weitzman was a champion of mine. He'd seen me in other readings, and invited me to be part of this new musical.

The show fit me like a glove. That first reading I did had Jon Cryer as Alan Swann. Then Jim Dale did a reading. And then Victor Garber. By that time, we were workshopping the show uptown at Lincoln Center. The show was changing a lot, and that whole regime of creatives, including Ira, moved from Playwrights to Lincoln Center.

I had done a production of *Lucky Stiff*, and Lynn Ahrens and Stephen Flaherty had come to see it. So they were somewhat familiar with me, and when I auditioned for them, I remember Lynn told me, "You walked in, and you were just different from everybody else." That meant a lot to me. Doing the show with them was wonderful.

I loved singing "Larger Than Life" in the show. I loved doing that big opening. I loved working opposite Lannyl Stephens. I couldn't wait to be onstage with her. I get weepy thinking about it.

In one scene, there was a sliding door to a balcony at the Waldorf. I would find these bottles in Alan's valise, and go hide them out on the balcony. One day, I went to open the door to the balcony, and it wouldn't open. The audience is watching me, and I'm just grunting, pulling at the handle. They thought it was part of the show. Finally, I found another place on the set to hide the bottles. Then Rookie, played by Tom Ikeda, came in and was supposed to open the door. I went, "No, that doesn't open!" to try to save it. But what happened is that the crew guys had fixed the problem—a latch they'd forgotten to undo before—so when Tom went to open it, it opened easily. The audience burst into hysterical laughter. It should've been in the show! Tom and I couldn't help it, and we started laughing.

There were things that didn't work about the show, but it's easy to remember the positive. I loved that company; we had a great time. What's sad about a show isn't that it is not well-received, but that you feel so attacked by the Broadway vultures. There are people who just can't wait to see things fail. And I come from another school. I want things to succeed. Everybody thinks they can always do it better, but you can't go to shows thinking like that. I find that kind of thinking exhausting.

You work so hard on a show. You see such potential. And look, if someone doesn't like it, that's fine. But the vulture attacks...

Also, we opened in the fall. Shows really weren't doing that then. I think if we had waited until the spring, it could've gone a bit differently. Lynn and Stephen's score was awfully good. And there were so many amazing people in the cast, who went on to do even more amazing work. Katie Finneran was in it, and Andrea Martin. Rob Ashford was a swing! I think we could've run longer.

When a show has some bad word-of-mouth, it's really hard on the cast. After all that work, you just feel awful. How do you rise above it? How do you say, "No, I'm proud of the work"? It's difficult. You get influenced by people you talk to outside of the production. But then you just try to go, "F— them. We're proud of what we've created." Our business can be joyous, and it can be so difficult and hurtful.

1993/1996: Two Performances On Thanksgiving

James Maloney, Stagehand

My dad was the electrician at the Vivian Beaumont Theatre for a few years, and then he left and someone else took over—and after that, I took over. I was there for eight years. It's a beautiful theater, and I did a lot of plays there. In 1996, they closed the Beaumont for a little while and refurbished it. Shortly after that, I chose to leave to go work for Disney.

I remember doing *Abe Lincoln In Illinois* at the Vivian Beaumont, and we had two performances on Thanksgiving Day. There were more people onstage than in the audience, and it was really hard for everyone. But the family onstage and backstage gets you through. You do homemade dinners and a potluck, and celebrate the holiday between shows together.

Because the Beaumont is such a large space, all of the designers would come in and be building these immense productions. There was one show where the lighting designer, Kenny Posner, came to me because he wanted to make a chandelier look like a gas chandelier. We did it, and it was beautiful. We rewired it and made it with all of these flickering candles, and the creative team just fell in love with that chandelier.

On *Juan Darien*, I looked at Don Holder's lighting plot and said, "Don, you don't have enough light for this space!" Sure enough, he went back and redesigned it. The Beaumont is almost 90 feet deep, from the front of the thrust to the back of the stage, and it's 100 feet wide. On *Abe Lincoln*, we had a caboose in the show that the character of Abe would come out on, and make a speech. It was a real caboose! It took everyone on the crew to move it.

The Vivian Beaumont is quite the space. Every show is a challenge there, because every show is so large.

1994: Audra Ann McDonald

Ira Weitzman, Musical Theatre Associate Producer at Lincoln Center Theater

During the 1993-1994 season, we were working on two musicals at the same time. The first one was *Hello Again* by Michael John LaChiusa and the next was *Rodgers and Hammerstein's Carousel*. We were holding some general auditions, to meet people we didn't know to anticipate what roles they might be right for. A casting assistant asked, as a favor, if we would see her friend. Of course we said yes because we wanted to see new people.

We were sitting in one of the rehearsal rooms in the basement of the Beaumont, with a list of auditioners, none of whom we previously knew. The casting assistant's friend came in, and the name on the list was Audra Ann McDonald. She sang "Bill" from *Show Boat*, and that thing happened where I found my whole body leaning forward, because she was just so captivating. Her performance was electric and unexpected in every way. I asked her to sing something else and she went into Stephen Schwartz's "Meadowlark". At that point, it was just: *Holy Mother of God, who is this girl?*

After Audra Ann McDonald sang "Meadowlark", I asked her, "Do you have a little time? Can you stay?" All I could think was: *Everybody has to hear her! I've got to see who else is in the building!* I put a big star next to her name and ran around the building and found Graciela Daniele, who was director in residence at the time. She was working on *Hello Again* in her office and I pulled her into the audition room and asked Audra if she would kindly repeat her audition again.

We were super excited to cast her in one of the shows we were about to do. The role she was most right for in *Hello Again* was already cast. That's when I started to think about *Carousel*. We had her come in for the director, Nick Hytner, and we decided we wanted her to be Carrie Pipperidge in *Carousel*.

We all wanted Audra to play Carrie but we needed approval from various representatives of the Rodgers & Hammerstein estate. So we had callbacks, and used the Mitzi Newhouse Theater to show everyone our final three choices for Carrie. Audra flew in from *The Secret Garden* tour early in the morning and she sang "Mister Snow" spectacularly for us on the Newhouse stage. As soon as she was done singing, she promptly fainted! She just fell to the floor. Mary Rodgers Guettel ran up to Audra instantly, concerned, and asked, "Honey, did you eat breakfast? Are you alright? What can we do?"

Of course she got the part. It was an extraordinary occasion and the beginning of the Broadway career of Audra McDonald.

———————

I had the privilege of interviewing both Ira Weitzman and André Bishop in their offices at Lincoln Center. Ira's office is filled to the brim with scripts from both past musicals and possible future musicals, and André's office has an impressive wall of hanging mugs from every production he's worked on at Lincoln Center. Both men, luminaries of their field, spoke with emotion about the shows they loved bringing to audiences, the shows they wished had gone differently, and the shows they hoped to do in the future. It was inspiring to sit and talk to two mid-career professionals who still had all of the enthusiasm and drive typically associated with people who are just starting out.

Even when my interviews didn't take place at Lincoln Center, a certain love for the Beaumont emerged that seemed to conjure it all around the interviewees. I interviewed John Weidman in his apartment and he sporadically got up and gestured, pointed, and knelt to explain the layout of the Lincoln Center Theater complex. Ted Chapin had a similar approach in his office, mapping out on a desk in front of him where the scenery was stored behind the Beaumont stage, how the orchestra pit was created, where he stood in the wings. The Beaumont is not a classically built Broadway house, with a proscenium and boxes and intricate, gilded décor. It is not a typical location, being so isolated from the other Broadway houses. Yet, the theater seems to exhilarate theatre professionals from stagehands to producers to directors and beyond for different reasons, and also for one unifying reason: there's an almost-constant energy that people are happy to be working there.

———————

1994: The Next Thing I Knew, They Were Picking Children For Audra And Me

Eddie Korbich, Actor

Doing *Carousel* at the Beaumont was glorious—and it was a challenge.

After the "If I Loved You" sequence, the mound from that scene just kept being drawn farther and farther away from the audience. The stage was so big that you could do that kind of thing. It looked like this place where they had sung was going into the ether. It was so beautiful that you just wept. One night we were told that Frank Rich and Wendy Wasserstein were sitting next to each other in the front row. Our director Nick Hytner joked, "Apparently it got downright unsanitary!"

Before Broadway, I had done *Carousel* at the Forestburgh Playhouse. I played Mr. Snow and, oh, I sucked. I could sing it, but I was just horrible; because I was young, I didn't get it, understand it.

Then, the show was coming to Broadway and I was told that they weren't seeing "musical theatre people" at all—they wanted "Juilliard-types." They were also going for a big guy to play Mr. Snow. The actor who had originated the role in the London revival was a large man, and they liked that.

Unfortunately—or not, as it turns out for me—they couldn't find what they were looking for. The creative team was sitting there in auditions, not knowing what to do, because they didn't have a Mr. Snow. And I'm told that Nick Hytner at one point said quietly, "Maybe Mr. Snow is only big and blustery in Carrie's eyes?" And at that point Ted Chapin, the head of The Rodgers & Hammerstein Organization, turned to Nick and said, "Have you thought of seeing Eddie Korbich?" Thank you, Ted.

They brought me in, and I sang it. But I was still doing the Forestburgh Playhouse version. I didn't know quite what to do. Nick looked at me and said, "Alright Eddie. I'm just going to say this. It's bad, it's 'bad American musical theatre acting'. It's bad. I want you to do it again, but just imagine you're the biggest capitalist you know." I did, and the next thing I knew, they were picking children for Audra and me.

We got into rehearsal, and I still didn't feel like I was doing a good job. I could sing it very well, but I wasn't the character of Mr. Snow yet.

Nick was wonderful to me. He was very patient, and never dismissive, even though I could see that he was getting discouraged. One day during rehearsal, he said, "We're going to do the end of the first act. There are some props over there for the picnic: food and oars and things. See if you can find something that suits you, to use for the scene."

I walked over there, and I saw this little wicker basket. I was struck by it. I picked it up, and ran over and said, "Nick! What if Mr. Snow can't eat the food at the clam bake? I can't eat it, because I have allergies. I have to bring my own food from home. Everyone else is happy about the clam bake, but I'm stuck with my own basket."

He looked me in the eyes, and then he stopped what he was doing. He announced: "Ladies and gentlemen of the ensemble: this wicker basket is Mr. Snow's personal property which he is bringing to the clambake because of dietary restrictions. He can't eat what the rest of you are eating." Then he turned to me and said, "Yes, Eddie. Yes. Well done."

From that moment on, it was a completely different show for me. I started to find the character more and more. Every scene changed. Inspiration comes sometimes, if you just keep working and trying. That wicker basket made the whole character—that he was different, that he was an outsider in their community—click.

1994: Modern Relevance

Tim Federle, Actor

I was a spastic theatre kid growing up in Pittsburgh, Pennsylvania. When I was 14 years old, my mom flew us to New York to see *Carousel* at Lincoln Center.

Eddie Korbich and I had done *Oliver!* together at Pittsburgh Civic Light Opera, and I had kept in touch with him. I told him, "My mother is taking me to see a Broadway show." And he responded, "You should come see our show, it's in previews!" Because of Eddie, I actually had house seats to the very first Broadway show I ever saw.

I was excited, but I thought that *Carousel* might be kind of a stodgy, old-person show. It was anything but. Seeing that revival informed my career. I learned that with the right lens and the right kind of respect for the material, you can inject modern relevance and a big breath of fresh air into a show that happens to be old.

Up until that point, my theatrical life had taken place in a series of very straightforward, Midwestern proscenium theaters, with red seats. My mind was blown by the Vivian Beaumont, with its thrust stage, extraordinary slanted audience area, and neon set. "Oh my God. Broadway is so different than theatre back home." That's actually not true. Of course, Broadway had a lot of very traditional shows running in traditional spaces. But at the time, I thought all of Broadway would be like the Vivian Beaumont.

My mom and I started elbowing each other during "Mister Snow". Who is this Audra Ann McDonald? The show had not yet been reviewed, and it felt like we were watching a star being born.

Afterward, we got a backstage tour, and I was astonished to see that this Broadway theater backstage was kind of clunky and rundown and cement-lined. I thought I was supposed to turn a corner and see Liza Minnelli playing the harp.

———————

Tim Federle appeared on Broadway in Gypsy, Chitty Chitty Bang Bang, *and* The Little Mermaid, *before taking on a behind-the-scenes role working with the children of* Billy Elliot. *This was partially responsible for inspiring him to pursue a new career, as an author of books for both adults and children. His young adult novels,* Better Nate Than Ever *and* Five, Six, Seven, Nate! *have been praised by the* New York Times *and* Publishers Weekly, *and the latter won the American Booksellers Association Award for Best Children's Book of 2014. The* Nate *books revolve around a middle-schooler dreaming of Broadway, who happens to be gay—and as such, the books have received recognition for their inclusive approach. The books have also been banned from several schools, and several school visits by the author have been cancelled due to faculty or parents being offended by the presence of homosexuality in a young adult book.*

In a 2013 piece for The Huffington Post, *Federle wrote:*

> *When we support books that feature diverse kids, we're telling those kids that we support them too, that they are, more than anything, okay. The opposite is true when we shut those kinds of books down… Happily, there are many more educators, booksellers, young readers and parents who have been supportive of this book and books like it, books that tell stories that star diverse characters who aren't just relegated to the sidelines as the sassy sidekick or the tomboy cousin. And some of* Better Nate Than Ever's *most noted reviewers celebrated its "inclusive" storyline or didn't even mention the gay thing at all, which I kind of loved… Despite meaningful support, I still think about those canceled visits. There has to be at least one kid at a junior high school much like mine who wonders, like I once wondered, whether there's anyone else like him on Earth (or at least in the library). I wish that kid could pick up my book and read the answer for himself.[107]*

If you are a young adult or have one in your life, run and grab one or both of the Nate *books. You'll be transported to a world of youthful theatrical adventure, where just like 14-year-old Tim Federle once thought, you might turn a backstage corner and see Liza Minnelli playing the harp.*

———————

1994: The Snow Globe Sitzprobe

Bert Fink, Press Agent/Senior Vice-President of The Rodgers & Hammerstein Organization

In February of 1994, when *Carousel* was in pre-production at Lincoln Center, there was a sitzprobe[108] scheduled for a Friday afternoon. They couldn't do the sitzprobe in the actual theater, because they were loading in the set, and there was no rehearsal room large enough for the entire cast of actors and the orchestra, because it was a very big group.

———————

[107] Federle, Tim. "Book for Kids Raises Eyebrows Over Young Gay Character." *The Huffington Post.* 23 Sep. 2013. Retrieved from huffingtonpost.com.
[108] sitzprobe: the rehearsal where the performers sing with the full orchestra for the first time

So they decided to have the sitzprobe in the lobby of the Vivian Beaumont. That day, there was suddenly a blinding snowstorm. It was one of those amazing New York Friday afternoons, where snow just blankets the entire city for the weekend.

Ted Chapin and I were in the Rodgers & Hammerstein Organization office, which was on 50th and Broadway at the time. We went downstairs and right into the subway, rode underground, stepped out at the Lincoln Center stop, and walked underground until we stepped up right into the lobby of the theater.

I remember the moment that we entered the huge, cavernous glass lobby of the Vivian Beaumont, with snow swirling all around, and a 30-piece orchestra right in the middle of it all. It suddenly felt like we were all in a Christmas card or a snow globe of Lincoln Center.

1994: The Carriage House

Michael Berresse, Actor/Director

When I was at the end of my contract at *Damn Yankees* at the Marquis, I had a vacation planned with my boyfriend at the time. The show asked me to stay on after my contract ended, and I said that I would, if I could have those few days for a vacation. They refused to give them to me, and I decided that the right thing for me to do was to take the trip. I told them I was going to do that and end my contract when I was supposed to, but I don't think they believed me. I did it, and I left.

The day I came home from the vacation, I got an audition for *Carousel*. I got the job, and three days after I started, the guy who replaced me in *Damn Yankees* started performances. They had taken that long to get him into the show; I would've been back in by the time they hired him! But because of those circumstances, I got another Broadway show.

I was only in *Carousel* for the last six or seven weeks of the run, but it was my introduction to Lincoln Center, and I understood that it was something very different and special. There was a whole different world of Broadway that was happening at Lincoln Center. If Broadway is a royal manor, the Beaumont is like the carriage house. It's its own separate residence with its own separate staff. It's still part of the manor, but it's also its own little world.

At the Beaumont, everyone has their own couch, a heated toilet seat, shower… it's all modern and gorgeous and beautiful and super comfortable. I think of the Beaumont as sort of like my grandmother, because my grandmother lived to be 107 years old. She never had a stressful day in her life. She was very well provided for and never struggled. Just like her, the Beaumont feels very stress-free. It has this energy about it, like it has a solid foundation of safety. Their huge subscription base lends itself to this confidence among people who work there. It's a very confident, secure theater.

––––––––––––––

When I started working on The Untold Stories of Broadway, *I knew that some of the stories I'd hear would be Broadway lore only known to inner circles. But I never imagined that one of the most secretive subjects whispered about would be the Vivian Beaumont Theatre's bathrooms! At one point, I interviewed a Tony Award winner who hadn't ever worked at the Beaumont, and told him about another interviewee I was speaking with later that day. "Oh my God!" he exclaimed. "You have got to ask him to tell you about the Beaumont backstage bathrooms."*

The bathrooms at the Beaumont are legendary and all the actors that have had shows there mentioned them to me. After hearing so many stories about how beat up the backstages of some of the historical theaters are, it was nice to hear about the luxurious accommodations and heated toilet seats at the Beaumont!

––––––––––––––

1995: I Got To Sing Eight Bars At The Beaumont

Hunter Bell, Actor/Writer

I lived in Atlanta as a teenager, and then I went to Webster University in St. Louis. After college, I flew back to Atlanta, and got my Equity card at the Alliance Theatre. Then, in 1995, I moved to New York.

I slept on friends' couches, and temped, and did tons of weird, odd jobs. And I auditioned for everything! I didn't have an agent; I would just wake up at the crack of dawn and go to every single audition.

I remember auditioning for the revival of *Carousel* at Lincoln Center. You got to go into the theater and sing on the Vivian Beaumont stage! I somehow wasn't typed out, and got to sing about eight bars. I remember it very well, because every other audition I'd been to had been at a rehearsal studio: 890 Broadway or 440 Lafayette, usually.

————————

The opening credits of the iconic television show That Girl *(1966-1971) feature Marlo Thomas strolling through Lincoln Center wearing a purple frock and matching parasol. Throughout the years, the plaza that leads to the Beaumont has provided a setting for many movie and television moments, including in* The Wiz *(1978),* Moonstruck *(1987),* In & Out *(1997) and* Center Stage *(2000).*

————————

1996: I've Had Something In Every Single Space At Lincoln Center

Julie Taymor, Director

Juan Darien started out in the St. Clement's Church, where it was very intimate and beautiful. Then the show made plans to transfer to the Vivian Beaumont, which was perfect. I love that big thrust stage, and it played into the circus/carnival aspect of *Juan Darien* very well. We were able to expand the concept by creating a circus tent canopy, and making more banners, and expanding the piece physically in other ways too. It was exciting.

Instead of one skeleton dance for the character of Mr. Bones, I had 12 puppets attached to humans dancing. The new theater made the piece bigger, and, I thought, better. But really, that's up to your audience. I loved *Juan Darien* at the Vivian Beaumont. It just fit beautifully there.

I've had something in every single space in Lincoln Center. I've had an exhibition at the Library of the Performing Arts, I've had films in both of the movie theaters, I've had an opera at the Met, and a show at the New York State Theater, I've worked at Avery Fisher, I did a show that moved to the Mitzi Newhouse. So for me, Lincoln Center is a home, in every sense.

At one point, I was sitting with Peter Gelb, former General Manager of the Met, in the movie theater across the street, watching the simulcast of our version of *The Magic Flute*, when he said, "Oh my God, we have to go!" He grabbed my hand and we ran underneath the parking lot so that I could come up into the Met and take a curtain call at the live show. All of a sudden, we went from watching the film version of the live show, to onstage taking a bow at the real thing.

I think that when you're working on a play like *Juan Darien* as a director though, you're just so busy that you're not thinking about what else is going on in the complex. You're just trying to get your show up on time and with all of the elements correct.

1997: She's Too Short

André Bishop, Producing Artistic Director of Lincoln Center Theater

When we were doing *The Little Foxes* with Stockard Channing, she and director Jack O'Brien decided that they wanted to present the character of Regina in a warm, feminine way. They didn't just want the standard Talullah Bankhead, Bette Davis, growly sort of tough bitch.

I'm not always the bravest sort of person about listening to audience members talking at intermission about our shows. We read books where all the great writers and directors talk about going out into the lobby and getting these great ideas from eavesdropping on the audience. But I don't know if that actually happens. I guess perhaps it used to in the past more than it does now, because now creatives can just read what audience members say on the Internet. But this time, it did. And I remember at the end of a preview, I overhead an audience member saying to her friends, "She's too short! She's too short!" I thought: *What does that even mean? What do you know?*

Later, after the play had opened and was a mixed success, I realized that this woman had actually encapsulated what was wrong with the production. It had nothing to do with how tall Stockard was—it was that she makes her affects in a small way; she's a subtle actress. And we'd surrounded her with an enormous two-story set. The play is supposed to be about this woman who feels trapped and confined and claustrophobic in this house, and what we had done in fact was put her in an enormous structure in which she did, in fact, seem very small. That was a big problem with the production. And this audience member sensed that. Even if I had realized at the time why she was saying it, nothing could really have been done at that point—we couldn't have changed the set. But it was a fascinating observation that really changed the way I thought about the production, once I processed it.

1998: The Beginning And The End Of An Era

Jason Robert Brown, Writer

Parade was my debut on Broadway as a writer. I was thrilled for the show to be happening at the Beaumont.

About a week before tech started, the director Hal Prince decided that he was going to make a big change at the end of the show, and that it was going to end in a World War I parade. Tech was very slow, and through the whole thing, we were building up to this parade that was going to be the conclusion. Alfred Uhry, the bookwriter, and I were not keen on the idea, but we went with it.

Finally the World War I parade moment came. The cast entered in doughboy costumes and then a huge cannon was rolled out to the middle of the stage. It pointed toward the audience and shot white confetti all over the stage. By this point, Alfred and I were in hysterics. It was unbelievably bad. Hal was looking at us, going, "What's so funny? Why is it funny?" I said, "Hal! We can't do this." He said, "Well, what are we supposed to do?" And I said, "Well, we can do what we wrote…" The cannon and doughboy outfits went away, with all of the other parade accoutrements. It was probably $30,000 down the toilet for that idea, but I'm grateful to the theatre gods every day that we didn't end our show with that particular image.

We didn't make a lot of changes during previews. It's hard to do that with a show as large as *Parade* was. It's technically difficult to make changes.

People walked out. The subscriber audience at Lincoln Center is very elderly, and when they don't like something, they walk out. There was one night early in previews when Jessica Molaskey was onstage singing

"My Child Will Forgive Me". That song ends with the character singing, "…and so I forgive you, Jew." At that point, a woman in the front row got up and walked out of the theater. I wanted to yell, "You know, you've only got eight more minutes until the act is over!"

After "Where Will You Stand When The Flood Comes," an actor had to push a large set piece off the stage. First, he would have to take his foot off this particular trap, and the stage managers would call the cue for the trap to go, as soon as his foot moved. It was in the dark, so there was an infrared camera trained on the actor's foot, to see the exact moment it would leave. Meanwhile, as soon as the foot moved, this actor would have to push a very heavy piece of scenery all the way off the stage. If the stage manager called the cue too early, the actor would've gone down under the stage. No one in the audience would ever have noticed this series of events unless there was a mistake, but every night, I would watch in the blackout to make sure everything happened correctly. I would get hives.

For *Parade*, our percussionist, Dean, had to be in a different room. There wasn't enough room for him in the orchestra pit, because there were all of these traps taking up space. So we put him in this office downstairs at Lincoln Center. He was connected to the orchestra pit remotely via a video camera. Every night before the show, Eric Stern our conductor would pick up the phone and call Dean in his percussion room. Then Dean would wave at the camera, and that's how they would know that everything was ready and they could start the show.

One night during the run, Eric picked up his phone and looked down at the camera and he didn't see Dean. It was time for the show to start, so Eric was getting a little nervous, and didn't know what to do. He turned around to look at the stage managers in the booth for help, and as he turned around he saw that Dean was sitting there, in the 5th row of the audience! Eric turned back to the pit, and suddenly there was Dean, on the video monitor, waving. He turned back toward the audience in disbelief, and Dean was still in the audience.

Dean had not told Eric that he had an identical twin who was coming to see the show that night. This was an evil prank that Dean and his brother would play on people all the time!

What always means the most to me is when other writers come to see my shows. I remember being in the pit of *Parade*, having played a performance, and looking up, and seeing Charles Strouse. Charles Strouse himself was leaning down into the pit! He caught my eye and he said, "Jason, that was fantastic! And Sebesky did an incredible job." Don Sebesky had orchestrated the show. It meant so much to me that Charles Strouse had come and had appreciated what we were doing. When other writers come, that matters a lot.

Parade meant an awful lot to a small number of people. I remember sitting in the audience during the final performance, crying, thinking: *This is the last time I'll ever get to see this show, and no one appreciated it, and this was my Broadway debut so now what?* There was a lot of emotion around it. It was a beautiful show to watch.

Carolee Carmello and everybody were giving magnificent performances, and I really didn't want to be sad about it. I wanted to celebrate the fantastic show we had created. I think everyone was acknowledging in their own way that the experience wasn't what they'd hoped it would be. And of course it wasn't what I'd hoped it would be, but it was something. It was something very big, and I just wanted to be able to be proud of it without *NY Times* critic Ben Brantley tainting my experience of it, which is something he does all the time. That was the first time I had experienced that, and I had to push all that away, and remember to celebrate the show. My mom was there with me. That show closing was a big event. It seems to me more and more now that it was the last of its kind. At the Beaumont, there weren't too many other shows that were original musicals with 20 people in the orchestra and 36 people onstage. There was an era that was ending then, and I don't know how many of us really knew it at the time.

1998: I've Never Done A Show That Polarizing

Evan Pappas, Actor

When I came back to the Beaumont to do *Parade*, I was put in the same dressing room that I had for *My Favorite Year*! It was filled with memories. And all of the IATSE crew guys were still there, more than half a decade later. They came up to me, and said, "How are you doing? You know, *My Favorite Year* is our favorite show we've had here, still." That meant so much. They said, "It's great to have you back, we loved that show." It was the best welcome I could have imagined.

A lot of the ushers were the same, and I loved talking to them. That started for me on my first Broadway show, *A Chorus Line*. I knew all of our ushers, and years later, I'd still go back to the Shubert and see them.

Be nice to everybody. Just be nice. It's a good rule. But honestly, I don't even think about it. I come from a large Greek family. I just like people. I want to talk to everybody. I want to know what they're about, where they came from. And ushers remember everything about the shows, so it's great to talk to them about that, too.

What was interesting about *Parade* is that people whose opinions I highly respect loved it with a passion, and people whose opinions I highly respect hated it with a vengeance. There was no in-between. I've never done a show that was that polarizing.

I was in *Parade* for the entire developmental process. My character, Britt Craig started out as far more present in act two, and wound up really only in act one. There were so many changes to the show. When it started out, you really didn't know if Leo Frank committed the crime or not. The situation was a little grayer, and it made the audience wonder: *Could he have?* I thought that was interesting and exciting. By the time we got to Lincoln Center, it was clear in the writing that Leo was innocent. The audience was not kept guessing or wondering. What was wonderful about the way Brent Carver played the role is that in his performance, he was so eccentric and odd that you almost thought he might be guilty. Watching that change within the production was interesting.

My big number in *Parade*, "Big News" was actually cut from the revival. So if they ever record the show again, that song won't be on it. Mine will be the only recording! And what was cool is that we did it in one take. One thing that was funny about doing the show onstage is that afterward, the actor J.B. Adams would throw me out of the bar and then throw my jacket and each shoe after me. But J.B. had a terrible arm. Three out of four times, the stuff would end up in the wrong place. One time, a shoe landed all the way in the netting on the pit, and I couldn't get to it, so I did the whole next scene wearing one shoe.

Parade has some of Jason Robert Brown's best music. And a lot of new numbers came and went. When we were in Toronto, there was this telephone number that opened act two. It was a really cool idea, and it was kind of centered around my character. But there were all these wires everywhere, and the song was so fast. The audience couldn't get all of the information. Jason and I had some tense moments working on it, and it was eventually cut.

I think the world of Jason, as a person and a writer. After my car accident, he was a person who really reached out to me. He was doing a reading of *Honeymoon in Vegas*. He called me and said, "Look, I know you're still recovering, and I want to help. Let's get you back, get your chops going. Would you come and just read the stage directions for me for this reading?" I was so flattered, but I couldn't. I still didn't have myself back together. I had so many broken bones, and they were still healing. I couldn't sit on a stool for three hours. I told Jason, "I owe you one. Thank you so much for thinking of me, and trying to help." It meant a lot.

1998: An Important Story To Tell

Patricia Birch, Director/Choreographer/Actor

I think one of my favorite shows that I did was *Parade*. I loved *Parade*. I first worked with Hal Prince in 1960 when I played Anybodys in *West Side Story*. It was one of his first shows as a producer, and he liked my audition and put me into the show.

13 years later, he chose me to collaborate with on *A Little Night Music*, as his choreographer. He always trusted my sense of how to help the story along. After that, we did *Candide* in the round, then *Pacific Overtures*, then *Roza*, then another *Candide* together, all on Broadway. *Parade* was next, in 1998.

The Beaumont was a great home for *Parade*, because it was big, just like the story was. Sometimes with serious shows, audiences don't appreciate them until they see them in a smaller space. Rob Ashford did a smaller production of *Parade* in London a little over a decade later which was more critically acclaimed.

With a brand-new serious musical, people don't always respond the first time around. I thought our production was gorgeous in lots of ways, but it was also overwhelming. We had to stage a hanging. I've never shied away from topics like that, and neither has Hal, but audiences were taken aback. *Parade* was a great collaboration and an important story to tell and I'm proud of my work on it.

1998: A Masterwork

Harold Prince, Producer/Director

Parade was terrific. It was an absolutely great production experience, and a show I'm very proud of in every way. The *New York Times* critic didn't get it, and that was that. I think it's wonderful material, a masterwork. And at this moment in time, I think that Jason Robert Brown hasn't yet been appreciated to the extent that he should be.

His *The Last 5 Years* is the best original musical I've seen since it premiered in 2002, with my daughter directing it. And yet again, when there was a revival at Second Stage in 2013... the critics didn't get it. With *Parade*, Alfred did a brilliant job with the book, we cast it beautifully, the score is wonderful, and I like very much what I did. I guess they'll catch up with it someday.

1998: A Note From Hal

John Hickok, Actor

During the summer of 1995, I directed a play called *Burning Blue* on the West End. A lot of people came to see it, and one of them was Hal Prince. I was back in the United States when I got a call from my stage manager saying, "Hal Prince was here this evening. He left a note for you."

The note was faxed to me, and I was amazed: Hal had loved the show, and he asked if I could come see him when he was back in New York. We met at his office, and he graciously spoke to me about the show and recommended it to a number of people. We became friends, and I did a couple workshops with him.

In 1996, when they were casting the first reading of *Parade*, I got a call for it, and came by car from Westchester, where I lived at the time. There was terrible traffic, and it was a hot summer day, and I ended up going to the wrong audition studio. When I finally got to the right one, luckily they were running late so I hadn't

277

missed my appointment. I paced around for an hour in a hot waiting room filled with a lot of actors, and finally I thought: *You know, this is crazy. I'm too stressed out. I'm just going to leave.* I literally got up, and that's when they said, "John Hickok?"

I went into the room, and I sang for Hal, and everything else went out the window. The first reading of *Parade* in 1996 was in Philadelphia and we all knew it was pretty special. Later, we did a reading in New York starring Matthew Broderick.

At one point, my song, "Pretty Music", had a massive amount of dance choreography. The show evolved. I remember that after three different readings over the course of several years, with just piano, we finally got into the studio in Toronto with a full orchestra, and the sound was just amazing. If you know that score, you know how lush and beautiful it is right from the opening chords. I couldn't sing. I was crying. It was too emotional. It was too amazing to hear that sound.

We came to Broadway and it didn't last as long as we'd hoped. I had a fever of 103 during the last preview week before opening, when all the critics were there. I called in sick and Hal called me and said "John, we have critics here tonight. Is there any way you can come in?" I said, "Uh, okay," and I experienced the power of theatre firsthand. Each time I went onstage, I'm sure my temperature went back to normal, and the minute I got off, I fell on my bed and it would spike up to 104 again and I was miserable.

I was very sad when *Parade* closed. It was my first Broadway musical and it was a very emotional experience.

1998: People Were Really Booing

Jessica Molaskey, Actor

Hal Prince is my hero. I listened to every record of every Broadway show he ever did, thinking: *Someday, I'm going to come to New York and I'm going to work with Hal Prince.* And I did.

I first met Hal through his daughter, Daisy. She hired me for a show, and we became friends. We actually had babies within months of each other; that was really nice. Then I did a show called *3hree* with Hal, which was supposed to come to Broadway but didn't. That was sad, because it was such a great piece, but I was still so grateful to have worked with him. And then *Parade* happened!

Parade was one of those pieces I love being in, where there's a real ensemble. Everyone was so strong in terms of what they could do. The funeral section was so powerful with that group singing Jason's music. And I remember the trial scene having the challenge of being very long, with all of us onstage the whole time, and not being able to smile or laugh.

I was pregnant when we did the original *Parade* workshop. By the time we started Broadway previews, my daughter was about a year old. There's this green, squishy, soft floor backstage at the Beaumont, which she used to play on all the time. If she fell, she wouldn't get hurt. My daughter learned to walk by holding the tops of the seats in the rows of the theater. You'd just see this little hand coming over the top. Everybody was really sweet about letting me have her there for those long, long tech days. She learned to walk at the Beaumont.

During *Parade*, Hal kept changing my costume. He'd bring me into a room and say, "You look like Maria Callas, and you're supposed to look like Betty." He wanted me to look like a farm worker. He'd say things like, "I want your hands to look gnarly! You look too chic." I didn't know what to do!

Also, they asked me to understudy the female lead, Carolee Carmello's role. I think understudying is a great thing to do when you're younger; it teaches you so much. But I was done doing it. Hal told me it was something to do with the Lincoln Center contracts, and the kind of money they had. He told me that they needed me to understudy her until the first of the year, and then it would kick over and they'd get another contract. I told him, "Hal, I can't do it: understudying Carolee! That's huge, and I'm tired, and I have this perfect little part, and it's just right." He told me, "You're never going to have to go on. She's a tank." And I replied, "No, I am. I'm going to go on on Christmas Eve."

We opened a week or so before Christmas. Two days after we opened, the day I was going to do all of my Christmas shopping, I got the call. Carolee, for the first time in her life, couldn't sing. She just had nothing. I had had no rehearsal for her role. The night before was the first time I had thought: *Tonight, I should just watch her.* So I did. I watched her once. And then I went on! I don't know how I did it. I remember in the song "This Is Not Over Yet", writing letters to the Governor, picking up pens and putting them on the table, thinking: *How did I get here?!*

After the show, Jason and Hal came backstage and were laughing, like, "That was really fun!" It was crazy! I think that at the end of my life, I could've maybe lived a few more days, if that hadn't happened. It was terrifying.

Parade inspired a lot of really wild audience participation. At the end of the first act one night, the lights came down, and we were all exiting, when we heard a sound. It was sort of like, "Booo!" I thought: *That can't be right.*

The next night, I heard it again, and it registered. People were really booing! I had never experienced anything like that in a production. I don't believe they were booing the quality of the show—there was something in the subject matter that they were reacting to.

Hal Prince had people running up to him in the audience and yelling at him. I went to a couple parties at the time where people said to me, "I don't know how you're doing that show."

I guess that in a way, that's what you want theatre to do. But it was still hard. We were so in love with the piece. When we were in rehearsals, it felt like it was going to be *West Side Story* or something. Then we got in front of audiences, and they didn't have the reaction we were expecting. To this day, I still don't completely understand why.

1999: Nobody In Between

Michael John LaChiusa, Writer

The Vivian Beaumont wasn't really built for musicals, so it never had an orchestra pit. However, it did have a giant circular elevator shaft that could go up and down and fill the thrust stage. It broke years and years ago, and was never fixed. So for dozens of shows, it was used as a storage space for props, tech equipment, and scenery.

Then *Marie Christine* came to the Beaumont, and we were trying to figure out where to put our 17-piece orchestra. I asked Bernie Gersten, "Could we dig out the elevator shaft?" And that's what we ended up doing. Lincoln Center turned the old broken elevator shaft into an orchestra pit, and that's what it's been ever since.

The Vivian Beaumont is utterly vast. The real estate covers an entire city block! Director/choreographer Graciela Daniele and scenic designer Christopher Barreca did amazing things with the space; they really used it. There was one moment when the actress playing Marie Christine's mother entered, and they had a tiny pin light on her face, shining from all the way in the back of the theater. As she came forward, there was this long stretch of time where her face got more and more huge. It was exciting to use the theater for its vastness in that way. A lot of shows at that time, like *Contact*, were cutting the stage off, and using it as a simple proscenium. It's such a great space to utilize as a thrust, when it suits the show.

I live in the audience during my shows. I like to go stand near audience members at intermission; I have to hear what they're saying. I'm entranced by the audience and their reactions. They truly are the final collaborators on the work. Sometimes they're nice collaborators and sometimes they're not—and during *Marie Christine*, a lot of audience members at intermission were angry. What was interesting is that they always came back for act two. I was amazed by that. And then at the end, they were polarized. Some audience members were deeply touched and had a very visceral emotional reaction to *Marie Christine*, and some absolutely hated it. There was nobody in between. I never heard, "Oh, I liked it." After the shows, I always heard audience members muttering with disgust, "Terrible," or people turning to their friends and saying, "That is truly the most amazing show I've seen in so long." I loved that. I loved those responses. I never wanted to have the "I liked it" response, because, to me, that's not important.

————————————

Marie Christine was the last musical to open on Broadway during the 20th century, with an opening night of December 2, 1999. A daring new musical, Marie Christine *was the classic story of* Medea *with a setting transplanted to 1890s New Orleans. Audra McDonald played the woman who chose to murder her own children as punishment toward her white ex-husband who left her for someone of his own race. In contrast, the first musical to open on Broadway during the 20th century was* Chris And The Wonderful Lamp, *with music by John Philip Sousa and song titles like "Fourth of July" and "The College of Hoop-Dee-Doo." We've come a long way!*

Lincoln Center received a notable amount of hate mail during Marie Christine *from patrons who were offended by the mixed-race relationship. Every letter was anonymous. A few seasons later, Lincoln Center would remind audience members that they never shied away from this kind of content by producing* South Pacific. *Through the years, many of the Beaumont's shows have addressed issues of race.*

Michael John LaChiusa decided he wanted to write a new musical for Audra McDonald after seeing her audition at Lincoln Center in 1994. From that audition, she walked away with her first Broadway role, in Carousel, *and she planted the seeds for her first leading Broadway role as well.*

————————————

1999: Getting His Due

Mary Testa, Actor

I've worked at Lincoln Center a couple of times, at the Beaumont and the Newhouse. Lincoln Center is so… clean. The dressing rooms, the theaters, everywhere.

Marie Christine was a beautiful piece. Audra's performance was wonderful, and people loved her. Graciela Daniele did amazing work, and Michael John created an exquisite score. As with a lot of Michael John's shows, there were people who didn't get it, and there were people who were enthralled by it.

Graci staged the show almost like it was a three ring circus. My character didn't come in until the second act, but we were all onstage the whole time. I was in the bleachers each night watching everyone in the playing field. I loved watching *Marie Christine* every night. I thought it was an extraordinary show. It was a joy to be part of, and a great pleasure to watch.

Michael John will not get his due until he's dead. People just will not recognize his brilliance yet. We recently went to see a student production of *Marie Christine* at NYU, and it was great to revisit that score. I just sat there and cried because I think it's the most magnificent score.

280

2000/2006: Backstage Can Be A Dangerous Place

Fritz Frizsell, Stagehand

The second part of *Contact* was titled "Did You Move?" and it was about an extremely abusive Mafia-type husband played by Jason Antoon taking his meek wife played by Karen Ziemba out for dinner. At one point, the husband returns to the table to find his wife dancing with the waiter. Angered, he pulls out a gun, which is knocked from his hand. Three waiters trap the gun under one of three chafing dish covers.

Every performance, a shell game ensued as the waiters moved the covers around while the husband tried to pick which cover the gun is under. When the husband was distracted, one of the waiters slid the gun to the wife, who hid it under her skirt. When the waiters simultaneously lifted all three covers to show there was no gun, he turned on his wife in a murderous rage and she shot him, to much applause.

One night, though, the gun slid past Ziemba, and well beyond the curtain upstage of her. Because of the angle, the audience did not see this, but we were all wondering how she was going to shoot him without the gun. When the moment came, Antoon rushed at her, and Ziemba shot him. Given the how suddenly the "gun" appeared, the sound effect of the gun going off, and Antoon's noisy and histrionic death, I'm pretty sure that no one noticed that Ziemba had shot him with her thumb and forefinger.

Backstage can be a dangerous place. It's dark, sets are moving and people are running around. You get used to where things and people are and when scenery is moving, but anything out of the ordinary can be hazardous. The night of the Live From Lincoln Center *Light in the Piazza* broadcast, I was working as an extra person backstage. I was, of course, dressed entirely in black, and was standing by to move a light (in a place where no one usually was) when Victoria Clark, who was running to make an entrance, nearly bowled me over. I flattened myself against the scenery just in time. "Sorry!" she called over her shoulder. I breathed a sigh of relief—just as Michael Berresse barreled around the corner, barely missing me as well. I decided to find another place to stand after that.

2001: A Secret Passageway From Juilliard

Michael Arden, Actor

When I was in school at Juilliard, I found a secret passageway underneath the school into the Beaumont.

During my first year of school, we were working on *A Winter's Tale*. And every night, after rehearsal, my friend and I would sneak over to the Beaumont and pretend to be in line at the bathroom. We would grab a Playbill, and we would walk in and we would second-act *Contact*. I think we saw "The Girl in the Yellow Dress," that whole section, probably... I wanna say 25 times. The cast started to recognize us, and they would wink at us during the show! I loved it. I could probably do the dance for you!

We just found a way in through the parking garage. I don't think it exists now that they've done the remodeling, but we went every night. I loved it. I loved it so much. And I thought, *I'm here at Juilliard, and I can end my night, every night, by being in the theater?!* It was such fun.

My dream is absolutely to work at the Beaumont, because I love the space itself. As an actor, the three-quarter thrust means that you always have to be aware of your audience, and make every angle of your body available to them. It's truly the closest thing we have to the first theaters.

But I also want to work there someday because I just love Lincoln Center.

The Vivian Beaumont was not actually the first attempt at Broadway theater in the area that was known as Lincoln Square. In 1906, even before they built the Shubert, the Shuberts managed a Broadway house called the Lincoln Square Theatre on Broadway and 66th Street. Only about a dozen Broadway shows called the Lincoln Square Theatre home before it turned to vaudeville, then movies, then became a CBS television studio and was then demolished, ironically, right around when Lincoln Center was being built. The Juilliard School stands where Lincoln Square's first Broadway house once did.

The David H. Koch Theater at Lincoln Center, at times home to opera or ballet, also housed three shows considered Broadway productions from 1978 to 1981. Through special temporary jurisdiction, the venue, at the time known as the New York State Theatre, was home to Stop The World-I Want To Get Off *(1978),* Camelot *(1980), and* Fiddler on the Roof *(1981). In the 1960s, the theater presented revivals of classic musicals as well, under the umbrella of Music Theater of Lincoln Center and their president, Richard Rodgers. These weren't considered "Broadway" productions, but one,* Annie Get Your Gun *(1966), did transfer to an official Broadway run at the Broadway Theatre.*

2005: Classical Singing

Jay Armstrong Johnson, Actor

I saw *The Light in the Piazza* when I was in college. I was studying Voice at NYU Steinhardt, and I was learning a lot about classical singing for the first time. Before, I had really only studied singing for theatre, but I started finding a love for classical music. It was right then that I saw that show, and the performances, that set, that score... it absolutely blew me away. I saw Kelli O'Hara's understudy, Jennifer Hughes, and she was amazing.

2005/2008: We Knew That Was In Our Show All Along

Kelli O'Hara, Actor

I don't always say that audiences need to be told how to feel, but sometimes it's true. The music in *Light in the Piazza* is challenging. It begs another listen. In the beginning of previews, we were also trying to get our sea legs with the show. We were still searching for exactly what my character, Clara, needed to be, so we made a lot of changes. We weren't completely solid by the time we opened, and I think that showed.

I don't read any reviews, but I know that things were mixed. The audience kind of went with that, and they were mixed too when they were watching the show. Some people loved the show, and some didn't. Then as people came back again, and as the show got more solid and started to become what it became, people started taking a different approach to it.

We had some critics retract their stories and rewrite their reviews into new ones that were glowing. All of a sudden, the audience was on that bandwagon, and came with a more open mind to see the show. After that and after the Tony Awards, all of a sudden people started respecting the show. People started feeling like *Light in the Piazza* was this brilliant moment in time.

It had been very different in the beginning. It was confusing to people, like: *What exactly is this? I'm not sure how to feel about it.* All of a sudden it was like: *This is amazing, this is brilliant!* But we knew that was in our show all along. We always loved it, and knew it was growing. We just did it.

Maybe audience members also need more time with something brand-new. Our ears aren't as geared to listen, the way they may have once been. That's interesting to me. *Light in the Piazza* also taught us all a lesson: don't get too discouraged right away, keep doing what you're doing and give it time.

My first trip ever to New York, I remember coming to Lincoln Center. There's a picture of my sister and me, standing right there in the middle of the plaza. I was really there to see the opera. I took a picture in front of the Met Opera and just looked at that place, this magical, crazy place that I could only dream of being a part of. Even just being there to see something was such a dream of mine, coming from Oklahoma.

There were many days when I was walking to work at Lincoln Center, and it would hit me that I was entering one of those buildings I had stared at. I was walking across that same plaza to go to work, where I had once taken a picture, when I was dreaming of performing in New York.

It never became mundane. I went from wanting to belong there, to actually being a part of Lincoln Center. There really is something going on in every single crevice of those buildings. Everywhere you look, in between shows on a Saturday, you see artists. You can walk across the parking deck to the Met cafeteria, and sit with some opera singers and musicians, and then see some ballet dancers walking around the fountain. It's unbelievable. I never went to a conservatory, but Lincoln Center must be what a conservatory feels like. It's a whole world of artists, a whole place dedicated to the thing you're passionate about. It really feels like a small country of art, that you get to be part of.

I've always thought of Lincoln Center as being kind of a family. In the theatre, you get to work with the same people in different shows over multiple years, and I've gotten to have that at the Beaumont. A lot of the same people worked on *Light in the Piazza* and then *South Pacific*, so we got to be back together again.

It makes you feel like you belong, and sometimes New York makes it hard to feel that way. I look forward to getting back to Lincoln Center.

2005: What The Sunlight Can Be

Michael Berresse, Actor/Director

I remember Meryl Streep coming to see us in *The Light in the Piazza*. I have always been enamored with her work. She is a real actress of integrity who loves the craft and what it means to do it. And she came to see *Piazza* repeatedly! She was never particularly visible, but I did see her at the stage door once. There was just something about that show. My impression is that for people like that, it might be hard to feel truly inspired, because they themselves have done so much inspirational work that people are constantly praising them for. So it's hard to be invisible enough to go and have an intimate experience with a piece of work. But I feel like she found a way to do that with *Piazza*. And there was something about the structure and content and integrity of the piece that I think appealed to her in particular. She came back with her daughters.

Theatre is the great equalizer. If you're the President, or a movie star, or a kid from Queens, everyone is in the same boat, experiencing the same story at the same time. As a person onstage in a situation like that, with all different kinds of people in the audience, you just feel grateful. I don't get any more nervous for the President than I do for the kid from Queens. I just want to make sure I'm telling the story as well as I can.

When *Piazza* came along, I had been dying to do a new piece, and I was so grateful. I was not involved in either of the productions prior to Broadway, in Seattle or Chicago, so I didn't have a history with the show. Out-of-town, my character had been kind of peripheral. I had just finished doing a project with Martha Clark, where I had to speak peasant Sicilian, so I had an Italian song ready. I came in for *Piazza*, and did that, and got to be both sexy and funny, which was the first time in my life I got to play a character like that. I was so happy to land that role.

Director Bart Sher, composer-lyricist Adam Guettel, and bookwriter Craig Lucas were all very available in the rehearsal room, to work on anything that came up. And Joseph Siravo, my cast mate, helped me a lot with the Italian moments. My character never spoke English; he only spoke Italian. It was interesting to see how that changed and informed the story. Sometimes I would throw in a moment in Italian and it would stick. They ended up expanding the character because it was a way of expanding the Italian part of the story.

When everyone is on the same page in a rehearsal/developmental process, you can take instincts that are personal and work together to see how they can impact the storytelling overall. One of my favorite moments ever onstage in a Broadway musical was standing in the churchyard at the end of *Light in the Piazza* and having the privilege of being part of the story while Vicki Clark sang "Fable". I cried literally every single night for months and months, for over a year. I felt like I was part of something that was so beautiful and true. *Light in the Piazza* will always be a seminal moment of my career and my life—being part of that particular story changed me.

————————

Both Michael Berresse and Kelli O'Hara have performed both a musical by Richard Rodgers and a musical by his grandson, Adam Guettel, at the Beaumont.

————————

2005: Part Of It All

Jeff Bowen, Writer/Actor

I started working in talent management, for Davis/Spylios in 1996. My first year with them was the year of *Titanic*, *The Life*, all of those shows from the 1997 Tony Awards. I loved getting to see everything, and a lot of the time, they had clients in the new shows, so we'd get to go backstage and say hi to people. I remember trying to keep my cool, trying to be like, "Oh whatever. This is nothing."... but secretly being totally excited.

I remember we went backstage at *Putting It Together* at the Barrymore because the managers were really good friends with George Hearn. Dale Davis took me back to George Hearn's dressing room, and Lauren Bacall was in there. She was just sitting there, hanging out. It was bizarre. I remember thinking: *Oh, I guess Lauren Bacall just hangs out here with the stars after the show.* It was mind-blowing to me.

That happened all season. It was both exciting and not-exciting because it happened so much. It was a crazy year, and I just took it all in. I still have so much fun when I get to go backstage at different theaters. If I'm doing a Gypsy of the Year, or have a friend in a show, it's fun to see what each backstage is like.

And of course, my partner Michael Berresse has been in so many shows, so I've been backstage at a lot of theaters to visit him. I don't really like to hang around in those situations, because I know it's such a private world, and people are doing their work. People backstage usually say, "Oh, come back and sit by the potato chips!" or whatever, and I'm always like, "No, you guys are doing your thing and I don't want to be in the way."

I remember feeling like that changed when we were doing [title of show] off-Broadway and Michael was doing *The Light in the Piazza* at the Vivian Beaumont. Suddenly I felt welcome in a different way, because I had something under my belt with [title of show]. I felt like part of the community. I also just knew his coworkers well on that show, because it was a social group who had dinner parties together. It was a nice to feel like even though I wasn't in that show, and I didn't really have anything to do with it, I was welcome to be there. I was allowed to be backstage at the Beaumont. At the time, you had to cut through the Lincoln Center offices to get to the dressing rooms, and I'd always pass this one person's desk who had the most amazing snow globe collection. I would slow down, because I wanted to see them. And the bathrooms are off the chart!

The Coast of Utopia is the straight play that holds the record for most Tony Award wins ever. In 2007, the Tom Stoppard trilogy was awarded seven Tonys, including one for Best Play. The next year, the Beaumont helped set another Tony Award record, when South Pacific *won the most awards of any musical revival (also seven).*

Several plays at the Beaumont had been nominated for the Tony Award for Best Play before. In 1968, Brian Friel's nominated duo of plays called Lovers *consisted of* Winners, *about a young couple who conceive out of wedlock and commit joint suicide and* Losers, *about an older couple in a loveless marriage. In 1970,* Operation Sidewinder *by Sam Shepard used a deadly military device let loose to illustrate the effects of technology and war on society. In 1973, David Rabe's* Boom Boom Room *told the story of a troubled, sexually abused go-go dancer. Also in 1973,* The au Pair Man *by Hugh Leonard illustrated the troubled relationship between the Irish and the English. In 1974, the prison drama* Short Eyes *by Miguel Piñero was only nominated for Best Play and no other awards, a rare occurence for any production. Three John Guare plays at the Beaumont were nominated for Best Play:* The House of Blue Leaves *in 1986,* Six Degrees of Separation *in 1991 and* Four Baboons Adoring The Sun *in 1992. (While his* A Free Man of Color *in 2010 did receive a nomination for the Pulitzer Prize for Drama, it did not receive a Tony nomination.) In 1995, Tom Stoppard's academic epic involving the past and present and the idea of uncertainty,* Arcadia *was nominated, and in 1996, David Hare's* Racing Demon, *involving gays in the Church of England, was given a nod.*

Before The Coast of Utopia, *in over 40 years of original plays at the Beaumont, not a single Best Play nominee had won the coveted prize. After* Coast of Utopia *won seven in 2007, the Beaumont's gorgeous production of* War Horse, *about World War I, won six awards including Best Play in 2011. In 2014, the production based on Moss Hart's seminal autobiography,* Act One, *received a nomination.*

Awards aside, it is clear that the Beaumont and those involved in its artistic decisions have never avoided presenting meaningful work containing controversial social and political themes.

2008: *South Pacific* Auditions

Ira Weitzman, Musical Theatre Associate Producer at Lincoln Center Theater

Another very memorable audition I remember in this building was Paulo Szot's, for *South Pacific*. We felt we needed to cast Emile first, because his age would impact who our Nellie should be. There was a very small category of qualified people who could play Emile, who had the voice, acting ability, likability and gravitas. Paulo came in among a bevy of opera singers and blew us away with his voice and beauty, but because we hadn't gained any perspective yet on the role or what our production was calling for, we thought he was too young and maybe his acting was a bit too much in the opera world. Sometimes opera singers can be a little bit stiff for musical theatre. That was that or so we thought.

Later on, we still hadn't cast the role and were realizing it was even more difficult than we initially anticipated! We remembered Paulo and asked him to come in again. We loved him, and thought: *Well, why couldn't Emile be a bit younger than we originally thought?* There's a line that says, "I'm much older than you," but does he have to say "much"? There was some age difference between Paulo and Kelli O'Hara, who by then we knew we wanted as our Nellie. It was workable.

Paulo's acting was still rooted in the opera world, where there's lots of singing while standing very still, with arms to the side or folded. While we were auditioning other people, we asked if he could stay and work for a little bit. We sent him into another room with a member of the creative team to work on the audition scene.

Part of my job is to facilitate the work of the team and I find it helpful to observe every part of the production process. As Paulo was working in the other room, I snuck in and sat down. The assistant director whispered to him, "You want to have sex with this woman," and a switch turned on in his head. Of course, he's the sexiest opera singer, but that just wasn't where he was coming at the role from. After that, he started to read again and loosen up and naturally exude that sex appeal that was so right for the character. I ran out of the room and got casting director Bernie Telsey, who was still in the main audition room. "Bernie, this is it! Come here." We snuck in and watched. We brought Paulo back into the main room and he gave the most passionate, open audition you could imagine. We found our Emile and the rest is history.

When we decided to produce *South Pacific* it began a very emotional time for me. I grew up in a home where my mother cherished the theater and shared her original cast albums with me. Her favorite and soon to be mine was *South Pacific*. I fell in love with that record. Every song was a winner! My mother was a great New York lefty liberal for whom *South Pacific* really meant something philosophically and she imparted that to me at a young age. To actually work on the first Broadway revival was a great fulfillment of my childhood fantasies and inspiration. It was also a great responsibility as we knew many people of all generations shared the love of this show. Our production not only had to be wonderful but it had to be perfect. I think we succeeded at making the best revival of the great *South Pacific* that we possibly could and I am very proud that it could be done so beautifully in the Beaumont.

2008: Veterans

Danny Burstein, Actor

There was a lot of crying that happened *after* the show at *South Pacific*.

People would come back in uniform. Old veterans would bring their hats and their medals and things, to see the show. Sometimes they were very stoic or tight-lipped afterward, but their spouse or their son would talk for them a little bit. That was a beautiful thing. That was lovely.

———————

In 1949, everyone onstage in South Pacific *was directly connected to a World War II veteran or was one. The war had ended just four years earlier, and here was a musical on Broadway set around it. In recent history, this would be as though a musical set around the September 11 attacks opened on Broadway in 2005. In 2008, many World War II veterans made their way to* South Pacific *at Lincoln Center with their children, grandchildren, and great-grandchildren.*

Richard Rodgers' daughter, Mary Rodgers Guettel, and Oscar Hammerstein's daughter, Alice Hammerstein Mathias, watched over their father's work in their stead, taking an active role in the production. In The New Yorker, *Mary noted that she had brought her friend Hal Prince, who was scared of getting drafted, to the original opening in 1949. That night, she introduced him to her other friend Stephen Sondheim. Alice could not attend the original opening, but she did have a significant wartime experience in the theatre when her father gave her a job on the original production of* Oklahoma! *supervising all of the noisy G.I.s in the standing room section.[109]*

The 2008 production of South Pacific *at the Vivian Beaumont became the longest-running Rodgers and Hammerstein revival on Broadway.*

———————

[109] Ross, Lillian. "Enchanted Evening." *The New Yorker*. 7 Apr. 2008. Retrieved from newyorker.com.

2008: Some Enchanted Evening

Michael John LaChiusa, Writer

All I did was cry through *South Pacific*. I cried and I cried and I cried. It was so moving to me, every single beat, and the lovely, simple way it was staged, and the wonderful performances by a perfect cast. The music-making was spectacular. The story was dark and dangerous. It was heartbreaking, and at the end you really felt destroyed. *South Pacific* was tremendous.

2000/2009: Replacement

Laura Osnes, Actor

The first Broadway show I ever saw was *Contact* at Lincoln Center. It was on a trip to New York with my 9th grade class. Then I ended up playing Nellie in *South Pacific* at the same theater eight years later.

I replaced Kelli O'Hara, and that was a new experience for me, joining a huge musical like that. I'm still shocked and honored that the creative team and casting director even considered me for the role. It seemed like such a longshot to me at the time, and I was overjoyed and so grateful I got the offer to do it. It was a perfect scenario because Kelli was having a baby, so she was leaving under very happy circumstances, and I had a nice, short contract of six months before she would come back. After baby Owen was born, Kelli returned to complete the final three months of her initial contract, then I took over the role again for the final eight months of the run.

Getting to replace in a show was interesting, because I only worked with the stage manager and dance captain for most of the time. We used mock-ups of the furniture on the set, but we didn't have the thrust stage to work with. I never heard the orchestra before my first night on! There were just so many elements I never experienced until my first performance in front of 1000 people! I did have a put-in at the theater, where I was in costume but the rest of the cast wasn't. It was scary because for the first time, everyone was watching to see how I was performing. I was very aware everyone would be ready to judge, and of course, I wanted to do a good job. However, the cast couldn't have been nicer, and I felt extremely welcome, even though I was the new kid. It made me very cognizant of show replacements and what they go through. Now if there's a replacement in any show I do, I really make a point to reach out to them.

Another unique thing about *South Pacific* was washing my hair onstage! The showers were going, the soap was flying, and we were all wet and dancing in bathing suits. By the time I got there, they had everything figured out, but I heard stories about the tech process. Kelli had tried to use her real hair, but they couldn't dry it and style it on time for the next scene. The only choice was to use wigs. The shampoo used onstage was that strawberry kids' bathroom foam, which was easy on eyes but hard on the wigs. They had to be replaced every three weeks, which was crazy, because those wigs are expensive! We'd use the nice, new wig for act two, and then cycle it into act one to be shampooed night after night, then they'd eventually have to be tossed. Somewhere at Lincoln Center, there are tons of blonde bobs just hanging out.

Fleet Week was a huge deal during *South Pacific*. I was there for two of them, where we had tons of real seabees and marines in the audience. I was also there for the performance given on the 60th Anniversary of *South Pacific*, when original cast members came. It was really special. My grandma was becoming a nurse during the time of World War II, but she was too young to be sent overseas. I kept a picture of her in her uniform in my dressing room. Lots of cast members had photos backstage of their grandparents or parents in service uniforms.

Knowing there was other art going on in the same building was amazing. My friend Bobby Steggert was in *The Grand Manner* downstairs at the Newhouse, and I'd go visit him, or he'd come to my dressing room at intermission. Jenny Powers was in a show, so I'd see her. And Victoria Clark! Victoria Clark said to me later, "Laura, we always heard your voice over the monitors singing *South Pacific*. We loved hearing it!" Who knew our monitors played down there?!

Bernard Gersten and André Bishop, who run Lincoln Center, are just wonderful. They often sent me handwritten notes and flowers. I felt so respected and honored and loved and embraced by the Lincoln Center family, which is somewhat rare. They really reached out. I would love to work there again; it's so beautiful! And I live really close, so it's also convenient. And to top it off, Lincoln Center has these decadent bathrooms. Almost all of the other Broadway theaters are old, which is great and gives them a lot of character, but at Lincoln Center you can really get spoiled by the amenities. I was treated like royalty there.

———————————

Lincoln Center Theater revolutionized the strategy for not-for-profits with Broadway houses when they began frequently producing shows outside of the Vivian Beaumont. Each season at the Beaumont would be planned out, but if a production proved to be a hit that could continue its run, provisions would be made to do the rest of the season elsewhere. For example, with South Pacific *occupying the Beaumont, Lincoln Center presented* Dividing The Estate *at the Booth in 2008,* Joe Turner's Come and *Gone at the Belasco in 2009,* In The Next Room *at the Lyceum in 2009, and* Women on the Verge of a Nervous Breakdown *at the Belasco in 2010. By not halting all Broadway operations to yield to one show, Lincoln Center Theater was able to gain new audiences at long-running hit and also continue patronage to subscribers with new productions.*

Another way that the Beaumont opted for new experiments in programming under Bernard Gersten's and André Bishop's leadership was by presenting a run of concerts during the off-nights of a production. Both the Beaumont and Mitzi began utilizing Sunday and Monday nights for once or twice-a-week engagements of solo concerts by artists including Patti LuPone, Brian Stokes Mitchell, and Barbara Cook. Other weekly fare included a one-man play featuring Alan Alda and several pieces by Spalding Gray.

———————————

2010: Political And Personal

André Bishop, Producing Artistic Director of Lincoln Center Theater

I'll never forget the closing performance of *South Pacific*. We had gotten Paulo Szot and Kelli O'Hara back for the last few weeks, because we were doing a television broadcast of the production. A lot of cast members returned, so the cast was virtually the same as it had been two years earlier.

South Pacific is a show that means a great deal to the people who love it, and I'm one of them. I was always determined that we were going to do *South Pacific* someday. I don't know quite why the elements of *South Pacific* mean so much to the people who love it, besides for the fact that it's obviously a great show and has a beautiful score. There's something extra about it that gets to people. It might be the political angle, or the personal angle of two people from different worlds finding each other, or the war, or the idea of America at its most optimistic. All of it, maybe.

That closing performance was the most emotional performance of the show. Audience members who were huge fans and had seen the show before came back. There were speeches, which we don't usually do here. I spoke at the end. There was a famous speech when the original Broadway production of *South Pacific* closed on Broadway in 1954, where they didn't lower the curtain at the end. They wanted to make the point that the curtain would never be lowered on *South Pacific*. We don't have a curtain, but I came out and made the same kind of speech, and shared the same sentiment.

That show meant so much to me. Sometimes you think these closing performances are going to be amazing, incredible and they're not. But *South Pacific* exceeded all of our already-high expectations, every step of the way.

2010: A Wondrous Insane Monster Of A Play

George C. Wolfe, Director/Writer/Producer

We planned to do *A Free Man of Color* at the Public, but weeks before we were supposed to go into rehearsal, we were told that there was no money and so John Guare and I went looking for a home. We checked with Lincoln Center and they said, "Come do a reading." At the end of our reading at Lincoln Center, André Bishop said, "We have to figure out how to do this." And so they did.

It was fun playing around with scenic designer David Rockwell, crafting a visual language that worked perfectly for the Beaumont. I think it looked stunning and was a gorgeous production; the cast was brilliantly smart. There would have been pros to doing *A Free Man of Color* in a proscenium house, as I think plays with multiple realities can benefit from a rigid box encasing them. But the Beaumont is a beautiful space to work in, and I had a lot of fun. I want to work there again.

When I was first appointed producer of the Public Theater in 1993, I did this interview with *Newsweek* where they asked me to describe what I thought would be happening in the theatre in five years. Among the things I told them, I said there would be a restoration comedy with an astonishing cast in the Newman Theatre. So even then I was obsessed with the genre. Originally I wanted to take the plots of *The Country Wife, Way of the World*, and *The Rivals* and combine them into one play, set in an American city pre-Civil War. I spoke to John about it and he went off into this mad demon research frenzy and came back with a wondrous insane monster of a play. The first reading we did at the Public, years earlier, was six hours long. It was a marathon. It was glorious!

I'm not sure if there's something in collaborating with me that inspires people to write six-hour plays. I think I engender trust with a lot of the artists that I work with. Once during part two of *Angels in America*, Tony Kushner told me, "I feel so much pressure from everyone!" And I said something to the effect, "To hell with all of that! Go write. Go create. I'll take care of everything else."

If you're panicked, you're not going to do your job well. I am ferocious about making sure everyone who is creating has the room they need so that the work can grow. That's all I care about. I have a very big ego, but my ego doesn't need to be fed at all. If one person tells me I'm brilliant, I can live on that for 20 years. I like making stuff and I like playing. I like working with smart people, and a lot of the time, smart people have interesting levels of damage. They are hostile because very frequently they've been in creative situations where their collaborators haven't respected their journey. So I feel it's my job to make every show I work on a safe place for every member of the team. If you make a safe place, the child will grow up well.

Under One Roof

Ira Weitzman, Musical Theatre Associate Producer at Lincoln Center Theater

When we were walking down to my office, you marveled at all of the posters on the walls. Over the last 20 plus years, we've had this tradition of putting up every Lincoln Center Theater poster backstage. Everyone I escort down the stairs and through the labyrinth remarks how warm they feel being surrounded by all these theater posters, particularly ones of shows that they've seen or worked on or had a personal relationship with.

It's a unique setup we have at Lincoln Center Theater because we have rehearsal rooms, offices and theaters all in the same building—everything is right here. For most shows produced in New York, you rehearse in one place, do the show in a theater many blocks away, and anyone working on the show has an office someplace else entirely. When you work on something at Lincoln Center Theater, everyone is in one building. It gives people a real feeling of family. And theatre is, after all, a family. When you work here, there are familiar faces and familiar surroundings each time. Having all of this under one roof has facilitated our work in so many incredible ways.

———————

In April of 2015, a new Broadway revival of Rodgers and Hammerstein's The King & I, *starring Ken Watanbe and Kelli O'Hara, will open at the Vivian Beaumont Theatre.*

The Nederlander Theatre

Built: 1921
Location: 208 West 41st Street
Owner: The Nederlander Organization
Formerly Named: National Theatre, Billy Rose Theatre, Trafalgar Theatre
Longest-Running Show: *Rent* (1996-2008)
Shortest-Running Show: *Broadway Bound* revival (closed before its first preview in 2009)
Number of Productions: 210

Introduction: The Fate Of The Nederlander

Austin Nathaniel, House Manager

The 41st Street location has a lot to do with the fate of the Nederlander. That block of that street used to be terrible! You didn't want to be there at night. It was not a good location, and it was the southernmost point of Broadway. Producers didn't want their shows there because you wouldn't get a lot of foot traffic.

When *Rent* moved in in 1996, there was a hole in the roof of the Nederlander, and the creative team said, "Don't close that up; we love how it looks!" They had to weatherproof it from the top, but they did leave the hole in the ceiling. The theater wasn't in great shape.

It had gotten down to the wire by the end of *Rent*'s run, and the theater had to have a major renovation before *Guys and Dolls* went in next. The entire interior of the building was redone. They worked really hard with a lot of the old architectural photos of the space. They paid attention to every last thing: what the proscenium used to look like, the boxes, the light fixtures. They wanted to use the source materials to bring it back to what it had been, and make the Nederlander authentic to its original design. It's gorgeous. They did a brilliant job.

During *Rent*, that area around the theater changed a lot. The block is thriving now, and the theater itself is glowing and gorgeous. It's a very sought-after theater these days, and I'm not surprised that Disney snapped it up for *Newsies* after *Million Dollar Quartet* closed. For two years, they had *Newsies* right across the street from their offices at the New Amsterdam.

The Nederlander was a fantastic place for *Rent*. When you walked into the theater, you felt like you were in a club on the Lower East Side, no question. You couldn't have put anything else into that theater the way they put *Rent* in. It fit.

The *Rent* wall is still there, in the alley. All through *Million Dollar Quartet*'s run, we had *Rent* fans showing up, asking if it was still there and if they could take a look. Of course I would always walk people back there to check it out. I loved that.

———————————

In 1921, The National—a new Broadway theater—opened on 41st Street. 41st Street was not an out-of-the-way place for a legit house at that time. In fact, as the theatre district had recently begun to migrate from Herald Square to Longacre (now Times) Square, 41st Street was right in the middle of the action. There was still the Empire on 40th Street, the Casino on 39th Street, and other playhouses in the high 30s and early 40s. New theaters like the New Amsterdam, Shubert and Booth were starting to loom to the north.

Prior to becoming a theater, the building had been a large, multi-level carpenter's shop that also had club rooms, showers, apartments and a tennis court. When the venue was renovated to become the National, a new fire escape had to be built to comply with fire laws, hence why the National's fire escape doesn't seem to match the rest of the exterior. The National cost $950,000 to build and opened on September 1, 1921, with a short-lived play called Swords *written by Sidney Howard, who later went on to write the screen adaptation of* Gone with the Wind.

While the first few shows at the National failed to catch on, the house soon became a favorite to present thrillers in. This was probably due to the precedent-setting hit 1922 horror play, The Cat and the Canary, *about a group of potential heirs in a mansion. It was first in that genre that would later spawn stories from* Clue *to* Gosford Park. *In 1926, the inarguable king of thrills appeared for a special engagement at the National: Harry Houdini. It was his only Broadway appearance in a theater that's still standing, and his last. Also in 1926, a melodrama called* Yellow *featured a supporting performance from a 26-year-old Spencer Tracy.*

Both The Trial of Mary Dugan *(1927) and* Inherit the Wind *(1955) were huge hits involving courtroom cases— the former about a showgirl accused of murdering her lover and the latter about creationism versus evolution.* The Trial of Mary Dugan *and its subsequent movie adaptation were such a hit with the homosexual community that gay men began referring to and identifying each other by saying, "Hey Mary Dugan!" This was later simplified to "Hey, Mary!"*

After the Stock Market crash of 1929, many Broadway theaters floundered. Dozens of legit houses became movie theaters or just fell into disrepair. By 1929, the National had become just successful enough to avoid this fate.

In 1930, the theater was home for 459 performances to the play Grand Hotel, *the epic story of a hotel in Berlin. That play would later be adapted into a musical of the same name. It was the first production on Broadway to use a revolving stage. Both* Grand Hotel *and* Within the Gates *(1934) were a huge help in keeping the theatre lit and thriving during the Great Depression.* Within the Gates *received rave reviews and starred Lillian Gish in the role of "The Young Whore," where she likely made her own costumes! Perhaps the most glamorous show of the 1930s was* Tonight at 8:30, *which reunited Noël Coward and Gertrude Lawrence in 1936. It boasted several celebrities in the audience every week.*

In 1938, Orson Welles and John Houseman transferred their hit productions of The Shoemakers' Holiday *and* Julius Caesar *from the Mercury Theatre to the National, where they played extended and acclaimed runs. In 1947, the National housed Broadway's longest running revival of* Medea, *featuring a performance from 19-year-old Marian Seldes in her Broadway debut.*

1948: A Press Agent Never Knows...

Harvey Sabinson, Press Agent

Gower Champion was a dear friend of mine, and we did a lot of shows together. My press partner had handled Gower and Marge Champion when they were dancers, before Gower became a great director, but I met Gower in 1948 when I was still an apprentice to Sam Friedman. He choreographed his first Broadway show, which was *Lend an Ear*. That opened at the National, which is now the Nederlander. It was my first show as a press rep rather than an assistant.

Not only was it my first show as a press rep and Gower's first show as a choreographer, *Lend an Ear* was the show that made a star out of Carol Channing! It was really an ensemble cast, but she stood out head and shoulders above everyone else, and the critics recognized that. She became a star overnight. The next show she did was *Gentlemen Prefer Blondes*.

I knew that *Lend an Ear* and Carol would both be hits. In my career, when a show was going to be a failure, I often knew that too. And I knew well in advance, even when the producer didn't.

But once, I turned down a show based on my reading of the script, and I was stupid enough to tell the producer who asked me what I thought of it. It was actually Gower Champion's *Bye Bye Birdie*.

The National was built by renowned theatrical agent Walter C. Jordan, who worked with the Shuberts on its first few productions. The Shuberts bought the house in 1927 and kept it alive until 1956.

In the mid-1950s, the Shuberts were forced to sell several of their Broadway houses, including the National and St. James, in order to comply with an anti-trust legal decision. Harry Fromkes, a real estate lawyer and passionate theatre fan purchased the National for $900,000 in 1956. He announced that he was beginning his own syndicate and would build a large musical house somewhere between 49th and 52nd Streets next. Due to Fromkes' premature death in 1959, after accidentally falling out a window, that never materialized. Neither did a planned renaming of the National to the George M. Cohan Theatre. After his death, the theater was sold to Billy Rose at auction for $849,500.

Billy Rose was a theatrical impresario, a multi-hyphenate in the style of Florenz Ziegfeld and Oscar Hammerstein I. The writer of songs such as "It's Only a Paper Moon" and "Me and My Shadow," Rose was also a producer of Broadway shows, proprietor of the Diamond Horseshoe Nightclub, one-time husband of Fanny Brice and, now a theater owner as well. Rose spared no expense in renovating the new theater he renamed after himself on 41st Street. In its first four decades, the place had slowly become run-down. Rose gave it a new marquee, an expanded lobby and had paintings and sculptures placed around the public areas.

Before Rose, the only physical change made to the National in 48 years was during the original production of The Little Foxes *in 1939. Tallulah Bankhead got into a heated argument with the show's producer over not having enough room to play a scene and used a screwdriver to personally unscrew two of the seats in the front row!*

In 1953, the National became Broadway's southern-most theater when the beloved Empire Theatre on Broadway near 40th Street was torn down. It has been the Broadway house lowest on the map for over 60 years.

1962: A Legendary Collaboration Begins

Harold Prince, Producer/Director

A Family Affair was at the Billy Rose, which is now the Nederlander. It was my first directing job. I went to Philadelphia because the show needed help, and I agreed to take over for Word Baker. We opened on Broadway a few weeks later… and then we found out the show would close after just a couple days.

Somehow, the producers got their affairs together to run for another week, and during that time, I kept working on the production. It picked up some momentum and ended up running for eight weeks!

I had said I wouldn't take billing at first. Then, I got so immersed in the show, and excited from working on it, that I took my first billing as a director. The show got quite good reviews, even though it didn't run. That was swell and, immediately, the word was out: *Oh, there's a new young director out there.*

I had been such a successful producer that everyone said, "Oh, why doesn't he just do that? Why doesn't he just settle and produce? Why does he *have* to have directing, too?"

A Family Affair was the first Broadway musical composed by John Kander, and his only one written without Fred Ebb. The show sparked a collaboration between 34-year-old Kander and 33-year-old Prince that would continue next with Flora the Red Menace *and then the landmark* Cabaret. *A Family Affair was about a young betrothed couple planning a wedding while coping with meddling family from every direction—a distant ancestor of the 2008 musical* A Catered Affair.*

The National was also the home of the first Broadway musical that golden age writers Alan Jay Lerner and Frederick Loewe collaborated on. It was called What's Up?, *and it closed in 1944 after only 63 performances. The show was about pilots who wound up stuck in an all-girls school. The following year, Lerner and Loewe had their second Broadway musical also play the National and also flop: a show called* The Day Before Spring, *about a college reunion. A few years later, they returned to Broadway with a string of hits:* Brigadoon, Paint Your Wagon, My Fair Lady, *and* Camelot.

1968: My Broadway Debut In *The House of Atreus*

Len Cariou, Actor

I made my Broadway debut in *The House of Atreus*. We did the production in full Greek style. It was directed by Tyrone Guthrie, and it was an extraordinary piece. We did it at the Billy Rose, which is now the Nederlander, in rep with a play called *The Resistable Rise of Arturo Ui*.

It's always hard when one has to learn how to work with masks, and that show was no exception. I also had these Greek-style stilt boots. I was 6'3" and on stilts. We felt like huge, larger-than-life creatures. I think everyone was stunned and amazed by how the show looked.

The Billy Rose was too small for what we were doing with *Atreus*. The show had to do a lot of maneuvering with sets, and the crew had to fly stuff just to store it. They do that a lot now, but I believe this was one of the early instances where they had to figure out a way to deal with scenery in that way.

In the 1960s, the Billy Rose might have been renamed "the Edward Albee" for all of his work that played there. Albee's first full-length play and Broadway debut, Who's Afraid of Virginia Woolf? *made a huge alcoholic splash in 1962, and he followed it with* Tiny Alice *in 1964, as well as a series of short plays in 1968, including* The Zoo Story *and* The American Dream.

1971: *Earl of Ruston*

Peter Link, Writer/Actor

Earl of Ruston was a horrible experience, my worst one on Broadway. The show broke up my writing partnership. C.C. Courtney and I had just done *Salvation* off-Broadway, which was a huge hit. With *Earl of Ruston*, we ended up with a terrible show that deserved to get killed, and the critics killed it. I left before it opened.

Billy Rose died in 1966, and his estate and management team carried on with the theater in his name until 1978. During those 12 years, there was no clear leader who could make all decisions on repairs and upkeep, so the theater fell into disrepair.

In 1978, the Nederlanders—new theater owners in the city—made a bid on the house. They bought the Billy Rose in partnership with Cooney-Marsh, owners of several London theaters, for $475,000, and repainted it gold and maroon. The theater was "worth" less in 1978 than it had been in the 1950s! Rumor was that the theater might now only present British productions. The theater was even given the British tinged name The Trafalgar. The first show it housed was Whose Life Is It Anyway?, *a British drama, and the second was* Betrayal, *penned by Brit scribe Harold Pinter.*

Whose Life is it Anyway? *was notable for starring Tom Conti, in his Broadway debut, at the center of a story about the moral questions surrounding euthanasia. A few months later, the same play was done at the Royale (now Jacobs) starring Mary Tyler Moore in the lead role, a rare gender reversal.* Betrayal *starred Raul Julia, Blythe Danner, and Roy Scheider in a complex exploration of an extramarital affair told through partial reverse chronology.*

Those two productions were it for the Trafalgar. In 1980, the theater was renamed the Nederlander in honor of the late patriarch of the theatrical family, David T. Nederlander.

1981: Sharing The Street With The Prostitutes

Michael Mayer, Director

I remember seeing Lena Horne play the Nederlander. I loved the way she talked about her relationship to the theater. It was 1981, before it had been renovated, and she talked about doing the show with water dripping down from the ceiling, and tons of prostitutes on 41st Street.

It was part of the show. She so respected that everyone made it over there to 41st, and she wanted audiences to know. It was all kind of fun, but there was something true about it. She was just grateful to be on Broadway.

There used to be an alley behind the Billy Rose—the Nederlander—that was open. You had to circle around to get to it, but you could peek right in.

41st Street was a different place in the 1970s and 1980s than it is today. The "New 42nd Street" renovation hadn't yet happened, and Times Square was dirty and dangerous. There was an adult theater or sex shop or dive bar where every souvenir store and Starbucks is today. The Nederlander, tucked away south of seedy 42nd Street, near Port Authority, was the haunted basement of the mansion of Broadway. Shows didn't want to play there, tourists wouldn't go there...

1981: Respect For 41st

Alex Rybeck, Musical Director

When Lena Horne did *The Lady And Her Music*, hers was the first big show to play The Nederlander in a long time. That block had deteriorated dramatically, and had become the territory of hookers and pimps.

As Lena herself told her audience, she made a point of meeting the ladies who worked the street, and said to them, "I just want you to know, I'm working here now. I respect you've got your job and I hope you'll respect mine. So I'm not going to work your side of the street, and I'd like you to respect MY customers between 7:30 and 8pm as they're coming into the theater."

And they did!

1986: *Raggedy Ann*

Patricia Birch, Director/Choreographer/Actor

The original story and doll, Raggedy Ann, were created by Johnny Gruelle for his daughter, Marcella, in the 1910s. Marcella tragically died at the age of 13. Our librettist Bill Gibson drew from that to create the story for a musical about Raggedy Ann. The idea was that a father is telling his very sick daughter, Marcella, this story about a rag doll. In the musical, Marcella has to go on all of these adventures to get to a hospital in California where she can be cured. Raggedy Ann is the force of good in the fable, and there's a villain named General D. A fantasy-land full of adolescent nightmares come to life with different creatures.

We did the show first in Albany, at the Empire State Institution for the Performing Arts. We were well-received there, except for one outraged parent who was upset that she had taken children to see a show with themes of darkness and death in it. She filed a public complaint and got on television to speak about it, so all of the Albany schools cancelled their tickets. Nevertheless, through a cultural exchange, we did *Raggedy Ann* in Russia next. The show was a huge hit there. It was an amazing experience, and every Russian audience was going crazy for it.

Because of the successful run in Russia, we were picked up to do the show on Broadway. First, we had to go to the Kennedy Center. A lot of changes happened. Some people on the team wanted to fire cast members who had been with the show because they weren't good enough singers and dancers. But they were fantastic storytellers! I didn't want to lose them, because they were the heart of the piece. Then I learned that Joe Raposo, our composer-lyricist, was sick with cancer. It was the only Broadway musical he'd ever get to write.

We were supposed to go into the Mark Hellinger Theatre, but we lost it because some special dance engagement was booked there. So we ended up going into the Nederlander, which was just a dump at the time. It was run-down, and people didn't want to go there—audience or cast.

Raggedy Ann completely bombed on Broadway. I was so proud of my work on the show and thought we were presenting a dark interesting fable that wasn't like other musicals. At the time, some friends said to me, "This is your *A Chorus Line*." I don't know about that. I'd had big hits with *Grease* and *A Little Night Music* and other shows. But they're right in that there was a stamp I put on this show that I was especially proud of. It was my kind of story. It was unique; it gave audiences joy and fear. We closed after 15 previews and five performances.

From 1987 to 1989, the Nederlander was leased to the Times Square Church. The church was looking for a midtown location, and after talks with the Nederlander Organization, they set up shop on 41st Street. By 1989, they were looking for a semi-permanent lease on a bigger space and the Nederlanders were open to leasing them the Mark Hellinger on 51st Street after a string of flops there. We mourn the loss of the Hellinger, no longer a Broadway house[110]—but if a few conversations in 1989 had gone differently, we might have wound up with the Nederlander turned into a church for 99 years or more, and the Mark Hellinger open to whatever offer came next.

The Nederlander is still not landmarked by the city.[111]

---

[110] Check out *The Untold Stories of Broadway, Volume 1* for more on this.

[111] After the Great Theater Massacre of 1982, many New Yorkers began campaigning for the remaining Broadway theaters to be landmarked. The majority of houses are now protected by landmark status, although some have only their interior *or* exterior landmarked, and not both. The most recently built theaters, including the Gershwin and Circle in the Square, are not landmarked at all. The Palace has a landmarked interior but not exterior, since its exterior had already been changed before the movement begun. The Barrymore and Shubert are landmarked, inside and out.

1992: A Dead House

Artie Gaffin, Stage Manager

I worked on a play called *Solitary Confinement* at the Nederlander back in the day. The tricky thing was walking from 42nd Street to 41st Street on Broadway. There were tons of anti-abortion people there every single day. They had graphic photos and would scream at you as you walked by.

That was just one group of many who made the area unpleasant. Nobody really went below 42nd Street in 1992. It was not safe and dignified as it is now. The streets were littered with all these mini syringes with colorful points. There was a lot of heroin use on the block. Once you got to the theater, it was a lovely place to be, but even the alley leading into it was pretty grungy. The neighborhood was not the best.

There are always theaters that get reputations for being dead houses. Before *Rent*, the Nederlander was considered a dead house. At times, east of Broadway has been called the "sad side of Broadway," and the Belasco, Cort, and Lyceum have been seen as dead houses. Even the Broadway Theatre, which now gets lots of shows, once had a bad reputation in the 1950s and 1960s, because it was said that no one wanted to go above 52nd Street.

It gets to the point sometimes where if the theater isn't on 44th or 45th Street, people say the theater itself caused their show to close. Everyone is always looking for excuses. Some of it is true, but most isn't. If you have a show people want to see, they'll go anywhere.

Solitary Confinement was a one-man show starring Stacy Keach. He played a sort-of witch man who was trapped in his home and spoke to all of these different characters on a video screen—but the surprise at the end was that he played all the characters. Rupert Holmes, who wrote it, is a master of those kinds of inventive shows, such as *The Mystery of Edwin Drood* and *Accomplice*. The audience was really tricked, and then at the curtain call they found out that every character was Stacy Keach.

It was a very clever show, but it was not a success. A lot of people blamed the location of the theater.

After being given the name Nederlander, there weren't many notable productions in the house before Rent. *Other than* Lena Horne, *one of the rare gems was* 84 Charing Cross Road. *Helene Hanff adapted her novel about her own 20-year correspondence with a British book-seller into a play. The show starred Ellen Burstyn as Hanff. Directly following Lena Horne into the Nederlander in 1982,* 84 Charing Cross Road *was well-received, and it was Hanff's long-awaited Broadway debut.[112]*

---

[112] *84 Charing Cross Road* was Helene Hanff's long-awaited Broadway debut. One of my favorite books of all time is *Underfoot in Show Business*, the memoir Helene wrote in 1961 about her adventures in the theatre as a dreamer new to New York. The first page says: "Each year, hundreds of stage-struck kids arrive in New York determined to crash the theatre, firmly convinced they're destined to be famous Broadway stars or playwrights. One in a thousand turns out to be Noël Coward. This book is about life among the other 999. By one of them." *Underfoot in Show Business* is out-of-print, but I highly recommend doing whatever you can to get your hands on a copy!

1994/2010: Coming Back To 41st Street

Hunter Foster, Actor

We rehearsed the 1994 revival of *Grease* at the Nederlander. That was my first experience ever performing on a Broadway stage—rehearsing on one.

The Nederlander couldn't get Broadway shows at that time. The house was dark very often, sometimes for years. Tommy Tune used it for rehearsals of several of his shows: *Grease*, and also *Best Little Whorehouse Goes Public* and *Busker Alley*. It was great to be in that space, even though it wasn't our real theater, the Eugene O'Neill. It was an amazing to actually rehearse your show on a Broadway stage. I don't think that will ever happen again. Actors today aren't lucky enough to get to do that.

When I moved back into the Nederlander for *Million Dollar Quartet*, I had history with that theater, because I had spent four weeks rehearsing in it when I was just starting out. It was great to come back to it.

I don't ever think of roles being musical or not. I just think of them as being characters. It never even occurred to me that my character in *Million Dollar Quartet* didn't sing. I just thought of him as a part of the story. During the run of that show, people asked me, "Do you miss it?" I didn't, not at all. If a character doesn't sing, he doesn't sing.

Certain shows are more difficult than others as far as vocal preparation. It just depends on exactly what you're doing. Certainly, *Million Dollar Quartet* was easy in that regard. *Bridges of Madison County* wasn't particularly difficult for me, but a show like *Urinetown* was very hard to sing eight times a week. You have to make sure you're in the right vocal shape to do that kind of role. *Hands on a Hardbody* wasn't that hard vocally, but it was challenging athletically. We really had to stretch because we were pushing that truck around. Each show requires its own different form of preparation.

The Nederlander is a quirky little theater. And it's nicer now than it was when I rehearsed there almost two decades earlier. During *Million Dollar Quartet*, I definitely noticed every bit of renovation, inside and outside. In 1994, 41st Street was a terrible street to be on. It's still not the greatest street, but it's definitely not what it was when there were drug dealers and hookers everywhere.

You always feel a little bit away from everything at the Nederlander, which I kind of like. The busy streets, 44th and 45th, are just too hectic. Especially on matinee days, it's hard to walk down the street just to get to your own show. The Nederlander is always uncongested. It was weird to come back to the place where I started and nice to be back on 41st Street.

1994: *The Best Little Whorehouse Goes Public* Callbacks

Casey Nicholaw, Director/Choreographer/Actor

When I auditioned for *Best Little Whorehouse Goes Public*, the callback was on the stage of the Nederlander. At the end of the audition, they told us we had the job. They just kept narrowing it down. We were all on the stage, and they had six and six, and said, "You guys are it!"

———————————

The Best Little Whorehouse Goes Public *was co-directed and choreographed by Tommy Tune, who loved to have auditions and rehearsals at the Nederlander Theatre during this time. Since shows didn't want the theater, he could book it instead of a rehearsal studio. It was cheaper, too!*

———————————

298

1995: Rehearsing In No Man's Land

Michael Berresse, Actor/Director

We rehearsed *Busker Alley* there, before the Nederlander was the Nederlander again... It was in that weird period of time where it was sort of a no man's land.

Tommy Tune decided to rent out the Nederlander so that we could do a full workshop of *Busker Alley* on a stage, before we went on tour. We rehearsed the entire show and performed it for backers there.

At the time, the show was called *Busker Alley*, and then at the presentation, producers Barry and Fran Weissler got up onstage and made the announcement that the show was now called *Stage Door Charley*. None of us knew that in advance. That show's title... it started as *Busker Alley,* went to *Stage Door Charley,* went to *Buskers,* and then came back to *Busker Alley*!

At the time, the theater was dilapidated. It was also lonely. I don't mean that it felt lonely for us to be inside, but the theater itself felt lonely. Walking in, you could feel that it had had better days. If I could personify that theater, I would say it was like it had a bad cold. It couldn't quite breathe, there was a lot of dust... it was sad and lonely and waiting for a revival of some sort.

When the Nederlander became what it became with *Rent*... I remember being really happy for that theater. It was essentially revived. It became legitimized again and had all that life in it and all those voices: onstage and in the house. I was so happy for it.

————————

Busker Alley *was set to open on Broadway in the fall of 1995. It was the most anticipated musical of the season, helmed by Broadway legend Tommy Tune. The marquee and posters were up at the St. James when Tune broke his foot on tour, and the plug was pulled on the entire production.* Busker Alley's *front-of-house was still up at the empty St. James, when* Rent *opened three blocks southward, in what had been* Busker Alley's *rehearsal hall.*

In fall of 1995, a show was announced for the Nederlander in spring of 1996: a Royal Shakespeare Company production of A Midsummer Night's Dream. *When a third Broadway outing of Carol Channing starring in* Hello, Dolly! *wasn't quite the success its producers had hoped, it closed early at the Lunt-Fontanne, and the Nederlanders shuffled* Midsummer *to that theater instead, leaving the Nederlander open.*

————————

1990s: Showing People The Nederlander

Tim Pettolina, House Manager

When I started working at the Nederlander Organization, the Nederlander Theatre was in disrepair. They used to have me go and show it to people. A lot of people would go see the space to see if they could do something to it.

My bosses had acquired the theater after it had already gone a little bit downhill. Economic times in New York were different, and not a lot of people who saw the theater were interested in it, either because of its size or location. Below 42nd Street? In the 1970s and 1980s and even the 1990s, you really had to watch your back.

I didn't have a lot of experiences in the Nederlander with people though. Just with ghosts.

1996: No Day But Today

Kevin McCollum, Producer

We had this show called *Rent* that was about to open, off-Broadway. Then we lost the writer, Jonathan Larson, which was absolutely devastating. My producing partner, Jeffrey Seller, and I had known Jonathan for years. I went to a few dinner parties with Jonathan where people would ask him about his work, and he'd say, "I'm writing the next *Hair*." I would turn to him and whisper, "Let other people say that. That's why I'm here!" He was brilliant and everyone who knew him was just waiting for him to have that breakthrough opportunity to prove it.

On opening night off-Broadway at New York Theatre Workshop, *New York Times* critic Ben Brantley said *Rent* "shimmers with hope for the future of the American musical."[113] He ended his *New York Times* review: "People who complain about the demise of the American musical have simply been looking in the wrong places." Every news outlet was telling people to remember Jonathan Larson's name because he wrote this landmark show. We knew we needed to move the show to Broadway, and we needed to open before the Tony cut-off that year.

While searching for a Broadway home for *Rent*, we looked at this broken-down theater on 42nd Street called the Selwyn. Jujamcyn, MTC, and Roundabout were looking at it, too. Roundabout made a bid on the theater and eventually turned it into the American Airlines, so that was out of the picture for us. We saw the Broadhurst, but it turned out that wouldn't be available to us. The Shuberts had another show they wanted to move into it.

Then we looked at the Nederlander. No one played the Nederlander. The last real show they'd had there closed after a few weeks four years earlier. But the Nederlander did have a tenant: mice and mold and leaking ceilings. Plus, the Nederlander was run on DC power. They had never changed over to AC power;[114] that's how behind that house was. In order to bring in the equipment to do *Rent* there, millions of dollars would need to be spent to renovate the theater. After discussing, we got a commitment from the Nederlanders that they would do that. So not only were we moving *Rent* to Broadway, we were rebuilding this theater together.

It's a credit to the Nederlanders that they got behind this. And even though they were investing in this expensive renovation, they gave us a great deal on rent for *Rent*. Nobody knew if the show was going to work on Broadway, so they invested in us, too, by giving us a deal that would help us try to get our footing.

I think the neatest thing about the Nederlander was the transformative process. Most times, you get the theater and that's it. It's done. You move in. This time, we weren't given a theater; we were given a canvas. We got to create a space. The Nederlanders let us and our designers play. I wish that there was more of that. It's hard, because real estate is so expensive in New York, and there are rules and unions. But the perfect storm of events and people and space really made the Nederlander like that barn in old movie musicals where everyone is like, "Let's put on a show! Grab a paintbrush!" We even got to hire our own stagehands and box office treasurers because the theater had been dark for so long that there was no regular house staff. We were lucky in that we got to put together a team of people who we wanted to work with. As a producer you don't often get to "cast" the house staff.

We wanted the Nederlander to feel like a club, like a downtown gallery or performance space. It doesn't sound crazy now, because lots of shows have started to do that to the theaters they move into. At the time, it was revolutionary. Jeffrey Seller and I were just making it up as we went along. And we had a great creative team who really knew and were from the Village. We knew we had a job to do. We wanted to present the best version of *Rent* that we could, but we also wanted Jonathan's ethic, his spirit, to come out in the surroundings.

---

113 Brantley, Ben. "East Village Rock Opera A La '*Boheme*' And '*Hair*.'" *The New York Times*. 14 Feb. 1996.
114 Check out *The Untold Stories of Broadway, Volume 1* for more on this.

We wanted the time and people he was writing about to sort of "happen" to you as soon as you got to the theater. We had a big story to tell, and that was the story of *Rent*, but it was also the story of Jonathan Larson.

Everyone said we were crazy for going to 41st Street. Everyone said nobody went there. I said, "How about everybody who goes to the Port Authority?" "Yeah, but that's not Broadway." I said, "If the show is right, people will find the theater." We ended up watching 41st Street change tremendously. We were the only thing on that block when we put those green doors on, and Paul Clay started directing a crew in painting the exterior.

Just as the staff was finishing painting the ceiling, our scenic designer came in and yelled, "Stop, stop!" He asked them to stop painting, because an unfinished ceiling would be part of the environment that would be right for *Rent*. The landlords called me and said, "Is your designer crazy? We're finishing the theater." I explained that we wanted it to look like the performance space wasn't done. And that's why the Nederlander ceiling was half-redone in 1996 and half-redone in 2008.

I remember vividly the day that tickets went on sale at the Nederlander box office. I actually lived in the Village at the time, so I took a cab uptown. The cab drove up 8th Avenue, and when I looked to my right, there was a line of people lined up down the block. We ran to Ticketmaster, and the phones were ringing off the hook for *Rent* tickets. It was remarkable.

Rent wasn't finished when Jonathan died. People tried to get us to change the show a lot, rewrite this and that, but we wanted his version to be what was in the world. We wanted *Rent* to be what it was: beautiful and remarkable and unfinished. Michael Greif and Tim Weil did a great job of making that happen, and the Larson family was very cooperative in letting us move around the few puzzle pieces that we needed to.

I'm still so proud of how we handled our move to the Nederlander. It was a key moment in the history of *Rent*. The theater really worked well in every way for the show. It seats 1200, so it's an intimate house for a musical, and the stage feels like it's right there, close to every seat. I think the immediacy of the story was even more powerful on Broadway than it was at NYTW. A lot of times, shows will go down in quality or intimacy when they move to Broadway, but I actually felt like our ideas were too big for the space at NYTW. It was a great place to start the show, but *Rent* was meant to fill the Nederlander. So that's what we did.

My favorite theater on Broadway is the Nederlander. It's a choice driven by emotions. I helped resurrect that theater. We brought it back to Broadway.

———————————

While rumors of a possible Broadway transfer for Rent *swirled around New York, the* New York Times *wrote: "Maybe* Rent *will jolt Broadway." Meanwhile, Jonathan Larson's family and friends mourned. Jonathan's close friend Victoria Leacock came back to America from a trip abroad to speak at his memorial. She then returned to her home to find mail from Jonathan that had been waiting for her: two tickets to* Rent *and a note, referring to two friends they'd recently lost to AIDS: "Darling Vix, '96 will be our year. (No more funerals.)"[115]*

For years, Jonathan knew he would someday make his mark on the theatre. In Anthony Rapp's memoir Without You, *he tells the story that at his 24th birthday party, a few weeks before* Rent *started rehearsals for its off-Broadway run, a friend came up to him and pointed to Jonathan Larson. "Who's that guy?" he asked, perplexed. Anthony told him that was Jonathan, who wrote the show he was about to be in. "I asked Jonathan what he did for a living," the friend said. "And he told me he was the future of musical theatre."[116]*

In the late 1980s, Jonathan Larson, dissatisfied with the current state of theatre on Broadway wrote a song called "Theatre Is Dead," intended for his autobiographical musical Boho Days. *The song was later used in, and cut from*

———————————

[115] Tommasini, Anthony. "The Seven-Year Odyssey That Led To Rent." *The New York Times.* 17 Mar. 1996.
[116] Rapp, Anthony. *Without You.* New York: Simon & Schuster, 2006.

tick, tick... BOOM! *A lyric went:*

"Walk through Times Square, what do you see
Ugliness where architecture used to be...
So-called producers run the show
Used to make plays, now its real-estate they know
Jack up the price, give 'em chandeliers
Blame it on the union, the show'll run for years
That's the Play Game, why do I want to play the Play Game?"

———————————

1996: Bringing The East Village To 41st Street

Michael Greif, Director

Initially, I thought that *Rent* would be great at the Lyceum. I loved that center doorway that goes down the whole block, and I thought we could restage the show using that doorway effectively. Because the original set utilized the architecture of NYTW, I naively assumed that I would restage the show for whatever space we moved into. As it turned out, other people who might have been a bit wiser and a bit more pragmatic got me to believe that the show wasn't broken so we shouldn't fix it.

Our move to the Nederlander was fast and furious, but I remember it being a very calm and focused time. When the show opened downtown, we were all still so raw from Jonathan's death. We were confused because there was so much joy from the show and its reception banging up against the unbelievable sorrow we were feeling. The next few months were a blur for me. I had just begun my time as artistic director of La Jolla Playhouse, so I was flying back and forth from New York to California, just as everyone was figuring out what was going to happen next.

When we got the Nederlander, a two week rehearsal period at NYTW was arranged before we moved to Broadway. I remember that it was around Passover time. After one rehearsal, Idina Menzel, her father, and I all got caught in traffic for hours on our way to our seders. So after we closed the show, we went back into rehearsal, worked on small cuts, restaged, and solidified so many beats. Every performance met with so much adulation and grew so extraordinarily during that downtown run. It was great to have another rehearsal process after the initial tumultuous one. When we moved into the Nederlander, tech was a joy. Blake Burba's lights were exquisite. It was wonderful to see them in a larger space with great height.

It was great that our commercial producers allowed Paul Clay, our really terrific scenic designer to affect the entire venue as well as the stage. He brought *Rent* to all of the public spaces at the Nederlander. I loved the leopard-print carpet and the metal tables he designed for the upstairs bar. The Nederlander had a lot of fun nooks and crannies. We had all of our notes at that upstairs bar. I continued to enjoy being in that space throughout the run.

Paul also designed a new proscenium arch for the stage. It was the only significant addition we made to the stage picture for Broadway; we framed the action of the show in this beautiful collage of mosaic tiles, reminiscent of the East Village shattered pottery installations.

An unexpected pleasure during our tech process was the affection and support we felt from the community. People would visit us at the Nederlander, and one of our most cherished visitors was Tommy Tune. I was a big fan. I thought both *Grand Hotel* and *Nine* were magnificently directed, and I especially loved his production of *Cloud Nine* that I'd seen years earlier. It was remarkable to be sitting there with him. I remember him being around a lot, happy that the theater he used as a rehearsal space was being revitalized.

During tech, I remember watching the crew at the Nederlander slowly being won over by the show. At first, they didn't know what to make of it, but the first time Daphne Rubin-Vega sang "Out Tonight", we all watched them see that something unusual was going on here. We were also in tech when *Rent* won the Pulitzer. It was sweet, sad, and surreal.

That original group was quite extraordinary. They handled everything about that experience, including the whole "overnight sensation" phenomenon, with unbelievable grace, generosity, and sweetness, without ever forgetting their debt to Jonathan.

Over the years, I continued to be impressed with them. When the 10th anniversary of *Rent* opening came around, a reunion performance was planned. It was incredible that every single person from the original cast was responsive, willing, and got themselves to New York from some far-flung places. Especially impressive were and are those cast members that the commercial system deems "ensemble." When we were building the show, there were 15 cast members and everyone had a very significant part to play. No distinctions were made between principals and ensemble. When a show moves to Broadway, contracts, dressing room assignments, and publicity demands all work to put wedges between cast members, and this group never let it happen to them.

41st Street changed very gradually over our 12-year occupancy. We were thrilled when the hotel and its bar opened next door. When *The Lion King* moved into the New Amsterdam, we really had neighbors. We watched the street change from the back-end of Port Authority to a busy part of Times Square. Ironically, scruffy *Rent* moved in just as the clean-up of Times Square was finishing up, and by the time we closed, we could see the "questionable" results.

The world also changed during the time *Rent* was running. With the onset of the new anti-viral medications for the first time in the late 1990s, we became aware of friends and relatives living longer and healthier lives with HIV. This was in terrible contrast to the time Jonathan was writing the show and I was developing the show with him, as well as the time we originally rehearsed the show. At that time, we had horrible first-hand awareness of the disease's devastation. As years went by, the young company members stopped having that immediate understanding of what it meant to be diagnosed with AIDS during the 1980s and early 1990s. To compensate, we distributed memoirs and plays from that time and had the company watch movies like *Long Time Companion* and *Paris is Burning*. Those books and movies became a very important part of the process of understanding the characters and headspace of the musical.

About the wall... when we moved in, we heard that the Nederlander had a tradition of celebrities signing the wall in the back alley. That seemed a little elitist to me, so after a couple of previews in which only celebrities signed the wall, I forged a couple of notes and signatures from some "ordinary" theatergoers. I think one was "Mrs. Field," a 5th grade teacher from Brooklyn, New York. After that, everyone felt free to contribute to the wall.

When Billy Rose took over the house in 1959, he brought along theatrical designer Oliver Messel, known for shows like House of Flowers *and that past season's* Rashomon. *Rose told reporters, "[The new dark garlands of flowers painted on the ceiling were] designed by Oliver Messel, one of the most gifted designers in the business. I believe it is one of the few times that a scenic designer has been called in to redesign a theatre. Essentially, the theatre's décor will be cherry red and gold and no sense will it be a moderne theatre. It will not look like a powder room at Schrafft's."*[117] *Showing distaste for the simple, uncolorful style of theater design that became in vogue during the 1950s and 1960s, Rose proved his theater would be different by having Messel install new chandeliers and sconces as well as a great deal of carpet and color.*

---

[117] Calta, Louis. "Billy Rose Talks Of His Theatre." *The New York Times.* 10 Sep. 1959.

Almost four decades later, Paul Clay carried on this tradition at the house on 41st Street, as a scenic designer looking at the building itself as part of the theatrical experience. One option the producers of Rent *considered after NYTW was claiming a non-performance space in the city and taking it over. This proved to be too expensive. There was also the idea that the show might move to a commercial off-Broadway house. Seller, McCollum and their producing partner Allan Gordon heard from every established producer that the audiences they were looking for, the audiences who would love* Rent, *were not audiences that would go to Broadway. Seller defended the show, "Our response [to the nay-sayers] has been, they haven't gone to Broadway because there hasn't been anything to see. We think they'll come to Broadway for this."[118]*

Once it became clear the Nederlander would be the home of Rent, *Paul Clay's transformation of the theater became key in making it the right home for the show. While Messel had brought his theatrical design expertise to the house, and other shows like* The Who's Tommy *(1993) and the* Grease *revival (1994) had taken over their theaters with personalized splashes of color paint, this was the first full-theater takeover and redesign for a specific show.*

In addition to the lime green paint and images of instruments, cast members, and NYC skyline that covered the exterior, there were murals and artwork all over the interior, including the ceilings. The paintbrushes even extended next door, where the windows of an abandoned hotel were covered in plywood and orange spray-painted signs reminiscent of the Village. The team went so far as to install silver grease vents, an image associated with East Village diners, in the back of the orchestra section, and funky mesh-covered lamps seen in East Houston nightspots in the upper lobby. Lime green, purple, and bright maroon were the colors of choice in installing seat cushions in the upstairs bar, décor around staircases, and new detailing around doorways. The mosaics of the proscenium also decorated the box office windows. The chandeliers that Messel had installed decades before had become broken and dusty, and Clay embraced this, adding mismatched light bulbs.

Now a part of Rent *lore, one piece of artwork bore a secret code of sorts. In the midst of flyers for Alphabet City happenings, an elaborate painting on one lobby door featured a line graph with four seemingly random numbers. Only those who came to know the Nederlander very well carried the knowledge that the four numbers were the birthdate of Giacomo Puccini (who had written the opera* La Bohème, *Larson's original inspiration), the birthdate of Jonathan Larson, the date* Rent *opened at NYTW, and the latitude and longitude of New York.*

It was only because the Nederlander didn't have landmark status that the Rent *team was able to create this unprecedented new physical space. The lack of landmark status had almost spelled doom, but now it was an asset and inspired a new beginning for the theater.*

1996: Finding The Cast Of *Rent*

Bernie Telsey, Casting Director

I started out as a casting assistant for Meg Simon and Fran Kumin. I was mostly in their office—I did books and organization. After I left, I worked at Lincoln Center. Then, on my own, I did a project called *I Was Looking at the Ceiling and Then I Saw the Sky*, a John Adams and Peter Sellars rock opera, about eight multi-racial young people. The show was made of rock 'n' roll opera singers. That was a big challenge, a really hard thing to find. Working on musicals was new for me, and we had to find unbelievable voices, and young, edgy performers for a rock opera.

It got me the *Rent* job.

---

[118] Marks, Peter. "Looking On Broadway For A Bohemian Home." *The New York Times*. 26 Feb. 1996.

Rent was being done at New York Theatre Workshop, which was a not-for-profit institution. Jim Nicola, the artistic director, called me up. They knew I was in touch with young, multi-racial performers, because of the other project I'd just done. They were doing a musical, *Rent* written by a new writer and directed by Michael Greif.

NYTW wanted to know if I would come and do *Rent* and also a play called *Quills*—and I really liked *Quills*! To be honest, I was a little hesitant about working on *Rent*, having just done the rock opera, which was really challenging—but it was a two-for-one, so I did it.

All that existed was a demo tape of a handful of songs, and they were going to be doing the show in eight months. I didn't know what I was getting into! It was so hard. Jonathan, Michael, Tim Weil, the musical supervisor, and Jim had done readings of *Rent* in-house, so they knew what they wanted, even if all the material wasn't there yet.

Casting off-Broadway musicals wasn't really happening at the time. And this was an off-Broadway musical by unknown people paying $300 a week! Even people who worked in musical theatre weren't going to give up being in the ensemble of a Broadway show to do this. Sometimes, people work on a piece because they think, "It's no money, but it's going to be a lot of visibility." No one knew *anything* about this, except that the people who worked on it believed in it.

On top of that, Jonathan and Michael were really specific about what they wanted. There were a *lot* of auditions where it was: "No, no, no, no." And I was young and just starting out. We just didn't know where we were going to find these people. It wasn't like you could do a ton of non-Equity open calls,[119] because we didn't have the money.

Seven of the parts were just impossible to find. At the time, I was just opening my own office, and we did mostly commercials. The two guys I worked with were like, "Get out of this job. It's never happening, we're never finding what they want."

They didn't want to settle for standard musical theatre-type performers; they *really* wanted something new. Now, every year, it feels like there's a musical that has that kind of sound. But back then, there wasn't. Except for *Hair*, which was already 30 years earlier, there weren't the same kind of pop-rock pieces happening in musical theatre.

We would do an open call for a rock 'n' roll guy, and no one would show up! We did some bizarre open call where we put an ad in the back of the Village Voice, near the rock 'n' roll vocal coaches, thinking maybe the right people would see that. 25 people showed up, and they all looked like Alice Cooper, except for one. Adam Pascal. This was four days before starting! It was a diamond in the rough. Like, *Oh my God, who is* that *guy? If only he can sing*. And then Adam opened up his mouth.

I'll never forget calling Michael and Jim and Jonathan and saying, "I have one! I have one! Tomorrow morning at ten. We can do this. He can't open his eyes when he sings, but who cares? You can teach him how to do that."

What was so thrilling is that it was so collaborative. The process actually made me fall in love with casting, not only because I got to see so many young, talented people, but because I realized then how the process of casting could really help change a piece, a collaboration, people's histories. And Jonathan, Michael and Jim were so welcoming and supportive of my input. It was a joy.

---

[119] non-Equity open calls: auditions that everyone is welcome to attend, regardless of Equity status or current representation

Then, when *Rent* became what it became, we'd do open calls and 5000 people would show up! We'd go around the world, and every time we did an open call, no matter what state, we'd find someone to go into one of the five *Rent* companies. The whole thing put me on the map as a casting director. It was unreal.

By opening night on Broadway, it was already "the *Rent* sensation." There was the great buzz from downtown and the horrible, devastating thing of Jonathan passing.

Opening night itself was out of control. There was such a joy. I remember having a little moment to myself and thinking: *Oh my God, I'm on Broadway. I'm participating in something, and I used to sit up here and have no connection to anybody.* I remember vividly sitting up there in the front row mezzanine, nail-biting—not because I was worried about reviews. It was already a hit. It was just that feeling of: *Oh my God, don't take this for granted. This is happening to you.* And that cast… it was like that for all of them, too. Everybody was practically making their Broadway debut.

Later on, there were great moments, as an audience member, of getting to see an understudy perform. I got to experience other people doing these roles I'd been working on, and often I then felt like I wanted to champion them, in my capacity as a casting director.

Norbert Leo Butz first started out as the standby for Roger in *Rent*. He was different than Adam. It's not that I didn't think it was going to work, but I didn't have that feeling that it was a shoo-in… and then I saw that artist do what he does, and magic happened. Norbert was genius. And he wasn't "Broadway's Norbert Leo Butz" at the time—it was his Broadway debut! He was so great that we gave him the replacement job. There were so many of those stories. Specifically on *Rent*, it happened a lot. If someone was a fantastic cover, they got the part on one of the national tours or on Broadway.

Those first few years of *Rent*, no one liked going there, to 41st Street. Even if *Rent* was the grooviest thing in the world, and the bathrooms had leopard-print carpet, and the theater looked awesome, you still got outside and were like: *Oh my God.* But it's true: *Rent* really redefined that whole area. How great that theatre can do that, gentrify a street corner. But it's truly a great theater, inside. I love seeing *Newsies* and other shows there now.

Rent closing was special. Maybe it was because it was my first Broadway show as a casting director in my own office, or maybe it was bringing my younger son, who wasn't even born yet when it opened. I have a 24-year-old and a 14-year-old son. When the show started, Danny was seven and now the show's closing and Felix is about seven. My family lived through it all with me. Opening the office, everything that happened, going from three people to 15 people. *Rent* will always be the one for me.

———————

In 1921, there were ornate cornucopia motifs that decorated the 24 exit signs of the theater. By the time Rent *closed in 2008, there was one lone sculpture left, over a rear mezzanine door. Now, the motifs are reconstructed over every exit in the theater.*

———————

1992/1996-2001: It Was Crazy For Years

Brig Berney, Company Manager

I did four shows with Kevin McCollum and Jeffrey Seller: *Rent, High Fidelity, La Bohème*, and *In the Heights*. At times, we had two or three shows running on Broadway simultaneously, and if you were out of ice packs, you'd call your "sister show" down the street.

My first time at the Nederlander was before *Rent*, working on a show called *Solitary Confinement*, which was a murder mystery. It was produced by the Nederlanders themselves, and one memory I have is of Gladys

306

Nederlander coming up to me and wanting to make sure there was a comfortable couch in the ladies' bathroom. That was very important to her.

I was so new to company management that the theater didn't seem in bad shape to me. I just remember the dressing rooms all being very small, and that Stacy Keach took one to get ready in, and another to greet guests in.

I worked on *Rent* for the first six years and four months of its run. At that point, I do remember the theater being filthy. Kevin and Jeffrey and Paul Clay, the set designer, had this vision of what the theater should look like. They had the lobby done over in mosaics as well as the proscenium, and the beautiful molding was painted funny colors. They found interesting East Village artists to hang their original works in the theater.

There was scaffolding in the boxes when we got there, and the theater told us they were working on getting it down. Someone said, "No! Leave it. It just adds to the East Village feel of the show." You could still have a couple chairs below, and people climbed through to get to them. It added to the atmosphere.

The mosaic around the proscenium had all kinds of crazy things in it: broken pieces of mugs and plates, the little smiley face from "Have A Nice Day," a *Cats* logo that had been smashed and reassembled. They built that. We kept it when the show closed and put it in storage.

They put in leopard-print carpeting. It turned out it wasn't quality carpeting, so it eventually became threadbare, and we had to make more industrial carpeting. But at the beginning, it looked really neat.

The show closed off-Broadway on a Sunday. On Monday we started rehearsals for Broadway, and two weeks later was the first preview. It was a very tight turnaround and there was so much to do to get the show ready. It was like trying to hold onto a rocket with your fingernails.

We made a green room area in the middle of the basement, out of cabinets and duplicate props and understudy costumes and cleaning supplies. We just sort of arranged things to create a space. Wardrobe was on one end, and some of the house crew had offices down there. Then there was an area with a large round table and two couches that people would sleep on in between shows. Because there were no wings to hang out in, because the show was so open, you could be seen standing there if you weren't on. So we had to make the basement a place where people would hang out.

Basements aren't made into green rooms as much as they used to be. Part of it is because there is more and more technical equipment that needs space in the basement. Right now at *Cinderella*, we have so much sound and lighting equipment, and so much automation, that there's just a table in a corner for birthday cakes, but it's not a separate room. At *Rent*, we only had five musicians, and they had a dressing room on top of the theater. On a Broadway show like *Cinderella,* with around 20 musicians, you have to have a basement area with lockers where they can lock up their instruments and black clothes.

We had a mice infestation in the basement of the Nederlander. We found out they were living in a nest in a couch in the green room, feeding off of birthday cake crumbs. There were things like that. Since the Nederlander hadn't been actively used in a long time, we had to replace all of these really old washing machines. A lot of the power had to be redone so we could do things like plug in coffee pots. The wiring was so old that it didn't have the strength to support a show in 1996 and all that it entailed.

We were sold out for so long. For many years into the run, it was crazy in the theater every single night.

The cast of *Rent* as a group could get in anywhere they wanted: any club or big party. So many people in our cast were Broadway babies. Very few of them had been in a Broadway show before, and Adam had never been in a play in his life! They were enjoying all of that, which was great—but in any job, you can't do that every night and then also come in and do a show the next day. It was my job to help these people deal with the immediate fame, the fans, developing the discipline to do the show eight times a week. I remember Daphne coming in one Saturday and saying to me, "I'm so tired!" I asked, "Are you getting sleep?" and she responded, "Well you know, we're out every night." I told her, "You need to eat well, you need to exercise, you need to know when you can go out and when you need to say: *I'm sorry, I have to go home and lay low.*" There was a lot of helping each of the cast members through that.

It was busy. I loved it. One thing that was weird was that I didn't get to see the show for weeks! There was so much to do that I could never get inside the theater while the show was going on.

There was nothing on our block except a parking garage and a bodega that did not have good food. Everything else opened during the run of *Rent*.

Of course, people were sleeping outside to wait for the seats in the front row that were $20. The block was shady. The *New York Times* hadn't taken over the end of the block, and the New Amsterdam hadn't reopened yet with *Lion King*, so we had to have a security person sitting in a car there all night, with teenagers on the sidewalk. Can you imagine all those teenagers sleeping on the New York City street in the middle of winter to get a ticket to *Rent*? It was really something.

After a while, we changed the system and made it a lottery, to make things fairer and safer. Kevin and Jeffrey really wanted theater to be accessible to young people and to people who couldn't afford a full price ticket. Our top ticket price at the time was around $65.

There were celebrities there all the time, so I spent a lot of time dealing with those folks. Tom Cruise and Nicole Kidman came when they were as white-hot as they ever were. There were cameras like crazy and people screaming and rock stars and Barbara Walters and fashion models and Calvin Klein and a slew of designers. The show was such an event! Adam Pascal and Daphne Rubin-Vega were on the cover of Newsweek!

Our wonderful director, Michael Greif, would want to come to the show, but without the cast finding out. Sometimes people change their performances when they know the director is watching, and he didn't want that. So he'd come very early and hide up in the mezzanine, or he'd walk in after the opening number had started so the actors couldn't see him.

I believe the signing of the wall in the alley started at the very first preview. Originally, it was going to really be a place for celebrities to leave notes of how much they'd enjoyed the show, but then members of the general public found that they could walk into the alley, and they started writing things on it as well. It took on a life all its own. There were signatures from John Travolta and Al and Tipper Gore and then all of these people who came through. People started signing on top of each other. Thankfully, the shows that have come in since have not painted over it. It's very faded, but you can still read a lot of them.

People started writing on the doors on the front of the theater, too. Audiences were given the license to express the joy that the show brought to them. It added to the atmosphere of the theater. Sometimes I'd walk in the stage door before a performance and there would be people back there, just reading the wall. It affected people of all ages and backgrounds.

One hot summer day, I got a call from the Nederlander Theatre. We had been having these flash thunderstorms where the rain just came down in buckets, and they said, "You might want to get over here. There's a hole in the ceiling, and rain is pouring into the mezzanine. I ran down there and found that a drain on the roof had gotten clogged, and it looked like somebody had turned on a gigantic fire hose and shoved it through a hole in the ceiling.

Suddenly you're thinking: *What are we going to do? We have a sold out show tonight, in six hours!* We finally got the Nederlander engineers to get the water to stop. The hole was plugged, and we all ran around getting wet vacs, heat lamps—even hair dryers from the hair room. We put towels on all of the seats, we opened the doors of the theater to let the humidity out. It was that true experience of: *The show must go on.* We got these huge fans. We did everything we could and just waited to let the audience in.

September 11 was a crazy day on so many levels. Amidst the horrible tragedy, we didn't really know what was going to happen with *Rent*. We ended up cancelling the show that Tuesday night. I walked up to the office and started calling our stage managers and everyone, saying, "The show is cancelled, stay home. I'll be in touch when I know more." Then Jeffrey called me and said, "What are you doing in the office? Get out of that area, Times Square might be the next target."

We resumed performances on Thursday, and only about 200 people came. The actor playing Mark Cohen, Trey Ellett, came out at the beginning and said to the audience, "Thank you for coming. We know this is difficult. We hope we lift your spirits."

I felt it was part of my job to be sure all of our younger performers were mentally okay. "Yes, this is a horrible, horrible, horrible event, and I know it seems strange that we're going to sing and dance for two hours, but hopefully it will have a healing effect on other people and on you. Anything we can do to take people's minds off what's happening for two hours is good. It's a good thing to have a routine to get back into, to have something to focus on."

Kevin and Jeffrey wanted *Rent* to be a different kind of Broadway show, and the Nederlander was a different kind of theater.

A lot of people told Kevin, Jeffrey, and Alan Gordon that the show should not move to Broadway at all. They were told over and over that it should play the Minetta Lane or sit down somewhere else off-Broadway. But they had the foresight to bring it to Broadway, and they knew: *Rent* should be at the Nederlander. It ran for more than 12 years.

Jonathan Larson's father, Al, made a wooden carving that hung backstage. It became a Rent *tradition to touch the carving before each performance. When* Rent *began touring and productions started all over the world, Mr. Larson made carvings for those productions as well. Caissie Levy, who did* Rent *on tour, remembered that each cast member from her production would touch the plaque at a different time before they went onstage. "It always felt like we were connecting to him," she told me. A canvas often traveled with each tour as well, to replicate the* Rent *wall in different cities.*

The Rent *"rush tickets" traveled from city to city on tour as well, and many credit* Rent *with re-enlivening the road, bringing a new generation to the theatre all over America.*

1996/2006-2008: I Can Do This

Telly Leung, Actor

The first show that made me feel like: *Oh my God, I want to do this*—or rather, *I can do this* was *Rent*. I was in high school, and I loved Broadway. Earlier that season, I had seen *Hello, Dolly!* and I loved it.

But *Rent* was different. First of all, I could afford it myself: I slept with the bums on 41st Street, and I got my own rush seat. That was the first show that ever did anything like that. It was sold out and impossible to get a seat otherwise! I remember getting there at 5am and waiting for the rush seat and hanging out with the bums. It was when 41st Street was still kind of scary, but it was fine. We all looked out for each other on the line.

I sat in the front row, and I looked up at the stage and I didn't quite understand it all. *Rent* is a pretty dense, wordy show. But I do remember that whole passage between "Another Day" into "Will I?", because that was the first time I ever cried in a theater. I was like: *Why am I crying? I don't have AIDS. I don't do drugs. I don't go to the East Village. Why am I uncontrollably crying at this moment?* It was just one of those moments where there was the perfect mesh of story, music, words... and you just felt it. I was there with my friend from high school, and we were just like: *We're both crying. This is very weird that we're both having an emotional reaction, and we're not even processing it, we're just in it.*

There was something about seeing such a diverse cast onstage, too. I looked up at that stage and, being a New Yorker, I was like: *Oh, this looks like New York!* I had seen Broadway shows before, like *Cats*, where everybody was a cat. And I'd seen *Crazy for You*. That was the other Broadway show I saw before I saw *Rent*, and it was very homogenous-looking. There were a couple of ethnic people onstage, but the dancers were mostly Caucasian, and everyone was the same height and the same size. I was like, *I don't know if I fit in this.*

When I saw *Rent*, I was like, *I fit there somewhere! There are young, old, black, white, Asian, Latin, gay, straight, different body types, everything people onstage!* And the music spoke to me. I thought, *I sing like this. This sounds like music that I dig and that I could do. I could really do this.*

In 2006, *Rent* was still running at the Nederlander—and I was cast as Steve and the Angel understudy.

I saw the show in 1996, and you fast-forward ten years and I'm standing there, doing "Seasons of Love" on the Nederlander stage. I stood on that line on my first night and I looked at the seat where I had sat, in the front row.

I was also in *Rent* when Anthony Rapp and Adam Pascal came back to play Mark and Roger toward the end of the run. When I was in high school, back when America Online chatrooms were big, there were theatre chatrooms where you could trade bootlegs. Well, before the *Rent* album came out, there was a frenzy for *Rent* bootlegs. VHS bootlegs, cassette bootlegs. I got online, and I was like, "I want a *Rent* bootleg! I'll trade you a *Sunset Boulevard* bootleg for a *Rent* bootleg!"

Anyway, I remember when Anthony Rapp and Adam Pascal came back into the show towards the end of the run. I remember being onstage, doing "Rent," the title number, and suddenly having this huge realization: *Oh my GOD. I'm in my own bootleg! This is crazy! I'm in my own bootleg of the original cast!*

Arrest me now with my illegal cassettes from somebody else sitting in the 12th row of the balcony with their old tape recorder, capturing *Rent* in 1996! I know it was illegal, but I love that story.

Through the 13 years that *Rent* ran on Broadway, the walls backstage became filled with pictures and memories and fan art. John Vivian was one of our stage managers, and he was with the show for the entire run, from the very beginning. We felt like his kids, because he saw all of us grow up in that building in a lot of ways. I just remember John taking each piece of the wall down. He took each photo down one at a time, slowly, absorbing every memory before he put it in a manila envelope. It took him almost the entire last month of the run to do it, little by little. That was his goodbye.

I don't think anybody ever notices that I do it, but as I exit a theater for the last time, I always bend down and I kiss the stage somehow. That's one of my personal traditions.

The final performance of *Rent* was a little bit of a pressure cooker because we knew they were filming it for a Sony Cinecast that was going to be broadcast all over the country. We were very emotional, but we couldn't be overly emotional because we were still on. We had to do the performance that was going to represent the show on record forever, so we had to keep it together.

The day after *Rent* closed, I went back to get my stuff in the theater and so did Will Chase. I saw Will sitting on the stage, and he said to me, "I have to grieve the show now because I didn't have time to last night. I was still on. I had to work. I had to be Roger." And I think I felt the same way. I never really got to kiss it goodbye until the day after it was over. And the one picture that remained on the Nederlander wall was Jonathan Larson's.

I was so blessed in that after *Rent* closed on Broadway, I got to do the tour with Anthony and Adam that went around the country and around the world. *Rent* is one of those shows that I could still do. I could do it forever. I get why people stayed in *Rent* for such a long time.

Rent gave birth to rush tickets as we know them today. As one way of reaching out to younger, less conventional audiences, the producers of Rent *arranged to have the entire front row of 34 tickets sold for $20 for every performance. 41st Street was constantly filled with a line of people, often under 40 years old, who might not have gone to a Broadway theater otherwise. The policy became so successful at nurturing new audiences that gradually, each new show began to offer cheaper "rush" tickets available the day of performance, usually to students or patrons under a certain age.*

The "rush ticket culture" rang in a new era on Broadway, and the young stars of Rent *did their part as well. Stage-dooring as we know it was born during* Rent. *Before, patrons might wait to get a glimpse of a star outside a Broadway house, or occasionally meet a favorite performer, but* Rent, *with its youthful audiences, was the first show to create a post-concert-like atmosphere on the street following the show. Fans with Sharpies would get every actor's autograph. Michael Greif and his team took* A Chorus Line *one step farther and throughout the run, there was like a third act on the sidewalk, as fans hollered for understudies, replacements, everyone who was part of* Rent.

1998: My First Lesson As A Young Actor

Jose Llana, Actor

Going into *Rent*, you want to be creative, but at the same time you need to hit the marks someone else left for you. I was lucky in that when I went in, Michael Greif directed me. I felt like I got to create my own Angel, as opposed to trying to duplicate anyone. The company at that point was in a major transition from the original cast into the second and third cast.

They had actually offered me the opportunity to originate the role of Angel in the Canadian cast, but I turned down *Rent* to do *Street Corner Symphony* which ended up running for three months. And the weird thing is, I thought I had given up the chance to go into *Rent*, and then six months later they came to me and said, "Hey, the New York company is open!" To go into *Rent* when it was that popular and to play Angel, it was a dream come true.

But that's not the full story... I had booked *The King and I* in September of 1995. We were supposed to start rehearsal in November, but then Lou Diamond Phillips got a movie, so they pushed us to February. Suddenly, I had all this time free, because I had left school already. I had just gotten an agent, and he said, "You know, there's this other show they're auditioning, at New York Theatre Workshop. It's an adaptation of *La Bohème*. They want to see you for this drag queen character."

I was a 19-year-old actor in 1995... And I was out at that point, but I was not comfortable. I had *just* started working. I went into that *La Bohème* adaptation audition and I got a callback, but I remember thinking to myself, "Who's gonna come down to this East Village theater for a nobody writer?" I was so young and stupid. I was that big headed, 19-year-old who had just booked his first Broadway show, and thought: *Maybe I'll do your off-Broadway show until my February Broadway show comes.* Of course, I didn't book it.

And then, while we were rehearsing *The King and I* in February, all anyone was talking about was *Rent, Rent, Rent.* I asked, "What's *Rent*?" and they said, "It's this thing at New York Theatre Workshop." "...What?!"

They won Best Musical that year at the Tony Awards, and we won Best Revival. It was my first lesson as a young actor. I realized I did the stupid thing of judging a piece out of arrogance, instead of actually looking at the material from a critical perspective. To be honest, I was so young that I didn't know anything about the world of Broadway versus off-Broadway. I thought then what my father still thinks today: off-Broadway isn't real Broadway. It was all about money.

My *Rent* story is that I auditioned for New York Theatre Workshop, probably gave a horrible audition out of arrogance, and then later ended up getting the chance to do the role proud.

———————

Rent played at the Nederlander over 4500 times. Between 1950 and 1996, 17 musicals opened at the Nederlander Theatre. None of them made it past 75 performances.

In fact, prior to Rent, *the Nederlander had a terrible overall track record for musicals. The theater's first musical,* Bye Bye Barbara, *came in 1924, and barely eked out two weeks of performances before closing at a loss. The* New York Times *told its readers: "There were some pretty tunes, some beautiful chorus girls, some agile dancers, and those who left before the final curtain are hereby assured that their fears are groundless and that Stanley is going to marry Barbara."[120]*

A number of Nederlander musicals closed on opening night: Here's Where I Belong *(1968),* Billy *(1969),* Heathen! *(1972), and* Broadway Follies *(1981). In addition to those, the following all played ten or less performances:* Hairpin Harmony *(1943),* Maggie *(1953),* Earl of Ruston *(1971),* Wind in the Willows *(1985),* Raggedy Ann *(1986),* Dangerous Games *(1989), and* One Night Stand, *which closed during previews in 1980.*

Why have so many musicals met a swift and early death in this house on 41st Street? Several theories arise. Since the theater was a producer's last resort for many years, it also was stuck with shows that were the least likely candidates for success, since they couldn't get a "better" theater. There's also the fact that with its 1200 seats, the Nederlander provides a great home for a small or mid-sized musical, and these weren't often palatable to a 20th century audiences, mostly preferring their musicals big and grand.

Since Rent *reinvigorated the Nederlander, it has been home to three musicals, two of them—Million Dollar Quartet and Newsies—huge hits that ran for over two years. The Nederlander is now poised as a popular house just as likely to bring its audiences hit musicals as the Shubert or the St. James.*

There was one *mega-hit musical at the Nederlander prior to* Rent: Call Me Mister. *In 1946, this good-natured revue celebrated servicemen and women coming home from World War II with songs and sketches—they even held a contest so veterans in hospitals could submit material for inclusion. All creative team members had been in the services, and audience members were overjoyed at the chance to finally laugh at the ins and outs of the war years.*

———————

---

[120] *"Bye Bye, Barbara* Arrives." *The New York Times.* 26 Aug. 1924.

2005: I Was Working At Bubba Gump

Robin De Jesús, Actor

I had never even been backstage at a Broadway theater before I booked *Rent*. I had just turned 21, and I was working at Bubba Gump Shrimp Company. I was trying to get acting work, and I was very unhappy.

I didn't want to audition for *Rent*. I felt typecast as a gay character actor. Then one day, Shaun Earl, an actor who was in *Rent* came up to me while I was working at Bubba Gump. He said, "I have to talk to you. I saw *Camp*, and I'm a fan of yours. I'm in *Rent*, and you should be in *Rent*." I told him, "It's not my thing right now. I'm trying to see if I can get a couple straight roles under my belt." He said, "Well, if you need money and you're waiting tables, it's gotta be better than that..."

I thought I was making a good career decision, but then I really thought about it and realized: *Maybe I've been wrong. I'd love to do* Rent. *I'm ready to do this if it's ready for me.* A month later, an audition came up, and I went.

I went in to audition for *Rent* on November 10th, had my callback the same day, and then I got the phone call on November 11th that I got it. It was a Friday morning at 10:30, and I had to be at the theater that night. I was going to be covering Angel. When I got the job and walked into that theater, Shaun Earl was one of the first people I saw. He said, "It happened!!!"

I remember walking through the alleyway of the Nederlander for the first time. There are these double doors, and then you have to go outside again, and then there's the stage door. It was winter, and I thought: *I gotta go outside again? I thought I was getting out of the ghetto!*

Then I saw the beautiful wall with everyone's writing on it. I didn't know what it was yet; it hadn't been explained to me, but it was beautiful. I thought I would open the stage door and a pool of light would just shine out. Then I opened the door, and the Nederlander door man was just like, "Yo! What's up?"

I watched the show every night for three weeks, from the sound board. Every night when the audience left, I would see mice all throughout the Nederlander aisles. Those mice knew that the audience had just left, and they were ready to play!

When it was finally time for me to go check out my dressing room, I remember thinking: *I've gotta climb all of these stairs?* It's so ungrateful! But it's reality. You never feel like you're in a Broadway theater until you go to Paper Mill Playhouse in New Jersey: it's so big, and it's what you imagine a Broadway house would look like. There are six floors of dressing rooms at the Nederlander and lots of stairs to climb.

At *Rent*, we had a tradition where every night before we went to the stage, we'd touch this piece of wood above the call board. It had Jonathan's name on it and was given to the company by his family. Some people would choose to touch it for good luck before they went onstage, and some wouldn't. Karmine Alers rubbed it each night, and she had a personal relationship with Jonathan; she had known him before *Rent*. The piece of wood was a tradition, a little connection with Jonathan.

One challenge of *Rent* was to do "Today 4 U" without breathing heavily—because you had to coat your lips in glitter, and if you breathed in hard, you would choke on it. The glitter got everywhere!

I also remember always looking up at the ceiling and going, "There are holes in the ceiling of this Broadway theater! Can someone patch them? I have an uncle who could do this. Can I please call my uncle, Miguel? This roof looks crazy."

———————

It was originally announced that the National would be called the Times Square Theatre, but the Selwyns, theater owners one block over, claimed they had a previous right to use this name. The Selwyns opened their Times Square Theatre on 42nd Street in 1920. It was a Broadway house for only 13 years, before it was seized by the bank during the Great Depression. After that, the Times Square was a movie theatre for many decades before falling into disuse. Plans were in progress recently to re-open the theater with "Broadway 4D," a special attraction that would incorporate both 3-D film and live performance. Much like several of the plans to save the Times Square Theatre, that one fell through. It is currently the only Broadway theater on 42nd Street that is fully intact, but completely shut off from the world, waiting for a resurrection of its own.

2007: The *Rent* Family

Justin Scribner, Stage Manager

I was stage managing at *Rent* for the last year of the run. When we found out the show was closing, I got another job, working on the *A Chorus Line* revival. Then, *Rent* extended, and I was the only one who had to leave on the original closing day! I was sad about that, but I had wanted to make sure I had a job.

Rent was my first experience working on a long-running show. It really cemented for me that I enjoy this lifestyle, and I enjoy being a stage manager. Parts of it felt like an off-Broadway show because I was doing so many different tasks all the time—but that's part of what made it so wonderful and charming. I felt like I was really a part of the *Rent* family. They instantly embraced me. I was their age, and the other two stage managers were older. They had, like, a mother-father relationship with them, and I got to feel like I was their cousin or sibling. And I got chills almost every day. *Rent* was just so influential to me. I would tear up calling the show.

I was in full view of stage-left, I could see everything. I often interacted with the actors as they came on and off stage. There's a moment in the show with the line, "Kiss Mimi." Whoever was playing Mimi would kiss the stage manager script every night, so there were a lot of kiss marks. Some of the scripts were old and used, and the pages became circular and rounded on the edges.

There's a moment in every show where the stage managers release the swings. If you're a swing and you don't go on, it's standard practice that once all of the characters you cover go on for their last entrance, you can leave. One night, after all the swings had been released, we were finishing the show. Karmine Alers was playing Mimi, and in the middle of the second act, she finished "Goodbye Love", and ran underneath the Christmas tree straight into a pole. It knocked her out, and she was just laying there onstage. Another actor had to pull her off!

Dana Dawson, who had swung in *Rent* and was coming back to the show, was in the audience watching. She was getting reacquainted, because she'd left to do another show. We had to run into the house and whisper to Dana, "You're going on as Mimi for the end of the show!" We brought her backstage and had just enough time to throw pants and that Mimi coat on her. She put the microphone over her ear, but had to carry the mic pack-there wasn't even time for a mic belt. And she went on! It might have actually been her first time ever playing Mimi.

Dana passed away from cancer a few years ago. She was an amazing person, and so young. Her family was incredible through the whole thing. And then there was also her *Rent* family. And we're all pretty young, so it was really upsetting to see someone pass away. It felt so sudden because she kept it to herself. It was a really upsetting funeral, of course, but then it was also so heartwarming to see this *Rent* family. The lasting experience on *Rent* was that we had a family. *Rent* just generated familial love and closeness and intimacy.

2008: "To Days Of Inspiration"

Nick Blaemire, Actor/Writer

I was in 7th grade when *Rent* came out. My mom gave me the CD and showed me the *New York Times* article and was like, "I think you'd be into this." I obviously didn't think so because my mom had given it to me. Then she wouldn't even play me all the songs because there was so much cursing!

Then this girl named Sarah in my 7th grade class was like, "What's your favorite part of *Rent*? I love it so much." Sarah Grey. I responded, "I just love, 'December 24th, 9pm'!" She said, "*That's* your favorite line?" And I was like, "Uh, yeah."

Then I saw *Rent* nine times. I saw it at Wolf Trap in D.C. I saw it at the Warner. I saw it on Broadway later, when I was writing *Glory Days*. I would go to see it so I could watch it and cry and figure out how to finish *Glory Days*.

I saw *Rent* three times when I was working on *Glory Days*. $20 tickets. It was before they started stunt casting, when Matt Caplan was playing the role for several years. I still think he's one of the best actors I've ever seen. I would sit there in the Nederlander, and I would literally sob to myself in the back of the audience listening to *Rent*. It was the show that made me understand the idea of dramatically induced pop options in music. I would think: *Oh, you made this choice, not because it's fancy, but because when Mimi went to sing "Goodbye Love", she couldn't control her emotions.* It was just the best. That was the best show to grow up with, and that theater was the perfect theater.

———————

In 2008, the cult movie musical Hamlet 2—*starring Skylar Astin, Amy Poehler, and Elisabeth Shue, among others—filmed several scenes at the Nederlander.* Rent's *final performance on Broadway was also filmed that year and includes documentary footage of the evening as well.*

Jonathan Larson gets a lot of credit for saving the American musical. And he did. But he also saved the Nederlander.

In 1996, right after Rent *opened off-Broadway, Frank Rich wrote in the* New York Times:

> *Two weeks ago, at a 150-seat theater in the East Village, a rock opera called* Rent, *written and performed by unknowns, came out of nowhere to earn the most ecstatic raves of any American musical in the two decades since* A Chorus Line. *And now the world is rushing to catch up:* Rent *will quickly move to Broadway to accommodate the insatiable demand for tickets....*
>
> *As Michael Greif, who directed* Rent, *recalled in an interview punctuated by tears this week, Mr. Larson had sacrificed his life to his work, waiting on tables for years, sustaining himself with the "sunny belief" that his talent would one day lead to his breakthrough. "He wanted it so bad," said Mr. Greif. "It's cruel that he's not here to enjoy it..." At so divisive a time in our country's culture,* Rent *shows signs of revealing a large, untapped appetite for something better. It's too early to tell. What is certain is that Jonathan Larson's brief life belies the size of his spirit. In the staying power of his songs, he lingers, refusing to let anyone who hears his voice abandon hope.*[121]

Rent *did jolt Broadway. It inspired a new generation of writers to create modern musicals in their own voice. It inspired producers to nurture and bring rock musicals to Broadway. It inspired audiences to look to Broadway for fresh new work. It inspired performers of different races to see Broadway as a place for them. Jonathan Larson knew he was the future of musical theatre. And now the world knew it, too.*

———

[121] Rich, Frank. "East Village Story." *The New York Times*. 2 Mar. 1996.

2009: Recession, Renovation, And "Rocking The Boat"

Steve Rosen, Actor

The day we started rehearsal for *Guys and Dolls*, there was a big announcement in the news about how bad the recession was. To get into the room on the first day of rehearsal and see that we were doing a big Broadway remount of a big beautiful show, that Des McAnuff was setting in the time when Damon Runyon lived, the 1930s during the Great Depression... that all felt so right on that first day. It felt like a *Guys and Dolls* for our time. These people were in a bad way, making the best of a bad situation.

There was a lot of very interesting reimagining involved to try to make our production grittier. During previews, the audiences sincerely seemed to love it. They leaped to their feet every night.

Then we opened.

The critics didn't respond warmly. That's putting it nicely (nicely). Our *Guys and Dolls* was lambasted.

Instantly, our enthusiastic audiences were replaced by people who had read reviews. They had formed an opinion about the show before the gloriously re-orchestrated overture began. People were just plain mean. And they weren't shy about telling us as we exited, because at the Nederlander there's no stage door! We had to walk all the way through the lobby because there's no street access to backstage.

For *Newsies,* after us, they figured out a plan to walk out a door on the side. We hadn't thought of that genius, unbelievably easy idea!

So after the show, we'd have to walk back through the lobby, and there would just be grumbling, shuffling feet, and the occasional, "Where was Nathan Lane?"

Lots of people expected to see the Nathan Lane/Faith Prince production which opened almost two decades earlier. That Jerry Zaks production was so iconic, that every review compared us negatively to it. With reviews like the ones we got, our producers could have easily closed up shop immediately. But to our producers' credit, they had faith in the show and ran it.

Like the characters in our reimagined production, the performers were trying to make the best out of a rough situation.

At the end of the day, I made some amazing friends on that show.

Oh, and the Tony Awards! Our producers were very clear about our show's need for a dramatic spike in ticket sales based on our performance at the Tonys. The thought was that if people could just see one of our imaginatively and athletically staged numbers, they'd buy a ticket immediately. And what better way to ensure success than having the incredible Tituss Burgess, the man I truly believe has the most amazing voice in the world, open up his golden throat on national television and slay everyone with an amazing gospel rendition of the textbook 11 o'clock number, "Sit Down You're Rocking The Boat". What could go wrong?

We went out on that stage that for the Tony Awards and took our seats in the Save-a-Soul-Mission. We knew that this was our shot and it had to go perfectly if we wanted to save our jobs. The lights in the house dimmed, the red lights on the camera went on and Tituss started talking... and there was no Tituss. His microphone went out. We heard people yelling everywhere. Onstage, off stage, and behind me, I heard someone whisper, "...And that's the sound of our show closing." Someone brought out a handheld microphone and Tituss did an incredible job... considering the circumstances.

The front page of the *New York Times* the next day was a picture Tituss holding a microphone shrugging as if to say "We did what we could... we did our best."

The producers called us the morning after to tell us that we were closing at the end of the week.

Rent was the show before us at the Nederlander and the place needed a renovation even before that show moved in. They were finally redoing the front-of-house simultaneously as we were teching onstage. The construction crew in the lobby was racing the show to see who would be ready first. The ultimate renovation was absolutely beautiful but we had to wear surgical masks during tech because of all the dust.

The alley between the lobby and the stage door still had the loving graffiti created by *Rent* fans. We thought they were going to paint over that before we moved in, but they didn't, and rightfully so. It's a loving testament to a beloved show that had made a mark on many people's lives. So on our closing night, our cast partied in the alley and we left our mark: "*Guys and Dolls* was here, too. Briefly."

After Rent *closed,* Guys and Dolls *booked the Nederlander. They were set to start performances five months later—so the Nederlanders needed to do extensive renovations, and fast. A real new roof. A cleaned-up façade. Everything updated, from the all-new grid, to the marquees, to the seating in the house.*

A 1921 New York Times *"Gossip of the Rialto" column read: "Those who have inspected the theatre declare that it is a good-looking theatre and a distinct addition to this town's huge and ever-growing list."[122] Every article and announcement of the new theater mentioned that it would be "just in back of the New Amsterdam." More than 80 years later, the New Amsterdam and the Nederlander would return to life around the same time.*

2009: Red-Headed Stepchild

Mary Testa, Actor

What do I remember about the Nederlander? A lot of sawdust.

I was there for so little time with *Guys and Dolls*. It's a fine theater. I had a sweet little dressing room all to myself. But it's a weird place to be. It's weird to be on 41st Street. You feel like the action starts on 42nd. It's like you're the red-headed stepchild of Broadway.

2012: The Perfect House For *Newsies*

Alan Menken, Writer

In between the Paper Mill production and the Broadway production, we wrote quite a bit of new material for *Newsies*. It doesn't happen as often as it used to, because it's expensive: but we did have that classic thing of going out to the hotel and writing a new song and breaking it in out-of-town.

---

[122] "Gossip of the Rialto." *The New York Times*. 31 July 1921.

Then we moved into the Nederlander, and it's just the perfect house for *Newsies*. I love it. I love being in that house. I loved being at Papermill, but when Newsies came into the Nederlander, it was: *Oh my God. We really have a Broadway show.*

2012: The *Newsies* And The Fansies

Andrew Keenan-Bolger, Actor

I think *Newsies* changed the way that the fanbase can mobilize and be connected. The show used social media so well to connect people from all around the country. I've never felt that supported by fans. I remember when Celia and I were doing Broadway For Obama, a lot of fans started volunteering for it, and they became friends. We would all just be in the same room, calling swing voters in Ohio.

Of course, *Rent* is the show that made the Nederlander really famous. There's a lot of *Rent* still in that theater, and a lot of that spirit. There's an alleyway that leads from the lobby to our stage door that has thousands of signatures and notes from people who were in the cast of *Rent* over the years, as well as all of the fans who waited for these stars to come out. It's truly floor-to-ceiling tagged with all these messages. It was always a fun thing to go out with the *Newsies* boys and try to pick out names.

We were like, "There's Anthony Rapp's signature! He wrote 'No Day But Today' and then signed it in 1996!" I also saw that original cast in 1996, when I was really young. It was definitely life-changing. I also have some friends who did *Rent*, and I found out that one of my best friends, Colin Hanlon, had my dressing room when he was in *Rent*! We were even in the same spot, using the same mirror, six or seven years apart.

There were a lot of rituals that happened at *Newsies*. Since it was so many people's first show, we made new traditions up. On Saturdays, you had to take your #SIP, your Saturday Intermission Picture, and post it online, and that's a tradition that still happens over there.

"Seize the Day" is one of the greatest musical numbers ever. It's so exciting. I'm not a dancer, and as Crutchie, I would get to hobble off to the side of the stage and cheer the Newsies on. I got to watch the number, not even from the wings, but from right at the proscenium. Every night, I'd be so amazed at what the boys could do. We were just like each other, but they could do something that was so remarkable and out-of-this-world, that I can't do. I would watch every night, with my jaw dropped.

———————

In Ben Brantley's review of Rent, *he wrote: "The leit-motif of the show is the image of time evaporating; its credo, quite unabashedly, 'Seize the day.'"*[123] Newsies *carried on this credo, quite literally, with a song of that exact name. Some also have jokingly referred to the Nederlander as "the Santa Fe Theatre," since both shows have songs titled "Santa Fe."*

While Rent *and* Newsies *both helped to bring younger audiences to the theatre, the majority of the* Newsies *cast had not hit elementary school yet when* Rent *opened. A whole new generation was bringing life to the Nederlander, and* Newsies *was the first time since* Rent *closed that found fans lining up around the block for tickets and autographs.*

———————

2012: Like 20 Billy Elliots

Chris Gattelli, Choreographer/Actor

———————

[123] Brantley, Ben. "East Village Rock Opera A La '*Boheme*' And '*Hair*.'" *The New York Times.* 14 Feb. 1996.

318

The Nederlander is so intimate and so beautiful. It's clean now.

They kept the *Rent* wall in the alley in back, but the theater was completely renovated. I remember going in there for the first time, when we were told that it would be our *Newsies* theater. I thought: *The boys are going to be dancing this close to us?! From any seat?!* I was thrilled.

The choreography didn't change much from Paper Mill, but being at the Nederlander made it all feel even better. It felt like the boys were now dancing on your lap. Paper Mill is a great theater, but the pit is very large, so that creates a barrier between the stage and audience. And the audience area is very wide and feels open. It was beautiful, and it gave more space to appreciate the set, but at the Nederlander, you really feel like you're *in* the story. You're looking up at all of it, and I always say it feels like you get the "David's perspective" of the event. My favorite seat to watch the show from is in the front row of the mezzanine. The towers feel like they're coming right at you. It's exciting.

When I went in to pitch the show to Disney, I told them how intense I wanted the dancing to be. I said, "It's like 20 Billy Elliots." It's 20 guys physicalizing their youth and their strength in all of these different ways. I knew I wanted 20 really special guys who could do a lot and who could really fly through the air.

The boys represent the next generation. That's what the show is about. It's about what President Roosevelt says at the end, about the next generation coming into power. "Everyone, this is our future. And we're in such good hands." So I wanted to put that in the dancing: *Look at what they're doing. Look at the talent. Look at the care involved in training to do that part.*

I thought I was talented as a dancer and at the top of my game, but I look at what I've choreographed these boys to do... and I wouldn't have even made it into the show! They're incredible. That's thrilling and inspiring as a choreographer. I think to myself: *Wow. This business, and dance in general, is in such good hands.* Because I know choreographers are going to come out of this show. They're going to push the form and take it to a different level. I can tell that not because they can do tricks and fancy stuff, but because of the care and time and strength and will I see them put into all of it. People see the spectacle of the dancing, which is exciting, but I see the process behind it, and that's what's exciting to me.

There were three different Billy Elliots at any given time, and each had their own thing: he's the tapping Billy, he's the ballet Billy, and so forth. They each had their own specialty, and the show was shaped for them. I said, "That's what this will be. The dancers are all stars and the show should change for them." If someone came in and could do something well, we should let them enjoy that, because it represents who they are as a person and as a performer.

By our year anniversary, about 30% of the cast had not been there when we opened. I went back in and worked with everyone. "You can do your spin here that you came in with." "He's doing flips here, so that moves you to here, and now you can do that move you've always wanted to do." We reconfigured some of the dances, and it made the group feel new again. It gave the new and old cast members respect for each other. I didn't want anyone to feel put into someone else's track. In the original company of *Dreamgirls*, Lillias White did not do the same riffs Jennifer Holliday did. It was about what came out of each of them as individuals. And I wanted the same thing for my dancers.

———————

In 1935, the National Theatre's neighbors were Mooney's Bar & Eating Place, the 41st Street Hotel with rooms for $1 a night, a shop called Fred's selling waiter's outfits, and a drugstore with signs advertising soda and candy in its windows. Today, the Nederlander's neighbors are Red Lobster, New York Sports Club, and a parking garage. A chic women's clothing store called New York Look stands where the drugstore once was and Hotel 41 with red neon lights has long occupied the space that was the 41st Street Hotel. Bar 41, where actors and staff from the

Nederlander grab a drink after their shows, was once Mooney's. All of the buildings, whether open or condemned, have been the same on the south side of 41st Street between Broadway and 8th Avenue for decades. That's about to change—the parking garage to the right of the theater is being turned into a high-rise hotel at this very moment.

2000/2012: If I Ain't Got Santa Fe

Jeremy Jordan, Actor

I'm originally from Corpus Christi, Texas. The first time I ever came to New York was when I was a freshman in high school. I was in choir, and we were invited to sing at Carnegie Hall. My aunt lived here so she showed us around New York, and then I saw my first two Broadway shows in one day: *Chicago* and *Rent.*

I thought *Chicago* was fine; I remember there was a TV star in it, but I was kind of indifferent to the show. And *Rent* blew me away. I loved every second of it. I never realized that an entire story could be told through rock music like that. I brought home the cast recording and was just obsessed with it. I remember sitting in the back of the Nederlander mezzanine, because we had the cheap seats.

Then I got to do *Newsies* at the Nederlander. There's no star dressing room at the theater. I was the lead, so I had first pick at a dressing room, and it was still the smallest one I've ever had. I picked it because it was the only one with a bathroom in it. It was a fine room, but I could barely lie down on the floor and nap if I wanted, because I didn't fit!

Because *Newsies* was a challenging show for me vocally, I kept to myself before performances. I really had to shut everybody out in order to do eight shows a week and sing the show correctly. I'd leave my door cracked in case anyone wanted to come in, but I wasn't running around the theater participating in games and things. Around my last two months in *Newsies*, I became obsessed with *Breaking Bad*, so I'd get to the Nederlander at 45 minutes to curtain and do fight call, and then go up to my dressing room and watch *Breaking Bad* on Netflix until places. I'd get two thirds of the way through an episode, pause it and perform act one, and then finish the episode at intermission. I was doing *Newsies* fueled on *Breaking Bad.*

I always stood in the wings to watch "King Of New York". What a cool number. I am in awe of big Broadway dance numbers, and even when I was Tony in *West Side Story*, I'd be onstage during "Dance at the Gym" going: *Wow, how are you guys doing this?!*

There were definitely more kids in the audience at *Newsies* than any other show I've done. That was great. And our standing ovations always felt genuine. Nowadays, people give a standing ovation for every show on Broadway. If four people stand, everyone stands. That's ridiculous, because as an actor, you want to really connect with the audience and know if they really enjoyed the show. No one wants a standing ovation just because the audience feels like they're supposed to do it. At *Newsies*, it really felt like the audience was filled with energy and wanted to stand for the show at the end, and that was meaningful.

Hands down my favorite memory of *Newsies* was getting to sing "Santa Fe" to close out the first act. What an incredible experience as an actor to get to stand onstage and deliver that number, hit that note, and then have the lights fade to black as the audience erupts. It was actually my idea to end on that high note. Alan Menken wrote the ending with three of the same notes, and I said, "Alan, we can't end the act like that. I gotta go up." He had me try it, and we never went back.

I would pause up there in the dark, taking it all in—being exhausted and taking in the joy from the audience. We left them on such a high that their energy gave *us* the energy to do act two. As Jack Kelly, I was filled with this mix of sadness and anger and passion, and when you add the audience's energy on top of that... it was just the greatest. I can't imagine recreating exactly that in any other show.

When I did my last show of *Newsies* at Paper Mill, I thought it was going to be the last show of *Newsies* ever. I was about to do *Bonnie & Clyde* on Broadway, and we knew something was going to happen with *Newsies* soon. I was positive that *Bonnie & Clyde* was going to be a hit, and so our closing show of *Newsies* at Paper Mill was rough for me. Every lyric, every moment, I thought: *This my the last time as Jack Kelly*. Then when I was waiting to start rehearsals for *Bonnie & Clyde*, they were auditioning for the new Jack Kelly in *Newsies*. I was powerless. Then fate intervened and *Bonnie & Clyde* closed, and I ended up getting to originate the role of Jack Kelly in *Newsies* after all.

We opened *Newsies* during Tony season, just as the Broadway Show League was starting. Disney didn't want us playing softball because it was on our one day off and they wanted us to rest. But our whole cast wanted to, and I said, "We're *Newsies*! If anybody should have the right to do this, it's us." So I started this petition, and we handed it to our company manager, saying: "We would all like to play softball please, thank you very much." The company manager loved that, and Disney saw our side of things and paid for us to be part of the softball league. It really bonded us; it felt like our first act as *Newsies* on Broadway was almost going on strike!

I started becoming fairly close with some of our stagehands when we all played softball together and then did a fantasy football league. Up until *Newsies*, I hadn't really learned to cherish those relationships, of all of the people on the crew in the theater. I never intentionally ignored anyone, but thinking back, it might have come off that I was. *Newsies* made me understand that it makes a huge difference when you make the effort to communicate with every single person in the theater. I didn't realize, but I'll always do that from now on.

I had some issues with people following me home after *Newsies*. I often took the bus home, and people followed me a couple of times. After that started happening, the security guard from *Mary Poppins* would pick me up and escort me across the street through the New Amsterdam stage door, down near their dressing rooms, up through the theater where their show was still happening, and out the front door. Almost every night, I would silently walk through *Mary Poppins* just as the dad character was having a change of heart in the bank.

When I got *Smash*, I decided to both film the TV show and continue doing *Newsies* at the same time. I would wake up at the crack of dawn, head to set, and if we were finished by 5pm, I would head to midtown and do *Newsies*, get home after midnight, and then start the whole thing again the next day. I didn't sleep; I didn't have a day off for 33 days. And almost every day, I was doing both jobs, except for days when I had two performances of *Newsies* or when we filmed *Smash* all day and all night. After 33 days, I had 12 days off to get married and go on my honeymoon, and when I came back, it was just *Smash*. I thought I could do both, but it was nearly impossible so I had to leave *Newsies*.

When the Nederlander was built, everyone in the theatre was impressed by its palatial attributes. Each dressing room backstage had a bath! Over the years, a lot of aspects of the house changed. Even worse than losing the private baths, the theater lost its stage door.

Step into the Nederlander lobby through the front doors and stand at the box office—you'll see a set of doors to your right. These were originally more of an entrance into the auditorium. The theater's original stage door was to the left—what is now the foyer that leads to the main entrance to the auditorium. In order for actors to leave the Nederlander, they have to walk through a back alley that leads to the front foyer hallway, and exit through the front doors. But in the early part of the 20th century, the left half of the front doors were the stage door. The foyer was expanded over the years, robbing the stage door of a true private hallway.

Jeremy Jordan's storyline on Smash *was a partially fictionalized version of Jonathan Larson's story.*

2014: Carrying The Banner

Ben Fankhauser, Actor

I moved to New York City in the spring of 2011 after graduating from Ithaca College. Around the end of the time I was in college, Telsey and Company started sending flyers to all of the musical theatre schools saying that they needed young guys to audition for *Newsies*. I thought: *I have to be in this show.* I had loved the movie for so long.

I didn't have an agent at the time, so I wasn't able to get an appointment. Then a couple months later, I was in the city, I had gotten an agent, and I had an audition for another project that Justin Huff from Telsey was casting. He told me that I wasn't right for it, but that he wanted to bring me in for *Newsies*. After that, I went in on a Monday afternoon to read, they called me back that night to dance, and then I got asked to be at the final callback the next morning. I didn't know this at the time, but Davey was the last role they had to cast.

When I got to the final callback, Jeremy Jordan was there. I knew him because he'd gone to Ithaca, too, although he was a few years ahead of me. He read Jack and I read Davey, and I thought: *Oh, isn't that funny that Telsey hires Jeremy to be a reader. He's so good.* I had no idea what was happening. I left, and half an hour later, I found out that I was going to be Davey in the Paper Mill Playhouse production of *Newsies*.

We were told that the Paper Mill production was the only plan for the show. It might be licensed or go on tour, but the producing team was not committing to anything yet. So we did *Newsies* at Paper Mill, and a week before closing, everyone on crew and all of the dressers were given these packets to fill out. They had to take extensive notes on the backstage goings-on throughout each performance. They started taking pictures of our costumes and reminding us not to keep any props as memorabilia. That's when the rumors began.

Then we had a luncheon before our final show at Paper Mill and Tom Schumacher, head of Disney Theatricals, announced, "We don't have any information we can tell you right now, except for one piece of exciting news. We will be performing on the 2011 Macy's Thanksgiving Day Parade." That was such a cool opportunity! I had grown up watching and loving the parade. But I still didn't think this necessarily meant we were going to Broadway, even though by that point Michael Riedel had written that we were rumored to be going into a Nederlander theater.

That's when the website went live. NewsiesTheMusicalOnBroadway.com was on the internet. I had not gotten an offer. None of my friends had gotten an offer. Jeremy was doing *Bonnie & Clyde*! Everyone was calling each other, going: *What's happening? The website said that* Newsies *was opening at the Nederlander in March 2012!*

That night, a bunch of us who had done *Newsies* at Paper Mill went to get drinks on 8th Avenue. We got drunk and walked down to 41st and stood in front of the Nederlander. It was snowing, and the *Million Dollar Quartet* marquee was still up.

We had a couple rehearsals for the parade, and then my agent called me. "You have an offer to make your Broadway debut in *Newsies*. They're going to put out the breakdown for all of the roles except yours and whoever else they decide to keep, tomorrow."

It seemed right to transfer *Newsies* to New York. It's a New York musical, a good ol' American story. All of the dancing in the show is driven toward Pulitzer. The dancing all comes from the intention of: *We can do things that you can't. You might be diminishing our rights, but look what we can do!* Chris Gatelli's choreography is all about what would elevate the storytelling, and how we could root dancing in our characters' goals and emotions.

Since Jeremy was in *Bonnie & Clyde* and couldn't come with *Newsies* to Broadway, they auditioned for his replacement. My friend Corey Cott was one of the people who auditioned. I remember him texting me to ask if I thought he should use an accent or not. I've known Corey for ten years. He and I grew up together in Cleveland, Ohio. We did shows together in community theatre as kids: *Les Mis, Jesus Christ Superstar, Sweeney Todd, Urinetown*. We did show choir together. We had the same voice teacher.

Then *Bonnie & Clyde* closed and Jeremy ended up being able to originate the role of Jack Kelly. When Jeremy booked *Smash*, they needed a standby for him, and Corey got the job! In the middle of the show one night I got a message from Corey: *I'm going to be doing* Newsies *with you*. It was unbelievable. And when Jeremy left the show, Corey became Jack Kelly full-time. The last show Corey and I did together in community theatre in Cleveland was *Rent*. We played Roger and Mark when we were kids and then we got to play leads together on Broadway in the theater *Rent* ran in for ten years.

Our first six months on Broadway were unbelievable. We opened in the spring, and we had these great audiences all through the summer. Then when we hit our first fall and winter, I got a good taste of what that dip in the Broadway grosses and audience energy is like. Our show is very energetic, and sometimes you feel like you want to rely on the audience giving back to you so you can continue to give back to them. It was a good lesson in how to tell the same story at the same level, no matter what the audience is giving to you.

Some of our crew members at the Nederlander have told me *Rent* stories. Billy Jr. says things like, "Oh yeah, this is where I used to light Mimi's candle." If you watch the *Rent* DVD of the final company, you can see Billy Sr. sweeping the stage at intermission. Those guys have been at the Nederlander for years. I was surprised to learn that when you go into a Broadway theater, you're basically in their home. They taught me what it meant to join and be part of their union, and that was great to learn since we were doing a show about strikes and unions.

There are a few of us who have been with *Newsies* from Paper Mill all the way through the final performance on Broadway. That's three full years of performing *Newsies*. I've done over 1000 performances! John Dossett has been here from the beginning, just like me. Before each performance, he goes around to every single person that works at this theater, offering them a mint and giving them a handshake or kiss on the cheek, saying, "Good show." Eight times a week, he wishes everyone in the building a good show. Every dresser, every actor, every crew member. The stage manager, the door man. Then at the end of act one, John always stands directly off stage right and as we run off stage sweating, he gives every person a high five. Three years of mints and high fives.

We were lucky to find out we were closing with a couple months' notice. We all love the show and are sad to see it go, but at least we've had ample time to say goodbye. Mostly, I'm sad to see the show go from New York. The relationships we've formed here, those will go on. But the message of *Newsies* won't get to reach new people at the Nederlander anymore. We get to tell people from all over the country and all over the world who are coming to New York this story of these brave boys who stood up for themselves and made a difference.

I can't wait to see *Newsies* in schools and community theaters. When I was growing up doing shows, I would always listen to the cast recordings of the shows I was doing and relate to the people who originated the roles. I can't believe people are going to be playing Davey and listening to me on the recording. Davey is such a huge part of who I am, and I think that people who play him in the future will be similar to me, brainy guys. I know we'll all share a bond. And I hope to direct a production of *Newsies* one day.

I haven't signed the wall. I don't know if I'll sign the wall. I feel like it belongs to *Rent*, and it should. I feel no obligation to make the wall my own; I just love admiring the history. "Great Job, Jonathan Larson." That was one of the first things I remember seeing written on it when I walked in. I'll probably write my name under my dressing room table. There's a signature from *Brighton Beach Memoirs* underneath my dressing room table.

We had a potluck to celebrate our final week in the mezzanine lobby area. We set up tables and food, and everyone ate together—cast, crew, ushers, musicians. On Sunday afternoon, we're going to come in and do our last show. There'll be a party then, too, and then that's it. A couple weeks from now, the tour cast starts rehearsals, and the whole thing will be reborn again. Even if New York doesn't have *Newsies*, people will get to hear the story in their own theaters all over America.

The day before Newsies *played its 1004th and final performance at the Nederlander, I sat with Ben Fankhauser in the mid-mezzanine and listened to his stories while watching the crew set up for their last show. After the interview, Ben took me inside the bowels of the mezzanine, through a maze-like set of stairs that lead to the mail room, the physical therapy room, the ushers' quarters, the house manager's office, and the VIP room where understudy costumes are stored. We went through pass doors to an area never seen by the public, where ushers were stuffing Playbills and the walls were covered in photos of the cast in rehearsal. Every corner of the Nederlander was jam-packed. Ben introduced me to the door man Joaquin, who told me that he thought the crew at the Nederlander was tighter than at any other theater he'd ever worked at. I asked him why, and he said, "Because we're like a little ant colony!"*

The Nederlander was the first Broadway theater I ever saw. I remember coming to New York when I was 15 and walking around with my family. I saw a huge green behemoth of a theater gleaming down a street corner, and when I squinted at it, I was sure: That was it. The Nederlander. The images on the front of the theater matched exactly the images on the liner notes that I'd memorized. This was Broadway! I didn't see Rent *until a few days later, but in my heart, the Nederlander still remains the first Broadway theater I ever "met."*

I saw each of the four shows that followed Rent *into the theater during their early previews. At* Guys and Dolls, *I was astonished by the total transformation the theater had undertaken. When* Brighton Beach Memoirs *and* Broadway Bound *were set to play in repertory as "The Neil Simon Plays," I was thrilled. I love those plays, and one of the most talented actors I know, Josh Grisetti, was going to make his Broadway debut in the latter. When the shows closed in previews,* Broadway Bound *gained the distinction of closing during previews without ever having played one, and so did he. This seemed so brutally unfair to me that one night at 3am, my friends and I stole an entire door decal off the Nederlander. It's six feet tall and hangs on my living room wall. I will remember you, ill-fated* Brighton Beach Memoirs *and* Broadway Bound *revival.*

I stood in the rain at the first Million Dollar Quartet *lottery and won front row tickets. I saw* Newsies *during its first week of previews, when the boys were just starting to make their mark on NYC. At the time of print,* Honeymoon in Vegas— *the new Jason Robert Brown/Andrew Bergman musical, starring Tony Danza, Brynn O'Malley, and Rob McClure—is in rehearsals to become the 211th production at the Nederlander Theatre. It's serendipitous that the next hope of the Nederlander is set to launch on the very same night as the book you are holding.*

As Ben led me all around the southernmost theater on Broadway, I memorized the doors and staircases and touched the walls—until we got to The Wall. At the back of the foyer was a door that led to the alley that I'd heard about for years. Thousands of messages overlapped, in different colors, different handwriting. I knew some of them had been written years apart. There was "We love you, Daphne!" and "We'll never forget you, Rent. *1996-2008." It was a shrine to a show that had been gone for six years. I winced when I saw that one part of the wall had been erased, wiped away by a fresh coat of beige paint. During the run of* Rent, *thousands of people had started signing the outside doors of the theater, too, and all of that was already gone. I knew the Nederlander would keep changing, just as it always had.*

The Wall

Kevin McCollum, Producer

I was sad that we couldn't take the *Rent* wall in the back alley with us when we closed, or that it couldn't stay the same and just live there forever. But that's the thing about the theatre that makes it beautiful: it all dies. As soon as you make it and share it, it goes away. That's what makes theatre so human and so humbling.

I'm glad I was alive and experienced that time at the Nederlander and got to be part of it. I understand why we couldn't preserve the wall. Even though a part of me wanted to, I'm not in the museum business. I'm in the life business. That wall celebrated life, and it happened, and it lives in people's memories just like the show does. Our time with *Rent* at the Nederlander was documented and it will be in books and it will live beyond us. We were just the ones who were lucky enough to experience it happening firsthand.

———————

On August 1, 2014, it was announced that a starry revival of the A.R. Gurney two-hander Love Letters *would open at the Nederlander Theatre in the fall. The likes of Carol Burnett, Mia Farrow, Anjelica Huston and more would move into the house on 41st Street. Two weeks later, a rare theater switch was made within the Nederlander Organization.* Honeymoon in Vegas *had been set for the Brooks Atkinson.* Honeymoon *and* Love Letters *would swap houses so that the musical could play the larger theater, the Nederlander.*

With two shows fighting over the Nederlander this fall, it's fair to say that the southern-most Broadway theater won't be empty for a long time.

———————

2014: *Honeymoon In Vegas*

Brynn O'Malley, Actor

Honeymoon in Vegas had an unusual journey to the Nederlander.

It was initially announced that we were going to the Brooks Atkinson—and then several weeks later we were switched to the Nederlander. Text messages from a few apprehensive cast members were fired off (mainly because of the theater's southernmost location). David Josefsberg had the best response: "Gee, guys, I dunno… how did *Rent* do? How did *Newsies* do? Can somebody look that up?"

Needless to say, it's an honor to be occupying the stage where shows like *Inherit The Wind* and *Who's Afraid of Virginia Woolf?* once debuted. And you cannot *imagine* what a gift it is for us to *not* have to cut through Times Square everyday to get to work! Also, the Nederlander is the closest Broadway house to my apartment, so this will absolutely be the greatest year of my life.

The company of *Honeymoon in Vegas* believes in our show with a near-religious fervor. We worked our tails off at Paper Mill to give this piece the production it deserves and, as a result, we grew freakishly close. If this cast could all sleep under the same roof, we would do it in a heartbeat. Sometimes in Broadway houses, people get separated by what feels like miles due to the dressing room layout. Once you get into a long run, there are cast mates you might not even *see* again if you don't have easy access to each other.

We were afraid we might lose that backstage intimacy we had at Paper Mill when we got to Broadway. When I first toured the Nederlander to pick my room, I was so thrilled to report back to my friends that we would be piled on top of each other once again. When you're doing a show with Tony Danza, you don't want to be out of ear-shot. The stories are too good.

———————

The Untold Stories of Broadway is about how Broadway shows have been affected by the theaters they've played in. It's also about how the theaters have been changed forever by the shows. The Nederlander was saved by Rent. *Even though the house on 41st Street looks very different now than it did in* Rent*'s heyday, the spirit of that show and the people who made it is a legacy that will always live inside the theater.*

———————————

I'll Cover You

Jonathan Burkhart, Producer

I met Jonathan Larson in 1984 in Nantucket. We were both in our mid-twenties. At the end of that summer, he said to me: "Don't go back to Boston, move to New York." Because of Jonathan, I moved to New York in the fall of 1984, and right away, through friends we made, we started seeing theatre. We started out seeing a small play here or there, nothing major. Then one day in October of 1986, we got offered free tickets to opening night of this new musical *Raggedy Ann*, at the Nederlander Theatre.

I had never been to a Broadway show before! It was my first one. Before the show started, there were tons of people outside under the marquee, and the energy was electric. I was completely intoxicated. We sat together in the front row center of the mezzanine of the Nederlander. The show began, and I was completely taken in by the dancing and the music and the colors and the lights. The whole thing just blew me away. When *Raggedy Ann* ended, people were standing and cheering and clapping, and Jonathan grabbed me and sat me down. "Don't leave," he says. "We're not leaving."

We sat there in the Nederlander as the audience was filing out, and he looked at me and went, "Oh my God, that was a complete piece of shit." And I was like, "Jonathan, that was the greatest thing ever!" And at that moment, he started explaining to me the entire history of Broadway, going back 100 years. He referenced the creation of opera, which of course is a whole other story. He gave me a whole lesson on musicals specifically, and the old Jewish vaudeville houses on the Lower East Side and how Broadway became Broadway. He explained the Broadway district to me, the physical street parameters, going from 41st Street to 53rd Street at the time. He even explained the process of how someone writes a musical. At this point, Jonathan and I had been close friends for several years, and he was a prolific writer. He was always creating stories. But until that night, I didn't understand how Broadway and musicals and being a musical theatre writer worked. He taught me that night, and it was all part of his explanation leading up to why he thought this specific show would be a bomb.

We were roommates at the time, and the next morning we got up and went down to Canal Street to eat breakfast at a diner. We were broke. We had no money, and you could get breakfast for a buck and a half at this one diner. We had a routine: we'd pick up the *New York Times* on the way to breakfast, then we'd each get a couple eggs and some toast and split the paper. This morning, he went right for the reviews. Three bites into his eggs, he started laughing. He said, "Yeah, I was right." Frank Rich had written the most horrific review of *Raggedy Ann*. The show ended up posting its closing notice the next day. They did five performances at the Nederlander, and then they were gone. I still remember the feeling I had sitting in the diner that morning: I was devastated. *How is this possible?! And who the f— is this guy, Frank Rich? How dare he!* I didn't know. Jonathan was correct about the show, and I was blown away by the process he taught me about that week. I learned about Frank Rich, the power of the pen, how Broadway evolved into this place where shows could close so quickly or run forever. And it was all because of the first Broadway show I ever saw, with Jonathan, at the Nederlander.

There was a period of time in the 1980s and 1990s when Broadway was not as strong as it is now and has been for the last 15 years. Jonathan and I used to ride our bikes past all of the Broadway houses that were closed— some had been closed for years, and some were just barely used. There was a time when easily a third to a half of the Broadway houses we'd ride past were closed on a regular basis. The theaters didn't have much of a life.

326

Jonathan was always trying to write new shows and get them on. We used to write letters to all the theater owners: Jujamcyn, the Nederlanders, the Shuberts. He'd write: *Can you just give us a theater? I've written a show, my friend Jonathan will produce it. Just give us a theater for a couple of weeks. They're empty. We don't need anyone to turn on one light, we can do the whole thing ourselves. We just want to put on a show.* We did that for years, and of course it never happened. No one ever responded.

Around 1992, Jonathan met Jim Nicola, artistic director of New York Theatre Workshop, and he said, "Bring me some of your work." At the time, NYTW was in a building on 41st Street, across the street from the Nederlander Theatre. So Jonathan and I rode our bikes to 41st Street. It was a hot, hot summer day. We went upstairs so that Jonathan could deliver his script, and while we were waiting, he started flirting with the secretary. I got bored, so I went back downstairs and outside. I started looking around. 41st Street at that time was a shithole! If it was on fire, I wouldn't have pissed on it. It was a mess. It was full of vagrants, drug dealers, prostitutes. It's basically the back end of 42nd Street, which had been very seedy for a while, although gentrification was starting to take place. But 41st Street hadn't caught up yet. The whole street smelled terrible. It was a mess. The Nederlander was totally abandoned, no longer cared for or used by anyone.

Jonathan finally came downstairs, and he saw that I was looking at the Nederlander. As he typically did, he went into his whole dialogue of "See? See that theater? It's empty, and there could be a show right here. I don't understand why we're not allowed to put on shows..." He was almost yelling, so upset about why this theater was closed. We had crossed the street while he was saying this, and we were about to get on our bikes and leave. I had been pulling on the doors of theater though, and just as we were about to leave, I pulled on one of the doors so hard that it opened about six inches. You could see inside. I pulled even harder, and I busted the door. We went in.

Jonathan and I had a habit of breaking into buildings. We had a goal: we wanted to get to all of the rooftops of the tallest buildings in New York. We would roll a joint, ride to the Woolworth Building or somewhere downtown, and find a way to get to the top floor and break onto the roof. We succeeded about half of the time.

On this day, we broke into the Nederlander Theatre. It was very musty and dirty. When we got inside, Jonathan ran up to the stage and jumped onto it. He used to do this thing where he'd clap. He did it all of the time and it annoyed the shit out of me. So of course, Jonathan stood center stage and clapped really loudly. Then he started barking, to hear the noise echo. I told him to be quiet, because we were being too loud and would draw attention. He said a few things about being onstage there, at the Nederlander, and then we got the hell out of there before we got caught.

After Jonathan died, I was in the group of his friends and family who toured the Broadway houses with *Rent*'s producers, looking at a bunch of possible theaters for the show. This was March of 1996, after the show had been at NYTW for a little while. After we had seen maybe eight or nine theaters, we got to 41st Street. The last theater we were looking at was the Nederlander.

We got inside, and I remember just starting to cry. I went: "Oh my God." The Nederlander had to be it. It was perfect. Jonathan always thought that if he ever got to put on a show, having it downtown, out of the Broadway district, would help get a new young vibrant audience to finally come to the theater. And that was a consideration of all of ours after he died; we thought about whether or not it was right to be downtown for *Rent*'s commercial run. But the NYTW run did so well that it got financing to move to Broadway. So I felt: *Okay, so here we are at the furthest out, southern-most Broadway house in the theatre district. The theater is on the most dilapidated, piece-of-shit street that's almost equivalent to streets we'd find in the East Village. It's a shithole. It has to be this theater.* And it became that theater.

Of all of the Broadway houses I've been in since that time, the Nederlander is very special to me. I've actually produced a couple of shows on Broadway now, including *Laugh Whore,* with Mario Cantone at the Cort. I fully developed and financed that show and put it on Broadway, and it was successful. I was so proud of it. I wished so much that Jonathan was around to see that. Because I never intended to put shows onstage. I'm a filmmaker. I make movies. But he brought me into the theatre.

I was with Jonathan almost every day of our lives for 12 years, until the day he died, on January 25, 1996. We were best friends. For me, *Rent* is a very true story in a lot of ways. A lot of the show is our lives and the people we knew. And it got to play at the Nederlander, on 41st Street for 12 years.

New York is different now. 41st Street is different. It's not dirty. It's happening, it's busy. It's filled with people, especially the Nederlander Theatre. It's changed so much.

Timelines

Shows featured in The Untold Stories of Broadway, Volume 2

1. Palace

1913	Sarah Bernhardt
1915	Weber and Fields
1916	Will Rogers
1917	Palmer and Hayden
	Palace Theatre Overseas
1918	Entertainment recruiting rally
1924	Woodrow Wilson's Memorial
	Cathedral of St. John the Divine
1925	Benefit
1927	Fanny Brice
1928	Fur Fashion Pageant and Revue
1932	Sophie Tucker
1936	Broadway Heat Wave
1941	Citizen Kane world premiere
1946	Song of the South protests

2. Barrymore

1936	The Women
1938	Knickerbocker Holiday
1940	Pal Joey
1943	Tomorrow the World
1945	Pygmalion
1946	Cyrano de Bergerac
1947	A Streetcar Named Desire

Year		Year	
1951	Judy Garland at the Palace "Two-A-Day"	1951	The Fourposter
		1953	Tea and Sympathy
1956	Judy Garland		
		1957	The Greatest Man Alive; Look Homeward, Angel
		1959	A Raisin in the Sun
		1962	Step on a Crack, Moby Dick
		1964	The Passion of Josef D.
1966	Sweet Charity		
1967	Judy Garland "At Home at the Palace"; Henry, Sweet Henry		
1968	George M!	1968	Don't Drink the Water, Happiness Is Just A Thing Called a Rolls Royce, The Goodbye People
1970	Applause	1970	A Place For Polly
		1971	Ain't Supposed to Die a Natural Death, Inner City
1972	From Israel with Love	1972	Don't Play Us Cheap!
1973	Bette Midler		
1974	Lorelei		
1975	Goodtime Charley	1975	The Night That Made America Famous, Travesties
1976	Home Sweet Homer, Shirley MacLaine, An Evening with Diana Ross		
1977	Man of La Mancha	1977	American Buffalo, I Love My Wife
1978	All That Jazz Filming		
1979	The Grand Tour, A Meeting by the River, Break a Leg, Oklahoma!		
1981	Frankenstein, Woman of the Year		
		1982	is there life after high school?
1983	Parade of Stars Playing the Palace, La Cage aux Folles	1983	Baby
		1984	Hurlyburly
		1986	Social Security
1987	George Abbott's 100th Birthday Celebration, Bob Fosse's Memorial		
		1988	Joe Turner's Come and Gone

330

1991	The Will Rogers Follies	1990	Lettice and Lovage
		1992	A Streetcar Named Desire
		1993	The Sisters Rosensweig
1994	Beauty and the Beast		
		1997	The Life
		1999	Putting It Together
2000	Aida	2000	The Real Thing, The Tale of the Allergist's Wife
		2002	Imaginary Friends
2004	Vanessa Williams: Silver & Gold; Linda Eder: The Holiday Concert		
2005	All Shook Up	2005	The Glass Menagerie
2006	Lestat	2006	Company
2007	Legally Blonde	2007	
2008	Liza's at the Palace....	2008	Speed-the-Plow
2009	West Side Story	2009	Exit the King, Race
		2010	Elling
2011	Priscilla Queen of the Desert	2011	Arcadia
2012	Annie	2012	Death of a Salesman, Chaplin
		2013	Smash Filming, Macbeth, Betrayal
2014	Holler If Ya Hear Me	2014	A Raisin in the Sun, The Curious Incident of the Dog in the Night-Time
2015	An American in Paris		

3. Gershwin

1972	Via Galactica
1973	Seesaw, The Desert Song, Gigi
	Sammy, Anthony Newley/Henry Mancini, The Fifth Dimension with
1974	Jo Jo's Dance Factory
1975	Treemonisha
1976	Porgy and Bess
1977	The King and I
1979	Sweeney Todd
1981	The Pirates of Penzance, My Fair Lady, Annie
1983	Show Boat, Mame
1984	Cyrano de Bergerac/Much Ado About Nothing
1985	Singin' in the Rain
1987	Starlight Express
1990	Bugs Bunny on Broadway, Fiddler on the Roof
1993	Raffi, Yanni, The Red Shoes
1994	Show Boat
1995	Something Wonderful: A Celebration of Oscar Hammerstein II on His 100th Birthday
1997	Candide, 1776
1998	On the Town
1999	Peter Pan
2002	Oklahoma!, Something Good: A Broadway Salute to Richard Rodgers on His 100th Birthday
2003	Wicked

4. Circle in the Square

1972	Mourning Becomes Electra
1973	Uncle Vanya, The Iceman Cometh
1974	Where's Charley?
1976	Pal Joey
1977	Saint Joan
1978	Once in a Lifetime, The Inspector General
1982	Present Laughter
1983	The Caine Mutiny Court-Martial, Heartbreak House
1984	Design For Living
1985	Arms and the Man
1987	Coastal Disturbances
1989	Sweeney Todd
1992	Anna Karenina
1995	Holiday
1996	Hughie
1997	Stanley
1999	Not About Nightingales, The Chris Rock Show
2000	True West, The Rocky Horror Show
2002	Metamorphoses
2003	Life (x) 3
2004	Frozen
2005	The 25th Annual Putnam County Spelling Bee

2008	Glory Days
2009	The Norman Conquests
2010	The Miracle Worker, Lombardi
2011	Godspell
2013	Soul Doctor
2014	Bronx Bombers, Lady Day at Emerson's Bar & Grill
2015	Fun Home

5. Shubert

1913	Othello, The Merchant of Venice, Hamlet, The Sacrament of Judas, The Passing of the Third Floor Back, Caesar and Cleopatra, The Light That Failed, Mice and Men
1914	The Belle of Bond Street, Madam Moselle
1917	Maytime
1918	The Copperhead, Sometime
1919	A Lonely Romeo
1927	Padlocks of 1927
1928	Ups-a Daisy
1932	Americana
1933	Gay Divorce
1937	Babes in Arms
1938	I Married An Angel
1939	The Philadelphia Story
1940	Higher and Higher
1941	Pal Joey
1942	By Jupiter
1948	My Romance
1950	Kiss Me, Kate
1953	Can-Can

1955	Pipe Dream
1956	Bells Are Ringing
1958	Whoop-Up
1959	Take Me Along
1961	Bye Bye Birdie
1962	I Can Get It for You Wholesale
1963	Here's Love
1964	Bajour
1966	The Apple Tree
1968	Golden Rainbow; Promises, Promises
1972	The Selling of the President
1973	A Little Night Music
1974	Over Here!
1975	The Constant Wife, A Chorus Line

1990	Buddy
1992	Crazy for You
1996	Big
1997	Chicago

6. Criterion Center

1989	Starmites, Mastergate
1990	Stand-Up Tragedy
1991	The Homecoming
1992	The Price
1993	Anna Christie, She Loves Me, White Lies/Black Comedy, A Grand Night for Singing
1994	No Man's Land, Picnic, Hedda Gabler, The Glass Menagerie
1995	A Month in the Country, Company
1996	The Father, The Rehearsal
1997	The Three Sisters, London Assurance, 1776, A

	View From the Bridge
1998	The Deep Blue Sea, Side Man, Little Me
1999	The Lion in Winter

| 2003 | Gypsy |
| 2005 | Spamalot |

| 2009 | Blithe Spirit, Memphis |

| 2013 | Matilda |

8. Nederlander

1921	Swords
1922	The Cat and the Canary
1924	Bye, Bye, Barbara
1926	Harry Houdini, Yellow
1927	The Trial of Mary Dugan
1930	Grand Hotel
1934	Within the Gates
1936	Tonight at 8:30
1938	The Shoemakers' Holiday, Julius Caesar
1939	The Little Foxes
1943	Hairpin Harmony, What's Up?
1945	The Day Before Spring
1946	Call Me Mister
1947	Medea
1948	Lend an Ear
1953	Maggie
1955	Inherit the Wind
1962	A Family Affair, Who's Afraid of Virginia Woolf?
1964	Tiny Alice

7. Beaumont

1965	Danton's Death

337

1967	Galileo, The Unknown Soldier and His Wife		
		1968	Here's Where I Belong, The American Dream, The Zoo Story, The House of Atreus, The Resistable Rise of Arturo Ui
1968	Lovers		
		1969	Billy
1970	Operation Sidewinder		
		1971	Earl of Ruston
		1972	Heathen!
1973	Boom Boom Room, The au Pair Man		
1974	Short Eyes		
1976	Threepenny Opera		
1977	The Cherry Orchard		
		1979	Whose Life is it Anyway?
1980	The Philadelphia Story	1980	Betrayal, One Night Stand
		1981	Broadway Follies, Lena Horne: "The Lady and Her Music"
		1982	84 Charing Cross Road
1983	La Tragedie de Carmen		
		1985	Wind in the Willows
1986	The House of Blue Leaves, The Front Page	1986	Raggedy Ann
1987	Anything Goes		
		1989	Dangerous Games
1990	Six Degrees of Separation		
1991	Monster in a Box		
1992	My Favorite Year, Four Baboons Adoring the Sun	1992	Solitary Confinement
1993	In The Summer House, Gray's Anatomy, Abe Lincoln in Illinois		
1994	Carousel, Gray's Anatomy		
1995	Arcadia, Racing Demon		
1996	It's a Slippery Slope, Juan Darien	1996	Rent
1997	The Little Foxes		
1998	Parade		
1999	Morning, Noon and Night; Marie Christine		
2000	Contact		
2001	QED		
2002	Mostly Sondheim		
2004	Barbara Cook's Broadway!, The Frogs		
2005	The Light in the Piazza, Love/Life		

2006	The Lady with the Torch, The Coast of Utopia
2008	South Pacific
2010	A Free Man of Color
2011	War Horse
2013	Ann
2014	Act One
2015	The King and I

2009	Guys and Dolls, Brighton Beach Memoirs, Broadway Bound
2010	Million Dollar Quartet
2012	Newsies
2014	Honeymoon in Vegas

Acknowledgements

Just like it takes an army to make a show, it takes an army to make a book series like *The Untold Stories of Broadway*. I am grateful to the hundreds of generous interviewees who contributed their stories, and to many other people whose energy, heart and skills made this snapshot of history possible.

When I declared I would write this book, people began connecting me to others. Immediately, there was an outpouring of folks being generous with their time, their smarts, and their connections. I was blown away by the selflessness and helpfulness of the community. Every step of the way, people were connecting me to their friends, calling and emailing on my behalf. I want to thank all of the countless people who opened up their hearts and their address books for me.

This book would not have been possible without the hard work and dedication of an indefatigable team of helpers, who transcribed, researched, co-interviewed, and gave invaluable insight as the book came together. Sierra Fox was the most outstanding assistant imaginable. Her knowledge and passion for theatre inspired me every step of the way, and her personal handprint is all over this book. From dressing room drawers to landmarkings, Anna Marie Ray was always passionate and on top of a good research project. Thank you Allie Glickman for your attention to detail, from Judy Garland to Kevin McCollum. Thank you Andrew Greenberg for your excitement and tears that match mine. Thank you Larry Owens for valuable suggestions and thoughts. Thank you Julia Castellanos for taking good care with sensitive stories. Thank you Nathan Hunter Bell for your reliability, perseverance and huge heart. Thank you Drew Factor and Jess McGinty for jumping in like true Broadway troupers. This book would not have been possible in any way without the skills and passion of the names above. Go back and read those names again, and remember them, because you're going to be hearing a lot from them in the future.

I want to deeply thank all of the authors, teachers, and mentors who inspired this stagestruck kid as she was growing up.

I also need to thank colleagues, family, and good friends who were a constant source of support. First, thank you to my best friend Joe Iconis—for everything and for *Elling*. Thank you to my "musical theatre Godmother" Mana Allen for your wisdom, your kind heart, and your willingness to talk theatre for hours at the Cafe Edison, over a bowl of matzo ball soup! Thank you to Richard Frankel, Tom Viertel, Steve Baruch, and everyone else at 54 Below who I am so happy to be working with every day in Broadway's living room. Thank you to Matt Murphy, whose generosity as a person is matched only by his brilliance as a photographer. Thank you to Justin "Squigs" Robertson, who lent his own unique brand of creativity to this project. Thank you to Hannah Ehrenberg for being a rock star in every way—I'm not sure how *Volume 1* ever happened without you! Thank you to Blair Ingenthron for always being game to talk through a Shubert avocado logic puzzle. Thank you to all of the interviewees not featured in this volume who have shared their stories as part of this book series.

Thank you to those who made a great deal of this work possible in so many different ways, from discussing Jonathan Larson at 3am to discussing vaudeville at 8am: Aaron Simon Gross, Ben Rauhala, Ben Skinner, Blake Joseph, Charlie Rosen, Danny Abosch, Dylan Bustamante, Elin Flack, Emily Essig, Eric Price, Hunter Arnold, Jason SweetTooth Williams, Jeff Heimbrock, Josh Safran, Julia Brownell, Julie Larson, Justin Braun, Kayla Greenspan, Kevin Michael Murphy, Lauren Marcus, Leah Harris, Maggie Larkin, Max Blake Friedman, Michael Gioia, Michael Growler, Nic Rouleau, Rachel Sussman, Shoshana Feinstein, Steven Tartick, Tess Harkin, and Zack Zadek. Thank you to my family, and especially to Zephrem Tepper, Jessica Kent, Leigh-Ann Tepper, my father Larry Tepper and my mother Janis Tepper.

Thank you to Brisa Trinchero and Roberta Pereira and everybody at Dress Circle Publishing, who were as excited about this project as I was, from my first pitch to the last draft, whose unwavering support, energy, and ideas made this book what it is. You are the reason that hundreds of people of Broadway, including me, got a platform to tell their stories, and I will always be grateful from the bottom of my heart.

Special thanks to all the people at the Shubert Organization, the Nederlander Organization, Jujamcyn Theaters, the Ambassador Theatre Group, the Little Theatre Group, Lincoln Center, Manhattan Theatre Club, Roundabout Theatre Company and Disney Theatrical Productions who are such excellent stewards of Broadway's iconic theater buildings.

Part of the proceeds of The Untold Stories of Broadway, Volume 2 *will benefit will benefit the Dress Circle Publishing Scholarship Fund.*

Volume 2 Complete List of Interviewees

Deborah Abramson

Loni Ackerman

Lynn Ahrens

Rose M. Alaio

Mana Allen

Charlie Alterman

Michael Arden

Brittnye Batchelor

Bryan Batt

Hunter Bell

Marty Bell

Brig Berney

Michael Berresse

Ken Billington

Sandy Binion

Patricia Birch

André Bishop

Nick Blaemire

Corbin Bleu

Heidi Blickenstaff

Walter Bobbie

Anne Bobby

Chris Boneau

Beowulf Boritt

Christian Borle

Jeff Bowen

Jason Robert Brown

Jeb Brown

Laura Bell Bundy

Todd Buonopane

Jonathan Burkhart

Danny Burstein

Liz Callaway

Liz Caplan

Len Cariou

Craig Carnelia

Eileen Casey

Harrison Chad

Ted Chapin

Nancy Coyne

Gavin Creel

Charlotte d'Amboise

Ken Davenport

Penny Davis

Carmel Dean

Robin De Jesús

Ed Dixon

Christopher Durang

James Dybas

Jake Epstein

Raúl Esparza

Ben Fankhauser

Tim Federle

Philip Feller

Bert Fink

Terry Finn

Stephen Flaherty

Merwin Foard

Shannon Ford

Hunter Foster

Fritz Frizsell

Larry Fuller

Artie Gaffin

Jack Gale

David Gallo

Irene Gandy

Chris Gattelli

Joanna Gleason

Annie Golden

Jason Graae

Todd Graff

Randy Graff

Ilene Graff

Amanda Green

Michael Greif

Harry Groener

Jonathan Groff

Julie Halston

Ann Harada

F. Michael Haynie

Diane Heatherington

Laura Heller

Tom Hewitt

John Hickok

Larry Hochman

Abe Jacob

Sally J. Jacobs

Jay Armstrong Johnson

Jeremy Jordan

Doug Katsaros

Andrew Keenan-Bolger

Celia Keenan-Bolger

Steve C. Kennedy

Chad Kimball

Eddie Korbich

Michael John LaChiusa

Liz Larsen

Baayork Lee

Telly Leung

Caissie Levy

Peter Link

Laura Linney

Jose Llana

William Ivey Long

David Loud

Anna Louizos

Hal Luftig

Arielle Tepper Madover

James Maloney

Richard Maltby Jr.

Joe Mantello

Josh Marquette

Kathleen Marshall

Mel Marvin

Tony Massey

Michael Mayer

Neil Mazzella

Elizabeth McCann

Kevin McCollum

Donna McKechnie

John McMartin

Lindsay Mendez

Michael Mendez

Alan Menken

Joanna Merlin

Lin-Manuel Miranda

Jessica Molaskey

Eric William Morris

Randy Morrison

Robert Morse

Julia Murney

Austin Nathaniel

George Nestor

Casey Nicholaw

Jack O'Brien

Kelli O'Hara

Brynn O'Malley

Laura Osnes

Evan Pappas

Michon Peacock

Tim Pettolina

Hayley Podschun

Red Press

Lonny Price

Harold Prince

Ben Rappaport

Krysta Rodriguez

Steve Rosen

Daryl Roth

Michael Rupert

Alex Rybeck

Harvey Sabinson

Sarah Saltzberg

Don Scardino

Justin Scribner

Joan Shepard

David Shire

Rick Sordelet

Louis St. Louis

Michael Starobin

Don Stitt

David Stone

Charles Strouse

Julie Taymor

Bernie Telsey

Mary Testa

Joe Traina

Taylor Trensch

Mike VanPraagh

Donna Vivino

Frank Vlastnik

Jim Walton

Tony Walton

Robert E. Wankel

John Weidman

Ira Weitzman

George C. Wolfe

Amy Wolk

Greg Woolard

James Woolley

Nick Wyman

Maury Yeston

Brian Yorkey

Jerry Zaks

In Upcoming Volumes of The Untold Stories Of Broadway

The Ambassador Theatre
The American Airlines Theatre
The Belasco Theatre
The Bernard B. Jacobs Theatre
The Bijou Theatre
The Booth Theatre
The Broadhurst Theatre
The Broadway Theatre
The Brooks Atkinson Theatre
The Cort Theatre
The Edison Theatre
The Eugene O'Neill Theatre
The Fulton Theatre
The Gerald Schoenfeld Theatre
The George Abbott Theatre
The Golden Theatre
The Harkness Theatre

The Helen Hayes Theatre
The Imperial Theatre
The Latin Quarter
The Longacre Theatre
The Lunt-Fontanne Theatre
The Lyric Theatre
The Majestic Theatre
The Minskoff Theatre
The Morosco Theatre
The Music Box Theatre
The New Amsterdam Theatre
The Rialto Theatre
The Samuel J. Friedman Theatre
The St. James Theatre
Studio 54
The Stephen Sondheim Theatre
The Walter Kerr Theatre

Also From Dress Circle Publishing

By Jennifer Ashley Tepper
Untold Stories of Broadway Volume 1
Untold Stories of Broadway Volume 2

By Ruby Preston
Showbiz
Staged
Broadway Academy

By Seth Rudetsky
Seth's Broadway Diary, Volume 1

By Jeremy Scott Blaustein
The Home For Wayward Ladies

By Joanna Parson
Emily's Tour Diary: And Other Tragedies of the Stage (2014 Release)

Founded in 2011 by Brisa Trinchero and Roberta Pereira, Dress Circle Publishing is commited to taking readers "behind the curtain" through our catalog of books about Broadway written by members of the Broadway community.

Made in the USA
Middletown, DE
06 May 2015